A-Z NOTTINGHAM & DERBY

Key to Map Pages
Large Scale Nottingham City Centre   216-303
Large Scale Derby City Centre
Map Pages   304

REFERENCE

Motorway	**M1**	Car Park (selected)	P
A Road	A611	Church or Chapel	†
Under Construction		Cycleway (selected)	
Proposed		Fire Station	■
B Road	B6004	Hospital	H
Dual Carriageway		House Numbers (A & B Roads only)	18 25
One-way Street	→	Information Centre	i
Traffic flow on A Roads is also indicated by a heavy line on the driver's left.	→	National Grid Reference	340
Restricted Access		Park & Ride (Bus)	P+
Pedestrianized Road		Park & Ride (NET)	P+
Track / Footpath	----	Police Station	▲
Residential Walkway	··········	Post Office	★

Railway — Station, Heritage Station, Tunnel, Level Crossing

Nottingham Express Transit (NET)
The boarding of NET trams at stops may be limited to a single direction, indicated by the arrow.   Stop

Built-up Area   DORIS RD.

Local Authority Boundary — · — · —

Posttown Boundary

Postcode Boundary (within Posttown) — — —

Map Continuation 18   Large Scale 4

Toilet: without facilities for the Disabled / with facilities for the Disabled / Disabled facilities only	▽ ▽ ▽
Educational Establishment	
Hospital or Hospice	
Industrial Building	
Leisure or Recreational Facility	
Place of Interest	
Public Building	
Shopping Centre or Market	
Other Selected Buildings	

SCALE

Map Pages 8-215
1:15840

¼   ½ Mile
250   500   750 Metres
4 inches (10.16cm) to 1 mile   6.31cm to 1km

Large Scale City Centre Pages 4-7
1:7920

⅛   ¼ Mile
125   250   375 Metres
8 inches (20.32cm) to 1 mile   12.63cm to 1km

Copyright of Geographers' A-Z Map Company Limited

Fairfield Road, Borough ...   ping data licensed
Telephone: 01732 78...   ...with the permission of
01732 78...   ...sty's Stationery Office.
www.a-zmaps.co.uk

Copyright © Geogr...

Every possible car...   ...atlas is accurate
at the date of publica...   ...ateful to learn of any
inaccuracies, we do n...   ...within this publication.

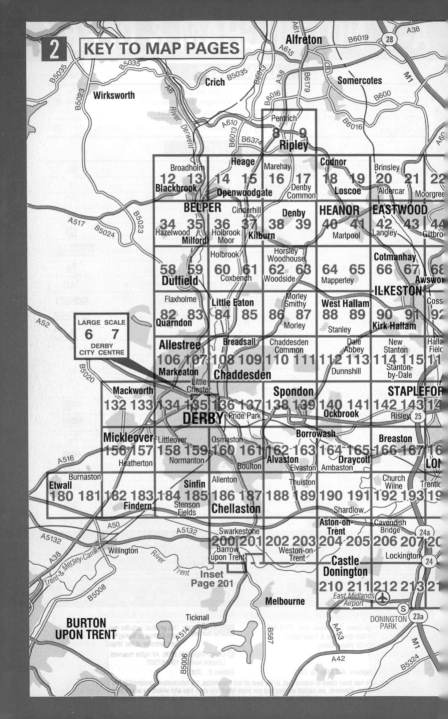

KEY TO MAP PAGES

2

Alfreton

Somercotes

Wirksworth

Crich

Pentrich

8 9
Ripley

Broadholm
12 13
Blackbrook

Heage
14 15
Openwoodgate

Marehay
16 17
Denby
Common

Codnor
18 19
Loscoe

Brinsley
20 21
Aldercar

22
Moorgree

BELPER
34 35
Hazelwood
Milford

Cinderhill
36 37
Holbrook
Moor Kilburn

Denby
38 39

HEANOR
40 41
Marlpool

EASTWOOD
42 43 44
Langley Giltbro

58 59
Duffield

Holbrook
60 61
Coxbench

Horsley
Woodhouse
62 63
Woodside

64 65
Mapperley

Cotmanhay
66 67 68
Awswo

ILKESTON

Flaxholme
82 83
Quarndon

Little Eaton
84 85

Morley
Smithy
86 87
Morley

West Hallam
88 89
Stanley

90 91 92
Kirk Hallam

Coss

Allestree
106 107 108 109 110 111 112 113 114 115 11
Markeaton
Little
Chester
Breadsall
Chaddesden
Common
Dale
Abbey
Dunnshill
New
Stanton
Stanton-
by-Dale
Halla
Field
Chaddesden

Mackworth
132 133 134 135 136 137 138 139 140 141 142 143 14
DERBY Pride Park
Spondon
Ockbrook
Risley 25
STAPLEFOR

Mickleover
156 157 158 159 160 161 162 163 164 165 166 167 16
Littleover Osmaston
Heatherton Normanton
Boulton
Alvaston
Elvaston Ambaston
Borrowash
Draycott
Church
Wilne
Trentlo
Breaston
LON

Burnaston
Etwall
180 181 182 183 184 185 186 187 188 189 190 191 192 193 19
Findern
Sinfin
Stenson
Fields
Allenton
Chellaston
Thulston
Shardlow
Aston-on-
Trent
Cavendish
Bridge
Castle
Donington

200 201 202 203 204 205 206 207 20
210 211 212 213 21

Swarkestone
Barrow
upon Trent
Weston-on-
Trent
Lockington 24

Inset
Page 201

Willington

Melbourne

East Midlands
Airport (S) 23a

BURTON
UPON TRENT

Ticknall

DONINGTON
PARK

LARGE SCALE
6 7
DERBY
CITY CENTRE

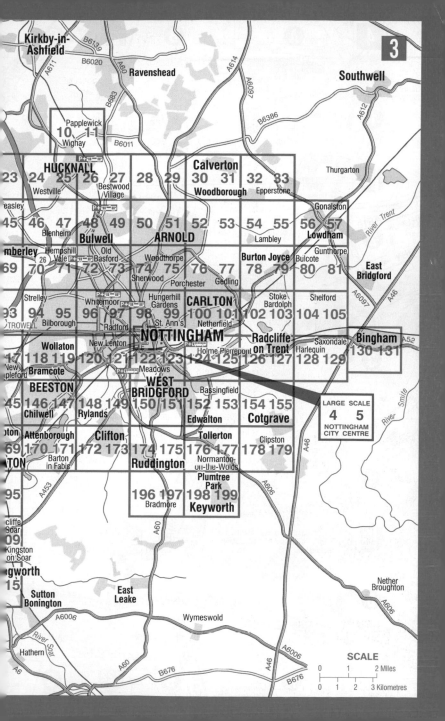

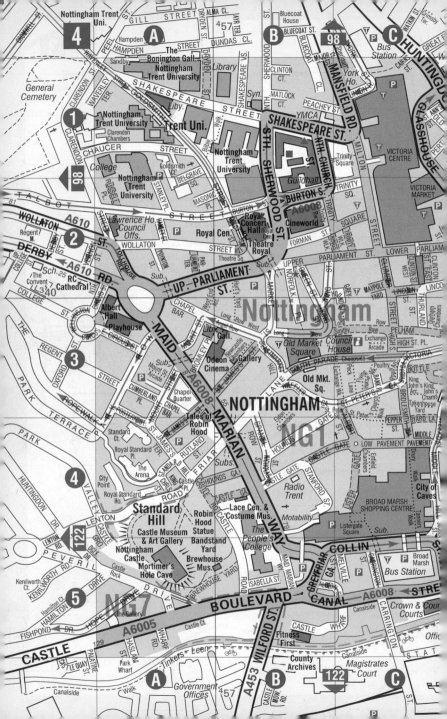

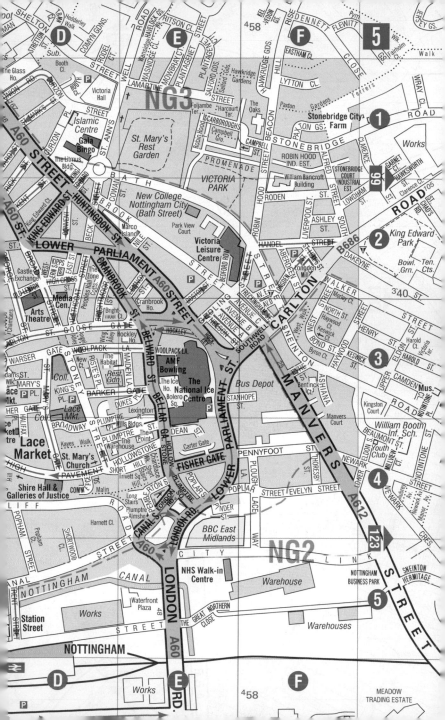

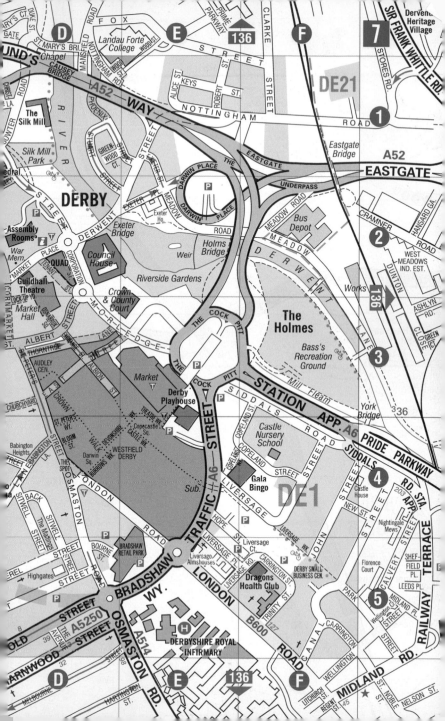

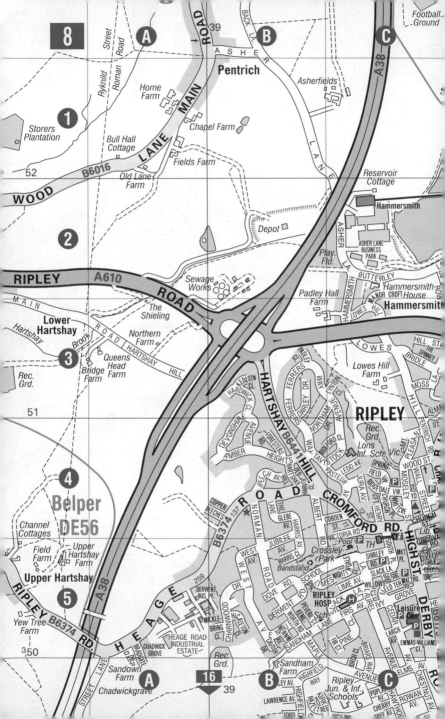

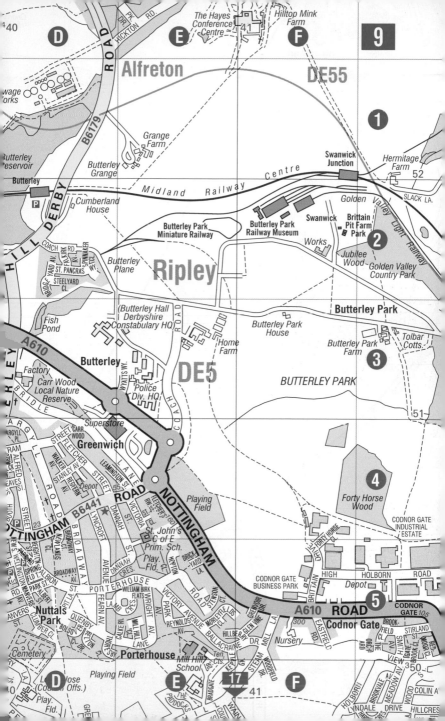

D
E
F

Newstead Grange 4 55

WAYE

Quarry (disused)

Kiln

Quarry

Jack o'Sherwood

Ford

B683

The Firs

1

BLIDWORTH

BREAK LA.

52

.Banks

Keeper's Lodge

Fish Pond

Old Quarry Banks

HALL

The Hermitage

Ten. Cts.

Top Farm

LANE

Weir Mills Farm

Fish Pond

Summerhouse Wood

Home Farm

Ten. Cts.

Nottingham

Iron Car Wood

Strawberry Hill Plantation

Play. Fld.

Pav.

BLIDWORTH

2

Quarry

Gray's Monument

HALL

King Edward's Plantation

Mason's Monument

Weirs

Papplewick Hall

WAYE

Weir

River

Weir

NG15

STREET

The Lodge

Mill Pond Plantation

Mortons Farm

Linby-cum-Papplewick C of E Prim. Sch.

School Plantation

Church Plantation

West View Court

West View Farm

3

B683

Papplewick

QUARRY

LINBY

Leen

B6011

BLACKSMITHS CT.

MAIN

LANE

The Poplars

FOREST B6011 LANE

51

Linby

Linby House

Castle Mill Farm

Dam Banks

Playgrd.

MOOR

4

Pump House

Weir

Moor Pond Wood

Papplewick Moor

The Mill House

LANE

HAYDEN

LANE

Victoria Gro.

CHURCH

ROAD

Great Northern Cotts.

OBEY CL.

BERNARD

FRANCES GRO.

SUSAN CL.

HAYDEN AV.

ALEXANDER

DAWN CL.

ETHEL

AVENUE

MARION AV.

DEVITT

CHRISTINE

DR.

LANE

PAPPLEWICK

B683

Grange Cottages

5

THE DRIFT

THE GATE

PARK LA.

CHURCH LANE

PRIM. Sch.

VAUGHAN

LEEN MILLS LA.

DRIVE

AVENUE

LYNMOOR CT.

Grange Farm

Papplewick Grange

GRANGE-MOOR

ROAD

BECK RD.

LINBY RD.

ICHLEY

WK.

ST. MICHAELS

BISHOPS

ROSSLYN PR.

DRIVE

BALMORAL

WIND

WAY

Leen Mills Prim. Sch.

Congel Hill

350

D
E
F

4 55

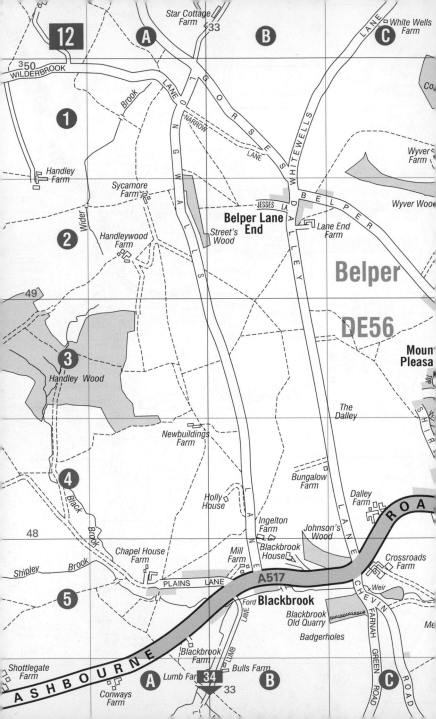

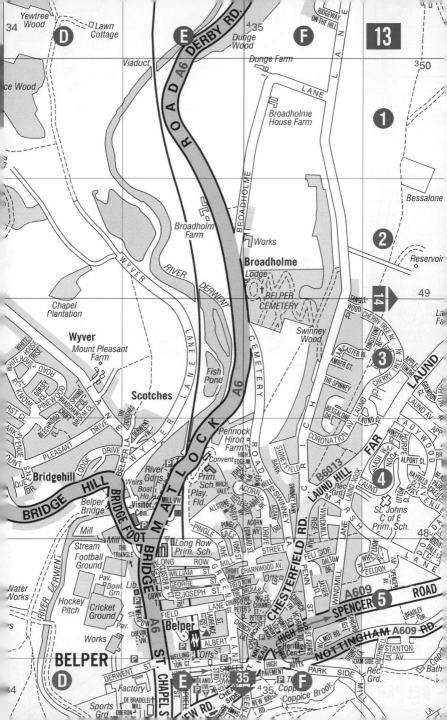

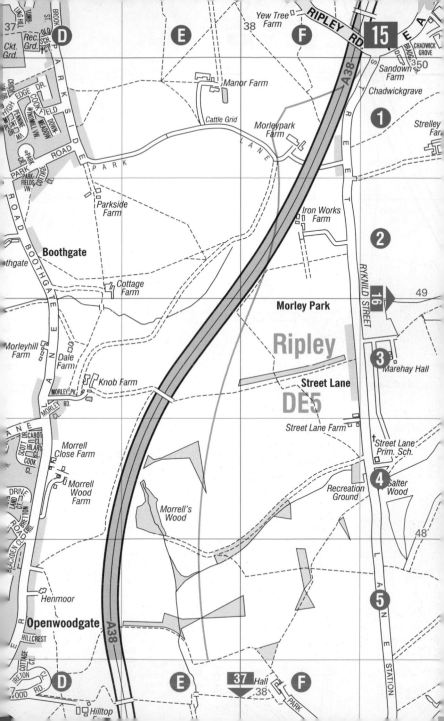

A
B
C

DHEAG

A38

DUDSLEY ROAD

HEAGE ROAD INDUSTRIAL ESTATE
CHADWICK GROVE
BRADGATE DR.

350

Sandown Farm
Chadwickgrave

1

Strelley Court Farm

Iron Works Farm

2

49

15

Morley Park

3

Street Lane

Street Lane Farm

† Street Lane Prim. Sch.

Salter Wood

4
Rec. Grd.

48

5

MICKLE...
39
OODROW

Rec. Grd.

Sandham Farm
STRELLEY AV.
LAWRENCE AV.
HIGHFIELD WAY
HIGHFIELD WAY
FORD CL.
HIGH MEADOW CL.
PEAR TREE WAY

DERWEN
PERIV...
FIRS AV.
SANDHAM
WORTH RD.
PINE
MAPLE

Ripley Jun. & Inf. Schools
POPLAR AV.
CHERRY TREE AV.
HOLLY AV.

HOSP...
Sch...
BIRCH RD.
BRIARS WAY
ELMS AVENUE

LAUREL
CEDAR
AVENUE
EMMAS-WILLIAMS CT.

Leisure Cen...
DERBY

CHESTNUT AV.

The Elms
HAWTHORN AV.
ROWAN AV.
SAMUEL CT.
SYCA...

AVENUE
CRESCENT
ASH
WILLOW
OAK AVENUE

Old Farm

ALMOND
SPOT CL.

Ckt. Grd.
Weston-spot.
BROOK
POPPYFI...
Bowl. Grn.

Norman Court Farm

WARMWELLS
BOWLER
THE GARDENS
BAMFORD S...

DOVEDALE CL.
LATHKIL
PEAKDO...
SWALLOW CT.
†

Rec. Grd.

UPPER
MAREHAY
BELLE VUE AV.
MULBERRY MEWS
BORDER BANK
PYGATE CL.
Works
ROAD

Marehay Hall

B6179

Sewage W...
Moun...

Slaughter Hou...

Stables

DERBY

A
38
39
B

Denby Pottery Visitor Centre

Pottery Works

C

THE COLLEGE

PARK

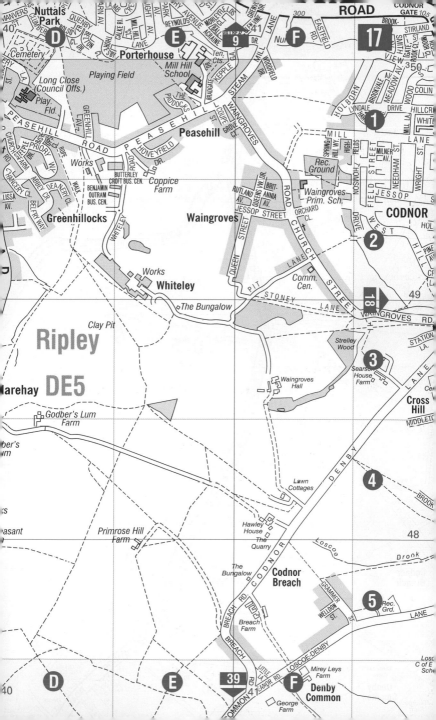

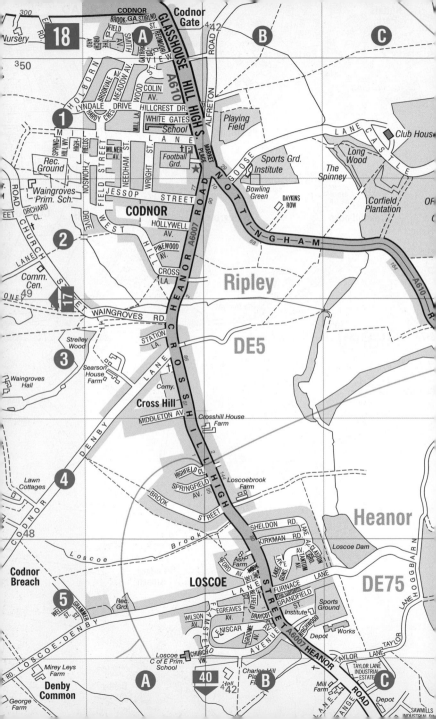

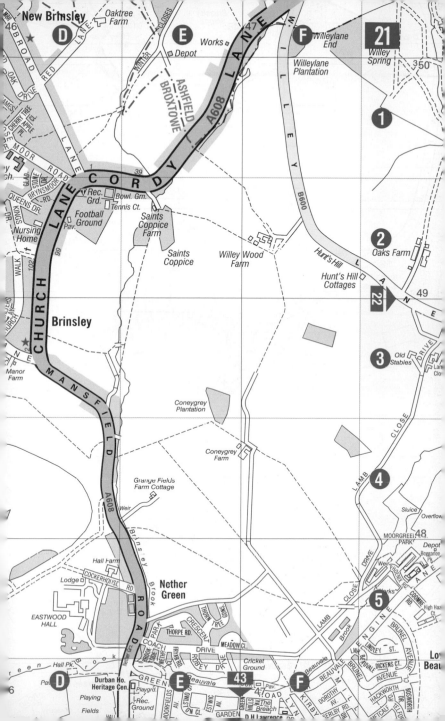

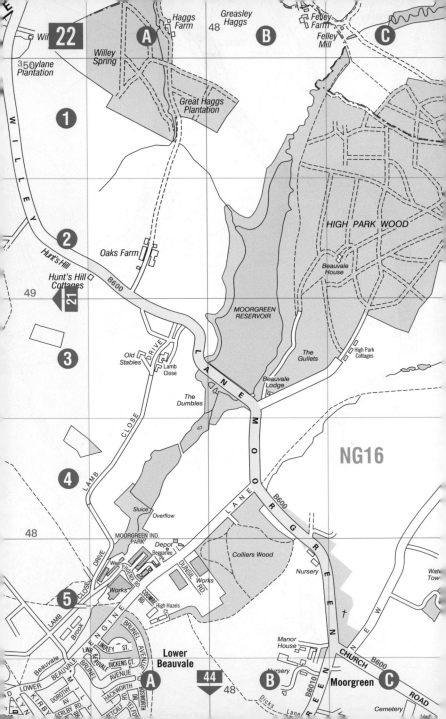

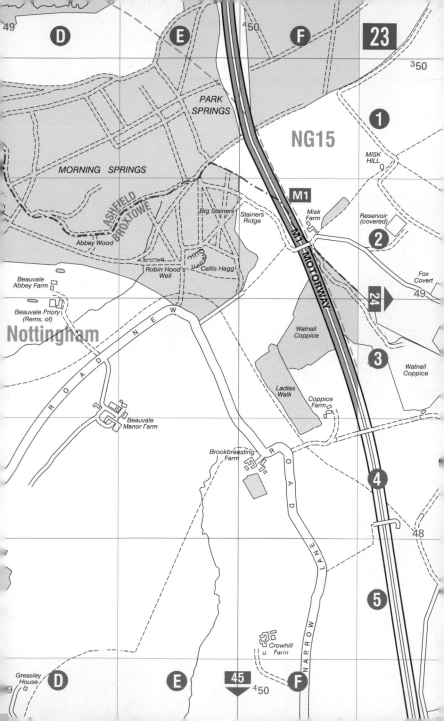

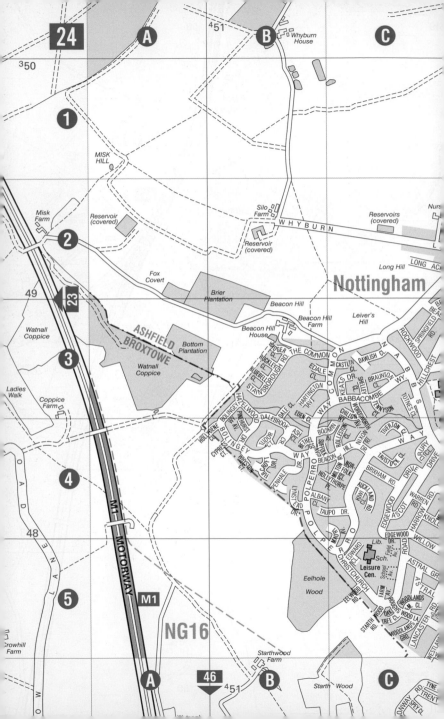

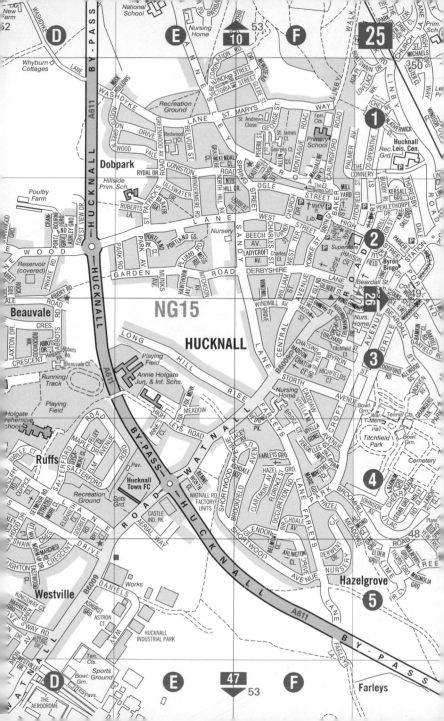

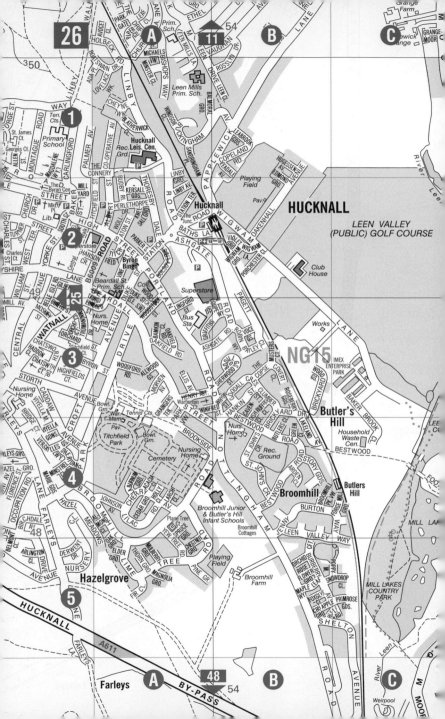

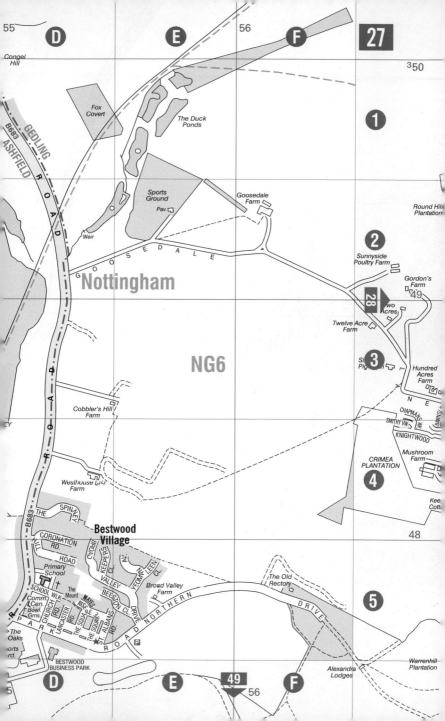

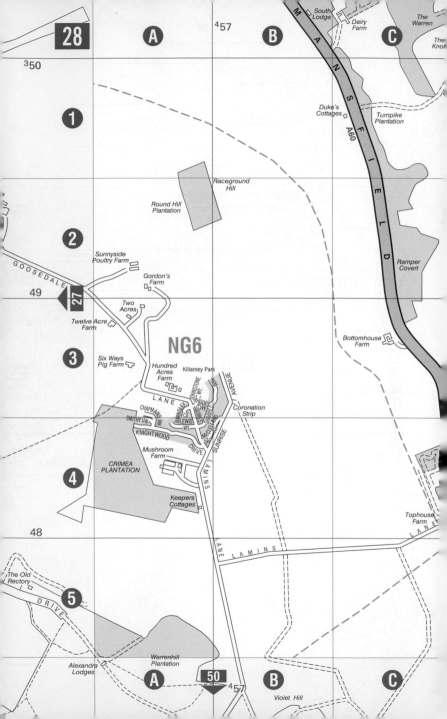

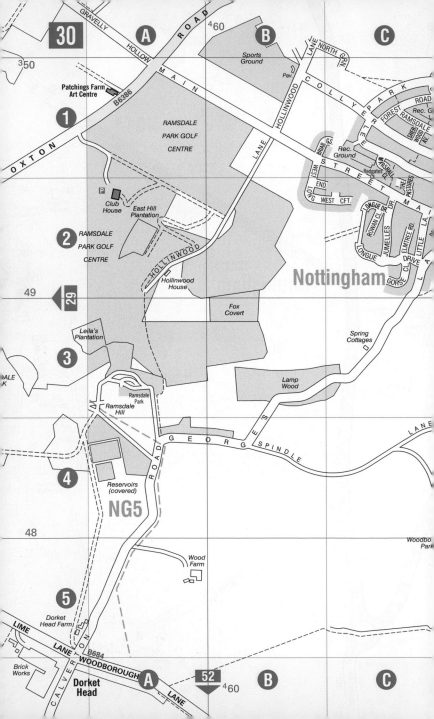

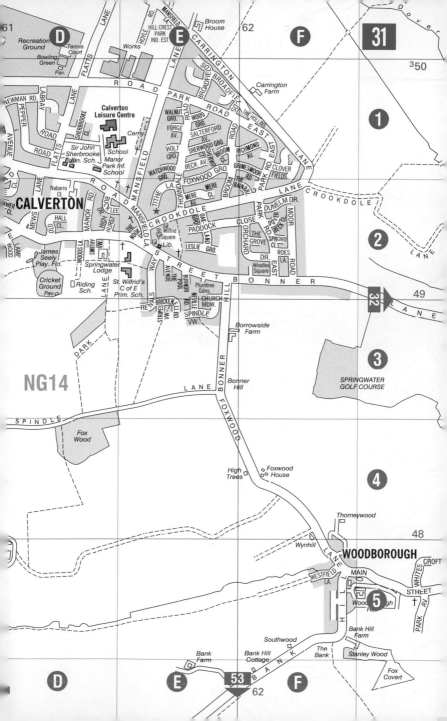

Hill Farm
Cottage

³50

Hill
Farm

1

Order

Beck

Cottage
Farm

Greenacres

2

Slaughter
House

Kennels

49

Nottingham

Chapel

NG14

Hill
House

Hill
House

Chapel
Farm

NEEPS
CFT.

3

CHURCH LA.

LANE

HAGG LANE

MAIN

EPPERSTONE

Epperstone Manor
(Notts. Constabulary HQ)

PADDOCK
FARM
COTTS.

Pav.

BLAND LA.

TOAD LA.

STREET

Sports
Ground

PARK LA.

Epperstone

The Old
House

HAGG

Shelt
Hill Farm

Fox
Covert

GONALSTON

4

Rifle
Range

Beck

Village
Hall Pav.

Epperstone
Playing
Field

48
LA.

Dover

LOWDHAM

Order

Wash Bridge

ROAD

Beck

A6097 BY-PASS

5

ROAD

Nursery

LANE

EPPERSTONE

AM

Woodlands

Eliment
Hill Farm

Nurs

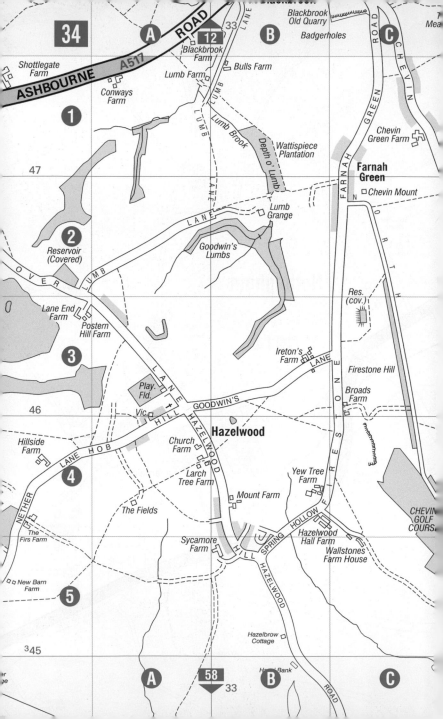

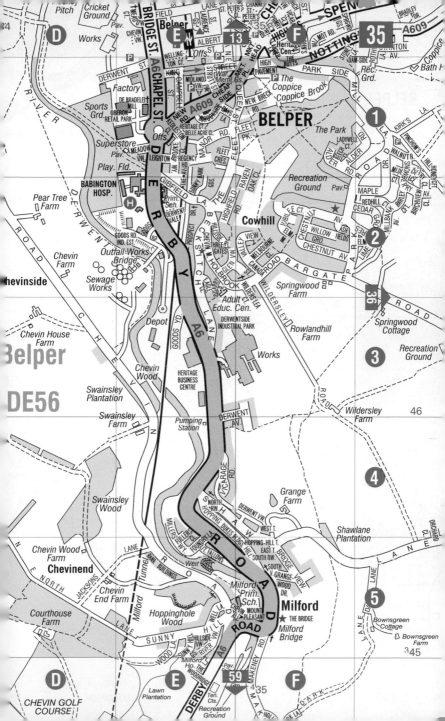

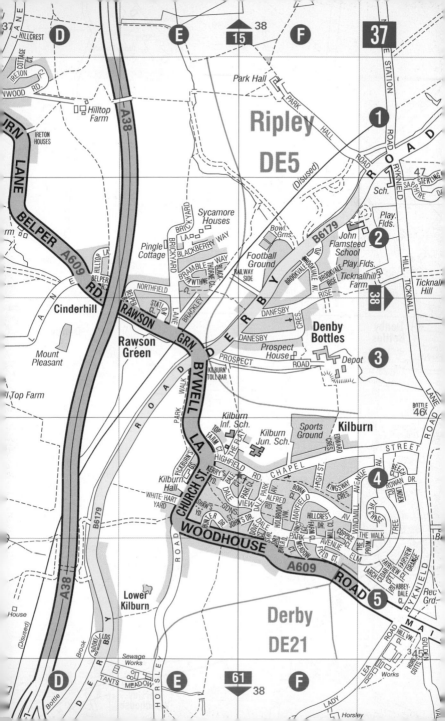

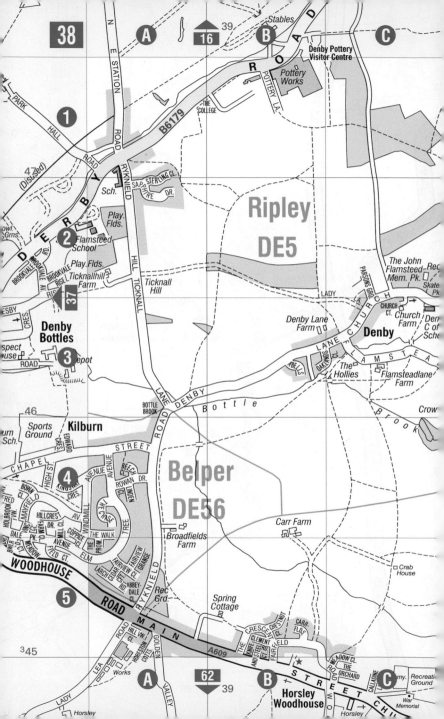

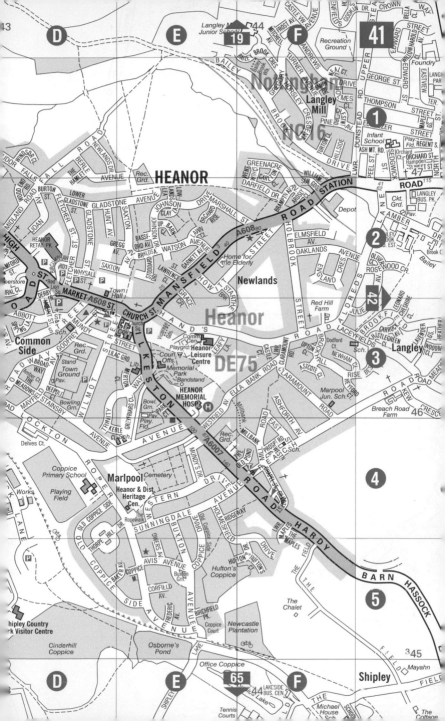

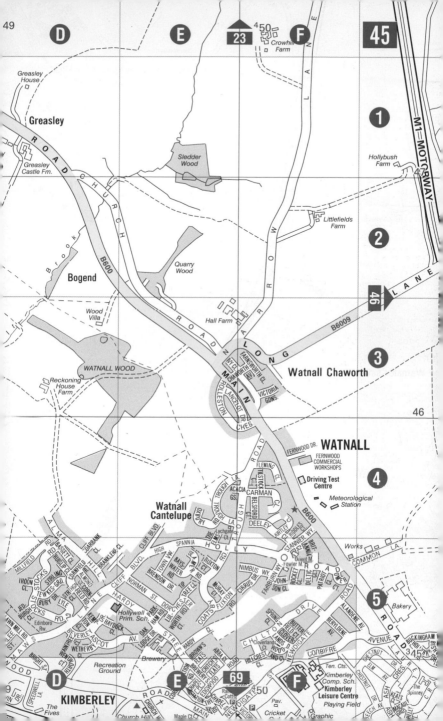

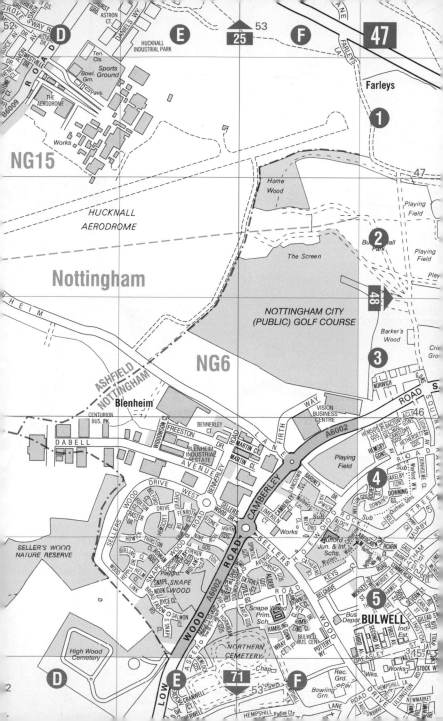

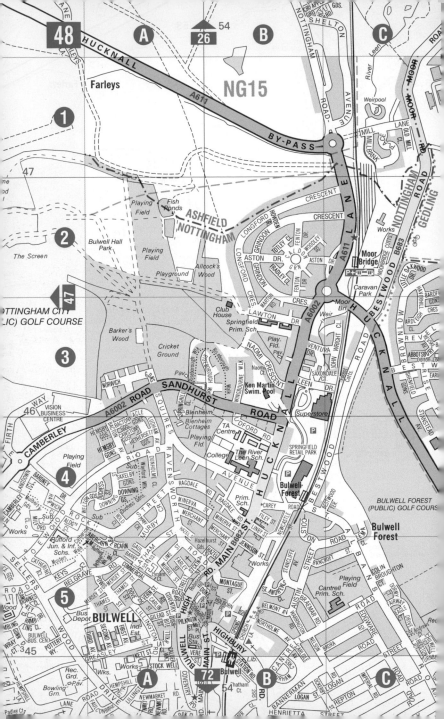

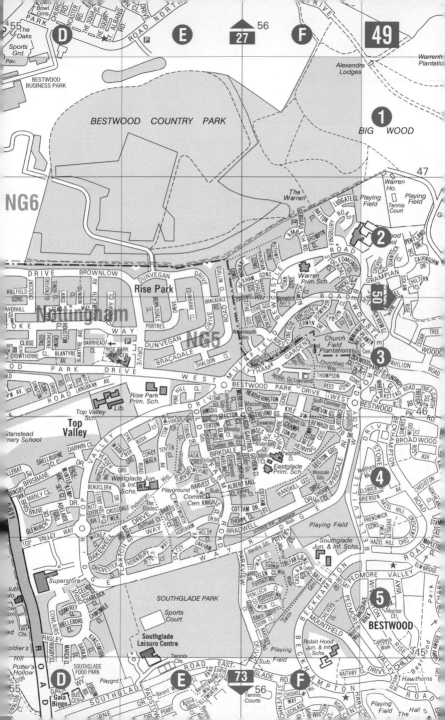

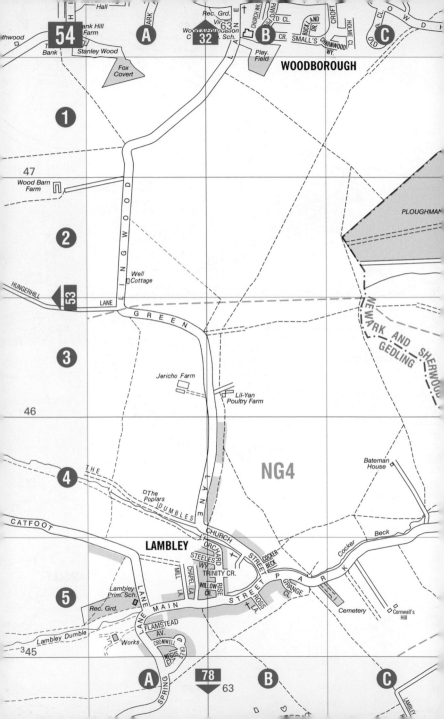

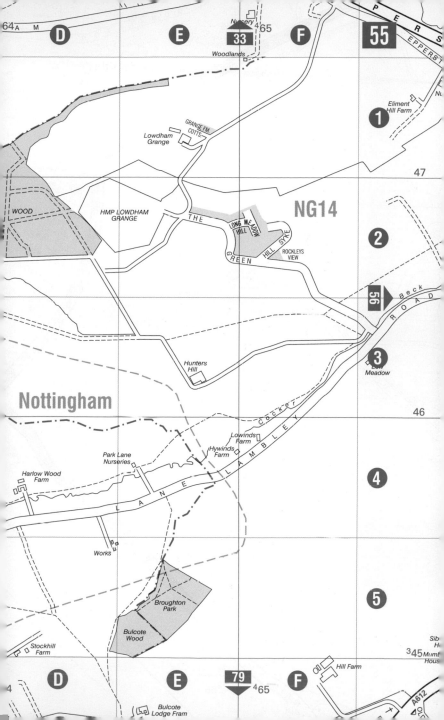

A

B

C

34 33

³45

Hazel
Cottage

Hazel Bank

1

Lapwing
Farm

Disused Railway

HAZELWOOD

Belper

BINK
NAY
CHEV

RICHMO

W I R K S W O R T H

2

Windley
Meadows

River

Ecclesbourne

DE56

Ceme

44

Brook
House

B5023

Duffield
Meadows

Meadows
Farm

ECCLESBOURNE
SEFTON WAY
MOULBOURN
WILLIAM
CL
CORNHILL
CL
MEADOWS

3

SNE

DUFFIELD

Duffield
The Meadows
Prim Sch

MEADOW
CR
PEPPERS
Meadows
Croft
BROOM
R
SPRIN
FIELD
HILL

Tennis
Court

FAIRLANKS

The Kirkstyles

VALE

WIRKS

4

Spring
Carr

Farnah
House

R O A D

B

Derby

W

CURZON

CAVEN
DISH

43

DE22

ROAD

CUMBERHILLS
GRANGE

5

Champion
Farm

A

82 33

B

CUMBERHILLS

Park
Leys

Celadon

C

Cumberhill
Farm

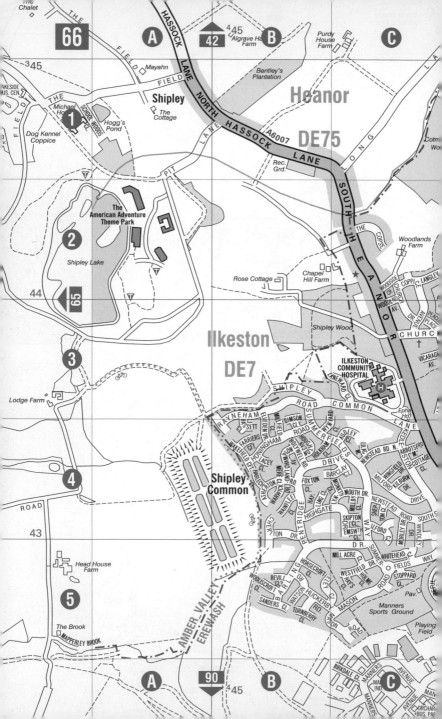

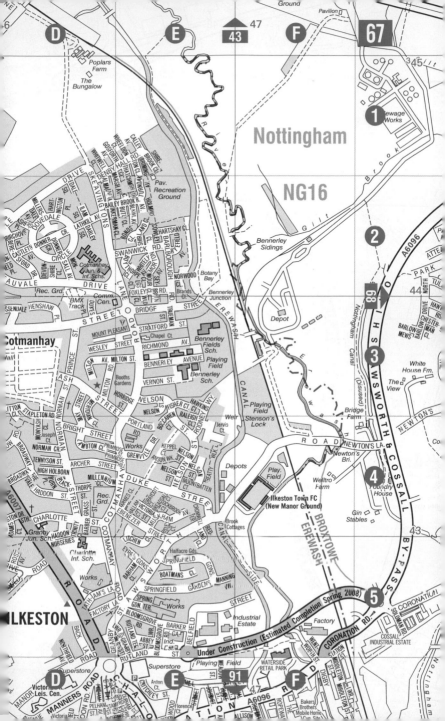

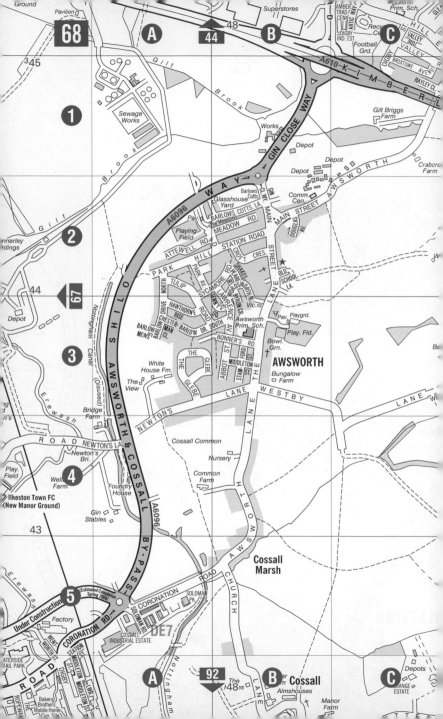

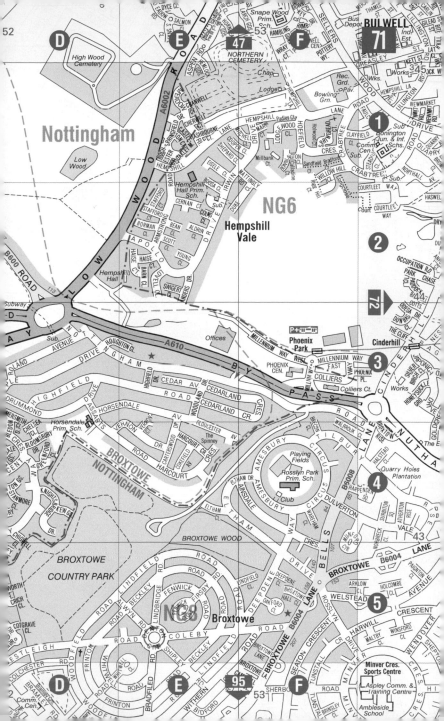

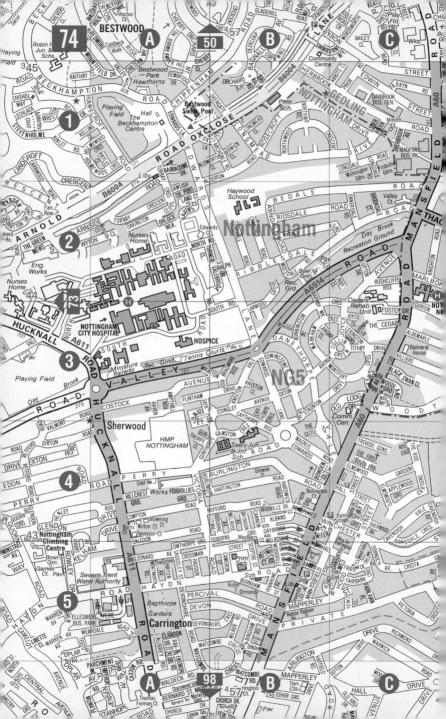

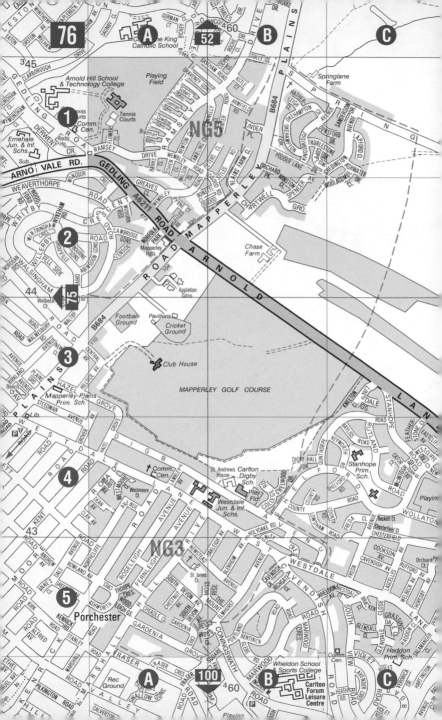

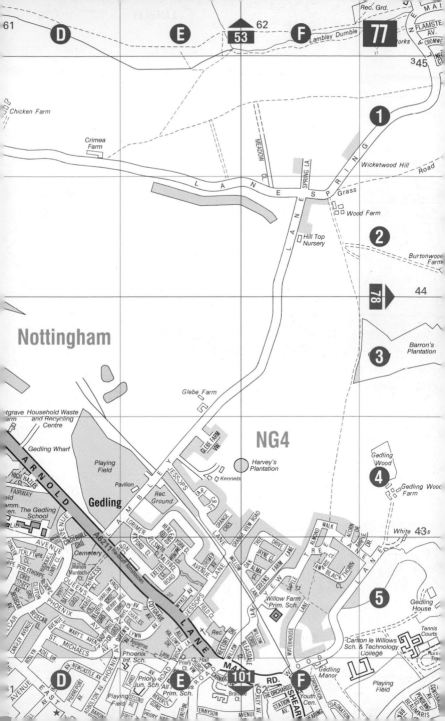

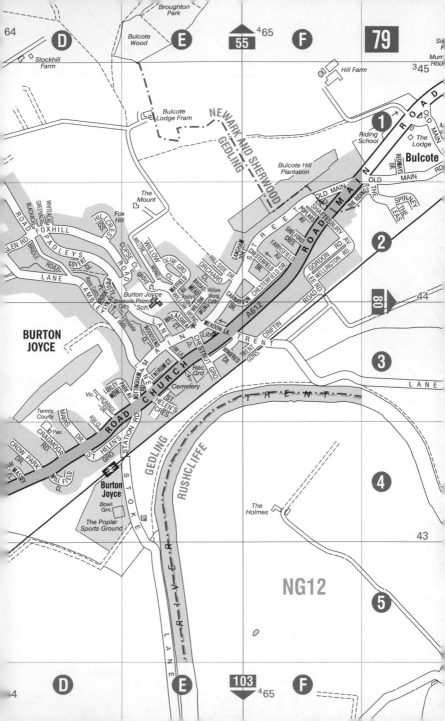

Silv
Mum
Hou

Broughton
Park

Bulcote
Wood

Stockhill
Farm

Hill Farm

Bulcote
Lodge Fram

NEWARK AND SHERWOOD
GEDLING

Riding
School

OLD MAIN ROAD

The
Lodge

Bulcote

REDMAYS DR.

OLD MAIN RD.

SPINNEY
THE LEAS

Bulcote Hill
Plantation

The
Mount

Fox
Hill

HILLCREST

WHITELAWS
GREENACRES
BLACKMOOR

ROAD

FOXHILL

PADLEYS

GLEN RD.
BRIDLE
ROAD
LANE
LAMBLEY

COVERT CL.
MISTY
CL.
PILTON

COPSE CL.

GROVE CL.

WILLOW CL.

WILLOW
WONG

OLIVE GRO.

ORCHARD
CL.

MAYFIELD
GRO.
Roslyn
BROAD
MEAD

CARNARVON
DR.

HILLSIDE DR.

LANGHAM
DR.

CHESTERFIELD
DR.

SHAFTESBURY AV.

POPLARS
AV.

SHELFORD
CRES.

FARNSFIELD
AV.

STREET

ROAD

OLD MAIN RD.

THE RIDINGS

GORDON RD.

WELLINGTON RD.

Burton Joyce
Brookside Prim.
Sch.

Rose Cottage

Fernside
Tennis
Cts.

WHEATSHEAF
CT.

WOODSEND
CL.

LIME LA.

Willow Wong
Cotts.

MEADOW LA.

Lib.

CHESTERFIELD DR.

CRIFTIN

A612

TRENT

TRENT GDNS.

WINIFRED
CR.

BURTON
JOYCE

80 ◄ 44

2

44

Vic.
LOXLEY DR.
VICARAGE CL.

CHESTNUT GRO.

PARK AV.

LENDRUM CT.

Hec.
Grd.

Cemetery

ST. HELEN'S CRES.

ROAD

CHURCH

ABBEY
MEWS

MAIN
WRIGHTSON
GDNS.

TRENT

LANE

3

Tennis
Courts

CRAGMOOR RD.

CROW PARK DR.

MASSEY DR.

Pav.

MILL FLD.
CL.

ST. HELEN'S GRO.

STATION RD.

GEDLING

RUSHCLIFFE

LANE

The
Holmes

4

43

Burton
Joyce

Bowl.
Grn.

The Poplar
Sports Ground

P

RIVER

LANE

STOKE

NG12

5

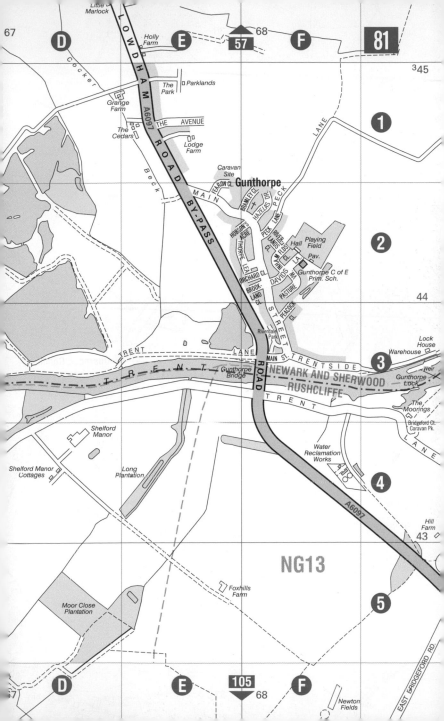

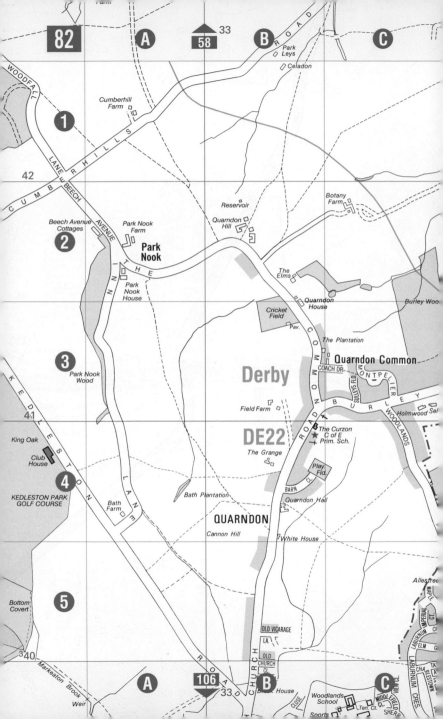

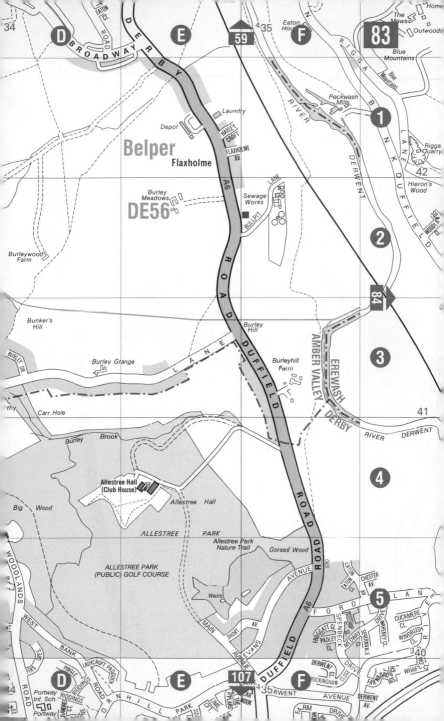

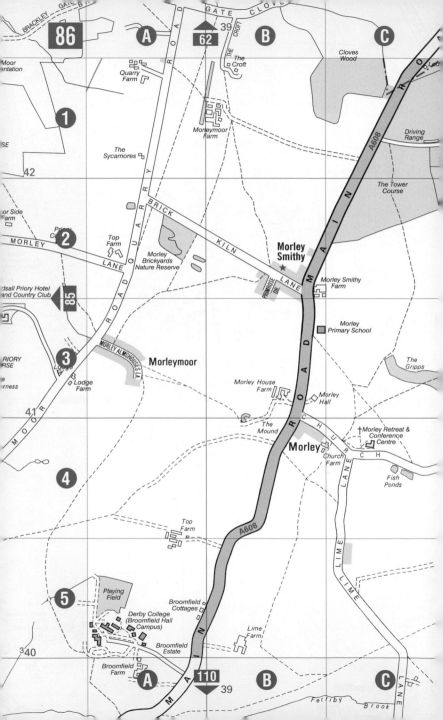

Tudor Lodge

Morley Manor

40

D

Feran Hayes

E

Club Room Farm

41

63

SPENCER ST.

GLENDON DR.

WILLOW CL.

BLUNT CL.

SNARDALE CL.

DANEFIELD CT.

STREET

BELPER

F

COMMON FIELDS CL.

TANGLEY AV.

A609

87

Morleyhayes Wood

Smalley Common

A609

ROAD

THE HOPEWALK

Club House

MORLEY HAYES GOLF COURSE
The Manor Course

★

1

Stanley Common C of E Prim. Sch.

HAYESWOOD

HILL CL.

VALLEY VIEW DR.

BARKER CL.

THE LANE

Rec. Grd.

42

CR. WY. CH.

Hayes Wood Lodge Farm

Stanley Common

Little Wood

Hayeswood Farm

Stanley Lodge Farm

2

Vall Cotta

88

Ilkeston

Hayes Park Farm

Park Farm

Briggswood Farm

3

COMMON

LANE

41

DE7

MOSES LANE

4

MORLEY

COMMON LA.

Spring Oak Farm

Brook House Farm

Whitehouse Farm

LANE S

ROAD

Jesse Farm

Stanley Farm

Th. H.

5

DAL

40

D

E

111

41

F

Ma Farm

40

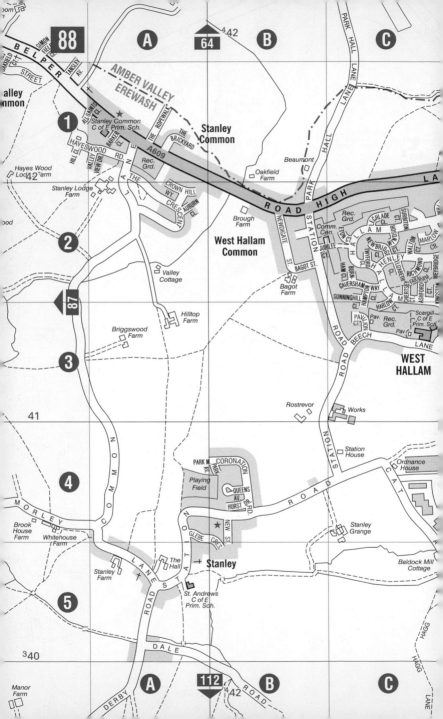

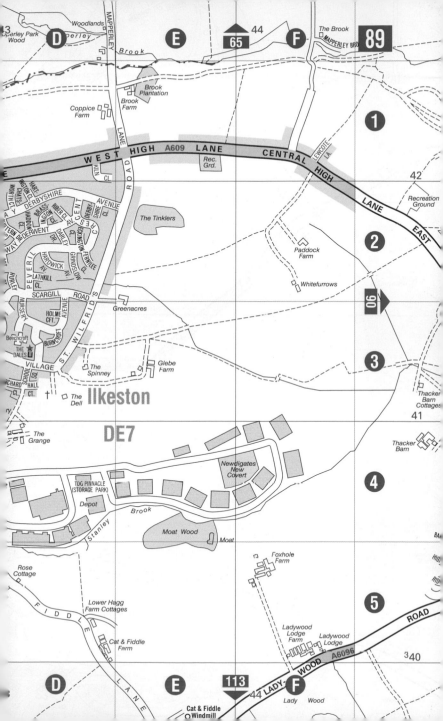

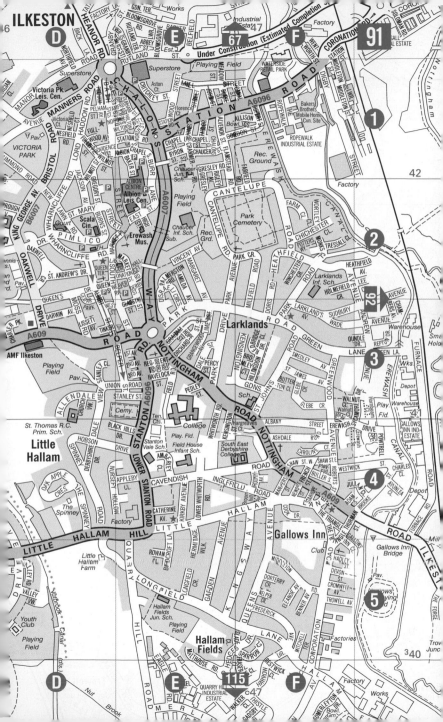

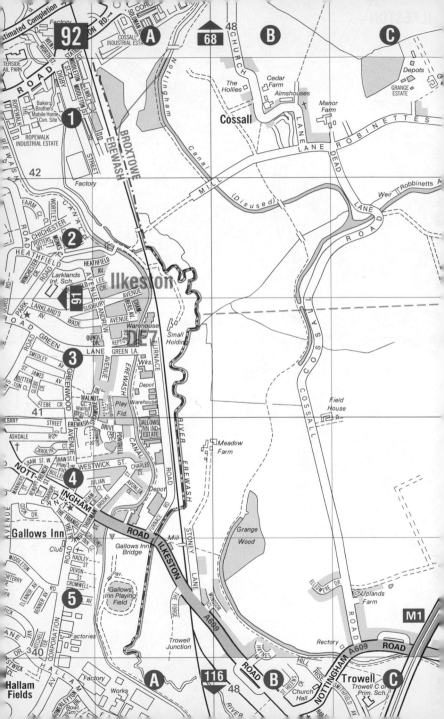

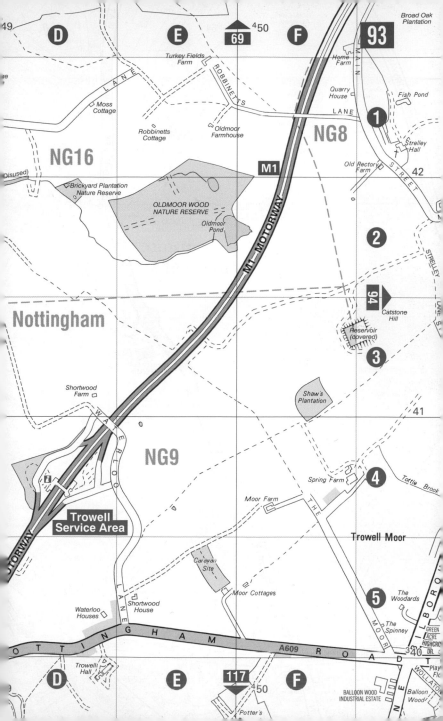

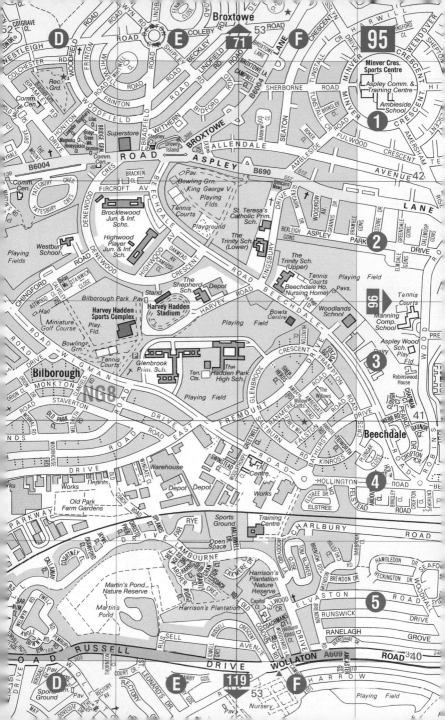

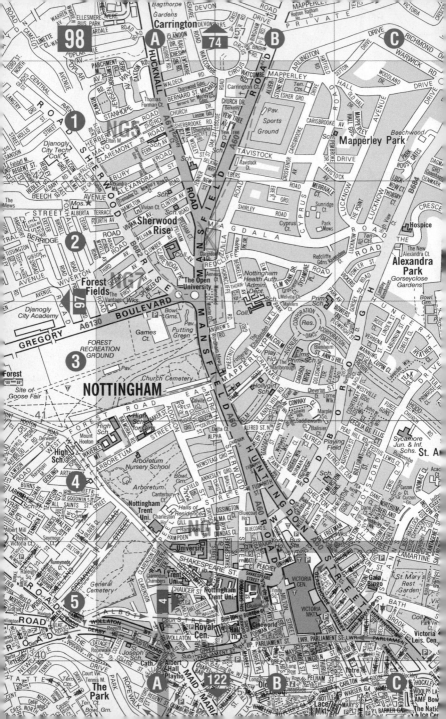

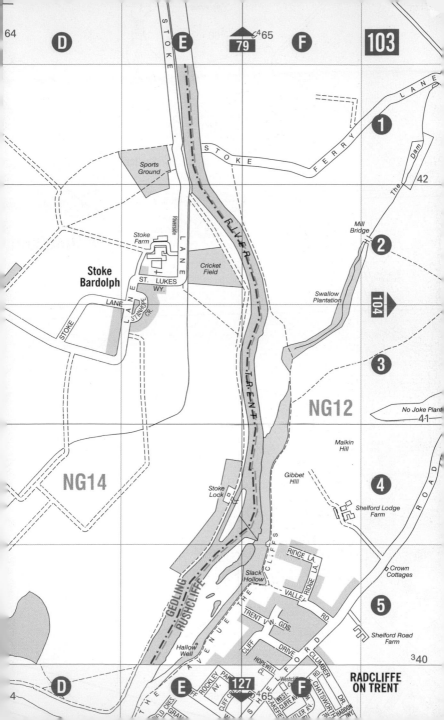

Sports Ground

STOKE FERRY LANE

1

The Dam

42

Mill Bridge

2

STOKE

RIVERSIDE LANE

Stoke Farm

Stoke Bardolph

Cricket Field

ST. LUKES WY.

STANHOPE CR.

STOKE LANE

LANE

R I V E R

Swallow Plantation

104

3

NG12

No Joke Plant

41

Malkin Hill

Gibbet Hill

NG14

Stoke Lock

T R E N T

4

Shelford Lodge Farm

Crown Cottages

5

Shelford Road Farm

GEDLING

RUSHCLIFFE

Hallow Well

Slack Hollow

THE CLIFFS

RIDGE LA.

RIDGE LA.

VALLEY RD.

TRENT VW. GDS.

CLIFF DRIVE

THE AVENUE

CLUMBER RD

ROAD

340

HOPEWELL CL.

Westcliffe

RADCLIFFE ON TRENT

ROCKLEY AV.

PARK AV.

CLIFF CRES.

CHATSWORTH RD

BUTLER AV.

WEST CLIFFE AV.

HADDON TWY.

DR.

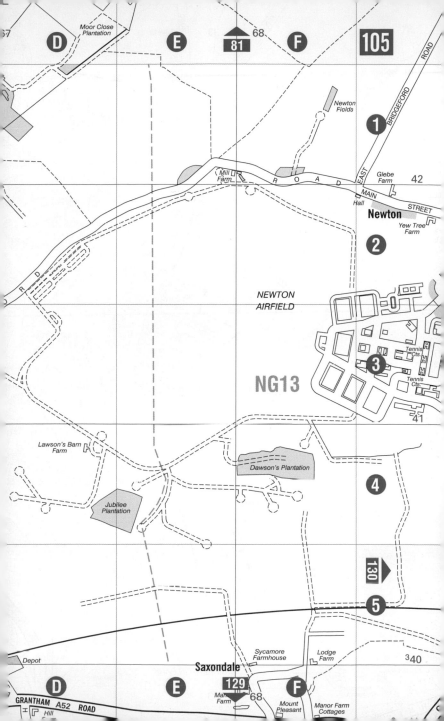

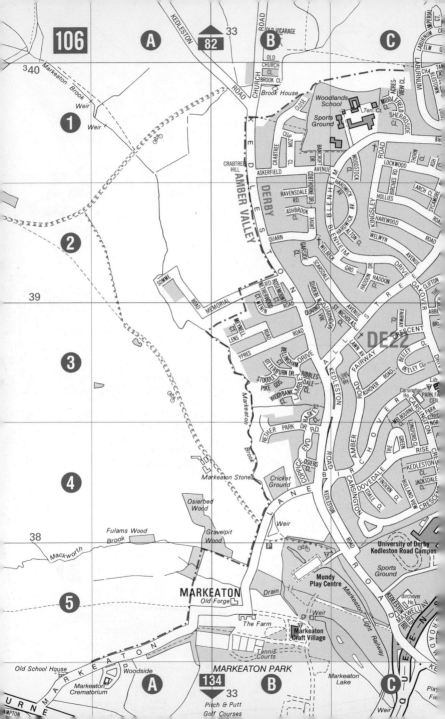

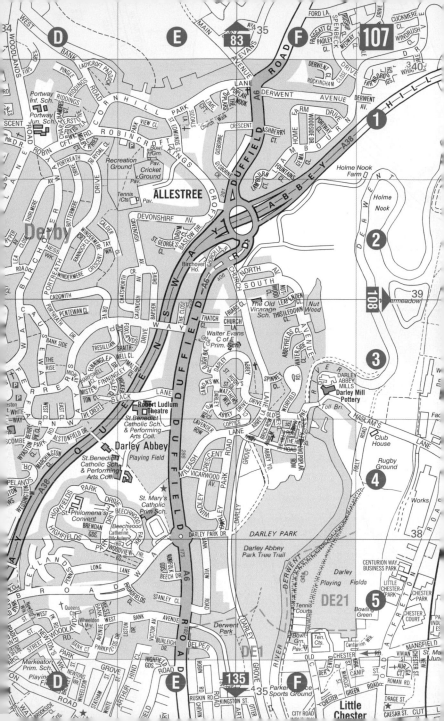

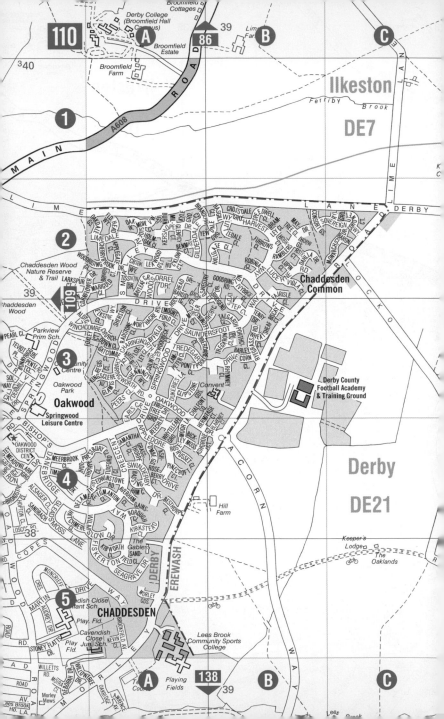

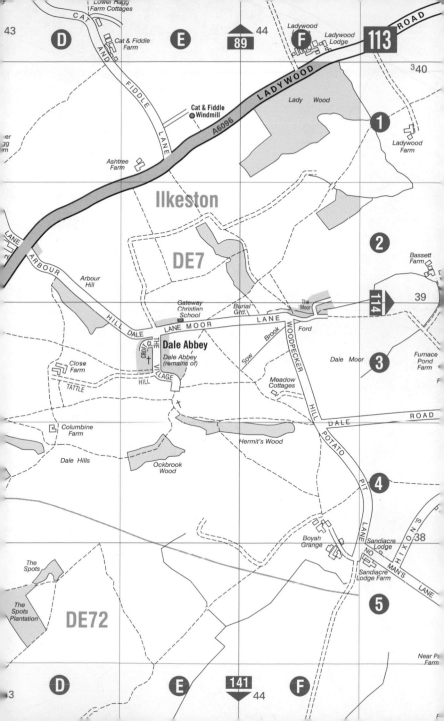

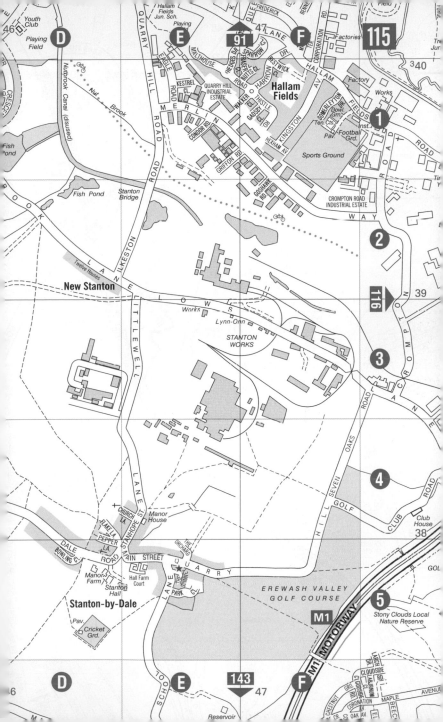

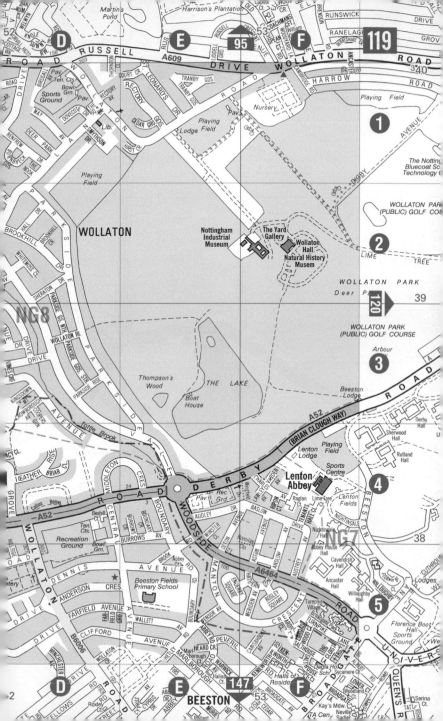

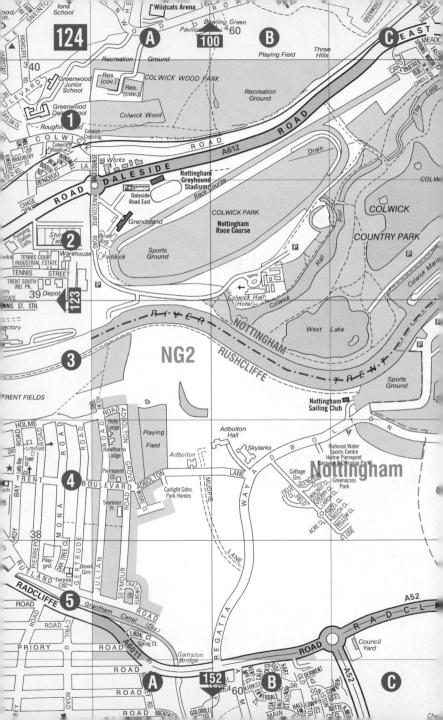

A

102 63

B

C

PRIVATE ROAD

NG4

1

Water Ski
Lagoon

GEDLING

RIVER

RUSHCLIFFE

Viaduct

Brook

ISLAND

HOLME PIERREPONT
COUNTRY PARK

Polser

LAN

2

Holme
Pierrepont
Hall

The Firs

HOLME

HOLME
PIERREPONT

Home Farm

Nottingham

SANDY

39
ADBOLTON

125

LANE

The Rectory

3

RSPCA
Animal Shelter

Nottingham

ROAD

GRA

Polser Brook

Cedar Lodge
Caravan Park

LEES

BAR

LANE

Pav.
Sports
Ground

4

A52

Holme
House

Lamcote
Field

Polser
Bridge

RADCLIFFE

STRAGGLETHORPE

38

5

Landfill Waste Site

Thorntons Holt
Camping Park

Polser

MAIN

Shepherd's
Houses

ROAD

A

154 63

B

C

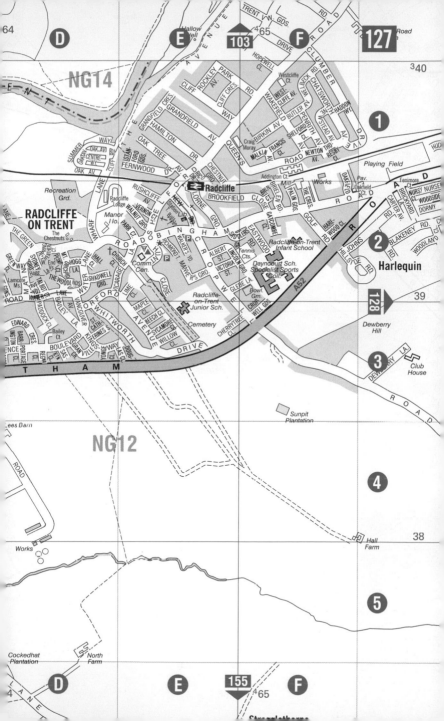

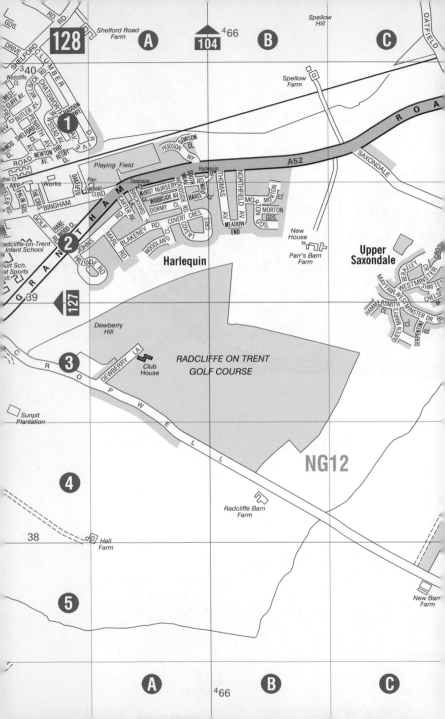

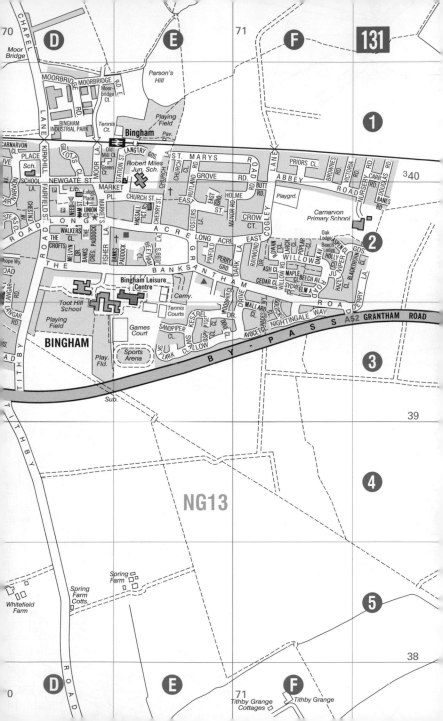

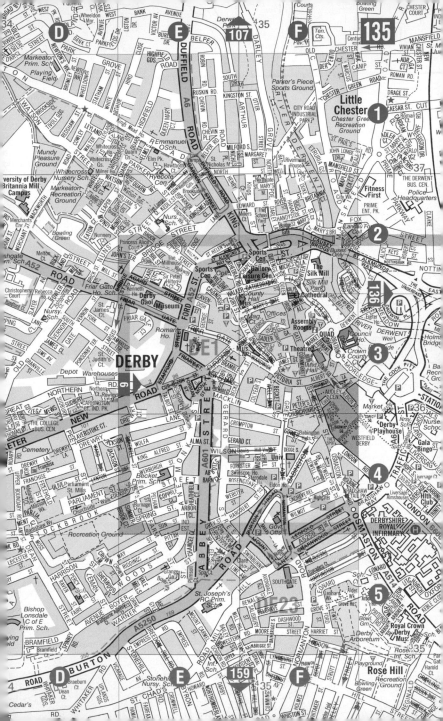

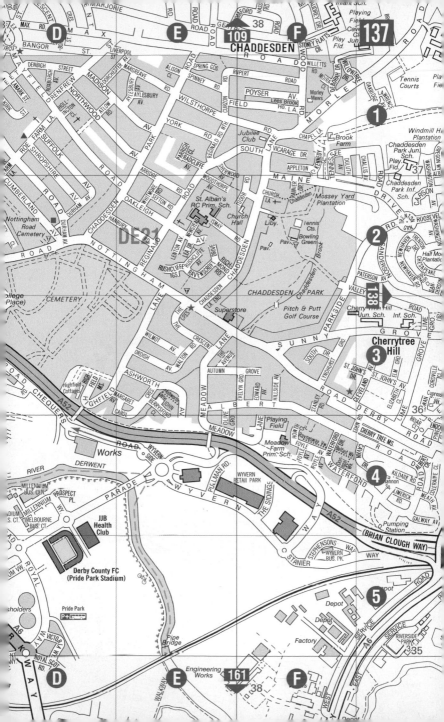

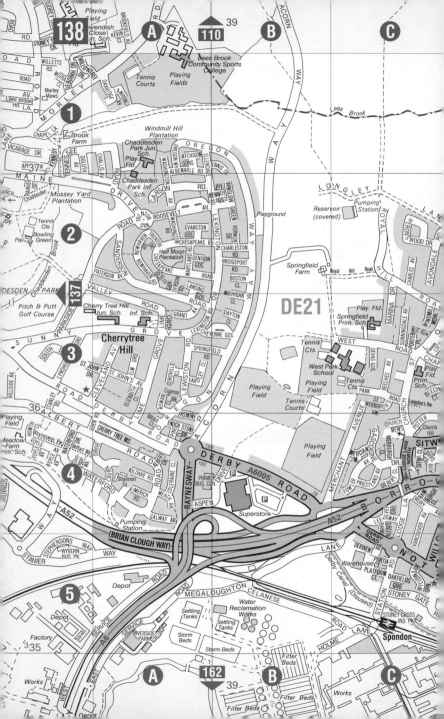

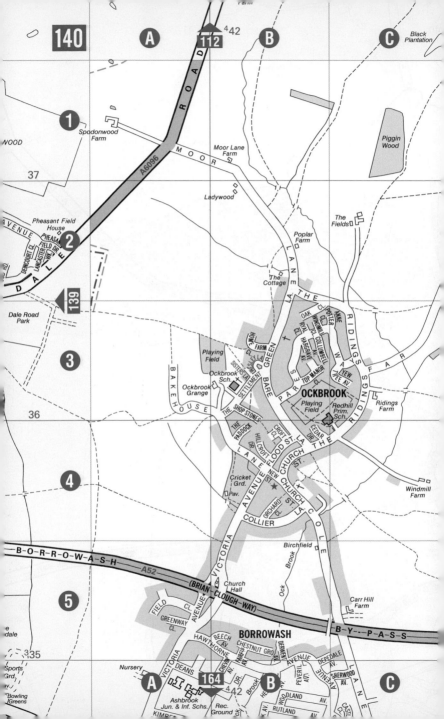

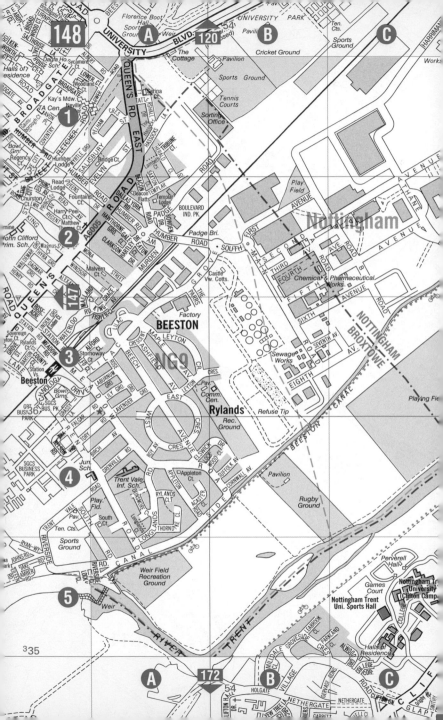

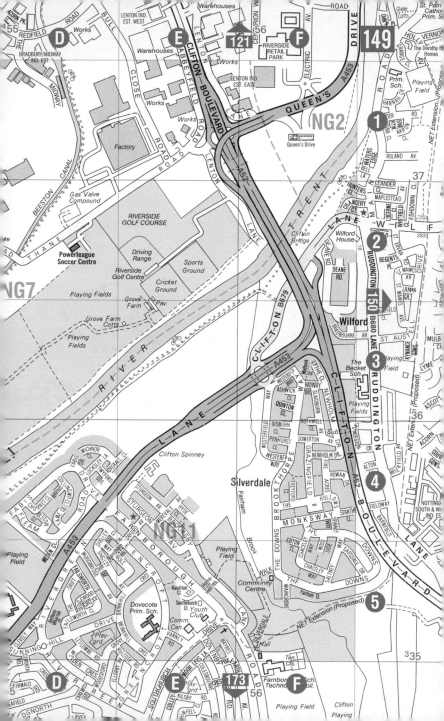

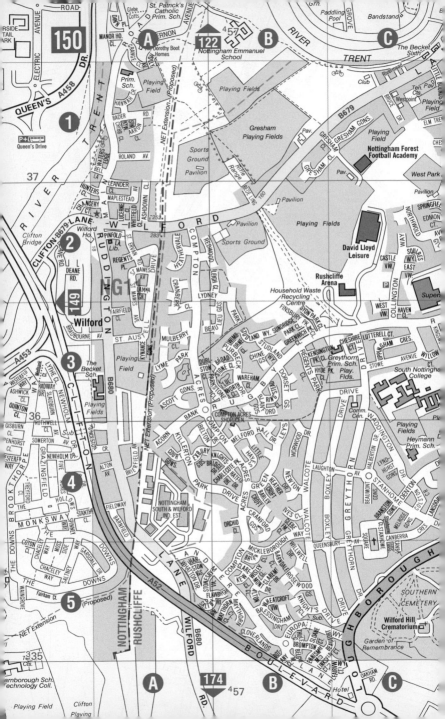

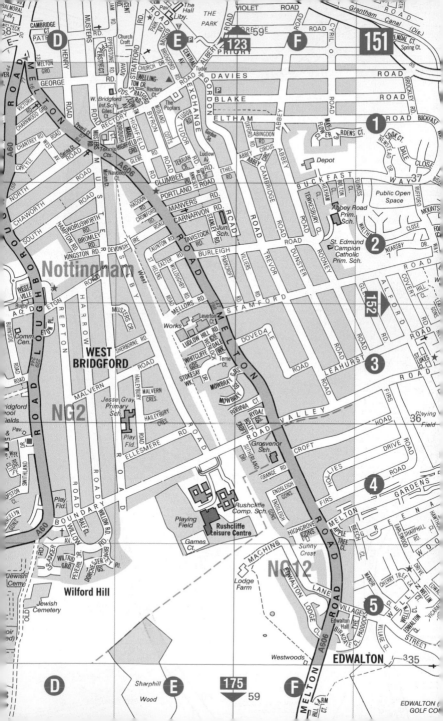

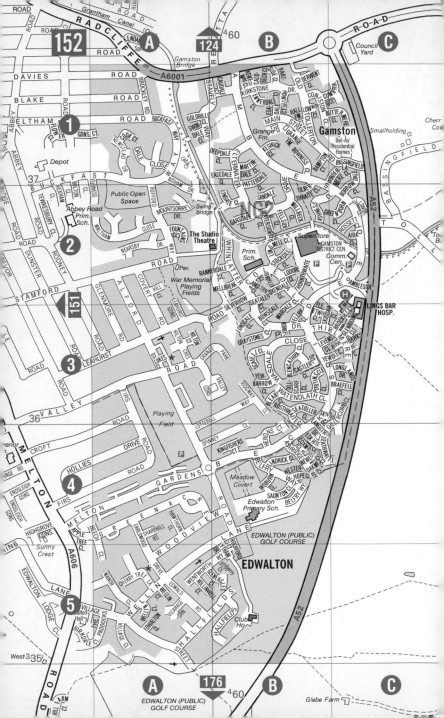

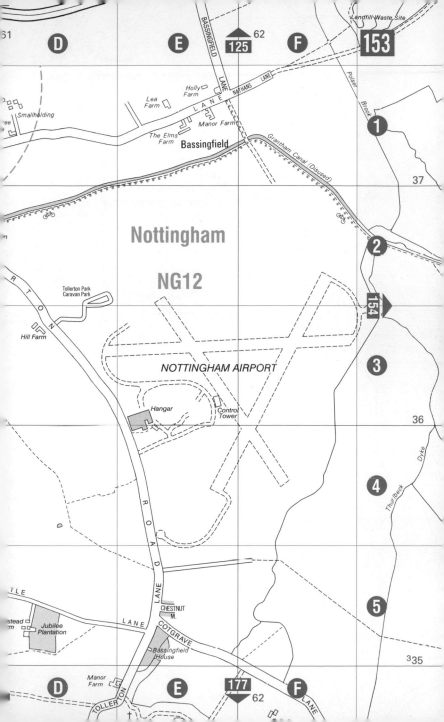

154

A

126 63

B

C Thorntons Holt Camping Park

Landfill Waste Site

S T R A G G L E

Shepherd's Houses

M A I N

Polser Brook

1

Grantham Canal (Disused)

37

Cotgrave Place

Club House

COTGRAVE PLACE

GOLF & COUNTRY CLUB

R O A D

2

153

Lock House

LAN

3

PEASHILL

36

Peashill Farm

Dyke

Thulibeck

4

WOODGATE

Sev Wel

5

335

A

178 63

B

C PLUM

D

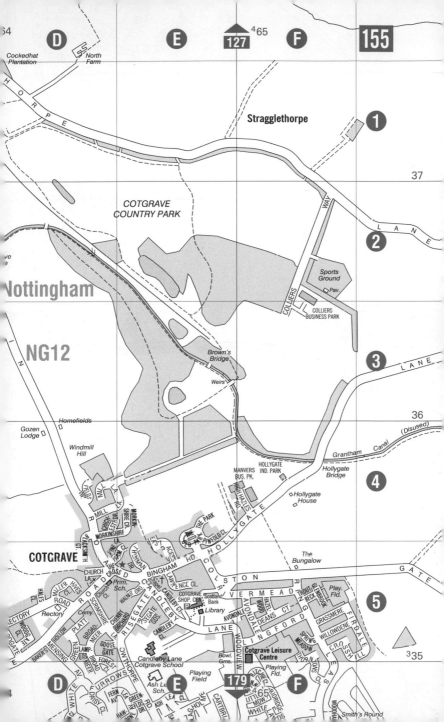

D **E** 127 465 **F**

1

Cockedhat Plantation

North Farm

THORPE

Stragglethorpe

37

WAY

LANE

2

COTGRAVE COUNTRY PARK

Sports Ground

Pav.

COLLIERS

COLLIERS BUSINESS PARK

Nottingham

NG12

Brown's Bridge

Weirs

3

LANE

36

(Disused)

Homefields

Gozen Lodge

Windmill Hill

Grantham Canal

Hollygate Bridge

MANVERS BUS. PK.

HOLLYGATE IND. PARK

Hollygate House

4

Hollygate

MILL

MORKIN-SHIRE CR.

MORKINSHIRE LA.

THE PARK

PINFOLD CL.

HOLLYGATE

COTGRAVE

CHURCH LA.

Prim. Sch.

BINGHAM

CANDLEBY

COLSTON

The Bungalow

GATE

CROSS

NCE. CL.

COTGRAVE SHOP. CEN.

Scotland Bank

Library

VERMEAD

AVONDALE

HAZEL WOOD

DEANS CT.

Play. Fld.

5

RISEGATE

RECTORY

Rectory

Cerny

HALES

MILLER CL.

ROAD

CHERRY ORCHARD

WALNUT GR.

PYGATE

CANDLEBY

AVONDALE

LANE

WOODVIEW

LINGFORD

SPRING MEADOW

GRASSMERE

WILLOWDENE

FIRDALE

CRO SSHILL

335

WOODS

HALES

WOODCROFT

PLATT

BROAD-MEER

GREEN

CHERRY CL.

LOS

FOREST

GOOSE GATE

COWTHORPE

Candleby Lane Cotgrave School

Bowl. Grns.

Cotgrave Leisure Centre

SPRINGS

THORNS

D

FURROWS

WHITE

DAISY CL.

BAKER'S

HENSING

GREEN

FERN AV.

GREEN-FLDS. DR.

Ash Le. Sch.

E

Playing Field

179 465

ATCHLE

WHA

CART-BRID

Playing Fld.

F

WHITE

MDW.

LITTLE

WHITE

LEAS

WOODH

Smith's Round

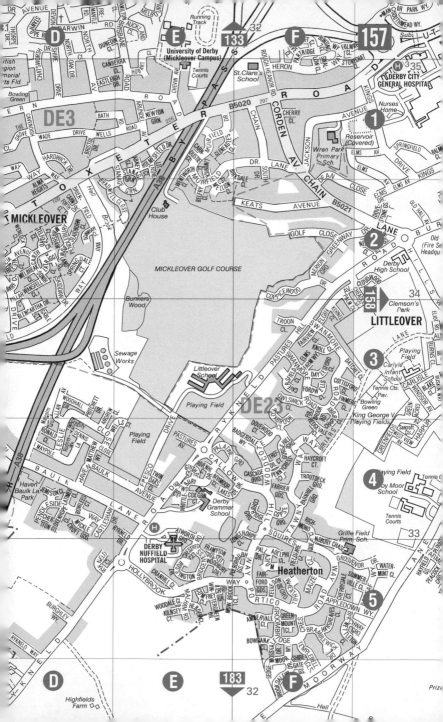

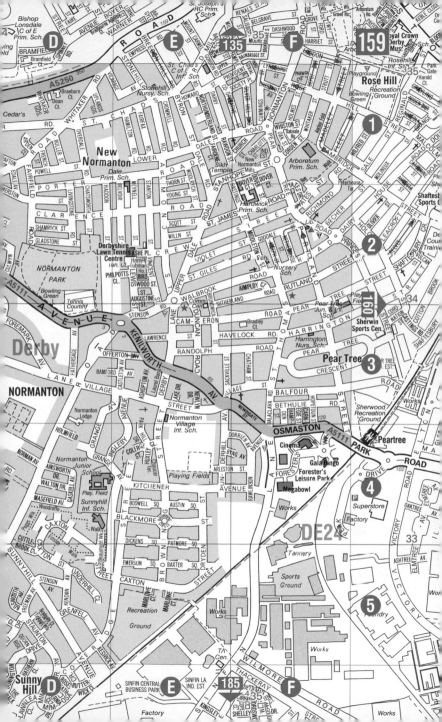

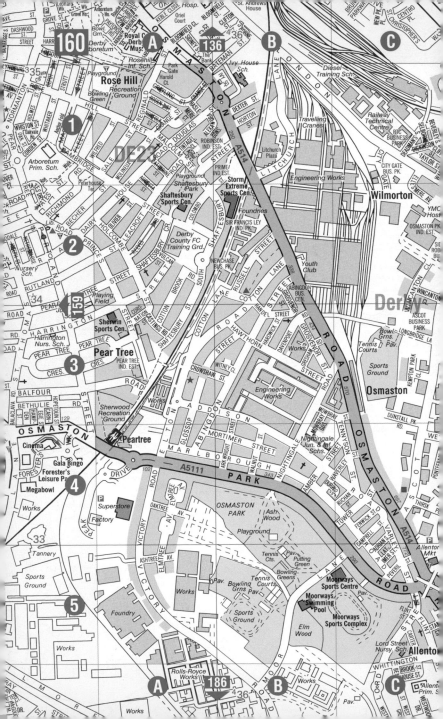

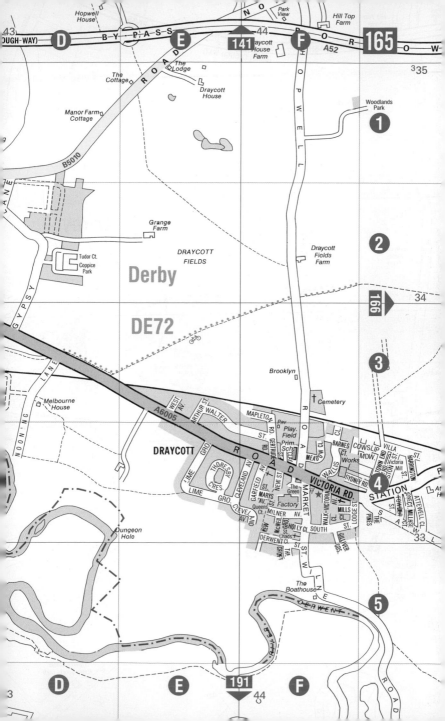

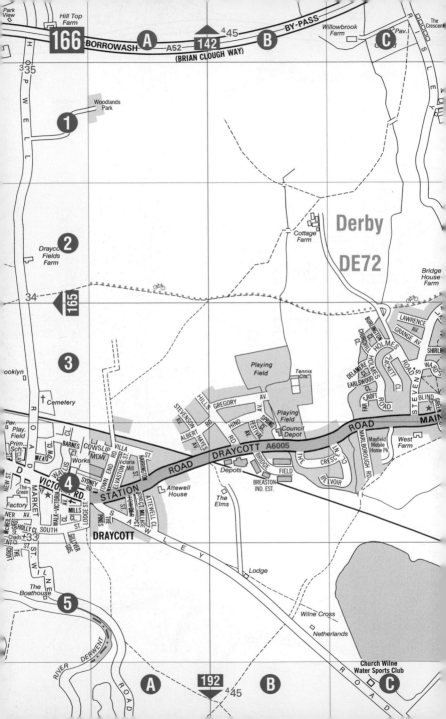

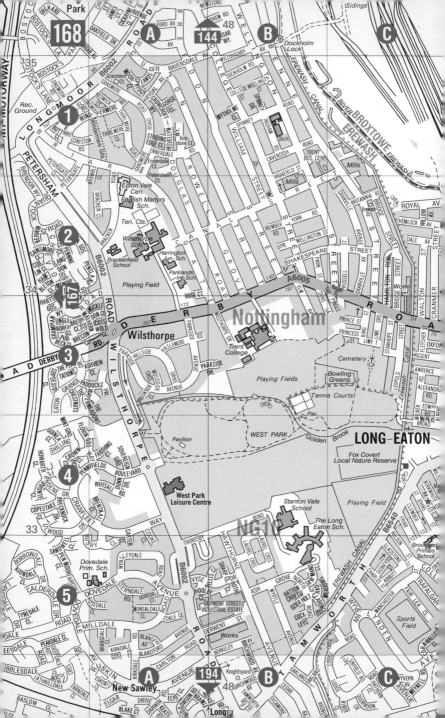

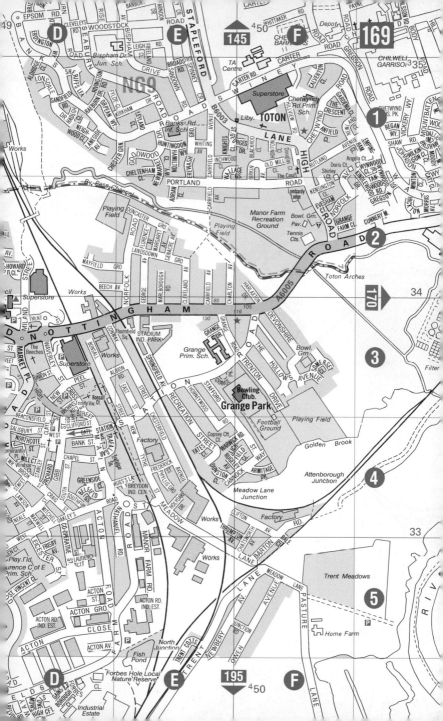

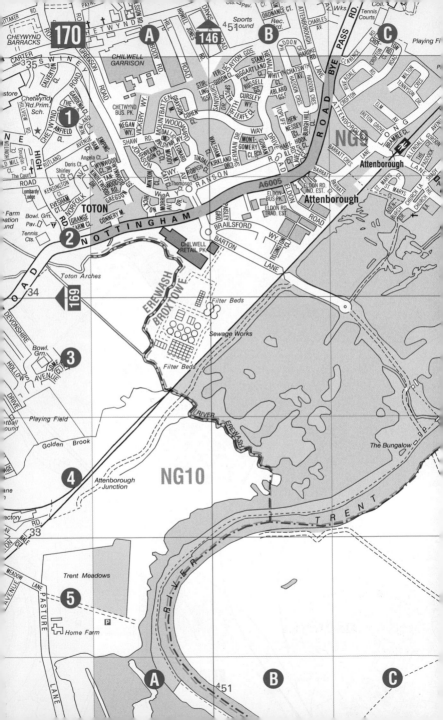

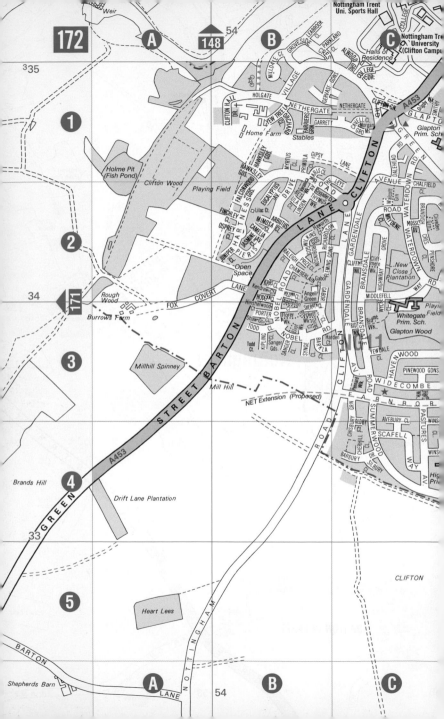

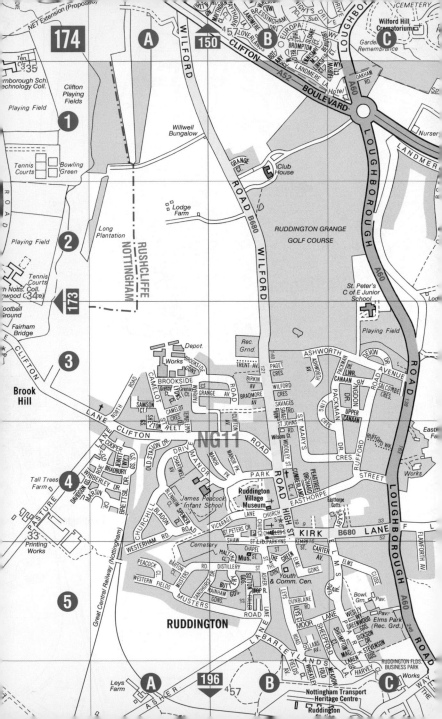

176

EDWALTON

Westwoods
335

152

460

Club Ho.

B

C

ROAD

HILL FARM CT.

1

EDWALTON (PUBLIC)
GOLF COURSE

Glebe Farm

A52

A606

MELTON

Sewage
Works

Play.
Field

TOLLERTON

PRIORY
CIRCUS

PRIORY
AVENUE

BURNSIDE

LOTHIAN RD.

LENTON

FRANKLIN DR.

HIGH

Toll Bar
House

LANE

2

M E L T O N

A606

175

34

3

BENTINCK

STANSTEAD

STELLA AV.

STELLA
GRO.

STELLA
AV.

SEDGLEY

ORCHARD CL.

MUIR

Nottingham

4

ire
rm

Flawford
House

33

5

NG11

Barn
Farm

A

198

460

B

C

BRADMO

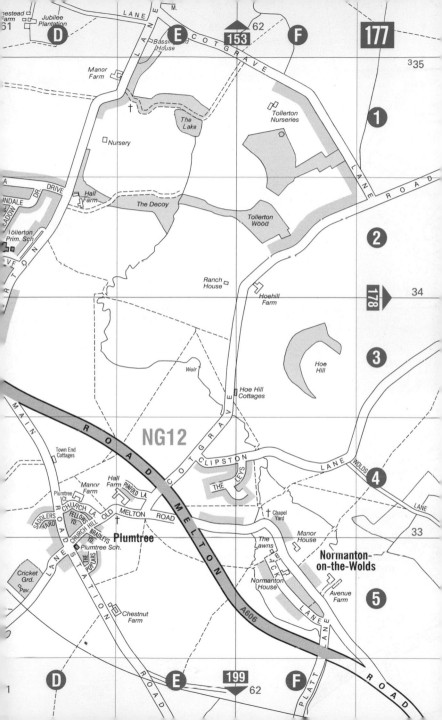

A **154** 63 **B** **C**

335

COTGRAVE

Tollerton
Nurseries

1

LANE

ROAD PLUMTRE

Boot
Pit

MILL LANE

M

2

COTGRAVE

Manor
Farm

RIVER LA

Nottingham

Clipston

34 **177**

GATE

Blackberry
Farm

Hall
Farm

CHURCH

Glebe
Farm

WOLDS

NG12

3

Hoe
Hill

LANE

4

LANE

WOLDS

Pasture
Plantation

Grange
Plantation

Chapel
Yard

33 nor
House

Wolds
Farm

**Normanton-
on-the-Wolds**

LANE

5

LANE

MELTON

Wolds
Plantation

A606 ROAD

A

63

B

PLUMTREE
WOLDS

C

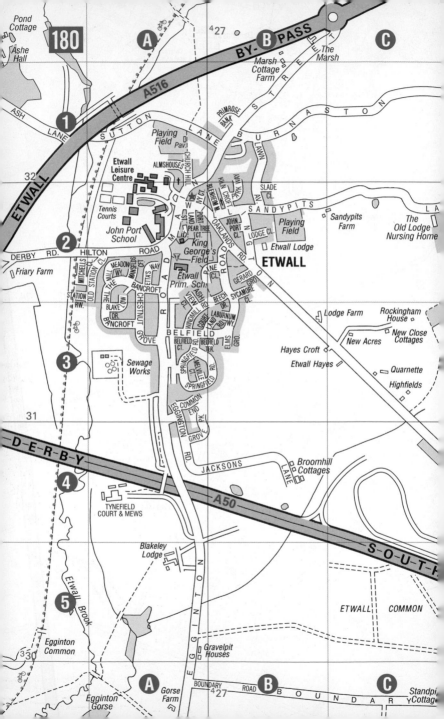

180

Pond Cottage
Ashe Hall
ASH LANE

A   ⁴27   BY- B PASS   C

A516
The Marsh
Marsh Cottage Farm
BURNASTON

1

SUTTON LANE
PRIMROSE BANK
STREET

ETWALL
32

Playing Field
Pav.
CHURCH HILL
ALMSHOUSES
Etwall Leisure Centre
IVY CT.
BLENHEIM
KILN CROFT
PARK
AV.
SANDYPITS
SLADE CL.
Sandypits Farm
The Old Lodge Nursing Home
LA

Tennis Courts
John Port School
PORT LAND CT.
PEAR TREE CT.
OAKLANDS
JOHN PORT CL.
LODGE CL.
Playing Field
Etwall Lodge

ETWALL

2
DERBY RD.   HILTON   ROAD
Friary Farm
MITCHELLS CL.
OLD STATION CL.
STATION RW.
THE MILL
MEADOW WY.
BANCROFT
MAWSINGS CT.
FETTAS WY.
King George's Field
Etwall Prim. Sch.
LANE
ASH
LANE (CL)
BEECH DR.
LABURNUM
SYCAMORE CL.
GERARD GRO.
ROTON
Lodge Farm
Rockingham House
New Close Cottages
New Acres

3
BLAKE DR.
BANCROFT
CHESTNUT
GROVE
VIEW
WINDMILL RD.
LOWRE
LAND
ROWY.
ELMS GRO.
Hayes Croft
Etwall Hayes
Quarnette
Highfields

Sewage Works
BELFIELD
BELFIELD CT.
BELFIELD TER.
SPRINGFIELD CT.
MELVILLE RD.
SPRINGFIELD RD.

31
COMMON END
EGGINTON GROVE PK.
GROVE

4
D- E- R- B- Y
JACKSONS
Broomhill Cottages
LANE
A50
S- O- U- T- H

TYNEFIELD COURT & MEWS

Blakeley Lodge

5
Etwall Brook
EGGINTON

ETWALL   COMMON

Eggington Common
³30

Gravelpit Houses

A   Gorse Farm   BOUNDARY   ⁴27   B ROAD B   BOUNDAR   C   Standpi Cottag

Eggington Gorse

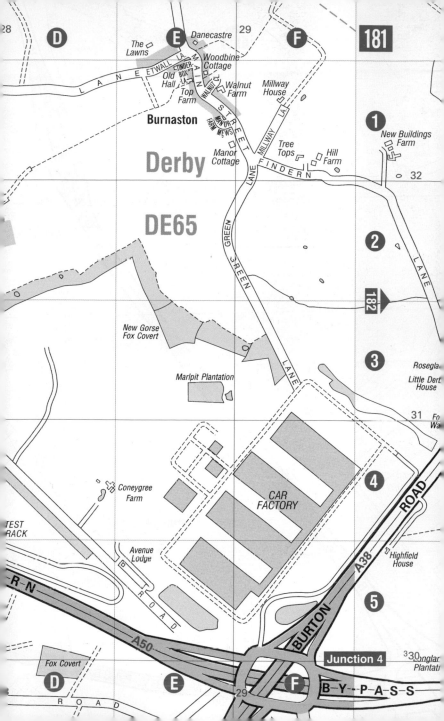

28

D

E Danecastre 29

F

The Lawns

LANE ETWALL LA. Woodbine Cottage

Old Hall

FINDER LA.

BOX

WALNUT CL.

Top Farm

Walnut Farm

Millway House

Burnaston

MANOR FARM MEWS

STREET

MILLWAY LA.

1 New Buildings Farm

MAIN

Tree Tops

Hill Farm

32

Derby

Manor Cottage

GREEN LANE

FINDERN

DE65

2

182

New Gorse Fox Covert

3 Rosegla

Little Dert House

Marlpit Plantation

GREEN LANE

31 Fo Wa

4

Coneygree Farm

CAR FACTORY

ROAD

A38

TEST TRACK

Avenue Lodge

ROAD

Highfield House

5

R N

BURTON

A50

Fox Covert

D

E 29

F

Junction 4

330 onglar Plantati

B Y - P A S S

ROAD

D | **E** | **157** | **F** | **183**

WOODALL
KILNSEY
CT.
HEADON DR.
GREEN DR.
AMBERVALE CL.
GROMBERG
GREEN MOUNT
HARGREAVES
BOWBANK
MOSS
MOOR
SHIRE GATE CL.
TEMPLE ST.
BROADDALE
BRIDLE
BROW
DRIVE
INN

SOUTH DERBYSHIRE

Highfields Farm

DE23

Hell Brook

1

Hall Pastures Farm

32

Derby

Thurston

2

Blakemere Farm

184

Hell Meadow

Brook

3

Hell

Stenson Fields Farm

31

DE73

4

Ash Plantation

BEECH DR.
COMMON
PIECE LA.
Clovermead

SOUTHERN — A50 — B-Y--P-A-S-S

DERBY

Sewage Works

5

Bank House

Stenson House

The Bungalow

Marina

Stenson Lock

330

Stenson

D | **E** | **F**

TRENT & MERSEY CANAL

Weir

Stenson Junction

eath House

32

Lower Farm

East Farm

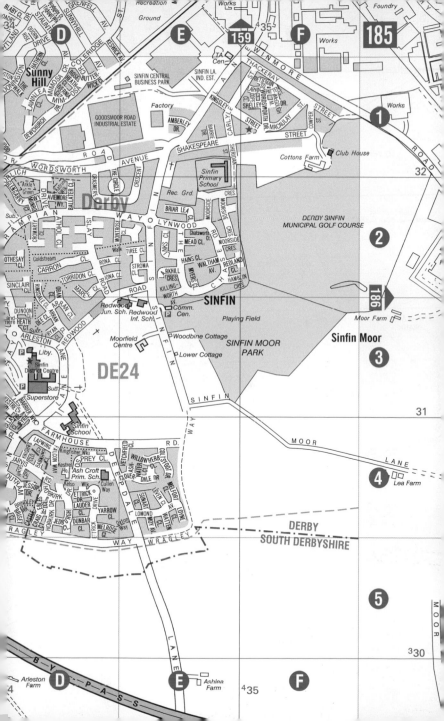

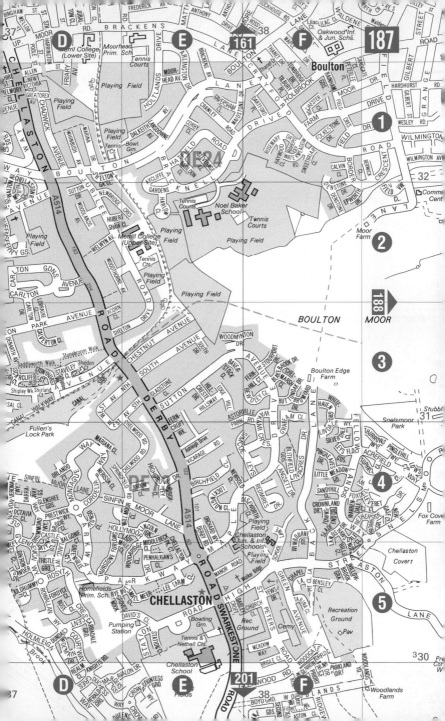

D   **E**   ▲ 165   **F**   **191**

1

Armis Cotta

Church Wilne
/32

St. Chads Water

River Derwent

SOUTH DERBYSHIRE

EREWASH

Ambaston Grange

2

Weir

192

WILNE MILL

Wilne Bridge

3

31

Great Wilne

Bottom Wood

4

GAVENDISH CL

...ROW

MILLFIELD

Shardlow Primary School

Playing Field

GLENN

CLOVER CT

INDIA WY

RED...

WEST END DR

WINFLYN CL

HODDER CL

COWLISHAW

Shardlow

Shardlow Hall Nursing Home

Shardlow Nurseries

Playing Field

THE WHARF

Mill Green

WILNE

P

5

Shardlow Marina

Shardlow Lock

CANAL BANK

CAVENDISH CT

Shardlow Heritage Centre

Roydon Hall Farm

TRENT & MERSEY CANAL

Shardlow Marina

330'

Cavendish Bridge

D   **E**   ▼ 205   44   **F**

Home Farm

D ACTON ROAD IND.

ACTON RD. IND. EST.

ACTON RD.
IND.

ACTON GRO

CLOSE

ACTON

ACTON AV.

E North Junction

TRENT COTS.

N E W B O U R N E

A V E N U E

O W E N

169

50

F

L A N E

P A S T U R E   L A N E

1

32

Fish Pond

Forbes Hole Local
Nature Reserve

GANS... BOROUGH
NICOLLS CL.
SNOW... CL.
HIGH CFT.

FORBES CL.

Industrial
Estate

Lodge

M
BAKEWELL RD.
BELVOIR RD.
LEYS...
FARM
HOS...
NEAR...
LETT...
BROOK CL.
WITTERING...
MEAD...
RD. CL.

2

ST. ALBANS CL.
SEDGMR...
FIELD...
WITTERING CL.
TEWKESBURY...
DUNBAR...
LUDFORD CL.

...FORD DR.
...CL.

HEXHAM CL.

South
Junction

T
R
E
N
T

Fish Ponds

Trent Rifle Range

Trent Valley
Sailing Club

Nottingham

Fish
Pond

Trent
Junction

Cranfleet
Farm

R.
S
O
A
R
T
R
E
N
T

E
R
E
W
A
S
H

R
U
S
H
C
L
I
F
F
E

3

Thrumpton
Hall

Trentlock

Cranfleet Canal

Trent Valley
Sailing Club

Weir

Pump
Ho.

THRUMPTON

PARK

Old
Wood

31

4

Wright's
Hill

S
O
A
R

Tunnel

Wood Hill

NG11

Redhill
Tunnels

Red Hill

Redhill
Lock

Weir

Ratcliffe
Junction

Redhill
Farm

Cooling
Towers

5

*RATCLIFFE ON SOAR
POWER STATION*

3 30

Coal Storage
Area

D

Middle Gate
Cottages

E

209

50

F

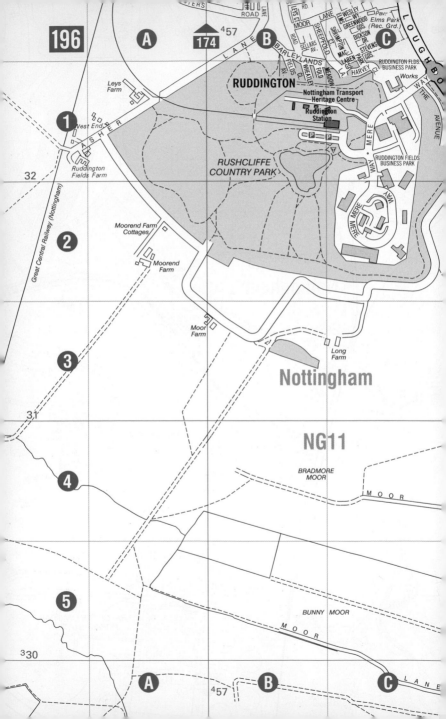

198

A

176 ⁴60

B

C

1

Barn Farm

LANE

32

Blackcliffe Hill

B R A D M O R E

L A N E

Nottingham

2

197

D E B D A

CROFT CT. SPINN GORSE RD.

PLANTA FARHAM

3

Cotton's Plantation

INTAKE RD.

CROFT PARK

NG11

PARK AV. WEST

AV.

31

Greenhays Farm

4

Rancliffe Wood

Woodfields

Lynwoo

PENDOCK LANE

B U N N Y

Wheatcroft Farm

KEYWORTH LANE

W Y S A L L

5

g Plantation

Sewage Works

³30

A

L A N E

⁴60

B

C

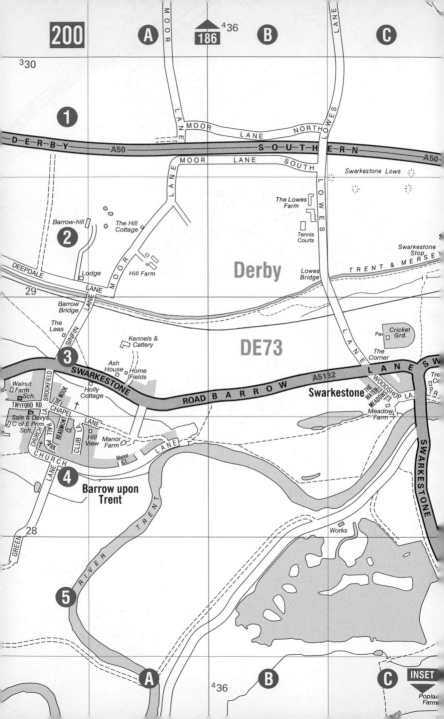

200

330

⌂ 186 ⁴36

A   **B**   **C**

MOOR LANE

LANE NORTHO

LOWES

1

D—E—R—B—Y A50 S—O—U—T—H—E—R—N A50

MOOR LANE SOUTH

LANE

LOWES

Swarkestone Lows

The Lowes Farm

Barrow-hill

The Hill Cottage

2

Tennis Courts

Derby

DEEPDALE

Lodge

Hill Farm

Lowes Bridge

Swarkestone Stop

T—R—E—N—T & M—E—R—S—E

29

LANE

MOOR

Barrow Bridge

SINFIN

The Leas

Kennels & Cattery

DE73

Cricket Grd.

Pav

The Corner

LANE

SW

3 SWARKESTONE

Ash House

Home Fields

Walnut Farm Sch.

BROOKFIELD

THE NOOK

Holly Cottage

ROAD B—A—R—R—O—W A5132 LANE

Swarkestone

THE WATER MEADOWS

WOODSHOP LA.

Tre Co

TWYFORD RD.

Sale & Davys C of E Prim Sch.

CHURCH

BEAUMONT CL.

CHAPEL

LANE

Hill View

Manor Farm

LANE

Meadow Farm

SWARKESTONE

CLUB

TILL PARK

Manor

4

Barrow upon Trent

C—H—U—R—C—H

28

GREEN

LANE

RIVER TRENT

Works

5

⁴36

A   **B**   **C** INSET

Popla Farm

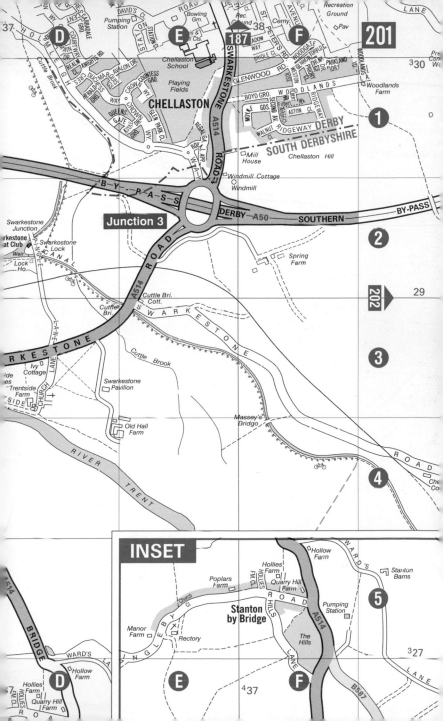

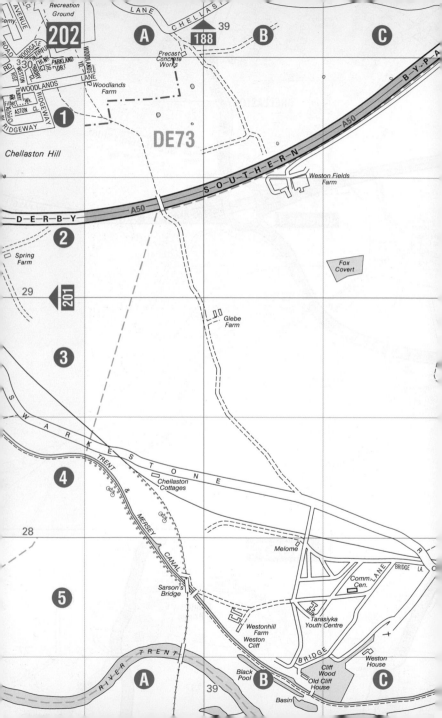

Recreation Ground

202

LANE CHELLAST

A

188 39

B

C

Precast Concrete Works

Woodlands Farm

WOODLANDS

1

DE73

Chellaston Hill

S O U T H E R N

B - Y - P - A

A50

Weston Fields Farm

D - E - R - B - Y

A50

2

Spring Farm

Fox Covert

29 **201**

Glebe Farm

3

S W A R K E S T O N E

TRENT

4

Chellaston Cottages

MERSEY CANAL

28

Melome

BRIDGE LA.

Comm. Cen.

Sarson's Bridge

5

Tarasiyka Youth Centre

Westonhill Farm Weston Cliff

BRIDGE

Cliff Wood

Weston House

TRENT

RIVER

A

39

Black Pool

B

Old Cliff House

Basin

C

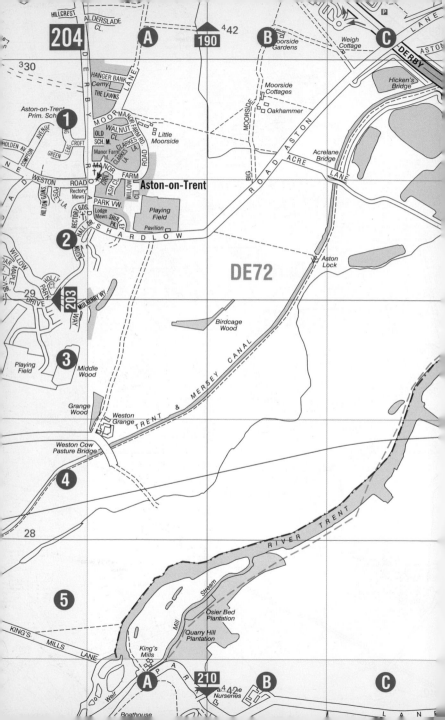

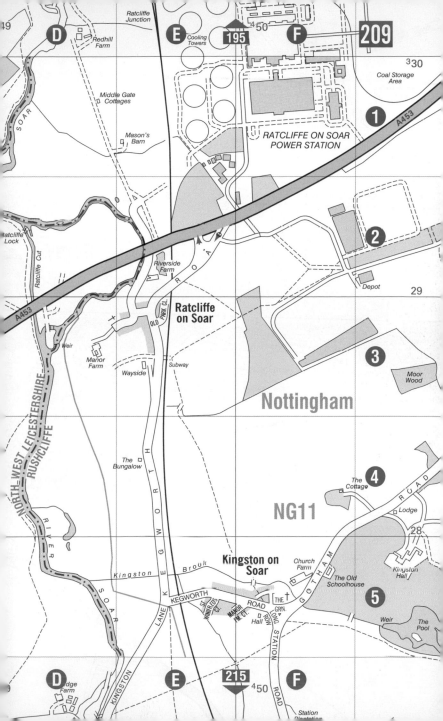

D **E** **195** 4 50 **F** **209**

Ratcliffe Junction

Redhill Farm

Cooling Towers

³30

Coal Storage Area

1 A453

Middle Gate Cottages

RATCLIFFE ON SOAR POWER STATION

SOAR

Mason's Barn

2

Ratcliffe Lock

Ratcliffe Cut

Depot

29

A453

Riverside Farm

OLD PARK CL.

Ratcliffe on Soar

Weir

Manor Farm

Wayside

Subway

3

Moor Wood

Nottingham

NORTH-WEST LEICESTERSHIRE

RUSHCLIFFE

KEGWORTH

The Bungalow

RIVER SOAR

The Cottage

4

ROAD

Lodge

28

NG11

Kingston Brook

Kingston on Soar

Church Farm

The Old Schoolhouse

Kingston Hall

KEGWORTH LANE

ST. WINIFRED'S CT.

MANOR FM. CT.

Hall

ROAD

LONG GRN.

THE GRN.

GOTHAM ROAD

5

Weir

The Pool

STATION ROAD

D Lodge Farm

KINGSTON

E **215** 4 50 **F**

Station

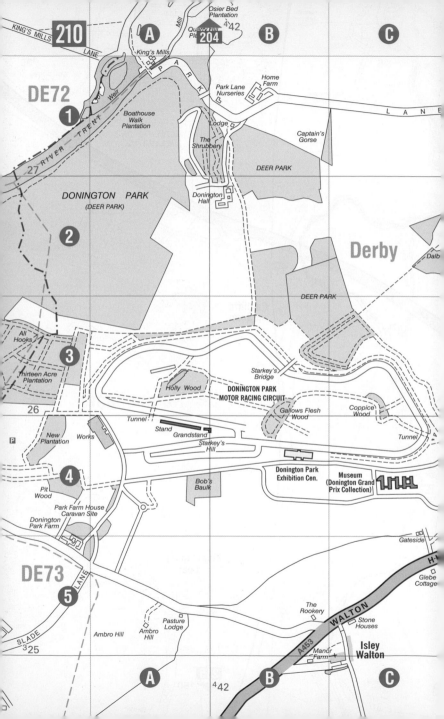

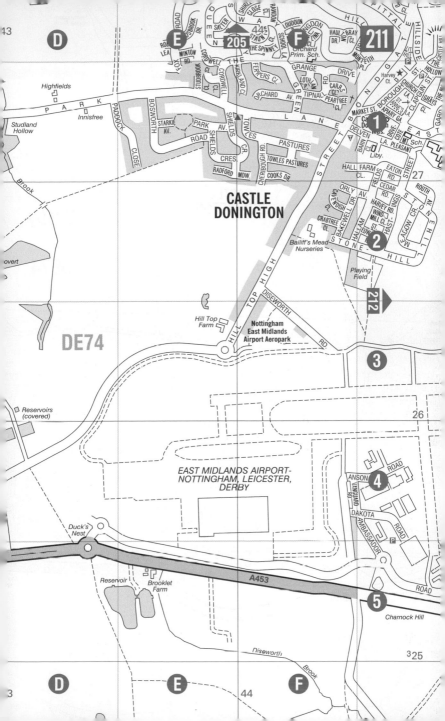

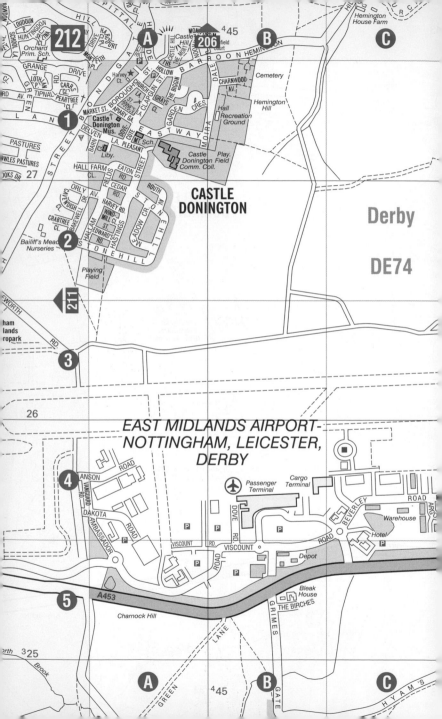

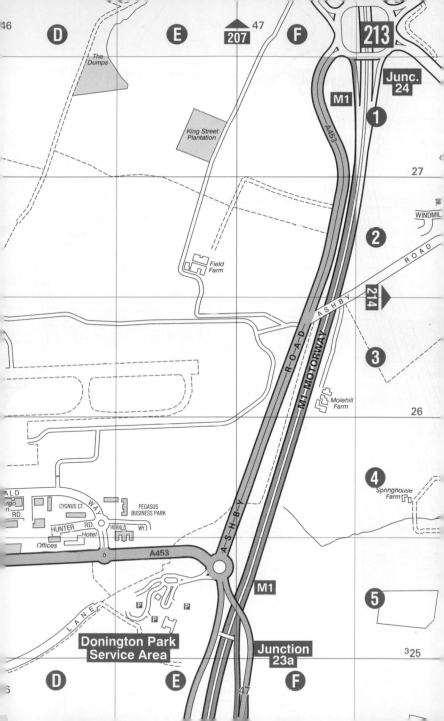

INDEX

Including Streets, Places & Areas, Industrial Estates,
Selected Flats & Walkways, Service Areas, Stations and
Selected Places of Interest.

HOW TO USE THIS INDEX

1. Each street name is followed by its Postcode District and then by its Locality abbreviation(s) and then by its map reference; e.g. **Abbey Bri.** NG7: Lent . . . .3D **121** is in the NG7 Postcode District and the Lenton Locality and is to be found in square 3D on page **121**. The page number is shown in bold type.

2. A strict alphabetical order is followed in which Av., Rd., St., etc. (though abbreviated) are read in full and as part of the street name; e.g. **Apple Tree Cl.** appears after **Appleton Rd.** but before **Appletree Cl.**

3. Streets and a selection of flats and walkways too small to be shown on the maps, appear in the index with the thoroughfare to which it is connected shown in brackets; e.g. **Albert Sq.** NG7: Lent . . . .2D **121** (off Church St.)

4. Addresses that are in more than one part are referred to as not continuous.

5. Places and areas are shown in the index in **BLUE TYPE** and the map reference is to the actual map square in which the town centre or area is located and not to the place name shown on the map; e.g. **ASPLEY** 2A **96**

6. An example of a selected place of interest is **DH Lawrence Birthplace Mus.** 1E **43**

7. An example of a station is **Attenborough Station (Rail)** 1C **170**
   Included are Rail **(Rail)**, Nottingham Express Transit **(NET)** and Park and Ride **(Park & Ride)**

8. Service Area names are shown in the index in **BOLD CAPITAL TYPE**; e.g. **DONINGTON PARK SERVICE** 5E **213**

9. Map references for entries that appear on large scale pages **4-7** are shown first, with small scale map references shown in brackets; e.g. **Abbey St.** DE22: Der 5B **6** (5E **135**)

GENERAL ABBREVIATIONS

All. : Alley	**Ent.** : Enterprise	**Nth.** : North
App. : Approach	**Est.** : Estate	**No.** : Number
Arc. : Arcade	**Fld.** : Field	**Pde.** : Parade
Av. : Avenue	**Flds.** : Fields	**Pk.** : Park
Bk. : Back	**Gdn.** : Garden	**Pas.** : Passage
Blvd. : Boulevard	**Gdns.** : Gardens	**Pl.** : Place
Bri. : Bridge	**Ga.** : Gate	**Prom.** : Promenade
Bldg. : Building	**Gt.** : Great	**Res.** : Residential
Bldgs. : Buildings	**Grn.** : Green	**Ri.** : Rise
Bus. : Business	**Gro.** : Grove	**Rd.** : Road
Cvn. : Caravan	**Hgts.** : Heights	**Shop.** : Shopping
Cen. : Centre	**Ho.** : House	**Sth.** : South
Chu. : Church	**Ho's.** : Houses	**Sq.** : Square
Chyd. : Churchyard	**Ind.** : Industrial	**Sta.** : Station
Circ. : Circle	**Info.** : Information	**St.** : Street
Cir. : Circus	**Intl.** : International	**Ter.** : Terrace
Cl. : Close	**La.** : Lane	**Trad.** : Trading
Comn. : Common	**Lit.** : Little	**Up.** : Upper
Cnr. : Corner	**Lwr.** : Lower	**Va.** : Vale
Cotts. : Cottages	**Mnr.** : Manor	**Vw.** : View
Ct. : Court	**Mkt.** : Market	**Vs.** : Villas
Cres. : Crescent	**Mdw.** : Meadow	**Vis.** : Visitors
Cft. : Croft	**Mdws.** : Meadows	**Wlk.** : Walk
Dr. : Drive	**M.** : Mews	**W.** : West
E. : East	**Mt.** : Mount	**Yd.** : Yard
Emb. : Embankment	**Mus.** : Museum	

LOCALITY ABBREVIATIONS

A'ton : **Allenton**	Atten : **Attenborough**	Bel : **Belper**
All : **Allestree**	Aws : **Awsworth**	Bestw : **Bestwood**
Alv : **Alvaston**	Babb : **Babbington**	Bestw V : **Bestwood Village**
Amba : **Ambaston**	Bar : **Bargate**	Bilb : **Bilborough**
Ambe : **Ambergate**	Bar T : **Barrow upon Trent**	Bing : **Bingham**
Arn : **Arnold**	Bart F : **Barton in Fabis**	B'ook : **Blackbrook**
Aspl : **Aspley**	Basf : **Basford**	Bor : **Borrowash**
Ast T : **Aston-on-Trent**	Bee : **Beeston**	Bram : **Bramcote**

Bre : **Breadsall**
Brea : **Breaston**
Brins : **Brinsley**
Brox : **Broxtowe**
Bulc : **Bulcote**
Bulw : **Bulwell**
Bunny : **Bunny**
Burn : **Burnaston**
Bur J : **Burton Joyce**
Calv : **Calverton**
Carl : **Carlton**
C Don : **Castle Donington**
Cayt : **Caythorpe**
Chad : **Chaddesden**
Chel : **Chellaston**
Chil : **Chilwell**
Cin : **Cinderhill**
Clif : **Clifton**
C'ton : **Clipston**
Cod : **Codnor**
Colw : **Colwick**
Coss : **Cossall**
Cotg : **Cotgrave**
Cox : **Coxbench**
Crop Bi : **Cropwell Bishop**
Crop Bu : **Cropwell Butler**
D Ab : **Dale Abbey**
D Abb : **Darley Abbey**
Den : **Denby**
Der : **Derby**
Dise : **Diseworth**
Dray : **Draycott**
Duff : **Duffield**
East B : **East Bridgford**
Eastw : **Eastwood**
Edwal : **Edwalton**
Egg : **Egginton**
Elv : **Elvaston**
Epp : **Epperstone**
Etw : **Etwall**
Find : **Findern**
Gam : **Gamston**
Ged : **Gedling**
Gilt : **Giltbrook**
Gon : **Gonalston**
Goth : **Gotham**
Grea : **Greasley**
Gun : **Gunthorpe**
Haz : **Hazelwood**
H'age : **Heage**
Hea : **Heanor**
Hem : **Hemington**
Hilt : **Hilton**
H'ook : **Holbrook**

Hol P : **Holme Pierrepont**
Hors : **Horsley**
H Woo : **Horsley Woodhouse**
Hove : **Hoveringham**
Huck : **Hucknall**
H Grn : **Hyson Green**
Ilk : **Ilkeston**
Iron : **Ironville**
I Wal : **Isley Walton**
Ked : **Kedleston**
Keg : **Kegworth**
Key : **Keyworth**
Kil : **Kilburn**
Kimb : **Kimberley**
King : **Kingston on Soar**
Kirk H : **Kirk Hallam**
Lamb : **Lambley**
Lang M : **Langley Mill**
Lent : **Lenton**
Lent A : **Lenton Abbey**
Lin : **Linby**
L Eat : **Little Eaton**
Lit : **Littleover**
Lock : **Lockington**
Long E : **Long Eaton**
Los : **Loscoe**
Lowd : **Lowdham**
L Har : **Lower Hartshay**
L Kil : **Lower Kilburn**
Mac : **Mackworth**
Mapp : **Mapperley**
Mapp P : **Mapperley Park**
Mare : **Marehay**
Mark : **Markeaton**
Mick : **Mickleover**
Mil : **Milford**
Mor : **Morley**
Neth : **Netherfield**
News : **Newstead**
Newth : **Newthorpe**
Newton : **Newton**
Norm W : **Normanton-on-the-Wolds**
Nott : **Nottingham**
N Air : **Nottingham East Midlands Airport**
Nuth : **Nuthall**
Oak : **Oakwood**
Ock : **Ockbrook**
Owt : **Owthorpe**
Oxt : **Oxton**
Pap : **Papplewick**
Pen : **Pentrich**
Plum : **Plumtree**
Quar : **Quarndon**

Rad : **Radbourne**
Rad T : **Radcliffe on Trent**
Radf : **Radford**
Rat : **Ratcliffe on Soar**
Redh : **Redhill**
Rid : **Riddings**
Rip : **Ripley**
Ris : **Risley**
Rudd : **Ruddington**
Sand : **Sandiacre**
Saxon : **Saxondale**
Shar : **Shardlow**
Shel : **Shelford**
S Loc : **Shelton Lock**
Sher : **Sherwood**
Ship : **Shipley**
Shot : **Shottle**
S'gate : **Shottlegate**
Sin : **Sinfin**
Smal : **Smalley**
Spon : **Spondon**
S'ley : **Stanley**
Stan C : **Stanley Common**
S Bri : **Stanton by Bridge**
Stan D : **Stanton-by-Dale**
Stan W : **Stanton-on-the-Wolds**
Stap : **Stapleford**
Sten : **Stenson**
S Flds : **Stenson Fields**
Sto B : **Stoke Bardolph**
Stre : **Strelley**
Sut B : **Sutton Bonington**
Swan : **Swanwick**
Swar : **Swarkestone**
Thru : **Thrumpton**
Thul : **Thulston**
Tith : **Tithby**
Toll : **Tollerton**
Top V : **Top Valley**
Toton : **Toton**
Trow : **Trowell**
Unde : **Underwood**
Want : **Watnall**
West Br : **West Bridgford**
West H : **West Hallam**
W Tre : **Weston-on-Trent**
Wilf : **Wilford**
Wils : **Wilson**
Woll : **Wollaton**
Woodbo : **Woodborough**
Woodt : **Woodthorpe**

A

Aaron Cl. NG11: Wilf 1A **150**
Abba Cl. NG16: Kimb 5E **45**
Abbey Bri. NG7: Lent 3D **121**
Abbey Cl. NG2: Woot Br . . . 1F **151**
Abbey Cl. NG15: Huck 2D **25**
Abbey Ct. NG7: Lent 1E **121**
NG9: Bee 5E **119**
Abbey Cres. DE5: Rip 2D **17**
Abbeydale Cl. DE56: Kil 5A **38**
Abbeydale Dr. DE56: Duff 4D **59**
Abbeydale Wlk.
DE24: Alv 5C **162**
(off Elvaston La., not continuous)
Abbey Dr. NG9: Bee 1E **147**
Abbeyfield Rd. NG7: Lent . . .5E **121**

Abbeyfields Cl.
DE22: D Abb 3F **107**
Abbey Gro. NG3: Nott 3E **99**
Abbey Hill DE22: D Abb 2F **107**
Abbey Hill Rd. DE22: All 3C **106**
Abbey Ho. Hall NG7: Nott 5F **119**
Abbey La. DE22: D Abb 4F **107**
Abbey Rd. NG2: West Br 1F **151**
NG9: Bee 5E **119**
NG13: Bing 1F **131**
NG15: News 1A **10**
NG16: Eastw 2A **44**
Abbey St. DE7: Ilk 5E **67**
DE22: Der 5B **6** (5E **135**)
NG7: Lent 3D **121**
Abbey Yd. DE22: D Abb 4F **107**
Abbot Cl. DE21: Oak 3D **109**
NG12: Key 2D **199**

Abbot M. DE22: D Abb 4F **107**
Abbot Rd. DE7: Kirk H 4B **90**
Abbotsbury Cl. NG5: Top V 3C **48**
Abbots Cl. NG5: Arn 1C **74**
Abbots Dr. NG15: Huck 3D **25**
Abbotsford Dr. NG3: Nott 4C **98**
Abbotsford M. DE7: Ilk 4C **66**
Abbots Gro. DE56: Bel 4F **13**
Abbots Rd. NG15: Huck 3D **25**
Abbot St. NG16: Aws 3B **38**
Abbots Wlk. NG15: Huck 3D **25**
Abbots Way NG8: Woll 1A **120**
Abbotts Barn Cl.
DE22: Der 4B **6** (4E **135**)
Abbott St. DE75: Hea 3D **41**
NG10: Long E 5C **160**
Abells DE5: Den 3B **38**
Abels Mill DE1: Der 1A **6**

Abercarn Cl. NG6: Bulw 5A **48**
Abercarn M. NG6: Bulw 5A **48**
Aberdare Cl. DE21: Oak 3A **110**
Aberdeen St.
  NG3: Nott 2F **5** (5D **99**)
Aberford Av. NG8: Basf 2C **96**
Abingdon Bus. Cen.
  DE24: Der 2B **160**
Abingdon Dr. NG11: Rudd . . .3C **174**
Abingdon Gdns. NG5: Woodt . . .2F **75**
  NG9: Chil 4C **146**
Abingdon Rd. NG2: West Br . . .1F **151**
Abingdon Sq. NG8: Aspl 1A **96**
Abingdon St. DE24: Der 4A **160**
Ablard Gdns. NG9: Chil 1B **170**
Abney Cl. DE3: Mick 1E **157**
Acacia Av. DE3: Mick 2D **157**
Acacia Cl. NG15: Huck 4A **26**
Acacia Ct. NG3: Nott 4C **98**
Acacia Cres. NG4: Carl 2E **101**
Acacia Gdns. NG5: Top V 4E **45**
Acacia Wlk. NG9: Bee 2E **147**
Academy Cl. NG6: Basf 4C **72**
Acaster Cl. NG9: Bee 4A **148**
Access 26 Bus. Pk.
  NG16: Lang M 1B **42**
Acer Cft. DE21: Oak 2D **109**
Acle Gdns. NG6: Bulw 3A **48**
Acorn Av. NG16: Gilt 4A **44**
  (not continuous)
Acorn Bank NG2: West Br 4A **150**
Acorn Cen. NG16: Lang M 1B **42**
Acorn Cl. DE24: S Loc 3D **187**
Acorn Dr. DE56: Bel 4F **13**
  NG4: Ged 4F **77**
Acorn Pk. NG7: Lent 5D **121**
Acorn Way DE21: Chad 4B **110**
  DE56: Bel 4F **13**
A'court St. NG7: H Grn 4E **97**
Acre Cl. NG2: West Br 4B **124**
Acrefield Way DE73: Chel 4A **188**
Acre La. DE72: Ast T 1B **204**
Acresview Cl. DE22: All 1C **106**
Acton Av. NG6: Basf 3C **72**
  NG10: Long E 5D **169**
Acton Cl. NG10: Long E 5D **169**
Acton Gro. NG10: Long E 5D **169**
Acton Rd. DE22: Mac 2E **133**
  NG5: Arn 4C **50**
  NG10: Long E 4D **169**
Acton Rd. Ind. Est.
  NG10: Long E 5D **169**
  (not continuous)
Acton St. NG10: Long E 5D **169**
Adale Rd. DE7: Smal 4A **40**
Adams Cl. DE75: Hea 4C **40**
Adams Ct. DE7: Ilk 4D **67**
Adams Hill NG7: Nott 3A **120**
  NG12: Key 3E **199**
Adam St. DE7: Ilk 4F **91**
Adams Wlk. NG1: Nott 3D **5**
Ada Pl. NG15: Huck 1F **25**
Adbolton Av. NG4: Ged 1D **101**
Adbolton Gro.
  NG2: West Br 3A **124**
Adbolton La. NG2: West Br 4A **124**
  NG12: Hol P 3E **125**
Adbolton Lodge NG4: Carl 4D **101**
Adderley Cl. NG5: Bestw 1F **73**
Addington Ct. NG12: Rad T 1F **127**
Addington Rd. NG7: Radf 4E **97**
Addison Dr. NG15: Huck 1D **25**
Addison Rd. DE24: Der 3A **160**
  NG4: Carl 2A **100**

Addison St. NG1: Nott 3A **98**
Addison Vs. NG16: Eastw 3D **43**
  (not continuous)
Adelaide Cl. DE3: Mick 4D **133**
  NG9: Stap 4E **117**
Adelaide Gro. NG5: Top V 4D **49**
Adel Dr. NG4: Ged 5D **77**
Adelphi Cl. DE23: Lit 5F **157**
Adenburgh Dr. NG9: Atten . . .2C **170**
Adler Cl. DE1: Der 1A **136**
Admiral Cl. DE75: Hea 2D **41**
Adrian Cl. NG9: Toton 2E **169**
Adrian St. DE24: Der 5C **160**
Adwick Cl. DE3: Mick 1B **156**
Aeneas Ct. NG5: Sher 2A **98**
Aerial Way NG15: Huck 4E **25**
Aerodrome, The
  NG15: Huck 1D **47**
Agard St. DE1: Der 1A **6** (2E **135**)
Agnes Vs. NG3: Mapp 5D **75**
Aidan Gdns. NG5: Top V 2F **45**
Aimploy Ct. DE23: Der 2F **159**
Ainley Cl. DE24: Alv 4E **161**
Ainsdale Cres. NG8: Cin 4F **71**
Ainsley Rd. NG8: Aspl 4C **96**
Ainsworth Dr. DE23: Der 4D **159**
  NG2: Nott 4A **122**
Aintree Cl. NG16: Kimb 5D **45**
Aira Cl. NG2: Gam 2C **152**
Airedale Cl. NG10: Long E 5F **167**
Airedale Cl. NG9: Chil 4F **145**
Airedale Wlk. DE24: Alv 5B **162**
  NG8: Woll 2B **118**
Aitchison Av. NG15: Huck 2E **25**
Alandene Av. NG16: Want 5F **45**
Albany Cl. NG5: Arn 5D **51**
  NG15: Huck 4B **24**
Albany Ct. NG9: Stap 4D **117**
Albany Rd. DE22: Der 4B **134**
  NG7: Basf 2F **97**
Albany St. DE7: Ilk 4F **91**
Albemarle Rd. DE21: Chad . . .1A **138**
  NG5: Woodt 3C **74**
Alberta Ter. NG7: H Grn 2F **97**
Albert Av. NG4: Carl 3A **100**
  NG8: Aspl 2C **96**
  NG9: Stap 1C **144**
  NG16: Nuth 5B **46**
Albert Ball Cl. NG5: Top V 4E **49**
Albert Cres. DE21: Chad 4A **138**
Albert Einstein Cen.
  NG7: Nott 4C **120**
Albert Gro. NG7: Lent, Radf . . .5E **97**
Albert Hall 3A **4** (1A **122**)
Albert Mill NG7: Radf 4F **97**
Albert Rd. DE5: Rip 4B **8**
  DE21: Chad 3E **137**
  DE72: Brea 4A **166**
  NG2: West Br 5E **123**
  NG3: Nott 1C **98**
  NG7: Lent 2E **121**
  NG9: Bee 5F **119**
  NG10: Long E 3C **168**
  NG10: Sand 2A **144**
  NG11: Bunny 5D **197**
Albert Sq. NG7: Lent 2D **121**
  (off Church St.)
Albert St. DE1: Der 3D **7** (3F **135**)
  DE5: Rip 5D **9**
  DE7: Ilk 2D **91**
  DE56: Bel 5E **13**
  NG1: Nott 4C **4** (1B **122**)
  NG4: Ged 1E **101**
  NG9: Stap 1C **144**

Albert St. NG12: Rad T 2E **127**
  NG15: Huck 2A **26**
  NG16: Eastw 1E **43**
  (not continuous)
Albion Cen. DE7: Ilk 2E **91**
Albion Leisure Cen. 2E **91**
Albion Ri. NG5: Arn 3E **51**
Albion Rd. NG10: Long E 3E **169**
Albion St. DE1: Der 3D **7** (3F **135**)
  DE5: Rip 5D **9**
  DE7: Ilk 1E **91**
  NG1: Nott 5B **4** (2B **122**)
  NG9: Bee 1E **147**
Albrighton Av.
  DE24: S Flds 4C **184**
Albury Dr. NG8: Aspl 1A **96**
Albury Sq. NG7: Nott 1F **121**
Alcester St. NG7: Lent 5D **121**
Aldene Ct. NG9: Chil 3C **146**
Aldene Way NG14: Woodbo . . .5B **32**
ALDERCAR 5A **20**
Aldercar La. NG16: Lang M 2E **19**
Alder Cl. DE21: Oak 2D **109**
Alderfen Cl. DE24: S Loc 3C **186**
Alder Gdns. NG6: Bulw 5F **47**
Alderley Cl. DE21: Oak 3F **109**
Aldermens Cl. NG2: Nott 3B **122**
Alderney St. NG7: Lent 2E **121**
Alder Rd. DE56: Bel 1F **35**
Aldersgate DE22: Mac 1E **133**
Alderslade Cl. DE72: Ast T . . .5A **190**
Aldersley Cl. DE65: Find 5B **182**
Alderton Rd. NG5: Bestw 1B **74**
Alder Wlk. DE23: Der 5F **135**
Alder Way NG12: Key 4F **199**
Aldgate Cl. NG6: Bulw 4F **47**
Aldred's La NG16: Lang M 2A **42**
Aldreds La. DE75: Hea 3F **41**
Aldridge Cl. NG9: Toton 1D **169**
Aldrin Cl. NG6: Bulw 2E **71**
Aldworth Cl. NG5: Bestw 1A **74**
Aldwych Cl. DE22: Mac 2F **133**
Aldwych Cl. NG5: Arn 3F **49**
  NG16: Nuth 5C **70**
Alexander Cl. NG15: Huck 5D **11**
Alexander Fleming Bldg.
  NG7: Nott 5C **120**
Alexander Rd. NG7: Nott 1F **121**
Alexandra Cres. NG9: Bee 2F **147**
Alexandra Gdns.
  DE23: Der 1A **160**
  NG5: Sher 1A **98**
Alexandra M. NG5: Sher 2A **98**
Alexandra Mills DE1: Der 3A **6**
ALEXANDRA PARK 2C **98**
Alexandra Rd.
  NG10: Long E 3C **168**
Alexandra St. NG5: Sher 2A **98**
  NG9: Stap 2C **144**
  NG16: Eastw 2E **43**
Alexandre Cl. DE23: Lit 5C **158**
Alford Cl. NG9: Bee 3F **147**
  (not continuous)
Alford Rd. NG2: West Br 2A **152**
  NG12: Edwal 2A **152**
Alfred Av. NG3: Mapp 5F **75**
Alfred Cl. NG3: Nott 4B **98**
Alfred Rd. DE56: Kil 4F **37**
Alfred St. DE5: Rip 4D **9**
Alfred St. Central
  NG3: Nott 4B **98**
Alfred St. Nth. NG3: Nott 4B **98**
Alfred St. Sth.
  NG3: Nott 1F **5** (5D **99**)

Alfreton Rd. DE5: Cod 1B 18
DE21: Bre 2B 108
DE21: Der 5A 108
NG7: H Grn, Radf 3D 97
Alice St. DE1: Der 1E 7 (2A 136)
Alison Av. NG15: Huck 5E 11
Alison Cl. DE21: Chad 1E 137
Alison Wlk. NG3: Nott 4C 98
Allan Av. DE23: Lit 3D 157
Allen Av. NG3: Mapp 1F 99
(not continuous)
Allendale DE7: Ilk 3D 91
Allendale Av. NG8: Aspl 1E 95
NG9: Atten 1C 170
Allendale Rd. DE75: Hea ...2C 40
Allen Fld. Ct. NG7: Lent 2E 121
Allen St. DE24: A'ton 1D 187
NG15: Huck 1F 25
Allen's Wlk. NG5: Arn 3E 51
ALLENTON 1D 187
ALLESTREE 1E 107
Allestree Cl. DE24: Alv 3D 161
Allestree Hall (Club House)
...................4D 83
Allestree La. DE22: All 3C 106
Allestree St. DE24: Alv 3D 161
All Hallows Dr. NG4: Ged 5E 77
Allington Av. NG7: Lent 2E 121
Allison Gdns. DE7: Ilk 1F 91
NG9: Chil 4C 146
Allissa Av. DE5: Rip 2D 17
All Saints Cl. DE7: Stan C ...1F 87
All Saints Ct. DE3: Mick 2C 156
All Saints St. NG7: Radf 4F 97
All Saints Ter. NG7: Radf ...4F 97
Allstone Lee DE56: Bel 4E 13
Allwood Dr. NG4: Carl 2D 101
Allwood Gdns. NG15: Huck ...3A 26
Alma Cl. DE7: Ilk 2D 67
NG1: Nott 1B 4 (4B 98)
NG4: Ged 5F 77
Alma Hgts. DE3: Mick 2D 157
Alma Hill NG16: Kimb 4D 45
Alma Rd. NG3: Nott 4E 99
Alma St. DE5: Rip 3C 8
DE22: Der 4B 6 (4E 135)
NG7: Basf 2F 97
Almond Av. DE5: Rip 1C 16
NG16: Kimb 5D 45
Almond Ct. NG2: Nott 3B 122
Almond St. DE23: Der 1E 159
Almond Wlk. NG4: Ged 5F 77
Almond Way NG8: Bilb 3C 94
Almshouses DE65: Etw 1A 180
Alnwick Cl. NG6: Bulw 1C 72
Alonso Cl. DE73: Chel 4D 187
Alpha Ter. NG1: Nott 4A 98
Alpine Cres. NG4: Carl 2D 101
Alpine St. NG6: Basf 5D 73
Alport Cl. DE56: Bel 4A 14
Alsager Cl. DE21: Oak 4F 109
Alstonfield Dr.
DE22: D Abb 4D 107
Althorpe St. NG7: Radf 5F 97
Alton Av. NG11: Wilf 4A 150
Alton Cl. DE22: All 2C 106
NG2: West Br 5B 150
Alton Dr. NG16: Gilt 4A 44
Alton Rd. DE56: Bel 5B 14
Alts Nook Way DE72: Shar ...5D 191
Alum Cl. DE24: Alv 4B 162
Alum Ct. NG5: Top V 4E 49
ALVASTON 4A 162

Alvaston Pk. Homes
DE24: Alv 2F 161
Alvaston St. DE24: Alv 3A 162
Alvenor St. DE7: Ilk 1E 91
Alverstone Rd. NG3: Mapp P ..1B 98
Alverton Cl. DE3: Mick 2B 156
Alvey Ter. NG7: Radf 5D 97
Alward's Cl. DE24: Alv 5F 161
Alward's Ct. DE24: Alv 5F 161
Alwood Gro. NG11: Clif 5C 148
Alwyn Ct. NG9: Bee 3E 147
Alwyn Rd. NG8: Brox 5E 71
Alyth Ct. NG6: Basf 4E 73
Ambassador Rd.
DE74: N Air 4A 212
AMBASTON 5C 164
Ambaston La.
DE72: Elv, Thul 1F 189
Amber Cl. DE56: Bel 3F 13
DE75: Hea 3D 41
Amber Dr. NG16: Lang M 2A 42
Ambergate Rd. NG8: Bilb ...3F 95
(not continuous)
Amber Hgts. DE5: Rip 4B 8
Amber Hill NG5: Bestw 5A 50
Amberley Cl. DE7: Ilk 4E 91
Amberley Dr. DE24: Sin 1E 185
Amber Rd. DE22: All 4C 106
NG3: Bee 5F 147
Amber St. DE24: Der 4B 160
Amber Trad. Cen.
NG16: Kimb 5C 44
Ambervale Cl. DE23: Lit 5F 157
Ambleside NG2: Gam 1B 152
Ambleside Dr. NG16: Eastw ..1C 42
Ambleside Rd. NG8: Aspl ...1F 95
Ambleside Way NG4: Ged ...2A 102
Ambrose Ter.
DE1: Der 2A 6 (3D 135)
Amen All. DE1: Der 2C 6 (3F 135)
American Adventure Theme Pk., The
...................2A 66
Amersham Rd. NG8: Aspl 1A 96
Amesbury Cir. NG8: Cin 4F 71
Amesbury La. DE21: Oak ...3D 109
AMF Bowling
Ilkeston 3D 91
Nottingham 3E 5 (1C 122)
Amilda Av. DE7: Ilk 2E 91
Ampthill Ri. NG5: Sher 3A 74
Amy St. DE22: Der 4D 135
Ancaster Gdns. NG8: Woll ...5F 95
Ancaster Hall NG7: Nott 5F 119
Anchor Cl. NG8: Aspl 5A 72
Anchor Ct. NG5: Bestw 5A 50
Anchor Fold DE23: Der 1F 159
Anchor Rd. NG16: Eastw 1B 42
Anders Dr. NG6: Bulw 2F 71
Anderson Cl. NG5: Top V 4F 49
Anderson Cres. NG9: Bee ...5D 119
Anderson St. DE24: Alv 1E 161
Andover Cl. NG8: Bilb 4A 96
Andover Rd. NG5: Bestw 1D 73
Andrew Av. DE7: Ilk 3A 92
NG3: Mapp 5F 75
Andrew Cl. DE23: Lit 3D 157
Andrews Cl. NG9: Chil 2B 146
Andrews Dr. DE7: Stan C 1F 87
NG16: Lang M 5F 19
Anfield Cl. NG9: Toton 1F 169
Anford Cl. NG6: Bulw 2A 72
Angela Cl. NG5: Arn 2D 51
Angela Ct. NG9: Toton 1F 169
Angel All. NG1: Nott 3D 5 (1C 122)

Angelica Ct. NG13: Bing 2B 130
Angell Grn. NG11: Clif 2B 172
Angel Row
NG1: Nott 3B 4 (1B 122)
Angel Row Art Gallery, The 3B 4
Anglers Bus. Cen.
DE21: Spon 5D 139
Anglers' La. DE21: Spon 5D 139
Anglesey St. DE21: Chad 5C 108
Angletarn Cl. NG2: West Br ..2B 152
Angrave Cl. NG3: Nott 3D 99
Angus Cl. NG5: Arn 3A 52
NG16: Kimb 2F 69
Anmer Cl. NG2: Nott 4A 122
Annan Ct. NG8: Aspl 2A 96
Anne Potter Cl. DE72: Ock ..3C 140
Anne's Cl. NG3: Mapp 5F 75
Annesley Gro. NG1: Nott 4A 98
Annesley Rd. NG2: West Br ..1E 151
NG15: Huck 3A 10
Annies Cl. NG15: Huck 4E 25
Anslow Av. NG9: Lent A 5F 119
Anson Rd. DE74: N Air 4F 211
Anson Ter. NG7: H Grn 3E 97
Anson Wlk. DE7: Ilk 4E 67
Anstee Rd. NG10: Long E 1B 194
Anstey Cl. DE21: Oak 4F 109
Anstey Ri. NG3: Nott 5E 99
Anthony Cres. DE24: Alv 5E 161
Anthony Dr. DE24: Alv 5E 161
Anthony Wharton Ct.
NG11: Clif 5D 149
Antill St. NG9: Stap 2C 144
Antony Ct. DE21: Spon 3D 139
Apiary Ga. DE74: C Don 1A 212
Apollo Dr. NG6: Bulw 2E 71
Appian Cl. DE72: Bor 2B 164
Appian Way DE24: Alv 5C 162
(not continuous)
Appleby Cl. DE7: Ilk 4E 91
Appleby Ct. DE22: Der 5D 135
Applecross Cl. DE24: Sin 3C 184
Appledore Av. NG8: Woll 3C 118
Appledore Dr. DE21: Oak 4A 110
Appledorne Way NG5: Arn 3D 51
Appledown Way DE23: Lit 5F 157
Applegate Cl. DE21: Oak 2A 110
Applemead Cl. DE21: Chad ...3D 109
Appleton Cl. DE21: Chad 1F 137
NG11: Clif 3B 172
Appleton Dr. DE56: Bel 3A 14
Appleton Gdns. NG3: Mapp ...2A 76
Appleton Rd. NG9: Bee 4A 148
Apple Tree Cl. NG12: Edwal ..4F 151
Appletree Cl. DE72: Bor 2B 164
Appletree La. NG4: Ged 5E 77
Appletree Wlk. DE3: Mick ...1C 156
Apple Wlk. NG3: Nott 2F 99
Applewood Cl. DE56: Bel 4A 14
Applewood Gro. NG5: Sher ...4C 74
Arbor Cl. DE22: Der 5B 6 (4E 135)
Arboretum Ho. DE23: Der 5A 136
Arboretum Sq. DE23: Der 5A 136
Arboretum St. DE23: Der 5A 136
NG1: Nott 4A 98
Arbour Hill DE7: D Ab 2D 113
Arbrook Dr. NG8: Aspl 4C 95
Arbutus Cl. NG11: Clif 2B 172
Archdale Rd. NG5: Bestw 1B 74
Archer Cres. NG8: Woll 5E 95
Archer Rd. NG9: Stap 3D 145
Archer St. DE7: Ilk 4D 67
DE24: Der 1D 161

Arch Hill NG5: Redh 1D 51
Archway Ct. *NG7: Radf* *4E 97*
  (off Limpenny St.)
Arden Cl. DE23: Der 1D 159
  NG9: Lent A 5F 119
  NG15: Huck 4B 26
Arden Gro. NG13: Bing 1B 130
Ardleigh Cl. DE3: Mick 3C 156
  NG5: Top V 3C 48
Ardmore Cl. NG2: Nott 2E 123
Ardsley Cl. DE75: Hea 2F 41
Arena, The
  NG1: Nott 4A 4 (1A 122)
Argosy Rd. DE74: N Air 4C 212
Argyle Ct. NG7: Radf 5E 97
Argyle M. NG16: Eastw 2E 43
Argyle St. DE22: Der 5E 135
  NG7: Radf 5E 97
  NG16: Lang M 5A 20
Argyll Cl. DE21: Spon 3E 139
Argyll Pl. DE5: Rip 4D 9
Argyll Rd. DE5: Rip 4D 9
Aria Ct. NG9: Stap 2C 144
Ariel Cl. NG6: Basf 2E 73
Arkendale Wlk. DE24: Alv 5B 162
Arkers Cl. NG6: Basf 4C 72
Arkle Grn. DE24: Sin 2D 185
Arklow Cl. NG8: Aspl 5F 71
Arkwright Av. DE56: Bel 3B 14
Arkwright St. DE24: Der 4B 160
  NG2: Nott 4C 122
Arkwright St. Nth.
  NG2: Nott 2B 122
Arkwright St. Sth.
  NG2: Nott 4C 122
Arkwright Wlk. NG2: Nott . . .3C 122
  (not continuous)
Arleston Dr. NG8: Woll 2C 118
Arleston La. DE24: S Flds 4C 184
  DE73: Bar T 5C 184
Arleston St. DE23: Der 4E 159
Arlington Cl. NG15: Huck 5F 25
Arlington Dr. DE24: Alv 5E 161
  NG3: Mapp P 1B 98
Arlington Rd. DE23: Der 2C 158
Armadale Cl. NG5: Arn 4B 52
Armes Cl. DE7: Ilk 4E 67
Armfield Rd. NG5: Arn 1B 76
Armitage Dr. NG10: Long E 4F 169
Armscote Cl. DE21: Oak 3A 110
Armstrong Rd. NG6: Bulw 2E 71
Armstrong Way NG7: Basf 1D 97
Arncliff Cl. NG8: Woll 1B 118
Arndale Rd. NG5: Sher 2B 74
Arne Ct. NG2: Nott 4B 122
Arnesby Rd. NG7: Lent 2C 120
Arnhem Ter. DE21: Spon 4D 139
Arno Av. NG7: H Grn 2A 98
ARNOLD 5E 51
Arnold Av. NG10: Long E 2F 193
Arnold Cres. NG10: Long E 2F 193
Arnold La. NG3: Ged, Mapp 2A 76
  NG4: Ged 4D 77
Arnold Rd. NG5: Bestw 2E 73
  NG6: Basf, Bestw 3D 73
Arnold Sports & Leisure Cen.
  . . . . .4E 51
Arnold St. DE22: Der 3C 134
Arnos Gro. NG16: Nuth 4C 70
Arnot Hill Pk. 1D 75
Arnot Hill Rd. NG5: Arn 5D 51
Arnot Ho. *NG4: Carl* *2D 101*
  (off Foxhill Rd. E.)
Arno Va. Gdns. NG5: Woodt . . .2E 75

Arno Va. Rd. NG5: Woodt 2D 75
Arnside NG9: Stap 3D 145
Arnside Cl. NG5: Bestw 2A 74
Arnside Rd. NG5: Bestw 2F 73
A Road NG7: Nott 2B 148
Arran Cl. DE24: Sin 3D 185
  NG9: Stap 3D 117
Arreton Ct. DE24: Alv 1B 188
Arridge Rd. DE21: Chad 1E 137
Arthur Av. NG7: Lent 1E 121
  NG9: Stap 5E 117
Arthur Ct. DE23: Der 1A 160
Arthur Cres. NG4: Carl 3B 100
Arthur Hind Cl. DE22: Der 1D 135
Arthur Mee Rd. NG9: Stap 3D 145
Arthur Neal Ho. DE22: Mac . . .2A 134
Arthur St. DE1: Der 1C 6 (1F 135)
  DE72: Dray 3E 165
  NG4: Neth 4F 101
  NG7: Radf 4F 97
Artic Way NG16: Kimb 5C 44
Arundel Av. DE3: Mick 1E 157
Arundel Cl. NG10: Sand 4A 144
Arundel Dr. DE21: Spon 3E 139
  NG9: Bram 3A 118
Arundel St. DE22: Der 5C 134
  NG7: Radf 5F 97
Ascot Av. NG16: Kimb 5D 45
Ascot Bus. Pk. DE24: Der 3C 160
Ascot Cl. DE7: West H 3C 88
Ascot Dr. DE24: Der 4C 160
  NG5: Redh 4C 50
  NG15: Huck 4C 24
Ascot Pk. Est. NG10: Sand 1B 144
Ascot Pl. DE7: Kirk H 5B 90
Ascot Rd. NG8: Aspl 3C 96
Ascott Gdns. NG2: West Br 3A 150
Ash Acre DE56: Bel 5C 14
Ashberry Cl. DE22: All 1F 107
Ashbourne Cl. NG9: Bram 4F 117
Ashbourne Ct. DE1: Der 3D 135
  NG6: Bulw 1E 71
Ashbourne Ho. *DE22: Spon* . . .*4D 139*
  (off Arnhem Ter.)
Ashbourne Rd. DE22: Der 2C 134
  DE22: Mac 1D 133
  DE56: S'gate 1A 34
Ashbourne St. NG7: Lent 5F 97
Ashbrook Av. DE72: Bor 1B 164
Ashbrook Cl. DE22: All 2B 106
Ashburnham Av. NG7: Lent . . .1E 121
Ashby Rd. DE74: Keg 5E 213
Ashby St. DE24: A'ton 5D 161
Ashchurch Dr. NG8: Woll 3C 118
Ash Cl. DE22: All 1C 106
  DE73: Ast T 2A 204
  NG13: Bing 2F 131
  NG14: Bur J 3D 79
  NG14: Woodbo 5B 32
  NG15: Huck 4B 24
Ashcombe Gdns.
  DE21: Oak 4A 110
Ash Ct. NG4: Carl 3C 100
Ash Cres. DE5: Rip 1C 16
  NG16: Nuth 1A 70
Ashcroft Cl. DE24: Alv 4E 161
Ashdale Av. NG15: Huck 4F 25
Ashdale Rd. DE7: Ilk 4F 91
  NG3: Nott 4A 100
  NG5: Arn 4F 51
Ashdene Gdns. DE56: Bel 4B 14
Ashdown Cl. NG11: Wilf 2A 150
Ashdown Gro. NG13: Bing 2C 130
Ashe Cl. NG5: Arn 5A 52

Ashe Pl. DE23: Der 2E 159
Asher La. DE5: Pen 1B 8
  NG11: Rudd 5B 174
Asher La. Bus. Pk. DE5: Rip 2C 8
Ashfield Av. DE21: Chad 5D 109
  NG9: Bee 3A 148
Ashfield Rd. NG2: Nott 1E 123
Ash Flds. DE56: Bel 2F 35
Ashford Cl. DE7: West H 2C 88
Ashford Pl. DE7: Ilk 2D 67
Ashford Ri. DE56: Bel 3B 14
  NG8: Woll 3C 118
Ashforth Av. DE75: Hea 3F 41
Ashforth Bus. Cen.
  NG3: Nott *4C 98*
  (off Ashforth St.)
Ashforth St. NG3: Nott 4C 98
Ashgate Rd. NG15: Huck 2A 26
Ash Gro. NG9: Stap 2C 144
  NG10: Long E 5B 168
  NG10: Sand 1F 143
  NG12: Key 4E 199
  NG14: Woodbo 4B 32
  NG16: Brins 1C 20
Ashgrove Ct. DE21: Oak 4A 110
Ashiana NG2: Nott 3F 5 (1D 123)
Ashington Dr. NG5: Arn 2F 51
Ash La. DE65: Etw 1A 180
Ash Lea Cl. NG12: Cotg 1E 179
Ashleigh Dr. NG73: Chel 4E 187
Ashley Cl. NG9: Chil 2C 146
Ashley Ct. NG9: Bee 2D 147
Ashley Cres. NG12: Key 3E 199
Ashley Gro. NG15: Huck 2D 25
Ashley Rd. NG12: Key 3D 199
Ashley St. DE22: Der 3B 134
  NG3: Nott 2F 5 (5D 99)
Ashling Ct. NG2: Nott 3D 123
Ashling St. NG2: Nott 3C 122
Ashlyn Rd.
  DE21: Der 3F 7 (3B 136)
Ashmeadow DE72: Bor 2A 164
Ash Mt. Rd. NG16: Lang M 1A 42
Ashness Cl. NG2: Gam 2B 152
Ashop Rd. DE56: Bel 4C 14
Ashopton Av. DE23: Der 3E 159
Ashover Cl. DE21: Chad 5E 109
  NG3: Nott 2D 99
Ashover Rd. DE21: Chad 5D 109
  DE22: All 3C 106
Ashridge Way NG12: Edwal 4B 152
Ash St. DE7: Ilk 3D 67
Ashton Av. NG5: Arn 2E 51
Ashton Cl. DE3: Mick 5B 132
Ashton Way DE56: Bel 5C 14
Ashtree Av. DE24: Der 5A 160
Ash Tree Cl. DE21: Bre 1D 109
  DE56: Duff 2D 59
Ash Tree Ct. NG8: Stre 5B 70
Ash Tree Sq. NG9: Bram 5A 118
Ashurst Gro. NG15: Huck 5D 25
Ash Vw. NG7: Radf 4E 97
Ash Vw. Cl. DE65: Etw 2A 180
Ashview Cl. NG10: Long E 3A 168
Ash Vs. NG5: Sher 1A 98
Ashville Cl. NG2: Nott 4F 121
Ashwater Cl. DE24: Sin 4E 185
Ashwater Dr. NG3: Mapp 1C 76
Ashwell Cl. NG5: Woodt 3D 75
Ashwell Gdns. NG7: H Grn 2D 97
Ashwell St. NG4: Neth 4E 101
Ashwick Cl. NG11: Wilf 3F 149
Ashworth Av. DE21: Chad 3E 137
  NG11: Rudd 3B 174

Ashworth Cl. NG3: Nott 5B **100**
Ashworth Cres. NG3: Mapp 5A **76**
Ashworth Wlk. DE21: Chad . . .3E **137**
Askeby Dr. NG8: Stre 1C **94**
Askerfield Av. DE22: All 1B **106**
Aslockton Dr. NG8: Aspl 5C **72**
Aspen Bus. Cen.
   DE21: Spon 4A **138**
Aspen Cl. NG13: Bing 2F **131**
Aspen Dr. DE21: Spon 4A **138**
Aspen Rd. NG6: Bulw 1E **71**
Asper St. NG4: Neth 3F **101**
Aspinall Ct. NG8: Woll 5B **96**
ASPLEY 2A **96**
Aspley La. NG8: Aspl, Bilb 1E **95**
Aspley Pk. Dr. NG8: Bilb 2F **95**
Aspley Pl. NG7: Radf 4E **97**
Assarts Rd. NG16: Nuth 3D **71**
Assembly Rooms 2D **7** (3F **135**)
Astcote Cl. DE75: Hea 3F **41**
Asterdale Vw. DE21: Spon 4E **139**
Aster Gdns. DE23: Lit 5A **158**
Aster Rd. NG3: Nott 3C **98**
Astle Ct. NG5: Arn 1B **76**
Astley Dr. NG3: Nott 1E **99**
Astlow Dr. DE56: Bel 3A **14**
Aston Av. NG9: Lent A 5F **119**
Aston Cl. DE73: Chel 1E **201**
Aston Ct. DE7: Ilk 1E **91**
   NG7: Lent 4D **121**
Aston Dr. NG6: Bulw 2B **48**
Aston Grn. NG9: Toton 5D **145**
Aston Hall Dr. DE72: Ast T . . .2F **203**
Aston La. DE72: Ast T 1B **204**
       (not continuous)
   DE73: Chel 5A **188**
ASTON-ON-TRENT 1F **203**
Aston Rd. DE23: Lit 1B **184**
Astorville Pk. Rd.
   DE73: Chel 4E **187**
Astral Dr. NG15: Huck 5D **25**
Astral Gro. NG15: Huck 5C **24**
       (not continuous)
Astrid Gdns. NG5: Bestw 1E **73**
Astron Ct. NG15: Huck 5D **25**
Astwood Cl. NG8: Bilb 3D **95**
Atchison Gdns. DE21: Chad . . .1A **138**
Atherfield Gdns.
   NG16: Eastw 1E **43**
Atherfield Wlk. DE24: Alv . . .1B **188**
Atherton Ri. NG8: Cin 4A **72**
Atherton Rd. DE7: Ilk 4B **66**
Athlone Ct. DE21: Chad 5C **108**
Athol Cl. DE24: Sin 2D **185**
Athorpe Gro. NG6: Basf 4D **73**
Atlas Way DE21: Spon 1E **163**
Atlow Rd. DE21: Chad 1D **137**
ATTENBOROUGH 1C **170**
Attenborough La.
   NG9: Atten, Chil 5B **146**
       (not continuous)
Attenborough Nature Reserve
       . . . . .1D **171**
Attenborough Station (Rail)
       . . . . .1C **170**
Attercliffe Ter. NG2: Nott 4B **122**
Attewell Cl. DE72: Dray 4A **166**
Attewell Rd. NG16: Aws 2A **68**
Attlebridge Cl. DE21: Chad . . .5C **108**
Atworth Gro. DE23: Lit 4E **157**
Aubrey Av.
   NG2: Nott 4F **5** (1D **123**)
Aubrey Rd. NG5: Sher 5A **74**
Auburn Cl. DE7: Stan C 2A **88**

Auckland Cl. DE3: Mick 5E **133**
   NG7: Radf 5D **97**
Auckland Rd. DE21: Chad 1E **137**
Auckland Pl. DE56: Duff 5D **59**
Auckland Rd. NG15: Huck 4C **24**
Audley Cen.
   DE1: Der 3D **7** (3F **135**)
Audley Cl. DE7: Ilk 4C **66**
Audon Av. NG9: Lent A 4E **119**
Audon Av. NG9: Chil 3D **147**
Audrey Dr. DE21: Chad 5F **109**
Augustine Gdns. NG5: Top V . . .3F **49**
Augusta St. DE23: Der 1A **160**
Aults Cl. DE65: Find 5B **182**
Auriga Ct. DE1: Der 1A **136**
Austen Av. DE23: Lit 3A **158**
   NG7: H Grn 3F **97**
   NG10: Long E 1B **194**
Austins Dr. NG10: Sand 4A **144**
Austin Sq. DE23: Der 4E **159**
Austin St. NG6: Bulw 5B **48**
Autrey Av. NG9: Lent A 5F **119**
Autumn Cl. NG15: Huck 3F **25**
Autumn Gro. DE21: Chad 3E **137**
Avalon Cl. NG6: Bulw 1D **73**
Avalon Dr. DE73: Chel 1D **201**
Avebury Cl. NG11: Clif 3C **172**
Aveline Cl. NG5: Top V 4E **49**
Avenue, The
   DE1: Der 5D **7** (4F **135**)
   DE21: Chad 3E **137**
   DE56: Bel 2E **35**
   DE72: W Tre 4E **203**
   NG11: Rudd 1C **196**
   NG12: Rad T 1E **127**
   NG14: Calv 2E **31**
   NG14: Gun 1E **81**
Avenue A NG1: Nott 3E **5** (1C **122**)
Avenue B NG1: Nott 3E **5** (1C **122**)
Avenue C NG1: Nott 3F **5** (1D **123**)
Avenue D NG1: Nott 3F **5** (1D **123**)
Avenue E NG1: Nott 2F **5** (5D **99**)
Avenue Rd. DE56: Duff 2D **59**
Averham Cl. DE21: Oak 4A **110**
Averton Sq. NG8: Woll 2C **120**
Aviemore Cl. NG5: Arn 3A **52**
Aviemore Way DE24: Sin 2D **185**
       (not continuous)
Avis Av. DE75: Hea 5E **41**
Avocet Cl. NG13: Bing 3F **131**
   NG15: Huck 5D **11**
Avocet Ct. DE24: Sin 2C **184**
Avocet Wharf NG7. Lent 3F **121**
Avon Av. NG15: Huck 1D **47**
Avonbridge Cl. NG5: Arn 3B **52**
Avondale NG12: Cotg 5F **155**
Avondale Cl. NG10: Long E . . .5F **167**
Avondale Rd. DE7: Kirk H 5B **90**
   DE21: Spon 2C **138**
   DE23: Der 5F **135**
   NG4: Carl 4C **100**
Avon Gdns. NG2: West Br 1E **151**
Avonlea Cl. DE7: Ilk 4A **92**
Avonmouth Dr. DE24. Alv 3D **161**
Avon Pl. NG9: Bee 1F **147**
Avon Rd. NG3: Nott 5A **100**
   NG4: Ged 5E **77**
Avon St. DE24: Alv 3D **161**
AWSWORTH 2B **68**
Awsworth & Cossall By-Pass
   NG16: Awo, Coco 3A **68**
Awsworth La. NG16: Coss 5B **68**
   NG16: Kimb 2C **68**
Agwsworth Rd. DE7: Ilk 5E **67**

Axford Cl. NG4: Ged 5E **77**
Aycliffe Gdns. DE24: Alv 1E **187**
Aylesbury Av. DE21: Chad . . .1E **137**
Aylesham Av. NG5: Arn 1E **75**
Aylestone Dr. NG8: Bilb 2A **96**
Ayr Cl. DE21: Spon 4C **138**
Ayr St. NG7: Radf 4F **97**
Ayscough Av. NG16: Nuth 1B **70**
Ayton Cl. NG2: Nott 3A **122**
Ayton Gdns. NG9: Chil 1B **170**
Azalea Ct. NG16: Gilt 4B **44**

B

Babbacombe Cl. DE24: Alv . . .4B **162**
Babbacombe Dr.
   NG5: Bestw 1A **74**
Babbacombe Way
   NG15: Huck 3C **24**
BABBINGTON 4D **69**
Babhington Cres. NG4: Ged . . .5D **77**
Babbington Dr. NG6: Cin 3A **72**
Babbington La.
   NG16: Kimb 3E **69**
Babington Ct. NG9: Chil 3B **146**
Babington Hgts.
   DE1: Der 4D **7** (4F **135**)
Babington La.
   DE1: Der 5C **6** (4F **135**)
Back La. DE5: Pen 1B **8**
   DE7: Ilk 5D **67**
   DE72: Shar 2F **205**
   DE73: Chel 5F **187**
   DE74: C Don 4F **205**
   NG12: Norm W 5F **177**
   NG16: Nuth 1C **70**
Bk. Sitwell St.
   DE1: Der 4D **7** (4F **135**)
Bk. Wyver La. DE56: Bel 4E **13**
       (off Wyver La.)
Bacon Cl. NG16: Gilt 4F **43**
Baconsfield Ho.
   DE21: Chad 4A **138**
       (off Coleraine Cl.)
Bacton Av. NG6: Bulw 4A **48**
Bacton Gdns. NG6: Bulw 4A **48**
Baden Powell Rd.
   NG2: Nott 1F **123**
Bader Rd. NG11: Wilf 1A **150**
Badger Cl. DE21: Spon 2E **139**
   NG4: Carl 2D **101**
   NG15: Huck 3B **24**
Badgerdale Way DE23: Lit 4F **157**
Bagnall Av. NG5: Arn 1B **74**
Bagnall Cotts. NG6: Bulw 2A **72**
Bagnall Rd. NG6: Basf, Cin . . .3A **72**
Bagot St. DE7: West H 2B **88**
Bagshaw St. DE24: Alv 3D **161**
Bagthorpe Cl. NG5: Sher 4F **73**
Baildon Cl. NG8: Woll 2D **120**
Bailey Brook Cres.
   NG16: Lang M 1F **41**
Boiloy Brook Dr.
   NG16: Lang M 1E **41**
Bailey Brook Ind. Est.
   NG16: Lang M 2A **42**
Bailey Brook Rd. DE7: Ilk 2D **67**
Bailey Brook Wlk.
   NG16: Lang M 1F **41**
Railey Cl. NG5: Arn 5C **50**
Bailey Ct. NG4: Neth 3F **101**
   NG12: Rad T 3D **127**
BAILEY GROVE 2C **42**

Bailey Gro. Rd.
NG16: Eastw 2C **42**
Bailey La. NG12: Rad T 3D **127**
Bailey St. DE23: Der 5E **135**
NG4: Neth 3F **101**
NG6: Basf 5D **73**
NG9: Stap 2B **144**
Bainbridge, The NG14: Calv . . .2F **31**
Bainbrigge St. DE23: Der 5F **135**
Bains Dr. DE72: Bor 2C **164**
Bainton Gro. NG11: Clif 2E **173**
Bakeacre La. DE65: Find 4C **182**
Bakehouse La. DE72: Ock . . .3A **140**
Baker Av. DE75: Hea 5E **41**
NG5: Arn 3F **51**
Baker Brook Cl. NG15: Huck . . .3C **26**
Bakerdale Rd. NG3: Nott 4A **100**
Baker Rd. NG16: Gilt, Newth . . .4B **44**
Bakers Brothers Mobile Home
Cvn. Site DE7: Ilk 1F **91**
Bakers Cl. NG7: Radf 4D **97**
BAKERS FIELDS 4A **100**
Baker's Hollow NG12: Cotg . . .5D **155**
Bakers La. DE1: Der . . .5C **6** (4F **135**)
Baker St. DE7: Ilk 1E **91**
DE24: Alv 3E **161**
NG1: Nott 3A **98**
NG15: Huck 2F **25**
Bakewell Av. NG4: Carl 1D **101**
Bakewell Cl. DE3: Mick 5D **133**
Bakewell Dr. DE74: C Don 2F **211**
NG5: Top V 5D **49**
Bakewell Rd.
NG10: Long E 1D **195**
Bakewell St.
DE22: Der 4A **6** (4E **135**)
Balaclava Rd. DE23: Der 3F **159**
Bala Dr. NG5: Bestw 5F **49**
Baldwin Ct. NG7: Radf 5E **97**
Baldwin St. NG7: Radf 5F **97**
NG16: Newth 3B **44**
Balfour Rd. DE23: Der 3F **159**
NG7: Lent, Radf 5E **97**
NG9: Stap 2C **144**
Balfron Gdns. NG2: Nott 3A **122**
Balgonie Ct. DE73: Chel 4D **187**
Balham Wlk. DE22: Mac 2F **133**
Balisier Cl. NG3: Nott 4B **98**
Ballacraine Dr. DE5: Rip 5E **9**
Ballantrae Cl. NG5: Arn 4A **52**
Ballards Way DE72: Bor 2C **164**
Ballater Cl. DE24: Sin 2D **185**
Balleny Cl. DE21: Oak 3E **109**
Ballerat Cres. NG5: Top V 4D **49**
Ball La. DE72: Elv 1F **189**
Balloon Wood Ind. Est.
NG9: Bram 1F **117**
Ball St. NG3: Nott 3E **99**
Balmoral Av. NG2: West Br . .5D **123**
Balmoral Cl. DE23: Lit 1A **158**
DE75: Hea 3B **40**
NG10: Sand 5A **144**
Balmoral Ct. DE74: Hem 4C **206**
Balmoral Cres. NG8: Woll 5B **94**
Balmoral Dr. NG9: Bram 3A **118**
Balmoral Gro. NG4: Colw . . .4E **101**
NG15: Huck 1A **26**
Balmoral Ho. NG5: Woodt 3C **74**
Balmoral Rd. DE7: Kirk H 5C **90**
DE72: Bor 2B **164**
NG1: Nott 4A **98**
NG4: Colw 4E **101**
NG13: Bing 2B **130**
Balshaw Way NG9: Chil 1A **170**

Bamburgh Cl. DE21: Spon 4C **138**
Bamford Av. DE23: Der 3D **159**
Bamford St. DE5: Rip 2C **16**
Bamkin Cl. NG15: Huck 3A **26**
Bampton Cl. NG2: Gam 1B **152**
Banbury Av. NG9: Toton 5E **145**
Bancroft, The NG14: Calv 2F **31**
Bancroft Dr. DE22: All 1B **106**
Bancroft St. NG6: Bulw 5B **48**
Bandstand Yard 5A **4**
Banes Rd. NG13: Bing 2F **131**
Bangor St. DE21: Chad 5D **109**
Bangor Wlk. NG3: Nott 3B **98**
Bank, The DE1: Der 5A **136**
Bank Bldgs. DE56: Mil 5E **35**
Bank Cl. DE22: Der 5D **107**
Bankfield Dr. DE7: Kirk H 4A **90**
DE21: Spon 4E **139**
NG6: Bram 4B **118**
Bank Hill NG14: Woodbo 1E **53**
Bankholmes Cl.
DE24: S Flds 4D **185**
Bank Pl. NG1: Nott . . .3C **4** (1B **122**)
Banks, The NG13: Bing 2D **131**
Banksburn Cl. DE75: Hea 3B **40**
Banks Cl. NG5: Arn 1A **76**
Banks Cres. NG13: Bing 2D **131**
Bank Side DE22: D Abb 3D **107**
Banksman Cl. NG3: Nott 3E **99**
Banks Paddock NG13: Bing . . .2E **131**
Banks Rd. NG9: Toton 5D **145**
Bank St. NG10: Long E 4D **169**
NG16: Lang M 5B **20**
Banks Yd. NG6: Bulw 5A **48**
(off Main St.)
Bank Vw. Rd. DE22: Der 5E **107**
Bankwood Cl. NG8: Aspl 1F **95**
Bannels Av. DE23: Lit 4A **158**
Bannerman Rd. NG6: Bulw . . .1B **72**
Banwell Cl. DE3: Mick 5B **132**
Barbara Sq. NG15: Huck 5B **10**
Barber Cl. DE7: Ilk 4D **67**
Barber St. NG16: Eastw 2F **43**
Barbrook Cl. NG8: Woll 5A **96**
Barbury Dr. NG11: Clif 4C **172**
Barcheston Cl. DE21: Oak . . .3A **110**
Barclay St. DE7: Ilk 4C **66**
Barden Dr. DE22: All 3E **107**
Barden Rd. NG3: Mapp 2F **75**
Bardfield Gdns. NG5: Top V . . .2C **48**
Bardney Dr. NG6: Bulw 4F **47**
Bardsey Ct. DE21: Oak 2A **110**
Bardsey Gdns. NG5: Bestw . . .5F **49**
Bare La. DE72: Ock 3B **140**
Barent Cl. NG5: Bestw 1E **73**
Barent Wlk. NG5: Bestw 1E **73**
Barf Cl. DE3: Mick 2D **157**
BARGATE 3B **36**
Bargate Cl. DE56: Bar 3B **36**
Bargate Rd. DE56: Bel 2F **35**
Barker Av. E. NG10: Sand 2A **144**
Barker Av. Nth. NG10: Sand . . .2F **143**
Barker Cl. DE7: Stan C 1A **88**
Barker Ga. DE7: Ilk 5E **67**
NG1: Nott 3D **5** (1C **122**)
NG15: Huck 2E **25**
Barker Hill NG14: Lowd 2C **56**
Barkers La. NG9: Chil 4E **147**
Barkla Cl. NG11: Clif 3B **172**
Bar La. NG6: Basf 5B **72**
Bar La. Ind. Pk. NG6: Basf . . .5C **72**
Barlborough Rd. DE7: Ilk 2E **67**
Barley Cl. DE21: L Eat 2B **84**
Barleycorn Cl. DE21: Oak . . .3B **110**

Barley Cft. DE56: Bel 2A **36**
DE73: Chel 5E **187**
NG2: West Br 4B **150**
Barleydale Dr. NG9: Trow 3C **116**
Barleylands NG11: Rudd 5B **174**
Barling Dr. DE7: Ilk 5B **66**
Barlock Rd. NG6: Basf 3D **73**
Barlow Dr. Nth. NG16: Aws . . .3A **68**
Barlow Dr. Sth. NG16: Aws . . .3A **68**
Barlows Cotts. NG16: Aws . . .2B **68**
Barlows Cotts. La.
NG16: Aws 2B **68**
Barlow St. DE1: Der 5A **136**
Barnard Rd. DE21: Chad 3C **108**
Barnby Wlk. NG5: Sher 2B **74**
Barn Cl. DE22: Quar 4B **82**
DE65: Find 4C **182**
DE74: C Don 1A **212**
NG6: Bulw 2E **71**
NG12: Cotg 1D **179**
Barn Cft. DE23: Lit 2B **158**
NG9: Chil 2A **146**
Barndale Cl. NG2: West Br . .5B **150**
Barnes Cft. DE75: Hea 4B **40**
Barnes Grn. DE22: Mac 1A **134**
Barnes Rd. NG5: Top V 4E **49**
Barnet Rd. NG3: Nott 3A **100**
Barnett Ct. NG12: Key 3D **199**
Barnfield NG11: Wilf 4A **150**
Barnhill Gro. DE23: Lit 4F **157**
Barnsley Cl. NG6: Bestw V . . .3A **28**
Barnsley Ter. NG2: Nott 4B **122**
Barnstaple Cl. DE21: Oak 3F **109**
Barnston Rd. NG2: Nott 5E **99**
Barnum Cl. NG8: Woll 5D **95**
Barnwood Cl. DE3: Mick 1B **156**
Baron Cl. DE21: Oak 2C **110**
Barons Cl. NG4: Ged 1D **101**
Barrack La. NG7: Nott 1E **121**
Barra M. NG2: Nott 3A **122**
Barratt Cl. NG9: Atten 2C **170**
Barratt Cres. NG9: Atten 1C **170**
Barratt La. NG9: Atten 1B **170**
Barrett St. DE24: Alv 4F **161**
Barrhead Cl. NG5: Top V 3D **49**
Barrie Dr. DE24: Sin 1E **185**
Barrington Cl.
NG12: Rad T 3D **127**
Barrique Rd. NG7: Lent 4D **121**
Barrons Ct. DE72: Brÿ 5F **163**
Barrons Way DE72: Bor 2B **164**
Barroon DE74: C Don 1A **212**
Barrow La. DE73: Swar 3B **200**
Barrow Slade NG12: Key 4D **199**
BARROW UPON TRENT 4A **200**
Barrydale Av. NG9: Bee 3E **147**
Barry St. NG6: Bulw 5A **48**
Bartlow Rd. NG8: Bilb 3C **94**
Barton Cl. DE21: Spon 2E **139**
NG11: Rudd 5A **174**
BARTON IN FABIS 5D **171**
Barton Knoll DE56: Bel 1C **36**
Barton Knowle DE56: Bel 5C **14**
Barton La. NG9: Atten 2B **170**
NG11: Bart F 5F **171**
NG11: Clif 3B **172**
Barton Rd. NG10: Long E 5F **169**
Bartons Cl. NG16: Newth 2B **44**
Barton St. NG9: Bee 3F **147**
Barton Way NG9: Chil 3D **147**
Barwell Dr. NG8: Stre 1C **94**
Basa Cres. NG5: Top V 4E **49**
Basford Rd. NG6: Basf 1C **96**
Basford Stop (NET) 4D **73**

Basildon Cl. DE24: Alv 1E **187**
Baskin La. NG9: Chil 4B **146**
Baslow Av. NG4: Carl 1C **100**
Baslow Cl. NG10: Long E 1F **193**
Baslow Dr. DE22: All 2E **107**
 NG9: Lent A 4F **119**
Bassett Cl. DE7: Ilk 4B **66**
 NG16: Kimb 5D **45**
Bassford Av. DE75: Hea 2E **41**
BASSINGFIELD 1E **153**
Bassingfield La.
 NG2: Gam 1C **152**
  (not continuous)
 NG12: Rad T 5E **125**
Bassingham Cl. DE21: Oak . . .4A **110**
Bass St. DE22: Der 2C **134**
Bastion St. NG7: Radf 5D **97**
Bateman Gdns. NG7: H Grn . . .3E **97**
Bateman St. DE23: Der 1B **160**
Bathley St. NG2: Nott 4B **122**
Bath Rd. DE3: Mick 1D **157**
Bath St. DE1: Der 1F **135**
 DE7: Ilk 1D **91**
 NG1: Nott 2E **5** (5C **98**)
Bathurst St. NG8: Bilb 4F **95**
Baulk La. NG9: Stap 5E **117**
Baverstock Cl. DE73: Chel 3E **187**
Bawtry Wlk. NG3: Nott 4E **99**
Baxter Sq. DE23: Der 5E **159**
Bayard Cl. NG8: Woll 5B **96**
Bayleaf Cres. DE21: Oak 2A **110**
Bayliss Rd. NG4: Ged 4C **76**
Bayswater Cl. DE22: Mac 2E **133**
Bayswater Rd. NG16: Kimb 5E **45**
Baythorn Rd. NG8: Bilb 4C **94**
Beacon Flatts NG9: Bee 2A **148**
Beacon Hill Dr. NG15: Huck . . .4B **24**
Beacon Hill Ri.
 NG3: Nott 1F **5** (5D **99**)
Beacon Rd. NG9: Bee 2A **148**
Beaconsfield St. NG7: H Grn . . .2E **97**
 NG10: Long E 4D **169**
Beaconsfield Street Stop (NET)
 . . . . .2E **97**
Beamwood Cl. DE21: Oak . . .4E **109**
Bean Cl. NG6: Bulw 2E **71**
Beardall St. NG15: Huck 2A **26**
Beardmore Cl. DE21: Oak . . .3E **109**
Beardsley Gdns. NG2: Nott . . .3A **122**
Beardsmore Gro.
 NG15: Huck 5D **10**
Beastmarket Hill
 NG1: Nott 3B **4** (1B **122**)
Beatty St. DE24: Alv 3E **161**
Beatty Wlk. DE7: Ilk 4E **67**
Beauclerk Dr. NG5: Top V 4D **49**
Beaufort Cl. DE21: Der 5B **108**
 NG2: West Br 5B **150**
Beaufort Dr. NG9: Chil 3B **146**
Beaufort Gdns. DE21: Chad . . .2C **136**
Beaufort Rd. DE24: S Flds 4B **184**
Beaufort St. DE21: Chad 5C **108**
Beaulieu Gdns.
 NG2: West Br 3B **150**
Beaumaris Ct. DE21: Spon . . .3E **139**
Beaumaris Dr. NG4: Ged 1A **102**
 NG9: Chil 4A **146**
Beaumont Cl. DE56: Bel 5C **14**
 DE73: Bar T 4A **200**
 NG9: Stap 4D **117**
 NG12: Key 2D **199**
Beaumont Gdns.
 NG2: West Br 5C **150**

Beaumont St.
 NG2: Nott 4F **5** (1D **123**)
Beaumont Wlk. DE23: Der 5D **159**
Beaurepaire Cres. DE56: Bel . .4A **14**
Beaureper Av. DE22: All 2D **107**
BEAUVALE
 NG15 . . . . .3C **24**
 NG16 . . . . .1A **44**
Beauvale NG16: Newth 2A **44**
Beauvale Ct. NG15: Huck 3D **25**
Beauvale Cres.
 NG15: Huck 3C **24**
Beauvale Dr. DE7: Ilk 2C **66**
Beauvale Ri. NG16: Eastw 1A **44**
Beauvale Rd. NG2: Nott 4B **122**
 NG15: Huck 3C **24**
Beaver Grn. NG2: West Br 1C **150**
Becher St. DE23: Der 2F **159**
Beck Av. NG14: Calv 1E **31**
Beckenham Rd. NG7: Radf 4E **97**
Beckenham Way
 DE22: Mac 2A **134**
Becket St. DE1: Der . . .3B **6** (3E **135**)
Beckett Ct. NG4: Ged 4C **76**
Becketwell La.
 DE1: Der 3C **6** (3F **135**)
Beckford Rd. NG2: Nott 2E **123**
Beckhampton Rd.
 NG5: Bestw 4A **50**
Beckitt Cl. DE24: Alv 3F **161**
Beckley Rd. NG8: Brox 5E **71**
Beckside NG2: West Br 4B **152**
 NG14: Lowd 3D **57**
Becksitch Ct. DE56: Bel 2E **35**
  (off Becksitch La.)
Becksitch La. DE56: Bel 2E **35**
Beck St. NG1: Nott 2D **5** (4B **98**)
 NG4: Carl 2C **100**
Bedale Cl. NG9: Chil 4F **145**
Bedale Rd. NG5: Sher 2B **74**
Bedarra Gro. NG7: Lent 1D **121**
Bede Ling DE7: Ilk 2B **150**
Bedford Cl. DE22: Der 5C **134**
 DE74: Keg 3C **214**
Bedford Ct. NG7: H Grn 2F **97**
 NG9: Stap 4D **117**
Bedford Gro. NG6: Bulw 2C **72**
Bedford Row
 NG1: Nott 2E **5** (5C **98**)
Bedford St. DE22: Der 4C **134**
Bedlington Gdns.
 NG3: Mapp 5D **75**
Beecham Av. NG3: Nott 4E **99**
Beech Av. DE5: Rip 4B **8**
 DE22: Quar 2A **82**
 DE24: Alv 3A **162**
 DE72: Bor 5B **140**
 DE72: Brea 3E **167**
 NG3: Mapp 3E **75**
 NG4: Neth 4E **101**
 NG7: Basf 2F **97**
 NG9: Bee 3A **148**
 NG10: Long E 2D **169**
 NG10: Sand 1A **144**
 NG12: Key 4E **199**
 NG13: Bing 2F **131**
 NG15: Huck 2F **25**
 NG16: Nuth 1A **70**
Beech Cl. DE56: Bel 1F **35**
 DE56: Kil 4A **38**
 NG2: West Br 4C **124**
 NG6: Cin 3B **72**
 NG12: Edwal 4A **152**
 NG12: Rad T 3E **127**

Beech Ct. DE21: Spon 3C **138**
 NG3: Mapp 3F **75**
Beechcroft DE7: West H 3D **89**
 DE21: Bre 1C **108**
BEECHDALE 4F **95**
Beechdale Rd.
 NG8: Aspl, Bilb 2E **95**
Beechdale Swimming Pool . . .4B **96**
Beech Dr. DE22: Der 5E **107**
 DE65: Etw 2B **180**
 DE65: Find 5D **183**
Beeches, The DE7: Smal 4B **40**
 NG3: Nott 2F **99**
 NG10: Long E 3D **169**
Beeches Av. DE21: Spon 3C **138**
Beech Gdns. DE24: Alv 4A **162**
Beech La. DE7: West H 3C **88**
Beechley Dr. DE21: Oak 4A **110**
Beech Lodge NG13: Bing 2F **131**
Beech Wlk. DE23: Lit 2C **159**
Beechwood Cl. DE56: Bel 4D **13**
Beechwood Cres. DE23: Lit . . .2B **158**
Beechwood Lodge Cvn. Pk.
 DE72: Elv 5F **163**
Beechwood Pk. Dr.
 DE22: D Abb 4E **107**
Beechwood Rd. NG5: Arn 4F **51**
Beeley Cl. DE21: Chad 3E **109**
 DE22: All 3C **106**
 DE56: Bel 3B **14**
BEESTON 1F **147**
Beeston Cl. NG6: Bestw V 5D **27**
Beeston Ct. NG6: Bulw 5C **48**
Beeston Flds. Dr.
 NG9: Bee, Bram 5B **118**
Beeston La. NG7: Nott 5A **120**
Beeston Marina Mobile Home Pk.
 NG9: Atten 5F **147**
Beeston Rd. NG7: Nott 4C **120**
Beeston Sailing Club 1F **171**
Beeston Station (Rail) 3F **147**
Beetham Cl. NG13: Bing 2E **131**
Beggarlee Pk. NG16: Newth . . .5A **22**
Beighton St. DE5: Rip 5D **9**
Bel-Air Res. Homes
 NG2: Gam 1C **152**
Belconnen Rd. NG5: Bestw . . .2E **73**
Belfast Wlk. DE21: Chad 4F **137**
Belfield Ct. DE65: Etw 3A **180**
 DE75: Los 5B **18**
Belfield Gdns.
 NG10: Long E 4D **169**
Belfield Rd. DE65: Etw 3A **180**
Belfield St. DE7: Ilk 5E **67**
Belfield Ter. DE65: Etw 3B **180**
Belford Cl. NG6: Bulw 4E **47**
Belfry Cl. DE3: Mick 2E **157**
Belfry Way DE5: Rip 2D **17**
 NG12: Edwal 4B **152**
Belgrave Cl. DE56: Bel 4B **14**
Belgrave M. NG2: West Br . . .5B **150**
Belgrave Rd. NG6: Bulw 5F **47**
Belgrave Sq.
 NG1: Nott 2A **4** (5A **98**)
Belgrave St. DE23: Der 5F **135**
Bella Cl. NG16: Lang M 5A **28**
Bellar Ga. NG1: Nott . . .3E **5** (1C **122**)
Bell Av. DE72: Ast T 2F **203**
Belle Acre Cl. DE56: Bel 1E **35**
Belle Isle Rd. NG15: Huck 3F **25**
Belleville Dr. NG5: Bestw 5A **50**
Belle Vue Av. DE5: Mare 4B **16**
Bellevue Ct. NG3: Nott 4D **99**
Belle Vue Ter. DE72: Bor 2A **164**

Bell Ho. NG7: Nott 5D **121**
Bellingham Ct. DE22: All 3B **106**
Bell La. DE7: Smal 3E **63**
  DE75: Ship 2C **64**
  NG11: Wilf 1A **150**
Bellmore Gdns. NG8: Bilb . . .5C **94**
Bells La. NG8: Cin 5F **71**
Bell St. NG4: Carl 2C **100**
Belmont Av. DE72: Brea . . .3D **167**
  NG6: Bulw 5B **48**
Belmont Cl. NG9: Chil 4A **146**
  NG15: Huck 5F **25**
Belmont Dr. DE72: Bor 1A **164**
BELPER 1E **35**
Belper Av. NG4: Carl 1C **100**
Belper Cres. NG4: Carl 1C **100**
Belper Ho. DE21: Spon 5D **139**
Belper La. DE56: Bel 2B **12**
BELPER LANE END 2B **12**
Belper Rd. DE1: Der 5E **107**
  DE7: Stan C, West H 5E **63**
  DE56: Bar, H'ook 3B **36**
  DE56: Kil 2D **37**
          (not continuous)
  NG7: H Grn 3E **97**
Belper St John's Chapel
  Heritage Cen. 5F **13**
Belper Station (Rail) 5E **13**
Belper St. DE7: Ilk 3E **91**
Belsay Rd. NG5: Bestw 5F **49**
Belsford Ct. NG16: Want 4F **45**
Belsize Cl. DE22: Mac 2E **133**
Belton Cl. NG10: Sand 4A **144**
Belton Dr. DE5: Rip 5D **9**
  NG2: West Br 4A **150**
Belton St. NG7: H Grn 2E **97**
Belvedere Av.
  NG7: H Grn 2E **97**
Belvedere Cl. DE3: Mick 4C **132**
  NG12: Key 2D **199**
Belvoir Cl. DE7: Kirk H 4C **90**
  DE72: Brea 4B **166**
  NG10: Long E 1D **195**
Belvoir Hill NG2: Nott 1E **123**
Belvoir Lodge NG4: Carl 4D **101**
Belvoir Rd. NG2: West Br . . .4F **123**
  NG4: Neth 3F **101**
Belvoir St. DE23: Der 1E **159**
  NG3: Mapp 5E **75**
  NG15: Huck 1E **25**
Belvoir Ter. NG2: Nott 1E **123**
Belward St.
  NG1: Nott 3E **5** (1C **122**)
Belwood Cl. NG11: Clif 1E **173**
Bembridge Ct.
  NG9: Bram 5F **117**
Bembridge Dr. DE24: Alv . . .1B **188**
  NG5: Bestw 1A **74**
          (not continuous)
Bemrose M. DE22: Der 4B **134**
Bemrose Rd. DE24: A'ton . . .4D **161**
Bendall Grn. DE23: Lit 1B **184**
Bendigo La. NG2: Nott 2F **123**
Benedict Ct. NG5: Top V 3F **49**
Benington Dr. NG8: Woll 2B **118**
Benjamin Outram Bus. Cen.
  DE5: Rip 2D **17**
Ben Mayo Ct. NG7: Radf 4E **97**
Benmore Ct. DE21: Oak 2A **110**
Benner Av. DE7: Ilk 5F **91**
Bennerley Av. DE7: Ilk 3E **67**
Bennerley Cl. NG6: Bulw 4E **47**
Bennerley Rd. NG6: Bulw . . .4E **47**
Bennett Rd. NG3: Mapp 4F **75**

Bennett St. DE24: A'ton 1C **186**
  NG3: Mapp 5E **75**
  NG10: Long E 5B **144**
  NG10: Sand 3A **144**
Benneworth Cl. NG15: Huck . . .4E **25**
Bensley Cl. DE73: Chel 5F **187**
Benson St. DE24: Alv 4E **161**
Ben St. NG7: Radf 4E **97**
Bentinck Av. NG12: Toll 2C **176**
Bentinck Ct. NG2: Nott 3F **5**
Bentinck Rd. NG4: Carl 5B **76**
  NG7: H Grn, Radf 4E **97**
Bentinck St. NG15: Huck 1E **25**
Bentley Av. NG3: Nott 4F **99**
Bentley Rd. DE74: C Don 5E **205**
Bentley St. DE24: A'ton 5D **161**
Bentwell Av. NG5: Arn 5F **51**
Beresford Dr. DE7: Ilk 2D **67**
  DE21: Spon 4D **139**
Beresford Rd.
  NG10: Long E 1F **193**
Beresford St. NG7: Radf 5D **97**
Berkeley Av. NG3: Mapp P . . .2B **98**
  NG10: Long E 5B **168**
Berkeley Cl. NG5: Sher 1B **98**
Berkeley Cres.
  NG12: Rad T 2C **128**
Berkshire St. DE21: Chad . . .5C **108**
Berle Av. DE75: Hea 1D **41**
Ber Mar Anda Res. Mobile Home Pk.
  NG16: Lang M 5A **20**
Bermuda Av. DE21: L Eat 4B **84**
Bernard Av. NG15: Huck 5D **11**
Bernard Boam Dwellings
  DE5: Rip 1C **16**
         (off Cedar Av.)
Bernard St. NG5: Sher 1A **98**
Bernard Ter. NG5: Sher 1A **98**
Bernisdale Cl. NG5: Top V . . .3E **49**
Berridge Rd. NG7: H Grn 2F **97**
Berridge Rd. Central
  NG7: H Grn 2E **97**
Berridge Rd. W. NG7: H Grn . .3D **97**
Berriedale Cl. NG5: Arn 3A **52**
Berrydown Cl. NG8: Aspl 1B **96**
Berry Hill Gro. NG4: Ged 5D **77**
Berry Pk. Cl. DE22: D Abb . . .4D **107**
Berwick Cl. DE21: Chad 1B **136**
Berwick Cl. DE24: Alv 1A **188**
  NG5: Bestw 1B **74**
Berwick Dr. DE24: S Flds 3C **184**
Berwin Cl. NG10: Long E 2F **167**
Beryldene Av. NG16: Want 5F **45**
Besecar Av. NG4: Ged 5D **77**
Besecar Cl. NG4: Ged 5D **77**
Bessalone Dr. DE56: Bel 3F **13**
Bessell La. NG9: Stap 3B **144**
Besthorpe Cl. DE21: Oak 4A **110**
Bestwick Av. DE75: Hea 3A **42**
Bestwick Cl. DE7: Ilk 1F **115**
BESTWOOD 5A **50**
Bestwood Av. NG5: Arn 4D **51**
Bestwood Bus. Pk.
  NG6: Bestw V 1D **49**
Bestwood Cl. NG5: Arn 4D **51**
Bestwood Country Pk. 1D **49**
Bestwood Footpath
  NG15: Huck 4C **26**
Bestwood Lodge Dr.
  NG5: Arn 3B **50**
Bestwood Lodge Stables
  NG5: Arn 2A **50**
Bestwood Pk. NG5: Arn 2A **50**

Bestwood Pk. Dr.
  NG5: Top V 3A **50**
Bestwood Pk. Dr. W.
  NG5: Top V 3C **48**
Bestwood Pk. Vw. NG5: Arn . .3D **51**
Bestwood Rd. NG6: Bulw 4B **48**
  NG15: Huck 4B **26**
Bestwood Swimming Pool . . .1A **74**
Bestwood Ter. NG6: Bulw 4C **48**
BESTWOOD VILLAGE 5D **27**
Bethel Gdns. NG15: Huck . . .4B **24**
Bethnal Wlk. NG6: Bulw 5A **48**
Bethulie Rd. DE23: Der 3F **159**
Betjeman Sq. DE24: Sin 1F **185**
Betony Cl. NG13: Bing 3B **130**
Betula Cl. NG11: Clif 2B **172**
Bevel St. NG7: H Grn 3E **97**
Beverley Cl. NG8: Woll 1A **118**
Beverley Dr. NG16: Kimb 5D **45**
Beverley Gdns. NG4: Ged 1E **101**
Beverley Rd. DE74: N Air 4C **212**
Beverley Sq. NG3: Nott 3D **99**
Beverley St. DE24: Der 1C **160**
Bewcastle Rd.
  NG5: Arn, Top V 3F **49**
Bewdley Cl. DE73: Chel 3F **187**
Bewick Dr. NG3: Nott 5B **100**
Bexhill Cl. NG9: Bee 4D **119**
Bexhill Wlk. DE21: Chad 4D **109**
Bexleigh Gdns. NG8: Bilb . . .2F **95**
Bexon Ct. NG4: Carl 3D **101**
Bexwell Cl. NG11: Clif 3D **173**
Biant Cl. NG8: Cin 4A **72**
Bicester Av. DE24: S Flds 4B **184**
Bickley Moss DE21: Oak 4A **110**
Bideford Cl. DE5: Rip 4B **8**
Bideford Dr. DE23: Der 5C **158**
Bidford Rd. NG8: Brox 1E **95**
Bidford St. NG8: Brox 1E **95**
Biggart Cl. NG9: Chil 1B **170**
Biggin, The DE74: C Don 1A **212**
Big Moorside DE72: Ast T . . .1B **204**
Biko Sq. NG7: H Grn 2E **97**
Bilberry Cl. DE21: Oak 4E **109**
Bilberry Wlk. NG3: Nott 4D **99**
Bibble Wlk. NG1: Nott . . .1A **4** (5A **98**)
BILBOROUGH 3C **94**
Bilborough College Sports Cen.
   . . . . .3B **94**
Bilborough Rd. NG8: Stre 5A **94**
Bilby Gdns. NG3: Nott 5E **99**
Billesdon Dr. NG5: Sher 3E **73**
BINGHAM 2D **131**
Bingham By-Pass
  NG13: Bing 2A **130**
Bingham Ind. Pk.
  NG13: Bing 1D **131**
Bingham Leisure Cen. 2E **131**
Bingham Rd. NG5: Sher 5B **74**
  NG12: Cotg 5E **155**
          (not continuous)
  NG12: Rad T 2E **127**
Bingham Station (Rail) 1E **131**
Bingham St. DE24: A'ton 5D **161**
Bingley Cl. NG8: Bilb 4A **96**
Binscombe La. DE21: Oak . . .2E **109**
Birch Av. DE7: Ilk 3F **91**
  NG4: Carl 3C **100**
  NG9: Bee 4A **148**
  NG16: Nuth 1A **70**
Birch Cl. DE5: Rip 1C **16**
  DE21: Spon 2F **139**
  NG16: Nuth 1A **70**
Birchdale Av. NG15: Huck 4F **25**
Birches, The DE74: Dise 5B **212**

Birches Rd. DE22: All 2C **106**
Birchfield Cl. DE73: Chel 4E **187**
Birchfield Pk. DE75: Hea 5E **41**
Birchfield Rd. NG5: Arn 4F **51**
Birch Lea NG5: Redh 4C **50**
Birchover Ho. DE22: D Abb ..2E **107**
  DE22: Mark 5C **106**
Birchover Pl. DE7: Ilk 2D **67**
Birchover Ri. DE21: Chad 4E **109**
Birchover Rd. NG8: Bilb 5B **94**
Birchover Way DE22: All 4B **106**
Birch Pk. NG16: Newth 5F **43**
Birch Pas. NG7: Radf 5F **97**
Birch Ri. NG14: Woodbo 4B **32**
Birchview Cl. DE56: Bel 2A **36**
Birch Va. DE56: Bel 4E **13**
Birchway Gro. DE23: Lit 5F **157**
Birchwood DE75: Los 5B **18**
Birchwood Av. DE23: Lit 5C **158**
  DE72: Brea 4E **167**
  NG10: Long E 5B **168**
Birchwood Rd. NG8: Woll 1B **118**
Bircumshaw Rd. DE75: Hea ..2D **41**
Birdcage Wlk. DE22: Mac ...2D **133**
  (not continuous)
Birdcroft La. DE7: Ilk 5E **91**
Birdsall Av. NG8: Woll 1D **119**
Birdwood St. DE23: Der 2E **159**
Birkdale Cl. DE3: Mick 1F **157**
  DE7: Ilk 1C **90**
  NG12: Edwal 5F **151**
Birkdale Way NG5: Top V ...4E **49**
Birkin Av. NG7: H Grn 3E **97**
  NG9: Toton 1F **169**
  NG11: Rudd 3B **174**
  NG12: Rad T 1F **127**
Birkland Av. NG1: Nott 4B **98**
  NG3: Mapp 3F **75**
Birley St. NG9: Stap 3C **145**
Birling Cl. NG6: Bulw 5E **47**
Birrell Rd. NG7: H Grn 2F **97**
Biscay Ct. DE21: Oak 3B **110**
Bisham Dr. NG2: West Br ...1A **152**
Bishopdale Cl.
  NG10: Long E 5F **167**
Bishopdale Dr. NG16: Want ..5A **46**
Bishops Cl. DE5: Rip 1D **17**
  NG12: Key 2D **199**
Bishop's Dr. DE21: Oak 3C **108**
Bishops Grn. DE22: Der 5B **134**
Bishops Rd. NG13: Bing 1C **130**
Bishop St. NG16: Eastw 2E **43**
Bishops Way NG15: Huck 5D **11**
Bispham Dr. NG9: Toton 5E **145**
Blaby Cl. DE23: Der 5D **159**
Blackacre NG14: Bur J 2D **79**
Blackberry Way DE56: Kil 2E **37**
Blackbird Row DE56: Bar 3B **36**
BLACKBROOK 5B **12**
Blackburn Pl. DE7: Ilk 4D **67**
Blackburn Way NG5: Bestw ..2F **73**
Blackcliffe Farm M.
  NG11: Rudd 3D **197**
Blackden Cl. DE56: Bel 5D **15**
Blackett's Wlk. NG11: Clif ...3B **172**
Blackfriars Cl. NG16: Nuth ..5C **70**
Blackhill Dr. NG4: Carl 2E **101**
Black Hills Dr. DE7: Ilk 4D **91**
Blackmore St. DE23: Der 4E **159**
Blackmount Ct. DE24: Sin ...3C **184**
Blackrod Cl. NG9: Toton 1F **169**
Blacksmith Ct. NG12: Cotg ..4D **155**
Blacksmith Cft. DE5: Rip 2C **16**

Blacksmiths Ct. NG15: Pap ...3F **11**
Blackstone Wlk.
  NG2: Nott 3B **122**
Black Swan Cl. NG5: Sher ...3C **74**
Blackthorn Cl. DE21: Oak 3D **109**
  NG4: Ged 5F **77**
  NG13: Bing 2F **131**
Blackthorn Dr. NG6: Cin 4A **72**
  NG14: Lowd 2C **56**
  NG16: Eastw 2D **43**
Blackthorne Cl. DE56: Kil 2E **37**
Blackwell Av. DE7: Ilk 2E **67**
Bladon Cl. NG3: Mapp 5D **75**
Bladon Rd. NG11: Rudd 4A **174**
Blagreaves Av. DE23: Lit 1B **184**
Blagreaves La. DE23: Lit 4B **158**
Blair Ct. NG2: Nott 4B **122**
Blair Gro. NG10: Sand 4F **143**
Blaise Cl. NG11: Clif 3D **173**
Blakebrook Dr. DE73: Chel ...3F **187**
Blake Cl. NG5: Arn 5F **51**
Blake Ct. NG10: Long E 1A **194**
Blakelow Dr. DE65: Etw 3A **180**
Blakeney Cl. DE7: Ilk 4B **110**
Blakeney Rd. NG12: Rad T ...2A **128**
Blakeney Wlk. NG5: Arn 2E **75**
Blake Rd. NG2: West Br 1E **151**
  NG9: Stap 2D **145**
Blake St. DE7: Ilk 1E **91**
Blandford Av.
  NG10: Long E 5A **168**
Blandford Cl. DE24: Alv 5C **162**
Blandford Rd. NG9: Chil 3B **146**
Bland La. NG14: Epp 4F **33**
Blanford Gdns.
  NG2: West Br 3B **150**
Blankney Cl. DE24: S Flds ...4C **184**
Blankney St. NG6: Basf 3D **73**
Blantyre Av. NG5: Top V 3D **49**
Blatherwick Dr. NG15: Huck ..1A **26**
Blatherwick's Yd. NG5: Arn ..4E **51**
Bleaberry Cl. NG2: West Br ..3B **152**
Bleachers Yd. NG7: Basf 1D **97**
Bleasby St. NG2: Nott 1E **123**
Bleasdale Cl. NG4: Ged 5F **77**
Blencathra Cl.
  NG2: West Br 3B **152**
Blencathra Dr. DE3: Mick ...3D **157**
BLENHEIM 3E **47**
Blenheim Cl. NG3: Nott 3B **98**
Blenheim Av. NG3: Mapp 5B **76**
  NG14: Lowd 3D **57**
Blenheim Cl. NG11: Rudd ...4A **174**
Blenheim Cl. DE56: Bel 4C **14**
  NG10: Sand 4A **144**
Blenheim Dr. DE22: All 2B **106**
  NG9: Chil 3B **146**
Blenheim Ind. Est.
  NG6: Bulw 4E **47**
Blenheim La. NG6: Bulw 2C **46**
Blenheim M. DE65: Etw 2B **180**
Blenheim Pde. DE22: All 1C **106**
Blidworth Cl. NG8: Stre 5D **71**
Blidworth Waye NG15: Pap ..2F **11**
Blind La. DE72: Brea 3C **166**
  NG12: Key 4D **199**
Blithfield Gdns. DE73: Chel ..4F **187**
Bloomfield Cl. DE1: Der 5A **136**
Bloomfield St. DE1: Der 5A **136**
Bloomsbury Ct. NG1: Nott ...2D **5**
  (off Beck St.)
Bloomsbury Dr. NG16: Nuth ..4D **71**
Bloomsbury M.
  NG12: Rad T 2D **129**

Bloomsgrove Ind. Est.
  NG7: Radf 5E **97**
Bloomsgrove Rd. DE7: Ilk ...5E **67**
Bloomsgrove St. NG7: Radf ..5E **97**
Bloom St. DE1: Der 4D **7** (4F **135**)
Bluebell Bank NG13: Bing ...3C **130**
Bluebell Cl. DE24: S Flds ...4B **184**
  NG15: Huck 3B **24**
Blue Bell Hill Rd. NG3: Nott ..4D **99**
Bluebell Way DE75: Hea 3A **42**
Bluebird Ct. DE24: Sin 2C **184**
Bluecoat Cl.
  NG1: Nott 1B **4** (4B **98**)
Bluecoat Ho.
  NG1: Nott 1B **4** (4B **98**)
Bluecoat St.
  NG1: Nott 1B **4** (4B **98**)
Blue Mountains DE56: Duff ..1A **84**
Blundell Cl. NG3: Nott 2E **99**
Blunt St. DE7: Stan C 5F **63**
Blyth Cl. DE74: C Don 5A **206**
Blyth St. NG3: Mapp 1D **99**
Blyton Wlk. NG5: Bestw 5A **50**
Boat La. NG16: Iron 2E **19**
Boatmans Cl. DE7: Ilk 5E **67**
Boatswain Dr. NG15: Huck ...1A **26**
Bobbers Mill NG7: H Grn 3D **97**
Bobbers Mill Bri.
  NG7: H Grn 3C **96**
  NG8: H Grn 3C **96**
Bobbers Mill Rd.
  NG7: H Grn 3D **97**
Bobbin Way DE56: Bel 4A **14**
Boden Dr. NG16: Nuth 1B **70**
Boden St. DE23: Der 1A **160**
  NG7: Radf 5E **97**
Bodill Gdns. NG15: Huck 3B **26**
Bodmin Av. NG15: Huck 4B **24**
Bodmin Cl. DE24: S Flds 3C **184**
Bodmin Dr. NG8: Aspl 5B **72**
Bodmin Grn. DE24: Alv 5A **162**
Body Rd. NG9: Chil 5A **146**
BOGEND 2D **45**
Bohem Rd. NG10: Long E ...5B **144**
Bolcote Ho. NG4: Carl 2D **101**
  (off Foxhill Rd. E.)
Bold Cl. NG6: Bulw 4A **48**
Bold La. DE1: Der 2C **6** (3F **135**)
Bolero Cl. NG8: Woll 5D **95**
Bolero Sq. NG1: Nott 3E **5**
Bolingey Way NG15: Huck ...4B **24**
Bollard's La. LE12: Sub B ...5F **215**
Bolsover Cl. DE5: Rip 5D **9**
Bolsover St. NG15: Huck 2A **26**
Bolton Av. NG9: Chil 4B **146**
Bolton Rd. NG2: West Br 2F **151**
Bolton Ter. NG12: Rad T 2E **127**
Bonchurch Cl. DE24: Alv 1B **188**
Bondgate DE74: C Don 1F **211**
Bonds Cl. DE7: Ilk 2E **67**
Bond St. NG2: Nott 3F **5** (1D **123**)
  NG5: Arn 4D **51**
Bonetti Cl. NG5: Arn 2A **76**
Boniface Gdns. NG5: Top V ..3F **49**
Bonington Dr. NG5: Arn 5E **51**
Bonington Gallery, The 1A **4**
Bonington Rd. NG3: Mapp ...3E **75**
Bonington Theatre 4E **51**
Bonner Hill NG14: Calv 3E **31**
Bonner La. NG14: Calv 2F **31**
Bonner's Rd. NG16: Aws 3B **68**
Bonnington Cl. NG6: Bulw ...1F **71**

Bonnington Cres. NG5: Sher . . .3B **74**
Bonnymead NG12: Cotg 1D **179**
Bonnyrigg Dr. DE21: Oak 3F **109**
Bonsall Av. DE23: Der 2C **158**
Bonsall Ct. NG10: Long E 3D **169**
Bonsall Dr. DE3: Mick 5D **133**
Bonsall St. NG10: Long E 3D **169**
Bonser Cl. NG4: Carl 3D **101**
Bonser Hedge Ct.
    NG10: Long E 2A **194**
Booth Cl. NG3: Nott 1D **5** (5C **98**)
BOOTHGATE 2D **15**
Boothgate DE56: Bel 2D **15**
Booths Gdns. DE7: Ilk 3E **67**
Booth St. DE5: Rip 4D **9**
    DE24: Alv 4E **161**
Border Bank DE5: Mare 3C **16**
Border Cres. DE24: Alv 1F **187**
Borlace Cres. NG9: Stap 2D **145**
Borman Cl. NG6: Bulw 2E **71**
Borough St. C Don 1A **212**
    DE74: Keg 2C **214**
BORROWASH 1A **164**
Borrowash Bri. DE72: Elv 3F **163**
Borrowash By-Pass
    DE21: Spon, Ris 4C **138**
Borrowash La. DE72: Elv 5F **163**
Borrowash Rd. DE21: Spon . . .5E **139**
Borrowdale Cl. NG2: Gam 2C **152**
Borrowdale Ct. NG9: Chil 4A **146**
Borrowdale Dr.
    NG10: Long E 5F **167**
Borrowell DE74: Keg 1B **214**
Borrowfield Rd. DE21: Spon . .5D **139**
Borrowfields DE72: Bor 2A **164**
Boscastle Rd. DE24: Alv 5A **162**
Boscawen Ct. DE7: Ilk 4E **67**
Bosden Cl. NG8: Bilb 4B **94**
Bosley M. DE56: Bel 4E **13**
Bosley Sq. NG9: Lent A 5F **119**
Bostock's La. DE72: Ris 4E **143**
    NG10: Sand 5F **143**
Boston Cl. DE21: Chad 2B **138**
Boston M. NG5: Sher 4E **73**
Boston St. NG1: Nott . . .2E **5** (5C **98**)
Boswell Sq. DE23: Der 4E **159**
Boswell St. NG7: Radf 5D **97**
Bosworth Av. DE23: Der 5D **159**
Bosworth Cl. NG12: Shel 2B **104**
Bosworth Dr. NG16: Newth . . .1A **44**
Bosworth Rd. DE74: C Don . . .1E **211**
Bosworth Wlk. NG2: Nott 4A **122**
Bosworth Way
    NG10: Long E 1C **194**
Botany Av. NG3: Nott 3E **99**
Botany Cl. NG2: West Br 5B **150**
Botany M. NG3: Nott 3E **99**
Bothe Cl. NG10: Long E 5B **168**
Bottle Brook DE5: Den 3A **38**
Bottle La. NG1: Nott . . .3C **4** (1B **122**)
Boulevard Ind. Pk.
    NG9: Bee 2A **148**
BOULTON 5F **161**
Boulton Dr. DE24: Alv 5F **161**
Boulton La.
    DE24: A'ton, Alv 1D **187**
    (not continuous)
Boundary Ct. DE74: C Don . . .3A **206**
Boundary Cres. NG9: Bee 4E **119**
Boundary La. NG16: Lang M . . .1B **42**
Boundary Rd. DE22: Der 4D **135**
    DE65: Egg 5B **180**
    NG2: West Br 4D **151**
    NG9: Bee 4E **119**

Bourne Cl. NG9: Bram 4C **118**
Bourne Dr. NG16: Lang M 1A **42**
Bourne M. NG4: Neth 4F **101**
Bourne Sq. DE72: Brea 3D **167**
Bourne St. DE1: Der . . .5D **7** (4F **135**)
    NG4: Neth 4F **101**
Bournmoor Av. NG11: Clif . . .2D **173**
Bovill St. NG7: Radf 4E **97**
Bowbank Cl. DE23: Lit 5F **157**
Bowbridge Av. DE23: Lit 1B **184**
Bowden Cl. NG5: Sher 4B **74**
Bowden Dr. NG9: Bee 2A **148**
Bowers Av. NG3: Mapp P 3C **98**
Bower St. DE24: Alv 3E **161**
Bowes Well Rd. DE7: Ilk 5D **67**
Bowland Cl. DE3: Mick 2D **157**
    NG3: Nott 3F **99**
Bowland Rd. NG13: Bing 2B **130**
Bowlees Ct. DE23: Lit 4D **157**
Bowler Dr. DE56: Kil 5F **37**
Bowler St. DE5: Rip 2C **16**
Bowling Cl. DE7: Stan D 5D **115**
Bowlwell Av. NG5: Top V 4E **49**
Bowmer Rd. DE24: Der 2D **161**
Bown Cl. DE56: Kil 4F **37**
Bowness Av. NG6: Basf 5B **72**
Bowness Cl. NG2: Gam 1B **152**
Bowscale Cl. NG2: West Br . .3B **152**
Boxley Dr. NG2: West Br 4B **150**
Boxmoor Cl. DE23: Lit 4E **157**
Boyce Gdns. NG3: Mapp 1E **99**
Boycroft Av. NG3: Nott 2E **99**
Boyd Cl. NG5: Arn 3A **52**
Boyd Gro. DE73: Chel 1E **201**
Boyer St. DE22: Der 5D **135**
Boyer Wlk.
    DE22: Der 5B **6** (5E **135**)
Boylestone Rd. DE23: Lit 1B **184**
Boynton Dr. NG3: Mapp 1E **99**
Boythorpe Cl. DE7: Ilk 2E **67**
Bracadale Rd. NG5: Top V . . .3E **49**
Bracebridge Dr. NG8: Bilb 4C **94**
Bracey Ri. NG2: West Br 5D **151**
Bracken Cl. NG4: Carl 5C **76**
    NG8: Bilb 1E **95**
    NG10: Long E 2A **168**
Brackendale Av. NG5: Arn 4E **51**
Brackenfield Dr. NG16: Gilt . . .4A **44**
Bracken Rd. NG10: Long E . . .2A **168**
Brackens Av. DE24: Alv 5E **161**
Brackensdale Av.
    DE22: Mac 3A **134**
Bracken's La. DE24: Alv 5D **161**
Brackley DE56: Kil 3E **37**
Brackley Dr. DE21: Spon 3D **139**
Brackley Ga. DE7: Mor 5F **61**
    DE21: Bre 5F **61**
Bracknell Cres. NG8: Basf 1C **96**
Bracknell Dr. DE24: Alv 1E **187**
Bracton Dr. NG3: Nott 4E **99**
Bradbourne Av. NG11: Wilf . . .3F **149**
Bradbourne Ct. DE22: Der . . .5D **135**
Bradbury Cl. DE72: Bor 2B **164**
Bradbury Gdns.
    NG11: Rudd 4A **174**
Bradbury/Midway Ind. Est.
    NG7: Lent 5D **121**
Bradbury St. NG2: Nott 1F **123**
Braddock Cl. NG7: Lent 1D **121**
Braddon Av. NG9: Stap 4D **117**
Bradfield Rd. NG8: Brox 1E **95**
Bradford Cl. NG6: Bulw 1F **71**
Bradgate Cl. NG10: Sand 4A **144**
Bradgate Ct. DE23: Der 5D **159**

Bradgate Dr. DE5: Rip 5A **8**
    (Heage Rd.)
    DE5: Rip 1E **17**
    (Peasehill)
Bradgate Rd. NG7: H Grn 2F **97**
Brading Cl. DE24: Alv 1C **188**
Bradley Ct. DE23: Der 3F **159**
    NG9: Bee 2F **147**
Bradley Dr. DE56: Bel 5A **14**
Bradley St. DE22: Der 5D **107**
    NG10: Sand 3B **144**
Bradleys Yd. NG12: Plum 4D **177**
Bradley Wlk. NG11: Clif 3E **173**
Bradman Gdns. NG5: Arn 1A **76**
Bradmoor Gro. DE73: Chel . . .4A **188**
BRADMORE 3D **197**
Bradmore Av. NG11: Rudd . . .3B **174**
Bradmore La. NG12: Plum . . .2B **198**
Bradmore Ri. NG5: Sher 3B **74**
Bradshaw Cft. DE56: Bel 3D **13**
Bradshaw Dr. DE56: H'ook . . .1B **60**
Bradshaw Retail Pk.
    DE1: Der 5E **7** (4F **135**)
Bradshaw St.
    NG10: Long E 1A **194**
Bradshaw Way
    DE1: Der 5E **7** (4A **136**)
Bradwell Cl. DE3: Mick 2D **157**
    NG16: Gilt 4B **44**
Bradwell Dr. NG5: Top V 4E **49**
Bradwell Way DE56: Bel 4A **14**
Braeburn Cl. DE23: Der 1D **159**
Braefell Cl. NG2: West Br 3C **152**
Braefield Cl. DE7: Kirk H 5B **90**
Braemar Av. NG16: Eastw 4E **43**
Braemar Cl. DE24: S Flds 3C **184**
Braemar Dr. NG4: Ged 1A **102**
Braemar M. NG6: Bulw 5B **48**
Brafield Cl. DE56: Bel 5C **14**
Braidwood Ct. NG7: H Grn 3E **97**
Brailsford Rd. DE21: Chad . . .5D **109**
    NG7: Lent 4D **121**
Brailsford Way NG9: Chil 2B **170**
Braintree Cl. DE21: Chad 3C **108**
Braithwell Cl. DE22: D Abb . . .3E **107**
Bramber Gro. NG11: Clif 4D **173**
Brambleberry Ct.
    DE21: Oak 2A **110**
Bramble Cl. NG6: Basf 4C **72**
    NG9: Atten 1C **170**
    NG10: Long E 2A **168**
Bramble Ct. NG4: Ged 1E **101**
Bramble Dr. NG3: Nott 3F **99**
Bramble Gdns. NG8: Bilb 2F **95**
Bramble M. DE3: Mick 2C **156**
Bramble St.
    DE1: Der 3B **6** (3E **135**)
Bramble Way DE56: Kil 2E **37**
    NG12: Cotg 1F **179**
Bramblewick Dr. DE23: Lit . . .5F **157**
Brambling Cres. DE3: Mick . . .4A **156**
BRAMCOTE 5F **117**
Bramcote Av. NG9: Chil 2B **146**
Bramcote Crematorium
    NG9: Bram 2E **117**
Bramcote Dr. NG8: Woll 2C **118**
    NG9: Bee 1D **147**
Bramcote Dr. W. NG9: Bee . . .2C **146**
BRAMCOTE HILLS 4B **118**
Bramcote La. NG8: Woll 3C **118**
    NG9: Chil 2B **146**
Bramcote Rd. NG9: Bee 1C **146**
Bramcote St. NG7: Radf 5D **97**
Bramcote Wlk. NG7: Radf 5D **97**

Bramerton Rd. NG8: Bilb 4B 94
Bramfield Av. DE22: Der 5D 135
Bramfield Ct. DE22: Der 5D 135
Bramhall Rd. NG8: Bilb 4B 94
Bramley Cl. DE21: Oak 2B 110
  NG14: Gun 2F 81
Bramley Ct. NG16: Kimb 1E 69
Bramley Grn. NG8: Brox 1D 95
Bramley Rd. NG8: Brox 1D 95
  NG10: Long E 1A 194
Brampton Av. DE75: Hea 2F 41
Brampton Cl. DE3: Mick 5B 132
  DE7: Ilk 2E 67
Brampton Ct. DE56: Bel 5C 14
Brampton Dr. NG9: Stap 3E 145
Brancaster Cl. NG6: Cin 3A 72
Brandelhow Ct. DE21: Oak . . .2A 110
Brandish Cres. NG11: Clif 2C 172
Brandreth Av. NG3: Nott 2E 99
Brandreth Dr. NG16: Gilt 4F 43
Brands Cl. DE7: Ilk 2E 67
Brand St. NG2: Nott 3E 123
Branklene Cl. NG16: Kimb 5D 45
Branksome Av. DE24: Alv 4B 162
Branksome Wlk. NG2: Nott . . .3B 122
Bransdale Cl.
  NG10: Long E 5A 168
Bransdale Rd. NG11: Clif 2C 172
Branston Gdns.
  NG2: West Br 4C 150
Branston Wlk. NG5: Sher 3B 74
Brantford Av. NG11: Clif 2E 173
Brassington Cl. DE7: West H . .2D 89
  NG16: Gilt 5A 44
Brassington Rd.
  DE21: Chad 4E 109
Bratton Dr. NG5: Bestw 2F 73
Braunton Cl. NG15: Huck 3C 24
Brayfield Av. DE23: Lit 3C 158
Brayfield Rd. DE23: Lit 3B 158
Brayton Cres. NG6: Bulw 2C 72
Breach Rd. DE5: Den 5E 17
  DE75: Hea 4F 41
BREADSALL 1D 109
Breadsall Ct. DE7: Ilk 4E 67
BREADSALL HILLTOP 2D 109
Break La. NG15: Pap 1F 11
BREASTON 3C 166
Breaston Ct. NG5: Top V 4F 49
       (off Erewash Gdns.)
Breaston Ind. Est.
  DE72: Dray 4B 166
Breaston La. DE72: Ris 5C 142
Brechin Cl. NG5: Arn 3A 52
Breckhill Rd. NG3: Mapp 2D 75
  NG5: Woodt 2D 75
Brecknock Dr.
  NG10: Long E 4F 167
Breckswood Dr. NG11: Clif . . .4D 173
Brecon Cl. DE21: Spon 2D 139
  NG8: Cin 4F 71
  NG10: Long E 3F 167
Bredon Cl. NG10: Long E 3F 167
Breedon Av. DE23: Lit 1C 104
Breedon Hill Rd. DE23: Der . . .5E 135
Breedon St. NG10: Long E 5A 144
Brendan Gdns.
  DE22: D Abb 4D 107
Brendon Ct. NG9: Bram 5A 118
Brendon Dr. NG8: Woll 5F 95
  NG16: Kimb 5F 45
Brendon Gdns. NG8: Woll 5F 95
Brendon Gro. NG13: Bing 1B 130
Brendon Rd. NG8: Woll 5F 95

Brendon Way NG10: Long E . . .1F 167
Brentcliffe Av. NG3: Nott 3F 99
Brentford Dr. DE22: Mac 2A 134
Brentnall Cl. NG10: Long E . . .4A 168
Brentnall Ct. NG9: Chil 5C 146
Bressingham Dr.
  NG2: West Br 5B 150
Bretby Sq. DE23: Lit 1B 184
Brett Cl. NG15: Huck 4D 25
Bretton Av. DE23: Lit 1B 158
Bretton Rd. DE56: Bel 4D 15
Brettsil Dr. NG11: Rudd 4A 174
Brewery St. NG16: Kimb 1E 69
Brewhouse Mus. 5A 4
Brewhouse Yd.
  NG7: Nott 5A 4 (2A 122)
Brewsters Cl. NG13: Bing 2D 131
Brewsters Rd. NG3: Nott 2D 99
Breydon Cl. DE24: S Loc 2C 186
Breydon Ind. Cen.
  NG10: Long E 4E 169
Brian Clough Way
  DE21: Chad, Der 3C 136
  DE72: Ock 5F 139
  NG7: Lent, Nott 1E 121
  NG9: Bram, Stap 2E 145
Briar Av. NG10: Sand 5F 143
Briarbank Av. NG3: Nott 2F 99
Briarbank Wlk. NG3: Nott 3F 99
Briar Cl. DE21: Chad 4A 138
  DE72: Bor 1B 164
  NG9: Bram 4D 119
  NG12: Key 2E 199
  NG15: Huck 4C 24
Briar Ct. NG2: Nott 4A 122
Briar Gdns. NG14: Calv 1B 30
Briar Ga. NG10: Long E 1F 167
  NG12: Cotg 1F 179
Briar Lea Cl. DE24: Sin 2E 185
Briar Rd. NG16: Newth 4A 44
Briarsgate DE22: All 3C 106
Briars La. DE23: Lit 4F 157
       (not continuous)
Briars Way DE5: Rip 5C 8
Briarwood Av. NG3: Nott 3F 99
Briarwood Ct. NG5: Sher 4D 75
Briarwood Way DE23: Lit 5B 158
Brickenell Rd. NG14: Calv 3E 31
Brick Kiln La. DE7: Mor 2A 86
Brick Row DE22: D Abb 4F 107
Brick St. DE1: Der 1A 6 (2D 135)
Brickyard NG15: Huck 3B 26
Brickyard, The DE7: Stan C . . .1A 88
Brickyard Cotts.
  NG16: Newth 3F 43
Brickyard Dr. NG15: Huck 4B 26
Brickyard La. DE5: Rip 5E 9
  DE56: Kil 2E 37
  NG12: Rad T 2A 128
Brickyard Plantation Nature Reserve
  . . . . .2D 93
Bridge, The DE56: Mil 5F 35
Bridge Av. NG9: Chil 3D 147
Bridge Ct. NG0: Boo 1A 148
  NG15: Huck 3F 25
Bri. Farm La. NG11: Clif 1D 173
Bridge Fld. DE72: Brea 4B 166
Bridge Flds. DE74: Keg 1D 215
Bridge Foot DE56: Bel 4D 13
Bridgeford Ct. Cvn. Pk.
  NG13: East B 4F 81
Bridge Ga. DE1: Der 1C 6 (2D 135)
Bridge Grn. NG8: Brox 1D 95
Bridge Grn. Wlk. NG8: Brox . . .1D 95

Bridge Gro. NG2: West Br 5D 123
BRIDGEHILL 4D 13
Bridge Hill DE56: Bel 4D 13
Bridge La. DE72: W Tre 5B 202
Bridgend Cl. NG9: Stap 3C 144
Bridgend Ct. DE21: Oak 3B 110
Bridgeness Rd. DE23: Lit 5E 157
Bridgeport Rd. DE21: Chad . . .2B 138
Bridge Rd. NG8: Woll 5C 94
Bridge St. DE1: Der 1A 6 (2E 135)
  DE7: Ilk 3E 67
  DE56: Bel 5E 13
  NG10: Long E 2C 168
  NG10: Sand 3B 144
  NG16: Lang M 1B 42
Bridge Vw. DE56: Mil 5F 35
Bridgeway Cen. NG2: Nott . . .3B 122
Bridgeway Ct. NG2: Nott 3C 122
Bridge Yard Av. DE5: Rip 2D 9
Bridgford Rd.
  NG2: West Br 4D 123
Bridgnorth Dr. NG11: Clif 1D 173
Bridgnorth Way NG9: Toton . .5D 145
Bridgwater Ct. DE24: Alv 4B 162
Bridle Cl. DE73: Chel 1E 201
Bridle Ga. La. DE24: Alv 4C 162
Bridle La. DE5: Rip 3C 8
Bridle Rd. NG9: Bram 4A 118
  NG14: Bur J 1C 78
Bridlesmith Ga.
  NG1: Nott 3C 4 (1B 122)
Bridlington St. NG7: H Grn 3D 97
Bridport Av. NG8: Radf 5C 96
Brielen Cl. NG12: Rad T 2F 127
Brielen Rd. NG12: Rad T 2F 127
Brierfield Av. NG11: Wilf 4A 150
Brierfield Way DE3: Mick 2D 157
Brierley Grn. NG4: Neth 3F 101
Brigden Av. DE24: A'ton 4D 161
Brighstone Cl. DE24: Alv 1B 188
Brightmoor Ct.
  NG1: Nott 3D 5 (1C 122)
Brightmoor St.
  NG1: Nott 3D 5 (1C 122)
Brighton Rd. DE24: Alv 2E 161
Bright St. DE7: Ilk 4D 67
  DE22: Der 3B 134
  NG7: Lent 5D 97
  NG16: Kimb 1D 69
Brigmor Wlk. DE22: Der 3C 134
Brimington Cl. DE7: Ilk 1E 67
Brindle Way DE23: Lit 1F 183
Brindley Cl. DE24: A'ton 5D 161
Brindley Rd. NG8: Bilb 5B 94
Brindley Wlk. DE24: S Flds . . .4D 185
Brinkhill Cres. NG11: Clif 5E 149
BRINSLEY 3D 21
Brinsley Cl. NG8: Aspl 1F 95
Brisbane Dr. NG5: Top V 4D 49
  NG9: Stap 4E 117
Brisbane Rd. DE3: Mick 4D 133
Briset Cl. DE24: S Flds 4D 185
Bristol Dr. DE3: Mick 1D 157
Bristol Rd. DE7: Ilk 1D 91
Britannia Av. DE5: Rip 2F 17
  NG6: Basf 2D 73
Britannia Cl. NG16: Want 5F 45
Britannia Ct. DE1: Der 2F 135
  NG4: Neth 4F 101
Britannia Rd.
  NG10: Long E 2C 168
British Geological Survey . . .2E 199
Brittain Dr. DE5: Rip 5F 9
Brittain Pit Farm Pk. 2F 9

Britten Gdns. NG3: Nott 4E **99**
Brixham Rd. NG15: Huck 4C **24**
Brixton Rd. NG7: Radf 5D **97**
B Road NG7: Nott 2C **148**
Broad Bank DE22: Der 5D **107**
Broad Cl. NG14: Woodbo 5B **32**
Broad Eadow Rd. NG6: Bulw . .5E **47**
Broadfields NG14: Calv 1E **31**
Broadfields Cl. DE22: Der 5E **107**
Broadgate NG9: Bee 1F **147**
Broadgate Av. NG9: Bee 1F **147**
Broadgate La. NG9: Bee 1F **147**
Broadgate Pk. NG9: Bee 5F **119**
Broadhill Rd. DE74: Keg 2B **214**
BROADHOLME 2E **13**
Broadholme La. DE56: Bel 2E **13**
Broadholme St. NG7: Lent 2E **121**
Broadhurst Av. NG6: Basf 5C **72**
Broadlands NG10: Sand 5A **144**
Broad La. DE72: Thul 2E **189**
NG16: Brins 1D **21**
Broadleaf Cl. DE21: Oak 3D **109**
Broadleigh Cl.
NG2: West Br 5B **150**
Broad Marsh
NG1: Nott 5C **4** (2B **122**)
Broad Marsh Shop. Cen.
NG1: Nott 4C **4** (1B **122**)
Broadmead NG14: Bur J 2E **79**
Broadmeer NG12: Cotg 5D **155**
Broadmere Ct. NG5: Arn 3A **52**
Broad Oak Cl. NG3: Nott 3D **99**
Broad Oak Dr. NG9: Stap 2C **144**
NG16: Brins 1C **20**
Broad Rushes DE74: C Don . .3A **206**
Broadstairs Rd. NG9: Toton . . .1E **169**
Broadstone Cl. DE21: Chad . . .4F **109**
NG2: West Br 3B **150**
Broad St. NG1: Nott . . .2D **5** (5C **98**)
NG10: Long E 4C **168**
Broad Valley Dr.
NG6: Bestw V 5D **27**
Broad Wlk. NG6: Basf 4B **72**
Broadway DE5: Rip 4D **9**
DE7: Ilk 4D **67**
DE22: Der 5C **106**
DE56: Duff 4C **58**
DE75: Hea 3D **41**
NG1: Nott 4D **5** (1C **122**)
Broadway Av. DE5: Rip 5D **9**
Broadway Ct. DE5: Rip 4D **9**
Broadway E. NG4: Carl 4C **100**
Broadway Media Cen. 3D **5**
Broadway Pk. Cl.
DE22: Der 5D **107**
Broadwood Ct. NG9: Bee 5F **119**
Broadwood Rd. NG5: Bestw . . .4A **50**
Brockdale Gdns.
NG12: Key 2D **199**
Brockenhurst Gdns.
NG3: Nott 4E **99**
Brockhall Ri. DE75: Hea 3F **41**
Brockhole Cl.
NG2: West Br 3C **152**
Brockley DE21: Spon 3D **139**
Brockley Rd. NG2: West Br . . .1A **152**
Brockwood Cres.
NG12: Key 2D **199**
Brodie Cl. DE73: Chel 4D **187**
Bromfield Cl. NG3: Nott 3B **100**
Bromley Cl. NG6: Bulw 1A **72**
Bromley Ct. DE7: Ilk 3F **91**
Bromley Pl.
NG1: Nott 3A **4** (1A **122**)

Bromley Rd. NG2: West Br . . .2D **151**
Bromley St. DE22: Der 1D **135**
Brompton Cl. NG5: Arn 2F **49**
Brompton Rd. DE22: Mac 2E **133**
(not continuous)
Brompton Way
NG2: West Br 5B **150**
Bromyard Dr. DE73: Chel 3F **187**
Bronte Cl. NG10: Long E 4F **167**
Bronte Ct. NG7: Radf 4F **97**
Bronte Pl. DE23: Lit 3A **158**
Brook Av. NG5: Arn 4A **52**
Brookbridge Ct.
DE1: Der 1A **6** (2E **135**)
Brook Cl. DE22: Quar 1B **106**
DE65: Find 5C **182**
NG6: Bulw 1A **72**
NG10: Long E 1D **195**
NG16: Newth 3A **44**
Brook Cotts. DE7: Ilk 4E **67**
Brook Ct. NG7: Radf 5E **97**
NG16: Lang M 2A **42**
Brookdale Ct. NG5: Sher 2C **74**
Brookdale Dr. DE23: Lit 1F **183**
Brooke Cl. DE56: Bel 1E **35**
Brooke St. DE7: Ilk 4A **92**
NG10: Sand 3A **144**
Brookfield DE73: Bar T 3A **200**
Brookfield Av. DE21: Chad . . .5A **110**
DE23: Der 5C **158**
NG15: Huck 4F **25**
Brookfield Cl. DE5: Cod 5F **51**
NG12: Rad T 2E **127**
Brookfield Ct. NG2: Nott 3B **122**
NG5: Arn 5F **51**
Brookfield Gdns. NG5: Arn . . .5F **51**
Brookfield M. NG10: Sand 2B **144**
Brookfield Rd. NG5: Arn 5E **51**
Brookfields DE56: L Kil 5D **37**
Brookfields Dr. DE21: Bre 1E **108**
Brookfield Way DE75: Hea 3A **42**
Brook Gdns.
DE1: Der 1A **6** (2D **135**)
NG5: Arn 4F **51**
BROOK HILL 3F **173**
Brookhill Cres. NG8: Woll 2D **119**
Brookhill Dr. NG8: Woll 2D **119**
Brookhill Leys Rd.
NG16: Eastw 3D **43**
Brookhill St. NG9: Stap 3B **144**
Brook Ho. DE1: Der 1A **6**
Brookhouse St. DE24: A'ton . . .1C **186**
Brookland Cl. NG14: Gun 2F **81**
Brookland Dr. NG9: Chil 3C **146**
Brooklands Av. DE75: Hea 2E **41**
Brooklands Cres. NG4: Ged . . .1F **101**
Brooklands Dr. DE23: Lit 3B **158**
NG4: Ged 1F **101**
Brooklands Rd. NG3: Nott 3A **100**
Brook La. DE5: Rip 2C **16**
Brooklyn Av. NG14: Bur J 3D **79**
Brooklyn Cl. NG6: Bulw 2C **72**
Brooklyn Rd. NG6: Bulw 1C **72**
Brook Rd. DE72: Bor 2A **164**
DE72: Thul 2E **189**
NG9: Bee 5E **119**
Brooksby La. NG11: Clif 4E **149**
Brooks Cotts. NG4: Carl 3B **100**
Brooks Hollow DE21: L Eat . . .3B **84**
Brookside DE1: Der 2E **135**
DE56: Bel 1E **35**
NG14: Lowd 3C **56**
NG15: Huck 4A **26**
NG16: Eastw 5E **21**

Brookside Av. NG8: Woll 3C **118**
Brookside Cl. DE1: Der 1D **135**
NG10: Long E 3A **168**
Brookside Cotts.
NG14: Bur J 2D **79**
Brookside Gdns.
NG11: Rudd 3A **174**
Brookside Ind. Units
NG9: Stap 5C **116**
Brookside Rd. DE21: Bre 1C **108**
NG11: Rudd 3A **174**
Brook St. DE1: Der 1A **6** (2E **135**)
DE56: H'age 1D **15**
DE75: Los 4A **18**
NG1: Nott 2D **5** (5C **98**)
NG15: Huck 1F **25**
Brookthorpe Way
NG11: Wilf 4F **149**
Brookvale Av. DE5: Cod 1A **18**
DE5: Den 2F **37**
Brookvale Ri. DE5: Den 2F **37**
Brookvale Rd. DE5: Den 2F **37**
NG16: Lang M 2B **42**
Brook Vw. Ct. NG12: Key 4D **199**
Brook Vw. Dr. NG12: Key 4D **199**
Brook Walkway
DE1: Der 1A **6** (2E **135**)
Brookwood Cres. NG4: Carl . . .3B **100**
Broom Cl. DE24: S Flds 4C **184**
DE56: Bel 4D **13**
DE56: Duff 4C **58**
DE73: Chel 4E **187**
NG14: Calv 1E **31**
Bromfield Cl. NG10: Sand 3F **143**
BROOMHILL 4B **26**
Broomhill Av. DE7: Ilk 4F **91**
(not continuous)
Broomhill Cl. DE3: Mick 5C **132**
Broomhill Cotts.
NG15: Huck 4B **26**
Broomhill Pk. Vw.
NG15: Huck 4B **26**
Broomhill Rd. NG6: Bulw 1B **72**
NG15: Huck 4F **25**
NG16: Kimb 1F **69**
Broom Rd. NG14: Calv 2E **31**
Broom Wlk. NG3: Nott 2A **100**
Brora Rd. NG6: Bulw 5C **48**
Brough St. DE22: Der 3C **134**
Broughton Av. DE23: Lit 2C **158**
Broughton Cl. DE7: Ilk 4D **67**
Broughton Dr. NG8: Woll 1B **120**
Broughton St. NG9: Bee 1E **147**
Brownes Rd. NG13: Bing 1F **131**
Browning Circ. DE23: Der 4E **159**
Browning Cl. NG5: Arn 5C **50**
Browning Ct. NG5: Sher 4A **74**
Browning St. DE23: Der 5E **159**
Brownlow Dr. NG5: Top V 3C **48**
Browns Cft. NG6: Basf 4C **72**
Brown's Flats NG16: Kimb 5E **45**
Brown's La. DE56: H'ook 5C **36**
Brown's Rd. NG10: Long E . . .3D **169**
Brown St. NG7: H Grn 3E **97**
BROXTOWE 5F **71**
Broxtowe Av. NG8: Aspl 5B **72**
NG16: Kimb 1C **68**
Broxtowe Country Pk. 5D **71**
Broxtowe Dr. NG15: Huck 5C **10**
Broxtowe Hall Cl. NG8: Brox . .5F **71**
Broxtowe La.
NG8: Aspl, Brox 1E **95**
Broxtowe Ri. NG8: Cin 4A **72**

Broxtowe St. NG5: Sher 5B 74
Bruce Cl. NG2: Nott 3C 122
Bruce Dr. NG2: West Br 1C 150
Brunel Av. NG16: Newth 5A 22
Brunel Parkway DE24: Der . . .5C 136
Brunel Ter. NG7: Lent 5F 97
Brun La. DE22: Mac 1A 132
Brunswick Dr. NG9: Stap 3D 145
Brunswick St. DE23: Der 2E 159
Brunswood Cl. DE21: Spon . . .3D 139
Brunton Cl. DE3: Mick 2B 156
Brushfield St. NG7: H Grn 3D 97
Brussells Ter. DE7: Ilk 1D 91
(off Bath St.)
Brusty Pl. NG14: Bur J 2D 79
Bryan Ct. NG8: Aspl 2B 96
Brynsmoor Rd. NG16: Brins . . .2D 21
Bryony Cl. DE21: Oak 4F 109
Buchanan St. DE1: Der 2F 135
Buchan St. DE24: Der 4C 160
Buckfast Way NG2: West Br . . .1F 151
Buckingham Av.
DE21: Chad 5C 108
NG15: Huck 1A 26
Buckingham Ct.
NG10: Sand 5F 143
Buckingham Dr. DE75: Hea . . .2B 40
NG12: Rad T 3C 128
Buckingham Rd.
NG5: Woodt 2D 75
NG10: Sand 5F 143
Buckingham Way
NG16: Want 5A 46
Buckland Cl. DE1: Der 2D 135
Buckland Dr. NG14: Woodbo . .5B 32
Bucklee Dr. NG14: Calv 2D 31
Bucklow Cl. NG8: Basf 1C 96
Buckminster Cl. DE21: Oak . . .3E 109
Buckminster Rd.
DE7: Kirk H 1B 114
Buck's La. LE12: Sut B 5F 215
Budby Ri. NG15: Huck 2A 26
BULCOTE 1A 80
Bulcote Dr. NG14: Bur J 4C 78
Bulcote Rd. NG11: Clif 5E 149
Bullace Rd. NG3: Nott 3E 99
Bull Cl. Rd. NG7: Lent 5D 121
Buller St. DE7: Ilk 4F 91
DE23: Der 1D 159
Buller Ter. NG5: Sher 4C 74
Bullfinch Rd. NG6: Basf 3C 72
Bullinc Cl. NG5: Arn 3B 50
Bullivant St. NG3: Nott 4C 98
Bullpit La. DE56: Duff 2F 83
BULLSMOOR 5A 14
Bullsmoor DE56: Bel 5B 14
Bulstrode Pl. DE74: Keg 2B 214
BULWELL 5A 48
Bulwell Bus. Cen. NG6: Bulw . .5F 47
BULWELL FOREST 4B 48
Bulwell Forest Stop (NET) 4B 48
Bulwell Hall Pk. 2A 48
Bulwell High Rd. NG6: Bulw . . .1A 72
Bulwell La. NG6: Basf 3C 72
Bulwell Station (Rail) 1B 72
Bulwell Stop (NET) 1B 72
Bulwer Rd. NG7: Radf 5E 97
Bunbury St. NG2: Nott 4C 122
BUNNY 5D 197
Bunny La. NG11: Bunny 4A 198
NG12: Key 4A 198
Bunting Cl. DE3: Mick 5F 133
DE7: Kirk H 4B 90
Buntings La. NG4: Carl 3B 100

Bunting St. NG7: Lent 4D 121
Burbage Cl. DE56: Bel 5C 14
Burbage Pl. DE24: Alv 4E 161
Burberry Av. NG15: Huck 5B 26
Burcot Cl. DE7: West H 2D 89
Burden La. NG12: Shel 1B 104
Burdock Cl. DE21: Oak 3D 109
Burford Rd. NG7: H Grn 2E 97
Burford St. NG5: Arn 4D 51
Burgass Rd. NG3: Nott 3F 99
Burge Cl. NG2: Nott 3B 122
Burgess Mill DE22: Der 2C 134
Burgh Hall Cl. NG9: Chil 1B 170
Burghley Cl. DE73: Chel 4E 187
Burghley Way DE23: Lit 5D 157
Burhill NG12: Cotg 1F 179
Burke St. NG7: Radf 5F 97
Burleigh Cl. NG4: Carl 3E 101
Burleigh Dr. DE22: Der 5E 107
Burleigh Rd. NG2: West Br 2E 151
Burleigh Sq. NG9: Chil 4B 146
Burleigh St. DE7: Ilk 1E 91
Burley Dr. DE22: Quar 3D 83
Burley La. DE22: Quar 3C 82
Burley Ri. DE74: Keg 3C 214
Burlington Av. NG5: Sher 4A 74
Burlington Cl. DE72: Brea 3C 166
Burlington Ct. NG5: Sher 4B 74
Burlington Rd. DE22: Mac 2E 133
NG4: Carl 2D 101
NG5: Sher 4B 74
Burlington Way DE3: Mick 2C 156
Burnaby St. DE24: Alv 3E 161
NG6: Basf 3C 72
Burnage Ct.
DE22: Der 5A 6 (4E 135)
BURNASTON 1E 181
Burnaston La. DE65: Etw 1B 180
Durnbank Cl. NG2: Woct Br . . .3C 152
Burnbreck Gdns. NG8: Woll . . .1D 119
Burncroft DE7: West H 3D 89
Burndale Wlk. NG5: Top V 4D 49
Burnham Av. NG9: Chil 4E 147
Burnham Cl. DE7: West H 2C 88
Burnham Dr. DE3: Mick 1B 156
Burnham Lodge NG5: Top V . . .3C 48
Burnham St. NG5: Sher 5B 74
Burnham Way NG2: Nott 2B 122
Burnor Pool NG14: Calv 2E 31
Burns Av. NG7: Radf 4F 97
Burns Cl. DE23: Lit 3A 158
Burns Ct. NG5: Sher 4A 74
Burnside DE24: Alv 3F 161
Burnside Cl. DE24: S Flds 3C 184
Burnside Dr. DE21: Spon 4E 139
NG9: Bram 3B 118
Burnside Grn. NG8: Bilb 4C 94
Burnside Gro. NG12: Toll 2B 176
Burnside Rd. NG2: West Br 3D 151
NG8: Bilb 4C 94
Burnside St. DE24: Alv 3E 161
Burns St. DE7: Ilk 2D 91
DE75: Hea 2C 40
NG7: Radf 4F 97
Burnthouse Rd. DE75: Hea 3C 40
Burnt Oak Cl. NG16: Nuth 4C 70
Burnwood Dr. NG8: Woll 5C 94
Burr La. DE7: Ilk 1E 91
Burrowfield M. DE21: Spon . . .1E 163
Burrows Av. NG9: Bee 4E 119
Burrows Ct. NG3: Nott 5E 99
Burrows Cres. NG9: Bee 4E 119
Burrows Wlk.
DE1: Der 4D 7 (4F 135)

Bursar Way NG10: Long E 5B 144
Burtness Rd. NG11: Clif 2D 173
Burton Av. NG4: Carl 2A 100
Burton Cl. NG4: Carl 1F 101
Burton Dr. NG9: Chil 4B 146
BURTON JOYCE 3E 79
Burton Joyce Station (Rail) . . .4D 79
Burton Manderfield Ct.
NG2: Nott 3B 122
Burton Rd. DE1: Der . . .5C 6 (4F 135)
DE23: Der, Lit 2A 158
DE65: Burn, Egg 5F 181
NG4: Carl, Ged 2E 101
NG4: Ged 5B 78
NG14: Bur J 5B 78
Burton St. DE75: Hea 2D 41
NG1: Nott 2B 4 (5B 98)
Burwell St. NG7: H Grn 4E 97
Bush Cl. NG5: Top V 4E 49
Bushy Cl. NG10: Long E 5F 167
Bute Av. NG7: Lent 1E 121
Bute Wlk. DE21: Chad 1B 136
Butler Av. NG12: Rad I 1F 127
Butlers Cl. NG15: Huck 4B 26
BUTLER'S HILL 3B 26
Butlers Hill Stop (NET) 4C 26
Butterfield Ct. NG16: Want 5F 45
BUTTERLEY 3D 9
Butterley Cl. DE7: Ilk 2E 67
Butterley Cft. Bus. Cen.
DE5: Rip 1E 17
Butterley Hill DE5: Rip 4C 8
Butterley La. DE5: Rip 2C 8
BUTTERLEY PARK 3F 9
Butterley Pk. 3F 9
Butterley Pk. Miniature Railway
. . . . .2E 9
Butterley Pk. Railway Mus. 2F 9
Butterley Row DE5: Rip 2C 8
Butterley Station
Midland Railway Cen. 2D 9
Buttermead Cl. NG9: Trow 3C 116
Buttermere Cl. NG2: Gam 1C 152
NG10: Long E 1F 167
Buttermere Ct. NG5: Sher 5B 74
Buttermere Dr. DE22: All 2D 107
NG9: Bram 5C 118
Butterton Cl. DE7: Ilk 3F 91
Butterwick Cl. DE23: Der 1D 185
Buttery Gdns. NG11: Rudd 5B 174
Butt Ho's. NG7: Lent 1D 121
Buttonoak Dr. DE73: Chel 3F 187
Butt Rd. NG13: Bing 2F 131
Butts, The DE56: Bel 1F 35
Butts Cl. DE7: Ilk 1F 115
Butt St. NG10: Sand 3A 144
Buxton Av. DE75: Hea 4E 41
NG4: Carl 1C 100
Buxton Dr. DE3: Mick 5D 133
DE21: L Eat 5C 60
Buxton Grn. DE75: Hea 5E 41
Buxton Ho. DE21: Spon 4D 139
(off Arnhem Ter.)
Buxton Rd. DE21: Chad 4E 109
Byard La. NG1: Nott . . .4C 4 (1B 122)
Bye Pass Rd. NG9: Chil 1C 170
Byfield Cl. DE21: Oak 3A 110
NG7: Radf 4E 97
Byford Cl. NG3: Mapp 5D 75
Byley Rd. NG8: Bilb 5A 94
Byng Av. DE23: Der 4E 159
By-Pass Rd. NG14: Gun 2E 81
Byrne Ct. NG5: Arn 2A 76
Byron Av. NG10: Long E 5A 144

Byron Bingo 2A 26
Byron Cen., The NG15: Huck 2F 25
Byron Ct. NG2: Nott . . .3F 5 (1D 123)
　NG9: Stap 4D 117
Byron Cres. NG16: Aws 3B 68
Byron Gro. NG5: Sher 4B 74
Byron Ind. Est. NG5: Arn 5F 51
Byron Pl. NG7: Lent 5D 97
　　　　　　　　(off Wragby Rd.)
Byron Rd. NG2: West Br 1E 151
Byron Sq. NG15: Huck 2F 25
　　　　　　　　(off Baker St.)
Byron St. DE7: Ilk 1E 91
　DE23: Der 1E 159
　NG5: Arn 5C 50
　NG15: Huck 3F 25
　NG15: News 1A 10
Bywell La. DE56: Kil 3E 37

C

Cabot Cl. DE56: Bel 4D 15
Caddaw Av. NG15: Huck 3F 25
Cadgwith Dr. DE22: All 2D 107
Cadlan Cl. NG5: Bestw 5F 49
Cadlan Ct. NG5: Bestw 5F 49
Cadwell Cl. DE24: Alv 5C 162
Caerhays Ct. DE24: S Flds 3C 184
Caernarvon Cl. DE21: Spon . . .3E 139
Caernarvon Pl. NG9: Chil 4A 146
Caesar St. DE1: Der 1A 136
Caincross Rd. NG8: Bilb 3C 94
Cairngorm Dr. DE24: Sin 3C 184
　NG5: Arn 2A 50
Cairns Cl. DE3: Mick 5D 133
　NG5: Bestw 2F 73
Cairnsmore Cl.
　NG10: Long E 2F 167
Cairns St. NG1: Nott 1C 4 (5B 98)
Cairo St. NG7: Basf 1E 97
Caister Rd. NG11: Clif 3D 173
Caithness Ct. NG5: Sher 1A 98
Calcroft Cl. NG8: Aspl 5B 72
Caldbeck Cl. NG2: Gam 1B 152
Caldbeck Ct. NG9: Chil 4A 146
Caldbeck Wlk. NG5: Bestw 5A 50
Calder Cl. DE22: All 2D 107
Calderdale NG8: Woll 2A 118
Calderdale Dr.
　NG10: Long E 5F 167
Calderhall Gdns.
　NG5: Bestw 4B 50
Caldermill Dr. DE21: Oak 3F 109
Calder Wlk. NG6: Bulw 5A 48
Caldon Grn. NG6: Bulw 2B 48
Caledon Rd. NG5: Sher 4A 74
CALIFORNIA 5D 135
California Gdns. DE22: Der 4B 134
Calke Ri. DE5: Rip 5E 9
Calladine Cl. DE75: Hea 2C 40
Calladine Ct. NG6: Bulw 1F 71
Calladine La. DE7: H Woo 1C 62
Callaway Cl. NG8: Woll 5D 95
Calley Av. DE7: Ilk 1E 67
Callow Hill Way DE23: Lit 4E 157
Calstock Rd. NG5: Woodt 2D 75
Calveley Rd. NG8: Bilb 2D 95
Calver Cl. DE21: Oak 2D 109
　DE56: Bel 3A 14
　NG8: Woll 1B 120
Calvert Cl. NG9: Chil 4C 146
　NG16: Lang M 1A 42
CALVERTON 2E 31

Calverton Av. NG4: Carl 1A 100
Calverton Cl. DE24: S Loc 3D 187
　NG9: Toton 1F 169
Calverton Dr. NG8: Stre 5C 70
Calverton Rd. NG5: Arn 3E 51
Calverton Sports & Leisure Cen.
　. . . . . .1D 31
Calvert St. DE1: Der 5F 7 (4B 136)
Calvin Cl. DE24: Alv 1F 187
Camberley Cl. NG6: Bulw 4F 47
Camberley Rd. NG6: Bulw 4F 47
Camberwell Av.
　DE22: Mac 2F 133
Camborne Cl. DE21: Chad 4D 109
Camborne Dr. NG8: Aspl 5B 72
Cambria M. NG3: Nott 3B 98
Cambridge Ct.
　NG2: West Br 5D 123
　NG7: Radf 4E 97
Cambridge Cres.
　NG9: Stap 3C 116
Cambridge Gdns.
　NG5: Woodt 2A 76
Cambridge Rd.
　NG2: West Br 1F 151
　NG8: Woll 1F 119
Cambridge St. DE21: Spon 4D 139
　DE23: Der 1F 159
　NG4: Carl 1D 101
Camdale Cl. NG9: Chil 2A 146
Camden Cl.
　NG2: Nott 3F 5 (1D 123)
Camden St. DE22: Der 4C 134
Camelia Av. NG11: Clif 2B 172
Camellia Cl. DE3: Mick 5C 132
Camelot Av. NG5: Sher 5F 73
Camelot Cres. NG11: Rudd 3A 174
Camelot St. NG11: Rudd 3A 174
Cameo Cl. NG4: Colw 4E 101
Camer Ct. NG9: Bee 2F 147
　　　　　　　(off Waverley Av.)
Cameron Rd. DE23: Der 3E 159
Cameron St. NG5: Sher 5B 74
Camomile Cl. NG8: Brox 1F 95
Camomile Gdns.
　NG7: H Grn 3D 97
Campbell Cl. NG8: Brox 1F 95
Campbell Dr. NG4: Carl 2B 100
Campbell Gdns. NG5: Arn 3B 52
Campbell Gro.
　NG3: Nott 1E 5 (5C 98)
Campbell St. DE24: Der 4C 160
　DE56: Bel 1E 35
　NG3: Nott 1F 5 (5D 99)
　NG16: Lang M 5B 20
Campden Grn. NG11: Clif 1D 173
Campion Hill DE74: C Don 5F 205
Campion St. DE22: Der 3C 134
　NG5: Arn 4D 51
Campion Way NG13: Bing 2C 130
Campsie Cl. DE24: Sin 3C 184
Camp St. DE1: Der 1F 135
　　　　　　　(not continuous)
Camp Wood Cl. DE21: L Eat . . .3B 84
Camrose Cl. NG8: Bilb 2E 95
Canada St. DE56: Bel 2F 35
Canal Bank DE72: Shar 5F 191
Canalgate Pk. DE21: Spon 1E 163
Canal Side DE7: Ilk 4E 67
　DE73: Chel 3D 187
　NG9: Bee 5A 148
Canalside Wlk.
　NG2: Nott 5A 4 (2B 122)

Canal St. DE1: Der 5F 7 (4A 136)
　DE7: Ilk 1F 91
　NG1: Nott 5B 4 (2B 122)
　NG10: Long E 2A 168
　NG10: Sand 3A 144
Canberra Cl. DE3: Mick 1D 157
　NG9: Stap 4D 117
Canberra Cres.
　NG2: West Br 4C 150
Canberra Gdns.
　NG2: West Br 5C 150
Candleby Cl. NG12: Cotg 5E 155
Candleby Ct. NG12: Cotg 5E 155
Candleby La. NG12: Cotg 5E 155
Candle Mdw. NG2: Colw 1C 124
Canning Cir. NG7: Nott 5F 97
Canning Ter. NG7: Nott 5F 97
Cannock Ct. DE22: Der 5B 134
Cannock Way
　NG10: Long E 4E 169
Cannon St. NG5: Sher 4B 74
Canonbie Cl. NG5: Arn 3A 52
Canon's Wlk. DE22: D Abb 3E 107
Cantabury Av. NG7: H Grn 2E 97
Cantelupe Gdns. NG16: Gilt . . .4B 44
Cantelupe Rd. DE7: Ilk 2E 91
Canterbury Cl. DE56: Duff 4C 58
　NG16: Nuth 3C 70
Canterbury Ct. NG1: Nott 4A 98
Canterbury Rd. NG3: Radf 5C 96
Canterbury St. DE21: Chad 4D 109
Cantley Av. NG4: Ged 5D 77
Cantley Cl. DE24: S Loc 3C 186
Cantrell Rd. NG6: Bulw 1B 72
Canver Cl. NG8: Bilb 4B 94
Canwick Cl. NG8: Bilb 5B 94
Capenwray Gdns.
　NG5: Bestw 4B 50
Capitol Cl. NG8: Woll 5F 95
Caporn Cl. NG6: Bulw 2B 72
Cardale Rd. NG3: Nott 4F 99
Cardales Cl. DE65: Find 4C 182
Cardean Cl. DE1: Der 1A 136
Cardiff St. NG3: Nott 5E 99
Cardigan St. DE21: Chad 1B 136
Cardinal Cl. DE21: Oak 3E 109
　NG3: Nott 4D 99
Cardington Cl. NG5: Top V 3D 49
Cardrona Cl. DE21: Oak 3E 109
Cardwell St. NG7: H Grn 2E 97
Carew Rd. NG11: Clif 1D 173
Carey Rd. NG6: Bulw 4B 48
Carisbrooke Av.
　NG3: Mapp P 1B 98
　NG4: Ged 1A 102
　NG9: Bee 5F 119
Carisbrooke Dr.
　NG3: Mapp P 1B 98
Carisbrooke Gdns.
　DE23: Lit 5B 158
Carlight Gdns. Pk. Homes
　NG2: West Br 4A 124
Carlin Cl. DE72: Brea 3D 167
Carlin Cl. DE72: Brea 3D 167
Carlingford Rd. NG15: Huck . . .1F 25
Carlisle Av. DE23: Lit 3A 158
　NG6: Bulw 5B 48
Carlswark Gdns. NG5: Top V . . .3E 49
CARLTON 3E 101
Carlton Av. DE24: S Loc 2D 187
Carlton Bus. Cen.
　NG4: Carl 3E 101
Carlton Cl. DE75: Hea 1F 41

Carlton Dr. DE24: S Loc 3D **187**
Carlton Fold NG2: Nott 2E **123**
Carlton Forum Leisure Cen.
. . . . .1B **100**
Carlton Gdns.
DE24: S Loc 2D **187**
Carlton Grange NG4: Carl . . .3B **100**
Carlton Hgts. NG4: Carl 3B **100**
Carlton Hill NG4: Carl 3A **100**
Carlton M. NG4: Carl 3B **100**
Carlton Rd. DE23: Der 2C **158**
NG3: Nott 3F **5** (1D **123**)
NG10: Long E 1A **194**
Carlton Sq. NG4: Carl 3D **101**
Carlton Station (Rail) 3E **101**
Carlton St.
NG1: Nott 3D **5** (1C **122**)
Carlton Va. Cl. NG4: Carl 1C **100**
Carlton Wlk. DE24: Alv 3F **161**
Carlyle Pl. DE75: Hea 1C **40**
Carlyle Rd. NG2: West Br 1D **151**
Carlyle St. DE24: Sin 1E **185**
DE75: Hea 1C **40**
Carman Cl. NG16: Want 4F **45**
Carmel Gdns. NG5: Arn 1E **75**
Carnaby Cl. DE22: Mac 3F **133**
NG12: Rad T 2D **129**
Carnarvon Cl. NG13: Bing . . .1D **131**
Carnarvon Dr. NG14: Bur J . .2E **79**
Carnarvon Gro. NG4: Carl . . .2C **100**
NG4: Ged 1E **101**
Carnarvon Pl. NG13: Bing . . .2C **130**
Carnarvon Rd.
NG2: West Br 2E **151**
Carnarvon St. NG4: Neth 4F **101**
Carnegie St. DE23: Der 3F **159**
Carnforth Cl. DE3: Mick 2D **157**
NG9: Stap 3C **144**
Carnforth Ct. NG5: Bestw . . .4B **50**
Carnival Way DE74: C Don . . .5A **206**
Carnwood Rd. NG5: Bestw . . .1F **73**
Carol Cres. DE21: Chad 3E **137**
Caroline Cl. DE24: Alv 4C **162**
Caroline Ct. DE7: Ilk 4F **91**
Caroline Wlk. NG3: Nott 4C **98**
Carradale Cl. NG5: Arn 4B **52**
Carradale Gro. DE73: Chel . . .5D **187**
Carrfield Av. NG9: Toton 1E **169**
NG10: Long E 2E **169**
Carrfields DE7: H Woo 5B **38**
CARRINGTON 5A **74**
Carrington Ct. NG5: Sher 1B **98**
Carrington Ct. Ind. Pk.
DE1: Der 3A **6** (3D **135**)
Carrington La. NG14: Calv . . .1E **31**
Carrington St NG2: Nott 2B **122**
Carrington St.
DE1: Der 5F **7** (4A **136**)
(not continuous)
NG1: Nott 5C **4** (2B **122**)
Carrock Av. DE75: Hea 3A **42**
Carroll Gdns. NG2: Nott 4B **122**
Carron Cl. DE24: Sin 2D **185**
Carr Rd. NG13: Bing 1F **131**
Carrs Cl. DE74: C Don 1F **211**
Carr Wood DE5: Rip 4D **9**
Carrwood Local Nature Reserve
. . . . .3D **9**
Carsington Cres. DE22: All . .3C **106**
Carsington Ho. DE22: All 3C **106**
Carsington M. DE22: All 4D **107**
Carson Rd. DE21: Chad 2A **138**
Cartbridge NG12: Cotg 1E **179**

Carter Av. NG11: Rudd 5B **174**
Carter Ga. NG1: Nott 2A **128**
Carter Cl. NG10: Long E 5A **168**
Carter Ga. NG1: Nott . . .4E **5** (1C **122**)
Carter Rd. NG9: Chil 5F **145**
(Readman Rd.)
NG9: Chil 1F **169**
(Swiney Way, not continuous)
Carter St. DE24: A'ton 5C **160**
Carterswood Dr. NG16: Nuth . .4E **71**
Carver St. NG7: H Grn 2E **97**
Carwood Rd. NG9: Bram 4C **118**
Cascade Gro. DE23: Lit 4F **157**
Casper Ct. NG5: Top V 4F **49**
(off Birkdale Way)
Casson Av. DE24: Alv 5F **161**
Castellan Ri. NG5: Bestw 4B **50**
Casterton Rd. NG5: Bestw . . .4A **50**
Castings Rd. DE23: Der 3A **160**
Castle Blvd.
NG7: Lent 5A **4** (2A **122**)
NG7: Lent, Nott 2E **121**
Castlebridge Office Village
NG7: Lent 3F **121**
Castle Bri. Rd. NG7: Lent 2F **121**
Castle Cl. DE72: Bor 1C **164**
NG14: Calv 2C **30**
Castle Ct. DE72: Elv 1E **189**
(not continuous)
DE75: Hea 3F **41**
NG7: Nott 5A **4** (2A **122**)
Castlecraig Ct. DE24: Sin 4D **185**
Castle Cft. DE24: Alv 1C **188**
CASTLE DONINGTON 1A **212**
Castle Donington Mus. 1A **212**
Castle Dr. DE5: Cod 1C **18**
Castle Exchange NG1: Nott 2D **5**
Castlefields NG2: Nott 3B **122**
Castle Gdns. NG7: Lent 2E **121**
Castle Ga.
NG1: Nott 4B **4** (1B **122**)
Castle Gro.
NG7: Nott 4A **4** (1A **122**)
Castle Hill DE56: Duff 3D **59**
DE65: Find 5C **182**
DE74: C Don 5A **206**
Castle Ho. DE1: Der . .4F **7** (4B **136**)
Castleland Way DE73: Chel . . .4D **187**
Castle Mdw. NG16: Iron 1D **19**
Castle Marina Pk.
NG7: Lent 2F **121**
Castle Marina Rd.
NG7: Lent 3F **121**
Castle Mdw. Retail Pk.
NG7: Lent 2A **122**
Castle Mdw. Rd.
NG2: Nott 5B **4** (2A **122**)
Castle M. NG7: Nott 2F **121**
Castle Mus. & Art Gallery
. . . . .4A **4** (2A **122**)
Castle Orchard DE56: Duff . . .2D **59**
Castle Pk. NG2: Nott 3A **122**
Castle Pl. NG1: Nott . . .4A **4** (1A **122**)
Castle Quay
NG7: Nott 5A **4** (2A **122**)
Castle Quay Cl. NG7: Lent 2F **121**
Castle Retail Pk. NG7: Radf . .4D **97**
Castlerigg Cl.
NG2: West Br 3B **152**
Castle Rd.
NG1: Nott 4A **4** (1A **122**)
Castle Rock
NG7: Nott 5A **4** (2A **122**)

Castleshaw Dr. DE23: Lit 4D **157**
Castle St. NG2: Nott 1E **123**
NG16: Eastw 3F **43**
Castleton Av. DE7: Ilk 2D **67**
DE23: Der 3E **159**
NG4: Carl 1D **101**
NG5: Arn 5E **51**
Castleton Cl. NG2: Nott 3A **122**
NG15: Huck 3C **24**
Castleton Ct. NG6: Bulw 1E **71**
Castle Vw. DE56: Duff 3D **59**
NG2: West Br 2C **150**
NG16: Lang M 5F **19**
Castle Vw. Cotts. NG9: Bee . .2B **148**
Castle Vs. NG2: Nott 1E **123**
Castle Wlk.
DE1: Der 4E **7** (4A **136**)
NG7: H Grn 3E **97**
Castle Wharf
NG1: Nott 5B **4** (2B **122**)
Cat & Fiddle La.
DE7: West H 4C **88**
Cat & Fiddle Windmill 1E **113**
Caterham Cl. NG8: Bilb 3C **94**
Catfoot La. NG4: Lamb 4C **52**
Cathedral Rd.
DE1: Der 1B **6** (2E **135**)
Cathedral Vw. DE22: Der 1C **158**
Catherine Av. DE7: Ilk 4E **91**
Catherine Cl. NG6: Bulw 5F **47**
Catherine McAuley Ho.
DE22: D Abb 4D **107**
Catherine St. DE23: Der 1A **160**
NG6: Bulw 5F **47**
Catkin Dr. NG16: Gilt 4B **44**
Catlow Wlk. NG5: Bestw 4B **50**
Cator Cl. NG4: Ged 4C **76**
Cator La. NG9: Chil 2C **146**
Cator La. Nth. NG9: Chil 2C **146**
Catriona Cres. NG5: Arn 2F **51**
Catt Cl. NG9: Chil 2A **170**
Catterick Dr. DE3: Mick 2B **156**
Catterley Hill Rd. NG3: Nott . .3F **99**
Cattle Mkt. Rd. NG2: Nott . . .3C **122**
Catton Rd. NG5: Arn 4F **51**
Caudale Ct. NG2: Gam 1B **152**
Caulton St. NG7: H Grn 4E **97**
(not continuous)
Caunton Av. NG3: Nott 1D **99**
Causeway DE22: D Abb 3D **107**
Causeway M. NG2: Nott 3A **122**
Causey Bri.
DE1: Der 1D **7** (2F **135**)
Cavan Ct. NG2: Nott 4B **122**
Cavan Dr. DE21: Chad 4A **138**
Cavell Cl. NG11: Clif 1C **172**
Cavell Ct. NG7: Nott 3C **120**
Cavendish Av. DE22: All 2E **107**
NG4: Ged 5C **76**
NG5: Sher 4C **74**
CAVENDISH BRIDGE 1A **206**
Cavendish Cl. DE56: Duff 4C **58**
DE72: Shar 4F **191**
DE74: C Don 2F **211**
NG15: Huck 4B **26**
Cavendish Ct.
DE1: Der 1B **6** (2E **135**)
DE72: Shar 5F **191**
NG3: Mapp 4E **75**
NG7: Nott 1F **121**
Cavendish Cres. NG4: Carl . . .5B **76**
NG9: Ctap 3C **116**
Cavendish Cres. Nth.
NG7: Nott 1F **121**

Cavendish Cres. Sth.
NG7: Nott 2F **121**
Cavendish Dr. DE5: Rip 5B **8**
NG4: Carl 2D **101**
Cavendish Hall NG7: Nott 5F **119**
Cavendish Ho. NG4: Carl 2D **101**
(off Foxhill Rd. E.)
Cavendish M. NG7: Nott 1F **121**
Cavendish Pl. NG7: Nott 2F **121**
NG9: Bee 2E **147**
Cavendish Rd. DE7: Ilk 4E **91**
NG4: Carl 5B **76**
NG10: Long E 1B **168**
Cavendish Rd. E.
NG7: Nott 1F **121**
Cavendish Rd. W.
NG7: Nott 1F **121**
Cavendish St.
DE1: Der 2B **6** (3E **135**)
NG5: Arn 4D **51**
NG7: Lent 4D **121**
Cavendish Va. NG5: Sher 4C **74**
Cavendish Way DE3: Mick 1D **157**
Caversfield Cl. DE23: Lit 3F **157**
Caversham Way
DE7: West H 2C **88**
Cawdron Wlk. NG11: Clif 1D **173**
Cawston Gdns. NG6: Bulw 4A **48**
Caxmere Dr. NG8: Woll 5E **95**
Caxton Cl. NG4: Neth 3F **101**
Caxton Rd. NG5: Sher 1A **98**
Caxton St. DE23: Der 4D **159**
CAYTHORPE 4F **57**
Caythorpe Cres. NG5: Sher 3B **74**
Caythorpe Ri. NG5: Sher 3B **74**
Caythorpe Rd.
NG14: Cayt, Lowd 4D **57**
Cecil St. DE22: Der 3C **134**
NG7: Lent 2E **121**
Cedar Av. DE5: Rip 5C **8**
NG9: Bee 1F **147**
NG10: Long E 1B **194**
NG16: Nuth 3E **71**
Cedar Cl. DE56: Duff 3C **58**
NG10: Sand 1A **144**
NG13: Bing 2F **131**
Cedar Ct. NG9: Bee 1F **147**
DE72: Ast T 2F **203**
Cedar Dr. DE72: Ock 4B **140**
NG12: Key 4D **199**
Cedar Gro. DE56: Bel 2A **36**
NG5: Arn 4A **52**
NG8: Woll 1E **119**
NG15: Huck 4A **26**
Cedarland Cres. NG16: Nuth . . .3E **71**
Cedar Lodge NG7: Nott 1F **121**
Cedar Lodge Cvn. Pk.
NG12: Hol P 3B **126**
Cedar Pk. DE7: Ilk 2D **91**
Cedar Rd. DE74: C Don 2A **212**
NG7: H Grn 2F **97**
NG9: Chil 3D **147**
Cedars, The NG5: Sher 3C **74**
Cedar St. DE22: Der 1D **135**
Cedar Tree Rd. NG5: Arn 3A **50**
Cedarwood Ct. DE21: Oak 3D **109**
Celandine Cl. DE21: Oak 3E **109**
NG5: Top V 5D **49**
Celandine Gdns.
NG13: Bing 2B **130**
Celanese Rd. DE21: Spon 5B **138**
Celia Dr. NG4: Carl 3C **100**
Cemetery La. DE5: Rip 5C **8**

Cemetery Rd. DE56: Bel 3F **13**
NG9: Stap 1D **145**
Central Av. DE72: Bor 2A **164**
NG2: West Br 5E **123**
NG3: Mapp 3A **76**
NG5: Arn 5E **51**
NG7: Basf 1F **97**
NG9: Bee 4D **119**
NG9: Chil 2C **146**
NG9: Stap 5D **117**
NG10: Sand 2A **144**
NG15: Huck 3F **25**
Central Av. Sth. NG5: Arn 5E **51**
Central Ct. NG7: Lent 4E **121**
Central St. NG3: Nott 4D **99**
Central Wlk. NG15: Huck 2F **25**
Centre Ct. DE1: Der 5A **136**
Centre Way NG12: Rad T 1D **127**
Centro Pl. DE24: Der 5C **136**
Centurion Bus. Pk.
NG6: Bulw 3D **47**
Centurion Wlk. DE1: Der 5F **107**
Centurion Way NG2: Nott 5F **121**
Centurion Way Bus. Pk.
DE21: Der 5A **108**
Century Ct. NG1: Nott 3A **98**
(off Nth. Sherwood St.)
Cernan Ct. NG6: Bulw 2E **71**
Cerne Cl. NG11: Clif 3E **173**
Chaceley Way NG11: Wilf 5F **149**
CHADDESDEN 5F **109**
Chaddesden DE21: Chad 2F **137**
Chaddesden, The
NG3: Mapp P 3B **98**
CHADDESDEN COMMON 2A **110**
Chaddesden La.
DE21: Chad 2E **137**
Chaddesden La. End
DE21: Chad 3E **137**
Chaddesden Pk. Rd.
DE21: Chad 2D **137**
Chaddesden Wood Nature Reserve
. . . . .2F **109**
Chadfield Rd. DE56: Duff 2D **59**
Chad Gdns. NG5: Top V 2F **49**
Chadwick Av. DE24: A'ton 1D **187**
Chadwick Gro. DE5: Rip 5A **8**
Chadwick Rd. NG7: H Grn 3D **97**
Chaffinch Cl. DE21: Spon 2E **139**
Chain La. DE3: Mick 1F **157**
DE23: Lit 2F **157**
NG7: Lent 4D **121**
Chalfield Cl. NG11: Clif 2C **172**
Chalfont Dr. NG8: Aspl 4B **96**
Chalfont Sq. DE21: Oak 3A **110**
Chalkley Cl. DE24: Alv 4E **161**
Challis Av. DE21: Chad 1A **138**
Challond Ct. NG5: Bestw 5B **50**
Chalons Cl. DE7: Ilk 1E **91**
Chalons Way DE7: Ilk 1E **91**
Chamberlain Cl.
NG11: Clif 2B **172**
Chambers Av. DE7: Ilk 3A **92**
Chambers St. DE24: Alv 3D **161**
Champion Av. DE7: Ilk 4B **66**
Champion Hill DE56: Duff 3D **59**
Chancel Pl.
DE22: Der 5B **6** (5E **135**)
Chancery, The NG9: Bram 1B **146**
Chancery Cl. DE5: Rip 1D **17**
Chancery Ct. NG11: Wilf 2F **149**
Chancery La. DE22: Mac 2F **133**
Chandlers Ford DE21: Oak 4E **109**
Chandos Av. NG4: Neth 2F **101**

Chandos Pole St.
DE22: Der 2C **134**
Chandos St. NG3: Nott 3D **99**
NG4: Neth 3F **101**
Chandres Ct. DE22: All 1D **107**
Chantrey Rd.
NG2: West Br 1D **151**
Chantry Cl. DE3: Mick 2C **156**
NG9: Chil 4C **146**
NG10: Long E 2F **193**
NG16: Kimb 2F **69**
Chapel Bar
NG1: Nott 3A **4** (1A **122**)
(not continuous)
Chapel Ct. DE7: Ilk 3E **67**
Chapel La. DE21: Chad 1F **137**
DE21: Spon 2D **139**
DE73: Bar T 3A **200**
DE73: Chel 5F **187**
NG4: Lamb 5A **54**
NG5: Arn 4D **51**
NG12: Cotg 5E **155**
NG13: Bing 1D **131**
NG14: Epp 3F **33**
Chapel M. Ct. NG9: Bram 5A **118**
Chapel Pl. NG16: Kimb 1E **69**
Chapel Quarter NG1: Nott 3A **4**
Chapel Row DE72: Bor 1A **164**
Chapel Side DE21: Spon 3D **139**
Chapel St. DE1: Der 1C **6** (2F **135**)
DE5: Rip 4C **8**
DE7: Ilk 1E **91**
(not continuous)
DE21: Spon 3C **138**
DE56: Bel 1E **35**
DE56: Duff 4E **59**
DE56: H'ook 5B **36**
DE56: Kil 4F **37**
DE75: Hea 4F **41**
NG7: Radf 5F **97**
NG9: Bram 5A **118**
NG10: Long E 4D **169**
NG11: Rudd 5B **174**
NG15: Huck 2F **25**
NG16: Eastw 3E **43**
NG16: Kimb 1E **69**
Chapel Yd.
NG12: Norm W 4F **177**
Chapman Av. DE24: Alv 5A **162**
Chapman Ct. NG8: Bilb 3A **96**
Chapmans Wlk.
NG6: Bestw V 3A **28**
Chapter Cl. DE21: Oak 3C **108**
Chapter Dr. NG16: Kimb 2F **69**
Chardlace Wlk. NG1: Nott 1C **122**
(off Hollowstone)
Chard St. NG7: Basf 5E **73**
Chard Ter. NG7: Basf 5E **73**
Charing Ct. DE1: Der 1A **136**
Charingworth Rd.
DE21: Oak 3A **110**
Chariot Cl. DE24: Alv 1C **188**
Charlbury Cl. DE23: Lit 4F **157**
Charlbury Ct. NG9: Bram 1A **118**
Charlbury Rd. NG8: Woll 4F **95**
Charlecote Dr. NG8: Woll 2B **118**
Charlecote Pk. Dr.
NG2: West Br 4B **150**
Charles Av. DE21: Spon 2C **138**
NG9: Chil 5B **146**
NG9: Lent A 4F **119**
NG9: Stap 5E **117**
NG10: Sand 2A **144**
NG16: Eastw 2A **44**

Charles Cl. DE7: Ilk 4A **92**
  NG4: Ged 5E **77**
Charles Ct. NG15: Huck 2F **25**
Charles Rd. DE24: Alv 2E **161**
Charles St. NG5: Arn 5D **51**
  NG10: Long E 5C **168**
  NG11: Rudd 4B **174**
  NG15: Huck 2F **25**
Charleston Ho. NG1: Nott 4A **98**
Charleston Rd. DE21: Chad . .2B **138**
Charlestown Dr. DE22: All 1C **106**
Charles Way NG6: Bulw 2A **72**
Charles Way Bus. Pk.
  NG6: Bulw 2B **72**
Charlesworth Av. NG7: Basf . . .2D **97**
Charlock Cl. NG5: Top V 5D **49**
Charlock Gdns. NG13: Bing . . .3C **130**
Charlotte Cl. NG5: Arn 2D **51**
Charlotte Ct. NG16: Eastw 1E **43**
Charlotte Gro. NG9: Bram . . .4C **118**
Charlotte St. DE7: Ilk 4D **67**
  DE23: Der 1F **159**
Charlton Av. NG10: Long E 2E **169**
Charlton Gro. NG9: Bee 4E **147**
Charnock Av. NG8: Woll 2C **120**
Charnwood Av. DE23: Lit 1C **184**
  DE56: Bel 5F **13**
  DE72: Bor 1B **164**
  DE74: C Don 1B **212**
  NG9: Bee 2C **146**
  NG10: Long E 2A **194**
  NG10: Sand 4F **143**
  NG12: Key 4D **199**
Charnwood Dr. DE5: Rip 5B **8**
Charnwood Gdns. NG5: Sher . . .1A **98**
Charnwood Gro.
  NG2: West Br 1D **151**
  NG13: Bing 2C **130**
  NG15: Huck 2D **25**
Charnwood La. NG5: Arn 1F **75**
Charnwood St.
  DE1: Der 5D **7** (5F **135**)
Charnwood Way
  NG14: Woodbo 5C **32**
Charta M. NG14: Lowd 3D **57**
Charterhouse Cl.
  DE21: Oak 2D **109**
Charter Pk. DE7: Ilk 3D **91**
Charterstone La. DE22: All 1D **107**
Chartwell Av. NG11: Rudd 4A **174**
Chartwell Dr. DE21: Der 3B **136**
Chartwell Gro. NG3: Mapp . . .2B **76**
Chase, The DE21: L Eat 5C **60**
  DE24: Sin 2E **185**
  DE56: Kil 4A **38**
Chase Cl. DE73: Chel 4A **188**
Chase Pk. NG2: Nott 2F **123**
Chatham Cl. DE56: Bel 5C **14**
  NG6: Bulw 1B **72**
Chatham St. DE23: Der 3F **159**
  NG1: Nott 4B **98**
Chatsworth Av. NG4: Carl . . .2D **101**
  NG7: Basf 5E **73**
  NG9: Chil 1B **170**
  NG10: Long E 5F **169**
  NG12: Rad T 1F **127**
Chatsworth Cl. NG10: Sand . . .4A **144**
Chatsworth Ct. DE7: West H . . .2D **89**
  DE24: Sin 2E **185**
  NG15: Huck 3F **25**
Chatsworth Cres. DE22: All . . .2E **107**
Chatsworth Dr. DE3: Mick 1D **151**
  DE21: L Eat 5C **60**
  NG15: Huck 3F **25**

Chatsworth Pl. DE7: Kirk H 5A **90**
Chatsworth Rd.
  NG2: West Br 5A **124**
Chatsworth St. DE23: Der 2D **159**
Chatsworth Way DE75: Hea . . .2B **40**
Chatteris Dr. NG21: Chad 4C **108**
Chatterley Ct. NG7: Lent 5D **97**
  (off Wragby Rd.)
Chatterley Parkway
  NG8: Stre 5B **70**
Chaucer Dr. DE7: Ilk 1E **91**
  NG1: Nott 1A **4** (5A **98**)
Chaucer Ter. DE23: Der 4E **159**
Chaworth Av. NG16: Want 3E **45**
Chaworth Rd.
  NG2: West Br 2D **151**
  NG4: Colw 4E **101**
  NG13: Bing 2C **130**
Cheadle Cl. DE23: Lit 2A **158**
  NG3: Mapp 5A **76**
  NG8: Bilb 2C **94**
Cheam Cl. DE22: Mac 2D **133**
Cheapside DE1: Der . . .2C **6** (3F **135**)
  DE56: Bel 1E **35**
  NG1: Nott 3C **4** (1B **122**)
Cheddar Rd. NG11: Clif 3D **173**
Chedington Av. NG3: Mapp . . .1C **76**
Chediston Va. NG5: Bestw 4A **50**
Chedworth Cl. NG3: Nott 5E **99**
Chedworth Dr. DE24: Alv 5C **162**
CHELLASTON 5E **187**
Chellaston La. DE72: Ast T . . .5D **189**
  DE73: Chel 5A **188**
Chellaston Pk. Ct.
  DE73: Chel 5E **187**
Chellaston Rd.
  DE24: A'ton, S Loc 1D **187**
  (not continuous)
Chelmarsh Cl. DE73: Chel 3F **187**
Chelmorton Pl. DE21: Chad . . .5E **109**
Chelmsford Cl. DE3: Mick 5B **132**
Chelmsford Rd. NG7: Basf 5E **73**
Chelmsford Ter. NG7: Basf 5E **73**
  (off Zulu Rd.)
Chelsbury Ct. NG5: Arn 5D **51**
Chelsea Cl. DE22: Mac 2E **133**
  NG16: Nuth 4D **71**
Chelsea M. NG12: Rad T 2C **128**
Chelsea St. NG7: Basf 1E **97**
Cheltenham Cl. NG9: Toton . . .1E **169**
Cheltenham St. NG6: Basf 3D **73**
Chelwood Dr. NG3: Mapp 4B **76**
Chelwood Rd. DE73: Chel 4E **187**
Chennel Nook NG12: Cotg 1F **179**
Chepstow Rd. NG11: Clif 3D **173**
Chequers La. DE21: Chad 2C **136**
Chequers Rd.
  DE21: Chad, Der 3B **136**
Cherhill Cl. NG11: Clif 4C **172**
Cheribough Rd.
  DE74: C Don 1F **211**
Cheriton Dr. DE7: Ilk 4B **66**
Cheriton Gdns. DE23: Lit 4D **157**
Cherry Av. NG15: Huck 4A **26**
Cherrybrook Dr. DE21: Oak . . .2A **110**
Cherry Cl. DE3: Mick 1F **157**
  DE72: Brea 3D **167**
  NG2: West Br 4B **124**
  NG5: Arn 4D **51**
  NG5: Bestw 1A **74**
Cherrydale Cl. DE23: Lit 5F **157**
Cherry Hill NG12: Key 3E **199**
Cherry Orchard
  NG12: Cotg 5D **155**

Cherry Orchard Mt.
  NG5: Bestw 1A **74**
Cherry St. NG13: Bing 2E **131**
  DE56: Bel 3A **14**
Cherry Tree Av. DE5: Rip 1C **16**
  DE56: Bel 3A **14**
Cherry Tree Cl. DE7: Kirk H . . .4C **90**
  DE22: Der 4A **134**
  DE72: Ris 4E **143**
  NG16: Brins 1D **21**
Cherrytree Cl. NG12: Rad T . . .3E **127**
CHERRYTREE HILL 3F **137**
Cherry Tree La.
  NG12: Edwal 5A **152**
Cherry Tree M. DE21: Chad . . .4A **138**
Cherry Tree Way
  NG16: Lang M 5B **20**
Cherry Wood Dr. NG8: Aspl . . .3A **96**
Cherrywood Gdns. NG3: Nott . .2F **99**
Chertsey Cl. NG3: Nott 1E **99**
Chertsey Ct. DE7: West H 2C **90**
Chertsey Rd. DE3: Mick 1B **156**
Cherwell Cl. NG6: Bulw 1E **71**
Chesapeake Rd.
  DE21: Chad 2A **138**
Chesham Dr. NG5: Sher 5A **74**
  NG9: Bram 2A **118**
Cheshire Ct.
  NG2: West Br 3C **150**
Cheshire St. DE24: A'ton 1C **186**
Chesil Av. NG8: Radf 5C **96**
Chesil Cotts. NG8: Radf 5C **96**
  (off Chesil Av.)
Cheslyn Dr. NG8: Aspl 2B **96**
Chesnuts, The NG4: Ged 1A **102**
Chester Av. DE22: All 5A **94**
Chester Ct. DE21: Der 5A **108**
  DE21: Spon 5D **139**
Chesterfield Av. NG4: Ged 4C **76**
  NG10: Long E 4E **169**
  NG13: Bing 2D **131**
Chesterfield Ct. NG4: Ged 4C **76**
Chesterfield Dr.
  NG14: Bur J 2F **79**
Chesterfield Ho.
  DE21: Spon 4D **139**
  (off Arnhem Ter.)
Chesterfield Rd. DE56: Bel 5F **13**
  (Belper)
  DE56: Bel 2B **14**
  (Far Laund)
Chesterfield St. NG4: Carl 3C **100**
Chesterford Ct. DE23: Lit 5E **157**
Chester Grn. NG9: Toton 1D **169**
Chester Grn. Rd. DE1: Der 1F **135**
  (not continuous)
Chesterman Cl. NG16: Aws . . .3A **68**
Chester Pk. DE21: Der 5A **108**
Chester Rd. NG3: Nott 5B **100**
Chesterton Av. DE23: Der 4D **159**
Chesterton Rd.
  DE21: Spon 2D **139**
Chestnut Av. DE3: Mick 5C **132**
  DE5: Rip 1C **16**
  DE23: Der 1F **159**
  DE56: Bel 2F **35**
  DE56: H'ook 5B **36**
  DE73: Chel 3E **187**
  NG3: Mapp 5A **76**
  NG9: Bee 2E **147**
  NG13: Bing 2D **131**
Chestnut Bank DE75: Hea 3C **40**
Chestnut Cl. DE7: D Woo 5B **38**
  DE56: Duff 5D **59**
Chestnut Dr. NG16: Nuth 5A **46**

Chestnut Gro.—Church St.

Chestnut Gro. DE65: Etw 2A **180**
DE72: Bor 5B **140**
NG2: West Br 1C **150**
NG3: Mapp P 3B **98**
NG4: Ged 1E **101**
NG5: Arn 3F **51**
NG10: Sand 1F **143**
NG12: Rad T 1E **127**
NG14: Bur J 3E **79**
NG15: Huck 5A **26**
Chestnut La. NG11: Bart F . . .5D **171**
Chestnut M. NG12: Toll 5E **153**
Chestnut Rd. NG16: Lang M . . .1F **41**
Chestnuts, The NG3: Nott 1E **99**
NG10: Long E 3F **167**
NG12: Rad T 2D **127**
Chestnuts Cl. LE12: Sut B . . .2F **215**
Chestnut Wlk. NG5: Sher 4D **75**
Chettles Ind. Est. NG7: Radf . . .5C **96**
Chetwind Rd. NG8: Bilb 5C **94**
Chetwynd Bus. Pk.
NG9: Chil 1A **170**
Chetwynd Rd. NG9: Chil 5A **146**
NG9: Toton 1F **169**
Cheveley Ct. DE21: Chad 5C **108**
Cheverton Cl. DE24: Alv 1C **188**
Cheverton Ct. NG3: Nott 3B **98**
Chevin All. DE56: Mil 5F **35**
Chevin Av. DE3: Mick 1E **157**
DE72: Bor 1B **164**
Chevin Bank DE56: Duff 1C **58**
CHEVINEND 5D **35**
Chevin Gdns. NG5: Top V 3F **49**
Chevin M. DE56: Bel 2E **35**
Chevin Pl. DE1: Der 1E **135**
Chevin Rd. DE1: Der 1E **135**
DE56: Bel, Mil 5C **12**
DE56: Duff 2D **59**
CHEVINSIDE 2D **35**
Chevin Va. DE56: Duff 2D **59**
Chevin Vw. DE56: Bel 5E **13**
Cheviot Cl. NG5: Arn 2A **50**
Cheviot Ct. NG9: Chil 5B **146**
Cheviot Dr. NG6: Bulw 4E **47**
Cheviot Rd. NG10: Long E . . .2F **167**
Cheviot St. DE22: Der 3B **134**
Chewton Av. NG16: Eastw 3F **43**
Chewton St. NG16: Eastw 3E **43**
Cheyenne Gdns.
DE21: Chad 3A **138**
Cheyne Wlk. DE22: Mac 2B **134**
NG15: Huck 1A **26**
Cheyny Cl. NG2: Nott 4B **122**
Chichester Cl. DE7: Ilk 2F **91**
NG5: Top V 5D **49**
Chichester Dr. NG12: Cotg . . .4D **155**
Chidlow Rd. NG8: Bilb 3C **94**
Chigwell Cl. NG16: Nuth 4D **71**
Chillon Way NG15: Huck 3C **24**
Chilson Dr. DE3: Mick 5B **132**
Chiltern Cl. NG5: Arn 2A **50**
Chiltern Dr. DE7: West H 2D **89**
Chiltern Gdns.
NG10: Long E 2F **167**
Chiltern Way NG5: Bestw 1A **74**
Chilton Dr. NG16: Want 5F **45**
Chilvers Cl. NG5: Bestw 5F **49**
CHILWELL 2B **146**
Chilwell Ct. NG6: Bulw 5C **48**
Chilwell La. NG9: Bram 1A **146**
Chilwell Meadows Nature Reserve
. . . . .4C **146**
Chilwell Olympia Leisure Cen.
. . . . .5C **146**

Chilwell Retail Pk.
NG9: Chil 2A **170**
(not continuous)
Chilwell Rd. NG9: Bee 3E **147**
(not continuous)
Chilwell St. NG7: Lent 2E **121**
Chime Cl. DE21: Oak 3D **109**
Chine Gdns.
NG2: West Br 3B **150**
Chingford Ct. DE22: Mac 2A **134**
Chingford Rd. NG8: Bilb 2D **95**
Chinley Rd. DE21: Chad 4F **109**
Chippendale St. NG7: Lent . . .2E **121**
Chippenham Rd.
NG5: Bestw 1A **74**
Chisbury Grn. NG11: Clif 4C **172**
Chisholm Way NG5: Bestw . . .1F **73**
Chiswick Cl. DE22: Mac 2E **133**
Chiswick Ct. NG5: Sher 4B **74**
Christchurch Ct.
DE1: Der 1D **7** (2F **135**)
Christchurch Rd.
NG15: Huck 5C **24**
Christina Av. NG6: Cin 3B **72**
Christina Cres. NG6: Cin 3B **72**
Christine Cl. NG15: Huck 5E **11**
Christine Ct. NG3: Nott 3F **99**
Christopher Cl. NG8: Woll 4E **95**
Chrysalis Way NG16: Eastw . . .1B **42**
Church Av. NG5: Arn 5D **51**
NG7: Lent 2E **121**
NG10: Long E 2F **193**
Church Cl. DE73: Chel 5F **187**
DE73: S Bri 5E **201**
NG5: Arn 5D **51**
NG9: Trow 1B **116**
NG12: Rad T 2D **127**
NG13: Bing 1E **131**
Church Ct. DE5: Den 3C **38**
NG12: Cotg 5D **155**
Church Cres. NG5: Arn 5C **50**
NG9: Chil 4F **145**
Church Cft. DE5: Rip 4C **8**
NG2: West Br 5E **123**
Churchdale Av. NG9: Stap 4D **117**
Churchdown Cl.
DE21: Oak 3A **110**
DE56: Duff 5E **59**
NG2: West Br 1E **151**
NG5: Arn 5C **50**
NG5: Sher 1A **98**
NG10: Sand 1A **144**
NG12: Key 3D **199**
NG15: Huck 2F **25**
Church Dr. E. NG5: Arn 5D **51**
Church Farm Rd. DE5: Rip 1D **17**
Churchfield Ct. NG5: Top V 3F **49**
Churchfield La. NG7: Radf 3D **97**
Churchfield Ter. NG6: Basf 5D **73**
Churchfield Way
NG5: Top V 3F **49**
Church Ga. DE74: Keg 2C **214**
NG12: C'ton 3B **178**
Church Gro. NG7: Lent 2D **121**
Church Hill DE21: Spon 4C **138**
DE65: Etw 1A **180**
NG12: Plum 5D **177**
NG16: Kimb 1E **69**
Churchill Cl. DE72: Brea 3C **166**
NG5: Arn 1E **75**
Churchill Dr. NG9: Stap 5D **117**
NG11: Rudd 4A **174**
Churchill Pk. NG4: Colw 5E **101**

Church La. DE7: H Woo 1C **62**
DE7: Mapp 5D **65**
DE7: Mor 4B **86**
DE7: Stan D 4E **115**
DE21: Bre 1D **109**
DE21: Chad 2F **137**
DE21: L Eat 3B **84**
DE22: D Abb 2E **107**
DE22: Mac 1E **133**
DE56: Bel 5E **13**
DE73: Bar T 4A **200**
DE73: Swar 3D **201**
DE74: C Don 1A **212**
DE74: Hem, Lock 5C **206**
DE74: Lock 5E **207**
NG5: Arn 3D **51**
NG6: Bulw 5B **48**
NG9: Atten 2C **170**
NG9: Stap 1C **144**
NG11: Bart F 5D **171**
NG12: Cotg 5D **155**
NG12: Plum 4D **177**
NG13: Bing 2E **131**
NG14: Epp 3F **33**
NG14: Lowd 2B **56**
NG15: Lin 4C **10**
NG16: Brins 3D **21**
NG16: Coss 5B **68**
Church La. Nth.
DE22: D Abb 2E **107**
Church Mdw. NG14: Calv 3E **31**
Church M. DE21: Spon 4C **138**
NG2: Nott 4C **122**
Churchmoor Ct. NG5: Arn 3D **51**
Churchmoor La. NG5: Arn 3D **51**
Church Rd. DE22: Quar 1B **106**
NG3: Nott 3C **98**
NG6: Bestw V 5D **27**
NG14: Bur J 3E **79**
NG16: Grea, Want 1C **44**
Churchside Gdns.
NG7: H Grn 2D **97**
Churchside Wlk.
DE22: Der 5A **6** (4D **135**)
Church Sq. DE75: Hea 3E **41**
NG7: Lent 2E **121**
Church St. DE5: Den 3C **38**
DE5: Rip 4C **8**
(Cromford Rd.)
DE5: Rip 2F **17**
(Jessop St.)
DE7: Ilk 3C **66**
DE21: Hors 1E **61**
DE21: Spon 4C **138**
DE23: Der 1F **159**
DE23: Lit 2B **158**
DE24: Alv 4B **162**
DE56: Bel 5F **13**
DE56: H'ook 1B **60**
DE56: Kil 4E **37**
DE72: Lock 4B **140**
DE74: Lock 5E **207**
DE75: Hea 3E **41**
NG4: Carl 3D **101**
NG4: Lamb 4B **54**
NG5: Arn 4E **51**
NG6: Basf 5D **73**
NG7: Lent 2D **121**
NG9: Bee 2E **147**
NG9: Bram 5A **118**
NG9: Stap 1C **144**
NG10: Sand 1A **144**
NG11: Rudd 4B **174**
NG12: Shel 1B **104**

234 A-Z Nottingham & Derby

Church St. NG13: Bing 2E **131**
  NG16: Eastw 3D **43**
Church Vw. DE7: Ilk 3D **91**
  DE56: Bel 5F **13**
  DE72: Brea 4C **166**
  DE75: Los 5A **18**
  NG4: Ged 1E **101**
Church Vw. Cl. NG5: Arn 3A **50**
Church Wlk. DE22: All 1E **107**
  DE23: Der 5E **135**
  DE56: Bel 5E **13**
  DE56: Duff 5E **59**
  NG4: Carl 3D **101**
  NG9: Stap 1C **144**
  NG14: Woodbo 5B **32**
  NG16: Brins 3D **21**
  NG16: Eastw 2E **43**
Church Way DE7: Ilk 3C **66**
CHURCH WILNE 1A **192**
Church Wilne Water Sports Club
  . . . . .1C **192**
Churnet Cl. NG11: Clif 4D **149**
Churston Ct. NG9: Bee 2F **147**
Cigar Factory, The
  NG7: Nott 5F **97**
  (off Derby Rd.)
CINDERHILL
  DE21 . . . . .3D **37**
  NG8 . . . . .3A **72**
Cinderhill Footway
  NG6: Bulw 3C **72**
Cinderhill Gro. NG4: Ged 5D **77**
Cinderhill Rd.
  NG6: Bulw, Cin 3A **72**
Cinderhill Stop (NET) 3A **72**
Cinderhill Wlk. NG6: Bulw . . .1A **72**
Cineworld
  Nottingham 5B **98**
Circle, The DE24: Sin 1D **185**
Cirrus Dr. NG16: Want 5F **45**
Citadel St. NG7: Radf 5D **97**
Citrus Gro. DE74: Keg 1B **214**
City, The NG9: Bee 2F **147**
  (not continuous)
City Ga. DE24: Der 1C **160**
City Ga. Bus. Pk.
  DE24: Der 1C **160**
City Ground 4D **123**
City Link NG2: Nott 5E **5** (2C **122**)
City of Caves 4C **4**
City Point NG1: Nott . . .4A **4** (1A **122**)
City Rd. DE1: Der 1F **135**
  NG7: Nott 4C **120**
  NG9: Bee 1F **147**
City Rd. Ind. Pk. DE1: Der 1F **135**
City Vw. NG3: Mapp 5E **75**
City Wlk. DE1: Der 2F **135**
Clandon Dr. NG5: Sher 5A **74**
Clanfield Rd. NG8: Bilb 3D **95**
Clapgun St. DE74: C Don . . .1A **212**
Clapham St. NG7: Radf 5D **97**
Claramount Rd. DE75: Hea . . .3F **41**
Clarborough Dr. NG5: Arn 1F **75**
Clare Cl. NG6: Basf 3D **73**
Clarehaven NG9: Stap 3D **145**
Clare Ho. DE1: Der 5F **135**
Claremont Av. NG9: Bram . . .5B **118**
  NG15: Huck 4F **25**
Claremont Dr.
  NG2: West Br 5B **150**
Claremont Gdns. NG5: Sher . . .1A **98**
Claremont Rd. NG5: Sher 1A **98**
Clarence Ct.
  NG3: Nott 2F **5** (5D **99**)

Clarence Rd. DE23: Der 2D **159**
  NG9: Chil 1C **170**
  NG10: Long E 5B **168**
Clarence St.
  NG3: Nott 1F **5** (5D **99**)
Clarendon Chambers
  NG1: Nott 1A **4** (5A **98**)
Clarendon Ct. NG5: Sher 2A **98**
Clarendon Pk. NG5: Sher 2A **98**
Clarendon St.
  NG1: Nott 1A **4** (5A **98**)
Clare St. NG1: Nott 2C **4** (5B **98**)
Clare Valley NG7: Nott 1A **122**
Clarewood Gro.
  NG11: Clif 4D **173**
Clarges St. NG6: Bulw 1B **72**
Clarke Av. DE75: Los 2B **40**
  NG5: Arn 4E **51**
Clarke Dr. NG10: Long E 2F **193**
Clarke Rd. NG2: Nott 3D **123**
Clarkes La. DE72: Ast T 1A **204**
  NG9: Chil 4C **146**
Clarke St. DE1: Der 1F **7** (2A **136**)
Clarkson Dr. NG9: Bee 2A **148**
Claude St. NG7: Lent 4D **121**
Claxton St. DE75: Hea 2C **40**
Claxton Ter. DE75: Hea 2C **40**
Clay Av. NG3: Mapp 4F **75**
Claye St. NG10: Long E 4D **169**
Clayfield Cl. NG6: Bulw 1F **71**
Claygate NG3: Nott 3F **99**
Clay La. DE75: Hea 2E **41**
Claypole Rd. NG7: H Grn 3E **97**
Clay St. DE72: Dray 4F **165**
Clayton Ct. NG7: Radf 5E **97**
  NG9: Bee 3F **147**
Clayton Gro. DE75: Los 5B **18**
Claytons Dr. NG7: Lent 3D **121**
Claytons Wharf
  NG7: Lent 3D **121**
Clement Rd. DE7: H Woo 5B **38**
Clether Rd. NG8: Bilb 4C **94**
Cleve Av. NG9: Toton 5D **145**
Clevedon Dr. NG5: Arn 3B **52**
Cleveland Av. DE21: Chad 3A **138**
  DE72: Dray 4E **165**
  NG10: Long E 2E **169**
Cleveland Cl. NG7: Radf 5D **97**
Cleveley's Rd. NG9: Toton . . .5D **145**
Clevely Way NG11: Clif 5D **149**
Cliff, The NG6: Bulw 3A **72**
Cliff Blvd. NG16: Kimb 5E **45**
  (not continuous)
Cliff Cres. NG12: Rad T 1E **127**
Cliff Dr. NG12: Rad T 5F **103**
Cliffe Hill Av. NG9: Stap 1C **144**
Cliffgrove Av. NG9: Chil 2C **146**
Cliffmere Wlk. NG11: Clif 2C **172**
  (not continuous)
Clifford Av. NG9: Bee 5D **119**
Clifford Cl. NG10: Long E 2F **193**
  NG12: Key 2E **199**
Clifford Ct. NG7: Radf 5E **97**
Clifford St. DE24: Der 1C **160**
  NG7: Radf 4E **97**
  NG10: Long E 4D **169**
Cliff Rd. NG1: Nott 4D **5** (1C **122**)
  NG4: Carl 4C **100**
  NG12: Rad T 1D **127**
Cliffs, The NG12: Rad T 5F **103**
Cliff Way NG12: Rad T 1E **127**
CLIFTON 2E **173**
Clifton Av. NG10: Long E 4F **169**
  NG11: Rudd 3B **174**

Clifton Blvd.
  NG7: Lent, Nott 3C **120**
  NG11: Rudd, Wilf 3F **149**
Clifton Cres. NG9: Atten 5D **147**
Clifton Dr. DE3: Mick 5D **133**
Clifton Grn. NG11: Clif 1C **172**
Clifton Gro. NG4: Ged 5D **77**
Clifton Hall Dr. NG11: Clif . .1B **172**
Clifton La. NG11: Clif, Wilf . .3C **172**
  NG11: Rudd 3F **173**
Clifton Leisure Cen. 2E **173**
Clifton M. NG7: Nott 1F **121**
Clifton Rd. DE22: All 2C **106**
  NG11: Rudd 4A **174**
Clifton St. DE1: Der 5B **136**
  NG9: Bee 2F **147**
Clifton Ter. NG7: Nott 2F **121**
Clinton Av. NG5: Sher 2A **98**
  NG16: Brins 3C **20**
Clinton Ct. NG1: Nott . . .1B **4** (5B **98**)
Clinton St. DE21: Chad 2C **136**
  NG5: Arn 5D **51**
  NG9: Bee 1D **147**
Clinton St. E.
  NG1: Nott 2C **4** (5B **98**)
Clinton St. W.
  NG1: Nott 2C **4** (5B **98**)
Clinton Ter. NG7: Nott 5F **97**
CLIPSTONE 2C **178**
Clipstone Av. NG1: Nott 4A **98**
  NG3: Mapp 3F **75**
Clipstone Ct. NG8: Stre 5C **70**
Clipstone Gdns.
  DE21: Oak 3A **110**
Clipston La.
  NG12: Norm W 4E **177**
Clive Cres. NG16: Kimb 2F **69**
Cliveden Grn. NG11: Clif 2C **172**
Clock Way DE21: Spon 5E **139**
Cloisters, The NG9: Bee 5F **119**
Cloisters Ct. DE21: Oak 2E **109**
Cloister St. NG7: Lent 3D **121**
Close, The DE22: D Abb 3E **107**
  DE23: Der 1C **158**
  NG5: Sher 4B **74**
  NG9: Chil 4C **146**
Close Quarters NG9: Bram . . .5B **118**
Cloud Av. NG9: Stap 1E **145**
Clouds Hill NG11: Clif 3D **173**
Cloudside Cl. NG10: Sand . . .1A **144**
Cloudside Rd. NG10: Sand . . .1F **143**
Cloudwood Cl. DE23: Lit 2A **158**
Clough Ct. NG8: Bilb 3A **96**
Clovelly Ct. DE22: Der 5C **106**
Clover Cl. DE21: Spon 3E **139**
Clover Ct. DE72: Shar 4D **191**
Cloverdale NG12: Cotg 1F **179**
Cloverdale Dr. DE24: Sin 4E **185**
Clover Flds. NG14: Calv 1F **31**
Clover Grn. NG6: Basf 4C **72**
Cloverlands NG2: West Br . . .5B **150**
Cloverlands Cl. NG16: Want . . .5F **45**
Cloverlands Dr. NG16: Want . . .5F **45**
Clover Ri. NG16: Newth 3A **44**
Cloverslade DE65: Find 5B **182**
Cloves Hill DE7: Mor 5B **62**
Club La. DE73: Bar T 4A **200**
Clumber Av. NG3: Mapp 3F **75**
  NG4: Neth 3F **101**
  NG5: Sher 2A **98**
  NG9: Chil 3C **146**
  NG16: Drins 1C **20**
  (not continuous)
Clumber Cl. DE5: Rip 5D **9**

Clumber Ct. NG7: Nott 2F **121**
Clumber Cres. Nth.
    NG7: Nott 1F **121**
Clumber Cres. Sth.
    NG7: Nott 2F **121**
Clumber Dr. NG12: Rad T 5F **103**
Clumber Rd. NG2: West Br . . .1E **151**
Clumber Rd. E. NG7: Nott 1F **121**
Clumber Rd. W. NG7: Nott 1F **121**
Clumber St.
    NG1: Nott 2C **4** (5B **98**)
    NG10: Long E 4C **168**
    NG15: Huck 3B **26**
Cluster Rd. DE56: Bel 5E **13**
Clusters Ct. DE56: Bel 5E **13**
Coach Dr. DE22: Quar 3C **82**
    NG16: Eastw 5E **21**
Coachmans Cft. NG8: Woll 5F **95**
Coach Rd. DE5: Rip 2D **9**
    (not continuous)
Coachways DE7: Mapp 4E **65**
Coates Av. NG15: Huck 5B **10**
Coatsby Rd. NG16: Kimb 5E **45**
Cobden Chambers
    NG1: Nott 3C **4** (1C **122**)
Cobden St. DE5: Rip 4C **8**
    DE22: Der 3C **134**
    (not continuous)
    NG7: Lent 5D **97**
    NG10: Long E 4C **168**
Cobham Cl. DE24: S Flds 3C **184**
Cobthorne Dr. DE22: All 1B **106**
Coburn Pl. DE1: Der . . .3B **6** (3E **135**)
Cockayne Cl. NG10: Sand 5A **144**
Cockayne St. Nth.
    DE24: A'ton 5D **161**
Cockayne St. Sth.
    DE24: A'ton 5D **161**
Cockcharme Gapp
    DE74: C Don 3A **206**
Cocker Beck NG4: Lamb 5B **54**
Cockerhouse Rd.
    NG16: Eastw 5D **21**
Cockington Rd. NG8: Bilb 5B **94**
Cockleys NG10: Long E 5B **168**
Cock Pitt, The
    DE1: Der 3E **7** (3A **136**)
Cod Beck Cl. DE24: Alv 5B **162**
CODNOR 1A **18**
CODNOR BREACH 5F **17**
Codnor Denby La.
    DE5: Cod, Den 5F **17**
CODNOR GATE 5F **9**
Codnor Ga. DE5: Cod 5F **9**
Codnor Ga. Bus. Pk. DE5: Rip . .5F **9**
Codnor Ga. Ind. Est. DE5: Rip . .4F **9**
Codrington Gdns.
    NG5: Bestw 4B **50**
Cogenhoe Wlk. NG5: Arn 2E **51**
Cogley La. NG13: Bing 2F **131**
Cohen Cl. NG5: Arn 1A **76**
    NG9: Chil 1A **170**
Cokefield Av. NG16: Nuth 4E **71**
Coke St. DE1: Der 3C **134**
Colborn St. NG3: Nott 3E **99**
Colbrook Pl. NG4: Carl 3E **101**
Colchester Rd. NG8: Brox 1D **95**
Coldstream Wlk. DE24: Sin . . .2D **185**
Coleby Av. NG7: Lent 3D **121**
Coleby Rd. NG8: Brox 5E **71**
Coledale DE7: Ilk 2B **152**
Cole La. DE72: Ock 4B **140**
Coleman St. DE24: Alv 4D **161**
Coleraine Cl. DE21: Chad 4A **138**

Coleridge Cres. NG5: Arn 5C **50**
Coleridge St. DE23: Der 1D **185**
    (not continuous)
    NG7: Radf 4D **97**
Colesbourne Rd. NG11: Clif . . .1E **173**
Colin Av. DE5: Cod 1A **18**
Colin Broughton Ct.
    NG6: Bulw 5C **48**
Colindale Gdns. NG16: Nuth . . .4D **71**
Colinwood Av. NG5: Top V 3D **49**
College, The DE5: Den 1A **38**
College Bus. Cen., The
    DE22: Der 4D **135**
College Dr. NG11: Clif 1C **172**
College M. DE1: Der 3E **135**
College Pl. DE1: Der . . .1C **6** (2F **135**)
College Rd. LE12: Sut B 2F **215**
    NG3: Mapp 4B **76**
    NG9: Chil 3D **147**
College St. NG1: Nott . . .2A **4** (5A **98**)
    NG10: Long E 5A **144**
College Way NG8: Bilb 3C **94**
Colleymoor Leys La.
    NG11: Clif 1E **173**
Collier La. DE72: Ock 4B **140**
Colliers Bus. Pk.
    NG12: Cotg 3F **155**
Colliers Way NG8: Cin 3F **71**
    NG12: Cotg 3F **155**
Colliery Cl. NG2: Nott 4A **122**
Collin Av. NG10: Sand 4A **144**
Collingham Gdns.
    DE22: Mac 3F **133**
Collin Grn. NG5: Sher 3C **74**
Collington St. NG9: Bee 2D **147**
Collington Way
    NG2: West Br 3C **150**
Collingwood Cl. NG11: Clif 4D **149**
Collingwood Rd.
    NG10: Long E 5C **168**
Collins Cl. NG6: Bulw 2E **71**
Collins Homes NG9: Bee 4D **119**
Collin St. NG1: Nott . . .5C **4** (2B **122**)
    NG9: Bee 2E **147**
Collis Cl. DE24: A'ton 4D **161**
Collison St. NG7: H Grn 4E **97**
Columbell Av. DE72: Ock 3B **140**
Collyer Rd. NG14: Calv 1B **30**
Colly Ga. NG16: Kimb 2F **69**
Collygate Rd. NG2: Nott 4C **122**
Colmon Cl. NG5: Bestw 5F **49**
Colmon Wlk. NG5: Bestw 5F **49**
Colombo St. DE23: Der 2A **160**
Colonsay Cl. NG9: Trow 2C **116**
Colston Cres.
    NG2: West Br 4C **150**
Colston Ga. NG12: Cotg 5E **155**
Colston Rd. NG6: Bulw 4B **48**
Coltsfoot Cl. NG13: Bing 3B **130**
Coltsfoot Dr. DE24: Sin 4E **185**
Columbine Cl. DE21: Oak 4F **109**
Colville Ct. NG1: Nott 3A **98**
Colville St. DE22: Der 2C **134**
    NG1: Nott 3A **98**
Colville Ter. NG1: Nott 4A **98**
Colville Vs. NG1: Nott 3A **98**
Colwell Dr. DE24: Alv 1B **188**
COLWICK 5D **101**
Colwick Bus. Pk. NG4: Colw . . .5E **101**
Colwick Country Pk. 2C **124**
Colwick Crossing NG2: Nott . . .1F **123**
Colwick Ind. Est.
    NG4: Colw 5D **101**
    (not continuous)

Colwick Lodge NG4: Carl 4E **101**
Colwick Loop Rd.
    NG4: Carl, Neth 2F **101**
    NG4: Colw, Neth 5D **101**
Colwick Mnr. Farm
    NG4: Colw 5D **101**
Colwick Pk. Cl. NG4: Colw . . .5D **101**
Colwick Quays Bus. Pk.
    NG4: Colw 5F **101**
Colwick Rd. NG2: Nott 2E **123**
    NG2: West Br 4D **123**
COLWICK VALE 4D **101**
Colwick Woods Ct.
    NG2: Nott 1F **123**
Colwyn Av. DE23: Der 2C **158**
Colyear St. DE1: Der . . .3C **6** (3F **135**)
Comery Av. NG3: Nott 4F **99**
Comet Dr. NG16: Eastw 2F **43**
Comfrey Cl. DE23: Lit 5E **157**
    NG5: Top V 5D **49**
Commerce Sq.
    NG1: Nott 4D **5** (1C **122**)
Commerce St. DE24: Alv 3E **161**
Commercial Av. NG9: Bee 2E **147**
Commercial Rd. NG6: Bulw . . .5A **48**
    NG12: Key 4D **199**
Commodore Ct. NG8: Aspl 5B **72**
Commodore Gdns.
    NG8: Aspl 5B **72**
Common, The DE22: Quar 2A **82**
    NG15: Huck 3B **24**
COMMON END 1C **156**
Common End DE65: Etw 3A **180**
Common La.
    DE7: S'ley, Stan C 4A **88**
    NG9: Bram 2F **145**
    NG15: Huck 3C **24**
    NG16: Want 5A **46**
Comn. Piece La.
    DE65: Find 5D **183**
Commons Cl. NG16: Newth 4F **43**
COMMON SIDE 3D **41**
Compton Acres
    NG2: West Br 2A **150**
Compton Acres Shop. Cen.
    NG2: West Br 3B **150**
Compton Av. DE72: Ast T 1F **203**
Compton Cl. DE24: Alv 5B **162**
Compton Rd. NG5: Sher 4A **74**
Comyn Gdns.
    NG3: Nott 1D **5** (4C **98**)
Condor Rd. DE7: Ilk 1E **115**
Conduit Cl. NG2: Nott 3B **122**
Coney Wlk. NG5: Top V 4E **49**
Conifer Cres. NG11: Clif 4D **173**
Conifer Wlk. NG3: Nott 3F **99**
Coningsby Gdns. E.
    NG5: Woodt 3E **75**
Coningsby Rd. NG5: Woodt 2E **75**
Coningswath Rd. NG4: Carl . . .5B **76**
Conisborough Ter.
    NG2: Nott 4B **122**
Conisbrough Av. NG4: Ged . . .1A **102**
Coniston Av. DE21: Spon 2D **139**
    NG6: Basf 5B **72**
Coniston Cl. NG2: Gam 1B **152**
Coniston Cres. DE21: Chad . . .3C **108**
Coniston Dr. DE7: Kirk H 5C **90**
Coniston Rd. NG9: Bram 4C **118**
    NG10: Long E 1F **167**
    NG15: Huck 1E **25**
Connaught Rd. DE22: Der 4B **134**
Connelly Cl. NG5: Arn 1B **76**
Connelly Ct. NG6: Bulw 2C **72**

Connery, The NG15: Huck 1A **26**
Connery M. NG9: Toton 2A **170**
Consett Cl. DE21: Chad 4C **108**
Consort Gdns. DE21: Oak ...2B **110**
Constable Av. DE23: Lit 5B **134**
Constable Dr. DE23: Lit 1A **158**
Constable La. DE23: Lit 1B **158**
Constance St. NG7: Basf 1F **97**
Convent, The NG1: Nott 2A **4**
Convent St.
    NG1: Nott 2D **5** (5C **98**)
Conway Av. DE72: Bor 1C **164**
    NG4: Carl 3F **101**
Conway Cl. NG3: Nott 3B **98**
Conway Cres. NG4: Carl 2F **101**
Conway Gdns. NG5: Arn 1D **75**
Conway Rd. NG4: Carl 3E **101**
    NG15: Huck 1C **46**
Conway St. NG10: Long E 3D **169**
Conway Wlk. NG3: Nott 3B **98**
Cook Cl. DE56: Bel 4D **15**
Cook Dr. DE7: Ilk 4F **91**
Cooke Cl. NG10: Long E 4A **168**
Cookfield DE56: H'age 1D **15**
Cookham Cl. DE3: Mick 1B **156**
Cooks Dr. DE74: C Don 1F **211**
Cookson Av. NG4: Ged 5C **76**
Coombe Cl. NG8: Woll 2B **120**
Coombe Rd. NG16: Newth 5A **22**
Co-operative Av.
    NG15: Huck 1A **26**
Co-operative St. DE23: Der ...1E **159**
    NG10: Long E 4D **169**
Cooper Cl. NG5: Arn 1B **76**
    NG6: Bulw 1E **71**
Cooper Gdns. NG11: Rudd ...4A **174**
Coopers Cl. DE72: Bor 2C **164**
Coopers Grn. NG8: Woll 3D **119**
Cooper St. DE5: Rip 5C **8**
    DE22: Der 2B **134**
    NG4: Neth 4F **101**
Copecastle Sq.
    DE1: Der 4E **7** (4A **136**)
Cope Cl. DE24: Sin 1F **185**
Copeland Av. NG9: Stap 5D **117**
Copeland Gro. NG13: Bing ...1B **130**
Copeland Rd. NG15: Huck 1B **26**
Copeland St.
    DE1: Der 4F **7** (4A **136**)
Copeland Wlk.
    DE1: Der 4E **7** (4A **136**)
Copenhagen Ct. NG3: Null ...1C **98**
Copestake Cl.
    NG10: Long E 4F **167**
Cope St. NG7: H Grn 4E **97**
Copes Way DE21: Chad 5F **109**
Copper Beeches DE5: Rip 4B **8**
Copperleaf Cl.
    DE22: Der 5A **6** (4E **135**)
Copper Yd. DE5: Den 2E **39**
Coppice Av. DE7: Ilk 2C **66**
Coppice Cl. DE22: D Abb 4E **107**
    DE56: Kil 4F **37**
    NG15: Huck 4D **25**
Coppice Ct. DE75: Hea 5E **41**
Coppice Dr. DE75: Hea 5E **41**
    NG16: Eastw 1C **42**
Coppice End Rd. DE22: All ...4B **106**
Coppice Ga. NG5: Arn 4E **51**
Coppice Gro. NG3: Mapp 5E **75**
Coppice M. DE75: Hea 5E **41**
Coppice Pk. DE72: Dray 2D **165**
Coppice Rd. NG5: Arn 4E **51**
Coppicewood Dr. DE23: Lit ...2F **157**

Copplestone Dr.
    NG3: Mapp 1B **76**
Copse, The DE7: Ilk 2C **66**
    NG9: Chil 2B **146**
    NG15: Huck 3B **26**
Copse Cl. NG14: Bur J 2E **79**
Copse Gro. DE23: Lit 4F **157**
Copseside Cl.
    NG10: Long E 3F **167**
Copsey Cft. Ct.
    NG10: Long E 4E **169**
Corbel Cl. DE21: Oak 3C **108**
Corben Gdns. NG6: Bulw 5E **47**
Corbiere Av. NG16: Want 5F **45**
Corbridge Gro. DE23: Lit 4F **157**
Corby Cl. DE24: Alv 1E **187**
Corby Rd. NG3: Nott 1D **99**
Cordelia Way DE73: Chel 4D **187**
Corden Av. DE3: Mick 1F **157**
Corden St. DE23: Der 1F **159**
Cordville Cl. DE21: Chad 3A **138**
Cordwell Cl. DE74: C Don 5F **205**
Cordy La. NG16: Brins 2D **21**
Corfe Cl. DE23: Lit 5C **158**
Corfield Av. DE75: Hea 5E **41**
Coriander Dr. NG6: Basf 4C **72**
Coriander Gdns. DE23: Lit 2C **184**
Corinium Cl. DE24: Alv 1C **188**
Corinth Rd. NG11: Clif 1D **173**
Corn Cl. NG12: Cotg 1D **179**
Corncrake Av. NG6: Basf 4C **72**
Corncrake Dr. NG5: Arn 5B **52**
Corn Cft. NG11: Clif 2E **173**
Cornell Dr. NG5: Arn 4A **52**
Corner, The NG14: Lowd 3C **56**
Cornfield Rd. NG16: Kimb 5D **45**
Cornfields, The NG5: Bestw ...4A **50**
Cornflower Dr. DE21: Oak 3F **109**
Cornhill DE22: All 1D **107**
Cornhill Cl. DE56: Duff 3C **58**
Cornhill Rd. NG4: Carl 2A **100**
Cornmarket
    DE1: Der 2D **7** (3F **135**)
Cornmill Cl. DE72: Elv 1C **188**
Cornwall Av. NG9: Bee 4B **148**
Cornwallis Cl.
    NG10: Long E 5C **168**
Cornwall Rd. DE21: Chad 1C **136**
    NG5: Arn 5B **50**
Cornwall's Hill NG4: Lamb ...5C **54**
Coronation Av. DE24: Alv 1B **188**
    DE56: Del 4F **13**
    NG10: Sand 1F **143**
    NG11: Wilf 4A **122**
Coronation Pk. 2F **43**
Coronation Rd. DE7: Ilk 5F **67**
    DE7: Mapp 4D **65**
        (not continuous)
    DE7: S'ley 4B **88**
    NG3: Mapp 4F **75**
    NG6: Bestw V 4D **27**
    NG15: Huck 1E **25**
    NG16: Nuth 2A **70**
Coronation St. DE7: Ilk 2E **91**
    DE23: Der 3A **160**
Coronation Wlk. NG4: Ged ...1F **101**
Coronet Ct. DE21: Oak 2C **110**
Corporation Cotts.
    NG14: Bulc 2A **80**
Corporation Oaks NG3: Nott ..3B **98**
Corporation Rd. DE7: Ilk 5F **91**
Corporation St.
    DE1: Der 2D **7** (3F **135**)
Corsham Gdns. NG3: Nott 3F **99**

Corve Dale Wlk.
    NG2: West Br 3E **151**
Cosby Rd. NG2: Nott 2E **123**
COSSALL 1B **92**
Cossall Ind. Est. DE7: Ilk 5A **68**
COSSALL MARSH 5B **68**
Cossall Rd. NG9: Coss, Trow ..3B **92**
    NG16: Coss 3B **92**
Costock Av. NG5: Sher 3A **74**
COTGRAVE 5E **155**
Cotgrave Av. NG4: Ged 5E **77**
Cotgrave Cl. NG8: Stre 5D **71**
Cotgrave Country Pk. 2E **155**
Cotgrave La. NG12: Toll 5E **153**
Cotgrave Leisure Cen. 5F **155**
Cotgrave Rd.
    NG12: C'ton, Plum 4E **177**
Cotgrave Shop. Cen.
    NG12: Cotg 5E **155**
COTMANHAY 3D **67**
Cotmanhay Rd. DE7: Ilk 4D **67**
Coton Cl. NG11: Wilf 5F **149**
Cotswold Cl. DE23: Lit 3B **158**
    NG10: Long E 3A **168**
Cotswold Ct. NG9: Bram 4C **118**
Cotswold Rd. NG8: Stre 1D **95**
Cottage Cl. DE7: Ilk 4C **66**
    DE56: H'age 2D **15**
Cottage Ct. DE56: Bel 1D **37**
Cottage Gdn. La. DE75: Hea ..2C **40**
Cottage Grn. NG2: West Br ...4B **124**
Cottage Mdw. NG4: Colw 1E **125**
Cottage Pasture La.
    NG14: Gun 5D **57**
Cottage Ter. NG1: Nott 5F **97**
Cottage Wlk. NG8: Woll 5D **95**
Cottam Dr. NG5: Top V 4E **49**
Cottam Gdns. NG5: Top V 4F **49**
Cottesmore Rd. NG7: Lent 1E **121**
Cottisford Cl. DE23: Lit 3F **157**
Cotton Brook Rd.
    DE23: Der 3A **160**
Cotton Ho. *NG7: Radf* *4D* **97**
        (off Radford Blvd.)
Cotton La. DE24: Der 3A **160**
Countess Gro. DE73: Chel 1D **201**
Countisbury Dr. DE21: Oak ...3F **109**
Country Bus. Pk. NG2: Nott ...3D **123**
County Archives 5B **4** (2B **122**)
County Cl. NG9: Bee 3F **147**
County Rd. NG2: Nott 3D **123**
    NG4: Ged 4B **76**
Coupe Gdns. NG15: Huck 3B **26**
Coupe St. DE5: Rip 1E **17**
    NG9: Toton 1F **169**
Court, The DE24: Alv 5A **162**
Court Cres. NG8: Woll 1E **119**
Courtenay Gdns. NG3: Nott ...3C **98**
Court Gdns. NG2: West Br 4A **150**
Courtland Dr. DE24: Alv 5F **161**
Courtland Gdns. DE24: Alv 4A **162**
Courtland Rd. DE65: Etw 3A **180**
Courtleet Way NG6: Bulw 2A **72**
Courtney Cl. NG8: Woll 5D **95**
Courtney Way DE56: Bel 4C **14**
Court St. NG7: H Grn 3E **97**
Court Vw. NG7: Nott 1F **121**
Courtway Cres. DE73: Chel ...5D **187**
Court Yd. NG9: Bram 5A **118**
Courtyard Pl. DE21: Spon 3D **139**
Covedale Rd. NG5: Sher 2B **74**
Covent Gdns. NG12: Rad T ...2D **129**
Coventry Ct. NG6: Bulw 2A **72**
Coventry La. NG9: Bram 4E **117**

Coventry Rd. NG6: Bulw 5A **48**
          (not continuous)
  NG9: Bee 1F **147**
Coverdale Wlk. *DE24: Alv 5B 162*
         (off Elvaston La.)
Covers, The NG2: West Br 4E **123**
Covert, The DE21: Spon 4D **139**
Covert Cl. NG12: Key 2E **199**
  NG14: Bur J 2D **79**
  NG15: Huck 3B **26**
Covert Cres. NG12: Shar . . .2A **128**
Covert Rd. NG2: West Br 2A **152**
Cowan St. NG1: Nott . .2D **5** (5C **98**)
Cowdray Cl. DE24: Sin 4C **184**
Cowdrey Gdns. NG5: Arn 1A **76**
COWHILL 2F **35**
Cowlairs NG5: Top V 5D **49**
Cow La. NG9: Bram 5A **118**
Cowley Cl. DE7: Ilk 2E **67**
Cowley St. DE1: Der 1D **135**
  NG6: Basf 4C **72**
Cowlishaw Cl. DE72: Shar . . .5D **191**
Cowper Rd. NG5: Woodt 3D **75**
  NG16: Newth 4F **43**
Cowper St. DE24: Sin 1F **185**
Cowsley Rd. DE21: Chad 5C **108**
Cowslip Cl. NG13: Bing 2B **130**
Cowslip Mdw. DE72: Dray . . .4F **165**
COXBENCH 3D **61**
Coxbench Rd.
  DE21: Cox, Hors 3D **61**
Cox Grn. Ct. DE23: Lit 4E **157**
Coxmoor Cl. NG12: Edwal . . .4B **152**
Coxmoor Ct. NG5: Top V 3F **49**
Coxon St. DE21: Spon 3D **139**
Crabapple Dr.
  NG16: Lang M 5B **20**
Crab Apple Gro.
  NG15: Huck 5B **26**
Crabtree Cl. DE22: All 1B **106**
  DE74: C Don 2F **211**
Crabtree Fld. NG2: Colw 1C **124**
Crab Tree Hill DE21: L Eat 2B **84**
Crabtree Rd. NG6: Bulw 1F **71**
Craddock Av. DE21: Spon 5D **139**
Cragdale Rd. NG5: Sher 2B **74**
Cragmoor Rd. NG14: Bur J . . .4D **79**
Craiglee Cl. DE24: Sin 2C **184**
Craig Moray NG12: Rad T . . .1F **127**
Craig St. NG10: Long E 4D **169**
Cramcote Leisure Cen. 4F **117**
Crammond Cl. NG2: Nott 3A **122**
Crampton Cl. NG5: Top V 4F **49**
Cramworth Gro. NG5: Sher . . .4C **74**
Cranberry Cl.
  NG2: West Br 2A **150**
Cranberry Gro. DE23: Lit 5E **157**
Cranborne Cl. NG9: Trow 3C **116**
Cranbourne Gro.
  NG15: Huck 2D **25**
Cranbrook Ho. NG1: Nott 3E **5**
Cranbrook St.
  NG1: Nott 2D **5** (5C **98**)
Cranfield Wlk. NG11: Clif 1E **173**
Cranfleet Way
  NG10: Long E 4F **167**
Cranford Gdns.
  NG2: West Br 4B **150**
Cranhill Cl. DE23: Lit 5E **157**
Cranleigh Dr. NG14: Lowd 3C **56**
Cranmer Gro. NG3: Nott 3B **98**
Cranmer Rd.
  DE21: Der 2F **7** (3B **136**)

Cranmer St. DE7: Ilk 1E **91**
  NG3: Nott 3B **98**
  NG10: Long E 3C **168**
Cranmer Wlk. NG3: Nott 3B **98**
Cranmore Cl. NG5: Arn 2F **51**
Cransley Av. NG8: Woll 3C **118**
Cranston Av. NG5: Arn 3E **51**
Cranston Rd. NG9: Bram 4B **118**
Cranthorne Dr. NG3: Nott 4B **100**
Crantock Gdns. NG12: Key . . .3E **199**
Cranwell Cl. NG6: Bulw 1E **71**
Cranwell Rd. NG8: Stre 1C **94**
Cranwood Cl. DE24: A'ton . . .1C **186**
Craster Dr. NG5: Arn 2F **51**
  NG6: Bulw 4E **47**
Craven Rd. NG7: H Grn 3D **97**
Crawford Av. NG9: Stap 5C **116**
Crawford Cl. NG8: Woll 5D **95**
Crawford Ri. NG5: Arn 4B **52**
Crawley Rd. DE24: Alv 1E **187**
Crayford Rd. DE24: Alv 1F **187**
Crecy Cl. DE22: Der 5B **134**
Creeton Grn. NG11: Clif 3E **173**
Crescent, The DE7: H Woo . . .5B **38**
  DE7: Stan C 1A **88**
  DE21: Chad 3E **137**
  DE24: Alv 5D **161**
  DE72: Brea 4B **166**
  DE72: Ris 5C **142**
  NG3: Nott 2C **98**
  NG5: Woodt 3D **75**
  NG9: Chil 5B **146**
  NG9: Stap 4D **117**
  NG9: Toton 1F **169**
  NG12: Rad T 2F **127**
  NG16: Eastw 2F **43**
Crescent Av. NG4: Carl 1D **101**
Cressbrook Way DE21: Oak . .2A **110**
Cressida Ct. DE73: Chel 4C **186**
Cresswell Rd. NG9: Chil 3A **146**
Cressy Rd. NG11: Clif 1E **173**
Crest, The DE22: D Abb 3D **107**
Cresta Gdns. NG3: Mapp 5C **74**
Cresta Gro. DE21: Chad 4E **109**
Crest Vw. NG5: Sher 4A **74**
Crewe Cl. NG7: Radf 4E **97**
Crewe St. DE23: Der 2E **159**
CREWTON 3F **161**
Crewton Way DE24: Alv 4E **161**
Cribb Cl. NG11: Wilf 1A **150**
Crich Av. DE23: Lit 1A **158**
Crich Circ. DE23: Lit 1B **158**
Crich La. DE56: Bel 4F **13**
Crich Vw. NG5: Sher 5B **74**
Crich Vw. Dr. DE56: H'age 1D **15**
Cricketers Ct. DE23: Lit 3C **158**
  NG2: West Br 4E **123**
Cricklewood Rd.
  DE22: Mac 2A **134**
Criftin Ent. Cen. NG14: Epp 1C **32**
Criftin Rd. NG14: Bur J 3F **79**
Cringle M. DE21: Oak 3D **109**
Cripps Hall NG7: Nott 3B **120**
Cripps Hill NG7: Nott 3B **120**
Critchley St. DE7: Ilk 1E **91**
Critch's Flats NG16: Kimb . . .1E **69**
Crocus Pl. NG2: Nott 2C **122**
Crocus St. NG2: Nott 3B **122**
Croft, The DE7: Mor 5B **62**
  DE23: Lit 3C **158**
  DE56: Bar 3B **36**
  DE72: Dray 5F **165**
  DE74: Keg 2C **214**
Croft Av. NG15: Huck 4F **25**

Croft Cl. DE7: D Ab 3E **113**
  DE21: Spon 2E **139**
  DE72: Ock 4B **140**
Croft Cres. NG16: Aws 2B **68**
Croft End DE21: L Eat 2B **84**
Crofters Ct. DE21: Oak 3D **109**
Croft La. DE21: Bre 2B **108**
Crofton Cl. NG8: Bilb 4A **96**
  NG9: Chil 5C **146**
Crofton Rd. NG9: Chil 1C **170**
Croft Rd. NG5: Arn 4E **51**
  NG12: Edwal 4F **151**
  NG12: Key 3C **198**
Crofts, The NG13: Bing 2D **131**
Cromarty Cl. DE24: Sin 2D **185**
Cromarty Ct. NG2: Nott 3A **122**
Cromdale Cl. NG5: Arn 3B **52**
Cromer Cl. DE3: Mick 2B **156**
Cromer Rd. NG3: Nott 3D **99**
Cromford Av. NG4: Carl 2C **100**
Cromford Cl.
  NG10: Long E 1F **193**
  NG16: Lang M 5A **20**
Cromford Dr. DE3: Mick 4D **133**
Cromford Rd. DE5: Rip 4C **8**
  DE21: Chad 5E **109**
  NG2: West Br 2E **151**
  NG16: Lang M 3D **19**
         (not continuous)
Cromford Rd. Ind. Est.
  NG16: Lang M 5A **20**
Crompton Rd.
  DE7: Ilk, Stan D 3A **116**
Crompton Rd. Ind. Est.
  DE7: Ilk 2F **115**
Crompton St.
  DE1: Der 4B **6** (4E **135**)
Cromwell Av. DE7: Ilk 5F **91**
  DE65: Find 4C **182**
Cromwell Cres. NG4: Lamb . . .5A **54**
Cromwell Rd. DE23: Der 1E **159**
  NG9: Bee 1D **147**
Cromwell St. NG4: Carl 3D **101**
  NG7: Radf 1A **4** (5F **97**)
  NG16: Gilt 4A **44**
Cromwell Ter. DE7: Ilk 4E **67**
Crookdole La. NG14: Calv 2E **31**
Cropton Cl. NG2: West Br 4D **151**
Cropton Cl. DE24: Alv 5B **162**
Cropton Cres. NG8: Bilb 4A **96**
Cropton Gro. NG13: Bing 2B **130**
Cropwell Gdns.
  NG12: Rad T 3F **127**
Cropwell Grn. NG3: Nott 4E **99**
Cropwell Rd. NG12: Rad T . . .2E **127**
Crosby Rd. NG2: West Br 4E **123**
Crosby St. DE22: Der 4C **134**
Cross, The NG12: Cotg 5D **155**
Cross Cl. DE23: Lit 3B **158**
Cross Cl. Wlk. DE23: Lit 3B **158**
Crossdale Gro. DE21: Oak . . .2B **110**
Crossdale Wlk. NG5: Top V . . .4D **49**
Crossfield Ct. NG5: Top V 4F **49**
Crossfield Dr. NG5: Top V 4F **49**
Crossgate Dr. NG2: Nott 5F **121**
CROSS HILL 3A **18**
Crosshill DE5: Cod 3A **18**
  NG12: Cotg 5F **155**
Crosshill Dr. DE7: Kirk H 5B **90**
Crossland Rd. NG5: Bestw . . .2F **73**
Crosslands Mdw.
  NG4: Colw 1E **125**
Cross La. DE5: Cod 2A **18**

Crossley St. DE5: Rip 5C 8
NG5: Sher 5A 74
Crossman St. NG5: Sher 5A 74
Cross St. DE22: Der 2C 134
NG4: Carl 2C 100
NG4: Neth 3F 101
NG5: Arn 4C 50
NG9: Bee 1E 147
NG10: Long E 3D 169
NG10: Sand 2B 144
NG16: Eastw 2F 43
Crowborough Av.
NG8: Woll 3D 119
Crow Ct. NG13: Bing 2F 131
Crowcroft Way
NG10: Long E 1A 168
Crow Hill Rd. NG4: Carl 3E 101
Crowley Cl. NG8: Bilb 4B 94
Crown Cl. NG10: Long E 4F 167
Crown Hill Way DE7: Stan C . . .2A 88
Crownland Dr. DE73: Der 4F 187
Crown M. DE22: Der . . .5A 6 (5D 135)
Crown St. DE22: Der 5D 135
DE56: Duff 3D 59
Crown Ter. DE56: Bel 5E 13
Crown Wlk.
DE1: Der 3D 7 (3F 135)
Crown Way DE73: Chel 1D 201
NG16: Lang M 5A 20
Crow Pk. Dr. NG14: Bur J 4D 79
Crowshaw St. DE24: Der 3A 160
Crowthorne Cl. NG5: Top V . . .3D 49
Crowthorne Gdns.
NG5: Top V 3D 49
Croxall Cl. NG11: Clif 4D 149
Croxley Gdns. NG16: Nuth 4C 70
Croydon Rd. NG7: Radf 5D 97
Croydon Wlk. DE22: Mac 2E 133
Crummock Cl. NG9: Bram . . .5B 118
Crusader Ct. NG11: Clif 2B 172
Crystal Cl. DE3: Mick 4C 132
Cubley Wlk. DE23: Lit 1B 184
Cuckmere Cl. DE22: All 5A 84
Cudworth Dr. NG3: Mapp 5E 75
Cuillin Cl. NG5: Top V 2E 49
NG10: Long E 2F 167
Culbert Lodge NG7: Basf 1E 97
Culbert Pl. NG7: Basf 1E 97
Cullens Ct. NG5: Sher 5B 74
Cullen Way DE24: Sin 4D 185
Culworth Cl. DE56: Bel 5C 14
Culworth Ct. DE21: Oak 3A 110
Cumberhills Grange
DE56: Duff 5C 58
Cumberhills Rd. DE22: Ked . . .2A 82
DE56: Duff 2A 82
Cumberland Av.
DE21: Chad 2D 137
NG9: Bee 2C 146
Cumberland Cl.
NG11: Rudd 4D 174
Cumberland Cres.
DE72: Bor 2A 164
Cumberland Pl.
NG1: Nott 3A 4 (1A 122)
Cumbria Grange NG2: Gam . . .1B 152
Cumbria Wlk. DE3: Mick 2B 156
Cummings St. DE23: Der 1F 159
Curborough Dr. DE24: Alv 5C 162
Curie Ct. NG7: Nott 3D 121
Curlew Cl. DE24: Sin 2C 184
NG3: Nott 5B 100
Curlew Wharf NG7: Lent 3F 121
Cursley Way NG9: Chil 1B 170

Curtis St. NG15: Huck 3F 25
Curzon Av. NG4: Carl 3A 100
Curzon Cl. DE22: All 1B 106
Curzon Ct. DE3: Mick 2C 156
DE56: Duff 4D 59
NG3: Nott 4C 98
Curzon Gdns. NG3: Nott 4C 98
Curzon La. DE24: Alv 3F 161
DE56: Duff 4C 58
Curzon Pl. NG3: Nott . . .1D 5 (5C 98)
Curzon Rd. DE21: Chad 1E 137
Curzon St.
DE1: Der 3A 6 (3E 135)
NG3: Nott 1D 5 (5C 98)
NG4: Neth 3F 101
NG10: Long E 1A 168
Cut La. DE1: Der 1A 136
DE21: Der 3E 139
Cutler Way DE3: Mick 4C 132
Cutthrough La. NG7: Nott 5A 120
Cuttlebrook Cl. DE23: Der 4D 159
Cuxton Cl. NG8: Stre 1C 94
Cycle Rd. NG7: Lent 1D 121
Cygnus Ct. DE74: N Air 4D 213
Cypress Ct. NG15: Huck 4B 24
Cypress Wlk. DE21: Chad 3A 138
Cyprus Av. NG9: Bee 1E 147
Cyprus Ct. NG3: Mapp P 2B 98
Cyprus Dr. NG9: Bee 1E 147
Cyprus Rd. NG3: Mapp P 2B 98
Cyril Av. NG8: Aspl 2C 96
NG9: Bee 1D 147
NG9: Stap 1C 144
Cyril Cotts. NG8: Aspl 2C 96
Cyril Rd. NG2: West Br 5F 123

D

Dabell Av. NG6: Bulw 4D 47
Dagmar Gro. NG3: Nott 1C 98
Dahlia Dr. DE21: Oak 2B 110
Dairy Ho. Rd. DE23: Der 2F 159
Daisy Cl. NG12: Cotg 1D 179
Daisy Farm Rd.
NG16: Newth 3A 44
Daisy Rd. NG3: Nott 1F 99
Dakeyne St.
NG3: Nott 2F 5 (5D 99)
Dakota Rd. DE74: N Air 4A 212
Dalbeattie Cl. NG5: Arn 4A 52
Dalbury Wlk. DE23: Lit 1B 184
Dalby Ho. DE22: Der 2B 134
Dalby Sq. NG8: Woll 2B 120
DALE ABBEY 3E 113
Daleacre Av. DE74: Lock 4E 207
Dale Av. NG3: Mapp 5F 75
NG4: Carl 3B 100
NG10: Long E 2C 168
Dalebrook Cres.
NG15: Huck 3B 24
Dale Cl. DE72: Brea 3C 166
NG2: West Br 1A 152
NG15: Huck 3B 24
Dale Ct. DE56: Kil 4E 37
Dale Farm Av. NG3: Nott 5F 99
Dale Gro. NG2: Nott 1E 123
Dalehead Rd. NG11: Clif 1C 172
Dale La. DE7: D Ab 3E 113
NG9: Chil 2D 147
Dalemoor Gdns.
NG8: Bilb 2A 96
Dale Pk. Av. DE56: Kil 4F 37

Dale Rd. DE7: D Ab, Stan D . . .4F 113
DE7: S'ley 5A 88
DE21: Spon 3E 139
DE23: Der 1E 159
DE24: Alv 4A 162
DE72: Ock 1A 140
NG4: Carl 3B 100
NG12: Key 3D 199
NG16: Kimb 2E 69
Dales, The DE7: West H 3D 89
Dalesgate Cl. DE23: Lit 1A 184
Daleside NG12: Cotg 1D 179
Daleside Rd. NG2: Nott 2E 123
Daleside Rd. E. NG2: Nott . . .1A 124
Dale St. DE7: Ilk 3E 91
NG2: Nott 1D 123
Dale Ter. NG2: Nott 1E 123
Dale Vw. DE7: Ilk 4D 91
Dale Vw. Gdns. DE56: Kil 4E 37
Dale Vw. Rd. NG3: Nott 3A 100
Dalkeith Av. DE24: Alv 1E 187
Dalkeith Ter. NG7: H Grn 3E 97
Dallaglio M. NG9: Chil 1A 170
Dallas York Rd. NG9: Bee 2A 148
Dalley Cl. NG9: Stap 1D 145
Dalley La. DE56: Bel 2B 12
Dallimore Rd. DE7: Kirk H 1C 114
Dalness Ct. DE24: Sin 3C 184
Dalton Av. DE22: Der 5B 134
Dalton Cl. NG9: Stap 3D 145
Dalton Dr. DE56: Ber 5F 13
Daltons Cl. NG16: Lang M 5F 19
Dam-Side DE56: Bel 1F 35
Damson Gro. DE24: Alv 3D 161
Damson Wlk. NG3: Nott 2A 100
Danebridge Cres.
DE21: Oak 4F 109
Dane Cl. NG3: Nott 4C 98
Dane Ct. NG3: Nott 4C 98
Danehurst Dr. NG4: Ged 1F 101
Danesby Cres. DE5: Den 3F 37
Danesby Ri. DE5: Den 3F 37
Danes Cl. NG5: Arn 4C 50
Danethorpe Va. NG5: Sher 3B 74
Daniel M. NG10: Sand 3F 143
Daniels Ct. NG16: Eastw 3E 43
Daniels Way NG15: Huck 5D 25
Dannah Cres. DE5: Rip 5E 9
Dannah St. DE5: Rip 4D 9
Dann Pl. NG11: Wilf 5A 122
Darby St. DE23: Der 1E 159
Darfield Dr. DE75: Hea 2F 41
Darkey La. NG9: Stap 3D 145
(not continuous)
Dark La. DE56: Mil 1F 59
NG13: Bing 2F 131
NG14: Calv 3D 31
DARLEY ABBEY 4E 107
Darley Abbey Dr.
DE22: D Abb 3E 107
Darley Abbey Mills
DE22: D Abb 3F 107
Darley Av. NG4: Carl 1D 101
NG7: H Grn 3D 97
NG9: Toton 5D 145
Darley Dr. DE5: Rip 3B 8
DE7: West H 2D 89
NG10: Long E 1F 193
Darley Gro. DE1: Der 5F 107
DE22: D Abb 4E 107
Darley La. DE1: Dor . . .1C 6 (2F 135)
Darley Mill Pottery 3F 107
Darley Pk. Dr. DE22: Der 4E 107

Darley Pk. Rd.
DE22: D Abb 4E **107**
Darley Rd. NG7: H Grn 3D **97**
Darley Sq. DE7: Ilk 2D **67**
Darley St. DE22: D Abb 4F **107**
Darlison St. *NG15: Huck* *1F 25*
(off Ogle St.)
Darlton Dr. NG5: Arn 5F **51**
Darnal Cl. NG5: Top V 5D **49**
Darnhall Cres. NG8: Bilb 3C **94**
Daron Gdns. NG5: Bestw 5F **49**
Darraway Gdns.
DE73: Chel 4D **187**
Darsway DE74: C Don 5E **205**
Dartford Pl. DE24: Alv 1F **187**
Dartmeet Ct. NG7: Radf 3C **96**
Darvel Cl. NG8: Bilb 4A **96**
Darwin Av. DE7: Ilk 3D **91**
DE24: A'ton 2C **186**
Darwin Cl. NG5: Top V 4D **49**
Darwin Pl. DE1: Der . . .2E **7** (3A **136**)
Darwin Rd. DE3: Mick 5D **133**
NG10: Long E 1A **194**
Darwin Sq. DE1: Der . . .4D **7** (4F **135**)
Dashwood St. DE23: Der 5F **135**
Datchet Cl. DE23: Lit 3F **157**
Davenport Rd. DE24: Der 3B **160**
Daventry Cl. DE3: Mick 5B **132**
David Gro. NG9: Bram 4C **118**
David La. NG6: Basf 4C **72**
David Lane Stop (NET) 4C **72**
David Lloyd Leisure
Derby 4C **136**
Nottingham 3C **96**
West Bridgeford 2C **150**
David's Cl. DE73: Chel 5E **187**
Davids La. NG14: Gun 2F **81**
Davidson Cl. NG5: Arn 5B **52**
Davidson Gdns.
NG11: Rudd 4F **173**
Davidson St. NG2: Nott 2E **123**
Davies Rd. NG2: West Br 1E **151**
Davies Way NG5: Bestw 2F **73**
Davis Ho. DE1: Der 4C **6** (4F **135**)
Davis Rd. NG9: Chil 5A **146**
Davy Cl. NG15: Lin 4D **11**
Dawes Way NG7: Lent 5D **97**
Dawlish Cl. NG15: Huck 3C **24**
Dawlish Ct. DE24: Alv 4B **162**
NG16: Eastw 1C **42**
Dawlish Dr. NG5: Bestw 2A **74**
Dawn Cl. NG15: Huck 5E **11**
Dawn Vw. NG9: Trow 3C **116**
Dawsmere Cl. DE21: Chad . . .4C **108**
Dawson Cl. NG16: Newth 3F **43**
Dawver Rd. NG16: Kimb 2E **69**
Daylesford Cl. DE23: Lit 3F **157**
Days La. DE56: Bel 1E **35**
Dayton Cl. DE21: Chad 3B **138**
Dayton Ct. DE22: Der 5D **107**
Deabill Cl. NG4: Neth 4F **101**
Deabill St. NG4: Neth 4F **101**
Deacon Cl. DE21: Oak 3D **109**
Dead La. NG16: Coss 1C **92**
Deadman's La. DE24: Der 1C **160**
Deakins Pl. NG7: Radf 5D **97**
Deal Gdns. NG6: Bulw 5E **47**

Dean Av. NG3: Mapp 4A **76**
Dean Cl. DE23: Lit 1F **157**
NG8: Woll 5C **94**
Dean Ct. DE23: Der 1D **159**
Deane Rd. NG11: Wilf 2F **149**
Deanery Cl. DE5: Rip 2D **17**
Dean Rd. NG5: Woodt 2D **75**
Deans Ct. NG12: Cotg 5F **155**
Deans Cft. NG9: Bram 4A **118**
Deans Dr. DE72: Bor 1A **164**
Dean St. DE22: Der 5D **135**
NG1: Nott 4E **5** (1C **122**)
NG16: Lang M 1B **42**
Debdale Ho. NG12: Key 3D **199**
Debdale La. NG12: Key 3C **198**
Deborah Dr. DE21: Chad 1F **137**
De Bradelei Mill DE56: Bel 1E **35**
Deddington La.
NG9: Bram 3A **118**
Dee Cl. DE24: Sin 3D **185**
Deeley Cl. NG16: Want 4F **45**
Deepdale Av. DE7: Kirk H 5C **90**
NG9: Stap 2C **144**
Deepdale Cl. NG2: Gam 1B **152**
Deepdale Ct. DE75: Hea 3D **41**
Deepdale La. DE24: Sin 4D **185**
DE73: Bar T 2A **200**
Deepdale Rd. DE21: Spon 5E **139**
DE56: Bel 4A **14**
NG8: Woll 1C **118**
NG10: Long E 5F **167**
Deepdene Cl. NG8: Brox 5F **71**
Deepdene Way
NG8: Brox, Cin 5F **71**
Deep Furrow Av. NG4: Carl . . .2C **100**
Deering Ct. NG2: Nott 3A **122**
Deerleap Dr. NG5: Arn 5B **50**
Deer Pk. NG8: Woll 1D **119**
Deer Pk. Dr. NG5: Arn 4A **50**
Deer Pk. Vw. DE21: Spon 2E **139**
De Ferrers Cl. DE56: Duff 4D **59**
Degge St. DE1: Der 4C **6** (4F **135**)
Deincourt Cl. DE21: Spon 2F **139**
Delamere Cl. DE21: Oak 4F **109**
DE72: Brea 3C **166**
Delia Av. NG15: Huck 5E **11**
Dell Way NG11: Clif 1E **173**
Dellwood Cl. NG4: Carl 5A **76**
Delta Cl. NG1: Nott 4B **98**
Delta St. NG7: Basf 1E **97**
Deltic Cl. NG16: Want 5F **45**
Delven La. DE74: C Don 1F **211**
Delves Ct. DE75: Hea 4D **41**
Delves Rd. DE75: Hea 4C **40**
Delville Av. NG12: Key 2D **199**
Denacre Av. NG10: Long E 2E **169**
Denarth Av. DE24: S Loc 3D **187**
Denbigh St. DE21: Chad 1D **137**
DENBY 3C **38**
DENBY BOTTLES 3F **37**
DENBY COMMON 1F **39**
Denby Comn. DE5: Den 1E **39**
Denby Ct. NG4: Neth 3F **101**
Denby Hall Rd. DE7: Ilk 1D **67**
Denby La. DE5: Den 3A **38**
Denby Pottery Vis. Cen. 5B **16**
Denehurst Av. NG8: Aspl 1B **96**
Denewood Av. NG9: Bram 3B **118**
Denewood Cres. NG8: Bilb 2D **95**
Denham St. Central
NG7: Radf 5E **97**
Denholme Rd. NG8: Bilb 5C **94**
Denison Ct. NG7: Radf 4E **97**
Denison Gdns. DE21: Chad . . .2A **138**

Denison St. NG7: Radf 4E **97**
NG9: Bee 1D **147**
Denman St. Central
NG7: Radf 5D **97**
(not continuous)
Denman St. E. NG7: Radf 5E **97**
Denmark Gro. NG3: Nott 1C **98**
Dennett Cl. NG3: Nott . . .1F **5** (4D **99**)
Dennis Av. NG9: Bee 5D **119**
Dennis Cl. DE23: Lit 4D **157**
Dennis St. NG4: Neth 3F **101**
Denstone Dr. DE24: Alv 2F **187**
Denstone Rd. NG3: Nott 5D **99**
Dentdale Ct. *DE24: Alv* *4B 162*
(off Hodge Beck Cl.)
Dentdale Dr. NG8: Woll 1A **118**
Denton Av. NG10: Sand 2F **143**
Denton Dr. NG2: West Br 4C **150**
Denton Grn. NG8: Brox 5E **71**
Denver Ct. NG9: Stap 4D **117**
Denver Rd. DE3: Mick 5C **132**
Depedale Av. DE72: Bor 5B **140**
Depot St. DE23: Der 1F **159**
Deptford Cres. NG6: Bulw 1B **72**
DERBY 3F **135**
Derby Arboretum 5A **136**
Derby Canal Walkway
DE24: A'ton, Der 4D **161**
DE24: Der 2E **161**
DE73: Chel 4C **186**
Derby Cathedral 1C **6** (3F **135**)
Derby College Fitness Cen. . . .3E **133**
Derby County FC 5D **137**
Derby County Football Academy &
Training Ground 3B **110**
Derby Dance Cen. 1C **6**
Derby Gaol 1A **6** (3E **135**)
Derby Golf Cen. 5E **139**
Derby Gro. NG7: Lent, Radf 5E **97**
Derby Hall NG7: Nott 3A **120**
Derby La. DE23: Der 3E **159**
Derby Mus. & Art Gallery
. . . . .2C **6** (3F **135**)
Derby Playhouse . . .3E **7** (4A **136**)
Derby Rd. DE5: Rip 5C **8**
DE7: Ilk 3B **90**
DE7: S'ley 2C **110**
DE21: Chad 2C **110**
DE21: Chad, Spon 3A **138**
DE21: Cox 2C **60**
DE21: L Eat 1C **84**
DE21: Spon 1E **163**
DE55: Swan 2D **9**
DE56: Ambe 1E **13**
DE56: Bel, Mil 2E **35**
DE56: Duff 5E **59**
DE56: Duff, Mil 2D **59**
DE56: L Kil 1D **61**
DE65: Etw, Hilt 2A **180**
DE72: Dray 2C **164**
DE72: Ris 4C **142**
DE72: Thul 3F **189**
DE73: Chel 3E **187**
(not continuous)
DE74: Keg 1B **214**
DE75: Hea 3C **40**
NG1: Nott 2A **4** (5F **97**)
NG7: Lent, Nott 3C **120**
NG9: Bee, Bram 5F **117**
NG9: Lent, Nott 4E **119**
NG9: Stap 3B **144**
NG10: Long E 3F **167**
NG10: Sand 3E **143**
NG16: Lang M 1B **42**

Derby Rd. Ind. Est.
DE75: Hea 3C **40**
NG10: Sand 3A **144**
Derbyshire Av. DE7: West H . . .2D **89**
NG9: Trow 1C **116**
Derbyshire Bus. Development Cen.
DE21: Chad 2C **136**
Derbyshire Cl. DE7: West H . . .2D **89**
Derbyshire Constabulary Memorabilia Mus.
. . . . .2C **6** (3F **135**)
Derbyshire County Cricket Ground
. . . . .2B **136**
Derbyshire Cres. NG8: Woll 5F **95**
Derbyshire Dr. DE7: Ilk 4D **91**
DE74: C Don 5A **206**
Derbyshire La. NG15: Huck 2F **25**
Derbyshire Lawn Tennis Cen.
. . . . .2E **159**
Derby Small Bus. Cen.
DE1: Der 5F **7**
Derby Southern By-Pass
DE65: Burn, Etw, Find, Hilt
. . . . .4A **180**
DE73: Bar T . . .5D **185** & 1A **200**
Derby Station (Rail) 5B **136**
Derby St. DE7: Ilk 2E **91**
NG1: Nott 2A **4** (5A **98**)
NG5: Arn 5E **51**
NG9: Bee 1E **147**
Derby Ter. NG7: Nott 5F **97**
Derby Trad. Est. DE21: Der . . .5A **108**
Dereham Pl. NG5: Arn 1E **75**
Derrington Leys DE24: Alv . . .5C **162**
Derry Dr. NG5: Arn 2E **51**
Derry Hill Rd. NG5: Arn 3D **51**
Derry La. NG13: Bing 3F **131**
Derventio Cl. DE1: Der 1F **135**
Derventio Heritage Village
. . . . .1F **7** (2B **136**)
Derwent Av. DE7: Ilk 5C **66**
DE7: West H 2D **89**
DE22: All 1F **107**
DE56: Mil 3E **35**
DE72: Bor 5B **140**
Derwent Bus. Cen., The
DE1: Der 2A **136**
Derwent Bus. Pk. DE5: Rip 5A **8**
Derwent Cl. DE22: All 1F **107**
NG2: Gam 1B **152**
NG9: Atten 5D **147**
Derwent Ct.
DE22: Der 3B **6** (3E **135**)
NG7: Radf 4F **97**
Derwent Cres. NG5: Arn 1F **75**
Derwent Dr. DE24: S Flds . . .4C **184**
NG15: Huck 5F **25**
Derwent Ho. DE21: Chad 2B **136**
Derwent Pde. DE24: Der 5C **136**
Derwent Ri. DE21: Spon 4E **139**
Derwent Rd. DE5: Rip 5B **8**
DE21: Spon 5C **138**
Derwentside Ind. Pk.
DE56: Bel 3E **35**
Derwent St.
DE1: Der 2D **7** (3F **135**)
DE56: Bel 1D **35**
DE72: Dray 4F **165**
NG10: Long E 5B **168**
Derwent St. Ind. Est.
NG10: Long E 5B **168**
Derwent Ter. NG5: Sher 5B **74**
Derwent Va. DE56: Bel 2E **35**
Derwent Valley Vis. Cen. 4E **13**

Derwent Vw. DE56: Bel 4E **13**
DE56: Mil 4F **35**
Derwent Way NG7: Lent 1C **120**
Desford Cl. NG5: Sher 3F **73**
Devas Gdns. DE21: Spon 3C **138**
De Vere Gdns. NG5: Woodt . . .2E **75**
Devitt Dr. NG15: Huck 5E **11**
Devon Cir. NG5: Redh 3C **50**
Devon Cl. DE21: Chad 1C **136**
NG10: Sand 3A **144**
NG16: Newth 2A **44**
Devon Dr. NG5: Sher 5A **74**
NG11: Rudd 3C **174**
Devonshire Av. DE5: Rip 4B **8**
DE22: All 2E **107**
DE72: Bor 1B **164**
NG9: Bee 2D **147**
NG10: Long E 3F **169**
Devonshire Cl. DE7: Ilk 2D **67**
Devonshire Cres. NG5: Sher . . .5A **74**
Devonshire Dr. DE3: Mick 5D **133**
DE56: Duff 4C **58**
NG9: Stap 3C **116**
NG16: Eastw 2E **43**
Devonshire Prom.
NG7: Lent 2D **121**
Devonshire Rd.
NG2: West Br 2D **151**
NG5: Sher 5A **74**
Devonshire Wlk.
DE1: Der 4D **7** (4F **135**)
Devon St. DE7: Ilk 5F **91**
NG3: Nott 5E **99**
Dewberry La. NG12: Rad T . . .3A **128**
Dewchurch Dr. DE23: Der 1D **185**
Dexter St. DE23: Der 1B **160**
DH Lawrence Birthplace Mus.
. . . . .1E **43**
DH Lawrence Craft Cen. 1E **43**
(off Victoria St.)
DH Lawrence 'Sons & Lovers' Cottage
. . . . .1F **43**
Dial, The NG12: Cotg 1D **179**
Diamond Dr. DE21: Oak 2E **109**
Dickens Ct. NG16: Newth 1A **44**
Dickens Sq. DE23: Der 4E **159**
Dickinson St. DE24: Der 1C **160**
Dicks La. NG16: Newth 1B **44**
Dickson Dr. NG11: Rudd 5C **174**
Didcot Ct. NG3: Basf 1C **96**
Digby Av. NG3: Mapp 4A **76**
NG8: Woll 1A **120**
Digby Ct. NG7: Lent 2E **121**
Digby Hall Dr. NG4: Ged 4B **76**
Digby Ind. Est.
NG16: Kimb 5C **44**
Digby St. DE7: Ilk 1F **91**
NG16: Kimb 1C **68**
Dirac Cl. NG11: Clif 3B **172**
Diseworth Cl. DE73: Chel 4F **187**
Diseworth Gro. NG2: Nott 4C **122**
Diseworth Rd. DE74: C Don . . .2F **211**
Disraeli Cres. DE7: Ilk 2E **91**
Distillery Ct. NG11: Rudd 5B **174**
Dix Av. DE7: Smal 1E **63**
Dobholes La. DE7: Smal 1E **63**
DOBPARK 1F **25**
Dockholm Rd. NG10: Long E . . .1B **168**
Dodburn Ct. DE24: Sin 2C **184**
Dodford Ct. DE75: Hea 3F **41**
Dogwood Av. NG6: Bulw 5E **47**
Doles La. DE65: Find 3C **182**
Dolphin Cl. DE21: Spon 2F **139**
Dolphin Ct. NG5: Top V 4F **49**

Domain Dr. DE73: Chel 5D **187**
Donald Hawley Way
DE56: Duff 4E **59**
Donbas Cl. NG6: Bulw 3A **72**
Doncaster Av. NG10: Sand . . .2A **144**
Doncaster Gro.
NG10: Long E 2E **169**
Doncaster Ter. NG2: Nott 4B **122**
Donegal Wlk. DE21: Chad 4F **137**
Donington Cl. DE23: Der 1C **184**
Donington Dr. DE23: Der 1D **185**
Donington Grand Prix Collection
(Mus.) 4C **210**
Donington La. DE72: Shar 2B **206**
DE74: C Don 2B **206**
Donington Pk. Exhibition Cen.
. . . . .4B **210**
Donington Pk. Motor Racing Circuit
. . . . .3B **210**
DONINGTON PARK SERVICE AREA
. . . . .5E **213**
Donington Rd. NG11: Clif 2D **173**
Donkey La. NG11: Rudd 3D **197**
Donner Cres. DE7: Ilk 2D **67**
Dooland Dr. NG3: Nott 1E **99**
Dorchester Av. DE21: Chad . . .1D **137**
Dorchester Gdns.
NG2: West Br 5D **151**
Dorchester Rd. NG16: Kimb . . .5E **45**
Doris Ct. NG9: Toton 1F **169**
Doris Rd. DE7: Ilk 3F **91**
Dorket Cl. NG5: Arn 3F **51**
Dorket Dr. NG8: Woll 2C **120**
DORKET HEAD 2D **51**
Dorket Ho. NG4: Carl 2D **101**
(off Foxhill Rd. E.)
Dorking Rd. DE22: Mac 2A **134**
NG7: Radf 4D **97**
Dormy Cl. NG9: Bram 1B **146**
NG12: Rad T 2A **128**
Dormy Ct. NG6: Bulw 5C **48**
Dornoch Av. NG5: Sher 5C **74**
Dorothy Av. NG10: Sand 3A **144**
NG15: Huck 5D **11**
NG16: Newth 1F **43**
Dorothy Boot Homes, The
NG11: Wilf 5A **122**
Dorothy Gro. NG8: Aspl 4B **96**
Dorrien Av. DE23: Der 4F **159**
Dorset Gdns. NG2: West Br . . .3B **150**
Dorset St. DE21: Chad 2C **136**
(not continuous)
NG8: Radf 5C **96**
Dorterry Cres. DE7: Ilk 5F **91**
Douglas Av. DE75: Hea 2B **40**
NG4: Carl 4C **100**
NG16: Aws 2B **68**
Douglas Cl. NG12: Rad T 3F **127**
Douglas Ct. NG9: Toton 1F **169**
Douglas Cres. NG4: Carl 4D **101**
Douglas Rd.
NG7: Lent, Radf 5E **97**
NG10: Long E 1A **168**
NG13: Bing 2F **131**
Douglas St. DE23: Der 1A **160**
Douro Dr. NG5: Arn 3A **52**
Dove Cl. DE3: Mick 5F **133**
DE56: Kil 4F **37**
NG13: Bing 3E **131**
Dovecote DE74: C Don 1A **212**
Dovecote, The DE21: Hors 1E **61**
Dovecote Dr. DE72: Bor 1A **164**
NG8: Woll 1D **119**
Dovecote La. NG9: Bee 2E **147**

Dovecote Rd.
  NG16: Eastw, Newth 2A **44**
Dovecotes, The NG9: Bee 3E **147**
Dovedale Av. DE24: Alv 4B **162**
  NG10: Long E 5F **167**
Dovedale Circ. DE7: Ilk 2D **67**
Dovedale Cl. DE5: Mare 3C **16**
Dovedale Ct. DE56: Bel 5A **14**
  NG10: Long E 5A **168**
Dovedale Cres. DE56: Bel 5A **14**
Dovedale Ri. DE22: All 4C **106**
Dovedale Rd. DE21: Spon 5E **139**
  NG2: West Br 3F **151**
  NG3: Nott 4B **100**
Dovedales, The DE3: Mick . . .2C **156**
Dove La. NG10: Long E 2B **168**
Dovenby Rd. NG11: Clif 5E **149**
Dover Beck Cl. NG14: Calv 2F **31**
Doverbeck Dr.
  NG14: Woodbo 5B **32**
Dover Ct. DE23: Der 1F **159**
  (not continuous)
Doveridge Av. NG4: Carl 2F **101**
Doveridge Rd. NG4: Carl 2E **101**
Doveridge Wlk. DE23: Lit 1B **184**
Dove Rd. DE5: Rip 5B **8**
  DE74: N Air 4B **212**
Dover St. DE23: Der 1F **159**
Dovestone Gdns. DE23: Lit . . .2A **158**
Dove St. NG6: Bulw 5A **48**
Dovewood Ct. DE23: Lit 4F **157**
Doveys Orchard NG14: Calv . . .2C **30**
Dower Cl. DE22: D Abb 3F **107**
Downes Cl. NG6: Bulw 5F **47**
Downham Cl. DE3: Mick 2D **157**
  NG5: Arn 1F **75**
Downing Cl. DE22: Mac 2E **133**
Downing Gdns. NG6: Bulw 4A **48**
Downing Rd. DE21: Der 3C **136**
Downing St. NG6: Bulw 4A **48**
Downmeadow DE56: H'age . . .1D **15**
Downs, The NG11: Wilf 5F **149**
Dowson Cl. NG12: Rad T 1A **128**
Dowson St. NG3: Nott 4E **99**
Doyne Ct. NG2: Nott 4B **122**
Drage St. DE1: Der 1A **136**
Dragons Health Club
  Derby 5F **7** (4A **136**)
Dragwell DE74: Keg 2C **214**
Drakemyre Cl. NG5: Arn 3A **52**
Drake Rd. NG4: Neth 4A **102**
DRAYCOTT 4F **165**
Draycott Cl. DE75: Los 5B **18**
Draycott Cl. DE7: Ilk 4E **67**
Draycott Dr. DE3: Mick 5B **132**
Draycott Rd. DE72: Bor 2B **164**
  DE72: Brea 4B **166**
  NG10: Long E 1E **193**
Draymans Ct. NG7: Basf 1E **97**
Drayton Av. DE22: Mac 2E **133**
Drayton St. NG5: Sher 5B **74**
Dresden Cl. DE3: Mick 1B **156**
Drewry Cl. DE22: Der . . .4A **6** (4E **135**)
Drewry Island NG8: Brox 1E **95**
Drewry La.
  DE22: Der 4A **6** (4D **135**)
Dreyfus Cl. DE21: Spon 3E **139**
Drift, The NG11: Clif 5D **149**
  NG15: Huck 5D **11**
Drill Hall Cotts. DE22: Der . . .2B **134**
Drive, The NG9: Atten 5D **147**
Driving Test Cen.
  Watnall 4F **45**
Dronfield Pl. DE7: Ilk 2D **67**

Drum Cl. DE22: All 2E **107**
Drummond Av. NG4: Neth 3A **102**
Drummond Dr. NG16: Nuth 3D **71**
Drummond Rd. DE7: Ilk 1D **91**
Drummond Way
  DE73: Chel 4D **187**
Drury Av. DE21: Spon 4C **138**
Drury Cl. NG15: Huck 4C **24**
Drury Wlk.
  NG1: Nott 4C **4** (1B **122**)
Dryden Cl. NG9: Stap 4D **117**
Dryden St. DE23: Der 5E **159**
  NG1: Nott 4A **98**
Drysdale Cl. NG6: Bulw 2A **72**
Drysdale Rd. DE3: Mick 5C **132**
Duchess Gdns. NG6: Bulw 4A **48**
Duchess St. NG6: Bulw 4A **48**
Duchess Way DE73: Chel 1D **201**
Duck Island DE56: Duff 4D **59**
Dudley Ct. NG9: Bram 5F **117**
Duesbury Cl. DE24: A'ton 4D **161**
Duesbury Ct. DE3: Mick 4A **156**
Duesbury Pl. DE3: Mick 4A **156**
DUFFIELD 4D **59**
DUFFIELDBANK 4F **59**
Duffield Bank DE56: Duff 4F **59**
Duffield Cl. NG10: Long E 1F **193**
Duffield Ct. DE56: Duff 4E **59**
  NG5: Top V 4E **49**
Duffield Rd. DE1: Der 1E **135**
  DE21: L Eat 2A **84**
  DE22: All 3F **83**
  DE22: All, D Abb, Der . . .4E **107**
Duffield Rd. Ind. Est.
  DE21: L Eat 4B **84**
Duffield Station (Rail) 3E **59**
Duke Cl. NG6: Bulw 2E **71**
Duke Cres. NG16: Gilt 3B **44**
Dukeries La. DE21: Oak 3A **110**
Dukes Bldgs. DE56: Mil 4E **35**
Dukes Pl. DE7: Ilk 3D **67**
  NG1: Nott 3E **5** (1C **122**)
Duke St. DE1: Der 1D **7** (2F **135**)
  DE7: Ilk 4E **67**
  NG5: Arn 5C **50**
  NG6: Bulw 5A **48**
  NG7: Basf 2E **97**
  NG15: Huck 2A **26**
Duke St. E. NG15: Huck 2A **26**
Duke William Mt.
  NG7: Nott 1F **121**
Duluth Av. DE21: Chad 1F **137**
Dulverton Av. DE24: S Flds . . .4B **184**
Dulverton Va. NG8: Cin 4F **71**
Dulwich Rd. DE22: Mac 2D **133**
  NG7: Radf 5D **97**
Dumbles, The NG4: Lamb 4A **54**
Dumbles Cl. DE7: Kirk H 4B **90**
Dumbles La. DE5: Den 2E **39**
Dunbar Cl. DE24: Sin 4D **185**
  NG10: Long E 2D **195**
Dunblane Rd. NG11: Rudd . . .5B **174**
Duncan Cl. DE56: Bel 3A **14**
Duncan Rd. DE23: Der 3E **159**
Duncombe Cl. NG3: Nott 3D **99**
Duncroft Av. NG4: Ged 1E **101**
Dundas Cl. NG1: Nott . . .1B **4** (4B **98**)
Dundas Way DE73: Chel 5D **187**
Dunedin Cl. DE3: Mick 5D **133**
Dunelm Dr. NG14: Calv 2F **31**
Dungannon Rd. NG11: Clif . . .3D **173**
Dunholme Cl. NG6: Bulw 4A **48**
Dunkery Ct. DE21: Oak 3F **109**
Dunkery Rd. NG11: Clif 3E **173**

DUNKIRK 3D **121**
Dunkirk DE22: Der 4B **6** (4E **135**)
Dunkirk Rd. NG7: Lent 4D **121**
Dunlin Wharf NG7: Lent 3F **121**
Dunlop Av. NG7: Lent 1D **121**
Dunn Dr. NG10: Long E 4A **168**
DUNNSHILL 4B **112**
Dunoon Cl. DE24: Sin 3D **185**
  NG5: Top V 2D **49**
Dunsby Cl. NG11: Clif 2D **173**
Dunsford Dr. NG3: Mapp 1B **76**
Dunsil Dr. NG2: Nott 5F **121**
Dunsil Rd. NG16: Newth 5A **22**
Dunsmore Cl. NG9: Bee 4A **148**
Dunsmore Dr. DE21: Oak 3E **109**
Dunstall Pk. Rd.
  DE24: Der 3C **160**
Dunstan St. NG4: Neth 3F **101**
  (not continuous)
Dunster Rd. NG2: West Br 2F **151**
  NG16: Newth 2A **44**
Dunston Cl. NG10: Long E 4E **169**
Dunton Cl.
  DE21: Der 2F **7** (3B **136**)
Dunvegan Cl. DE24: S Flds . . .4C **184**
Dunvegan Dr. NG5: Top V 2E **49**
Durban House Heritage Cen.
  .1D **43**
Durham Av. DE21: Chad 2D **137**
  NG2: Nott 1E **123**
Durham Chambers
  NG1: Nott 3C **4** (1B **122**)
Durham Cl. NG2: Nott 1E **123**
Durham Cres. NG6: Bulw 1B **72**
Durham St. DE7: Ilk 1E **91**
Durley Cl. DE24: Alv 4B **162**
Durlston Cl. NG2: West Br 3A **150**
Durnford St. NG7: Basf 5E **73**
Dursley Cl. NG6: Bulw 2A **72**
Durward Cl. DE24: Der 4B **160**
Dyce Cl. NG6: Bulw 5E **47**
Dylan M. NG8: Bilb 2D **95**
Dylan Thomas Rd.
  NG5: Bestw 4A **50**

E

Eagle Cl. DE56: Bel 2E **35**
  NG5: Arn 5F **51**
  NG9: Bee 5C **118**
Eagle Ct. NG6: Bulw 5C **48**
Eagle Rd. DE7: Ilk 1E **115**
Ealing Av. NG6: Basf 3C **72**
Ealing Cl. DE22: Mac 2A **134**
Eardley Cl. DE21: Chad 3A **138**
Eardley Rd. NG5: Bestw 1D **73**
Earl Cres. NG4: Ged 4E **77**
Earl Dr. NG16: Gilt 3B **44**
Earlham Cl. DE7: Kirk H 4B **90**
Earls Cl. NG8: Bilb 5B **94**
Earls Cres. DE21: Oak 3A **110**
Earlsfield Dr. NG5: Top V 3C **48**
Earlswood Ct. DE72: Brea 3C **166**
Earlswood Dr. DE3: Mick 4E **133**
  NG12: Edwal 4A **152**
Easedale Cl. NG2: Gam 1B **152**
Easegill Ct. NG5: Top V 4E **49**
  (off Avenue Cl.)
East Acres NG12: Cotg 5E **155**
East Av. DE3: Mick 5C **132**
Eastbrae Rd. DE23: Der 4C **158**
E. Bridgeford Rd.
  NG13: Newton 1F **105**

East Cir. St.
NG1: Nott 3A **4** (1A **122**)
Eastcliffe Av. NG4: Ged 4C **76**
East Cl. DE22: D Abb 3D **107**
NG12: Key 4D **199**
Eastcote Av. NG9: Bram 3A **118**
East Cres. DE56: H'ook 4B **36**
NG9: Bee 3A **148**
E. Croft Av. DE23: Lit 1C **184**
Eastdale Rd. NG3: Nott 4B **100**
East Dr. NG7: Nott 4B **120**
Easter Pk. NG7: Lent 3E **121**
Eastfield Rd. DE5: Rip 5F **9**
Eastgate DE1: Der 1F **7** (2A **136**)
DE21: Der 1F **7** (2A **136**)
Eastglade Rd. NG5: Bestw 1E **73**
East Gro. NG7: Basf 2F **97**
NG13: Bing 2E **131**
Eastham Cl.
NG3: Nott 1F **5** (4D **99**)
Eastham Rd. NG5: Arn 1A **76**
Eastholme NG2: Colw 5C **100**
Easthorpe Cotts.
NG11: Rudd 4C **174**
Easthorpe St. NG11: Rudd . . .4B **174**
East Lawn DE65: Find 4C **182**
Eastleigh Dr. DE3: Mick 1D **157**
EAST MIDLANDS
AIRPORT-NOTTINGHAM,
LEICESTER, DERBY 4B **212**
East Moor NG12: Cotg 2F **179**
Eastmoor Dr. NG4: Carl 2E **101**
E. Nelson St. NG7: Nott 1A **4**
East Rd. NG7: Nott . . : 3C **120**
E. Service Rd. DE21: Spon . . .1A **162**
East St. DE1: Der 3D **7** (3F **135**)
DE7: Ilk 2E **91**
DE75: Hea 4F **41**
NG1: Nott 2D **5** (5C **98**)
NG10: Long E 3E **169**
NG13: Bing 2E **131**
East Ter. DE56: Mil 5F **35**
East Vw. NG2: West Br 2C **150**
Eastview Ter. NG16: Lang M . . .1A **42**
Eastway DE74: C Don 1A **212**
Eastwell Ct. NG15: Huck 1F **25**
(off Allen St.)
Eastwell St. NG15: Huck 1F **25**
Eastwold NG12: Cotg 1F **179**
EASTWOOD 2E **43**
Eastwood Av. DE23: Lit 1B **158**
Eastwood Cl. NG16: Huck 5D **26**
Eastwood Community Sports Cen.
. . . . .1D **43**
Eastwood Dr. DE23: Lit 1B **158**
Eastwood Rd. NG12: Rad T . . .2F **127**
NG16: Kimb 5C **44**
Eastwood St. NG6: Bulw 2B **72**
Eastwood Town FC 2F **43**
Eaton Av. DE7: Kirk H 4C **90**
DE22: All 5F **83**
NG5: Arn 5F **51**
Eaton Bank DE56: Duff 5F **59**
Eaton Cl. DE22: All 5F **83**
NG9: Bee 2A **148**
Eaton Ct. DE1: Der . . .1A **6** (2D **135**)
DE56: Duff 5D **59**
Eaton Grange Dr.
NG10: Long E 3F **167**
Eaton Pl. NG13: Bing 2D **131**
Eaton Rd. DE74: C Don . . .1A **212**
Eatons Rd. NG9: Stap 2C **144**
Eaton St. NG3: Mapp 4E **75**
Eaton Ter. NG3: Mapp 5E **75**

Ebenezer St. DE7: Ilk 4E **67**
Ebers Gro. NG3: Mapp P 2B **98**
Ebers Rd. NG3: Mapp P 1B **98**
Ebony Wlk. NG3: Nott 2A **100**
Ebury Rd. NG5: Sher 1A **98**
Ecclesbourne Av. DE56: Duff . .4E **59**
Ecclesbourne Cl. DE56: Duff . . .4D **59**
Ecclesbourne Mdws.
DE56: Duff 3C **58**
Eccles Way NG3: Nott 3E **99**
Eckington Cl. DE7: West H . . .2D **89**
Eckington Ter. NG2: Nott 4B **122**
Ecton Cl. NG5: Top V 3E **49**
Edale Av. DE3: Mick 1C **156**
DE23: Der 1D **159**
DE24: Alv 4A **162**
Edale Cl. DE22: All 4C **106**
NG10: Long E 4A **168**
NG15: Huck 3B **24**
Edale Dr. DE21: Spon 5E **139**
Edale Ri. NG9: Toton 5D **145**
Edale Rd. NG2: Nott 5F **99**
Edale Sq. DE7: Ilk 2D **67**
Edale Way DE56: Bel 4E **13**
Eddlestone Dr. NG11: Clif 2E **173**
Edenbridge Ct. NG8: Woll 3C **118**
Eden Cl. NG5: Arn 1E **75**
NG15: Huck 3B **24**
Edenhall Gdns. NG11: Clif 1E **173**
Eden Rd. DE21: Chad 4F **137**
Edensor Dr. DE56: Bel 3B **14**
Edensor Sq.
DE22: Der 5A **6** (4D **135**)
Eden St. DE24: Alv 3F **161**
Edern Cl. NG5: Bestw 5F **49**
Edern Gdns. NG5: Bestw 5F **49**
Edgbaston Ct. DE23: Lit 3B **158**
Edgbaston Gdns. NG8: Aspl . . .2C **96**
Edgecote Way NG5: Bestw 1F **73**
Edge Hill DE73: Chel 3E **187**
Edge Hill Ct. NG10: Long E . . .2C **194**
Edgelaw Cl. DE24: Sin 3C **184**
Edgeway NG8: Stre 1C **94**
Edgewood Dr. NG15: Huck 4C **24**
Edgewood Leisure Cen. 5C **24**
Edgington Cl. NG12: Cotg 1F **179**
Edginton St. NG3: Nott 3E **99**
Edginton Ter. NG3: Nott 3E **99**
Edgware Rd. DE22: Mac 2E **133**
NG6: Bulw 5C **48**
Edgwood Rd. NG16: Kimb 1E **69**
Edinbane Cl. NG5: Top V 2E **49**
Edinboro Row NG16: Kimb . . .5D **45**
Edinburgh Cres.
DE24: A'ton 2D **187**
Edinburgh Dr. NG13: Bing 1C **130**
Edingale Ct. NG9: Bram 1A **118**
Edingley Av. NG5: Sher 3B **74**
Edingley Sq. NG5: Sher 3A **74**
Edison Village NG7: Nott 4D **121**
Edison Way NG5: Arn 5B **52**
Edith Ter. NG7: Radf 4D **97**
(off Hartley Rd.)
Edith Wood Cl. DE24: Alv 1A **188**
Edlington Dr. NG8: Woll 2B **118**
Edmond Gro. NG15: Huck 1B **26**
Edmonds Cl. NG5: Arn 2F **49**
Edmonstone Cres.
NG5: Bestw 2E **73**
Edmonton Ct.
NG2: West Br 2C **150**
Edmund Rd. DE21: Spon 5E **139**
Edmunds Sq. DE3: Mick 4A **156**

Ednaston Av. DE23: Lit 1C **184**
Ednaston Rd. NG7: Nott 4C **120**
Edwald Rd. NG12: Edwal 5A **152**
EDWALTON 5A **152**
Edwalton Av. NG2: West Br . . .1E **151**
Edwalton Cl. NG12: Edwal . . .5A **152**
Edwalton Ct. NG6: Bulw 1D **73**
Edwalton Hall NG12: Edwal . . .5F **151**
Edwalton Lodge Cl.
NG12: Edwal 5F **151**
Edward Av. DE21: Chad 3F **137**
NG8: Aspl 2C **96**
Edward Cl. NG15: Huck 5C **24**
Edward Ct. NG2: West Br 4E **123**
Edward Cres. DE56: Kil 4F **37**
Edward Rd. NG2: West Br 4E **123**
NG10: Long E 3C **168**
NG16: Eastw 2F **43**
NG16: Nuth 2B **70**
Edwards Ct. NG5: Sher 2A **74**
Edwards La.
NG5: Bestw, Sher 1A **74**
Edward St. DE1: Der 2F **135**
DE56: Bel 4F **13**
NG9: Stap 1C **144**
NG16: Lang M 5A **20**
Edwinstowe Av.
NG2: West Br 1E **151**
Edwinstowe Dr. NG5: Sher 3B **74**
Edwinstowe Rd. DE21: Oak . . .4F **109**
Edwin St. NG5: Arn 1C **74**
Eelwood Rd. NG15: Huck 5C **24**
Egerton Dr. NG9: Stap 3C **116**
Egerton Rd. NG5: Woodt 3C **74**
Egerton St. NG3: Nott 3B **98**
Egerton Wlk. NG3: Nott 3B **98**
Eggesford Rd. DE24: S Flds . . .4C **184**
Eggington Rd. DE65: Etw 3A **180**
Egginton Rd. DE65: Etw 5A **180**
Egling Cft. NG4: Colw 1E **125**
Egmanton Cl. DE21: Oak 4A **110**
Egmont Cl. NG2: Nott 3B **122**
Egreaves Av. DE75: Los 5B **18**
Egypt Rd. NG7: Basf 1E **97**
(not continuous)
Eighth Av. NG7: Nott 3B **148**
Eileen Rd. NG9: Bee 5F **147**
Eisele Cl. NG6: Bulw 1E **71**
Ekowe St. NG7: Basf 5E **73**
Eland Cl. DE21: Spon 2F **139**
Eland St. NG7: Basf 1E **97**
Elder Cl. NG5: Arn 3F **51**
Elder Gdns. NG5: Top V 4F **49**
Elder Gro. NG15: Huck 5A **26**
Elden Bus. Pk. NG9: Atten 2B **170**
Eldon Chambers
NG1: Nott 4B **4** (1B **122**)
Eldon Ho. DE1: Der 5C **6** (4F **135**)
Eldon Rd. NG9: Atten 2B **170**
Eldon Rd. Ind. Est.
NG9: Atten 2B **170**
Eldon Rd. Trad. Est.
NG9: Chil 2B **170**
Eleanor Av. DE7: Ilk 5F **91**
Eleanor Cres. NG9: Stap 1E **145**
Electric Av. NG2: Nott 1F **149**
Eley Cl. DE7: Ilk 5B **66**
Eley Wlk. DE1: Der 5B **6** (4E **135**)
Elford Ri. NG3: Nott 1E **123**
Elgar Dr. NG10: Long E 1A **194**
Elgar Gdns. NG3: Nott 4E **99**
Elgin Av. DE23: Lit 3F **157**
Eliot Cl. NG10: Long E 1A **194**
Eliot Dr. DE7: Kirk H 5C **90**

Eliot Rd. DE23: Lit 3A 158
Eliot Wlk. NG11: Clif 3B 172
Elizabeth Cl. DE7: West H 2C 88
  DE21: Chad 3A 138
  NG15: Huck 4D 25
Elizabeth Gro. NG4: Ged 5D 77
Elkstone Cl. DE21: Oak 3A 110
Ella Bank Rd. DE75: Hea 3E 41
Ella Rd. NG2: West Br 4E 123
Ellastone Av. NG5: Bestw 4B 50
Ellastone Gdns. DE24: Alv 4A 162
Ellendale Rd. DE21: Chad 1A 138
Ellerby Av. NG11: Clif 1D 173
Ellerslie Gro. NG10: Sand 3F 143
Ellesmere Av. DE24: Der 1C 160
Ellesmere Bus. Pk.
  NG5: Sher 5F 73
Ellesmere Cl. NG5: Arn 5A 52
Ellesmere Cres. NG5: Sher . . .5A 74
Ellesmere Dr. NG9: Trow 5B 92
Ellesmere Rd.
  NG2: West Br 4E 151
Ellington Rd. NG5: Arn 2F 51
Elliot St. NG7: Nott 5F 97
Elliott Durham Swimming Pool
  . . . . .1D 99
Ellis Av. NG15: Huck 3A 26
Ellis Cl. NG10: Long E 5B 168
Ellis Ct. NG3: Nott 4C 98
Ellis Gro. NG9: Bee 3E 147
Ellison Av. DE72: Ast T 2F 203
Ellsworth Ri. NG5: Bestw 1E 73
Ellwood Cres. NG8: Woll 5F 95
Elm Av. DE56: Bel 2A 36
  NG3: Nott 3B 98
  NG4: Carl 3E 101
  NG9: Atten 1C 170
  NG9: Bee 2D 147
  NG10: Long E 2B 168
  NG10: Sand 1A 144
  NG12: Key 4E 199
  NG13: Bing 2F 131
  NG15: Huck 4D 25
  NG16: Nuth 1A 70
Elm Bank NG3: Mapp P 2B 98
Elm Bank Dr. NG3: Mapp P . . .2B 98
Elmbridge NG5: Bestw 5A 50
Elm Cl. NG3: Mapp P 3B 98
  NG12: Key 4E 199
Elmdale Gdns. NG8: Bilb 2A 96
Elm Dr. NG4: Carl 3E 101
Elm Gro. DE21: Chad 3A 138
  DE22: All 5C 82
  NG5: Arn 3F 51
Elmhurst Av. NG3: Mapp 5B 76
Elmore Ct. NG7: Radf 4F 97
Elm Pk. Ct. DE1: Der 1E 135
ELMS, THE 1C 16
Elms, The NG4: Colw 4E 101
  NG16: Want 5E 45
Elms Av. DE5: Rip 1C 16
  DE23: Lit 1A 158
Elms Cl. NG11: Rudd 5C 174
Elmsdale Gdns. NG14: Bur J . .3E 79
Elms Dr. DE23: Lit 2A 158
Elms Farm Way DE23: Lit 3F 157
Elmsfield Av. DE75: Hea 2F 41
Elms Gdns. NG11: Rudd 5B 174
Elms Gro. DE65: Etw 3B 180
Elmsham Av. NG5: Top V 3D 49
Elms Pk. NG11: Rudd 5C 174
Elms St. DE1: Der 1E 135
Elmsthorpe Av. NG7: Lent . . .1D 121
Elm St. DE72: Bor 1A 164

Elmswood Gdns.
  NG5: Sher 4C 74
Elm Tree Av. DE56: Kil 5F 37
  NG2: West Br 1C 150
Elmtree Av. DE24: Der 4A 160
Elmtree Rd. NG14: Calv 2C 30
Elm Vw. NG7: Radf 4E 97
Elmwood Dr. DE21: Der 3B 108
Elnor St. NG16: Lang M 2B 42
Elsecar Cl. DE56: Bel 4C 14
Elson St. NG7: Basf 2E 97
Elston Gdns. NG11: Clif 4D 149
Elston M. NG3: Nott 3A 100
Elstree Dr. NG8: Bilb 4F 95
Elswick Cl. NG5: Bestw 4A 50
Elswick Dr. NG9: Bee 4A 148
Elterwater Dr. NG2: Gam 1B 152
Eltham Cl. NG8: Cin 4E 71
Eltham Dr. NG8: Cin 4E 71
Eltham Rd. NG2: West Br 1E 151
Elton Cl. NG9: Stap 5D 117
Elton M. NG5: Sher 1A 98
Elton Rd. DE24: Der 4A 160
Elton Rd. Nth. NG5: Sher 1A 98
Elton Ter. NG7: H Grn 3E 97
ELVASTON 5F 163
Elvaston Castle Cvn. Pk.
  DE72: Elv 4F 163
Elvaston Castle Country Pk.
  . . . . .4D 163
Elvaston Castle Mus. 4E 163
Elvaston Ct. NG5: Bestw 2E 73
Elvaston Dr. NG10: Long E . . .2E 193
Elvaston La. DE24: Alv 4A 162
Elvaston Rd. NG8: Woll 5F 95
Elvaston St. DE72: Dray 4A 166
Elveden Dr. DE7: Ilk 3B 66
Elwes Lodge NG4: Carl 4E 101
Elwin Dr. NG9: Bram 4B 118
Embankment Cl.
  DE22: Mac 1E 133
Emerald Cl. DE21: Oak 3E 109
Emerson Sq. DE23: Der 5E 159
Emerys Rd. NG4: Ged 2A 102
              (not continuous)
Emmanuel Av. NG3: Mapp . . .1F 99
  NG5: Arn 3F 49
Emmas-Williams Ct.
  DE5: Rip 5C 8
Emneth Cl. NG3: Nott 2E 99
Emperor Cl. NG5: Sher 1A 98
Empingham St. NG9: Toton . .1A 170
Empire Ct. DE75: Hea 2D 41
             (off Fletcher St.)
Empire Gallery, The 3B 4
Empress Rd. DE23: Der 5E 135
Emsworth Cl. DE7: Ilk 4C 66
Ena Av. NG2: Nott 5E 99
Enderby Gdns. NG5: Redh . . .3D 51
Enderby Sq. NG9: Lent A 5E 119
Endsleigh Gdns.
  DE22: Mac 2E 133
  NG9: Bee 1E 147
  NG12: Edwal 4F 151
Enfield Chambers
  NG1: Nott 4C 4 (1B 122)
Enfield Rd. DE22: Mac 2A 134
Enfield St. NG9: Bee 2D 147
Engine La. NG16: Newth 5A 22
England Cres. DE75: Hea 2F 41
England Ind. Est. DE1: Der . . .3C 134
Ennerdale Cl. NG2: Gam 1B 152
Ennerdale Ct.
  NG10: Long E 1A 168

Ennerdale Rd. NG5: Sher 2C 74
  NG10: Long E 1A 168
Ennerdale Wlk.
  DE21: Chad 3C 108
Ennis Cl. DE21: Chad 1B 138
Ennismore Gdns. NG8: Aspl . .4B 96
Ennismore M.
  NG2: West Br 5B 150
Enoch Stone Dr.
  DE21: Chad 4A 138
Enterprise Way DE21: Der . . .1A 136
  NG2: Nott 3F 121
  NG16: Lang M 1B 42
Enthorpe St. NG8: Bilb 4A 96
EPPERSTONE 4F 33
Epperstone By-Pass
  NG14: Woodbo 3D 33
Epperstone Ct.
  NG2: West Br 5D 123
Epperstone Rd.
  NG2: West Br 5D 123
  NG14: Lowd 1C 56
  NG25: Oxt 1B 32
Epping Cl. DE22: Mac 2D 133
Epsom Rd. NG9: Toton 5D 145
Epworth Dr. DE24: Alv 2F 187
Erdington Way NG9: Toton . . .5D 145
Erewash Ct. NG10: Long E . . .2C 168
Erewash Dr. DE7: Ilk 4F 91
Erewash Gdns. NG5: Top V . . .4F 49
Erewash Gro. NG9: Toton 1E 169
              (not continuous)
Erewash Indoor Bowling Club
  . . . . .3F 169
Erewash Mus. 2E 91
Erewash Sq. DE7: Ilk 4A 92
Eric Av. NG15: Huck 5B 10
Erith Cl. NG8: Stre 1C 94
Ernest Rd. NG4: Carl 2A 100
Ernhale Ct. NG5: Arn 4D 51
Erskine Rd. NG5: Sher 1A 98
Esher Gro. NG3: Mapp P 1B 98
Eskdale Cl. NG10: Long E 1A 194
Eskdale Ct. NG2: Gam 1B 152
Eskdale Dr. NG8: Aspl 2A 96
  NG9: Chil 3F 145
Eskdale Wlk. DE24: Alv 5C 162
           (off Whernside Cl.)
Esk Hause Cl.
  NG2: West Br 4B 152
Essex St. DE7: Ilk 1E 91
  DE21: Chad 2C 136
  NG16: Eastw 2E 43
Estwic Av. NG16: Eastw 1E 43
Ethel Av. NG3: Mapp 1F 99
  NG15: Huck 5D 11
Ethel Rd. NG2: West Br 1E 151
Eton Cl. DE7: West H 2C 88
Eton Gro. NG8: Woll 1A 120
Eton Pl. NG2: West Br 3D 151
Eton Rd. NG2: West Br 2D 151
  NG5: Sher 1A 98
         (off Claremont Rd.)
Eton St. DE24: Der 2D 161
Etruria Gdns. DE1: Der 1F 135
Etta's Way DE65: Etw 2A 180
Ettrick Dr. DE24: Sin 4D 185
ETWALL 2B 180
Etwall By-Pass DE65: Etw 2A 180
Etwall La. DE65: Burn 1E 181
Etwall Leisure Cen. 1A 180
Etwall Rd. DE3: Mick 3A 156
             (not continuous)
Etwall St. DE22: Der 3C 134

Eucalyptus Av. NG11: Clif 2B **172**
Eugene Gdns. NG2: Nott 3C **122**
Eugene St. NG2: Nott 2C **122**
Europa Way NG2: West Br 5B **150**
Euston Dr. DE1: Der 1A **136**
Evans Av. DE22: All 5F **83**
Evans Rd. NG6: Basf 4C **72**
Evanston Gdns.
 DE21: Chad 2A **138**
Evedon Wlk. NG5: Top V 3A **50**
Evelyn Gro. DE21: Chad 3F **137**
Evelyn St. NG2: Nott . . .4F **5** (1D **123**)
 NG9: Bee 1A **148**
Evergreen Cl. DE21: Oak . . .3F **109**
Eversley Wlk. NG5: Bestw 4A **50**
Evesham Cl. DE21: Chad 4D **109**
Evesham Ct. NG9: Toton 2F **169**
Ewart Rd. NG7: H Grn 2E **97**
Ewe Lamb Cl. NG9: Bram 4E **117**
Ewe Lamb La. NG9: Bram 4E **117**
Ewell Rd. NG8: Woll 5D **95**
Exbourne Rd. NG8: Aspl 1E **95**
Exbury Gdns. NG2: West Br . . .4A **150**
Excelsior Av. DE24: Alv 5E **161**
Exchange Arc. NG1: Nott 3C **4**
Exchange Rd.
 NG2: West Br 1E **151**
Exchange St.
 DE1: Der 3D **7** (3F **135**)
Exchange Wlk.
 NG1: Nott 3C **4** (1B **122**)
Excise Chambers NG1: Nott . . .3D **5**
Exeter Cl. NG4: Ged 5E **77**
Exeter Ho. DE1: Der . .2E **7** (3A **136**)
Exeter Pl. DE1: Der . . .2E **7** (3A **136**)
Exeter Rd. NG2: West Br 2E **151**
 NG7: H Grn 2F **97**
Exeter St. DE1: Der 1E **7** (3A **136**)
Experian Way NG2: Nott 3F **121**
Exton Rd. NG5: Sher 4F **73**
Eyam Cl. NG9: Bram 3B **118**
Eyam Wlk. DE56: Bel 4F **13**
Eyes Ct. DE56: Duff 4D **59**
 (off Town St.)
Eyre's Gdns. DE7: Ilk 5E **67**
Eyre St. NG2: Nott . . .3F **5** (1D **123**)
Eyrie, The DE24: S Flds 4D **185**

F

Fabis Dr. NG11: Clif 4D **149**
Factory La. DE7: Ilk 5D **67**
 NG9: Chil 3D **147**
Failsworth Cl. NG11: Clif 5D **149**
Fairbank Cres. NG5: Sher 5C **74**
Fairbourne Dr. DE3: Mick 4C **132**
Fairburn Cl. NG8: Woll 1B **118**
Fairburn Way NG16: Want 5F **45**
Faircroft Av. NG10: Sand 3A **144**
Fairdale Dr. NG16: Newth 2A **44**
Fairdene Ct. DE23: Der 1E **159**
Faires Cl. DE72: Bor 2C **164**
Faire St. DE22: Der 5D **135**
Fairfax Cl. NG5: Basf 5E **73**
Fairfax Rd. DE23: Der 1E **159**
Fairfield Av. DE72: Bor 5B **140**
Fairfield Cl. NG11: Wilf 3A **150**
Fairfield Cres.
 NG10: Long E 2F **193**
Fairfield Rd. DE7: H Woo 5B **38**
 DE23: Der 1D **159**
Fairfield St. NG13: Bing 2D **131**
Fairford Gdns. DE23: Lit 5F **157**

Fairham Brook Nature Reserve
 . . . . .3E **173**
Fairham Cl. NG11: Rudd 3A **174**
Fairham Ct. NG11: Wilf 5F **149**
Fairham Dr. NG8: Woll 1C **120**
Fairham Rd. NG12: Key 3C **198**
Fairholm Ct.
 NG3: Nott 1F **5** (4D **99**)
Fairisle Cl. DE21: Oak 2B **110**
Fairland Cres.
 NG2: West Br 4C **150**
Fairlawn Pl. NG5: Sher 5C **74**
Fairlawns DE56: Duff 4C **58**
Fair Lea Cl. NG10: Long E 5C **168**
Fairlight Way NG5: Bestw 5A **50**
Fairmaid Gro. NG11: Clif 1D **173**
Fairmead Cl. NG3: Nott 2F **99**
Fairney Cft. NG8: Bilb 2C **94**
Fairview Cl. DE23: Lit 3F **157**
 DE56: Kil 5A **38**
Fairview Ct. NG2: West Br 1C **174**
Fairview Grange DE56: Kil . . .5A **38**
Fairview Rd. NG5: Woodt 3D **75**
Fairway NG12: Key 3E **199**
Fairway, The NG4: Ged 4D **77**
Fairway Cl. DE22: All 3C **106**
Fairway Cres. DE22: All 3C **106**
Fairway Dr. NG4: Carl 2B **100**
 NG6: Bulw 5C **48**
 NG9: Chil 2C **146**
Fairwood Dr. DE24: Alv 5C **162**
Falcon Cl. NG7: Lent 1D **121**
Falconers Wlk. NG5: Arn 4B **50**
Falcon Gro. NG7: Basf 1F **97**
Falconside Dr. DE21: Spon . . .1E **163**
Falcons Ri. DE56: Bel 4B **14**
Falcon St. NG7: Basf 1F **97**
Falcon Way DE24: Sin 4D **185**
Falconwood Gdns.
 NG11: Clif 2B **172**
Falkirk Av. DE5: Rip 2D **9**
Fallow Cl. NG11: Clif 1D **173**
Fallow Rd. DE21: Spon 2E **139**
Fall Rd. DE75: Hea 1D **41**
Falmouth Rd. DE24: Alv 1B **188**
Falstaff M. NG7: Basf 1F **97**
Falston Rd. NG8: Bilb 4F **95**
Faraday Bldg. NG7: Nott 4C **120**
Faraday Ct. NG9: Stap 4D **117**
Faraday Rd. NG7: Lent 1D **121**
Far Cft. DE72: Brea 3C **166**
Farfield Av. NG9: Bee 5D **119**
Farfield Gro. NG9: Bee 5D **119**
Farfield Rd. DE7: Ilk 1F **91**
Far La. DE72: Ock 3C **140**
FAR LAUND 3B **14**
Far Laund DE56: Bel 4A **14**
Farley Rd. DE23: Der 1C **158**
FARLEYS 1A **48**
Farleys Gro. NG15: Huck 4F **25**
Farleys La. NG15: Huck 3F **25**
 (not continuous)
Farley St. NG6: Bulw 5A **48**
Farm Av. NG15: Huck 5C **24**
Farm Cl. DE7: Ilk 2F **91**
 DE56: Bel 5B **14**
 DE56: Kil 4F **37**
 NG10: Long E 1D **195**
 NG11: Clif 1D **173**
Farm Dr. DE24: Alv 1F **187**
Farmer St. NG11: Rudd 3D **197**
Farmhouse M. DE65: Find . . .4C **182**
Farmhouse Rd. DE24: Sin . . .4D **185**

Farmlands La. DE23: Lit 5A **158**
Farm Rd. NG5: Arn 5A **52**
 NG9: Chil 3B **146**
Farm St. DE22: Der 5A **6** (4E **135**)
FARNAH GREEN 1C **34**
Farnah Grn. Rd. DE56: Bel . . .2C **34**
Farnborough Gdns.
 DE22: All 1A **108**
Farnborough Rd.
 NG11: Clif 3C **172**
Farncombe La. DE21: Oak . . .2E **109**
Farndale Cl. NG10: Long E . . .1F **193**
Farndale Ct. DE24: Alv 5B **162**
Farndale Dr. NG8: Woll 1A **118**
Farndon Dr. NG9: Toton 5E **145**
Farndon Grn. NG8: Woll 1B **120**
Farndon M. NG3: Nott 2F **99**
Far New Cl. NG10: Sand 3A **144**
Farneworth Rd. DE3: Mick . . .1C **156**
Farnham Cl. DE3: Mick 2B **156**
Farnham Wlk. DE7: West H . . .2C **88**
Farningham Cl.
 DE21: Spon 3C **139**
Farnsfield Av. NG14: Bur J . . .2F **79**
Farnsworth Cl. NG16: Want . . .3F **45**
Farnway DE22: D Abb 3D **107**
Far Pastures Cl. NG12: Key . . .4D **199**
Farrier Gdns. DE23: Lit 4F **157**
Farriers Cft. DE7: Ilk 4B **66**
Farriers Grn. NG11: Clif 1B **172**
Farringdon Cl. DE22: Mac . . .2E **133**
 NG16: Nuth 4C **70**
Farrington Way
 NG16: Eastw 2D **43**
Farr Row NG5: Bestw 2F **73**
Far Rye NG8: Woll 4E **95**
Far St. NG11: Rudd 3D **197**
Farthing Ct. NG10: Long E . . .4A **168**
Farthings, The NG7: Lent 1D **121**
Farwells Cl. NG6: Basf 4B **72**
Faulconbridge Cl.
 NG6: Bulw 1A **72**
Faversham Cl. DE24: Alv 1E **187**
Fearn Av. DE5: Rip 5D **9**
Fearn Chase NG4: Carl 3D **101**
Fearn Cl. DE72: Brea 4F **167**
Fearnleigh Dr. NG6: Basf 5C **72**
Fearon Cl. NG14: Gun 2E **81**
Featherstone Cl. NG4: Ged . . .4C **76**
Feignies Ct. NG12: Key 3D **199**
Felen Cl. NG5: Bestw 5F **49**
Fellbarrow Cl.
 NG2: West Br 3B **152**
Felley Cl. NG15: Huck 4D **25**
Fellow Lands Way
 DE73: Chel 3F **187**
Fellows Rd. NG9: Bee 1D **147**
Fellows Yd. NG12: Plum 4D **177**
Fell Side NG5: Woodt 2F **75**
Fellside DE21: Spon 2E **139**
 DE56: Bel 5F **13**
Fellside Cl. NG2: Garn 2B **152**
Felstead Ct. NG9: Bram 4B **118**
Felstead Rd. NG8: Bilb 4F **95**
Felton Cl. NG9: Chil 3A **146**
Felton Rd. NG2: Nott 4C **122**
Fenchurch Cl. NG5: Arn 3F **49**
Fenchurch Wlk. DE22: Mac . . .2A **134**
Fenimore Cl. NG12: Rad T . . .1A **128**
Fenroth Cl. NG6: Bulw 4E **47**
Fenton Cl. NG5: Sher 3E **73**
Fenton Dr. NG6: Bulw 2B **48**
Fenton Rd. DE3: Mick 1B **156**
 NG5: Sher 3E **73**

Fenwick Cl. NG8: Brox 5E **71**
Fenwick Ct. NG4: Neth 3F **101**
Fenwick Rd. NG8: Brox 5E **71**
Fergus Cl. NG11: Clif 3E **173**
Ferguson Cl. NG9: Chil 1B **170**
Fern Av. NG5: Sher 1A **98**
Fern Cl. NG6: Bram 1A **146**
Fern Cres. NG16: Eastw 1D **43**
Ferncroft Wlk. DE73: Chel 4E **187**
Ferndale Cl. NG9: Atten 1C **170**
Ferndale Gro. NG3: Nott 4A **100**
Ferndale Rd. NG3: Nott 4A **100**
Ferndene Dr. NG10: Long E . . .4F **167**
Ferngill Cl. NG2: Nott 4A **122**
Fernhill Ct. DE73: Chel 3F **187**
Fernilee Cl. DE7: West H 2D **89**
Fernilee Gdns. DE21: Chad . . .4E **109**
Fern Lea Av. NG12: Cotg 1D **179**
Fernleigh Av. NG3: Mapp 5A **76**
Fernwood Cl. DE23: Lit 3B **158**
Fernwood Commercial Workshops
NG16: Want 4F **45**
Fernwood Cres. NG8: Woll 1B **118**
Fernwood Dr. NG12: Rad T . . .1E **127**
NG16: Want 4F **45**
Ferny Hollow Cl.
NG5: Top V 4D **49**
Ferrers Cl. DE74: C Don 1F **211**
Ferrers Cres. DE56: Duff 4C **58**
Ferrers Wlk.
NG3: Nott 1F **5** (5D **99**)
Ferrers Way DE5: Rip 3B **8**
DE22: D Abb 3D **107**
Ferriby Ter. NG2: Nott 4B **122**
Ferry Lodge NG4: Carl 4D **101**
Festival Av. DE72: Brea 4B **166**
Festival Rd. DE7: Kirk H 5B **90**
Festus Cl. NG3: Nott 4C **98**
Festus St. NG4: Neth 3F **101**
Field, The DE75: Ship 2E **65**
Field Av. NG15: Huck 5C **24**
Field Cl. DE72: Bor 5A **140**
DE72: Brea 4E **167**
NG2: West Br 4B **124**
NG4: Ged 5E **77**
NG9: Chil 4F **145**
Field Ct. DE56: Kil 5F **37**
Field Cres. DE24: Alv 1F **187**
Field Dr. DE24: Alv 1F **187**
Fieldfare Ct. DE23: Lit 5F **157**
Fieldgate Dr. DE21: Oak 3E **109**
Field Head Way DE21: Oak . .2A **110**
Field Ho. Cl. NG8: Woll 5C **94**
Field La. DE21: Chad 1E **137**
DE24: Alv 5A **162**
DE56: Bel 5E **13**
NG9: Chil 4F **145**
NG12: Shel 2B **104**
NG14: Woodbo 5B **32**
Field Maple Dr. NG7: H Grn . .2D **97**
Field Ri. DE23: Lit 4B **158**
Field Rd. DE7: Ilk 3E **91**
Field Row DE56: Bel 5E **13**
Fields Av. NG11: Rudd 1B **196**
Fields Farm Rd.
NG10: Long E 1B **194**
Field St. DE5: Cod 2A **18**
Fields Vw. NG12: Cotg 4D **155**
Fieldsway Dr. DE21: Chad 3C **108**
Field Ter. DE5: Rip 5C **8**
Field Vw. Cl. DE24: Alv 2A **188**
Fieldway NG11: Wilf 4A **150**
Fiennes Cres. NG7: Nott 2F **121**

Fife St. DE24: Alv 3D **161**
Fifth Av. NG7: Nott 2B **148**
Filbert Wlk. DE73: Chel 1E **201**
Filey St. NG6: Bulw 4B **48**
Filey Wlk. DE21: Chad 4C **108**
Fincham Cl. DE21: Chad 4C **108**
Finch Cl. NG7: Lent 5E **121**
Finch Cres. DE3: Mick 3B **156**
Finchley Av. DE22: Mac 2E **133**
Finchley Cl. NG11: Clif 2B **172**
FINDERN 5C **182**
Findern Cl. DE22: All 4C **106**
DE56: Bel 3A **14**
Findern Grn. NG3: Nott 4F **99**
Findern La. DE65: Burn 1F **181**
Findern St. DE22: Der 3C **134**
Fingal Cl. NG11: Clif 2E **173**
Finmere Cl. DE23: Lit 3F **157**
Finningley Dr.
DE22: D Abb 3D **107**
Finsbury Av. DE22: Mac 2A **134**
NG2: Nott 1E **123**
Finsbury Pk. Cl.
NG2: West Br 3B **150**
Finsbury Rd. NG5: Arn 2F **49**
NG9: Bram 2B **118**
Finsley Wlk. DE23: Der 4D **159**
Firbank Ct. NG9: Chil 3A **146**
Firbeck Rd. NG5: Arn 4F **51**
NG8: Woll 1A **118**
Fir Cl. NG6: Bulw 5E **47**
NG15: Huck 5A **26**
Fircroft Av. NG8: Bilb 2D **95**
Fircroft Dr. NG15: Huck 4B **24**
Firdale NG12: Cotg 5F **155**
Firecrest Way NG6: Basf 3C **72**
Fire House, The NG5: Arn . . .1D **75**
Firestone DE56: Haz 4C **34**
Firfield Av. DE72: Brea 3D **167**
Firs, The NG5: Sher 4C **74**
Firs Av. DE5: Rip 5C **8**
NG9: Bee 1E **147**
Firsby Rd. NG8: Brox 5E **71**
Firs Cres. DE22: All 1D **107**
Firs Rd. NG12: Edwal 4F **151**
Firs St. NG10: Long E 2F **193**
First Av. DE7: Ilk 3E **91**
DE72: Ris 3E **143**
NG4: Carl 3B **100**
NG4: Colw 5D **101**
NG4: Ged 1E **101**
NG6: Bulw 5A **48**
NG7: H Grn 2A **98**
NG7: Nott 2B **148**
Firth Cl. NG5: Arn 3B **52**
Firth Dr. NG9: Chil 1B **170**
Firth Way NG6: Bulw 4F **47**
Firtree Gro. DE21: Oak 3A **110**
Fir Wlk. NG3: Nott 3A **100**
Fisher Av. NG5: Woodt 2E **75**
Fisher Ct. DE7: Ilk 3E **67**
Fisher Ga.
NG1: Nott 4E **5** (1C **122**)
Fisher La. DE56: Duff 3D **59**
NG13: Bing 2D **131**
Fisher St. DE24: A'ton 5D **161**
NG7: Basf 2E **97**
(not continuous)
Fishpond Dr.
NG7: Nott 5A **4** (2F **121**)
Fiskerton Way DE21: Oak . . .5A **110**
Fitness First
Derby 2A **136**
Nottingham 5B **4**

Five Acres NG11: Wilf 4F **149**
Five Lamps DE1: Der 1E **135**
Five Lamps Ct. DE1: Der 2E **135**
Flagholme NG12: Cotg 1E **179**
Flake La. DE7: Stan D 4D **115**
Flamingo Ct. NG7: Lent 3F **121**
Flamstead Av. DE75: Los 5B **18**
NG4: Lamb 5A **54**
Flamstead La. DE5: Den 3C **38**
Flamstead Rd. DE7: Ilk 1E **91**
Flamstead St. DE24: A'ton 5D **161**
Flamsteed Rd. NG8: Stre 1C **94**
Flat, The DE56: Kil 4E **37**
Flatts, The NG9: Chil 3A **146**
Flatts La. NG14: Calv 1D **31**
Flawborough Ri.
NG2: West Br 5B **150**
Flawforth Av. NG11: Rudd 4C **174**
Flawforth La. NG11: Rudd 4C **174**
Flaxendale NG12: Cotg 1F **179**
FLAXHOLME 1E **83**
Flaxholme Av. DE56: Duff 1E **83**
Flaxton Way NG5: Top V 5E **49**
Fleam Rd. NG11: Clif 4D **149**
Fleeman Gro.
NG2: West Br 4F **123**
Fleet, The DE56: Bel 2E **35**
Fleet Cl. NG7: Radf 4C **96**
Fleet Cres. DE56: Bel 1E **35**
Fleet Pk. DE56: Bel 1F **35**
Fleet St. DE23: Der 1F **159**
Fleetway Cl. NG16: Newth 3A **44**
Fleetwith Cl. NG2: West Br . . .3B **152**
Fleming Cl. NG16: Want 4F **45**
Fleming Dr. NG4: Carl 3B **100**
Fleming Gdns. NG11: Clif 2B **172**
Fleming Ho. NG3: Mapp 5E **75**
Fletcher Ga.
NG1: Nott 3C **4** (1B **122**)
Fletcher Rd. NG9: Bee 1F **147**
Fletcher's Row DE5: Rip 4E **9**
Fletcher St. DE5: Rip 4D **9**
DE75: Hea 2D **41**
NG10: Long E 3C **168**
Fletcher Ter. NG3: Mapp 5D **75**
Flewitt Gdns.
NG3: Nott 1F **5** (4D **99**)
Flintham Dr. NG5: Sher 3A **74**
Flint St. DE24: A'ton 5C **160**
Flixton Rd. NG16: Kimb 5E **45**
Flood St. DE72: Ock 4B **140**
Florence Av. NG10: Long E . . .2E **169**
Florence Boot Cl.
NG7: Nott 5A **120**
Florence Ct.
DE1: Der 5F **7** (4B **136**)
DE7: Ilk 1E **91**
Florence Cres. NG4: Ged 2A **102**
Florence Gro. NG3: Nott 3F **99**
Florence Rd. NG2: West Br . . .5F **123**
NG3: Nott 1F **99**
NG4: Ged 1A **102**
Florence St. NG15: Huck 4F **25**
Florey Ct. NG7: Nott 3D **121**
Florey Wlk. NG11: Clif 3B **172**
Florimel Ct. NG5: Arn 5B **50**
Florin Gdns. NG10: Long E . . .4F **167**
Flowers Cl. NG5: Arn 1A **76**
Flying Horse Wlk.
NG1: Nott 3C **4** (1B **122**)
Foljambe Ter. NG3: Nott 1E **5**
Folkestone Dr. DE24: Alv 1F **187**
Folkton Gdns. NG3: Mapp 1E **99**
Folly Rd. DE22: D Abb 4A **108**

Forbes Cl. NG10: Long E 1D 195
Forbes Hole Local Nature Reserve
. . . . .1D 195
Ford Av. DE75: Los 5B 18
Ford Cl. DE5: Rip 1B 16
Fordham Grn. NG11: Clif 3D 173
Ford La. DE21: L Eat 5B 84
DE22: All 5F 83
(not continuous)
Ford St. DE1: Der 2B 6 (3E 135)
DE56: Bel 5E 13
NG7: Basf 1F 97
Ford St. Nth. NG7: Basf 1F 97
Fordwells Cl. DE23: Lit 3F 157
Fordyce Cl. DE73: Chel 5D 187
Foremark Av. DE23: Der 3D 159
Forest Cl. DE56: Bel 4A 14
NG12: Cotg 5D 155
Forest Cotts. NG6: Bulw 3C 48
Forest Ct. NG7: Radf 4F 97
Forester Cl. NG9: Chil 4B 146
Forester Gro. NG4: Carl 3C 100
Forester Rd. NG3: Nott 2F 99
Forester's Leisure Pk. 4F 159
Foresters Rd. DE5: Rip 4B 8
Forester St.
DE1: Der 4B 6 (4E 135)
NG4: Neth 3F 101
Forester's Way DE23: Der 4F 159
FOREST FIELDS 2F 97
Forest Gro. NG1: Nott 3A 98
NG7: Radf 4F 97
Forest La. NG15: Pap 3F 11
Forest Rd. NG13: Bing 2B 130
NG14: Calv 1C 30
Forest Rd. E. NG1: Nott 4F 97
Forest Rd. W. NG7: Radf 4F 97
Forest, The Stop (NET) 3F 97
Forest Vw. Dr. NG15: Huck . . .2D 25
Forge, The NG9: Trow 5A 92
NG14: Lowd 2C 56
Forge Av. NG14: Calv 1E 31
Forge Hill NG9: Chil 4C 146
Forge Mill Gro. NG15: Huck . . .4C 26
Forman St. DE1: Der . . .3B 6 (3E 135)
NG1: Nott 2B 4 (5B 98)
Forrester Av. DE72: W Tre 4E 203
Forster St. NG7: Radf 4D 97
(not continuous)
Forsythia Gdns. NG7: Lent . . .3D 121
Forty Horse Cl. DE5: Rip 5F 9
Forum Cl. DE24: Alv 1C 188
Forum Rd. NG5: Bestw 1D 73
Fosbrook Dr. DE74: C Don . . .5E 205
Fosbrooke Dr.
NG10: Long E 1C 194
Fosse, The
NG12: Cotg, Crop Bi, Owt
. . . . .4F 179
Fosse Cl. DE72: Bor 2B 164
Fosse Rd.
NG13: Bing, Newton, Saxon
. . . . .2A 130
Fosse Wlk. NG12: Cotg 1F 179
Foss Way NG12: Crop Bu 3F 129
NG13: Bing 3F 129
Foster Av. NG9: Bee 2E 147
Foster Dr. NG5: Sher 3C 74
Fosters La. NG13: Bing 2E 131
Fothergill Ct. NG3: Mapp P . . .3B 98
Foundry La. DE56: Mil 5E 35
Fountain Dale Ct. NG3: Nott . . .3C 98
Fountains Cl. DE22: All 1F 107
NG2: West Br 2A 152

Fountains Ct. NG9: Bee 2F 147
Fourth Av. NG4: Carl 2A 100
NG7: H Grn 2A 98
NG7: Nott 2B 148
Fowler Av. DE21: Spon 4C 138
Fowler M. NG16: Want 5F 45
Fowler St. DE1: Der 3D 135
DE72: Dray 4A 166
NG3: Mapp P 2C 98
Foxbrook Cl. DE23: Lit 3F 157
Fox Cl. DE24: S Flds 3C 184
NG10: Long E 1C 194
Fox Covert NG4: Colw 1E 125
Fox Covert La. NG11: Clif 3A 172
Fox Covert Local Nature Reserve
. . . . .4C 168
Foxdell Way DE73: Chel 4F 187
Foxearth Av. NG11: Clif 1F 173
Fox End NG5: Sher 5C 74
Foxes Cl. NG7: Nott 2F 121
(off Hermitage Wlk.)
Foxcs Wlk. DE22: All 1D 107
Foxfields Dr. DE21: Oak 3D 109
Foxglove Cl. NG15: Huck 5B 26
Foxglove Dr. DE21: Oak 2E 109
Foxglove Rd. NG16: Newth . . .4A 44
Foxgloves, The
NG13: Bing 3C 130
Fox Gro. NG5: Basf 4D 73
Fox Gro. Ct. NG5: Basf 4D 73
Foxhall Rd. NG7: H Grn 2F 97
Foxhill NG12: Cotg 1E 179
Foxhill Ct. NG4: Carl 2D 101
Foxhill Rd. NG4: Carl 2B 100
NG14: Bur J 2D 79
Foxhill Rd. Central
NG4: Carl 2A 100
Foxhill Rd. E. NG4: Carl 2C 100
Foxhill Rd. W. NG4: Carl 2F 99
Foxhills DE74: Keg 3B 214
Foxhollies Gro. NG5: Sher 4A 74
Foxlands Av. DE22: D Abb 3E 107
Foxley Ct. DE21: Oak 3A 110
Foxley Rd. DE7: Ilk 2E 67
Fox Mdw. NG15: Huck 3E 25
Fox Rd. DE74: C Don 1E 211
NG2: West Br 4E 123
Fox St. DE1: Der 1D 7 (2F 135)
Foxton Cl. DE7: Ilk 4B 66
NG6: Bulw 4E 47
Foxton Gdns. NG8: Bilb 3F 95
Fuxwood Gro. NG14: Calv 2F 31
Foxwood La. NG14: Woodbo . . .3E 31
Foyle Av. DE21: Chad 4F 137
Fradley Cl. NG6: Bulw 2B 48
Frampton Gdns. DE23: Lit 5E 157
Frampton Rd. NG8: Bilb 3F 95
Frances Gro. NG15: Huck 5D 11
Franchise Ct. DE22: Der 4D 135
Franchise St. DE22: Der 4D 135
Francis Gro. NG6: Basf 4D 73
Francis Rd. NG4: Carl 2E 101
Francis St. DE21: Chad 2C 136
NG7: Radf 4F 97
(not continuous)
Francklin Rd. NG14: Lowd 2C 56
Franklin Cl. NG5: Arn 4B 50
Franklin Dr. NG12: Toll 2C 176
Franklin Ho. NG3: Mapp 5E 75
(off Ockbrook Dr.)
Franklyn Dr. DE24: Alv 5F 161
Franklyn Gdns. NG8: Aspl 4B 96
NG12: Key 2D 199
Fraser Cres. NG4: Carl 1A 100

Fraser Rd. NG2: Nott 5C 122
NG4: Carl 5A 76
Fraser Sq. NG4: Carl 1A 100
Fraser St. NG15: News 1A 10
Frazer Cl. DE21: Spon 2D 139
Frearson Farm Ct.
NG16: Eastw 3E 43
Freckingham St.
NG1: Nott 2F 5 (5C 98)
Freda Av. NG4: Ged 5C 76
Freda Cl. NG4: Ged 4C 76
Frederic Av. DE75: Hea 5E 41
Frederick Av. DE7: Ilk 5F 91
DE24: Alv 5E 161
DE74: Keg 1B 214
NG4: Carl 3A 100
Frederick Gro. NG7: Lent 2E 121
Frederick Rd. NG9: Stap 1C 144
Frederick St. DE22: Der 2C 134
NG10: Long E 4E 169
Freehold St. DE22: Der 4D 135
Freeland Cl. NG9: Toton 5E 145
Freeman Av. DE23: Der 5D 159
Freemans Rd. NG4: Carl 2F 101
Freemans Ter. NG4: Carl 2E 101
Freemantle Wlk.
NG5: Top V 4D 49
Freesia Cl. DE3: Mick 2D 157
Freeston Dr. NG6: Bulw 4E 47
Freeth Ct. NG2: Nott 3E 123
Freeth St. NG2: Nott 3D 123
Freiston St. NG7: H Grn 3D 97
Fremantle Rd. DE3: Mick 5D 133
Fremount Dr. NG8: Bilb 4E 95
French La. DE21: Hors 2E 61
French St. DE7: Ilk 4F 91
DE23: Der 1D 159
Fresco Dr. DE23: Lit 4E 157
Freshwater Ho. DE24: Alv 4B 162
(off Durley Cl.)
Fretwell St. NG7: H Grn 3D 97
Friar Ga. DE1: Der 1A 6 (3E 135)
Friar Ga. Ct.
DE1: Der 2A 6 (3E 135)
Friargate M.
DE1: Der 3B 6 (3E 135)
Friar La. NG1: Nott 4A 4 (1A 122)
Friars Cl. DE22: D Abb 3E 107
Friars Ct. DE7: Kirk H 4B 90
NG7: Nott 2F 121
Friar St. NG7: Lent 3D 121
NG10: Long E 4C 168
Friary, The NG7: Lent 3D 121
Friary Av. DE24: A'ton 1D 187
Friary Cl. NG7: Lent 3D 121
Friary St. DE1: Der 3B 6 (3E 135)
Friday La. NG4: Ged 5E 77
Friesland Dr. NG10: Sand 3E 143
Frinton Rd. NG8: Brox 1D 95
Frisby Av. NG10: Long E 5D 169
Fritchley Cl. DE21: Chad 4F 109
Frobisher Gdns. NG5: Arn 1C 74
Froggatt Cl. DE22: All 5F 83
Frngmore St. NG1: Nott 4B 98
Front St. NG5: Arn 5E 51
Frost Av. NG16: Lang M 5F 19
Frost Flds. DE74: C Don 5A 206
Fryar Rd. NG16: Eastw 5E 21
Fulbrook Rd. DE23: Lit 3F 157
Fulforth St. NG1: Nott 4B 98
Fulham Rd. DE22: Mac 3F 133
Fullers Cl. DE56: Mil 5E 35
Fuller St. NG11: Rudd 5B 174
Full St. DE1: Der 1C 6 (2F 135)

Fullwood Av. DE7: Ilk 1D 91
Fullwood St. DE7: Ilk 1D 91
Fulmar Cl. DE3: Mick 5F 133
Fulwood Cl. NG9: Chil 4B 146
Fulwood Cres. NG8: Aspl 1F 95
Fulwood Dr. NG10: Long E 4F 167
Furleys Cotts. NG14: Lowd 1A 56
Furlong Av. NG5: Arn 4D 51
Furlong Cl. NG9: Stap 5C 116
Furlong Ct. NG5: Arn 4D 51
Furlong St. NG5: Arn 5D 51
(not continuous)
Furnace La. DE75: Los 5B 18
Furnace Rd. DE7: Ilk 3A 92
Furness Cl. NG2: West Br 1A 152
Furness Rd. NG6: Basf 4B 72
Furrows Cl. DE21: Oak 2B 110
Furzebrook Rd. NG4: Colw 5D 101
Furze Gdns. NG3: Nott 3C 98
Fylde Cl. NG9: Toton 1D 169
Fylingdale Way NG8: Woll 2A 118

G

Gable Ct. DE3: Mick 3D 157
Gables, The NG7: Basf 1F 97
Gable's Lea LE12: Sut B 5F 215
Gabor Cl. NG11: Clif 2B 172
Gabor Ct. NG11: Clif 2B 172
Gabrielle Cl. NG6: Bulw 3C 72
Gadd St. NG7: Radf 4E 97
Gadsby Cl. DE7: Ilk 1F 115
Gadwall Cres. NG7: Lent 3F 121
Gainsborough Cl.
   DE21: Oak 4A 110
   NG9: Stap 2D 145
   NG10: Long E 1D 195
Gainsborough Ct. NG9: Bee . . .1F 147
Gainsford Cl. NG5: Bestw 2E 73
Gainsford Cres. NG5: Bestw . . .2E 73
Gairloch Cl. DE24: S Flds 4C 184
Gala Bingo
   Bestwood 1D 73
   Derby, Forester's Leisure Pk.
   . . . . .4F 159
   Derby, Liversage St.
   . . . . .4F 7 (4A 136)
   Nottingham 1D 5 (5C 98)
   Old Radford 4D 97
Gala Dr. DE24: Alv 4E 161
Gala Way NG5: Bestw 1D 73
Gale Cl. NG9: Bee 2A 148
Galena Dr. NG3: Nott 3F 99
Galen Ct. NG7: Nott 3D 121
Galleries of Justice & Mus. of Law
   .4D 5
Gallery, The
   NG7: Nott 5A 4 (2A 122)
GALLOWS INN 4F 91
Gallows Inn Cl. DE7: Ilk 5F 91
Gallows Inn Ind. Est. DE7: Ilk . .4A 92
Galway Cl. DE21: Chad 4A 138
Galway Rd. NG5: Arn 4C 50
   NG7: Lent 2E 121
Gamble St. NG7: Radf 4F 97
GAMSTON 1B 152
Gamston Cres. NG5: Sher 4B 74
Gamston District Cen.
   NG2: West Br 2B 152
Gamston Lodge NG4: Carl 4D 101
Ganton Cl. NG3: Mapp 1E 99
Garden Av. DE7: Ilk 5E 91
   NG4: Carl 3C 100

Garden City NG4: Carl 2D 101
Garden Cres. DE74: C Don . . .1A 212
Gardendale Av. NG11: Clif 2C 172
Gardeners Wlk. NG5: Sher 3E 73
Gardenia Cl. NG9: Toton 1F 169
Gardenia Cres. NG3: Mapp . . .5A 76
Gardenia Gro. NG3: Mapp 5A 76
Garden Lodge Cl.
   DE23: Der 1C 158
Garden Rd. NG13: Bing 2C 130
   NG15: Huck 2E 25
   NG16: Eastw 1E 43
Garden Row DE74: Keg 1C 214
Gardens, The DE5: Rip 2C 16
   DE75: Los 5B 18
Gardens Cl. NG2: West Br 1F 151
Garden St. DE1: Der 1E 135
   NG7: Radf 5E 97
Garfield Av. DE72: Dray 4F 165
Garfield Cl. DE23: Lit 5B 158
   NG9: Stap 4D 117
Garfield Ct. NG7: Radf 5E 97
Garfield Rd. NG7: Radf 4D 97
   (not continuous)
Garforth Cl. NG8: Basf 2D 97
Garland, The NG7: Lent 3D 121
Garners Hill
   NG1: Nott 4C 4 (1C 122)
Garnet Cl. NG3: Nott . . .1F 5 (5D 99)
Garnet St. NG4: Neth 3E 101
Garnett Av. DE75: Hea 2B 18
Garrett Gro. NG11: Clif 1B 172
Garrick St. DE23: Lit 1C 184
Garry Cl. DE24: S Flds 4C 184
Garsdale Cl. NG2: Gam 2B 152
Garsdale Ct. DE24: Alv 5C 162
Garsdale Dr. NG11: Wilf 5F 149
Garth Cres. DE24: Alv 5A 162
Garthorpe Ct. DE21: Oak 3E 109
Garton Cl. NG6: Bulw 2A 72
   NG9: Chil 3A 146
Gary Cl. DE23: Lit 1C 184
Gascoigne Dr. DE21: Spon . . .4C 138
Gaskell Av. DE23: Der 4D 159
Gasny Av. DE74: C Don 4A 206
Gas St. NG10: Sand 2B 144
Gatcombe Cl. DE21: Oak 3A 110
   NG12: Rad T 2F 127
Gatcombe Gro. NG10: Sand . . .5F 143
Gate Brook Cl. DE5: Cod 5F 9
Gateford Cl. NG9: Bram 3B 118
Gatehouse Ct. NG9: Chil 3C 146
Gateside Rd. NG2: Nott 4F 121
Gatling St. NG7: Radf 5D 97
Gaul St. NG6: Bulw 5A 48
Gauntley Ct. NG7: Basf 2E 97
Gauntley St. NG7: Basf 2D 97
Gautries Cl. NG5: Top V 4F 49
Gavin M. NG7: H Grn 2E 97
Gawthorne St. NG7: Basf 1E 97
Gayhurst Grn. NG6: Bulw 2D 73
Gayhurst Rd. NG6: Bulw 2D 73
Gaynor Cl. NG8: Bilb 4A 96
Gayrigg Ct. NG9: Chil 3A 146
Gayton Av. DE23: Lit 5C 158
Gayton Cl. NG8: Bilb 2C 94
Gayton Rd. DE7: Ilk 2C 90
Gayton Thorpe Cl. DE23: Lit . . .4E 157
Gaywood Cl. NG11: Clif 3E 173
GEDLING 5E 77
Gedling Gro. NG5: Arn 5E 51
   NG7: Radf 4F 97
Gedling Rd. NG4: Carl 2E 101
   NG5: Arn 5E 51

Gedling St.
   NG1: Nott 3E 5 (1C 122)
Gedney Av. NG3: Nott 2E 99
Gell Rd. NG9: Chil 4F 145
Gema Cl. DE22: All 1F 107
Genesis Pk. NG7: Radf 5C 96
George Av. NG9: Bee 3E 147
   NG10: Long E 2E 169
George Grn. Ct. NG2: Nott . . .1E 123
   (off Sneinton Blvd.)
George Rd. NG2: West Br 1D 151
   NG4: Carl 3D 101
George's La.
   NG14: Calv, Woodbo 4A 30
George St. DE1: Der . . .2B 6 (3E 135)
   DE56: Bel 5E 13
   NG1: Nott 2D 5 (5C 98)
   NG5: Arn 1D 75
   NG15: Huck 1F 25
   NG16: Lang M 1A 42
George Yd. DE1: Der . . .2C 6 (3F 135)
Georgia Dr. NG5: Arn 2D 51
Georgina Cl. DE74: C Don 5A 206
Georgina Rd. NG9: Bee 3E 147
Gerard Cl. DE21: Spon 2E 139
Gerard Ct.
   DE1: Der 4B 6 (4E 135)
Gerard Gro. DE65: Etw 2B 180
Gerard St. DE1: Der . . .3B 6 (4E 135)
Gerrard Cl. NG5: Arn 2F 49
Gerrard Cres. DE74: Keg 3C 214
Gertrude Rd. DE21: Chad 5E 109
   DE72: Dray 4F 165
   NG2: West Br 5F 123
Gervase Gdns. NG11: Clif 1B 172
Ghost Ho. La. NG9: Chil 3A 146
   (not continuous)
Ghyll Cl. DE24: Alv 2F 161
Gibbons Av. NG9: Stap 2C 144
Gibbons St. NG7: Lent 5D 121
Gibb St. NG10: Long E 4D 169
Gibfield La. DE56: Bel 2E 35
Gibson Rd. NG7: H Grn 2F 97
Gifford Gdns. NG2: Nott 3B 122
Gilbert Blvd. NG5: Arn 5B 52
Gilbert Cl. DE21: Spon 4C 138
   NG5: Bestw 2F 73
Gilbert Cres. DE56: Duff 5D 59
Gilbert Gdns. NG3: Nott 4F 99
Gilbert St. DE24: Alv 1A 188
   (not continuous)
   NG15: Huck 2F 25
Gilderdale Way DE21: Oak 2A 110
Gilead St. NG6: Bulw 5A 48
Giles Av. NG2: West Br 2C 150
Giles Ct. NG2: West Br 1D 151
Gillamoor Ct. DE24: Alv 5B 162
Gillercomb Cl.
   NG2: West Br 3C 152
Gilliver Gdns. DE72: Dray 4F 165
Gilliver La. NG12: C'ton 2B 178
Gillotts Cl. NG13: Bing 1D 131
Gillott St. DE75: Hea 4F 41
Gill St. NG1: Nott 1A 4 (4A 98)
Gilpet Av. NG3: Nott 2E 99
GILTBROOK 4B 44
Giltbrook Cres. NG16: Gilt 4B 44
Giltbrook Ind. Est.
   NG16: Gilt 5B 44
Gilt Hill NG16: Kimb 5C 44
Giltway NG16: Gilt 5B 44
Gimson Cl. DE7: Ilk 4B 66
Gin Cl. Way NG16: Aws 2B 68
   NG16: Gilt 1B 68

Gipsy La. NG11: Clif 1B 172
  NG15: Huck 4A 10
Girton Rd. NG5: Sher 4F 73
Gisborne Cl. DE3: Mick 5D 133
Gisborne Cres. DE22: All 1E 107
Gisborne Grn. DE1: Der 2D 135
Gisburn Cl. NG11: Wilf 4F 149
Glade, The NG11: Clif 4D 173
Glade Av. NG8: Woll 5B 96
Glade Bus. Cen., The
  NG5: Bestw 1D 73
Gladehill Rd.
  NG5: Arn, Bestw 5B 50
Glades, The NG5: Top V 4E 49
Gladstone Av. DE75: Hea 2D 41
Gladstone Cl. DE73: Chel 3E 187
Gladstone Dr. NG16: Brins ...2D 21
Gladstone Rd. DE21: Spon ...3D 139
Gladstone St. DE7: Ilk 3E 91
  (not continuous)
  DE23: Der 2D 159
  DE75: Hea 2D 41
  NG4: Carl 3C 100
  NG7: Basf 2E 97
  (not continuous)
  NG9: Bee 3D 147
  NG10: Long E 5C 168
  NG16: Lang M 1B 42
Gladys St. NG7: Basf 1F 97
Glaisdale Dr. E. NG8: Bilb ...4C 94
Glaisdale Dr. W. NG8: Bilb ...5C 94
Glaisdale Nook DE24: Alv 5C 162
  (not continuous)
Glaisdale Pk. Ind. Est.
  NG8: Bilb 4C 94
Glaisdale Parkway NG8: Bilb ...5C 94
Glamis Cl. DE21: Oak 3A 110
Glamis Rd. NG5: Sher 5F 73
Glanton Way NG5: Arn 2F 51
Glapton La. NG11: Clif 1C 172
Glapton Rd. NG2: Nott 4B 122
Glaramara Cl. NG2: Nott 4A 122
Glass Ho., The
  NG3: Nott 1D 5 (5B 98)
Glasshouse Hill DE5: Cod ...1A 18
Glasshouse St.
  NG1: Nott 1C 4 (5B 98)
Glastonbury Dr. DE24: Alv ...4B 162
Gleadsmoss La. DE21: Oak ...4F 109
Glebe, The NG16: Coss 3A 68
Glebe Av. DE5: Rip 4B 8
  DE7: Smal 1E 63
Glebe Cotts. NG11: Wilf 5A 122
Glebe Cres. DE7: Ilk 3F 91
  DE7: S'ley 4A 88
Glebe Dr. NG14: Bur J 4C 78
Glebe Farm Cl
  NG2: West Br 4B 150
Glebe Farm Vw. NG4: Ged 4E 77
Glebe La. NG12: Rad T 2E 127
Glebe Ri. DE23: Lit 2B 158
Glebe Rd. NG2: West Br 1E 151
  NG4: Carl 5B 76
  NG16: Nuth 1B 70
Glebe St. NG9: Bee 2D 147
  NG15: Huck 1F 25
Glen, The NG11: Clif 2D 173
Glen Av. DE56: H'ook 5B 36
  NG16: Eastw 3A 44
Glenbrook NG12: Cotg 5F 155
Glenbrook Cres. NG10: Dilb ...3F 06
Glencairn Dr. NG8: Bilb 2F 95
Glencairn M. NG8: Bilb 2F 95
Glencoe Rd. NG11: Clif 2F 173

Glencoyne Rd. NG11: Clif 3D 173
Glencroft Dr. DE24: S Flds ...3C 184
Glencross Cl.
  NG2: West Br 4B 124
Glendale Cl. NG4: Carl 5C 76
Glendale Ct. NG9: Chil 5D 147
Glendale Gdns. NG5: Arn 5F 51
Glendevon Way DE73: Chel ...4D 187
Glendoe Gro. NG13: Bing ...2B 130
Glendon Dr. NG5: Sher 4F 73
  NG15: Huck 4F 25
Glendon Rd. DE7: Kirk H 1B 114
  DE24: S Flds 3C 184
Glendon St. DE7: Stan C 5F 63
Gleneagles Cl. DE3: Mick ...1E 157
Gleneagles Ct.
  NG12: Edwal 5A 152
Gleneagles Dr. NG5: Arn 3A 52
Glenfield Av. NG16: Kimb 5C 44
Glenfield Cres. DE3: Mick ...1B 156
Glenfield Rd.
  NG10: Long E 1C 194
Glengarry Way DE24: Sin 2D 185
Glen Helen NG4: Colw 4E 101
Glenlivet Gdns. NG11: Clif ...2E 173
  (not continuous)
Glenloch Dr. NG11: Clif 3E 173
Glenmore Dr. DE24: S Flds ...2C 184
Glenmore Rd.
  NG2: West Br 2A 152
Glenmoy Cl. DE23: Der 4C 158
Glenn Way DE72: Shar 5C 190
Glenorchy Ct. DE21: Oak 2A 110
Glenorchy Cres. NG5: Top V ...4D 49
Glen Pk. Cl. DE73: Chel 1D 201
Glen Parva Av. NG5: Redh ...3D 51
Glenridding Cl.
  NG2: West Br 3C 162
Glen Rd. NG14: Bur J 2D 79
Glensford Gdns. NG5: Top V ...2D 49
Glenshee Gdns.
  DE73: Chel 4D 187
Glenside NG5: Woodt 2A 76
Glenside Rd. NG9: Bram 4B 118
Glenstone Ct. NG7: H Grn ...2E 97
Glentworth Rd. NG7: Radf ...4D 97
Glen Vw. DE56: Bel 2E 35
Glen Vine DE5: Rip 5F 9
Glenwood Av. NG8: Woll 1C 118
Glenwood Rd. DE73: Chel ...1E 201
  (not continuous)
Glins Rd. NG5: Top V 4E 49
Glossop St. DE24: Der 4A 160
Gloster St. DE24: Der 1D 161
Gloucester Av. NG7: Lent 1D 121
  NG9: Chil 3E 147
  NG10: Sand 4F 143
  NG16: Nuth 4E 71
Glover Av. NG8: Woll 1C 118
Glover Ho. NG5: Arn 1F 75
  (off Derwent Cres.)
Glover Rd. DE74: C Don 5A 206
Glue La. DE75: Loo 2R 40
Goatchurch Ct. NG5: Top V ...4F 49
Goathland Cl. NG5: Bestw ...4A 50
Goathland Rd.
  DE24: S Flds 4C 184
Godber Rd. NG15: Huck 4D 25
Godfrey Dr. DE7: Kirk H 5B 90
Godfrey St. DE75: Hea 3D 41
  (not continuous)
  NG4: Neth 4F 101
Godkin Dr. NG16: Lang M ...5F 19

Goldcrest Cl. NG13: Bing 3F 131
Goldcrest Dr. DE21: Spon ...2E 139
Goldcrest Rd. NG6: Cin 4A 72
Golden Valley DE7: H Woo ...5A 38
Golden Valley Light Railway
  Swanwick Station 2F 9
Golders Grn. Wlk.
  DE22: Mac 2F 133
Goldham Rd. NG8: Stre 2C 94
Gold La. DE22: Mac 1D 133
Goldrill Cl. NG2: Gam 1A 152
Goldsmith Ct. NG1: Nott 1A 4
Goldsmith St.
  NG1: Nott 1A 4 (5A 98)
Goldstone Ct. DE21: Spon ...4D 139
Goldswong Ter. NG3: Nott ...3B 98
Golf Cl. DE23: Lit 2F 157
Golf Club Rd. DE7: Stan D ...4F 115
Golf Course Rd.
  NG12: Stan W 4F 199
Golf La. DE56: Duff 2D 59
Golf Rd. NG12: Rad T 2F 127
GONALSTON 1E 57
Gonalston La.
  NG14: Epp, Gon, Hove ...1B 56
Goodale St. DE23: Der 2F 159
Goodall Cres. NG15: Huck ...3B 26
Goodall St. NG7: H Grn 3E 97
Goodliffe St. NG7: H Grn 2E 97
Goodman Cl. NG16: Gilt 4B 44
Goodrington Rd. DE21: Oak ...2B 110
Goodsmoor Rd. DE23: Lit ...1C 184
  DE24: Sin 1C 184
Goodsmoor Rd. Ind. Est.
  DE24: Sin 1D 185
Goods Rd. DE56: Bel 2E 35
Goods Rd. Ind. Est.
  DE56: Bel 2E 35
Goods Yd. DE56: Bel 3E 35
Goodwin Cl. NG10: Sand 2F 143
Goodwin Dr. NG16: Kimb 1D 69
Goodwin's La. DE56: Haz 3A 34
Goodwin St. NG7: Radf 4F 97
Goodwood Av. NG5: Arn 4D 51
Goodwood Cres.
  DE7: Kirk H 1C 114
Goodwood Dr. DE24: Alv 5B 162
  NG9: Toton 1E 169
Goodwood Rd. NG8: Woll ...1C 118
Goole Av. DE7: Kirk H 5C 90
Goosedale La. NG6: Bestw V ...2D 27
Goose Ga.
  NG1: Nott 3D 5 (1C 122)
  NG12: Cotg 5D 155
Goose La. DE5: Cod 1B 18
Gordon Cl. NG9: Atten 1C 170
Gordon Gro. NG7: Basf 1E 97
Gordon Ri. NG3: Mapp 5D 75
Gordon Rd. DE23: Der 5E 135
  DE72: Bor 2A 164
  NG2: West Br 1E 151
  NG3: Nott 4D 99
  NG14: Bur J 2F 79
Gordon Sq. NG2: West Br ...1E 151
Gordon St. DE7: Ilk 1E 91
  NG6: Basf 3C 72
Gorman Ct. NG5: Arn 5A 52
Gorse Cl. DE23: Lit 5A 158
  NG10: Long E 1A 168
  NG14: Calv 2C 30
  NG16: Newth 3A 44
Gorse Ct. NG6: Bulw 2D 73
Gorsehill Gro. DE23: Lit 4F 157
Gorse Rd. NG12: Key 3C 198

Gorses DE56: Bel 1B **12**
Gorse Wlk. NG3: Nott 3A **100**
Gorsey Cl. DE56: Bel 3D **13**
Gorsey Rd. NG3: Mapp P 3C **98**
Gorsty Leys DE65: Find 5C **182**
Gosforth Av. DE7: Ilk 1D **67**
Gosforth Ct. NG2: Nott 4C **122**
Gosforth Rd. DE24: Der 4D **161**
Goshawk Rd. DE7: Ilk 2F **115**
Gotham Rd. NG11: King 5F **209**
Gothic Cl. NG6: Basf 3D **73**
Goverton Sq. NG6: Bulw 2C **72**
Gowan Cl. NG9: Chil 1B **170**
Gower St.
  DE1: Der 4C **6** (4F **135**)
Goyden Cl. NG5: Top V 4F **49**
GPT Bus. Pk. NG9: Bee 3F **147**
Grace Av. NG9: Bee 3A **148**
Grace Cres. DE75: Hea 2E **41**
Grace Dr. NG8: Aspl 2C **96**
Grafham Cl. DE73: Chel 4F **187**
Grafton Av. NG5: Woodt 2D **75**
Grafton Ct. NG7: Radf 5F **97**
Grafton St. DE23: Der 1D **159**
Graham St. DE7: Ilk 3E **91**
  NG7: Radf 5E **97**
Grainger Av. NG2: West Br . . .5D **151**
Graingers Ter.
  NG15: Huck 3A **26**
Grainger St. NG2: Nott 3D **123**
Grammer St. DE5: Den 5F **17**
Grampian Dr. NG5: Arn 2A **50**
Grampian Way
  DE24: S Flds 3C **184**
  NG10: Long E 3F **167**
Granby Ct. NG13: Bing 2C **130**
Granby St. DE7: Ilk 5D **67**
Granby Vs. NG2: Nott 1E **123**
Grandfield Av.
  NG12: Rad T 1E **127**
Grandfield Cres.
  NG12: Rad T 1E **127**
Grandfield St. DE75: Los 5B **18**
Grandstand Rd.
  DE21: Chad 2B **136**
Grange, The DE7: Smal 4B **40**
Grange Av. DE23: Der 4D **159**
  DE72: Brea 3C **166**
  NG9: Bee 2E **147**
  NG11: Rudd 3A **174**
Grange Cl. NG4: Lamb 5B **54**
  NG11: Wilf 5A **122**
Grange Ct. NG11: Rudd 1B **174**
Grange Cres. NG4: Ged 4E **77**
Grange Dr. DE74: C Don 1F **211**
  NG10: Long E 3E **169**
Grange Est. NG16: Coss 1C **92**
Grange Farm NG2: Gam 1B **152**
Grange Farm Cl.
  DE74: Hem 4B **206**
  NG9: Toton 2F **169**
Grange Farm Cotts.
  NG14: Lowd 1E **55**
Grange Gdns. DE75: Los 1B **40**
Grange Ga. DE22: Der 5E **135**
Grangelea Gdns.
  NG9: Bram 5A **118**
Grangemoor NG15: Pap 5F **11**
Grangeover Way
  DE22: Der 4B **134**
GRANGE PARK 3F **169**
Grange Pk. NG2: West Br . . .3A **152**
  NG10: Long E 3E **169**
  NG12: Crop Bu 5F **129**

Grange Rd. DE24: Alv 1A **188**
  NG5: Woodt 3D **75**
  NG6: Basf 4C **72**
  NG10: Long E 3E **169**
  NG12: Edwal 4F **151**
Grange St. DE23: Der 1A **160**
  (not continuous)
Grange Vw. NG16: Eastw 1E **43**
Grange Vw. Rd. NG4: Ged . . .5E **77**
Grangewood Av. DE7: Ilk 3E **91**
Grangewood Ct. NG8: Woll . . .2B **118**
Grangewood Dr. DE56: Mil . . .5F **35**
Grangewood Rd.
  NG8: Woll 2B **118**
Grannis Dr. NG8: Bilb 2F **95**
Grant Av. DE21: Chad 3A **138**
Grantham Av. DE21: Chad . . .4C **108**
Grantham Cl. NG16: Gilt 5B **44**
Grantham Rd. NG12: Rad T . . .3C **126**
Grantleigh Cl. NG8: Woll 5E **95**
  (not continuous)
Granton Av. NG11: Clif 3E **173**
Grant St. NG7: Radf 5E **97**
Granville Av. NG10: Long E . . .2C **168**
Granville Cl. DE56: Duff 4D **59**
Granville Ct. NG3: Nott 5E **99**
Granville Cres.
  NG12: Rad T 3D **127**
Granville Gro. NG3: Nott 5E **99**
Granville St. DE1: Der 3D **135**
Grasby Wlk. NG11: Clif 1C **172**
Grasmere Av. DE21: Spon . . .2D **139**
  NG8: Aspl 5B **72**
Grasmere Cl. NG15: Huck 1E **25**
Grasmere Ct.
  NG10: Long E 1A **168**
Grasmere Cres. DE24: Sin . . .2D **185**
Grasmere Rd. NG9: Bram . . .5C **118**
  NG10: Long E 1A **168**
Grasmere St. NG10: Sand . . .3A **144**
Grasmoor Cl. NG3: Nott 2E **99**
Grassingdale Cl. NG4: Carl . . .5C **76**
Grassington Rd. NG8: Aspl . . .4C **96**
Grassmere NG12: Cotg 5F **155**
Grass St. DE7: Ilk 4D **67**
Grassthorpe Cl. DE21: Oak . . .4A **110**
Grassy La. DE3: Mick 4A **156**
  DE23: Lit 4B **158**
  NG9: Bee 3F **147**
Gravelly Hollow NG14: Calv . . .1F **29**
Gravel Pit La. DE21: Spon . . .3D **139**
Graveney Gdns. NG5: Arn 1A **76**
Graylands Rd. NG8: Bilb 3C **94**
Grayling St. DE23: Der 1A **160**
Grays Cl. DE74: C Don 1A **212**
Grayson M. NG9: Chil 1A **170**
Graystones Cl.
  NG2: West Br 3B **152**
Grazingfield NG11: Wilf 4F **149**
GREASLEY 1D **45**
Greasley Av. NG16: Newth . . .2B **44**
Greasley Sports & Community Cen.
  . . . . .2A **44**
Greasley St. NG6: Bulw 5A **48**
Great Central Railway
  Ruddington Station 1C **196**
Gt. Freeman St.
  NG3: Nott 1C **4** (4B **98**)
Gt. Hoggett Dr. NG9: Chil 2F **145**
Gt. Northern Cl., The
  NG2: Nott 5E **5** (2C **122**)
Gt. Northern Cotts.
  NG15: Huck 5D **11**

Gt. Northern Rd.
  DE1: Der 3A **6** (3D **135**)
  NG16: Eastw 2C **42**
Gt. Northern Way
  NG4: Neth 4A **102**
Greatorex Av. DE24: A'ton 1D **187**
Greaves Cl. NG5: Arn 2A **76**
  NG8: Stre 1C **94**
Greaves St. DE5: Rip 4D **9**
Greek St. NG7: Radf 5F **97**
Green, The DE3: Mick 2C **156**
  DE21: Hors 1E **61**
  DE22: All 4C **106**
  DE56: Bel 4F **13**
  (off Cemetery Rd.)
  DE65: Find 5C **182**
  DE72: Ast T 1A **204**
  DE72: Brea 3C **166**
  DE72: Dray 4F **165**
  DE72: W Tre 4D **203**
  DE74: C Don 1E **211**
  NG4: Carl 2B **100**
  NG9: Chil 4D **147**
  NG11: King 5F **209**
  NG11: Rudd 5B **174**
  NG12: Rad T 2D **127**
  NG14: Lowd 2E **55**
Green Acre NG8: Woll 5A **94**
Greenacre NG12: Edwal 4A **152**
  NG14: Bur J 2D **79**
Greenacre Av. DE75: Hea 1F **41**
Greenacres DE23: Lit 3A **158**
Greenacres Cl. NG16: Newth . .2B **44**
Greenacres Pk.
  NG2: West Br 4C **124**
Green App. NG4: Carl 2B **100**
Green Av. DE73: Chel 5F **187**
  NG4: Neth 3F **101**
Green Bank DE21: Spon 4C **138**
Greenbank NG4: Carl 4C **100**
Greenbank Ct. NG5: Sher 5B **74**
Greenbanks NG5: Woodt 3D **75**
Greenburn Cl. DE23: Lit 5B **158**
  NG2: Gam 2C **152**
Green Cl. NG12: Key 2E **199**
  NG15: Huck 4B **26**
Green Ct. NG13: Bing 1D **131**
Greencroft NG11: Clif 1E **173**
Greendale Gdns. NG8: Bilb . . .2A **96**
Greendale Rd. NG3: Nott 4B **100**
  NG5: Arn 1E **75**
Greenfield Gro. NG4: Carl 2A **100**
Greenfields NG16: Lang M . . .5F **19**
Greenfields Av. DE23: Lit 4A **158**
Greenfields Dr. NG12: Cotg . . .1E **179**
Greenfield St. NG7: Nott 4C **120**
Greenfinch Cl. DE21: Spon . . .2E **139**
Greenford Cl. NG16: Nuth 4D **71**
Greengates Av. NG3: Mapp . . .4E **75**
Greenhill Av. DE5: Rip 1D **17**
Greenhill Cres. NG4: Carl 4D **101**
GREENHILLOCKS 2D **17**
Greenhill Ri. NG4: Carl 3D **101**
Greenhill Rd. NG4: Carl 4D **101**
Greenhills Av. NG16: Eastw . . .1F **43**
Greenhills Rd. NG16: Eastw . . .1E **43**
Greenland Av. DE22: Mac 3A **134**
Greenland Cres. NG9: Chil . . .4B **146**
Green La. DE1: Der 5C **6** (3F **135**)
  DE7: Ilk 3F **91**
  DE24: Alv 3A **162**
  DE56: Bel 5E **13**
  DE65: Burn 2E **181**
  DE72: Ock 3B **140**

Green La. DE73: Bar T 5A **200**
   DE74: Dise 5A **212**
   NG4: Lamb 3A **54**
   NG11: Clif 1C **172**
Green Leas DE72: Ast T 1F **203**
Green Leys NG2: West Br 4B **150**
Green M., The NG5: Bestw . . .2F **73**
Greenmount Cl. DE23: Lit 5F **157**
Green Pk. DE22: Mac 2F **133**
Green Platt NG12: Cotg 5D **155**
Greens Farm La. NG4: Ged 5F **77**
Greenside Cl.
   NG10: Long E 4D **169**
Greenside Ct. DE3: Mick 1B **156**
Greenside Vw. DE7: Smal 1E **63**
Greenside Wlk. NG3: Nott 4B **100**
Greens La. NG16: Kimb 1E **69**
Green St. NG2: Nott 4C **122**
   NG11: Bart F, Thru 5E **171**
Green's Windmill (Mus.) 1E **123**
Greenville Cft. DE73: Chel . . .5D **187**
Green Way DE65: Find 4C **102**
Greenway, The DE72: Elv 1C **188**
   NG10: Sand 2A **144**
Greenway Cl. DE72: Bor 5A **140**
   NG12: Rad T 2D **127**
Greenway Dr. DE23: Lit 2F **157**
GREENWICH 4D **9**
Greenwich Av. NG6: Basf 3B **72**
Greenwich Dr. Nth.
   DE22: Mac 2A **134**
Greenwich Dr. Sth.
   DE22: Mac 3F **133**
Greenwich Pk. Cl.
   NG2: West Br 3B **150**
Greenwood Av. DE7: Ilk 3F **91**
   DE21: Chad 5E **109**
   NG3: Nott 5C **100**
   NG15: Huck 1E **25**
Greenwood Ct.
   DE1: Der 1D **7** (2F **135**)
   NG9: Chil 3C **146**
Greenwood Cres.
   NG4: Carl 4D **101**
Greenwood Gdns.
   NG11: Rudd 5C **174**
Greenwood Rd. NG3: Nott 5F **99**
   NG4: Carl 5F **99**
Greenwood Va. NG15: Huck . . .1D **25**
Greet Ct. NG7: Radf 3C **96**
Greetwell Cl. NG8: Bilb 4F **95**
Gregg Av. DE75: Hea 2E **41**
Gregory Av. DE72: Brea 3B **166**
   NG3: Mapp 5F **75**
   NG7: Lent 2E **121**
   NG16: Lang M 1F **41**
Gregory Blvd. NG7: H Grn 3D **97**
Gregory Cl. NG8: Stap 5E **117**
Gregory Ct. NG7: H Grn 2E **97**
   NG7: Lent 2D **121**
   NG9: Chil 4A **146**
Gregory St. DE7: Ilk 2D **91**
   NG7: Lent 2D **121**
Gregorys Way DE23: Lit 4B **14**
Gregory Wlk. DE23: Lit 4D **157**
Gregson Gdns. NG9: Toton . . .2A **170**
Gregson Rd. NG9: Chil 5F **145**
Grenay Ct. NG11: Rudd 3A **174**
   (not continuous)
Grendon Cl. DE56: Bel 3A **14**
Grenfell Av. DE23: Der 5D **160**
Grenfell Ter. NG6: Basf 3D **73**
Grenville Dr. DE7: Ilk 4E **67**
   NG9: Stap 5D **117**

Grenville Ri. NG5: Arn 3E **51**
Grenville Rd. NG9: Bee 4A **148**
Grenvoir Dr. DE5: Rip 5F **9**
Gresham Cl. NG2: West Br . . .1B **150**
Gresham Gdns.
   NG2: West Br 1C **150**
   NG5: Woodt 2F **75**
Gresham Rd. DE24: Der 3B **160**
Gresley Dr. NG2: Nott 2E **123**
Gresley Rd. DE7: Ilk 1E **91**
Gretton Rd. NG3: Mapp 3F **75**
Greyfriar Ga.
   NG1: Nott 5B **4** (2B **122**)
Greyfriars Cl. DE75: Hea 4E **41**
Greyhound St.
   NG1: Nott 2C **4** (1B **122**)
Greys Rd. NG5: Woodt 3E **75**
Greystoke Dr. NG8: Bilb 3B **94**
Grey St. DE22: Der 5B **6** (4E **135**)
   NG16: Newth 3F **43**
Greythorn Dr. NG2: West Br . .4C **150**
Grierson Av. NG5: Bestw 4A **50**
Griffin Cl. DE24: Alv 4E **161**
Griffiths Way NG15: Huck 3A **26**
Griffon Rd. DE7: Ilk 1E **115**
Griffs Hollow NG4: Carl 3D **101**
Grimes Ga. DE74: Dise 5B **212**
Grimesmoor Rd. NG14: Calv . . .1F **31**
Grimsby Ter.
   NG3: Nott 1C **4** (4B **98**)
Grimshaw Av. DE24: Alv 4A **162**
Grimston Rd. NG7: Radf 4D **97**
Grindlow Rd. DE21: Chad 5F **109**
Grindon Cres. NG6: Bulw 2B **48**
Grindslow Av. DE7: West H . . .2D **89**
Grinsbrook NG7: Lent 1D **121**
Gripps, The NG12: Cotg 1E **179**
   (off Owthorpe Rd.)
Gripps Comn. NG12: Cotg 1E **179**
Grisedale Ct. NG9: Chil 4F **145**
Gritley M. NG2: Nott 3A **122**
Grizedale Gro. NG13: Bing . . .2A **130**
Groombridge Cres.
   DE23: Lit 5F **157**
Groome Av. DE75: Los 5B **18**
Grosvenor Av. DE72: Brea 3E **167**
   NG3: Mapp P 1B **98**
   NG10: Long E 2F **193**
Grosvenor Cl. NG12: Rad T . . .2C **128**
Grosvenor Ct. NG3: Mapp P . .2B **98**
Grosvenor Dr. DE23: Lit 5F **157**
Grosvenor Rd. DE5: Rip 5C **8**
   NG16: Eastw 1E **43**
Grosvenor St. DE24: Der 2B **160**
   (not continuous)
Grouville Dr. NG5: Woodt 2F **75**
Grove, The DE3: Mick 1D **157**
   DE5: Rip 5C **8**
   DE72: Brea 3E **167**
   NG5: Sher 5A **74**
   NG7: Radf 4E **97**
   NG14: Calv 2F **31**
Grove Av. NG7: Radf 4F **97**
   NG9: Chil 2D **147**
Grovebury Dr. DE23: Lit 1B **104**
Grove Cl. DE72: Thul 2E **189**
   NG14: Bur J 2E **79**
Grove Ct. DE5: Rip 1E **17**
   DE72: Thul 2E **189**
   NG9: Chil 2C **146**
Grove Ho DE23: Der 5F **135**
Grove M. NG16: Eastw 3D **43**
Grove Pk. DE65: Etw 4A **180**
Grover Av. NG3: Mapp 4F **75**

Grove Rd. NG7: Lent 2E **121**
   NG13: Bing 1E **131**
Groveside Cres. NG11: Clif . . .5B **148**
Groves Nook DE73: Chel 5D **187**
Grove St. DE23: Der 5F **135**
   NG9: Bee 3F **147**
Grundy St. NG7: H Grn 3D **97**
Gt Northern Ct.
   DE1: Der 3A **6** (3D **135**)
Guardian Ct. NG8: Aspl 2B **96**
Guildhall Theatre 2D **7** (3F **135**)
Guinea Cl. NG10: Long E 4F **167**
Gunn Cl. NG6: Bulw 5F **47**
Gunnersbury Way
   NG16: Nuth 4C **70**
GUNTHORPE 2F **81**
Gunthorpe Cl. NG5: Sher 4A **74**
Gunthorpe Dr. NG5: Sher 4A **74**
Gunthorpe Rd. NG4: Ged 4B **76**
   NG14: Lowd 4D **57**
Gurney Av. DE23: Der 5C **158**
Gutersloh Ct. NG9: Stap 5E **117**
Guy Cl. NG9: Stap 2D **145**
Gwenbrook Av. NG9: Chil 3D **147**
Gwenbrook Rd. NG9: Chil 3D **147**
Gwndy Gdns. NG5: Bestw 5F **49**
Gypsy La. DE72: Dray 3D **165**

Habitat, The NG1: Nott 3D **5**
Hackworth Cl. NG16: Newth . . .1A **44**
Hadbury Rd. NG5: Sher 4E **73**
Hadden Ct. NG8: Bilb 5C **94**
Haddon Cl. DE7: West H 2D **89**
   DE22: All 2C **106**
   DE75: Hea 2B **40**
   NG4: Carl 5C **76**
   NG15: Huck 3F **25**
Haddon Cres. NG9: Chil 5B **146**
Haddon Dr. DE3: Mick 5D **133**
   DE21: L Eat 5B **60**
   DE21: Spon 4E **139**
   DE22: All 2C **106**
Haddon Nurseries DE7: Ilk . . .4D **67**
Haddon Rd. NG2: West Br 2E **151**
Haddon St. DE7: Ilk 2D **91**
   DE23: Der 2D **159**
   NG5: Sher 5A **74**
Haddon Way NG10: Long E . . .2E **193**
   NG12: Rad T 1F **127**
Hadleigh Cl. NG9: Toton 1D **169**
Hadley St. DE7: Ilk 5F **91**
Hadrian Gdns. NG5: Top V 2F **49**
Hadstock Cl. NG10: Sand 4A **144**
Hagg La. DE7: D Ab, West H . . .5C **88**
   (not continuous)
   NG14: Epp 4F **33**
Hagley Cl. NG3: Nott 4F **99**
Haig St. DE24: Alv 3E **161**
Haileybury Cres.
   NG2: West Br 3E **151**
Haileybury Rd.
   NG2: West Br 3E **151**
Hailsham Cl. DE3: Mick 5C **132**
Hains Cl. DE24: Sin 2E **185**
Haise Ct. NG6: Bulw 2E **71**
Halberton Dr.
   NG2: West Br 4C **150**
Hales Cl. NG12: Cotg 5D **155**
Halfacre Gdns. DE7: Ilk 5E **67**
Halifax Cl. DE21: Chad 4B **108**
Halifax Ct. NG8: Stre 5C **70**

Halifax Pl.
 NG1: Nott 4D **5** (1C **122**)
Halina Ct. NG9: Bee 1E **147**
Hallam Ct. DE7: Ilk 4E **67**
HALLAM FIELDS 1F **115**
Hallam Flds.
 DE74: C Don 2F **211**
Hallam Flds. Rd. DE7: Ilk . . .1F **115**
Hallam Rd. NG3: Mapp 5F **75**
 NG9: Bee 2E **147**
Hallams La. NG5: Arn 5E **51**
 NG9: Chil 4B **146**
Hallam Way DE7: West H 2C **88**
 NG16: Lang M 1B **42**
Hall Ct. NG12: Rad T 2D **127**
Hall Ct. DE7: West H 3D **89**
Hall Cft. NG9: Bee 3E **147**
Hallcroft Ct. DE7: Ilk 2E **91**
Hallcroft Rd. DE7: Ilk 2E **91**
Hall Dr. NG8: Woll 2D **119**
 NG9: Chil 3B **146**
 NG10: Sand 2A **144**
Hall Dyke DE21: Spon 3C **138**
Hall Farm Cl.
 DE74: C Don 1F **211**
 NG12: Toll 2C **176**
Hall Farm Ct. DE7: Stan D . . .5E **115**
 NG2: Gam 1B **152**
Hall Farm Rd. DE56: Duff 5D **59**
Hall Farm Way DE7: Smal 5E **39**
Hallfields NG12: Edwal 5A **152**
Hall Gdns. DE74: Hem 5C **206**
 NG9: Bram 1A **146**
Hallgate DE21: Oak 2B **110**
Hallington Dr. DE75: Hea 3C **40**
Hall La. NG15: Pap 1F **11**
 NG16: Brins 2B **20**
Hall M. NG15: Pap 2F **11**
Hallowell Dr. NG8: Woll 4E **95**
Hall Pk. DE73: Bar T 4A **200**
Hall Pk. Cl. DE23: Lit 2A **158**
Hall Pk. Dr. NG16: Eastw 1D **43**
Hall Rd. NG16: Lang M 5B **20**
Halls La. NG16: Newth 4F **43**
Halls Rd. NG9: Stap 2C **144**
Hall St. DE24: Alv 4F **161**
 NG5: Sher 4C **74**
Hall Vw. Dr. NG8: Bilb 4C **94**
Halstead Cl. NG8: Cin 4A **72**
 NG9: Chil 4B **146**
Halstock Dr. DE24: Alv 3B **162**
Haltham Wlk. NG11: Clif 3C **172**
Hambledon Dr.
 DE24: S Flds 4C **184**
 NG8: Woll 5A **96**
Hambleton Cl.
 NG10: Long E 2F **167**
Hamblin Cres. DE24: Sin 2E **185**
Hambling Cl. NG6: Bulw 5F **47**
Hamilton, The *NG7: Lent 3D 121*
 (off Leen Ct.)
Hamilton Cl. DE3: Mick 5E **133**
 NG5: Arn 3B **52**
 NG9: Toton 1E **169**
Hamilton Ct.
 NG7: Nott 5A **4** (2A **122**)
 NG11: Clif 5E **149**
Hamilton Dr.
 NG7: Nott 5A **4** (2A **122**)
 NG12: Rad T 1E **127**
Hamilton Gdns.
 NG5: Sher 1A 98
 (off Alexandra St.)
Hamilton Pl. NG2: Nott 1E **123**

Hamilton Rd. DE21: Spon 2E **139**
 DE23: Der 1E **159**
 NG5: Sher 2A **98**
 NG10: Long E 2C **168**
Hamlet, The DE75: Hea 1D **41**
Hamlet Ct. DE73: Chel 5D **187**
HAMMERSMITH 2C **8**
Hammersmith Dr. DE75: Rip 3C **8**
Hammersmith Cl.
 NG12: Rad T 3C **128**
 NG16: Nuth 3D **71**
Hammersmith Station
 Midland Railway Cen. . . .2C **8**
Hampden NG1: Nott 1A **4** (4A **98**)
Hampden Gro. NG9: Bee 2D **147**
Hampden St. DE23: Der 3F **159**
 NG1: Nott 1A **4** (4A **98**)
 NG16: Gilt 4A **44**
 NG16: Lang M 1A **42**
Hampstead Ct. *NG5: Sher 4B 74*
 (off St Albans St.)
Hampstead Dr. DE22: Mac 2F **133**
Hampstead Rd. NG3: Nott 1D **99**
Hampton Cl. DE7: West H 2C **88**
 DE21: Spon 3E **139**
 NG9: Toton 5D **145**
Hampton Ct. DE75: Hea 2C **40**
Hampton Rd. NG2: West Br . . .2D **151**
Hanbury Rd. DE21: Chad 2D **137**
Handel St. DE24: Der 3B **160**
 NG3: Nott 2F **5** (5D **99**)
Handford Ct. DE1: Der 3D **135**
Handford St. DE22: Der 3C **134**
Hand's Rd. DE75: Hea 3E **41**
Handyside St.
 DE1: Der 1C **6** (2F **135**)
Hanger Bank DE72: Ast T 1A **204**
Hankin St. NG15: Huck 3B **26**
Hanley Av. NG9: Bram 5A **118**
Hanley St. NG1: Nott 2A **4** (5A **98**)
Hannah Cres. NG11: Wilf 1A **150**
Hanover Cl. NG8: Bilb 4C **94**
Hanover Sq. DE22: Mac 2F **133**
Hansard Ga.
 DE21: Der 2F **7** (3B **136**)
Hanslope Cres. NG8: Bilb 4C **94**
Hanslynn DE72: Thul 2E **189**
Hanson Cres. NG15: Huck 2F **25**
Hanwell Way DE22: Mac 2A **134**
Hanworth Gdns. NG5: Arn 4C **50**
Harberton Cl. NG5: Redh 3D **51**
Harby Dr. NG8: Woll 1B **120**
Harcourt Cl. DE7: Ilk 1C **90**
Harcourt Cres. NG16: Nuth 4E **71**
Harcourt Pl. DE74: C Don 5A **206**
Harcourt Rd. NG7: H Grn 2E **97**
Harcourt St.
 DE1: Der 5B **6** (4E **135**)
 NG9: Bee 2D **147**
Harcourt Ter. NG3: Nott 1E **5**
Harden Ct. NG11: Clif 3B **172**
Hardhurst Rd. DE24: Alv 1A **188**
Hardigate Rd.
 NG12: Crop Bu 5E **129**
Hardstaff Almshouses
 NG4: Ged 5D **77**
Hardstaff Homes, The
 NG16: Gilt 4B **44**
Hardstaff Rd. NG2: Nott 5F **99**
Hardwick Av. DE7: West H 2D **89**
 DE22: All 2C **106**
Hardwick Cl. DE5: Rip 3B **8**

Hardwick Ct. NG10: Long E . . .2E **193**
Hardwick Dr. DE3: Mick 1D **157**
Hardwicke Rd. NG9: Chil 5B **146**
Hardwick Gro.
 NG2: West Br 4E **123**
 NG7: Nott 1F **121**
 NG13: Bing 2C **130**
Hardwick Pl. DE7: Kirk H 5B **90**
Hardwick Rd. NG5: Sher 4B **74**
 NG7: Nott 2F **121**
Hardwick St. DE24: Der 3B **160**
Hardwood Cl. NG6: Bulw 5F **47**
Hardy Barn DE75: Ship 4F **41**
Hardy Cl. NG10: Long E 5C **168**
 NG16: Kimb 5E **45**
Hardy Cres. DE5: Cod 1A **18**
Hardy's Dr. NG4: Ged 1E **101**
Hardy St. NG7: Radf 4F **97**
 NG16: Kimb 5E **45**
Harebell Cl. DE21: Oak 2F **109**
Harebell Gdns. NG13: Bing . . .2B **130**
Harepit Cl. DE24: Alv 1F **187**
Harewood Av. NG6: Bulw 2C **72**
Harewood Cl. DE56: Bel 4C **14**
 NG10: Sand 4F **143**
 NG12: Rad T 2F **127**
Harewood Rd. DE22: All 2C **106**
Hargrave Av. DE72: Ock 3B **180**
Hargreaves Cl. DE23: Lit 5F **157**
Hargreaves St. DE7: Ilk 4F **91**
Harkstead Rd. NG5: Top V 3A **50**
Harlaxton Dr. NG7: Lent 1E **121**
 NG10: Long E 2F **169**
Harlaxton Wlk. NG3: Nott 4B **98**
Harlech Cl. DE7: Ilk 4B **66**
 DE21: Spon 3F **139**
Harlech Ri. NG9: Chil 4A **146**
HARLEQUIN 1A **128**
Harlequin Cl. NG12: Rad T 2A **128**
Harlequin Cl. NG16: Eastw 1C **42**
Harlequin M. NG12: Rad T 1A **128**
Harlesden Av. DE22: Mac 1F **133**
Harley St. NG7: Lent 2E **121**
Harlow Cl. DE24: Alv 2E **187**
Harlow Ct. DE7: West H 3C **88**
Harlow Gro. NG4: Ged 5D **77**
Harmston Ri. NG5: Sher 3E **73**
 (not continuous)
Harnett Cl.
 NG1: Nott 4D **5** (1C **122**)
Harold Av. NG16: Lang M 5A **20**
Harold Ct. DE23: Der 1A **160**
 NG2: Nott 3F **5** (1D **123**)
Harold St. NG2: Nott . . .3F **5** (1D **123**)
Harpenden Sq. NG8: Cin 4F **71**
Harpole Wlk. NG5: Arn 2E **51**
Harpswell Cl. DE22: D Abb . . .3D **107**
Harpur Av. DE23: Lit 4A **158**
Harrier Gro. NG15: Huck 5D **25**
Harrier Rd. DE56: Bel 4B **14**
Harrier Way DE24: Sin 3D **185**
Harriet St. DE23: Der 5F **135**
Harriett St. NG9: Stap 1C **144**
Harriet Tubman Ho.
 DE23: Der 2E **159**
Harrimans Dr.
 DE72: Brea 3E **167**
Harrimans La. NG7: Lent 5C **120**
Harringay Gdns.
 DE22: Mac 2B **134**
Harrington Av. DE72: Bor 1B **164**
Harrington Cl. NG4: Ged 1A **102**
Harrington Dr. NG7: Lent 1E **121**
Harrington Rd. DE23: Lit 2B **158**

Harrington St. DE23: Der 3F **159**
   DE24: A'ton 5D **161**
   DE72: Dray 4A **166**
   NG10: Long E 1A **194**
Harris Av. DE5: Rip 4B **8**
Harris Cl. DE5: Rip 5B **8**
   NG8: Woll 5E **95**
Harrison Ct. NG13: Bing 2B **130**
Harrison Rd. NG9: Stap 5C **116**
Harrison's Plantation Nature Reserve
   . . . . .5F **95**
Harrison St. DE22: Der 5D **135**
Harris Rd. NG9: Chil 2C **146**
Harrogate Cres.
   DE21: Chad 4C **108**
Harrogate Rd. NG3: Nott . . .5B **100**
Harrogate St. NG4: Neth . . .3E **101**
Harrowby Rd. NG7: Lent 1E **121**
Harrow Dr. DE7: Ilk 1F **115**
Harrow Gdns. NG8: Woll 1B **120**
Harrow Rd. NG2: West Br . . .3D **151**
   NG8: Woll 1F **119**
   NG15: Huck 4C **24**
Harrow St. DE24: Der 2D **161**
Harry Peel Ct. NG9: Bee 2F **147**
Harston Gdns.
   NG2: West Br 5A **150**
Hartcroft Rd. NG5: Bestw . . .1F **73**
Hartford Cl. NG2: Nott 3C **122**
Hartill Cl. NG9: Chil 1B **170**
Hartington Av. NG4: Carl 1C **100**
   NG15: Huck 3B **24**
Hartington Cl. DE7: West H . .2D **89**
Hartington Pl. DE7: Ilk 2D **67**
Hartington Rd. NG5: Sher 4B **74**
Hartington St.
   DE23: Der 5D **7** (5F **135**)
Hartington Way DE3: Mick . . .2C **156**
Hartland Dr. DE23: Der 5D **159**
Hart Lea NG10: Sand 2A **144**
Hartley Cl. NG7: Radf 4E **97**
Hartley Dr. NG9: Bee 2A **148**
Hartley Rd. NG7: Radf 4D **97**
Hartness Rd. NG11: Clif 2B **172**
Hartshay Cl. DE7: Ilk 2E **67**
Hartshay Hill DE5: L Har 3A **8**
   DE5: Rip 3B **8**
Hartshorne Rd. DE23: Lit . . .5B **158**
Hartside Cl. NG2: Gam 1B **152**
Hartside Gdns.
   NG10: Long E 3F **167**
Hartside Way DE75: Hea 3A **42**
Hart St. NG7: Lent 2E **121**
Hartwell St. NG3: Nott 4C **98**
Hartwood Dr. NG9: Stap 4C **116**
Harvest Cl. NG5: Top V 4E **49**
   NG13: Bing 2C **130**
Harvester Cl. DE5: Rip 4B **8**
Harvest Way DE21: Oak 2B **110**
Harvey Cl. NG11: Rudd 1C **196**
Harvey Ct. DE74: C Don 1A **212**
   NG7: Nott 3D **121**
Harvey Cft. NG9: Trow 1B **116**
Harvey Hadden Sports Cen. . . .3D **95**
Harvey Hadden Stadium 3E **95**
Harvey Rd. DE24: A'ton 5D **161**
   DE74: C Don 2A **212**
   NG7: Nott 3C **120**
   NG8: Bilb 3E **95**
Harwich Cl. NG6: Bulw 4F **47**
Harwill Cres. NG8: Aspl 5A **72**
Harwood Cl. NG5: Arn 4A **52**
Hasgill Cl. DE21: Oak 2B **110**

Haskeys Cl. DE22: All 3B **106**
Haslam's La.
   DE22: D Abb 4A **108**
Haslam St.
   NG7: Nott 5A **4** (2A **122**)
Haslemere Ct. DE23: Der 1A **160**
Haslemere Rd. NG8: Aspl 2C **96**
Hassall Ct. NG13: Bing 2E **131**
Hassock La. Nth.
   DE75: Ship 5A **42**
Hassock La. Sth.
   DE75: Ship 1B **66**
Hassocks, The NG9: Bee 1A **148**
Hassocks La. NG9: Bee 1A **148**
Hassop Rd. DE21: Chad 5F **109**
Hastings St. DE23: Der 2F **159**
   (not continuous)
   DE74: C Don 2A **212**
   NG4: Carl 3B **100**
Haswell Rd. NG6: Bulw 2A **72**
Hatchmere Cl. DE21: Oak . . .4F **109**
Hatfield Av. NG10: Sand 4A **144**
Hatfield Dr. NG2: West Br . . .4B **150**
Hatfield Rd. DE24: Alv 1E **187**
   NG3: Mapp P 1B **98**
Hatherleigh Cl. NG3: Mapp . .1B **76**
Hathern Cl. DE23: Der 1D **185**
   NG10: Long E 1C **194**
Hathern Grn. NG9: Lent A . . .5F **119**
Hathersage Av. DE23: Der . . .3D **159**
   NG10: Long E 1E **193**
Hatley Cl. NG2: Nott 4A **122**
Hatton Cl. NG5: Arn 2D **89**
Hatton Crofts NG10: Long E . .5B **168**
Hatton Gdns. NG16: Nuth . . .4D **71**
Haulton Dr. DE74: C Don 5F **205**
Havelock Gdns.
   NG3: Nott 1E **5** (4C **98**)
Havelock Rd. DE23: Der 3E **159**
Havelock St. DE5: Rip 4D **9**
   DE7: Ilk 3E **67**
Havenbaulk Av. DE23: Lit . . .4D **157**
Haven Baulk La. DE23: Lit . . .4C **156**
Haven Cl. NG2: West Br 3C **150**
Haven Ct. DE24: Alv 5C **162**
Havenwood Gro. DE23: Lit . . .1B **184**
Havenwood Ri. NG11: Clif . . .3C **172**
Haverhill Cres. NG5: Top V . . .2C **48**
Haversham Cl. NG5: Basf 5C **72**
Hawarden Ter. NG7: H Grn . . .3E **97**
Hawke St. DE22: Der 3B **134**
Hawkhurst Dr. NG8: Woll 3C **118**
Hawkins Ct. DE7: Ilk 3E **67**
Hawkridge Gdns.
   NG3: Nott 1E **5** (5D **99**)
Hawksdale Cl. DE73: Chel . . .4F **187**
Hawkshead Av. DE21: Chad . .4C **108**
Hawkshead Cl.
   NG2: West Br 3C **152**
Hawksley Gdns.
   NG11: Clif 1B **172**
Hawksley Rd. NG7: H Grn 3E **97**
Hawkswood Cl. NG9: Chil 4A **146**
Hawksworth Av. NG5: Sher . . .3C **74**
Hawksworth Rd.
   NG2: West Br 4E **123**
Hawksworth St.
   NG3: Nott 1F **5** (5D **99**)
Hawley Mt. NG5: Sher 4E **75**
Haworth Ct. NG11: Clif 2B **172**
Hawthorn Av. DE5: Rip 1C **16**
   DE72: Brea 3E **167**
   NG15: Huck 2E **25**

Hawthorn Cl. NG2: Nott 4A **122**
   NG12: Edwal 4A **152**
   NG12: Key 4D **199**
   NG14: Woodbo 5B **32**
Hawthorn Ct. DE1: Der 1E **135**
Hawthorn Cres. DE65: Find . .4C **182**
   NG5: Arn 3F **51**
Hawthorne Av. DE24: Alv . . .4F **161**
   DE72: Bor 5A **140**
   NG9: Stap 2C **144**
   NG10: Long E 5B **168**
   NG12: Cotg 1E **179**
Hawthorne Cl. DE56: Kil 2E **37**
Hawthorne Gro. NG9: Bee . . .2A **148**
Hawthorne Lodge
   NG2: West Br 4A **124**
Hawthorne Ri. NG16: Aws 3A **68**
Hawthorn Rd. DE74: C Don . . .4A **206**
Hawthorns, The DE21: L Eat . . .2C **84**
   DE56: Bel 4C **14**
Hawthorn St. DE24: Der 3B **160**
Hawthorn Vw. NG2: Nott 3A **122**
   (not continuous)
Hawthorn Wlk. NG3: Nott . . .3A **100**
Hawton Cres. NG8: Woll 1B **120**
Hawton Spinney NG8: Woll . .1B **120**
Hawtrey Gdns. DE24: Alv 5F **161**
Haycroft Ct. DE23: Lit 4F **157**
Hayden La. NG15: Lin 4D **11**
   (not continuous)
Haydn Av. NG5: Sher 5A **74**
Haydn Rd. DE21: Chad 5E **109**
   NG5: Sher 5F **73**
Haydock Cl. NG16: Kimb 5D **45**
Haydock Pk. Rd. DE24: Der . .3D **161**
Hayes, The DE65: Find 5B **182**
Hayes Av. DE23: Der 3C **158**
   DE72: Brea 4A **166**
Hayes Cl. DE7: West H 2D **89**
Hayes Rd. NG12: Key 3C **198**
Hayeswood Rd. DE7: Stan C . .1F **87**
Hayfield Cl. DE56: Bel 4A **14**
Hayfield Gdns. DE23: Lit 5A **158**
Hayford Pl. DE22: Der 4C **134**
Hayles Cl. NG5: Bestw 1A **74**
Hayley Cl. NG16: Kimb 1C **68**
Hayley Cft. DE56: Duff 1E **83**
Hayling Cl. DE7: Ilk 4B **66**
Hayling Dr. NG8: Basf 1C **96**
Haymarket DE1: Der 3C **6**
Haynes Av. NG9: Trow 5B **92**
Haynes Cl. NG11: Clif 5E **149**
Hay's Cl. DE7: Ilk 5C **66**
Haywood Cl. DE24: Alv 1F **187**
Haywood Ct.
   NG2: Nott 3F **5** (1D **123**)
Haywood Rd. NG3: Mapp 5E **75**
Haywood St.
   NG2: Nott 3F **5** (1D **123**)
Hayworth Rd. NG10: Sand . . .3A **144**
Hazelas Dr. NG14: Gun 2F **81**
Hazel Av. DE23: Lit 5C **158**
Hazelbank Av. NG3: Nott 1E **99**
Hazel Cl. DE65: Find 4D **183**
   DE75: Hea 3C **40**
   NG2: West Br 4B **124**
   NG13: Bing 2F **131**
Hazeldene Cl. DE56: Duff 2D **59**
Hazel Dr. DE21: Spon 2F **139**
   NG16: Nuth 1A **70**
HAZELGROVE 4F **25**
Hazel Gro. DE56: Duff 4D **59**
   NG3: Mapp 3F **75**
   NG15: Huck 4F **25**

Hazel Hill Cres. NG5: Bestw . . .4A **50**
Hazelhurst Gdns. NG6: Bulw . . .5A **48**
Hazel Mdws. NG15: Huck 4F **25**
Hazelmere Gro. NG7: Lent 1D **121**
Hazelrigg Cl. DE74: C Don . . .5E **205**
Hazel St. NG6: Bulw 4A **48**
(not continuous)
Hazeltree Cl. DE5: Rip 1B **16**
Hazel Way NG15: Lin 4D **11**
HAZELWOOD 4B **34**
Hazelwood NG12: Cotg 5F **155**
Hazelwood Cl. NG16: Newth . . .2A **44**
Hazelwood Dr. NG15: Huck 3B **24**
Hazelwood Hill DE56: Haz 4A **34**
Hazelwood Rd. DE21: Chad . . .5E **109**
DE56: Haz 5B **34**
NG7: H Grn 3D **97**
Headingley Ct. DE23: Lit 3B **158**
Headingley Gdns. NG8: Aspl . . .2C **96**
Heafield Dr. DE74: Keg 2C **214**
Heage Rd. DE5: Rip 5A **8**
Heage Rd. Ind. Est. DE5: Rip . .5A **8**
Healey Cl. NG2: Nott 3B **122**
HEANOR 2D **41**
Heanor & District Heritage Cen.
. . . . .4E **41**
HEANOR GATE 4B **40**
Heanor Ga. Ind. Est.
DE75: Hea 3C **40**
(not continuous)
Heanor Ga. Rd. DE75: Hea 3B **40**
Heanor Ho. DE21: Spon 5D **139**
Heanor Leisure Cen. 3E **41**
Heanor Retail Pk.
DE75: Hea 2D **41**
Heanor Rd. DE5: Cod 2A **18**
DE5: Den 1F **39**
DE7: Ilk 2C **66**
DE7: Smal 1E **63**
DE75: Hea 1E **63**
DE75: Los 5B **18**
Heard Cres. NG9: Bee 5E **119**
Heath, The NG16: Gilt 4F **43**
Heath Av. DE23: Lit 2B **158**
Heathcoat Bldg. NG7: Nott . . .4C **120**
Heathcoat St.
NG1: Nott 3D **5** (1C **122**)
Heathcote Cl. DE24: Alv 1A **188**
Heathcotes Cotts. DE1: Der . . .5F **135**
Heath Ct. DE24: Sin 3D **185**
Heather Cl. DE24: S Flds 4C **184**
NG3: Nott 3C **98**
NG16: Newth 3A **44**
Heather Ct. DE75: Hea 3A **42**
Heather Cres. DE23: Lit 5B **158**
DE72: Brea 3E **167**
Heather Cft. NG2: West Br 4B **150**
Heatherington Gdns.
NG5: Top V 3F **49**
Heatherley Dr. NG6: Basf 3E **73**
Heathermead Cl.
DE21: Oak 4E **109**
Heather Ri. NG9: Bram 4D **119**
Heather Rd. NG4: Carl 1C **100**
HEATHERTON 5F **157**
Heathervale NG2: West Br . . .2A **150**
Heathfield Av. DE7: Ilk 2F **91**
Heathfield Gro. NG9: Chil 5B **146**
Heathfield Rd. NG5: Sher 3E **73**
Heath Gdns. DE72: Brea 3F **167**
Heath La. DE65: Find 5C **182**
(not continuous)
Heath Rd. DE5: Rip 5C **8**
Heaton Cl. NG3: Nott 1E **99**

Hebden Cl. DE23: Lit 5E **157**
Hebrides Cl. DE24: Sin 3C **184**
Heckington Dr. NG8: Woll 5A **96**
Hedderley Wlk.
NG3: Nott 1D **5** (4C **98**)
Heddington Gdns.
NG5: Arn 4C **50**
Hedgebank Ct. DE21: Oak 2B **110**
Hedgerow Gdns.
DE21: Oak 2B **110**
Hedges Dr. DE7: Ilk 1E **115**
Hedgevale Cl. DE23: Lit 4F **157**
Hedingham Cl. DE7: Ilk 2C **90**
Hedingham Way DE3: Mick . . .2B **156**
Hedley St. NG7: Basf 2F **97**
Hedley Vs. NG7: Basf 1F **97**
Heigham Cl. DE24: S Loc 3C **186**
Helen Cl. NG9: Chil 2C **146**
Hellebore Cl. NG5: Top V 5D **49**
Helm Cl. NG6: Bulw 5E **47**
Helmsdale Cl. NG5: Arn 3A **52**
Helmsdale Gdns.
NG5: Top V 3E **49**
Helmsley Dr. NG16: Eastw 1C **42**
Helston Cl. DE24: Alv 5A **162**
Helston Dr. NG8: Stre 5C **70**
Helvellyn Cl. NG2: Nott 3B **122**
Helvellyn Way
NG10: Long E 1A **168**
HEMINGTON 4C **206**
Hemington Cl. DE74: Hem 5B **206**
Hemington Hill DE74: Hem 5B **206**
Hemington La. DE74: Lock 4D **207**
Hemingway Cl. NG4: Carl 3B **100**
NG16: Newth 3B **44**
Hemlock Av. NG9: Stap 5D **117**
NG10: Long E 2C **168**
Hemlock Cl. DE21: Oak 2F **109**
Hemlock Gdns. NG6: Bulw 1E **71**
Hemlock La. DE7: Kirk H 5C **90**
Hempshill La. NG6: Bulw 1E **71**
(Low Wood Rd.)
NG6: Bulw 1A **72**
(Sellers Wood Dr.)
HEMPSHILL VALE 2E **71**
Hemsby Gdns. NG6: Bulw 4A **48**
(not continuous)
Hemscott Cl. NG6: Bulw 4E **47**
Hemswell Cl. NG3: Nott 5F **99**
Hendon Ct. NG3: Nott 2E **99**
Hendon Ri. NG3: Nott 2E **99**
Hendon Way DE22: Mac 2A **134**
Hendre Gdns. NG5: Top V 5F **49**
Henley Cl. NG4: Neth 4F **101**
Henley Gdns. NG9: Stap 4D **117**
Henley Grn. DE22: Mac 2E **133**
Henley Ri. NG5: Sher 4F **73**
Henley Way DE7: West H 2C **88**
Hennessey Cl. NG9: Chil 1B **170**
Henning Gdns. NG5: Top V 4F **49**
Henrietta St. NG6: Bulw 1B **72**
Henry Ct. NG2: Nott 3B **122**
Henry Rd. NG2: West Br 5D **123**
NG7: Lent 2E **121**
NG9: Bee 2F **147**
Henry St. DE1: Der 2E **135**
(not continuous)
DE5: Rip 4C **8**
NG2: Nott 3F **5** (1D **123**)
NG5: Redh 2D **51**
NG15: Huck 3A **26**
Henshaw Av. DE7: Kirk H 5C **90**
Henshaw Pl. DE7: Ilk 3D **67**
Henson Cl. NG12: Rad T 2D **129**

Henson La.
NG12: Crop Bu, Rad T . . .1D **129**
Hensons Row NG6: Basf 5C **72**
Hensons Sq. NG9: Bram 5A **118**
(not continuous)
Hepple Dr. NG6: Bulw 5E **47**
Herald Cl. NG9: Bee 1A **148**
Herald Gro. DE73: Chel 1D **201**
Herald Way DE74: N Air 4C **212**
Herbert Buzzard Ct.
NG15: Huck 3B **26**
(off Hankin St.)
Herbert Rd. NG5: Sher 1A **98**
Hereford Rd. DE21: Chad 5C **108**
NG3: Nott 5A **100**
NG4: Ged 4E **77**
NG5: Woodt 2D **75**
Heritage Bus. Cen.
DE56: Bel 3E **35**
Heritage Ct. DE56: Bel 1E **35**
Hermitage Av. DE72: Bor 1B **164**
Hermitage Ct. DE21: Oak 4A **110**
Hermitage Sq. NG2: Nott 1E **123**
Hermitage Wlk. DE7: Ilk 5E **91**
NG7: Nott 2F **121**
Hermon St. NG7: Nott 5F **97**
Heron Dr. NG7: Lent 1D **121**
Herons Ct. NG2: West Br 4B **152**
Heronswood Dr.
DE21: Spon 2C **138**
Heron Way DE3: Mick 1F **157**
Heron Wharf NG7: Lent 3E **121**
Hervey Grn. NG11: Clif 1D **173**
Heskey Cl. NG3: Nott 4B **98**
Heskey Wlk. NG3: Nott 4B **98**
Heslington Av. NG8: Basf 2F **97**
Hethbeth Ct. NG2: Nott 3B **122**
Hethersett Gdns. NG6: Bulw . . .4A **48**
Hetley Rd. NG9: Bee 5E **119**
Hexham Av. DE7: Ilk 1F **115**
Hexham Cl. NG2: West Br 2F **151**
Hexham Gdns. NG5: Top V 2F **49**
Hexham Wlk. DE21: Chad 4D **109**
Heydon Cl. DE56: Bel 3A **14**
Heyes Yd. DE21: Spon 1D **163**
Heyford Ct. DE75: Hea 3F **41**
Hey St. NG10: Long E 2A **194**
Heyworth St. DE22: Der 2C **134**
Hicking Bldg, The
NG2: Nott 2C **122**
Hickings La. NG9: Stap 5D **117**
Hickleton Cl. DE5: Rip 5B **8**
Hickling Cl. DE24: S Loc 3C **186**
Hickling Rd. NG3: Mapp 5F **75**
Hickling Way NG12: Cotg 2F **179**
Hickton Dr. NG9: Chil 2A **170**
Hickton Rd. DE55: Swan 1E **9**
High Bank DE5: Den 2E **39**
Highbank Dr. NG11: Clif 3D **173**
Highbury Av. NG6: Bulw 2B **72**
Highbury Cl. DE22: Mac 2E **133**
NG16: Nuth 4C **70**
Highbury Rd. NG6: Bulw 5B **48**
NG12: Key 2D **199**
HIGHBURY VALE 3C **72**
Highbury Vale Stop (NET) 3C **72**
Highbury Wlk. NG6: Bulw 1B **72**
High Chu. St. NG7: Basf 1E **97**
(not continuous)
Highclere Dr. NG4: Carl 2E **101**
Highcliffe Rd. NG3: Nott 5B **86**
Highcroft NG3: Mapp 3E **75**
High Cft. Cl. NG10: Long E . . .1D **195**

Highcroft Dr. NG8: Woll 5A **94**
Highcross Ct. NG7: Radf 4E **97**
High Cross Leys NG3: Nott 4B **98**
High Cross St.
  NG1: Nott 2D **5** (5C **98**)
High Edge Dr.
  DE56: H'age 1D **15**
High Edge M. DE56: Bel 4E **13**
Highfield Cl. DE75: Los 4A **18**
Highfield Cotts.
  DE21: Chad 3D **137**
Highfield Ct. NG9: Bee 2E **147**
Highfield Dr. DE7: Kirk H 5A **90**
  NG4: Carl 3A **100**
  NG16: Nuth 3E **71**
Highfield Gdns. DE22: Der . . .1E **135**
Highfield Gro.
  NG2: West Br 1E **151**
Highfield La. DE21: Chad . . .3D **137**
Highfield M. DE21: Chad 3D **137**
Highfield Rd. DE21: L Eat 3B **84**
  DE22: Der 1E **135**
  DE23: Lit 4B **158**
  DE56: Bel 2E **35**
  DE56: Kil 4E **37**
  NG2: West Br 1E **151**
  NG7: Nott 4C **120**
  NG9: Chil 4F **145**
  NG12: Key 2D **199**
  NG16: Nuth 3D **71**
Highfields DE5: Cod 1F **17**
Highfields DE15: Huck 3F **25**
Highfields Pk. Dr.
  DE22: D Abb 4D **107**
Highfield St.
  NG10: Long E 1B **168**
Highfield Way DE5: Rip 1B **16**
Highgate Cl. NG4: Carl 5B **76**
Highgate Dr. DE7: Ilk 4B **66**
Highgate Grn. DE22: Mac . . .3F **133**
Highgates
  DE1: Der 5D **7** (4F **135**)
High Gro. DE56: Bel 5C **14**
Highgrove Av. NG9: Chil 2C **146**
Highgrove Ct. DE75: Hea 3B **40**
Highgrove Dr. DE73: Chel . . .4E **187**
Highgrove Gdns.
  NG12: Edwal 4F **151**
High Hazels Ct.
  NG16: Newth 5A **22**
High Hazles Cl. NG4: Ged 4D **77**
High Hazles Rd.
  NG12: Cotg 4F **155**
High Holborn DE7: Ilk 4D **67**
High Holborn Rd. DE5: Rip . . .5F **9**
High Hurst NG14: Calv 2D **31**
Highland Ct. NG5: Basf 5E **73**
High La. Central
  DE7: West H 1E **89**
High La. E. DE7: West H 1F **89**
High La. W. DE7: West H 2B **88**
High Leys Rd.
  NG15: Huck 3E **25**
High Mdw. NG12: Toll 2C **176**
High Mdw. Cl. DE5: Rip 1C **16**
High Pk. Cotts.
  NG16: Newth 3C **22**
High Pavement DE56: Bel 1F **35**
  NG1: Nott 4D **5** (1C **122**)
High Rd. NG9: Bee 2E **147**
  NG9: Chil 3D **147**
  NG9: Toton 1F **169**
High School Stop (NET) 4F **97**
High Spannia NG16: Kimb 5E **45**

High St. DE5: Cod 1A **18**
  DE5: Rip 5C **8**
  DE7: Ilk 2E **91**
  DE56: Bel 5F **13**
  DE56: Kil 4F **37**
  DE73: Chel 5E **187**
  DE74: C Don 2F **211**
  DE74: Keg 2B **214**
  DE75: Hea 2D **41**
  DE75: Los 4B **18**
  NG1: Nott 3C **4** (1B **122**)
  NG5: Arn 5D **51**
  NG9: Stap 1D **145**
  NG10: Long E 3D **169**
  NG11: Rudd 4B **174**
  NG15: Huck 2F **25**
  NG16: Kimb 1E **69**
High St. Av. NG5: Arn 5D **51**
High St. Pl.
  NG1: Nott 3C **4** (1B **122**)
Highurst Ct. NG7: Radf 5F **97**
Highurst St. NG7: Radf 5F **97**
High Vw. Av. NG12: Key 3E **199**
High Vw. Ct. NG3: Mapp P . . .2C **98**
Highwood Av. DE56: Bel 3A **36**
  NG8: Bilb 2E **95**
High Wood Bank
  DE56: Bel 3B **36**
Highwray Gro. NG11: Clif 2C **172**
Hilary Cl. DE56: Bel 4D **15**
  NG8: Woll 2C **118**
Hilcot Dr. NG8: Aspl 1A **96**
Hilderstone Cl. DE24: Alv 5C **162**
Hilditch Way NG7: Radf 5D **97**
Hill, The DE22: D Abb 4F **107**
Hillary Pl. DE7: Kirk H 5A **90**
Hillbeck Cres. NG8: Woll 1B **118**
Hillberry DE5: Rip 5E **9**
Hill Brow DE1: Der 4C **6** (4F **135**)
Hill Cl. DE7: Stan C 1F **87**
  DE21: Spon 4D **139**
  NG2: West Br 2A **152**
  NG16: Newth 3B **44**
Hillcrest DE56: Bel 5D **15**
  DE72: Ast T 5F **189**
Hillcrest Cl. NG16: Want 5F **45**
Hillcrest Dr. DE5: Cod 1A **18**
  DE56: Kil 4F **37**
  NG15: Huck 3C **24**
Hillcreste Dr. DE73: Chel 3E **187**
Hillcrest Gdns. NG14: Bur J . . .2D **79**
Hillcrest Gro. NG5: Sher 4A **74**
Hill Crest Pk. Ind. Est.
  NG14: Calv 1E **31**
Hillcrest Rd. DE21: Chad 1C **136**
  NG12: Key 2D **199**
Hillcrest Vw. NG4: Carl 1A **100**
Hillcroft Dr. DE72: Ock 4B **140**
HILLCROSS 5B **158**
Hill Cross Av. DE23: Lit 4B **158**
Hill Cross Dr. DE23: Lit 4A **158**
Hill Dr. NG13: Bing 1C **130**
Hill Farm Ct. NG12: Edwal 1F **175**
Hillfield Gdns. NG5: Top V 2D **49**
Hillfield Rd. NG9: Stap 5E **117**
Hillgrove Gdns. *NG5: Top V 4F 49*
(off Whitchurch Cl.)
Hilliers Ct. NG5: Top V 4E **49**
Hillingdon Av. NG16: Nuth 4C **70**
Hillingdon Dr. DE7: Ilk 3F **91**
Hillington Ri. NG5: Bestw 5B **50**
Hill Nook Cl. DE73: Chel 1E **201**
Hill Ri. NG9: Trow 1B **116**
Hill Ri. Cl. DE23: Lit 3C **158**

Hill Rd. DE75: Hea 3C **40**
  NG6: Bestw V 5D **27**
  NG9: Chil 5A **146**
Hillsdorn Cl. NG8: Woll 5F **95**
Hillside DE65: Find 5B **182**
  DE74: C Don 5A **206**
  DE74: Keg 3C **214**
  NG7: Nott 2C **120**
  NG16: Lang M 1F **41**
Hillside Av. DE21: Chad 3F **137**
  NG3: Mapp 3F **75**
Hillside Cres. DE21: Spon 4E **139**
  NG9: Bram 5D **119**
Hillside Dr. NG10: Long E 3A **168**
  NG14: Bur J 2E **79**
Hillside Gro. NG10: Sand 2F **143**
Hillside Ri. DE56: Bel 2E **35**
Hillside Rd. DE21: Spon 4D **139**
  NG9: Bram 4B **118**
  NG9: Chil 5F **145**
  NG12: Rad T 2F **127**
Hillside Vw. DE56: Mil 5E **35**
Hills La. DE73: S Bri 5F **201**
Hill Sq., The DE22: D Abb . . .4F **107**
Hills Rd. DE72: Brea 3A **166**
  NG5: Woodt 3D **75**
Hill St. DE5: Rip 3C **8**
Hillsway DE23: Lit 2A **158**
  DE73: Chel 3E **187**
Hill Syke NG14: Lowd 2F **55**
HILL TOP 2A **44**
Hill Top DE74: C Don 3E **211**
Hilltop DE21: Bre 2D **109**
Hilltop La. DE56: Kil 2D **37**
Hilltop Ri. NG16: Eastw 2A **44**
Hill Vw. DE56: Duff 4C **58**
Hillview Av. NG3: Mapp 5C **74**
Hill Vw. Cl. DE7: H Woo 5A **38**
Hill Vw. Gro. DE21: Spon 3D **139**
Hill Vw. Ho.
  DE1: Der 4C **6** (4F **135**)
Hillview Rd. NG4: Carl 1F **99**
  NG9: Toton 1F **169**
Hilton Cl. DE3: Mick 2C **156**
  NG10: Long E 2E **193**
Hilton Ct. NG2: West Br 3A **152**
Hilton Cres. NG2: West Br 3A **152**
Hilton Gdns. DE72: Ast T 2F **203**
Hilton Rd. DE65: Etw 2A **180**
  NG3: Mapp 5E **75**
Hinchin Brook NG7: Lent 1D **121**
Hind Av. DE72: Brea 3B **166**
Hindscarth Cres. DE3: Mick . . .2D **157**
Hine Hall NG3: Nott 1E **99**
Hinshelwood Ct. NG11: Clif . . .3B **172**
Hinsley Cl. NG5: Arn 4A **52**
Hinsley Ct. NG8: Bilb 5B **94**
Hirst Ct. NG7: Radf 5F **97**
Hirst Cres. NG8: Woll 1E **119**
Hixon's La. DE7: D Ab 5A **114**
HMP Lowdham Grange
  NG14: Lowd 2D **55**
HMP Nottingham NG5: Sher . . .4A **74**
Hobart Cl. DE3: Mick 1E **157**
  NG2: Nott 4B **122**
Hobart Dr. NG9: Stap 4E **117**
Hob Hill DE56: Haz 4A **34**
Hobkirk Dr. DE24: Sin 4D **185**
HOBSIC 1C **20**
Hobsic Cl. NG16: Brins 1C **20**
Hobson Dr. DE7: Ilk 4D **91**
  DE21: Spon 1E **163**
Hobson's Acre NG14: Gun 2E **81**
Hockerwood NG11: Clif 4D **149**

Hockley NG1: Nott 3E **5** (1C **122**)
Hockley Ho.
NG1: Nott 3E **5** (1C **122**)
Hodge Beck Cl. DE24: Alv 5B 162
Hodgkin Cl. NG11: Clif 2B 172
Hodgkinson St. NG4: Neth 4F 101
Hodson Ho. NG5: Sher 5B 74
Hodthorpe Cl. DE21: Oak 4F 109
Hoefield Cres. NG6: Bulw 1F 71
Hoe Hill Vw. NG12: Toll 2C 176
Hoewood Rd. NG6: Bulw 5F 47
Hogan Gdns. NG5: Top V 3F 49
Hogarth Cl. NG9: Stap 2D 145
Hogarth St. NG3: Nott 4E 99
Hoggbarn La. DE75: Los 5C 18
Hoggetts Cl. NG9: Chil 2A 146
Hogg La. NG12: Rad T 2D 127
(not continuous)
Hoggs Fld. NG16: Eastw 2E 43
Holbeck Rd. NG8: Aspl 4B 96
NG15: Huck 5D 11
Holborn Av. NG2: Nott 5E 99
Holborn Cl. NG16: Nuth 4C 70
Holborn Dr. DE22: Mac 1F 133
Holborn Pl. NG6: Bulw 5B 48
Holborn Vw. DE5: Cod 1F 17
HOLBROOK 1B 60
Holbrook Ct. NG11: Clif 3D 173
HOLBROOK MOOR 5B 36
Holbrook Rd. DE24: Alv 1F 187
DE56: Bel 2E 35
Holbrook St. DE75: Hea 2F 41
Holbrook Vw. DE56: Kil 4F 37
Holby Cl. NG5: Top V 4E 49
Holcombe Cl. NG8: Aspl 5A 72
Holcombe St. DE23: Der 2A 160
Holdale Rd. NG3: Nott 4A 100
Holden Av. DE72: Ast T 1F 203
Holden Ct. DE24: Alv 3F 161
NG7: Radf 5F 97
Holden Cres. NG16: Nuth 1B 70
Holden Gdns. NG9: Stap 2D 145
Holden Rd. NG9: Bee 1D 147
Holden St. NG7: Radf 5F 97
Holderness Cl.
DE24: S Flds 4C 184
Holgate NG11: Clif 1B 172
Holgate Rd. NG2: Nott 4B 122
Holgate Wlk. NG15: Huck 3D 25
Holkham Av. NG9: Chil 3B 146
Holkham Cl. DE7: Ilk 4B 66
NG5: Arn 1F 75
Holland Mdw.
NG10: Long E 1C 194
Holland St. NG7: H Grn 3E 97
Hollands Way DE74: Keg 2C 214
Holles Cres. NG7: Nott 2F 121
Hollies, The NG10: Sand 3F 143
NG16: Eastw 2E 43
Hollies Dr. NG12: Edwal 4F 151
Hollies Farm Cl.
DE73: S Bri 5F 201
Hollies Rd. DE22: All 2C 106
Hollington Cl. DE21: Chad . . .1D 137
Hollington Rd. NG8: Bilb 4F 95
Hollingworth Av.
NG10: Sand 5A 144
Hollins, The NG14: Calv 1F 31
Hollinwell Av. NG8: Woll 5A 96
Hollinwell Ct.
NG12: Edwal 5A 152
Hollinwood La. NG14: Calv . . .2A 30
Hollis St. DE24: Alv 3F 161
NG7: Basf 1F 97

Hollow, The DE3: Mick 2C 156
(not continuous)
DE23: Lit 2B 158
DE23: Mick 3C 156
DE74: C Don 1A 212
Holloway Rd. DE24: Alv 5E 161
DE56: Duff 3C 58
Hollowood Av. DE3: Lit 3B 158
Hollows, The NG10: Long E . . .3F 169
NG11: Wilf 4F 149
Hollowstone
NG1: Nott 4E **5** (1C **122**)
Holly Av. DE5: Rip 1C 16
DE72: Brea 2E 167
NG3: Nott 3F 99
NG4: Carl 3C 100
NG11: Wilf 5A 122
Hollybrook Gro. NG16: Want . . .5A 46
Hollybrook Way DE23: Lit 5E 157
Holly Bush La. DE56: Mil 1F 59
Holly Cl. DE72: Dray 4F 165
NG13: Bing 2F 131
NG15: Huck 4A 26
Holly Copse Nature Reserve
. . . . .5E 69
Holly Ct. DE3: Mick 2C 156
DE72: Ast T 2F 203
NG3: Nott 3E 99
NG9: Bram 5B 118
Hollycroft NG2: West Br 4F 151
Hollydale Rd. NG3: Nott 4A 100
Hollydene Cl. NG15: Huck 4A 24
Hollydene Cres. NG6: Cin 3A 72
Holly End Rd. DE3: Mick 2C 156
Holly Farm Cotts.
NG12: Key 5D 199
Holly Farm Ct. NG16: Newth . . .3B 44
Holly Gdns. NG3: Nott 3E 99
Hollygate Ind. Pk.
NG12: Cotg 4F 155
Hollygate La. NG12: Cotg 5E 155
Holly La. NG9: Chil 3D 147
Holly Leaf Rd. NG15: Huck 5B 26
Holly Lodge NG2: West Br 4A 124
Hollymoor Dr. DE73: Chel 4D 187
Holly Rd. NG16: Want 5E 45
Hollythorpe Pl. NG15: Huck . . .4B 24
Hollywell Av. DE5: Cod 2A 18
Holm Av. DE21: L Eat 3A 84
Holme Cl. DE7: Ilk 5C 66
NG14: Woodbo 5C 32
Holme Ct. DE7: West H 3D 89
Holmefield Cres. DE7: Ilk 2F 91
Holme Gro. NG2: West Br 3A 124
Holme La. DE21: Spon 5B 138
NG12: Hol P, Rad T 2A 126
Holme Lea NG10: Sand 2A 144
Holme Lodge NG4: Carl 4D 101
HOLME PIERREPONT 2F 125
Holme Pierrepont Cvn. &
Camping Pk.
NG2: West Br 4B 124
Holme Pierrepont Country Pk.
. . . . .2F 125
Holme Pierrepont Hall 2A 126
Holme Rd. NG2: West Br 4E 123
NG13: Bing 2E 131
HOLMES, THE 3F **7** (3A 136)
Holmes Cl. NG16: Lang M 1F 41
Holmesfield Dr. DE3: Mick . . .1E 157
DE75: Hea 4E 41
Holmes Rd. DE72: Brea 3C 166
Holmes St. DE23: Der 1F 159
DE75: Hea 2C 40

Holme St. NG2: Nott 3D 123
Holmewood Av. DE7: Ilk 2E 67
Holmewood Cres.
NG5: Bestw 1F 73
Holmewood Dr. NG16: Gilt 4A 44
Holmfield DE23: Der 4D 159
Holmfield Rd. NG9: Chil 5B 146
Holmleigh Way DE73: Chel . . .5D 187
Holmoak Cl. DE21: Oak 2A 110
Holmsfield NG12: Key 4D 199
Holroyd Av. NG2: Nott 1E 123
Holt Av. DE24: Alv 5B 162
Holt Gro. NG14: Calv 1E 31
Holtlands Dr. DE24: Alv 1E 187
Holwood Ct. NG6: Bulw 1F 71
Holyhead Dr. DE21: Oak 3A 110
Holyoake Dr. NG10: Long E . . .4E 169
Holyoake Rd. NG3: Mapp 4B 76
Holyoake Vs. NG4: Colw 4E 101
Holyrood Cl. DE21: Spon 3E 139
Holyrood Ct. NG9: Bram 4B 118
Holywell Rd. DE7: Ilk 4B 66
Home Cl. NG5: Arn 4C 50
Home Cft., The NG9: Bram . . .1A 146
Home Farm Cl. DE72: Ock 3B 140
Home Farm Dr. DE22: All 1F 107
Home Farm La.
NG12: Rad T 2D 129
Homefield Av. NG5: Arn 2F 51
Homefield Rd. NG8: Aspl 3C 96
Homestead NG16: Lang M 5F 19
Homewell Wlk. NG11: Clif 5E 149
Honeycroft Cl. DE56: Bel 1A 36
Honeyfield Dr. DE5: Rip 1E 17
Honeysuckle Cl. NG5: Brox . . .1D 95
Honeysuckle Gro. NG6: Cin . . .3A 72
NG13: Bing 3C 130
Honeywood Cl. NG3: Nott 3F 99
Honeywood Dr. NG3: Nott 3F 99
Honingham Cl. NG5: Arn 2E 75
Honingham Rd. DE7: Ilk 4B 66
Honister Cl. NG2: Gam 1B 152
NG11: Clif 4C 172
Honiton Cl. NG9: Toton 1F 169
Honiton Rd. NG8: Brox 1D 95
Hood Cotts. NG5: Sher 5C 74
Hood St. NG5: Sher 5C 74
Hook Cl. NG9: Chil 1B 170
Hooley Cl. NG10: Long E 5A 168
Hooley Pl. NG5: Sher 4C 74
Hoopers Wlk. NG2: Nott 3B 122
Hooton Rd. NG4: Carl 3B 100
Hooton St. NG3: Nott 5E 99
Hope Av. DE3: Mick 1C 156
Hope Cl. NG2: Nott 3A 122
Hopedale Cl. NG7: Radf 5D 97
Hope Dr. NG7: Nott 5A **4** (2A **122**)
Hope St. DE1: Der 4E **7** (4A **136**)
DE7: Ilk 3E 91
NG9: Bee 1D 147
Hopetoun St. DE23: Der 3F 159
Hopewell Cl. NG12: Rad T 5F 103
Hopkins Ct. NG16: Eastw 1E 43
Hopping Hill DE56: Mil 4E 35
Hopping Hill Ter. DE56: Mil . . .5F 35
Hopton Cl. DE5: Rip 5E 9
DE21: Chad 4F 109
Hopwell Rd. DE72: Dray 5F 141
Horace Av. NG9: Stap 1B 144
Horeston Cotts. DE7: H Woo . . .1A 62
Horizon Pl. NG8: Stre 5B 70
Hornbeam Cl. DE7: Ilk 3A 92
DE21: Oak 3D 109
Hornbeam Gdns. NG6: Bulw . . .5E 47

Hornbuckle Ct. NG7: Radf 5E 97
Horncastle Rd. DE21: Chad . . .4C 108
Hornchurch Rd. NG8: Bilb 2C 94
Hornsby Wlk. NG5: Top V 4D 49
Hornsea Rd. DE21: Chad 4C 108
Horridge St. DE7: Ilk 3E 67
Horsecroft Cl. DE7: Ilk 5B 66
Horsendale Av. NG16: Nuth . . .3D 71
Horse Shoes, The
  DE74: Hem 5B 206
Horsham Dr. NG5: Top V 4E 49
HORSLEY 2E 61
Horsley Cres. DE56: H'ook . . .5B 36
  NG16: Lang M 1F 41
Horsley La. DE21: Cox 3D 61
Horsley Rd. DE21: Hors 1E 61
  DE56: Kil 1E 61
HORSLEY WOODHOUSE 1B 62
Horton St. DE23: Der 1B 160
Horwood Av. DE23: Der 1C 158
Hoselett Fld. Rd.
  NG10: Long E 1D 195
Hospital La. DE3: Mick 4A 156
Hoten Rd. NG2: Nott 2E 123
Hotspur Cl. NG6: Basf 2D 73
Hotspur Dr. NG4: Colw 4D 101
Houghton Av. DE7: Ilk 4B 66
Houghton Cl. NG16: Nuth 3D 71
Houghton Ct. DE21: Oak 3E 109
Houldsworth Ri. NG5: Arn 2D 51
Hoult St. DE22: Der 4C 134
Hound Rd. NG2: West Br 5D 123
Hounds Ga.
  NG1: Nott 4A 4 (1B 122)
        (not continuous)
Hounslow Rd. DE22: Mac 2A 134
Houseman Gdns.
  NG2: Nott 3B 122
Houston Cl. DE21: Chad 2A 138
  NG5: Top V 3D 49
Hovenden Gdns. NG7: H Grn . .3D 97
Hove Rd. NG5: Bestw 2D 73
Hoveton Cl. DE24: S Loc 3C 186
Howard Cl. NG10: Long E 2D 169
Howard St. DE23: Der 1E 159
  NG1: Nott 1D 5 (5B 98)
Howarth Cl. NG10: Long E 4F 167
Howbeck Rd. NG5: Arn 4A 52
Howden Cl. DE3: Mick 2B 156
Howden Rd. NG6: Bulw 2B 48
Howell Jones Rd.
  NG9: Chil 5A 146
Howells Cl. NG5: Arn 4B 50
Howe St. DE22: Der 3C 134
Howick Dr. NG6: Bulw 5E 47
Howitt St. DE75: Hea 2E 41
  NG10: Long E 4D 169
Howth Cl. DE21: Chad 4F 137
Hoylake Cl. DE3: Mick 5B 132
Hoylake Cres. NG8: Bilb 3C 94
Hoylake Dr. DE3: Mick 5B 132
Hoyland Av. NG7: Lent 3D 121
Hoyland Cl. DE56: Bel 4D 15
Hoyle Rd. NG14: Calv 1E 31
Hubert Ct. NG7: H Grn 4E 97
Hubert Shaw Cl.
  DE24: S Loc 2D 187
Hubert St. NG7: H Grn 4E 97
Huckerby Rd. DE7: Ilk 5B 66
Huckerbys Fld. NG4: Carl 1B 100
Hucklow Ct. DE21: Oak 2A 110
HUCKNALL 2F 25
Hucknall By-Pass
  NG15: Huck 2D 25

Hucknall Cl. NG8: Stre 5C 70
Hucknall Cres. NG4: Ged 5D 77
Hucknall Ind. Pk.
  NG15: Huck 5E 25
Hucknall La. NG6: Bulw 4B 48
Hucknall Leisure Cen. 1A 26
Hucknall Rd.
  NG5: Bestw, Sher 1D 73
  NG5: Top V 3C 48
  NG6: Bulw 3C 48
  NG15: News . . . .2A 10 & 1A 10
Hucknall Station (Rail & NET)
  . . . . .2B 26
Hucknall Town FC 4E 25
Hudson St. NG3: Nott 4E 99
Hudson Way DE24: Der 5B 136
  NG12: Rad T 1A 128
Hufton's Ct. DE75: Hea 5F 41
Hufton's Dr. DE75: Hea 5E 41
Hugessen Av. NG15: Huck 1B 26
Huggett Gdns. NG5: Top V 4F 49
Hugh Stewart Hall
  NG7: Nott 4B 120
Hulland Cl. DE1: Der 5B 136
Hulland Vw. DE22: All 4C 106
Humber Cl. DE24: Alv 5B 162
  NG2: Nott 3B 122
Humber Lodge NG9: Bee 1F 147
Humber Rd. NG9: Bee 1F 147
  NG10: Long E 2B 168
Humber Rd. Sth. NG9: Bee . . .2A 148
Humberston Rd. NG8: Woll . . .2B 118
Humbleton Dr. DE22: Mac 3F 133
HUNGERHILL GARDENS 3C 98
Hungerhill La.
  NG14: Woodbo 2E 53
Hungerhill Rd. NG3: Nott 3C 98
Hungerton St. NG7: Lent 2E 121
Hunston Cl. NG8: Bilb 3F 95
Hunt Av. DE75: Hea 2D 41
Hunt Cl. NG12: Rad T 2E 127
Hunter Dr. DE56: Kil 4E 37
Hunter Rd. DE56: Bel 4C 14
  DE74: N Air 4D 213
  NG5: Arn 1B 76
Hunters Cl. NG11: Wilf 2F 149
Hunters Cft. DE24: S Flds 4D 185
Huntingdon Dr.
  DE74: C Don 5F 205
  NG7: Nott 4A 4 (1A 122)
Huntingdon Grn.
  DE21: Chad 2B 136
Huntingdon St.
  NG1: Nott 1C 4 (4B 98)
Huntingdon Wlk.
  NG10: Sand 3A 144
Huntingdon Way NG9: Toton . . .1E 169
Huntley Av. DE21: Spon 2E 139
Huntly Cl. NG11: Clif 2F 173
Hurcomb St. NG3: Nott 3E 99
Hurley Ct. DE7: West H 2D 89
Hurst Dr. DE7: S'ley 4B 88
Hurts Cft. NG9: Chil 4C 146
Hurt's Yd. NG1: Nott 2B 4 (5R 98)
Huss's La. NG10: Long E 4E 169
Hutchinson Grn. NG3: Nott 4E 98
Hutton Cl. NG9: Bram 4C 118
Hutton St. DE24: A'ton 5D 161
  NG2: Nott 2E 123
Huxley Cl. DE23: Der 4E 159
  NG8: Bilh 3C 94
Hyam's La. DE74: Dise 5C 212
Hyde Cl. NG11: Clif 4E 149
Hyde Pk. Cl. NG2: West Br . . .3B 150

Hyde Pk. Rd. DE22: Mac 2F 133
Hyson Cl. NG7: H Grn 2E 97
HYSON GREEN 2D 97
Hyson Green Market Stop (NET)
  .3E 97
Hyson St. NG7: H Grn 3E 97

I

Ian Gro. NG4: Carl 2E 101
Ibsley Cl. DE24: Alv 5B 162
Ice Ho., The NG1: Nott 3E 5
Ikea Way NG16: Gilt 5B 44
Ilam Sq. DE7: Ilk 2D 67
Ilford Cl. DE7: Ilk 4C 66
Ilford Rd. DE22: Mac 3F 133
Ilford Wlk. DE22: Mac 3F 133
ILKESTON 1D 91
Ilkeston Rd. DE7: Mor 5D 63
  DE7: Stan D 2E 115
  DE75: Hea 3E 41
  NG7: Lent, Nott, Radf 5C 96
  NG9: Stap 3D 117
  NG9: Trow 5A 92
  NG10: Sand 4B 116
Ilkeston Town FC 4F 67
Imex Ent. Pk. NG15: Huck 3C 26
Imperial Av. NG4: Ged 1D 101
  NG9: Bee 2D 147
Imperial Ct. DE22: All 5C 82
Imperial Rd. NG6: Bulw 1C 72
  NG9: Bee 2D 147
Incher M. NG4: Carl 1B 100
Inchwood Cl. NG9: Toton 1E 169
Incinerator Rd. NG2: Nott 3D 123
Independent St. NG7: Radf 4E 97
Industrial St. DE23: Der 1F 159
Ingham Dr. DE3: Mick 3C 156
Ingham Gro. NG7: Lent 2D 121
Ingham Rd. NG10: Long E 1B 168
Ingleborough Gdns.
  NG10: Long E 3F 167
Ingleby Av. DE23: Der 4E 159
Ingleby Cl. NG8: Woll 1A 118
  NG12: Cotg 1F 179
Ingleby Rd. DE73: S Bri 5E 201
  NG10: Long E 2E 193
Ingle Cl. DE21: Spon 3D 139
Ingledew Cl. DE31: Oak 4D 109
Inglefield Cl. DE7: Ilk 4E 91
Ingles Channel DE56: Bel 5F 13
Inglewood Av. DE3: Mick 5C 132
Inglewood Rd. NG11: Clif 2D 173
Ingliston Cl. DE24: Alv 5C 162
Ingram Rd. NG6: Bulw 1B 72
Ingram Ter. NG6: Bulw 1B 72
Inham Cir. NG9: Chil 2B 146
Inham Cl. NG9: Chil 3F 145
Inham Flds. Cl. NG14: Gun 2F 81
Inham Rd. NG9: Chil 3F 145
Inkerman Cl. DE7: Ilk 2D 67
Innes Cl. NG4: Carl 3B 100
Inn La. DE22: Quar 2A 82
Instow Dr. DE23: Der 1C 184
Instow Ri. NG3: Nott 4C 98
Intake Rd. NG12: Key 3C 198
Interchange 25 Bus. Pk.
  NG10: Sand 4F 143
Inveraray Cl. DE24: Sin 3C 184
Iona Cl. DE24: Sin 2D 185
Iona Dr. NG9: Trow 2C 116
Iona Gdns. NG5: Top V 3F 49
Ipswich Cir. NG3: Nott 5F 99

Ireland Av. NG9: Bee 3F 147
Ireland Av. NG9: Bee 3F 147
Iremonger Rd. NG2: Nott 3C 122
Irene Ter. NG7: Basf 5E 73
Ireton Cl. DE56: Bel 1D 37
Ireton Gro. NG9: Atten 1C 170
Ireton Ho's. NG56: Bel 1D 37
Ireton St. NG7: Radf 5F 97
    NG9: Bee 2D 147
Iron Ga. DE1: Der 2C 6 (3F 135)
Irvine Cl. DE24: S Flds 3C 184
Irving Pl. DE24: Alv 4E 161
Irwin Dr. NG6: Bulw 2E 71
Isaac Newton Cen.
    NG7: Nott 4C 120
Isaacs La. NG9: Stap 1C 144
Isabella St.
    NG1: Nott 5B 4 (2B 122)
Isandula Rd. NG7: Basf 5E 73
Island, The NG16: Eastw 3E 43
Island La. NG12: Rad T 1C 126
Islay Cl. NG5: Arn 3E 51
    NG9: Trow 2C 116
Islay Rd. DE24: Sin 2D 185
Isleworth Dr. DE22: Mac 2E 133
ISLEY WALTON 5C 210
Ismay Rd. DE21: Chad 2E 137
Ivatt Dr. NG2: Nott 2E 123
Ivernia Cl. DE23: Der 1D 185
Ives Cl. NG2: West Br 4B 150
Ivybridge Cl. DE21: Oak 2B 110
Ivy Cl. NG16: Want 3E 45
Ivy Ct. DE3: Mick 2C 156
    DE65: Etw 2A 180
    NG4: Carl 3C 100
Ivy Gro. DE5: Rip 5C 8
    NG4: Carl 3C 100
    NG7: Basf 2F 97
Ivy La. NG16: Eastw 2D 43
Ivyleaf Way DE23: Lit 5A 158
Ivy Sq. DE23: Der 1B 160

Jackdaw Cl. DE22: Der 3C 134
Jacklin Gdns. NG5: Top V 3F 49
Jacksdale Cl. DE22: All 4C 106
Jackson Av. DE3: Mick 1F 157
    DE7: Ilk 1D 91
    NG10: Sand 2F 143
Jacksons La. DE56: H'age 2C 14
    DE56: Mil 5D 35
    DE65: Etw 4B 180
Jackson St.
    DE22: Der 4A 6 (4D 135)
                    (not continuous)
Jaeger Cl. DE56: Bel 5F 13
Jakcson Dr. NG5: Bestw 2F 73
Jake Rd. NG9: Bee 5F 147
James Cl. DE1: Der 3D 135
James St. NG5: Arn 4D 51
    NG16: Kimb 1E 69
Japonica Dr. NG6: Cin 3A 72
Jardine Ct. DE72: Dray 4A 166
Jardines, The NG9: Bram 4B 118
Jarrow Gdns. NG5: Top V 2E 49
Jarvis Av. NG3: Nott 4A 100
Jarvis Rd. DE24: S Flds 4D 185
Jasmine Cl. DE21: Chad 4A 138
    NG8: Brox 1D 95
    NG9: Bram 4C 118
    NG11: Clif 2B 172
Jasmine Ct. DE75: Hea 3B 42
Jasmine Rd. NG5: Basf 4D 73

Jasper Cl. NG12: Rad T 3D 127
Jay Ct. DE22: Der 3C 134
Jayne Cl. NG4: Ged 5F 77
    NG8: Woll 4D 95
Jebb's La. NG13: Bing 2E 131
Jedburgh Cl. DE24: Sin 4D 185
    NG3: Nott 4C 98
    NG16: Kimb 5D 45
Jedburgh Wlk. NG3: Nott 4C 98
Jeffares Cl. DE74: Keg 1B 214
Jefferson Pl. DE24: Alv 4E 161
Jemison Cl. DE23: Lit 4D 157
Jenned Rd. NG5: Arn 2F 51
Jenner Ho. NG3: Mapp 5E 75
Jenner St. NG5: Sher 1A 98
Jenness Av. NG5: Top V 3D 49
Jennison St. NG6: Bulw 5B 48
Jenny Burton Way
    NG15: Huck 4B 26
Jenny's Ct. DE56: Bel 4B 14
Jensen Way NG5: Sher 1A 98
Jermyn Dr. NG5: Arn 3F 49
Jersey Gdns.
    NG3: Nott 1F 5 (4D 99)
Jervis Ct. DE7: Ilk 4E 67
Jesmond Rd. NG6: Bulw 1C 72
Jessamine Cl. NG9: Bee 2F 147
Jesse Boot Wildcats Arena . . .5A 100
Jesses La. DE56: Bel 2B 12
Jessop Dr. DE24: S Flds 4D 185
Jessops La. NG4: Ged 4E 77
Jessop St. DE5: Cod 2A 18
    DE5: Rip 2F 17
Jewitt Way NG11: Rudd 4A 174
Jill-iain Ct. NG9: Stap 2D 145
JJB Health Club
    Derby, Pride Pk. 4D 137
Joan Av. DE75: Hea 2D 41
Jodrell Av. DE56: Bel 5C 14
John Berrysford Cl.
    DE21: Chad 3E 137
John Carroll Ct. NG3: Nott 4E 99
John Carrol Leisure Cen. 5E 97
John F Kennedy Gdns.
    DE21: Chad 2B 138
John Lombe Dr. DE1: Der 1F 135
John O'Gaunts Way
    DE56: Bel 5B 14
John Port Cl. DE65: Etw 2B 180
John Quinn Ct. NG7: Basf 1E 97
Johnson Av. DE24: A'ton 4D 161
    NG15: Huck 4A 26
Johnson Cl. NG16: Want 5F 45
Johnson Dr. DE75: Hea 2E 41
Johnson Rd. NG7: Lent 1D 121
Johnson Way NG9: Chil 1A 170
John's Pl. DE75: Hea 3C 40
Johns Rd. NG9: Bee 5F 147
    NG12: Rad T 2F 127
Johnstone Way
    NG6: Bestw V 3A 28
John St. DE1: Der 5F 7 (4A 136)
    DE7: Ilk 1E 91
    DE75: Hea 2C 40
    NG7: Basf 1E 97
John Wright Cl. NG6: Bulw . . .3C 48
Joseph Cl. DE7: Ilk 4D 67
Joseph St. DE23: Der 2F 159
    DE56: Bel 5E 13
Joseph Wright Ter.
    DE1: Der 2F 135
                    (off Arthur St.)
Joshua Bus. Pk.
    NG16: Lang M 1B 42

Joyce Av. NG5: Sher 3C 74
    NG9: Toton 5E 145
Joyce Cl. NG5: Sher 3C 74
Jubalton Cl. DE24: A'ton 5D 161
Jubilee Av. DE5: Rip 5B 8
Jubilee Bus. Pk. DE21: Der . . .2A 136
Jubilee Ct. DE7: West H 2B 88
    DE56: Bel 2F 35
    NG8: Stre 1C 94
    NG15: Huck 4D 25
Jubilee Parkway DE21: Der . . .2A 136
Jubilee Rd. DE24: S Loc 2D 187
    NG5: Arn 1D 75
Jubilee St. NG2: Nott 1E 123
    NG16: Kimb 5D 45
Judson Av. NG9: Stap 2E 145
Julian Cl. DE7: Ilk 4A 92
Julian La. NG12: Shel 1B 104
Julian Rd. NG2: West Br 5A 124
Julie Av. DE75: Hea 3F 41
Julius Cl. NG16: Lang M 5A 20
Jumelles Dr. NG14: Calv 2C 30
Junction, The NG15: Huck 2A 26
Junction Rd. NG10: Long E . . .5F 169
Junction St. DE1: Der 4C 134
Juniper Cl. NG11: Clif 2B 172
Juniper Ct. NG7: Radf 4F 97
                    (off Waterloo Prom.)
    NG16: Gilt 4B 44
Juniper Gdns. NG13: Bing 2F 131
Jura Av. DE5: Rip 4C 8
Jury St. DE1: Der 2B 6 (3E 135)

K

Kappler Cl. NG4: Neth 3F 101
Karen Gdns. NG9: Chil 4C 146
Karen Ri. NG5: Arn 3F 51
Katherine Dr. NG9: Toton 4E 145
Katrine Wlk. DE24: Sin 2D 185
Kayes Ct. NG9: Stap 1C 144
Kayes Wlk.
    NG1: Nott 4D 5 (1C 122)
Kay's Mdw. NG9: Bee 1F 147
Kean Pl. DE24: Alv 4E 161
Keats Av. DE23: Lit 2F 157
Keats Cl. NG5: Arn 5C 50
    NG10: Long E 1A 194
    NG16: Nuth 1A 70
Keats Dr. NG15: Huck 3C 24
Keble Cl. DE1: Der 5A 136
    DE75: Hea 4D 41
Kedleston Cl. DE5: Rip 3B 8
    DE22: All 4C 106
    DE56: Bel 1E 35
    NG9: Chil 3B 146
    NG10: Long E 1F 193
Kedleston Ct. DE22: All 3D 107
Kedleston Dr. DE7: Ilk 4C 66
    DE75: Hea 2B 40
Kedleston Dr. Sth. DE7: Ilk 4D 67
Kedleston Gdns. DE1: Der 2E 135
Kedleston Old Rd.
    DE22: Mark 5C 106
Kedleston Rd.
    DE22: All, Der, Mark 1B 106
    DE22: Ked 3A 82
Kedleston St.
    DE1: Der 1A 6 (2E 135)
Keeling Cl. NG16: Newth 3A 44
Keepers Cl. NG6: Bestw V 5D 27
KEGWORTH 2C 214
Kegworth Av. DE23: Lit 5B 158

Kegworth Mus. 2B 214
Kegworth Rd.
  NG11: King, Rat 5E 209
Keighton Dr. NG7: Nott 4B 120
Keldholme La. DE24: Alv 4B 162
Kelfield Cl. NG6: Bulw 2D 73
Kelham Dr. NG5: Sher 5F 73
Kelham Grn. NG3: Nott 4E 99
Kelham M. NG3: Nott 2A 100
Kelham Way NG16: Eastw 1D 43
Kelling Cl. NG5: Bestw 1F 73
Kelly Wlk. NG11: Wilf 1A 150
Kelmoor Rd. DE24: Alv 4A 162
Kelsey Cl. NG9: Atten 5D 147
Kelso Gdns. NG2: Nott 3A 122
Kelso Wlk. DE24: Sin 4D 185
Kelstern Cl. NG8: Cin 4A 72
Kelvedon Dr. DE23: Lit 5F 157
Kelvedon Gdns.
  NG3: Nott 1F 5 (4D 99)
Kelvin Cl. NG9: Stap 3B 144
Kelvin Rd. NG3: Nott 3F 99
Kemble Pl. DE24: Alv 4E 161
Kemmel Rd. NG6: Bulw 2C 72
Kempsey Cl. NG5: Top V 4D 49
Kempson St. NG11: Rudd 4B 174
Kempton Cl. NG16: Kimb 5D 45
Kempton Dr. NG5: Arn 3F 51
Kempton Pk. Cl.
  DE24: Der 3C 160
Kendal Cl. NG15: Huck 1E 25
Kendal Ct. NG2: West Br 5A 124
Kendal Dr. NG9: Bram 5C 118
Kendale Ct. NG3: Nott 1E 99
Kendal Wlk. DE21: Chad 4C 108
Kendon Av. DE23: Der 5D 159
Kendray Cl. DE56: Bel 4C 14
Kendrew Ct. NG11: Clif 2B 172
Kenia Cl. NG4: Carl 2C 100
Kenilworth Av. DE23: Der 3E 159
Kenilworth Ct.
  NG7: Nott 5A 4 (2A 122)
  NG9: Bee 5F 119
Kenilworth Dr. DE7: Kirk H . . .5B 90
Kenilworth Rd. DE5: Rip 5B 8
  NG7: Nott 5A 4 (2A 122)
  NG9: Bee 1F 147
Ken Martin Swimming Pool . . .3B 48
Kenmore Gdns. NG3: Nott 4C 98
Kennedy Av. NG10: Long E . . .1B 194
Kennedy Cl. DE21: Chad 1F 137
  NG5: Arn 5C 50
Kennedy Dr. NG9: Stap 4D 117
Kenneth Ho.
  DE1: Der 1A 6 (2E 135)
Kenneth Rd. NG5: Arn 2E 51
Kennington Rd. NG8: Radf . . .5C 96
Ken Reid Gdns. NG6: Bulw . . .4B 48
  (off Minerva St.)
Kenrick Rd. NG3: Mapp 1F 99
  (not continuous)
Kenrick St. NG4: Neth 3F 101
Kensal Ct. NG2: West Br 5D 123
Kensal Ri. DE22: Mac 2A 134
Kensington Av. DE75: Hea 3B 40
Kensington Cl. NG9: Toton . . .2F 169
Kensington Ct. NG5: Sher 4B 74
  (off St Albans St.)
Kensington Gdns. DE7: Ilk 3F 91
  NG4: Carl 3D 101
Kensington Pk. Cl.
  NG2: West Br 3B 150
Kensington Rd.
  NG10: Sand 4F 143

Kensington St.
  DE1: Der 3A 6 (3E 135)
  DE7: Ilk 4E 91
Kenslow Av. NG7: H Grn 3D 97
Kent Av. NG9: Bee 4E 147
Kentish Ct. DE1: Der 1A 136
Kentmere Cl. NG2: Gam 1B 152
Kenton Av. NG16: Nuth 4C 70
Kenton Ct. NG2: Nott 4C 122
Kent Rd. NG3: Mapp 5E 75
  NG16: Gilt 3B 44
Kent St. DE21: Chad 1C 136
  NG1: Nott 2D 5 (5C 98)
Kentwood Rd. NG2: Nott 1E 123
Kenyon Rd. NG7: Lent 2C 120
Keppel Ct. DE7: Ilk 4E 67
Kepple Ga. DE5: Rip 1E 17
Kernel Cl. DE23: Lit 3F 157
Kerry Dr. DE7: Smal 1E 63
Kerry St. DE21: Chad 1C 136
  (not continuous)
Kerry's Yd. DE56: Kil 4E 37
Kersall Ct. NG6: Bulw 2C 72
Kersall Dr. NG6: Bulw 2C 72
Kersall Gdns. NG15: Huck 2A 26
Kershope Dr. DE21: Oak 2A 110
Kestrel Cl. DE3: Mick 4A 156
  DE7: Ilk 1E 115
  NG4: Carl 1A 100
Kestrel Dr. NG13: Bing 3E 131
Kestrel Ho. DE24: Sin 4D 185
Kestrels Cft. DE24: Sin 3D 185
Keswick Av. DE23: Der 5D 159
Keswick Cl. DE7: Kirk H 5C 90
  NG2: Gam 1B 152
  NG9: Bram 5C 118
Keswick Ct.
  NG2: Nott 3F 5 (1D 123)
  NG10: Long E 1A 168
Keswick St.
  NG2: Nott 3F 5 (1D 123)
Kettlewell Cl. DE24: A'ton 5D 161
Kett St. NG6: Bulw 5A 48
Keverne Cl. NG8: Aspl 5B 72
  (not continuous)
Kevin Cl. DE21: Chad 5A 110
Kevin Rd. NG8: Woll 3C 118
Kew Cl. NG2: West Br 5B 150
Kew Cres. DE75: Hea 3A 42
Kew Gdns. DE22: Mac 3A 134
  NG16: Nuth 4D 71
Keyhaven Cl. DE21: Chad 5C 108
Keynsham Cl. DE24: Alv 3D 161
Keys Cl. NG6: Bulw 5F 47
Keys St. DE1: Der 1E 7 (2A 136)
Key St. NG3: Nott 5E 99
Keyworth 4D 199
Keyworth La. NG11: Bunny . . .5E 187
Keyworth Leisure Cen. 3E 199
Keyworth Rd. NG4: Ged 4C 76
Kibworth Cl. DE21: Oak 5A 110
  NG5: Sher 3E 73
Kiddier Av. NG5: Arn 5A 52
Kielder Dr. NG13: Bing 2B 130
Kilbourne Rd. DE56: Bel 5B 14
  NG5: Arn 3A 52
Kilbourn St. NG3: Nott 4B 98
KILBURN 4F 37
Kilburn Cl. NG9: Bram 3A 118
Kilburn Dr. DE7: Ilk 4C 66
Kilburn La. DE56: Bel 1C 36
Kilburn Toll Bar DE56: Kil 3E 37
Kilby Av. NG3: Nott 4F 99
Kilby Ho. NG10: Long E 4C 168

Kildare Rd. DE21: Chad 4A 138
  NG3: Nott 2E 99
Kildonan Cl. NG8: Stre 5C 70
Kildrummy Cl. DE73: Chel . . .5D 187
Killarney Pk. NG6: Bestw V . . .3A 28
Killerton Grn. NG11: Clif 4E 173
Killerton Pk. Dr.
  NG2: West Br 4A 150
Killingworth Av. DE24: Sin . . .2E 185
Killisick Cl. NG5: Arn 4A 52
Killisick La. NG5: Arn 2A 52
Killisick Rd. NG5: Arn 4F 51
Killis La. DE56: Kil 4C 36
Kilnbrook Av. NG5: Arn 3A 52
Kiln Cl. DE7: West H 1D 89
Kiln Cft. DE65: Etw 2B 180
Kilnsey Ct. DE23: Lit 5E 157
Kilnwood Cl. NG3: Nott 3F 99
Kilsby Rd. NG11: Clif 1E 173
Kilverston Rd. NG10: Sand . . .2F 143
Kilverton Cl. NG8: Woll 1B 120
Kilvington Rd. NG5: Arn 5A 52
Kimber Cl. NG8: Dilb 4C 94
KIMBERLEY 1E 69
Kimberley Cl. NG16: Kimb 2E 69
Kimberley Eastwood By-Pass
  NG8: Cin 2A 70
  NG16: Eastw, Gilt, Kimb,
    Newth, Nuth 2C 42
Kimberley Leisure Cen. 1F 69
Kimberley Rd. DE72: Bor 1A 164
  NG16: Nuth 2A 70
Kimberley St. NG2: Nott 1F 99
Kimbolton Av.
  NG7: Lent, Radf 5E 97
Kinder Wlk. DE22: Der 4D 135
Kindlewood Dr. NG9: Toton . . .1A 170
King Alfred St.
  DE22: Der 4A 6 (4E 135)
King Charles St.
  NG1: Nott 4A 4 (1A 122)
King Edward Ct.
  NG1: Nott 2D 5 (5C 98)
King Edward Gdns.
  NG10: Sand 2A 144
King Edward St.
  NG1: Nott 2D 5 (5C 98)
  NG10: Sand 2A 144
  NG15: Huck 3F 25
Kingfisher Cl. DE3: Mick 4A 156
  NG6: Basf 3C 72
  NG9: Bee 3A 148
Kingfishers Ct.
  NG2: West Br 4B 152
Kingfisher Wlk. DE24: Sin . . .4D 185
Kingfisher Wharf NG7: Lent . . .3F 121
King George Av. DE7: Ilk 2D 91
King John's Arc. NG1: Nott 3C 4
King John's Chambers
  NG1: Nott 3C 4
Kinglake Pl. NG2: Nott 3B 122
Kingrove Av. NG9: Chil 2C 146
Kings Av. NG4: Ged 5D 77
Kingsbridge Av. NG3: Mapp . . .1B 76
Kingsbridge Way
  NG9: Bram 2B 146
Kingsbury Dr. NG8: Bilb 2F 95
Kingsbury Rd. DE22: Mac 2F 133
Kingsclere Av. DE21: Oak 3A 110
Kingsclere Av. DE21: Oak 3A 110
Kings Cl. DE75: Hea 3B 40
Kings Ct. DE1: Der 2F 135
Kings Cft. DE22: All 1E 107
Kingsdale Cl.
  NG10: Long E 1F 193

Kingsdale Gro. DE73: Chel 1D **201**
Kingsdown Mt. NG8: Woll 3D **119**
Kings Dr. DE23: Lit 1A **158**
  NG16: Brins 2D **21**
Kingsford Av. NG7: Radf 4D **97**
Kingsgate DE74: Lock 5E **207**
Kingsland Cl. DE21: Oak 3E **109**
Kingsley Cres.
  NG10: Long E 2A **194**
Kingsley Dr. NG4: Neth 4F **101**
Kingsley Rd. DE22: All 2C **106**
  NG2: Nott 1F **123**
Kingsley St. DE1: Der 1E **185**
Kingsmead Av. NG9: Trow . . .3C **116**
Kingsmead Cl. DE1: Der 2E **135**
King's Mead Ho. DE22: Der . . .1E **135**
Kingsmead Ind. Est.
  DE22: Der 2C **134**
Kingsmead Wlk.
  DE1: Der 1B **6** (2E **135**)
Kings Mills La.
  DE72: W Tre 4D **203**
Kingsmoor Cl. NG5: Top V . . .5D **49**
Kingsmuir Rd. DE3: Mick 5B **132**
King's Pl. NG1: Nott 3D **5** (1C **122**)
Kings Rd. NG10: Sand 2A **144**
Kingsthorpe Cl. NG3: Nott 1E **99**
Kingston Av. DE7: Ilk 1F **115**
Kingston Ct. DE7: West H 2E **88**
  NG2: Nott 3F **5** (1D **123**)
  *NG12: Rad T 2E **127***
    (off Bingham Rd.)
Kingston Dr. NG12: Cotg 2E **179**
Kingston La. DE74: Keg 1D **215**
KINGSTON ON SOAR 5F **209**
Kingston Rd. NG2: West Br . . .2D **151**
Kingston St. DE1: Der 1E **135**
King St. DE1: Der 1C **6** (2E **135**)
  DE7: Ilk 1E **91**
  DE56: Bel 1E **35**
  DE56: Duff 3D **59**
  NG1: Nott 2B **4** (1B **122**)
  NG9: Bee 2F **147**
  NG10: Long E 3C **168**
  NG16: Eastw 2E **43**
Kings Wlk. NG1: Nott . . .2B **4** (5B **98**)
Kingsway DE7: Ilk 5E **91**
  DE22: Der 3A **134**
  DE75: Hea 2C **40**
  NG12: Rad T 3D **127**
Kingsway Cres. DE56: Kil 4F **37**
Kingsway Gdns. NG15: Huck . .5D **25**
Kingsway Ind. Pk.
  DE22: Der 3B **134**
Kingsway Pk. Cl.
  DE22: Der 3A **134**
Kingsway Retail Pk.
  DE22: Der 4B **134**
Kingsway Rd. NG15: Huck . . .5D **25**
Kingswell Av. NG5: Arn 5E **51**
Kingswell Rd. NG5: Arn 5E **51**
Kingswood Av. DE56: Bel 3B **14**
Kingswood Cl.
  NG2: West Br 3C **150**
Kingswood Pl. DE23: Lit 2A **158**
Kingswood Rd.
  NG2: West Br 3C **150**
  NG8: Woll 5A **96**
Kinlet Rd. NG5: Bestw 1F **73**
Kinross Av. DE21: Chad 5B **108**
Kinross Cres. NG8: Bilb 4F **95**
Kinsale Wlk. NG11: Clif 1D **173**
Kintyre Dr. DE24: Sin 3C **184**
Kipling Cl. NG11: Clif 3B **172**

Kipling Dr. DE3: Mick 2C **156**
Kipps St. NG1: Nott 2D **5** (5C **98**)
Kirby Cl. NG16: Newth 1F **43**
Kirby Dr. DE74: Keg 3B **214**
Kirby Rd. NG16: Newth 1F **43**
Kirk Av. DE74: Keg 2C **214**
Kirkbride Ct. NG9: Chil 4A **146**
Kirkby Av. DE7: Ilk 4E **91**
Kirkby Gdns. NG2: Nott 3C **122**
Kirk Cl. DE5: Rip 1B **16**
  NG9: Chil 4C **146**
Kirkdale Av. DE21: Spon 5E **139**
Kirkdale Cl. NG8: Woll 1A **118**
Kirkdale Gdns.
  NG10: Long E 5A **168**
Kirkdale Rd. NG3: Nott 4A **100**
  NG10: Long E 1A **194**
Kirkewhite Ct. NG2: Nott 3C **122**
Kirkewhite St. W.
  NG2: Nott 3B **122**
Kirkewhite Wlk. NG2: Nott . . .3B **122**
Kirkfell Cl. NG2: West Br 3B **152**
Kirkfield Dr. DE72: Brea 3C **166**
KIRK HALLAM 5C **90**
Kirkham Cl. DE75: Hea 3C **40**
Kirkham Dr. NG9: Toton 1E **169**
Kirkhill NG13: Bing 1D **131**
Kirkistown Cl. DE24: Alv 5B **162**
Kirkland Cl. DE74: C Don 1F **211**
Kirkland Dr. NG9: Chil 1B **170**
Kirkland Way DE24: S Flds 3C **184**
Kirk La. NG11: Rudd 4B **174**
Kirkley Dr. DE75: Hea 3B **40**
Kirkley Gdns. NG5: Arn 4F **51**
Kirk Leys Av. Nth.
  DE21: Spon 4D **139**
Kirkleys Av. Sth.
  DE21: Spon 4D **139**
Kirkman Rd. DE75: Los 5B **18**
Kirk Rd. NG3: Mapp 5F **75**
Kirk's Bldgs. NG4: Carl 3C **100**
Kirk's La. DE56: Bel 1A **36**
Kirkstead Cl. DE21: Oak 4A **110**
Kirkstead Gdns. NG7: H Grn . . .3E **97**
Kirkstead St. NG7: H Grn 3E **97**
Kirkstone Av. DE75: Hea 3A **42**
Kirkstone Ct. NG10: Long E . . .1A **168**
Kirkstone Dr. NG2: Gam 1B **152**
Kirk St. DE1: Der 1F **135**
Kirkwhite Av.
  NG10: Long E 4C **168**
Kirtle Cl. NG8: Aspl 2A **96**
Kirtley Cl. NG16: Want 4F **45**
Kirtley Dr. NG7: Lent 3F **121**
Kirton Av. NG10: Long E 4C **168**
Kitchener Av. DE23: Der 4E **159**
Kittiwake M. NG7: Lent 1D **121**
Kiwi Cl. NG15: Huck 4C **24**
Kiwi Dr. DE24: Alv 3E **161**
Knapp Av. NG16: Eastw 3E **43**
Kneesall Gro. NG15: Huck 2A **26**
Kneeton Cl. NG4: Ged 3C **76**
  NG5: Sher 3B **74**
Kneeton Va. NG5: Sher 3B **74**
Knife and Steel Ct.
  DE7: H Woo 5B **38**
Knighton Av. NG7: Radf 4D **97**
Knighton Rd. NG5: Woodt 2C **74**
Knightsbridge DE22: Mac 2F **133**
Knightsbridge Ct. *NG5: Sher* . . .4B **74**
  (off Newstead St.)
Knightsbridge Dr.
  NG2: West Br 4B **150**
  NG16: Nuth 4D **71**

Knightsbridge Gdns.
  NG15: Huck 4B **10**
Knightsbridge Way
  NG15: Huck 5B **10**
Knights Cl. DE24: S Flds 4D **185**
  NG2: West Br 5B **150**
  NG5: Top V 4E **49**
  NG9: Toton 1E **169**
Knights Rd. DE73: Chel 1D **201**
Knight St. NG4: Neth 4E **101**
Knightsyard Ct.
  NG10: Long E 1B **194**
Knightwood Dr.
  NG6: Bestw V 4A **28**
Kniveton Pk. DE7: Ilk 3C **90**
Knole Rd. NG8: Woll 5D **95**
Knoll Av. NG15: Huck 4C **24**
Knoll Cl. DE23: Lit 3F **157**
Knowl Av. DE56: Bel 3D **13**
Knowle Hill NG16: Kimb 2F **69**
Knowle La. NG16: Kimb 3F **69**
Knowle Pk. NG16: Kimb 2F **69**
Knowles Wlk. NG5: Arn 4C **50**
Knutsford Grn. DE21: Chad . . .3C **108**
Kozi Kots NG4: Neth 3E **101**
Krebs Cl. NG11: Clif 2B **172**
Kyle Gro. DE21: Oak 2A **110**
Kyle Vw. NG5: Top V 3F **49**
Kyme St. NG7: Radf 5E **97**
Kynance Cl. DE24: Alv 1B **188**
Kynance Gdns. NG11: Wilf . . .3A **150**

L

Labray Rd. NG14: Calv 1D **31**
Laburnum Av. NG12: Key 4F **199**
Laburnum Cl. NG10: Sand 1A **144**
Laburnum Cres. DE22: All 5C **82**
Laburnum Gdns. NG6: Bulw . . .2D **73**
Laburnum Gro. DE22: Mac . . .3F **133**
  NG9: Bee 3A **148**
  NG15: Huck 4A **26**
Laburnum St. NG3: Nott 3C **98**
Laburnum Way DE65: Etw 3B **180**
Lace Cen. & Costume Mus.
  . . . . .4B **4** (1B **122**)
LACE MARKET 4D **5** (1C **122**)
Lace Market Stop (NET)
  . . . . .3C **4** (1B **122**)
Lace Market Theatre
  . . . . .4D **5** (1C **122**)
Lace Mill Ct. NG6: Basf 4C **72**
Lace Rd. NG9: Bee 1E **147**
Lace St. NG7: Nott 4C **120**
Lace Way NG1: Nott 4F **5** (1D **123**)
  NG2: Nott 4F **5** (1D **123**)
Lacey Av. NG15: Huck 4F **25**
Lacey Cl. DE7: Ilk 4B **66**
Laceyfields Rd. DE75: Hea 3F **41**
Ladbroke Gdns. DE22: Mac . . .2E **133**
Ladbrooke Cres. NG6: Basf . . .4B **72**
Ladybank Ri. NG5: Arn 4B **52**
Ladybank Rd. DE3: Mick 5B **132**
Lady Bay Av. NG2: West Br . . .4E **123**
Lady Bay Bri.
  NG2: Nott, West Br 3D **123**
Lady Bay Ct. NG2: West Br . . .4F **123**
Lady Bay Rd. NG2: West Br . . .4F **123**
Ladybay Workshops
  *NG2: West Br 4E **123***
    (off Ladybay Av.)
Ladybower Rd. DE21: Spon . . .4E **139**
Ladybridge Cl. NG9: Atten . . .5D **147**

Ladycroft Av. NG15: Huck 2F 25
Ladycroft Paddock
DE22: All 1D 107
Ladygrove Cotts.
DE23: Der 5A 136
Lady La. DE5: Den 3B 38
Lady Lea Rd. DE7: H Woo 1F 61
DE21: Hors 1F 61
Ladylea Rd. NG10: Long E . . .2F 193
Lady Mantle Cl. DE73: Chel . . .5E 187
Ladysmith Rd. DE72: Bor 1A 164
Ladysmith St. NG2: Nott 1F 123
Ladysmock Gdns.
NG2: Nott 3C 122
Ladywell Ct. DE56: Bel 1F 35
Ladywood Av. DE56: Bel 4A 14
Ladywood Rd.
DE7: D Ab, Kirk H 1F 113
Lake Av. DE75: Los 4B 18
Lake Dr. DE23: Der 3E 159
Lake Gdns. DE75: Los 5B 18
Lakehead Ho. NG11: Clif 2D 173
Lakeland Av. NG15: Huck 4B 26
Lakeside Av. NG10: Long E . . .2B 194
Lakeside Cres.
NG10: Long E 1C 194
Lakeside Dr. DE23: Lit 4E 157
Lake St. NG7: Radf 4E 97
Lamartine St.
NG3: Nott 1E 5 (5C 98)
Lamb Cl. NG16: Eastw 3A 22
Lamb Cl. Dr.
NG16: Eastw, Newth 5F 21
Lamb Cres. DE5: Rip 5D 9
Lambe Ct. DE23: Der 5A 136
Lambert Gdns. NG8: Aspl 2B 96
Lambert Hill NG15: Huck 2E 25
Lambert St. NG7: H Grn 3D 97
Lambeth Ct. NG9: Bee 1A 148
Lambeth Rd. NG5: Arn 2F 49
Lambie Cl. NG8: Woll 5B 96
LAMBLEY 5B 54
Lambley Almshouses
NG3: Nott 2C 98
Lambley Av. NG3: Mapp 4A 76
Lambley Bridle Rd.
NG14: Bur J 1C 78
Lambley Ct. NG3: Mapp 4E 75
Lambley Dr. DE22: All 3B 106
Lambley La. NG4: Ged 4D 77
NG14: Bur J 2C 78
Lambley Rd. NG14: Lowd 4F 55
Lambourn Ct. DE22: All 2F 107
Lambourn Dr. DE22: All 1F 107
Lambourne Cl. NG9: Bram . . .5B 118
Lambourne Cres.
NG14: Lowd 3D 57
Lambourne Dr. NG8: Woll . . .5E 95
Lambourne Gdns.
NG5: Woodt 2F 75
Lambrook Cl. DE3: Mick 1B 156
Lambton Cl. DE7: Ilk 4D 67
Lamcote Gdns.
NG12: Rad T 2D 127
Lamcote Gro. NG2: Nott 4C 122
Lamcote M. NG12: Rad T 2D 127
Lamcote St. NG2: Nott 4C 122
Lamins La. NG6: Bestw V 4A 28
Lammas Gdns. NG2: Nott 3C 122
Lamorna Gro. NG11: Wilf 2A 150
Lampeter Cl. DE21: Oak 3A 110
Lamplands NG12: Cotg 5D 155

Lamp Wood Cl. NG14: Calv . . .2D 31
Lanark Cl. NG8: Woll 2B 120
Lanark St. DE21: Chad 1D 137
Lancaster Av. NG9: Stap 2D 145
NG10: Sand 4F 143
Lancaster Ct. NG3: Nott 3A 100
Lancaster Ri. DE56: Bel 3F 13
Lancaster Rd. NG3: Nott 3A 100
NG6: Bestw V 5D 27
NG15: Huck 5C 24
Lancaster Sports Cen.
. . . . .1C 6 (2F 135)
Lancaster Wlk. DE21: Spon . . .2F 109
Lancaster Way NG8: Stre 5C 70
Lancelot Dr. NG16: Want 3E 45
Lancelyn Gdns.
NG2: West Br 4D 151
Landcroft Cres. NG5: Bestw . . .1F 73
Landcroft La. LE12: Sut B 4F 215
Lander La. DE56: Bel 5F 13
Landmere Cl. DE7: Ilk 4B 66
Landmere Gdns. NG3: Nott . . .1E 99
Landmere La.
NG2: West Br 5A 150
NG11: Rudd 1C 174
NG12: Edwal 2E 175
Landsdown Gro.
NG10: Long E 2E 169
Landseer Cl. NG7: Radf 4D 97
Lane, The DE5: Rip 4B 8
NG16: Aws 3B 68
Laneham Av. NG5: Arn 5F 51
Laneside Av. NG9: Toton 1D 169
Laneward Cl. DE7: Ilk 3C 66
Langar Cl. NG5: Sher 3B 74
Langar Rd. NG13: Bing 3D 131
Langbank Av. NG5: Top V 3D 49
Langdale Dr. DE21: Chad 4C 108
NG10: Long E 5F 167
Langdale Gro. NG13: Bing . . .2A 130
Langdale Rd. NG3: Nott 5A 100
Langdon Cl. NG10: Long E . . .2F 167
Langdown Cl. NG6: Bulw 4F 47
Langen Ct. NG10: Long E 5D 169
Langford Rd. DE3: Mick 5C 132
NG5: Arn 5A 52
Langham Av. NG3: Nott 4F 99
Langham Dr. NG14: Bur J 2E 79
Langham Pk. DE7: Stan D 3A 116
Langham Pk. Ind. Est.
DE74: C Don 4F 205
LANGLEY 3A 42
Langley Av. DE7: Ilk 2C 66
NG5: Arn 1E 75
Langley Bus. Pk.
NG16: Lang M 2A 42
Langley Dr. DE74: Keg 2B 214
LANGLEY MILL 1B 42
Langley Mill By-Pass
NG16: Lang M 4F 19
Langley Mill Station (Rail) . . .1A 42
Langley Pk. NG16: Lang M . . .1A 42
Langley Rd. DE21: Spon 5D 139
Langley St. DE22: Der 3C 134
Langsett Dr. DE73: Chel 4F 187
Langstrath Dr.
NG2: West Br 4B 152
Langstrath Rd. NG11: Clif . . .2D 173
Langton Cl. NG4: Colw 4D 101
Langtry Gdns. NG13: Bing . . .1E 131
Langtry Gro. NG7: Basf 1F 97
Langwith Cl. DE7: Ilk 2E 67

Lanscombe Pk. Rd.
DE22: D Abb 4D 107
Lansdown Cl. NG9: Chil 4A 146
Lansdowne Av. DE24: Alv 1E 187
Lansdowne Dr.
NG2: West Br 4C 150
Lansdowne Rd. NG6: Basf . . .3D 73
Lansing Cl. NG11: Clif 3E 173
Lansing Gdns. DE21: Chad . . .2A 138
Lantern Gro. DE3: Mick 4C 132
Lanthwaite Cl. NG11: Clif 2E 173
Lanthwaite Rd. NG11: Clif . . .2E 173
Lapford Cl. NG3: Mapp 1C 76
Lapwing Cl. DE24: Sin 4D 185
Larch Av. DE5: Rip 5C 8
Larch Cl. DE22: All 2C 106
NG2: West Br 4B 124
NG5: Arn 4B 50
NG13: Bing 2F 131
NG15: Huck 4A 26
Larch Cres. NG9: Bee 1D 147
NG16: Eastw 2D 43
Larchdene Av. NG8: Woll 2C 118
Larch Dr. NG10: Sand 1A 144
Larch Gdns. NG6: Bulw 5F 47
Larch Rd. DE56: Kil 5A 38
Larch Way NG12: Key 4F 199
Larges St. DE1: Der . . .2A 6 (3D 135)
Largs Cl. NG5: Top V 2D 49
Lark Cl. DE23: Lit 5B 158
NG9: Chil 3F 145
Larkdale St. NG7: Radf 4F 97
Larkfield Rd. NG16: Nuth 2A 70
LARKFIELDS 2A 70
Lark Hill DE3: Mick 4A 156
Larkhill Cres. DE24: Sin 2E 185
Larkin Cl. DE24: Sin 1F 185
LARKLANDS 3F 91
Larkland's Av. DE7: Ilk 3F 91
Larkspur Av. NG5: Redh 2D 51
Larkspur Ct. DE21: Oak 2F 109
Larwood Gro. NG5: Sher 3B 74
Lascelles Av. NG4: Ged 5C 76
Lashley Gdns. DE21: Oak 3E 109
Latham St. NG6: Bulw 5A 48
Lathbury Cl. DE21: Chad 4C 108
Lathkill Av. DE7: Ilk 2D 67
DE24: Alv 4B 162
Lathkill Cl. DE7: West H 2D 89
NG6: Bulw 5A 48
Lathkilldale Cres.
NG10: Long E 1F 193
Lathkill Dr. DE5: Mare 3C 10
Lathkill Rd. DE21: Chad 5E 109
Latimer Cl. DE23: Lit 4D 157
NG6: Bulw 1B 72
Latimer Dr. NG9: Bram 2A 118
Latimer St. DE24: Der 5C 160
Latrigg Cl. DE3: Mick 2D 157
Lauder Cl. DE24: Sin 4D 185
Laughton Av. NG2: West Br . . .4B 150
Laughton Cres. NG15: Huck . . .5D 25
Launceston Cres.
NG11: Wilf 4F 149
Launceston Rd. DE24: Alv 1A 188
Laund Av. DE56: Bel 3A 14
Laund Cl. DE56: Bel 3F 13
Launder St. NG2: Nott 3B 122
Laund Farm M. DE56: Bel 3B 14
Laund Hill DE56: Bel 4F 13
Laund Nook DE56: Bel 4F 13
Laurel Av. DE5: Rip 5C 8
NG12: Key 4E 199
Laurel Bank DE23: Der 3E 159

Laurel Cres. DE7: Smal 2E 63
  NG10: Long E 5B 168
  NG16: Nuth 5A 46
Laurel Dr. DE72: Ast T 2F 203
Laurel Rd. NG4: Carl 2C 100
Laurie Av. NG7: H Grn 2F 97
Laurie Cl. NG7: H Grn 2F 97
Laurie Pl. DE24: A'ton 4D 161
Lauriston Dr. NG6: Bulw 3C 72
Lavelle Ct. NG9: Chil 1B 170
Lavender Cl. NG8: Brox 1D 95
Lavender Cres. NG4: Carl 1C 100
Lavender Gdns. DE75: Hea . . .3A 42
Lavender Gro. NG9: Bee 3A 148
Lavender Row DE22: D Abb . .4E 107
Lavender Wlk. NG3: Nott 3C 98
Laver Cl. NG5: Arn 5A 52
Laverock Cl. NG16: Kimb 1E 69
Laverstoke Ct. DE22: Der 4D 135
Lawdon Rd. NG5: Arn 3F 51
Lawley Av. NG9: Lent A 4F 119
Lawn Av. DE22: All 3C 106
  DE65: Etw 1B 180
Lawn Cl. DE75: Hea 2E 41
Lawn Gro. NG4: Carl, Ged 1F 101
Lawn Heads Av. DE23: Lit . . .1B 158
Lawnlea Cl. DE23: Der 1D 185
Lawn Mill Rd. NG16: Kimb . . .5D 45
Lawns, The DE72: Ast T 1A 204
Lawnside DE21: Spon 3E 139
Lawnswood Cl. DE23: Lit 3B 158
Lawrence Av. DE5: Rip 1B 16
  DE21: Chad 1A 138
  DE72: Brea 3C 166
  NG4: Colw 5D 101
  NG16: Aws 2B 68
  NG16: Eastw 2E 43
Lawrence Cl. NG12: Cotg 5E 155
Lawrence Dr. NG8: Stre 5B 70
  NG16: Brins 1C 20
Lawrence M. NG12: Cotg 5E 155
    (off Lawrence Cl.)
Lawrence St. DE23: Der 3E 159
  NG9: Stap 2C 144
  NG10: Long E 3C 168
  NG10: Sand 1A 144
Lawrence Way NG7: Lent 3F 121
Lawson Av. NG10: Long E 4D 169
Lawson St. NG7: Radf 4F 97
Lawton Dr. NG6: Bulw 3B 48
Laxton Av. NG6: Bulw 2C 72
Laxton Dr. NG15: Huck 3D 25
Leabrook Cl. NG11: Clif 5B 148
Leabrook Gdns. NG15: Huck . . .1B 26
Lea Cl. DE22: All 2D 107
Leacroft Rd. DE23: Der 2A 160
  NG8: Aspl 3C 96
Leadale Av. NG15: Huck 1B 26
Lea Dr. DE3: Mick 5C 132
  DE21: Chad 2E 137
Leaf Cl. NG15: Huck 5D 11
Leafe Cl. NG9: Chil 1B 170
Leafenden Cl. DE22: D Abb . .3F 107
Leafgreen La. DE23: Lit 5B 158
Leafield Grn. NG11: Clif 1D 173
Leafy La. DE75: Hea 3E 41
Leahurst Gdns.
  NG2: West Br 3A 152
Leahurst Rd. NG2: West Br . . .3F 151
Leahy Gdns. NG5: Bestw 1E 73
Leake St. DE1: Der 3C 134
Leamington Cl. DE23: Der . . .2C 158
Leamington Dr. NG9: Chil . . .4B 146
Leamington St. DE5: Rip 4D 9

Leander Cl. DE23: Lit 4C 158
Leander Cl. NG11: Wilf 2A 150
Leaper St. DE1: Der . . .1A 6 (2D 135)
Leas, The NG14: Bulc 2A 80
Leatherlands DE74: Keg 1C 214
Leawood Gdns. DE21: Oak . . .2A 110
Leche Cft. DE56: Bel 5C 14
Lechlade Cl. DE7: West H 2C 88
Lechlade Rd. NG5: Bestw 1F 73
Ledbury Chase
  DE24: S Flds 4C 184
Ledbury Pl. DE21: Chad 4C 108
Ledbury Va. NG8: Aspl 2A 96
Ledger Wlk. *NG5: Sher* *1A 98*
    (off Jensen Way)
Ledo Av. DE5: Rip 4C 8
Leech Ct. NG16: Gilt 5A 44
Lee Cres. DE7: Ilk 2A 92
Leeds Pl. DE1: Der 5F 7 (4B 136)
Lee Farm Cl. DE73: Chel 5E 187
Lee La. DE75: Hea 3A 42
Leen Cl. NG6: Bestw V 5E 27
Leen Ct. NG15: Huck 1B 26
Leen Ct. NG7: Lent 3D 121
Leen Dr. NG6: Bulw 3B 48
  NG15: Huck 5D 11
Leen Ga. NG7: Lent 3C 120
Leen Mills La. NG15: Huck . . .5D 11
Leen Pl. NG7: Radf 5F 97
Leen Valley Country Pk. 4C 26
Leen Valley Way
  NG15: Huck 4B 26
Lee Rd. NG14: Bur J 2F 79
  NG14: Calv 1C 30
Lees, The DE72: Elv 1C 188
Lees Barn Rd.
  NG12: Rad T 3C 126
Lees Brook Ho. DE21: Chad . .1F 137
Lees Hill Footpath
  NG2: Nott 2D 123
Lees Hill St. NG2: Nott 1D 123
Leeside DE24: Alv 2F 161
Lees Rd. NG3: Mapp 1F 99
Leeway Dr. NG21: Spon 4C 138
Leicester Ho. NG9: Bram 5E 117
Leicester St. DE22: Der 5D 135
  NG10: Long E 5D 169
Leigh Cl. NG2: West Br 2B 150
Leigh Rd. NG9: Toton 5E 145
Leighton St. NG3: Nott 4E 99
Leighton Way DE56: Bel 1E 35
Leiston Gdns. NG5: Top V 4F 48
Leivers Av. NG5: Arn 4E 51
Leivers Ho. *NG5: Arn* *1F 75*
    (off Derwent Cl.)
Lema Cl. NG6: Bulw 4C 48
Leman St. DE22: Der 5D 135
Lendal Ct. NG7: Radf 5F 97
Lendrum Ct. NG14: Bur J 3E 79
Leniscar Av. DE75: Los 5B 18
Len Maynard Ct. NG3: Nott . . .4F 99
Lennox St. NG1: Nott . .2E 5 (5C 98)
Lens Rd. DE22: All 3B 106
LENTON ABBEY 4F 119
Lenton & Wortley Halls
  NG7: Nott 3A 120
Lenton Av. DE21: Chad 2E 137
  NG7: Nott 1F 121
  NG12: Toll 2B 176
Lenton Blvd. NG7: Lent 5E 97
Lenton Cir. NG12: Toll 2B 176
Lenton Ct. NG7: Lent 1E 121
  NG7: Nott 2F 121

Lenton Hall Dr. NG7: Nott 3B 120
Lenton Ind. Est. E.
  NG7: Lent 1E 149
Lenton Ind. Est. W.
  NG7: Lent 5E 121
Lenton La. NG7: Lent 3E 121
    (not continuous)
Lenton Leisure Cen. 2E 121
Lenton Mnr. NG7: Lent 2D 121
Lenton Rd.
  NG7: Nott 5A 4 (2F 121)
Lenton St. NG10: Sand 2B 144
Leominster Dr. DE21: Oak . . .3A 110
Leonard Av. NG5: Sher 5A 74
Leonard Cheshire Cl.
  DE75: Hea 3A 42
Leonard Cl. DE23: Der 5F 135
Leonard M. NG9: Chil 1A 170
Leonard St. DE23: Der 5A 136
  NG6: Bulw 2A 72
Leonard Wlk. DE23: Der 5F 135
Leopold St.
  DE1: Der 5C 6 (5F 135)
  NG10: Long E 3C 168
Le Page Ct. NG8: Bilb 2F 95
Leroy Wallace Av.
  NG7: Radf 4E 97
Lerwick Cl. NG11: Clif 2F 173
Leslie Av. NG7: H Grn 2F 97
  NG9: Bee 3E 147
  NG16: Kimb 2E 69
Leslie Cl. DE23: Lit 4D 157
Leslie Gro. NG14: Calv 2E 31
Leslie Rd. NG7: H Grn 2F 97
    (not continuous)
Letchworth Cres. NG9: Chil . .4B 146
Letcombe Rd. NG11: Clif 5D 149
Leven Cl. DE24: Sin 4E 185
Levens Cl. NG2: West Br 3B 152
Leveret Cl. DE73: Chel 4A 188
Leverton Ct. NG2: West Br 3E 151
Leverton Grn. NG11: Clif 1D 173
Leverton Wlk. NG5: Arn 4F 51
Levick Ct. NG2: Nott 3B 122
Lewcote La. DE7: West H 1F 89
Lewindon Ct. NG5: Woodt 3D 75
Lewis Cl. NG3: Nott 4C 98
Lewis Ellise Home, The
  DE22: Mac 2A 134
Lewis St. DE23: Der 2E 159
Lewiston Rd. DE21: Chad 3A 138
Lewis Way NG6: Bestw V 4A 28
Lexington Gdns. NG5: Sher . . .3C 74
Lexington Pl. NG1: Nott 3E 5
Lexington Rd. DE21: Chad . . .2B 138
Leybourne Dr. NG5: Bestw . . .1D 73
Leycote Way DE56: Bel 4F 13
Leyland Cl. NG9: Toton 1E 169
Leyland Ct. DE1: Der 1D 135
Leyland Gdns. DE1: Der 1D 135
Leylands DE22: Der 5D 107
Leyland St. DE1: Der 1D 135
Leys, The DE21: L Eat 5C 60
  NG11: Clif 2B 172
  NG12: Norm W 4E 177
  NG14: Lowd 2C 56
Leys Ct. DE56: Bel 4C 14
  NG11: Rudd 5B 174
Leys Fld. Gdns. DE73: Chel . . .4F 187
Leys Rd. NG11: Rudd 5B 174
Leys St. NG4: Neth 3F 101
Leyton Cres. NG9: Bee 3A 148
Leytonstone Dr. DE22: Mac . .3F 133
Library Rd. NG7: Nott 4B 120

Lichfield Cl. NG9: Toton 5D **145**
 NG10: Long E 4E **169**
Lichfield Dr. DE24: Alv 4F **161**
Lichfield Rd. NG2: Nott 1F **123**
Liddell Gro. NG8: Woll 5E **95**
Liddington St. NG7: Basf 1E **97**
Lidgate Cl. DE3: Mick 2B **156**
Lilac Av. DE22: Mac 3F **133**
 NG4: Carl 2B **100**
Lilac Cl. DE24: Alv 5F **161**
 NG8: Brox 1D **95**
 NG12: Key 4F **199**
Lilac Ct. DE24: Alv 5F **161**
 NG11: Clif 2B **172**
Lilac Cres. NG9: Bee 3A **148**
Lilac Gro. DE75: Hea 3D **41**
 NG9: Bee 3A **148**
Lilac M. DE7: Ilk 4C **66**
Lilac Rd. NG15: Huck 4A **26**
Lilacs, The NG9: Bee 2F **147**
Lilac Way DE22: All 3C **106**
Lilian Hind Cl. NG6: Bulw 4E **47**
Lilian Prime Cl. DE24: Alv . . .3A **162**
Lilleker Ri. NG5: Arn 3D **51**
Lilley St. DE24: Alv 5A **162**
Lillie Ter. NG2: Nott 1E **123**
Lillington Rd. NG6: Bulw 5A **48**
Lily Av. NG4: Neth 3F **101**
Lily Gro. NG9: Bee 3A **148**
Lime Av. DE1: Der 5E **135**
 DE5: Rip 5C **8**
 DE21: Bre 3C **108**
 DE56: Duff 3D **59**
 NG16: Lang M 2B **42**
Lime Cl. NG12: Rad T 2E **127**
 NG16: Nuth 1F **69**
Lime Cres. DE56: Bel 2A **36**
Lime Cft. DE22: All 1E **107**
Limedale Av. DE21: Oak 2A **110**
Limefield Ct. NG2: West Br . .4F **123**
Limegate M. DE23: Lit 1C **158**
Lime Gro. DE21: Chad 3A **138**
 DE72: Dray 4E **165**
 NG9: Stap 3C **144**
 NG10: Long E 3C **168**
 NG10: Sand 2A **144**
Lime Gro. Av. NG9: Chil 3D **147**
Limekiln Ct. NG6: Bulw 4F **47**
Lime La. DE7: Mor 2C **110**
 DE21: Oak 2F **109**
 (not continuous)
 NG5: Arn 4D **29**
Limerick Rd. DE21: Chad 4A **138**
Limes, The DE7: Mapp 4D **65**
 NG11: Bart F 5D **171**
Limes Av. DE3: Mick 2C **156**
Limes Cl. NG16: Lang M 5B **20**
Limes Pk. DE5: Rip 5B **8**
Lime St. DE7: Ilk 3E **91**
 NG6: Bulw 5A **48**
Lime Ter. NG10: Long E 3C **168**
Lime Tree Av. NG8: Cin 4A **72**
 NG8: Woll 2A **120**
Limetree Cl. NG12: Key 4E **199**
Lime Tree Ct. NG9: Nott 4F **119**
Limetree Ct. DE7: Kirk H 4B **90**
Lime Tree Gdns.
 NG14: Lowd 3D **57**
Lime Tree Ri. DE7: Kirk H 4B **90**
Lime Tree Rd. NG15: Huck . . .5A **26**
Lime Wlk. DE23: Lit 2C **158**
Limmen Gdns. NG3: Nott 4D **99**
Limpenny St. NG7: Radf 4F **97**
Linacres Dr. DE73: Chel 4F **187**

LINBY 3D **11**
Linby Av. NG15: Huck 2A **26**
Linby Cl. NG4: Ged 5D **77**
 NG5: Sher 2C **74**
Linby Dr. NG8: Stre 5C **70**
Linby Gro. NG15: Huck 1A **26**
Linby Rd. NG15: Huck 1A **26**
Linby St. NG6: Bulw 4B **48**
Linby Wlk. NG15: Huck 1F **25**
Lincoln Av. DE24: Alv 3F **161**
 NG10: Sand 4F **143**
Lincoln Cir. NG7: Nott 1F **121**
Lincoln Cl. NG9: Stap 4D **117**
Lincoln Ct. NG8: Bilb 3C **94**
Lincoln Grn. DE73: Chel 4E **187**
Lincoln Gro. NG12: Rad T . . .2E **127**
Lincoln Hall NG7: Nott 3A **122**
Lincoln St. NG1: Nott . . .2C **4** (5B **98**)
 NG6: Basf 4D **73**
Lindale Cl. NG2: Gam 2B **152**
Lindale Way DE73: Chel 4F **187**
Lindbridge Rd. NG8: Brox 5E **71**
Linden Av. NG11: Clif 2B **172**
Linden Cl. DE56: Kil 4A **38**
Linden Ct. NG9: Bee 3F **147**
Linden Gro. NG4: Ged 1A **102**
 NG9: Bee 3F **147**
 NG9: Stap 2D **145**
 NG10: Sand 1F **143**
Linden Pl. NG3: Mapp 1B **76**
Linden St. NG3: Nott 3C **98**
Lindfield Cl. NG8: Brox 5F **71**
Lindfield Rd. NG8: Brox 5E **71**
Lindford Cl. DE21: Oak 2E **109**
Lindisfarne Cl. DE24: Sin 3C **184**
Lindisfarne Gdns.
 NG5: Top V 3F **49**
Lindley St. NG16: Newth 5A **22**
Lindley Ter. NG7: H Grn 3D **97**
Lindon Dr. DE24: Alv 5B **162**
Lindrick Cl. DE3: Mick 1E **157**
 NG12: Edwal 4B **152**
Lindsay St. NG7: H Grn 3E **97**
Lindsey Cl. DE21: Chad 2D **137**
Lindum Gro. NG2: Nott 2E **123**
Lindum Rd. NG6: Basf 4C **72**
Linen Ho. NG7: Radf 4D **97**
 (off Hartley Rd.)
Linette Cl. NG5: Sher 5F **73**
Linford Ct. NG9: Bram 1A **118**
Ling Croc. NG11: Rudd 3B **174**
Lingfield Ct. NG8: Woll 2C **118**
Lingfield Ri. DE3: Mick 5B **132**
Lingford NG12: Cotg 5F **155**
Lingford St. NG15: Huck 3A **26**
Lingmell Cl. NG2: West Br 2B **152**
Lings Bar Rd. NG2: Gam 2C **152**
 (off Ambleside)
Lings Cl. DE7: Ilk 2E **67**
Lings La. NG12: Key 5D **199**
Lingwood La.
 NG14: Woodbo 2A **54**
Linkin Rd. NG9: Chil 2B **146**
Linkmel Cl. NG2: Nott 4F **121**
Linkmel Rd. NG16: Eastw 1B **42**
Links Cl. DE24: Sin 2E **185**
Linksfield Ct. NG2: West Br . . .1B **174**
Linley Dr. NG13: Bing 2D **131**
 (off Long Acre)
Linnell St. NG3: Nott 4E **99**
Linnet Cl. DE21: Spon 2E **139**
Linnet Hill DE3: Mick 4A **156**
Linsdale Cl. NG8: Bilb 5A **94**

Linsdale Gdns. NG4: Ged 3C **76**
Linton Ri. NG3: Nott 4F **99**
Linwood Cres. NG16: Eastw . .3E **43**
Lion Cl. NG8: Aspl 5B **72**
Liskeard Dr. DE22: All 1C **106**
Lismore Cl. NG7: Radf 5D **97**
Lismore Ct. DE24: Sin 3C **184**
Lissett Av. DE7: Ilk 3D **91**
Lister Cl. DE22: Der 5A **134**
Lister Ga. NG1: Nott . . .4C **4** (1B **122**)
Listergate Sq.
 NG1: Nott 4C **4** (1B **122**)
Lister Ho. NG3: Mapp 5E **75**
Lister Rd. NG7: Nott 3D **121**
Liston Dr. DE22: Der 5E **107**
Listowel Cres. NG11: Clif 3D **173**
Litchchurch St.
 DE1: Der 5F **7** (5A **136**)
Litchen Cl. DE7: Ilk 5E **67**
Litchfield Ri. NG5: Arn 2D **51**
Litchurch La. DE24: Der 1B **160**
Litchurch Plaza DE24: Der . . .1B **160**
Litchurch St. DE1: Der 5A **136**
Litmus Bldg., The NG1: Nott . . .1D **5**
Little Bounds NG2: West Br . . .1C **150**
Little Bri. St.
 DE1: Der 1A **6** (2E **135**)
LITTLE CHESTER 1A **136**
Lit. Chester Pk. DE21: Der . . .5A **108**
Littledale Cl. DE21: Oak 2B **110**
LITTLE EATON 2B **84**
Lit. Eaton By-Pass
 DE21: L Eat 5B **84**
 DE56: Cox, L Kil 1D **61**
Little Fallows DE56: Mil 5E **35**
Littlegreen Rd. NG5: Woodt . . .3D **75**
LITTLE HALLAM 4E **91**
Lit. Hallam Hill DE7: Ilk 5D **91**
Lit. Hallam La. DE7: Ilk 4E **91**
Little Hayes NG2: West Br 4B **150**
Little Hill DE74: C Don 5A **206**
Lit. Holland Gdns.
 NG16: Nuth 1A **70**
Lit. John Wlk. NG3: Nott 3C **98**
Little La. DE5: Den 1F **39**
 NG12: Toll 5D **153**
 NG14: Calv 2C **30**
 NG16: Kimb 2E **69**
Lit. Lime La. NG5: Arn 4D **29**
 (not continuous)
Lit. Longstone Cl.
 DE3: Mick 1E **157**
Little Lunnon NG11: Bart F . . .5D **171**
Little Mdw. NG12: Cotg 1F **179**
Little Mdw. Rd. DE73: Chel . . .4F **187**
Littlemoor La. NG11: Rudd . . .3D **197**
Lit. Oakwood Dr. NG5: Top V . .2C **48**
LITTLEOVER 3F **157**
Littleover Cres. DE23: Der . . .3C **158**
Littleover La. DE23: Der 3C **158**
Little Ox NG4: Colw 1F **125**
Lit. Parliament St.
 DE22: Der 5A **6** (4E **135**)
Lit. Tennis St. NG2: Nott 2F **123**
Lit. Tennis St. Sth.
 NG2: Nott 2F **123**
Littlewell La. DE7: Stan D 3E **115**
Lit. Woodbury Dr. DE23: Lit . . .5E **157**
Lit. Wood Ct. NG15: Huck 4D **25**
Littlewood Gdns. NG8: Bilb . . .5B **94**
Litton Cl. DE7: Ilk 3D **67**
 DE56: Bel 4A **14**
 NG5: Woodt 3D **75**
Litton Dr. DE21: Spon 5E **139**

Liverpool St. DE21: Chad 5D **109**
  NG3: Nott 2F **5** (5D **99**)
Liversage Almshouses
  DE1: Der 5E **7** (4A **136**)
Liversage Ct.
  DE1: Der 5F **7** (4A **136**)
Liversage Pl.
  DE1: Der 5E **7** (4A **136**)
Liversage Rd.
  DE1: Der 5E **7** (4A **136**)
Liversage St.
  DE1: Der 4E **7** (4A **136**)
Liversage Wlk.
  DE1: Der 4F **7** (4A **136**)
Livingstone Rd. DE23: Der . . .2D **159**
Livingstone St.
  NG15: News 1A **10**
Llanberis Gro. NG8: Aspl 5B **72**
Lloyd St. DE22: Der 3C **134**
  NG5: Sher 5B **74**
Loach Ct. NG8: Woll 5B **96**
Lobelia Cl. NG3: Nott 3C **98**
Lochinvar Cl. DE21: Spon 4E **139**
Lock Cl. DE7: Kirk H 4B **90**
  NG9: Bee 5F **147**
Lockerbie St. NG4: Colw 4E **101**
LOCKINGTON 5E **207**
Lockington Cl. DE73: Chel 4E **187**
Lockington Hall
  DE74: Lock 4E **207**
Lockington La. DE74: Hem . . .4C **206**
Lock La. NG10: Long E 2A **194**
  NG10: Sand 3A **144**
Locko Ct. DE21: Spon 3C **138**
Locko Rd. DE21: Chad 2C **110**
Locksley La. NG11: Clif 4D **149**
Lockton Av. DE75: Hea 4D **41**
Lock-Up Yd.
  DE1: Der 3D **7** (3F **135**)
Lockwood Cl. NG5: Top V 3F **49**
  NG9: Bee 4B **148**
Lockwood Rd. DE22: All 1C **106**
Locomotive Way
  DE24: Der 5C **136**
Lodge Cl. DE56: Duff 4D **59**
  DE65: Etw 2B **180**
  NG5: Redh 2D **51**
  NG8: Aspl 2C **96**
Lodge Dr. DE56: Bel 4D **13**
Lodge Farm La. NG5: Arn 3D **51**
Lodge La. DE1: Der . . .1B **6** (2E **135**)
  DE21: Spon 4C **138**
  NG16: Lang M 3D **19**
Lodge La. Nth.
  DE21: Spon 4C **138**
Lodge M. DE72: Ast T 2A **204**
Lodge Rd. DE7: Mapp 4E **65**
  NG10: Long E 1C **194**
  NG16: Newth 4F **43**
Lodge Row DE7: Mapp 4D **65**
Lodge St. DE72: Dray 4F **165**
Lodge Way DE3: Mick 2C **156**
Lodgewood Cl.
  NG6: Bulw 1F **71**
Lodore Cl. NG2: West Br 2B **152**
Loganberry Ct. DE24: Alv 3D **161**
Logan Ct. NG6: Basf 2D **73**
Logan St. NG6: Bulw 1B **72**
Lois Av. NG7: Lent 2E **121**
Lombard Cl. NG7: Lent 2E **121**
Lombard St. DE22: Mac 2E **133**
Lombardy Lodge
  NG9: Toton 2F **169**
Lomond Av. DE24: Sin 4E **185**

London Rd.
  DE1: Der 4D **7** (4F **135**)
  DE24: Alv, Der 2D **161**
  DE72: Shar 4D **191**
  DE74: Keg 3B **214**
  NG2: Nott 4E **5** (1C **122**)
      (not continuous)
Long Acre NG13: Bing 2D **131**
  NG15: Huck 2C **24**
Longacre NG5: Woodt 3E **75**
Long Acre E. NG13: Bing 2E **131**
Longbeck Av. NG3: Nott 1F **99**
Longbridge La. DE24: Der . . .3C **160**
  DE75: Los 1C **40**
Longclose Ct. NG6: Bulw 1F **71**
Longcliffe Ct. DE72: Ast T 1F **203**
Longcroft Av. DE7: Ilk 2D **67**
Longdale Rd. NG5: Arn 1E **74**
Longden Cl. NG9: Bram 3E **117**
Longden Mill NG3: Nott 2F **5**
Longden St.
  NG3: Nott 2F **5** (5D **99**)
Longdon's Row
  DE1: Spon 3C **138**
LONG EATON 4D **169**
Long Eaton Stadium 3E **169**
Long Eaton Station (Rail) . . .1B **194**
Longfellows Cl. NG5: Bestw 4A **50**
Longfield Av. NG8: Bilb 3B **94**
Longfield Cres. DE7: Ilk 5E **91**
Longfield La. DE7: Ilk 5E **91**
Longford Cl. DE22: All 4C **106**
Longford Cres. NG6: Bulw 2B **48**
Longford St. DE22: Der 5C **106**
Long Hill Ri. NG15: Huck 3E **25**
Longlands Cl. NG9: Bee 4A **148**
Longlands Dr.
  NG2: West Br 3C **152**
Longlands La. DE65: Find 5B **182**
Longlands Rd. NG9: Bee 4A **148**
Long La. DE74: Keg 3C **208**
  DE75: Ship 5C **42**
  NG9: Atten 1C **170**
  NG16: Want 3F **45**
Longleat Cres. NG9: Chil 3B **146**
Longley La. DE21: Spon 2C **138**
Longmead Cl. NG5: Bestw 1B **74**
Longmead Dr. NG5: Bestw 1B **74**
Long Mdw. Hill NG14: Lowd . . .2E **55**
Longmoor Av. NG14: Lowd 4D **57**
Longmoor Gdns.
  NG10: Long E 1F **167**
Longmoor La. DE72: Brea 2D **167**
  NG10: Long E 1F **167**
Longmoor Rd.
  NG10: Long E 1F **167**
Longore Sq. NG8: Woll 1C **120**
Longridge Rd. NG5: Woodt 3E **75**
Long Row DE56: Bel 5E **13**
  DE72: Shar 4A **192**
  NG1: Nott 3B **4** (1B **122**)
      (not continuous)
  NG11: King 5F **209**
Long Row W.
  NG1: Nott 3B **4** (1B **122**)
Longshaw Gdns. DE24: Alv . . .5F **161**
Longs Mill DE1: Der 1B **6**
Long Stairs NG1: Nott 4E **5**
Longstock Cl. DE21: Oak 4D **109**
Longstone Ri. DE56: Bel 3A **14**
Longstone Wlk.
  DE1: Der 5B **6** (4E **135**)
Longthorpe Cl. DE23: Lit 4F **157**
Longthorpe Ct. NG5: Arn 5E **51**

Longue Dr. NG14: Calv 2C **30**
      (not continuous)
Longwall Av. NG2: Nott 4F **121**
Longwalls La. DE56: Bel 1A **12**
Long W. Cft. NG14: Calv 2B **30**
Longwood Ct. NG5: Top V 4E **49**
Lonscale Cl. NG2: West Br . . .3B **152**
Lonsdale Dr. NG9: Toton 1D **169**
Lonsdale Hall DE22: Der 4C **134**
Lonsdale Pl. DE22: Der 4C **134**
Lonsdale Rd. NG7: Radf 4D **97**
Loom Cl. DE56: Bel 4B **14**
Lord Haddon Rd. DE7: Ilk 1D **91**
Lord Nelson St. NG2: Nott 1E **123**
Lord St. DE24: A'ton 1C **186**
  NG2: Nott 1E **123**
Lorimer Av. NG4: Ged 4E **77**
Lorna Ct. NG3: Nott 1C **98**
Lorne Gro. NG12: Rad T 2E **127**
Lorne St. DE22: Der 5E **135**
Lorne Wlk. NG3: Nott 3B **98**
Lorraine Cl. DE24: S Loc 3D **187**
Lortas Rd. NG5: Sher 5E **73**
LOSCOE 5B **18**
Loscoe-Denby La. DE5: Den . . .1F **39**
  DE75: Los 5A **18**
Loscoe Gdns. NG5: Sher 1A **98**
Loscoe Grange DE75: Los 1B **40**
Loscoe Mt. Rd. NG5: Sher . . .5B **74**
Loscoe Rd. DE21: Chad 4F **109**
  DE75: Hea 1C **40**
  NG5: Sher 1B **98**
Lothian Pl. DE21: Chad 1C **136**
  DE74: C Don 1F **211**
Lothian Rd. NG12: Toll 2B **176**
Lothlorien Cl. DE23: Lit 4A **158**
Lothmore Ct. NG2: Nott 3A **122**
Lotus Cl. NG3: Nott 3D **99**
Loudon St. DE23: Der 5F **135**
Loudoun Pl. DE74: C Don 5F **205**
Loughborough Av.
  NG2: Nott 1E **123**
Loughborough Rd.
  NG2: West Br 2D **151**
  NG11: Bunny, Rudd 1C **174**
Loughrigg Cl. NG2: Nott 4A **122**
Louis Av. NG9: Bee 1D **147**
Louise Av. NG4: Neth 2F **101**
Louise Greaves La.
  DE21: Spon 2D **139**
Louvain Rd. DE22: Der 5B **134**
  DE23: Der 5B **134**
Lovelace Wlk. NG15: Huck 1A **26**
Lovell Cl. NG6: Bulw 2E **71**
Lowater Pl. NG4: Carl 3A **100**
Lowater St. NG4: Carl 3A **100**
Lowcroft NG5: Woodt 3E **75**
LOWDHAM 2C **56**
Lowdham La.
  NG14: Woodbo 5C **32**
Lowdham Rd. NG4: Ged 4B **76**
  NG14: Epp 5F **33**
  NG14: Gun 4D **57**
Lowdham Station (Rail) 4D **57**
Lowdham St.
  NG3: Nott 2F **5** (5D **99**)
LOWER BEAUVALE 5A **22**
Lower Beauvale
  NG16: Newth 1F **43**
Lwr. Bloomsgrove Rd.
  DE7: Ilk 5E **67**
Lwr. Brook St.
  NG10: Long E 4D **169**
Lower Canaan NG11: Rudd . . .3C **174**

Lwr. Chapel St. DE7: Ilk 1E 91
Lwr. Claramount Rd.
    DE75: Hea 3F 41
Lower Ct. NG9: Bee 1F 147
Lwr. Dale Rd. DE23: Der 1E 159
Lwr. Dunstead Rd.
    NG16: Lang M 1F 41
Lwr. Eldon St.
    NG2: Nott 4F 5 (1D 123)
Lwr. Eley St.
    DE1: Der 5B 6 (5E 135)
Lwr. Gladstone St.
    DE75: Hea 2D 41
Lwr. Granby St. DE7: Ilk 5E 67
Lower Grn. DE65: Find 5C 182
Lwr. Hall Cl. DE56: H'ook 1B 60
LOWER HARTSHAY 3A 8
LOWER KILBURN 5E 37
Lower Maples DE75: Ship 4F 41
Lwr. Middleton St. DE7: Ilk 1F 91
Lower Mill DE5: Rip 5D 9
Lwr. Orchard St.
    NG9: Stap 1C 144
Lower Pk. St. NG9: Stap 2B 144
Lwr. Parliament St.
    NG1: Nott 2C 4 (5B 98)
Lwr. Regent St. NG9: Bee 2F 147
Lower Rd. DE22: Mac 1E 133
    NG9: Bee 1A 148
Lwr. Stanton Rd. DE7: Ilk 4E 91
Lwr. Whitworth Rd. DE7: Ilk . . .4E 91
Lowes Hill DE5: Rip 3C 8
                        (not continuous)
Lowes La. DE73: Swar 1B 200
Lowe St. DE24: A'ton 5D 161
Loweswater Ct. NG2: Gam . . .1B 152
Lowlands Dr. NG12: Key 2E 199
Lowlands Lea DE75: Hea 2E 41
Lowlands Rd. DE56: Bel 4A 14
Low Pavement
    NG1: Nott 4C 4 (1B 122)
Lows Cl. DE73: Chel 4A 188
Lows La. DE7: Stan D 3E 115
                        (not continuous)
Low Wood Rd. NG6: Bulw 2D 71
Loxley Cl. DE21: Oak 3A 110
    NG15: Huck 4D 25
Loxley Mdw. NG14: Bur J 3D 79
Loxton Ct. DE3: Mick 5C 132
Loyne Cl. DE24: Sin 4E 185
Luccombe Dr. DE24: Alv 1C 188
Lucerne Cl. NG11: Wilf 2A 150
Lucerne Rd. DE21: Oak 2B 110
Lucknow Av. NG3: Mapp P . . .2C 98
Lucknow Ct. NG3: Mapp P . . .1C 98
Lucknow Dr. NG3: Mapp P . . .2C 98
Lucknow Rd. NG3: Mapp P . . .2C 98
Ludford Cl. NG10: Long E 1D 195
Ludford Rd. NG6: Bulw 4B 48
Ludgate Cl. NG5: Arn 2F 49
Ludgate Wlk. DE22: Mac 3D 133
Ludham Av. NG6: Bulw 4A 48
Ludlam Av. NG16: Gilt 5F 43
Ludlow Av. NG2: West Br 1E 151
    NG9: Bram 4C 118
Ludlow Hill Rd.
    NG2: West Br 3E 151
Lulworth Cl. DE23: Lit 5C 158
    NG2: West Br 3B 150
Lulworth Ct. NG16: Kimb 5E 45
Lumb La. DE56: B'ook 1A 34
Lundie Cl. DE24: S Flds 4C 184
Lune Cl. NG9: Atten 5D 147

Lupin Cl. DE21: Oak 2B 110
    NG3: Nott 3C 98
Luther Cl. NG3: Nott 3D 99
Luton Cl. NG8: Aspl 1C 96
Lutterell Ct. NG2: West Br 3C 150
Lutterell Way
    NG2: West Br 3A 152
Lybster M. NG2: Nott 3A 122
Lychgate Cl. DE21: Oak 3C 108
Lychgate Cl. NG16: Want 4E 45
Lydia Gdns. NG16: Eastw 3D 43
Lydney Pk. NG2: West Br 2A 150
Lydstep Cl. DE21: Oak 3B 110
Lyle Cl. NG16: Kimb 5D 45
Lyme Pk. NG2: West Br 3A 150
Lymington Gdns. NG3: Nott . . .4E 99
Lymn Av. NG4: Ged 5E 77
Lynam Ct. NG6: Bulw 5A 48
Lyncombe Gdns.
    NG12: Key 2E 199
Lyncroft Av. DE5: Rip 4D 9
Lyndale Dr. DE5: Cod 1A 18
Lyndale Rd. NG9: Bram 5F 117
Lynden Av. NG10: Long E 5C 168
Lyndhurst Gdns.
    NG2: West Br 4C 150
Lyndhurst Gro. DE21: Chad . . .3F 137
Lyndhurst Rd. NG2: Nott 1E 123
Lyndhurst St. DE23: Der 1F 159
Lynmoor Ct. NG15: Huck 5E 11
Lynmouth Cres. NG7: Radf . . .3D 97
Lynmouth Dr. DE7: Ilk 4C 66
Lynncroft NG16: Eastw 1F 43
Lynnstead Dr. NG15: Huck . . .4B 24
Lynton Cl. DE5: Rip 3C 8
Lynton Ct. NG3: Nott 3E 99
Lynton Gdns. NG5: Arn 4F 51
Lynton Rd. NG9: Chil 2B 146
Lynton St.
    DE22: Der 5A 6 (4D 135)
Lynwood Rd. DE24: Sin 2E 185
Lyons Cl. NG11: Rudd 3A 174
Lysander Dr. DE73: Chel 5D 187
Lytham Cl. DE21: Chad 4C 108
Lytham Dr. NG12: Edwal 5B 152
Lytham Gdns. NG5: Top V 3F 49
Lythe Cl. NG11: Wilf 3F 149
Lyttelton St. DE22: Der 3B 134
Lytton Cl. NG3: Nott 1F 5 (5D 99)

M

Mabel Gro. NG2: West Br 5F 123
Mabel St. NG2: Nott 3C 122
Macaulay Gro. NG16: Nuth . . .1A 70
Macaulay St. DE24: Sin 1F 185
McClelland Av.
    NG6: Bestw V 4A 28
Macdonald Sq. DE7: Kirk H . . .5B 90
McGough M. DE24: Sin 1F 185
Machins La. NG12: Edwal 5F 151
McIntosh Rd. NG4: Ged 4C 76
Mackenzie St. DE22: Der 2B 134
Mackinley Av. NG9: Stap 4D 117
Macklin St.
    DE22: Der 3B 6 (3E 135)
MACKWORTH 2F 133
Mackworth Rd. DE22: Der 2D 135
Maclaren Gdns.
    NG11: Rudd 5C 174
Maclean Rd. NG4: Carl 3B 100
Macmillan Cl. NG3: Mapp 5E 75
McNeil Gro. DE72: Dray 4F 165

Macready Pl. DE24: Alv 4E 161
Madden Cl. NG5: Bestw 2E 73
Madeley Cl. DE3: Mick 2C 156
Madeley St. DE23: Der 1F 159
Madford Bus. Pk. NG5: Arn . . .1C 74
Madison Av. DE21: Chad 1D 137
Madison Ct. NG7: Lent 1C 120
Madryn Wlk. NG5: Bestw 5F 49
Mafeking St. NG2: Nott 1F 123
Magdala Rd. NG3: Mapp P . . .2B 98
Magdalene Way NG15: Huck . . .1F 25
Magna Cl. NG14: Lowd 3D 57
Magnolia Cl. NG8: Brox 1D 95
Magnolia Cl. NG9: Bram 4C 118
Magnolia Gro. NG15: Huck . . .5A 26
Magnus Ct. NG9: Bee 2F 147
Magnus Rd. NG5: Sher 4B 74
Magson Cl. NG3: Nott 5D 99
Maiden La.
    NG1: Nott 3E 5 (1C 122)
Maidens Dale NG5: Arn 4C 50
Maid Marian Way
    NG1: Nott 3A 4 (1A 122)
Maidstone Dr. DE24: Alv 1E 187
    NG8: Woll 3C 118
Maidwell Cl. DE56: Bel 3A 14
Main Av. DE22: All 5E 83
Maine Dr. DE21: Chad 2F 137
Main Rd. DE5: L Har 3A 8
    DE5: Pen 1A 8
    DE7: Mor 1F 109
    DE72: Elv 1F 189
    NG4: Ged 1E 101
    NG7: Nott 2B 148
    NG11: Wilf 2A 150
    NG12: Cotg, Rad T 1C 154
    NG12: Plum 3D 177
    NG12: Rad T 2D 127
    NG12: Shel 2B 104
    NG14: Bulc 2F 79
    NG16: Want 3E 45
Main St. DE7: H Woo 5A 38
    DE7: Mapp 4D 65
    DE7: Stan D 5E 115
    DE65: Burn 1E 181
    DE65: Etw 2A 180
    DE65: Find 5C 182
    DE72: Amba 5C 164
    DE72: Brea 3C 166
    DE72: W Tre 5D 203
    DE74: Hem 5C 206
    DE74: Lock 5E 207
    LE12: Sut B 4F 215
    NG2: Gam 1B 152
    NG4: Lamb 5A 54
    NG6: Bulw 1A 72
    NG8: Stre 5A 70
    NG10: Long E 4D 169
    NG11: Rudd 3D 197
    NG12: Key 5D 199
    NG12: Shel 1B 104
    NG13: Newton 2F 105
    NG14: Bur J 3E 79
    NG14: Calv 1A 30
    NG14: Cayt 4F 57
    NG14: Epp 3D 33
    NG14: Gun 2E 81
    NG14: Lowd 2C 56
    NG14: Woodbo 5A 32
    NG15: Lin 3C 10
    NG15: Pap 3F 11
    NG16: Aws 2B 68
    NG16: Brins 1C 20
    NG16: Eastw 3E 43

Main St. NG16: Kimb 1E **69**	**Manns Leys** NG12: Cotg 1D **179**	**Manvers St.** DE5: Rip 5D **9**
NG16: Newth 2B **44**	**Mann St.** NG7: Basf 2E **97**	NG2: Nott 3F **5** (1D **123**)
Maitland Av. NG5: Woodt 3E **75**	**Manor Av.** DE23: Lit 5B **134**	NG4: Neth 4F **101**
Maitland Rd. NG5: Woodt 3E **75**	NG2: Nott 4F **5** (1D **123**)	**Manville Cl.** NG8: Aspl 4B **96**
Maize Cl. DE23: Lit 5F **157**	NG9: Atten 5D **147**	NG9: Bram 2A **118**
Major St. NG1: Nott 1B **4** (5B **98**)	NG9: Bee 2E **147**	**Maori Av.** NG15: Huck 4C **24**
MAKENEY 1F **59**	NG9: Stap 5C **116**	**Maple Av.** DE5: Rip 5B **8**
Makeney Rd. DE56: Duff 5E **59**	**Manor Cl.** NG12: Edwal 5A **152**	DE23: Lit 5C **158**
DE56: H'ook 1A **60**	**Manor Ct.** DE72: Brea 3D **167**	NG9: Bee 3A **148**
DE56: Mil 1F **59**	DE73: Bar T 4A **200**	NG10: Sand 1A **144**
Malbon Cl. NG3: Nott 2E **99**	NG4: Carl 3E **101**	**Maplebeck Ct.** DE1: Der 2F **135**
Malcolm Cl. NG3: Mapp P 3B **98**	NG9: Bram 1B **146**	**Maplebeck Rd.** NG5: Arn 5F **51**
Malcolm Gro. DE23: Lit 3D **157**	**Manor Cres.** NG4: Carl 2E **101**	**Maple Cl.** NG12: Key 4F **199**
Malcolm St. DE23: Der 1A **160**	**Manor Cft.** DE5: Rip 2C **8**	NG12: Rad T 3E **127**
Maldon Cl. NG9: Chil 4B **146**	NG6: Basf 4D **73**	NG13: Bing 2F **131**
NG10: Long E 1D **195**	**Mnr. Farm Cl.** NG11: Rudd . .3D **197**	**Maple Ct.** NG16: Kimb 1E **69**
Malham Rd. DE23: Lit 5E **157**	**Mnr. Farm Ct.** NG11: King . . .5E **209**	**Mapledene Cres.**
Malin Cl. DE24: Alv 1A **188**	**Mnr. Farm La.** NG11: Clif 1D **173**	NG8: Woll 2B **118**
NG5: Arn 4A **52**	**Mnr. Farm M.** DE65: Burn . . .1E **181**	**Maple Dr.** DE24: Alv 5F **161**
Malin Hill NG1: Nott 4D **5**	DE72: Ast T 1A **204**	DE56: Bel 2A **36**
Malkin Av. NG12: Rad T 1F **127**	**Mnr. Farm Rd.** DE72: Ast T . .1A **204**	DE72: Ast T 2F **203**
Mallard Cl. NG6: Basf 3E **73**	NG10: Long E 5E **169**	DE73: Chel 5E **187**
NG13: Bing 3F **131**	**Manor Flds. Dr.** DE7: Ilk 3C **90**	NG4: Ged 5A **78**
Mallard Ct. NG9: Bee 3F **147**	**Manor Grn.** NG4: Carl 2E **101**	NG15: Huck 4D **25**
Mallard Rd. NG4: Neth 4A **102**	**Manor Grn. Wlk.** NG4: Carl . .2E **101**	NG16: Nuth 1A **70**
Mallard Wlk. DE3: Mick 4B **156**	**Manor Ho. Cl.** NG11: Wilf . . .5A **122**	**Maple Gdns.** DE75: Hea 3C **40**
Mallow Way NG13: Bing 2B **130**	NG14: Lowd 2C **56**	NG16: Lang M 1A **42**
(not continuous)	**Manor La.** NG12: Shel 1B **104**	**Maple Gro.** DE22: All 5C **82**
Malmesbury Rd. NG3: Mapp . .3F **75**	**Manorleigh** DE72: Brea 3D **167**	DE72: Brea 3E **167**
NG8: Aspl 5A **72**	**Manor Pk.** DE72: Bor 2F **163**	**Maple Leaf Way**
Maltby Cl. DE22: D Abb 3E **107**	NG11: Rudd 4A **174**	NG15: Huck 5B **26**
Maltby Rd. NG3: Mapp 3F **75**	**Manor Pk. Ct.** DE22: Der 5A **134**	**Maple Rd.** DE74: C Don 4F **205**
Malt Cotts. NG7: Basf 1E **97**	**Manor Pk. Way** DE22: Der . . .5A **134**	**Maples, The** DE75: Ship 4F **41**
Malthouse Cl. NG16: Eastw . . .3E **43**	**Manor Rd.** DE7: Ilk 1D **91**	**Maples St.** NG7: H Grn 3E **97**
Malthouse Rd. DE7: Ilk 5E **91**	DE22: Der 5B **134**	**Maplestead Av.** NG11: Wilf . . .2A **150**
Malthouse Yd. DE5: Rip 5C **8**	DE23: Der 5B **134**	**Mapleton Av.** DE21: Chad 4E **109**
Malting Cl. NG11: Rudd 5B **174**	DE56: Bel 1E **35**	**Mapleton Rd.** DE72: Dray 3F **165**
Maltings, The	DE72: Bor 1F **163**	**Mapletree Cl.** NG5: Bestw 5A **50**
DE1: Der 4D **7** (4F **135**)	DE73: Chel 5E **187**	**Maple Way** NG2: West Br 4D **151**
DE22: Der 2C **134**	NG4: Carl 2E **101**	MAPPERLEY
DE72: Shar 5F **191**	NG11: Bart F 5D **171**	DE7 . . . . .4D **65**
NG3: Nott 3E **99**	NG12: Key 3D **199**	NG5 . . . . .4E **75**
NG6: Basf 5D **73**	NG13: Bing 2E **131**	**Mapperley Brook** DE7: Mapp . .5F **65**
Maltmill La.	NG14: Calv 2D **31**	**Mapperley Cres.** NG3: Mapp . .5D **75**
NG1: Nott 4C **4** (1C **122**)	NG16: Eastw 3E **43**	**Mapperley Hall Dr.**
Malton Pl. DE21: Chad 4C **108**	**Manor St.** NG2: Nott 1D **123**	NG3: Mapp P 1B **98**
Malton Rd. NG5: Sher 5E **73**	**Manorwood Rd.**	**Mapperley Hall Gdns.**
Malvern Cl. DE3: Mick 5C **132**	NG12: Cotg 1E **179**	NG3: Mapp P 1C **98**
NG3: Nott 1D **99**	**Mansell Cl.** NG16: Eastw 3A **44**	**Mapperley Hgts.**
Malvern Ct. NG3: Mapp P 3B **98**	**Mansfield Ct.** NG5: Sher 2A **98**	NG5: Woodt 2A **76**
NG9: Bee 2A **148**	**Mansfield Gro.** NG1: Nott 4A **98**	**Mapperley La.** DE7: Mapp 5D **65**
Malvern Cres.	**Mansfield La.** NG14: Calv 1E **31**	**Mapperley Orchard**
NG2: West Br 3E **151**	**Mansfield Rd.**	NG5: Arn 5A **52**
Malvern Gdns.	DE1: Der 1D **7** (2F **135**)	MAPPERLEY PARK
NG10: Long E 3F **167**	DE21: Bre 2E **109**	DE7 . . . . .4B **64**
Malvern Rd. NG2: West Br . . .3D **151**	DE21: Der 5A **108**	NG3 . . . . .1B **98**
NG3: Nott 1D **99**	DE75: Hea 2E **41**	**Mapperley Pk. Dr.**
Malvern Way DE21: Chad 4C **108**	NG1: Nott 1C **4** (2A **98**)	NG3: Mapp P 2B **98**
NG10: Long E 5C **168**	NG5: Arn, Redh, Sher 1B **28**	**Mapperley Plains**
Manchester St. DE22: Der 2C **134**	NG5: Sher 2A **98**	NG3: Mapp 2A **76**
Mandalay St. NG6: Basf 3C **72**	NG16: Brins, Eastw 3D **21**	**Mapperley Ri.** NG3: Mapp 5D **75**
Mandarin Way DE24: Alv 4E **161**	**Mansfields Cft.** DE65: Etw 2A **180**	**Mapperley Rd.** NG3: Mapp P . .3B **98**
Manesty Cres. NG11: Clif 4D **173**	**Mansfield St.** DE1: Der 1F **135**	**Mapperley St.** NG5: Sher 5B **74**
Manifold Dr. DE24: Alv 3A **162**	NG5: Sher 5B **74**	**Mapperley Wood**
Manifold Gdns. NG2: Nott 3B **122**	**Manston M.** NG7: Radf 4E **97**	Local Nature Reserve 4E **65**
Manly Cl. NG5: Top V 4D **49**	**Manthorpe Cres.** NG5: Sher . . .4E **75**	**March Cl.** NG5: Top V 5D **49**
Manners Av. DE7: Ilk 1C **90**	**Manton Cres.** NG9: Lent A 5E **119**	**Marchesi Cl.** NG15: Huck 5D **25**
Manners Ind. Est. DE7: Ilk 1C **90**	**Manvers Av.** DE5: Rip 5D **9**	**Marchington Cl.**
Manners Rd. DE7: Ilk 1D **91**	**Manvers Bus. Pk.**	DE22: D Abb 4D **107**
Manners St. DE7: Ilk 4F **91**	NG12: Cotg 4F **155**	**Marchwood Cl.** NG8: Radf 5C **96**
Manning St. NG3: Nott 3C **98**	**Manvers Ct.**	**Marco Island** NG1: Nott 2E **5**
Manning Vw. DE7: Ilk 5E **67**	NG2: Nott 3F **5** (1D **123**)	**Marcus St.** DE1: Der 1F **135**
Mannion Cres.	**Manvers Gro.** NG12: Rad T . . .2E **127**	**Mardale Cl.** NG2: West Br 3B **152**
NG10: Long E 1A **194**	**Manvers Rd.** NG2: West Br . . .2E **151**	**Mardling Av.** NG5: Bestw 2F **73**

Maree Cl. DE24: Sin 2D **185**
MAREHAY 3C **16**
Marfleet Cl. DE3: Mick 5C **132**
Margaret Av. DE7: Ilk 2E **91**
   DE21: Chad 3E **137**
   NG10: Long E 2E **169**
   NG10: Sand 4A **144**
Margaret Cres. NG4: Ged 5D **77**
Margaret Pl. NG13: Bing 1C **130**
Margarets Ct. NG9: Bram . . .5F **117**
Margaret St. DE1: Der 1F **135**
Margreave Rd. DE21: Chad . . .1E **137**
Marham Cl. NG2: Nott 2D **123**
Marhill Rd. NG4: Carl 3E **101**
Maria Ct. NG7: Nott 2F **121**
Mariana Cl. DE73: Chel 4D **187**
Marie Gdns. NG15: Huck 4F **25**
Marigold Cl. DE21: Oak 2A **110**
Marina Av. NG9: Bee 3E **147**
Marina Dr. DE21: Spon 3C **138**
   DE24: A'ton 1D **187**
Marina Rd. DE7: Smal 4A **40**
Mariner Ct. NG6: Bulw 1F **71**
Marion Av. NG15: Huck 5E **11**
Maris Cl. NG11: Clif 1B **172**
Maris Dr. NG14: Bur J 3D **79**
Marjorie Rd. DE21: Chad 5D **109**
MARKEATON 5B **106**
Markeaton Craft Village 5B **106**
Markeaton Crematorium
   DE22: Mark 1F **133**
Markeaton La.
   DE22: Mark 1F **133**
Markeaton Light Railway
   Markeaton Station 1B **134**
Markeaton Pk. 1B **134**
Markeaton Station
   Markeaton Light Railway
   . . . . .1B **134**
Markeaton St.
   DE1: Der 1A **6** (1C **134**)
Market Head DE56: Bel 5F **13**
Market Pl. DE1: Der . .2D **7** (3F **135**)
   DE5: Cod 1B **18**
   DE5: Rip 5C **8**
   DE7: Ilk 2D **91**
   DE56: Bel 1F **35**
   DE75: Hea 3D **41**
   (off Market St.)
   NG5: Arn 5E **51**
   NG6: Dulw 5A **48**
   NG10: Long E 3D **169**
   NG13: Bing 2D **131**
   NG15: Huck 2F **25**
Market Side *NG6: Bulw* 5A **48**
   (off Duke St.)
Market St. DE7: Ilk 2E **91**
   DE72: Dray 4F **165**
   DE74: C Don 1A **212**
   DE75: Hea 2D **41**
   NG1: Nott 2B **4** (5B **98**)
   NG13: Bing 2D **131**
Markham Ct. DE21: Oak 3E **109**
Markham Cres. NG5: Sher 3B **74**
Markham Rd. NG9: Bram 4C **118**
Mark's Cl. DE23: Der 5C **158**
Mark St. NG10: Sand 3B **144**
Marlborough, The
   NG3: Nott 3B **98**
Marlborough Ct.
   NG2: West Br 1E **151**
   NG9: Bee 5E **119**
Marlborough Dr. DE56: Bel . . .4B **14**

Marlborough Rd.
   DE24: Der 4A **160**
   DE72: Brea 4C **166**
   NG5: Woodt 2C **74**
   NG9: Bee 5E **119**
   NG10: Long E 2E **169**
Marlborough St. NG7: Lent . .4D **121**
Marldon Cl. NG8: Bilb 5A **94**
Marle Pit Hill LE12: Sut B 4F **215**
Marlow Av. NG6: Basf 5D **73**
Marlow Cres. DE7: West H . . .2C **88**
Marlowe Ct. DE23: Der 5E **159**
   (not continuous)
MARLPOOL 5E **41**
Marl Rd. NG12: Rad T 2A **128**
Marlwood Cl. NG12: Cotg 2F **179**
Marmion Rd. NG3: Nott 3F **99**
Marnham Dr. NG3: Nott 1D **99**
Marple Sq. NG3: Nott 3B **98**
Marquis Gdns. DE73: Chel . . .1D **201**
Marriott Av. NG9: Chil 3F **145**
Marriott Cl. NG9: Chil 3F **145**
Marsant Cl. NG8: Woll 5B **96**
Marsden Cl. DE56: Duff 4D **59**
   NG6: Bulw 2D **73**
Marsden St. DE24: A'ton 4D **161**
Marshall Cl. NG14: Calv 1C **30**
Marshall Dr. NG9: Bram 5E **117**
Marshall Hill Dr.
   NG3: Mapp 1A **100**
Marshall Rd. NG3: Mapp 1F **99**
Marshall St. DE75: Hea 2E **41**
   NG5: Sher 5B **74**
Marshall Way DE7: Kirk H 4B **90**
Marsh Av. DE7: Ilk 2D **67**
Marshaw Cl. DE3: Mick 2D **157**
Marshgreen Cl. DE24: Alv . . .1C **188**
Marsh La. DE56: Bel 4F **13**
Marsh La. Cres. DE56: Bel . . .5A **14**
Marston Cl. DE23: Lit 1C **184**
   DE56: Bel 3B **14**
Marston Rd. NG3: Nott 3A **100**
Martell Ct. NG9: Chil 5B **146**
Martin Cl. NG6: Bulw 4E **47**
Martin Ct. NG6: Bulw 4F **47**
Martin Cres. NG11: Rudd 4A **174**
Martindale Cl. NG2: Gam 1B **152**
Martindale Ct. DE56: Bel 4C **14**
Martin Dr. DE21: Chad 5F **109**
Martinmass Cl. NG7: Lent 2D **121**
Martin's Hill NG4: Carl 3D **101**
Martin's Pond Nature Reserve
   . . . . .5D **95**
Marton Rd. NG6: Bulw 3B **48**
   NG9: Chil 5B **146**
Marvin Rd. NG9: Bee 2E **147**
Marvyn Cl. NG6: Bulw 1D **73**
Marwood Crcs. NG4: Carl 5B **76**
Marwood Rd. NG4: Carl 1B **100**
Mary Ct. NG3: Nott 1D **99**
Maryland Ct. NG9: Stap 4D **117**
Maryland Rd. DE21: Chad 2A **138**
Marylebone Cres.
   DE22: Mac 2E **133**
Mary Rd. NG16: Eastw 3A **44**
Masefield Av. DE23: Der 4D **159**
Masonic Pl.
   NG1: Nott 2A **4** (5A **98**)
Mason Rd. DE7: Ilk 5C **66**
Masons Pl. Bus. Pk.
   DE21: Chad 2C **136**
Massey Cl. NG14: Bur J 4D **79**
Massey Gdns. NG3: Nott 4D **99**
Masson Ct. NG5: Top V 3F **49**

Masson Wlk. DE22: Der 4D **135**
Matlock Cl. NG1: Nott . .1B **4** (5B **98**)
   NG10: Long E 1E **193**
Matlock Ho. DE21: Spon 5D **139**
Matlock Rd. DE21: Chad 4E **109**
   DE56: Bel 4E **13**
Matlock St. NG4: Neth 3E **101**
Matthews Ct. NG9: Stap 3E **117**
Matthew St. DE24: Alv 5E **161**
Matthew Thomas Ct.
   NG9: Bee 2F **147**
Matthew Way DE23: Lit 4D **157**
Mattingly Rd. NG6: Bulw 1F **71**
Maud St. NG7: Basf 1F **97**
Maun Av. NG7: Radf 4C **96**
Maun Gdns. NG7: Radf 4C **96**
Maurice Dr. NG3: Mapp 5D **75**
Maws La. NG16: Kimb 5D **45**
Max Rd. DE21: Chad 5D **109**
Maxtoke Rd. NG7: Nott 2F **121**
Maxwell Av. DE22: Marn 5C **106**
Maxwell Cl. NG7: Lent 2E **121**
Maxwell St. DE72: Brea 3E **167**
   NG10: Long E 4D **169**
May Av. NG8: Woll 1D **119**
May Ct. NG5: Sher 1A **98**
Maycroft Gdns. NG3: Nott 3F **99**
Maydene Cl. NG11: Clif 2C **172**
Mayes Rd. NG6: Bestw V 5D **27**
Mayfair NG12: Rad T 2C **128**
Mayfair Cl. DE56: Duff 3D **59**
Mayfair Cres. DE22: Mac 2D **133**
Mayfair Gdns. NG5: Sher 2E **73**
Mayfield Av. DE56: Kil 4F **37**
   DE75: Hea 3D **41**
   NG14: Bur J 2E **79**
Mayfield Cl. NG2: Nott 3B **122**
Mayfield Dr. NG9: Stap 3E **117**
Mayfield Gro.
   NG10: Long E 2D **169**
Mayfield Mobile Home Pk.
   DE72: Brea 4C **166**
Mayfield Rd. DE21: Chad 1D **137**
   NG4: Carl 3A **100**
Mayflower Cl.
   NG2: West Br 1F **151**
Mayflower Rd.
   NG16: Newth 4A **44**
Mayland Cl. NG8: Bilb 4B **94**
Maylands DE72: Bor 2A **164**
Maylands Av. DE72: Brea 3D **167**
Mayo Rd. NG5: Sher 1A **98**
Maypole NG11: Clif 5D **149**
Maypole La. DE23: Lit 4D **157**
Maypole Yd.
   NG1: Nott 2C **4** (5B **98**)
May's Av. NG4: Carl 4B **100**
Mays Cl. NG4: Carl 4B **100**
May St. DE7: Ilk 4D **67**
   DE22: Der 5A **6** (5E **135**)
Maythorn Cl. NG2: West Br . . .5B **150**
Maythorne Wlk. NG5: Bestw . .4B **50**
Mayvale Gro. DE22: Der 4B **134**
Mead Cl. DE24: Sin 2E **185**
Meadow Av. DE5: Cod 1A **18**
Meadowbank Ct.
   NG16: Eastw 1C **42**
Meadowbank Way
   NG9: Bee 3F **147**
   (off Queen's Rd.)
   NG16: Eastw 1C **42**
Meadow Brook Cl.
   DE23: Lit 5E **157**

Meadow Brown Rd.
NG7: H Grn 2D **97**
Meadow Cl. DE7: H Woo 1C **62**
DE21: Spon 4D **139**
DE65: Find 4C **182**
DE72: Brea 4D **167**
DE72: Dray 4F **165**
NG2: Nott 3D **123**
NG4: Lamb 1F **77**
NG15: Huck 4C **24**
NG16: Eastw 5E **21**
Meadow Cotts. NG4: Neth 3E **101**
Meadow Ct. DE56: Bel 5E **13**
DE56: Kil 5F **37**
DE72: Amba 5C **164**
NG2: Nott 3E **123**
(Brand St.)
NG2: Nott 3E **123**
(Meadow Cl.)
Meadow Cres.
DE74: C Don 2A **212**
Meadow Dr. NG12: Key 3F **199**
Meadow End NG12: Rad T . . .2B **128**
Meadow Gdns. DE75: Hea 3A **42**
NG9: Chil 4D **147**
Meadowgrass Cl. DE23: Lit . . .5A **158**
Meadow Gro. NG2: Nott 3D **123**
Meadow Lane 3D **123**
Meadow La.
DE1: Der 2F **7** (3A **136**)
DE21: Chad 4E **137**
DE24: Alv 2E **161**
NG2: Nott 4D **123**
(not continuous)
NG9: Chil 3D **147**
NG10: Long E 4E **169**
(not continuous)
NG14: Bur J 3E **79**
Meadowlark Gro.
DE21: Oak 4F **109**
Meadow Nook DE24: Alv 2B **188**
Meadow Ri. NG6: Bulw 1E **71**
Meadow Rd.
DE1: Der 2E **7** (3A **136**)
DE5: Rip 5C **8**
NG4: Neth 4E **101**
NG9: Bee 3F **147**
NG16: Aws 2B **68**
MEADOWS 3B **122**
Meadows, The DE21: Der 3B **136**
DE75: Hea 3D **41**
NG14: Woodbo 5A **32**
NG16: Aws 2B **68**
Meadows Cft. DE56: Duff 4C **58**
Meadows Ind. Est., The
DE21: Der 3C **136**
Meadow St. DE7: Ilk 1E **91**
Meadows Way NG2: Nott 4A **122**
Meadowsweet Hill
NG13: Bing 2B **130**
Meadow Trad. Est.
NG2: Nott 5F **5** (2D **123**)
Meadow Va. DE56: Duff 4C **58**
Meadowvale Cres.
NG11: Clif 2D **173**
Meadow Vw. DE56: Bel 1E **35**
Meadow Vw. Cl. DE21: Oak . . .2A **110**
Meadow Way DE73: Chel 5F **187**
Mear Dr. DE72: Bor 2A **164**
Meath Av. DE21: Chad 4A **138**
Medawar Cl. NG11: Clif 2B **172**
Medbank Ct. NG11: Wilf 3F **149**
Meden Cl. NG11: Clif 5D **149**
Meden Gdns. NG7: H Grn 3C **96**

Medina Cl. DE24: Alv 1B **188**
Medina Dr. NG12: Toll 2C **176**
Medway Cl. NG9: Chil 3B **146**
Medway Dr. DE22: All 5F **83**
Medway St. NG8: Radf 5C **96**
Meeks Rd. NG5: Arn 4A **52**
Meerbrook Cl. DE21: Oak 4F **109**
Meerbrook Pl. DE7: Kirk H 5B **90**
Meer Rd. NG9: Chil 3F **145**
Megabowl
Derby 4F **159**
Nottingham 4D **121**
Megaloughton La.
DE21: Spon 5A **138**
Melandra Ct. DE22: Der 4D **135**
Melbourn Cl. DE56: Duff 5D **59**
Melbourne Bus. Ct.
DE24: Der 4D **137**
Melbourne Cl. DE3: Mick 5E **133**
DE22: All 3C **106**
DE56: Bel 2F **35**
Melbourne Ct. NG8: Aspl 1B **96**
NG10: Long E 2E **193**
Melbourne Ho. DE21: Spon . . .5D **139**
Melbourne Rd.
NG2: West Br 4E **123**
NG8: Aspl 2A **96**
NG9: Stap 3D **117**
Melbourne St.
DE1: Der 5D **7** (5F **135**)
Melbreak Cl. DE3: Mick 2D **157**
Melbury Rd. NG5: Woodt 3E **75**
NG8: Bilb 2C **94**
Meldreth Rd. NG8: Bilb 4D **95**
Melford Hall Dr.
NG2: West Br 4B **150**
Melford Rd. NG8: Bilb 2C **94**
Melfort Cl. DE24: Sin 4E **185**
Melksham Rd. NG5: Bestw 4B **50**
Mellbreak Cl.
NG2: West Br 2B **152**
Mellers Ct. NG3: Nott 3F **99**
Mellor's La. DE56: H'ook 1B **60**
Mellors Rd. NG2: West Br 3E **151**
NG5: Arn 3E **51**
Mellor St. DE24: A'ton 5D **161**
Mellors Way NG8: Stre 5B **70**
NG9: Bee 3F **147**
Melrose Av. NG5: Sher 4B **74**
NG9: Bee 3F **147**
Melrose Cl. DE24: Sin 4D **185**
Melrose Gdns.
NG2: West Br 4C **150**
Melrose St. NG5: Sher 4B **74**
Melton Av. DE23: Lit 5B **158**
Melton Ct. DE22: Der 2D **135**
NG10: Sand 3F **143**
Melton Gdns. NG12: Edwal . . .4F **151**
Melton Gro. NG2: West Br . . .1D **151**
Melton Hall NG8: Woll 1B **120**
Melton La. LE12: Sut B 2F **215**
Melton Rd. NG2: West Br 1D **151**
NG12: Edwal, Key, Plum, Stan W
. . . . .2F **175**
Melville Ct. NG3: Mapp P 2B **98**
NG3: Mapp P 2B **98**
Melville Gdns. NG3: Nott 4D **99**
Melville St.
NG1: Nott 5C **4** (2B **122**)
Melvyn Dr. NG13: Bing 2D **131**
Memorial Rd. DE22: All 3B **106**
Mendip Cl. NG10: Long E 2F **167**
Mendip Ct. DE21: Oak 3D **109**
NG5: Top V 4E **49**
Menin Rd. DE22: All 3B **106**

Mensing Av. NG12: Cotg 5D **155**
Mercaston Rd. DE21: Chad . . .5E **109**
Merchant Av. DE21: Spon 4C **138**
Merchants Cnr. DE22: Der . . .2D **135**
Merchant St. DE22: Der 2D **135**
NG6: Bulw 4A **48**
(not continuous)
Mercia Cl. NG16: Gilt 4F **43**
Mercian Cl. DE7: Ilk 1D **91**
Mercian M. DE21: Spon 4C **138**
Mercury Cl. NG6: Basf 2D **73**
Mere Av. NG14: Calv 2E **31**
Mere Beck DE72: Amba 5C **164**
Mere Cl. NG14: Calv 2E **31**
Meredith Cl. NG2: Nott 4A **122**
Meredith Ct. NG9: Stap 3D **117**
Meregill Cl. NG5: Top V 3E **49**
Merevale Av. NG11: Clif 4E **149**
Merevale Cl. NG14: Lowd 3D **57**
Mere Way NG11: Rudd 2C **196**
Meriac Cl. NG5: Top V 4E **49**
Meriden Av. NG9: Lent A 5F **119**
Meridian Cl. DE7: Ilk 3D **67**
NG5: Sher 4F **73**
Merion Gro. DE23: Lit 2F **157**
Merlin Cl. DE56: Bel 4B **14**
NG11: Clif 1D **173**
Merlin Dr. NG15: Huck 5D **25**
Merlin Grn. DE24: Sin 2C **184**
Merlin Way DE3: Mick 4A **156**
DE7: Ilk 1E **115**
Merridale Rd. DE23: Lit 4B **158**
Merrill Way DE24: A'ton 1C **186**
(not continuous)
Merrivale Ct. NG3: Mapp P 2B **98**
Merrybower Cl.
DE24: S Flds 3B **184**
Mersey St. NG6: Bulw 5A **48**
Merthyr Ct. DE21: Oak 3A **110**
Merton Cl. DE75: Hea 3E **41**
NG5: Arn 3A **52**
Merton Ct. NG9: Stap 4D **117**
Metcalfe Cl. DE24: Alv 3A **162**
Metcalf Rd. NG16: Newth 1A **44**
Meteor Bus. Pk. DE21: Der . . .4A **108**
Meteor Retail Pk.
DE21: Der 4B **108**
Metro Cinema 4C **6**
Mettham St. NG7: Lent 2E **121**
Mevell Ct. NG7: Nott 1F **121**
Mews, The DE56: Duff 4D **59**
NG7: Basf 2F **97**
Mews Ct. DE3: Mick 4C **132**
Mews La. NG14: Calv 2D **31**
Meynell Cl. DE22: All 3B **106**
Meynell Gro. NG7: Basf 1F **97**
Meynell Rd. NG10: Long E . . .1C **194**
Meynell St. DE23: Der 2E **159**
Miall Cl. NG7: Lent 5D **97**
Miall St. NG7: Lent 5D **97**
Michael Gdns. NG5: Sher 1A **98**
Michael Rayner Ct.
NG6: Basf 4C **72**
Michelle Cl. DE24: S Flds 3B **184**
Michigan Cl. DE21: Chad 3B **138**
Mickleborough Av.
NG3: Nott 2E **99**
Mickleborough Way
NG2: West Br 5B **150**
Micklebring Cl. DE5: Rip 5B **8**
Micklecroft Gdns.
DE23: Lit 4D **157**
Mickledon Cl. NG2: Nott 3A **122**
NG10: Long E 3A **168**

MICKLEOVER 2D 157
Mickleover By-Pass
   DE3: Mick 5C 156
   DE22: Der 5C 156
Mickleover Manor
   DE3: Mick 2B 156
Mickleross Cl. DE3: Mick 4C 132
Middle Av. NG4: Carl 2B 100
Middlebeck Av. NG5: Arn 4B 52
Middlebeck Cl. DE73: Chel . .4E 187
Middlebeck Dr. NG5: Arn 4A 52
Middledale Rd. NG4: Carl . .4B 100
Middlefell Way NG11: Clif . . .2C 172
Middlefield Cl. DE22: All 1C 106
Middle Furlong Gdns.
   NG2: Nott 3A 122
Middle Furlong M.
   NG2: Nott 3A 122
Middle Hill
   NG1: Nott 4C 4 (1B 122)
Middle La. NG9: Chil 3D 147
Middle Mill DE1: Der 1B 6
Middle Nook *NG8: Woll* *5D 95*
   (off Cottage Wlk.)
Middle Orchard St.
   NG9: Stap 1C 144
Middle Pavement
   NG1: Nott 4C 4 (1B 122)
Middle St. NG9: Bee 2E 147
Middleton Av. DE5: Cod 4A 18
   DE23: Lit 1B 158
Middleton Blvd. NG8: Woll . . .1B 120
Middleton Ct. NG16: Nuth 1B 70
Middleton Ct. NG8: Bilb 5C 94
Middleton Cres. NG9: Bee . . .4D 119
Middleton Dr. DE23: Lit 1B 158
Middleton Rd. DE7: Ilk 5F 91
Middleton St. DE7: Ilk 1F 91
   DE23: Der 2F 159
   NG7: Lent 5D 97
   NG9: Bee 1D 147
   NG16: Aws 3B 68
Midhurst Cl. NG9: Chil 4B 146
Midhurst Way NG11: Clif 1D 173
Midlame Gdns. NG6: Bulw . . .5E 47
Midland Av. NG4: Neth 3F 101
   NG7: Lent 2D 121
   NG9: Stap 3B 144
Midland Cotts.
   NG2: West Br 1E 151
Midland Ct. NG8: Aspl 4C 96
Midland Cres. NG4: Carl 3E 101
Midland Gro. NG4: Neth 2F 101
Midland Pl.
   DE1: Der 5F 7 (4B 136)
Midland Railway Cen.
   Butterley Station 2D 9
   Hammersmith Station 2C 8
   Swanwick Junction Station
   . . . . .1F 9
Midland Rd.
   DE1: Der 5F 7 (5A 136)
   DE75: Hea 2D 41
   NG4: Carl 3E 101
   NG16: Eastw 2E 43
Midland St. NG10: Long E . . .3D 169
Midland Vw. DE56: Bel 1E 35
Midland Way NG7: Radf 5C 96
Midway DE22: D Abb 3D 107
Midway, The NG7: Lent 5D 121
Mikado Rd. NG10: Long E 1R 194
Milburn Gdns. DE21: Oak . . .2A 110
Milburn Gro. NG13: Bing 2B 130
Milbury Cl. DE21: Oak 3E 109

Mildenhall Cres.
   NG5: Bestw 4B 50
Mileash La. DE22: D Abb 4E 107
Mile End Rd. NG4: Colw . . .5D 101
MILFORD 5F 35
Milford Av. NG10: Long E . . .5A 144
Milford Cl. NG6: Bulw 4F 47
Milford Ct. NG5: Arn 1C 74
Milford Dr. DE7: Ilk 4C 66
Milford Rd. NG3: Nott 3B 100
Milford St. DE56: Duff 2D 59
Milford St. DE1: Der 1E 135
Milk Acre Cl. DE7: Ilk 5C 66
Millbank DE75: Hea 3F 41
   (not continuous)
Millbank Av. DE56: Bel 2A 36
Millbank Cl. DE7: Ilk 4C 66
   DE22: Mac 2D 133
Millbank Ct. NG6: Bulw 1F 71
Millbank Pl. NG6: Bestw V 1C 48
Millbeck Av. NG8: Woll 1B 118
Millbeck Cl. NG2: Gam 2B 152
Millbrook Dr. NG4: Carl 1B 100
Mill Cl. DE56: Kil 4F 37
   DE65: Find 4C 182
   DE72: Bor 2B 164
Mill Cl., The NG6: Basf 4D 73
Mill Ct. NG10: Long E 4D 169
Mill Cres. NG5: Arn 4D 51
Mill Cft. DE3: Mick 4C 132
Milldale Cl. DE5: Mare 3C 16
   NG11: Clif 1B 172
Milldale Ct. DE56: Bel 1A 36
Milldale Rd. DE21: Spon 5E 139
   NG10: Long E 5A 168
Millenium Bus. Cen.
   DE24: Der 4D 137
Millenium Cl. DE7: Ilk 4D 67
Millennium Ct. NG6: Bulw 2C 72
Millennium Way DE24: Der . .4D 137
   NG8: Cin 3F 71
Millennium Way E.
   NG8: Cin 3F 71
Millennium Way W.
   NG8: Cin 3F 71
Miller Hives Cl.
   NG12: Cotg 5D 155
Millers Bri. NG12: Cotg 1D 179
Millers Cl. NG12: Shel 1B 104
Millers Ct. DE1: Der 2F 135
   NG7: Radf 4D 97
Millersdale Av. DE7: Ilk 2D 67
Millersdale Cl. DE56: Bel 4A 14
Millers Grn. NG2: Nott 1F 123
Millers Way DE56: Mil 4E 35
Millfield DE72: Shar 4A 192
Mill Fld. Cl. NG14: Bur J 4D 79
Millfield Cl. DE7: Ilk 3B 66
Millfield Rd. DE7: Ilk 3F 91
   NG16: Kimb 5D 45
Mill Ga. DE22: Der 2D 135
Mill Grn. DE72: Shar 5F 191
Mill Hill DE24: Alv 2B 188
Mill Hill Cl. DE5: Rip 5E 9
Mill Hill La.
   DE23: Der 5C 6 (5E 135)
   DE72: Brea 2D 167
Mill Hill Rd. DE23: Der 5E 135
   NG13: Bing 3C 130
Mill Ho. *NG1: Nott* *4D 5*
   (off Stoney St.)
Millhouse, The
   DE1: Der 1A 6 (2E 135)
Millhouse Ct. DE72: Dray 4A 166

Millicent Gro.
   NG2: West Br 5E 123
Millicent Rd. NG2: West Br . . .5D 123
Mill Lakes Country Pk. 5C 26
Mill La. DE3: Mick 4C 132
   DE5: Cod 1F 17
   DE56: Bel 1F 35
   DE74: Keg 2C 214
   NG4: Lamb 5A 54
   NG5: Arn 4D 51
   NG6: Bestw V 1C 48
   NG10: Sand 2B 144
   NG11: Rudd 2E 197
   NG12: Cotg 4D 155
   NG12: C'ton, Cotg 2C 178
   NG16: Coss 2A 92
Mill Mdw. Way DE65: Etw . . .2A 180
Mill Moor Cl. DE73: Chel 4E 187
Millom Pl. DE21: Chad 4C 108
Mill Rd. DE75: Hea 4F 41
   NG9: Stap 5C 116
   NG16: Newth 1F 43
Mill Row DE21: Spon 3C 138
Mills Bldg. NG1: Nott 4E 5
Mills Cl. DE72: Dray 4F 165
Mill Stream Grange
   DE72: Bor 2A 164
Mill St. DE1: Der 1A 6 (2D 135)
   DE7: Ilk 1E 91
   DE56: Bel 5E 13
   NG6: Basf 4C 72
Mill Vw. DE56: Bel 4E 13
Mill Vw. Cl. NG2: Nott 1E 123
Millview Ct.
   NG2: Nott 4F 5 (1D 123)
Millway La. DE65: Burn 1F 181
Mill Yd. NG15: Huck 2F 25
Milner Av. DE5: Cod 1A 18
   DE72: Dray 4F 165
Milner Ho. DE1: Der 1D 135
Milner Rd. NG5: Sher 5B 74
   NG10: Long E 3C 168
Milnhay Rd. DE75: Hea 3B 42
   NG16: Lang M 2B 42
Milton Av. DE7: Ilk 3D 67
Milton Cl. DE3: Mick 5B 132
Milton Ct. NG5: Arn 5A 52
   NG5: Sher 4A 74
Milton Cres. NG9: Atten 1C 170
Milton Ri. NG15: Huck 4C 24
Milton Rd. DE7: Ilk 3D 67
Milton St. DE7: Ilk 3E 67
   DE22: Der 4D 135
   NG1: Nott 1C 4 (5B 98)
   NG10: Long E 4C 168
Milton Ter. NG10: Long E 4C 168
Milverton Rd. NG5: Bestw . . .4B 50
Milward Rd. DE75: Los 2C 40
Mimosa Cl. NG11: Clif 2B 172
Mimosa Cres. DE23: Der 1D 185
Minerva St. NG6: Bulw 4A 48
   (not continuous)
Minkley Dr. NG16: Lang M 5B 24
Minster Cl. NG15: Huck 1A 26
Minster Ct. NG5: Sher 3A 98
Minster Gdns. NG16: Newth . . .3A 44
Minster Rd. DE21: Oak 3D 109
Minstrel Av. NG5: Sher 5F 73
Minstrel Cl. NG15: Huck 4F 25
Mint Gro. NG10: Long E 4F 167
Minton Cl. NG9: Chil 2A 170
Minton Rd. DE74: C Don 5E 205
Minver Cres. NG8: Aspl 1F 95

Minver Crescent Sports Cen.
    . . . .**1A 96**
Mirberry M. NG7: Lent 2D **121**
Miriam Ct. NG2: West Br 1D **151**
Misk Hollows NG15: Huck 1E **25**
Misk Vw. NG16: Eastw 2A **44**
Mission St. NG3: Mapp 5D **75**
Misterton Cl. DE22: D Abb . . .3D **107**
Mitcham Wlk. DE22: Mac 2F **133**
Mitchell Av. NG16: Lang M 5F **19**
Mitchell Cl. NG6: Bulw 1F **71**
Mitchells Cl. DE65: Etw 2A **180**
Mitchell St. NG10: Long E . . .4D **169**
Mitchell Ter. DE7: Ilk 5F **91**
Moat, The DE74: C Don 5A **206**
Moffat Cl. NG3: Nott 3E **99**
Moira Cl. DE21: Chad 1F **137**
Moira Dale DE74: C Don 1A **212**
Molineux St. DE23: Der 1A **160**
Mollington Sq. NG6: Cin 3A **72**
Monarch Dr. DE21: Oak 2C **110**
Monarch Way DE75: Hea 2C **40**
Mona Rd. NG2: West Br 4F **123**
Mona St. NG9: Bee 2F **147**
Moncrieff Cres. DE21: Chad . .5F **109**
Mondello Dr. DE24: Alv 5B **162**
Monks Cl. DE7: Ilk 2F **91**
    DE24: S Flds 3C **184**
Monk St. DE22: Der 4A **6** (4E **135**)
Monksway NG11: Wilf 4F **149**
Monkton Cl. DE7: Ilk 4C **66**
Monkton Dr. NG8: Bilb 3D **95**
Monmouth Cl. NG8: Woll 1A **118**
Monmouth St. DE21: Chad . . .2C **136**
Monroe Wlk. NG5: Bestw 5F **49**
Monsaldale Cl.
    NG10: Long E 5A **168**
Monsal Dr. DE21: Spon 5E **139**
Monsall Av. DE7: Ilk 2D **67**
Monsall St. NG7: Basf 1E **97**
Monsell Dr. NG5: Redh 3D **51**
Montague Rd. NG15: Huck 1F **25**
Montague St. NG6: Bulw 5B **48**
    NG9: Bee 1D **147**
Montague Way DE73: Chel . . .4D **187**
Monteith Pl. DE74: C Don . . .5A **206**
Montford St. DE74: C Don . . .5A **206**
Montfort Cres. NG5: Sher 3C **74**
Montfort St. NG7: Radf 5F **97**
Montgomery Cl. NG9: Chil . . .1B **170**
Montgomery St. NG7: Radf . . .4F **97**
Montpelier DE22: Quar 3C **82**
Montpelier Rd. NG7: Lent . . .4D **121**
Montrose Cl. DE24: Sin 2D **185**
Montrose Ct. NG9: Stap 4D **117**
Monyash Cl. DE7: Ilk 4D **67**
    DE21: Chad 5F **109**
Monyash Way DE56: Bel 4A **14**
Moody Cl. NG9: Chil 1A **170**
Moor, The DE7: D Ab 3F **113**
    NG8: Trow 4F **93**
    NG16: Brins 1C **20**
Moorbridge Cotts.
    NG6: Bulw 2C **48**
Moorbridge Ct. NG13: Bing . . .1D **131**
Moorbridge La. NG9: Stap . . .4C **116**
Moorbridge Rd.
    NG13: Bing 1D **131**
Moorbridge Rd. E.
    NG13: Bing 1D **131**
Moor Bridge Stop (NET) 2C **48**
Moor Dr. DE24: Alv 1F **187**
Moore Av. DE74: Keg 1C **214**
Moore Cl. NG2: West Br 4A **124**

Moore Ga. NG9: Bee 2E **147**
Moor End DE21: Spon 3D **139**
Moore Rd. NG3: Mapp 5F **75**
Moores Av. NG10: Sand 1B **144**
Moore St. DE23: Der 5F **135**
    NG6: Bulw 2B **72**
Moor Farm Holiday & Home Pk.
    NG14: Calv 3B **32**
Moor Farm Inn La.
    NG9: Bram 3F **117**
Moorfield Ct. NG9: Stap 4D **117**
Moorfield Cres.
    NG10: Sand 3A **144**
Moorfield Rd. DE56: H'ook . . .5B **36**
Moorfields Av. NG16: Eastw . . .1E **43**
Moorgate DE22: Mac 2D **133**
Moorgate St. NG7: Radf 5F **97**
MOORGREEN 1C **44**
Moorgreen NG16: Newth 4B **22**
Moorgreen Dr. NG8: Stre 5C **70**
Moorgreen Ind. Pk.
    NG16: Newth 4A **22**
Moorhead Av. DE24: Alv 1E **187**
Moorhouse Rd. NG8: Bilb 4D **95**
Moorings, The NG7: Lent 3E **121**
Moorland Av. NG9: Stap 2C **144**
Moorland Rd. DE3: Mick 5C **132**
Moorlands Cl.
    NG10: Long E 1A **168**
Moor La. DE7: D Ab 3E **113**
    DE21: L Eat 1C **84**
            (not continuous)
    DE24: A'ton 1B **186**
    DE72: Ast T 1A **204**
    DE72: Ock 1A **140**
    DE73: Bar T 2A **200**
            (not continuous)
    NG9: Bram 3A **118**
    NG11: Bunny 5B **196**
    NG11: Rudd 4C **196**
            (Bradmore)
    NG11: Rudd 5B **174**
            (Ruddington)
    NG13: Bing 1D **131**
    NG14: Calv 3B **32**
Moor La. Nth. DE73: Bar T . . .1A **200**
Moor La. Sth. DE73: Swar . . .1A **200**
Moorpool Cres. DE56: H'ook . .5B **36**
Moor Ri. DE56: H'ook 4B **36**
Moor Rd. DE7: Mor 1D **109**
    DE21: Bre 1D **109**
    NG6: Bestw V 1C **48**
    NG8: Stre 1C **94**
    NG14: Calv 2F **31**
    NG15: Pap 4F **11**
    NG16: Brins 1D **21**
Moorsholm Dr. NG8: Woll 1B **118**
Moorside Cres. DE24: Sin 2E **185**
Moorside La. DE56: H'ook 4B **36**
Moor St. DE21: Spon 3D **139**
    NG4: Neth 3E **101**
Moorway DE21: Bre 1D **109**
Moorway Cft. DE21: Bre 4A **158**
Moorway La. DE23: Lit 1F **183**
Moorways Sports Cen. 5B **160**
Moorways Sports Complex
    .5C **160**
Moorways Swimming Pool
    .5B **160**
Moray Ct. NG16: Kimb 5E **45**
Moray Wlk. DE21: Chad 5B **108**
Morden Cl. NG8: Bilb 2C **94**
Morden Grn. DE22: Mac 2F **133**
Morden Rd. NG16: Gilt 4B **44**

Morefern Dr. DE21: Oak 3E **109**
Moreland Ct. NG2: Nott 2E **123**
    NG4: Carl 3B **100**
Moreland Pl. NG2: Nott 2E **123**
Moreland St. NG2: Nott 2E **123**
Morello Av. NG4: Carl 3E **101**
Moreton Rd. NG11: Clif 4D **173**
Morgan M. NG11: Clif 1C **172**
Morkinshire Cres.
    NG12: Cotg 4E **155**
Morkinshire La.
    NG12: Cotg 4D **155**
Morledge DE1: Der 3D **7** (3F **135**)
MORLEY 4C **86**
Morleston St. DE23: Der 5A **136**
Morley Almshouses La.
    DE7: Mor 3A **86**
Morley Av. NG3: Mapp 5D **75**
Morley Brickyards Nature Reserve
    .2A **86**
Morley Cl. DE56: Bel 3D **15**
Morley Ct.
    NG2: Nott 2F **5** (1D **123**)
Morley Dr. DE7: Ilk 4C **66**
Morleyfields Cl. DE5: Rip 5E **9**
Morley Gdns. DE21: Oak 5A **110**
    NG5: Sher 1A **98**
Morley La. DE7: Mor 2C **84**
    DE7: S'ley 4F **87**
    DE21: L Eat 2C **84**
Morley M. DE21: Chad 1F **137**
MORLEYMOOR 3A **86**
MORLEY PARK 3F **15**
Morley Pk. Rd. DE56: Bel 3D **15**
Morley Rd.
    DE21: Chad, Oak 1F **137**
    NG3: Nott 1F **99**
Morley's Cl. NG14: Lowd 3D **57**
MORLEY SMITHY 2B **86**
Morley St. DE22: Der 2B **134**
    NG5: Arn 1C **74**
Morlich Dr. DE24: Sin 2D **185**
Morningside Cl.
    DE24: A'ton 2C **186**
Mornington Cl. NG10: Sand . .2B **144**
Mornington Cres.
    DE22: Mac 2F **133**
    NG16: Nuth 4C **70**
Morpeth Gdns. DE21: Chad . . .3C **108**
Morrell Bank NG5: Bestw 1E **73**
Morrell Wood Dr.
    DE56: Bel 4C **14**
Morris Av. NG9: Chil 2A **170**
Morris Rd. NG8: Stre 1C **94**
Morris St. NG4: Neth 3F **101**
Mortimer's Hole Cave 5A **4**
Mortimer St. DE24: Der 4B **160**
Morton Av. DE7: Ilk 2E **67**
Morton Cl. NG12: Rad T 2B **128**
Morton Gdns. NG12: Rad T . .2B **128**
Morval Rd. NG8: Bilb 3D **95**
Morven Av. NG15: Huck 3A **26**
Moscow DE56: Mil 2E **59**
Mosedale Cl. DE24: Alv 3E **161**
Moseley St. DE5: Rip 4C **8**
Moses La. DE7: Mor 4D **87**
Mosley St. NG7: Basf 2E **97**
    NG15: Huck 3F **25**
Moss Cl. NG5: Arn 4B **50**
Mosscroft Av. NG11: Clif 2C **172**
Mossdale Rd. NG5: Sher 2B **74**
Moss Dr. NG9: Bram 1A **146**
Moss La. DE5: Rip 3C **8**
Moss Ri. NG3: Mapp 5A **76**

Moss Rd. DE7: Ilk 3D **91**
  NG15: Huck 2E **25**
Moss Side NG11: Wilf 5F **149**
Moss St. DE22: Der 5D **135**
Mossvale Dr. DE23: Lit 5F **157**
Mosswood Cres.
  NG5: Bestw 5A **50**
Mostyn Av. DE23: Lit 2C **158**
Mottistone Cl. DE24: Alv 1C **188**
Mottram Rd. NG9: Chil 2B **146**
Moulbourn Dr. DE56: Duff 3C **58**
Moult Av. DE21: Spon 4D **139**
Moulton Cl. DE56: Bel 4C **14**
Mount, The NG3: Mapp 5B **76**
  NG5: Redh 3C **50**
  NG6: Bestw V 5D **27**
  NG8: Stre 1D **95**
  NG9: Stap 2C **144**
Mountbatten Cl.
  DE24: A'ton 2D **187**
Mountbatten Ct. DE7: Ilk 4E **67**
Mountbatten Gro.
  NG4: Ged 5D **77**
Mountbatten Way
  NG9: Chil 1A **170**
Mt. Carmel St. DE23: Der 5E **135**
Mountfield Av. NG10: Sand . . .4F **143**
Mountfield Dr. NG5: Bestw . . .5F **49**
Mountfield Way DE24: Alv 2C **188**
Mountford Cl. DE21: Oak 3A **110**
Mount Hgts. NG7: Basf 1F **97**
Mount Hooton NG1: Nott 4F **97**
Mt. Hooton Rd. NG7: Radf 3F **97**
MOUNT PLEASANT 4D **13**
Mt. Pleasant DE5: Rip 4C **8**
  DE7: Ilk 3D **67**
  DE56: Mil 5F **35**
  DE74: C Don 1A **212**
  DE74: Keg 2B **214**
  NG4: Carl 3D **101**
  NG6: Basf 5C **72**
  NG12: Key 3E **199**
  NG12: Rad T 2D **127**
  NG14: Lowd 2C **56**
Mt. Pleasant Dr. DE56: Bel 4D **13**
  DE56: H'age 1D **15**
Mountsorrel Dr.
  NG2: West Br 2A **152**
Mount St. DE1: Der 5C **6** (5F **135**)
  DE72: Brea 4E **167**
  DE75: Hea 3D **41**
  NG1: Nott 3A **4** (1A **122**)
  (not continuous)
  NG7: Basf 1E **97**
  NG9: Stap 1D **145**
Mount St. Arc. NG1: Nott 3A **4**
Mowbray Ct.
  NG3: Nott 1E **5** (5C **98**)
Mowbray Gdns. DE24: Der . . .4B **160**
  NG2: West Br 3E **151**
Mowbray Ri. NG5: Arn 3E **51**
Mowbray St. DE24: Der 3B **160**
Moy Av. DE24: Sin 4E **185**
Moyne Gdns. DE73: Chel 1E **201**
Moyra Dr. NG5: Arn 5B **50**
Moyra Ho. NG5: Arn 5D **51**
Mozart Cl. NG7: Radf 5D **97**
Mudpie La. NG2: West Br 4A **124**
Muir Av. NG12: Toll 3C **176**
Muirfield Dr. DE3: Mick 1E **157**
Muirfield Rd. NG6: Top V 3E **48**
Mulberries Ct. DE22: All 1D **107**
Mulberry Cl. DE56: Bel 1A **36**
  NG2: West Br 3A **150**

Mulberry Gdns. DE74: Keg . . .2C **214**
  NG6: Bulw 4F **47**
Mulberry Gro. NG15: Huck 5A **26**
Mulberry M. DE5: Mare 3B **16**
Mulberry Way DE72: Ast T 3F **203**
Mull Ct. DE24: Sin 3C **184**
Mullion Pl. DE24: Alv 1A **188**
Mundella Rd. NG2: Nott 4C **122**
Mundy Cl. DE1: Der 2D **135**
Mundy Play Cen. 5B **106**
Mundy's Dr. DE75: Hea 4E **41**
Mundy St. DE1: Der . . .1A **6** (2D **135**)
  DE7: Ilk 5E **67**
  DE75: Hea 3D **41**
Munford Cir. NG8: Cin 4F **71**
Munks Av. NG15: Huck 2E **25**
Munnmoore Cl. DE74: Keg . . .2B **214**
Munro Ct. DE24: Sin 2D **185**
Murby Cres. NG6: Bulw 4A **48**
Murden Way NG9: Bee 2A **148**
Muriel Rd. NG9: Bee 1E **147**
Muriel St. NG6: Bulw 5A **48**
Murray Cl. NG5: Bestw 2E **73**
Murray Rd. DE3: Mick 4E **133**
Murray St. DE24: Alv 3E **161**
Mushroom Farm Ct.
  NG16: Eastw 1C **42**
Muskham Av. DE7: Ilk 4E **67**
Muskham St. NG2: Nott 4C **122**
Musters Ct. NG2: West Br 5D **123**
  NG15: Huck 3B **26**
Musters Cres.
  NG2: West Br 3E **151**
Musters Cft. NG4: Colw 2E **125**
Musters Rd. NG2: West Br 5D **123**
  NG11: Rudd 5A **174**
  NG13: Bing 2C **130**
  NG15: News 1A **10**
Musters Wlk. NG6: Bulw 5F **47**
Muston Cl. NG3: Mapp 1E **99**
Muswell Rd. DE22: Mac 2D **133**
Myers Cl. DE24: Sin 2E **185**
Myrtle Av. NG7: H Grn 2A **98**
  NG9: Stap 2D **145**
  NG10: Long E 5B **168**
Myrtle Gro. NG9: Bee 1F **147**
Myrtle Rd. NG4: Carl 2B **100**
Myrtus Cl. NG11: Clif 1B **172**
Mytholme Cl.
  NG10: Long E 1B **168**

N

Nabarro Ct. NG14: Calv 2D **31**
Nabbs La. NG15: Huck 3C **24**
Naburn Ct. NG8: Basf 1C **96**
Nailers Way DE56: Bel 4D **14**
Nairn Av. DE21: Chad 1C **136**
Nairn Cl. DE24: S Flds 3C **184**
  NG5: Arn 3A **52**
Nairn M. NG4: Carl 3D **101**
Namur Cl. DE22: Der 5B **134**
Nansen Gdns. NG5: Bootw 1E **73**
Nansen St. NG6: Bulw 1B **72**
Naomi Cl. NG6: Bulw 3B **48**
Naomi Cres. NG6: Bulw 3B **48**
Napier Cl. DE3: Mick 4D **133**
Napier St. DE22: Der 3B **134**
Naranjan M. NG7: Radf 4F **97**
Narrow La. DE56: Bel 1A **12**
  NG16: Want 3E **45**
Naseby Cl. DE3: Mick 5A **132**
  NG5: Sher 3E **73**

Naseby Dr. NG10: Long E 1D **195**
Naseby Rd. DE56: Bel 5C **14**
Nathaniel Rd.
  NG10: Long E 4E **169**
Nathans La. NG12: Rad T 1F **153**
National Ice Cen., The
  . . . . .3E **5** (1C **122**)
National Water Sports Cen.
  . . . . .3D **125**
Natural History Mus. 2F **119**
Navdeep Ct. NG2: West Br . . .1D **151**
Navenby Wlk. NG11: Clif 1D **173**
Navigation Home Pk.
  DE24: Der 2D **161**
Navigation Pk. DE24: Alv 2D **161**
Naworth Cl. NG6: Bulw 2D **73**
Naylor Ho. NG5: Arn 1F **75**
  (off Derwent Cres.)
Nazareth Ct. NG7: Lent 3D **121**
Nazareth Rd. NG7: Lent 3D **121**
Neal Ct. NG16: Lang M 1F **41**
Neale St. NG10: Long E 4D **169**
Near Mdw. NG10: Long E 1D **195**
Nearsby Dr. NG2: West Br 2A **152**
Nearwood Dr. DE21: Oak 2D **109**
Needham Rd. NG5: Arn 4F **51**
Needham St. DE5: Cod 1A **18**
  NG13: Bing 2D **131**
Needwood Av. NG9: Trow 3C **116**
Neeps Cl. NG14: Epp 3F **33**
Negus Ct. NG4: Lamb 5A **54**
Neighbours La. NG14: Lowd . . .3D **57**
Neighwood Cl. NG9: Toton 1D **169**
Neilson St. DE24: Alv 4E **161**
Nell Gwyn Cres. NG5: Arn 3B **50**
Nelper Cres. DE7: Ilk 5F **91**
Nelson Cl. DE3: Mick 5D **133**
Nelson Rd. NG5: Arn 5D **51**
  NG6: Bulw 5B **48**
  NG9: Bee 4F **147**
Nelson St. DE1: Der 5F **7** (5B **136**)
  (not continuous)
  DE7: Ilk 3E **67**
  DE75: Hea 2C **40**
  NG1: Nott 3E **5** (1C **122**)
  NG10: Long E 5C **168**
Nene Cl. NG15: Huck 1D **47**
Nerissa Cl. DE73: Chel 4D **187**
Nesfield Cl. DE24: Alv 4B **162**
Nesfield Ct. DE7: Ilk 1D **91**
Nesfield Rd. DE7: Ilk 1D **91**
Ness Wlk. DE22: All 2D **107**
Neston Dr. NG6: Cin 3A **72**
Nestor Cl. DE73: Chel 4C **186**
Nether Cl. DE56: Duff 2C **58**
  NG3: Nott 4F **99**
  NG16: Eastw 5E **21**
Netherclose St. DE23: Der 2F **159**
NETHERFIELD 4E **101**
Netherfield La. DE72: Shar . . .2D **207**
  DE74: Hem 2D **207**
Netherfield Rd.
  NG10: Long E 2A **194**
  NG10: Sand 3A **144**
Netherfield Station (Rail) 4E **101**
Nethergate NG11: Clif 1B **172**
NETHER GREEN 5E **21**
Nether Grn. NG16: Eastw 1E **43**
Nether La. DE56: Haz 4A **34**
  DE56: H'ook 2C **60**
Nether Pk. Dr. DE22: All 4B **106**
Nether Pasture NG4: Neth 4F **101**
Netherside Dr. DE73: Chel 4F **187**
Nether St. NG9: Bee 2F **147**

Netherwood Ct. DE22: All 2B 106
Nettlecliff Wlk. NG5: Top V 4D 49
Nettleton Cl. DE23: Lit 5F 157
Neville Rd. NG14: Calv 3E 31
Neville Sadler Ct.
  NG9: Bee 1F 147
Nevinson Av. DE23: Der 4C 158
Nevinson Dr. DE23: Der 4C 158
Nevis Cl. DE24: S Flds 4C 184
New Alexandra Ct., The
  NG3: Nott 2C 98
Newall Dr. NG9: Chil 1B 170
Newark Av.
  NG2: Nott 4F 5 (1D 123)
Newark Ct. NG5: Bestw 2E 73
Newark Cres.
  NG2: Nott 4F 5 (1D 123)
Newark Hall NG8: Woll 1C 120
Newark Rd. DE21: Chad 3C 108
Newark St.
  NG2: Nott 4F 5 (1D 123)
NEW BASFORD 1E 97
New Basford Bus. Area
  NG7: Basf 1E 97
         (off Palm St.)
Newbery Av. NG10: Long E . . .5E 169
Newbold Av. DE72: Bor 2B 164
Newbold Cl. DE73: Chel 4E 187
Newbold Dr. DE74: C Don 4A 206
Newborough Rd. DE24: Alv . . .5B 162
New Breck Rd. DE56: Bel 1F 35
New Brickyard La.
  DE74: Keg 3C 214
Newbridge Cl. DE7: West H . . .2C 88
Newbridge Cres.
  DE24: S Loc 2D 187
NEW BRINSLEY 1D 21
Newbury Cl. NG3: Mapp 3F 75
Newbury Ct. NG5: Sher 2A 98
Newbury Dr. NG16: Nuth 4C 70
Newbury St. DE24: Der 3D 161
Newcastle Av. NG4: Ged 1D 101
  NG9: Bee 2E 147
Newcastle Chambers
  NG1: Nott 3B 4 (1B 122)
Newcastle Cir. NG7: Nott 1F 121
Newcastle Ct. NG7: Nott 1F 121
Newcastle Dr. NG7: Nott 1F 121
Newcastle Farm Dr.
  NG8: Aspl 1B 96
Newcastle St. NG6: Bulw 4B 48
Newcastle Ter. NG7: Nott 5F 97
  NG8: Aspl 1C 96
Newchase Bus. Pk.
  DE23: Der 2B 160
New Chester St. DE1: Der 5A 108
New City Pk. Homes
  DE24: Alv 3F 161
Newcombe Dr. NG5: Arn 5B 52
New Ct. NG1: Nott 3D 5
Newcrest Cl. DE23: Lit 2A 158
New Derby Rd. NG16: Eastw . . .1C 42
Newdigate Rd. NG16: Want 5F 45
Newdigate St. DE7: Ilk 4F 91
  DE7: West H 2B 88
  DE23: Der 3F 159
  NG7: Radf 5F 97
  NG16: Kimb 1E 69
Newdigate Vs. NG7: Radf 5F 97
NEW EASTWOOD 3E 43
New Eaton Rd. NG9: Stap 3D 145
Newel Wlk. DE3: Mick 2B 156
New Farm La. NG16: Nuth 1B 70
Newfield Rd. NG5: Sher 4E 73

Newgate Cl. DE73: Chel 4A 188
  NG4: Carl 3D 101
Newgate Ct. NG7: Lent 1E 121
Newgate St. NG13: Bing 1D 131
Newhall Gro. NG2: West Br . . .4E 123
Newham Cl. DE75: Hea 3F 41
Newhaven Rd. DE21: Chad . . .2A 138
Newholm Dr. NG11: Wilf 3F 149
New Inn La. DE21: L Eat 3B 84
Newland Cl. NG8: Aspl 5B 96
  NG9: Toton 1F 169
NEWLANDS 2F 41
Newlands Cl. DE5: Rip 5D 9
  NG12: Edwal 4B 152
Newlands Dr. DE75: Hea 1D 41
  NG4: Ged 1E 101
Newland St.
  DE1: Der 3B 6 (3E 135)
New Lawn Rd. DE7: Ilk 2D 91
NEW LENTON 2E 121
Newlyn Dr. DE23: Der 3E 159
  NG8: Aspl 2C 96
Newlyn Gdns. NG8: Aspl 2C 96
Newmanleys Rd.
  NG16: Eastw 4D 43
Newmanleys Rd. Sth.
  NG16: Eastw 3D 43
New Manor Ground 4F 67
Newman Rd. NG14: Calv 1D 31
Newmarket Ct. DE24: Der 2D 161
Newmarket Dr. DE24: Der 3C 160
Newmarket Rd. NG6: Bulw . . .1A 72
Newmarket Way
  NG9: Toton 2E 169
New Mt. Cl. DE23: Lit 1C 184
Newnham Av. DE5: Rip 5B 8
NEW NORMANTON 1D 159
New Normanton Mills
  DE23: Der 1F 159
NEW NUTHALL 1B 70
New Orchard Pl. DE3: Mick . . .1C 156
New Pk. Pl. DE24: Der 5C 136
Newport Cl. DE24: Alv 1B 188
Newport Dr. NG8: Basf 1C 96
Newquay Av. NG7: Radf 3D 97
Newquay Pl. DE24: Alv 1B 188
New Rd. DE22: D Abb 4F 107
  DE56: Bel 1E 35
  DE56: H'age 2C 14
  NG7: Radf 4C 96
  NG9: Stap 4C 116
  NG11: Bart F 5D 171
  NG12: Rad T 2E 127
  NG16: Newth, Want 5C 22
New Row NG4: Carl 3C 100
  NG14: Woodbo 5B 32
NEW SAWLEY 1A 194
NEW STANTON 2D 115
NEW STAPLEFORD 4D 117
NEWSTEAD 1A 10
Newstead Av. DE21: Chad 2E 137
  NG3: Mapp 5A 76
  NG12: Rad T 1F 127
Newstead Ct. NG5: Woodt 2F 75
Newstead Dr.
  NG2: West Br 1A 152
Newstead Gro. NG1: Nott 4A 98
  NG13: Bing 2B 130
Newstead Ind. Est. NG5: Arn . .5F 51
Newstead Rd.
  NG10: Long E 5B 144
Newstead Rd. Nth. DE7: Ilk . . .4C 66
Newstead Rd. Sth. DE7: Ilk . . .4C 66
Newstead St. NG5: Sher 4B 74

Newstead Ter. NG15: Huck 1F 25
Newstead Way NG8: Stre 5C 70
New St. DE1: Der 4F 7 (4A 136)
  DE5: Rip 5D 9
  DE7: S'ley 4B 88
  DE21: L Eat 2B 84
  DE72: Dray 4F 165
         (not continuous)
  DE72: Ock 4B 140
  DE74: Keg 1D 215
  NG5: Redh 3D 51
  NG5: Sher 1A 98
  NG10: Long E 3D 169
New Ter. NG10: Sand 2A 144
NEWTHORPE 3B 44
NEWTHORPE COMMON 4A 44
Newthorpe Comn.
  NG16: Newth 3F 43
Newthorpe St. NG2: Nott 3C 122
NEWTON 2F 105
Newton Av. NG12: Rad T 1F 127
  NG13: Bing 2C 130
         (not continuous)
Newton Cl. DE56: Bel 3B 14
  NG5: Arn 1A 76
  NG14: Lowd 3D 57
Newtondale Cl. NG8: Aspl 1C 96
Newton Dr. NG2: West Br 4B 150
  NG9: Stap 2D 145
Newton Gdns.
  NG13: Newton 1B 130
Newton Grn. DE3: Mick 1E 157
Newton Rd. NG4: Ged 4C 76
Newton's La. NG16: Coss 4F 67
         (not continuous)
Newton St. NG7: Lent 5D 121
  NG9: Bee 2D 147
Newton's Wlk. DE22: Der 5D 107
         (not continuous)
New Tythe St.
  NG10: Long E 4E 169
New Va. Rd. NG4: Colw 5C 100
New Victoria Ct.
  DE24: A'ton 1D 187
New Windmill Ct.
  NG2: Nott 1E 123
New Works Cotts.
  NG14: Sto B 2B 102
New Zealand La. DE56: Duff . . .5D 59
New Zealand Sq.
  DE22: Der 3B 134
NG2 Bus. Pk. NG2: Nott 3F 121
Nicholas Cl. DE21: Spon 2D 139
Nicholas Rd. NG9: Bram 4C 118
Nicker Hill NG12: Key 2E 199
Nicklaus Ct. NG5: Top V 4F 49
       (off Crossfield Dr.)
Nicola Gdns. DE23: Lit 2C 184
Nidderdale NG8: Woll 1B 118
Nidderdale Cl. NG8: Woll 2B 118
Nidderdale Dr. DE24: Alv 5C 162
Nightingale Cl. DE5: Rip 5C 8
  NG7: Nott 4F 119
  NG16: Nuth 1C 70
Nightingale Hall NG7: Nott . . .4F 119
Nightingale Ho. NG3: Mapp . . .5E 75
Nightingale M.
  DE1: Der 4F 7 (4B 136)
Nightingale Rd. DE24: Der 4B 160
Nightingale Way
  NG13: Bing 3F 131
Nile St. NG1: Nott 2E 5 (5C 98)
Nilsson Rd. NG9: Chil 5A 146
Nimbus Way NG16: Want 5F 45

Nine Acre Gdns. NG6: Bulw 5E **47**
Nine Acres DE74: Keg 2B **214**
Nine Corners NG16: Kimb 1E **69**
Nixon Ri. NG15: Huck 4C **24**
Nobel Rd. NG11: Clif 3B **172**
Noble St. DE1: Der 5F **7** (5B **136**)
Noel St. DE22: Der 2C **134**
   NG7: H Grn 2E **97**
   NG16: Kimb 1F **69**
Noel Street Leisure Cen. 2E **97**
Noel Street Stop (NET) 3E **97**
No Man's La. DE7: D Ab 5A **114**
   DE72: Ris 5A **114**
   NG10: Sand 1E **143**
Nook, The DE56: H'ook 5B **36**
   DE73: Bar T 3A **200**
   DE75: Los 5B **18**
   NG8: Woll 1D **119**
   NG9: Bee 1F **147**
   NG9: Chil 4D **147**
   NG14: Calv 2E **31**
   NG16: Kimb 2F **69**
Nook End Rd. DE75: Hea 3C **40**
Nooning La. DE72: Dray 4D **165**
Norbett Cl. NG9: Chil 5B **146**
Norbett Ct. NG5: Arn 3F **51**
Norbett Rd. NG5: Arn 4F **51**
Norbreck Cl. NG8: Cin 4A **72**
Norburn Cres. NG6: Basf 4E **73**
Norbury Cl. DE22: All 4C **106**
Norbury Ct. DE22: All 3C **106**
Norbury Cres. DE23: Lit 1B **184**
Norbury Way DE56: Bel 3B **14**
   NG10: Sand 2F **143**
Nordean Rd. NG5: Woodt 2F **75**
Norfolk Av. NG9: Toton 2F **169**
Norfolk Cl. NG15: Huck 4C **24**
Norfolk Gdns. DE22: Der 5E **107**
Norfolk Pk. NG5: Arn 2A **76**
Norfolk Pl. NG1: Nott . . .2B **4** (5B **98**)
Norfolk Rd.
   NG10: Long E 2E **169**
Norfolk St. DE23: Der 1A **160**
Norfolk Wlk. NG10: Sand 3A **144**
Norland Cl. NG3: Nott 3D **99**
            (not continuous)
Norman Av. DE23: Der 4D **159**
Normanby Rd. NG8: Woll 2B **118**
Norman Cl. NG3: Nott 4B **98**
   NG9: Chil 3B **146**
Norman Ct. DE74: Keg 3C **214**
Norman Cres. DE7: Ilk 4D **67**
Norman Dr. NG15: Huck 5D **25**
   NG16: Eastw 2A **44**
Norman Rd. DE5: Rip 4B **8**
   NG3: Nott 2F **99**
Norman St. DE7: Ilk 3D **67**
   NG4: Neth 4F **101**
   NG16: Kimb 5E **45**
NORMANTON 3D **159**
Normanton La. DE23: Lit 2B **158**
   NG12: Key 3E **199**
Normanton Lodge
   DE23: Der 3D **159**
NORMANTON-ON-THE-WOLDS
   . . . . .5F **177**
Normanton Rd.
   DE1: Der 5C **6** (4F **135**)
   DE23: Der 1F **159**
Northacre Rd. DE21: Oak . . .3A **110**
Northall Av. NG6: Bulw 1A **72**
Northam Dr. DE5: Rip 4B **8**
Northampton St.
   NG3: Nott 4D **99**

North Av. DE3: Mick 5D **133**
   DE22: D Abb 2F **107**
   NG10: Sand 2F **143**
Nth. Church St.
   NG1: Nott 1B **4** (5B **98**)
Nth. Circus St.
   NG1: Nott 2A **4** (1A **122**)
Northcliffe Av. NG3: Mapp 5A **76**
North Cl. DE3: Mick 5D **133**
Northcote St.
   NG10: Long E 4D **169**
Northcote Way NG6: Bulw 2B **72**
Northdale Rd. NG3: Nott 3A **100**
Northdown Dr. NG9: Chil 4B **146**
Northdown Rd. NG8: Aspl 4C **96**
North Dr. NG9: Chil 2D **147**
Northern Ct. NG6: Basf 3C **72**
Northern Dr. NG6: Bestw V 5E **27**
   NG9: Trow 2C **116**
Northern Rd. DE75: Hea 2C **40**
Northfield DE24: S Flds 3C **184**
   DE56: Kil 2E **37**
Northfield Av. DE7: Ilk 5D **67**
   NG10: Long E 2A **194**
   NG12: Rad T 1B **128**
Northfield Cres. NG9: Chil 4E **145**
Northfield Rd. NG9: Chil 4F **145**
Northfields NG10: Long E 2A **194**
North Ga. NG7: Basf 1E **97**
Northgate DE1: Der 2F **135**
North Ga. Pl. *NG7: Basf* 1E **97**
           (off High Chu. St.)
Northgate St. DE7: Ilk 1D **91**
North Grn. NG14: Calv 1C **30**
Nth. Hill Av. NG15: Huck 2E **25**
Nth. Hill Cres. NG15: Huck . . .2E **25**
North La. DE56: Bel, Mil 2C **34**
Northmead Dr. DE22: Der 5A **134**
Northolme Av. NG6: Bulw 5B **48**
Northolt Dr. NG16: Nuth 4C **70**
North Pde. DE1: Der 1F **135**
North Rd. NG2: West Br 2D **151**
   NG5: Sher 3F **73**
   NG7: Nott 3C **120**
              (West Rd.)
   NG7: Nott 1F **121**
            (Western Ter.)
   NG10: Long E 5B **168**
   NG11: Rudd 3A **174**
North Row DE22: D Abb 4F **107**
   DE56: Mil 4E **35**
Nth. Sherwood St.
   NG1: Nott 1B **4** (3A **98**)
Northside Wlk. NG5: Arn 2E **51**
North St. DE1: Der 1E **135**
   DE7: Ilk 1E **91**
   DE23: Lit 1B **158**
   NG2: Nott 3F **5** (1D **123**)
   NG9: Bee 2D **147**
   NG16: Kimb 2F **69**
   NG16: Lang M 1A **42**
   NG16: Newth 2B **44**
North Ter. DE56: Bel 5F **13**
Northumberland Cl.
   NG3: Nott 4C **98**
Northumberland St.
   DE23: Der 1E **159**
North Vw. DE23: Lit 2B **158**
Northville Ct. NG3: Nott 3C **98**
Northway Dr. DE1: Der 4D **135**
Northwold Av.
   NG2: West Br 2C **150**
Northwood Av.
   DE21: Chad 1D **137**

Northwood Cres.
   NG5: Bestw 1B **74**
Northwood Rd.
   NG5: Bestw 1B **74**
Northwood St. NG9: Stap 5C **116**
Norton Ct. NG7: Radf 4D **97**
Norton St. NG7: Radf 4D **97**
Norwich Gdns. NG6: Bulw . . .3A **48**
Norwich St. DE21: Chad 1C **136**
Norwood Cl. DE7: Ilk 2E **67**
   DE22: Mac 3F **133**
Norwood Rd. NG7: Radf 5D **97**
Nothills Cl. DE73: Chel 5F **187**
Notintone Pl.
   NG2: Nott 3F **5** (1D **123**)
Notintone St.
   NG2: Nott 4F **5** (1D **123**)
NOTTINGHAM 3C **4** (1B **122**)
NOTTINGHAM AIRPORT 3E **153**
Nottingham Arts Theatre
   . . . . .3D **5** (1C **122**)
Nottingham Bus. Pk.
   NG2: Nott 5F **5** (2D **123**)
   NG8: Stre 5B **70**
Nottingham Castle
   . . . . .5A **4** (1A **122**)
Nottingham Climbing Cen. 4F **73**
Nottingham East Midlands
   Airport Aeropark 3F **211**
Nottingham Forest FC 4D **123**
Nottingham Forest Football Academy
   . . . . .1C **150**
Nottingham Greyhound Stadium
   . . . . .1A **124**
Nottingham Industrial Mus.
   . . . . .2E **119**
Nottingham Intl. Clothing Cen.
   NG15: Huck 4A **10**
Nottingham Playhouse
   . . . . .3A **4** (1A **122**)
Nottingham Race Course 2B **124**
Nottingham Rd.
   DE1: Der 1D **7** (2F **135**)
            (not continuous)
   DE5: Cod 2B **18**
   DE5: Rip 4D **9**
   DE7: Ilk 3E **91**
   DE21: Chad 2B **136**
   DE21: Spon 5C **120**
   DE56: Bel 5F **13**
   DE72: Bor, Ris 2A **164**
            (not continuous)
   DE74: Keg 1C **214**
   NG5: Arn 1D **75**
   NG6: Basf 4D **73**
            (not continuous)
   NG7: Basf 5E **73**
   NG8: Cin 3D **71**
   NG9: Chil, Toton 3D **169**
   NG9: Stap 1C **144**
   NG9: Trow 1B **116**
   NG10: Long E 3D **169**
   NG11: Goth 5A **172**
   NG12: Key 4D **199**
   NG12: Rad T 3C **126**
   NG13: Bing 2A **130**
   NG14: Bur J 4C **78**
   NG14: Lowd 4C **56**
   NG14: Woodbo 2C **52**
   NG15: Huck 4B **26**
   NG16: Cin, Nuth 2C **70**
   NG16: Eastw 2E **43**
   NG16: Gilt, Newth 3A **44**
   NG16: Kimb 1F **69**

Nottingham Rd. E.
  NG16: Eastw, Gilt, Newth
  . . . . .3A **44**
Nottingham Sailing Club 3B **124**
Nottingham Science &
  Technology Pk.
  NG7: Nott 4C **120**
Nottinghamshire County
  Cricket Ground 4D **123**
Nottingham Sth. & Wilford Ind. Est.
  NG11: Wilf 4A **150**
Nottingham Station (Rail)
  . . . . .5D **5** (2C **122**)
Nottingham Tennis Cen. 5C **120**
Nottingham Transport Heritage Cen.
  .1B **196**
Nottingham Trent University
  City Campus 1A **4** (5A **98**)
  Clifton Campus 5C **148**
Nottingham Trent University
  Sports Hall 5C **148**
Nottingham Trent University Stop
  (NET) 1A **4** (5A **98**)
Notts County FC 3D **123**
Nuart Rd. NG9: Bee 2E **147**
Nugent Gdns. NG3: Nott 4D **99**
Nunnery Ct.
  DE1: Der 1A **6** (2D **135**)
Nunsfield Dr. DE24: Alv 4A **162**
Nuns' St. DE1: Der . . .1A **6** (2D **135**)
Nurseries, The NG16: Eastw . .2F **43**
Nursery Av. DE7: West H 3D **89**
  NG9: Chil 3B **146**
  NG10: Sand 3E **143**
Nursery Cl. DE72: Bor 1A **164**
  NG12: Rad T 2A **128**
  NG15: Huck 5F **25**
Nursery Dr. NG4: Carl 2C **100**
Nursery Gdns.
  NG14: Lowd 2C **56**
Nursery Hollow DE7: Ilk 4D **91**
Nursery La. NG6: Basf 3D **73**
Nursery Rd. NG5: Arn 5E **51**
  NG12: Rad T 2A **128**
  NG13: Bing 2A **128**
Nutbrook Cres. DE7: Kirk H . . .1C **114**
NUTHALL 2C **70**
Nuthall Circ. DE7: Kirk H 1B **114**
Nuthall Gdns. NG8: Aspl 2C **96**
Nuthall Rd. NG8: Aspl, Cin . . .4A **72**
NUTTALS PARK 5D **9**
Nutwood Cl. DE22: D Abb . . .2F **107**

O

Oadby Ri. DE23: Der 5D **159**
Oak Acres NG9: Chil 3F **145**
Oak Apple Cres. DE7: Ilk 4D **91**
Oakash Ct. NG16: Nuth 1A **70**
Oak Av. DE5: Rip 2C **16**
  NG10: Sand 1F **143**
  NG12: Rad T 1D **127**
  NG13: Bing 2F **131**
  NG16: Lang M 4A **20**
Oak Cl. DE22: All 1D **107**
  DE56: Duff 4D **59**
  DE72: Ock 3B **140**
Oak Cres. DE23: Lit 3B **158**
Oakdale Dr. NG9: Chil 4B **146**
Oakdale Gdns. DE21: Oak . . .2A **110**
Oakdale Rd. NG3: Nott 4A **100**
  NG4: Carl 4C **100**
  NG5: Arn 4A **52**

Oak Dr. DE3: Mick 1D **157**
  DE24: Alv 5F **161**
  NG16: Eastw 2D **43**
  NG16: Nuth 1A **70**
Oakenhall Av. NG15: Huck . . .3B **26**
Oakfield NG12: Rad T 1F **127**
Oakfield Cl. NG8: Woll 2B **118**
Oakfield Ct. DE7: Stan C 1F **87**
  NG12: Rad T 2A **128**
Oakfield Dr. NG10: Sand 5A **144**
Oakfield Rd. NG8: Woll 2B **118**
  NG9: Stap 1C **144**
  NG15: Huck 3A **26**
Oakfields Gro. DE21: Spon . . .5C **138**
Oakfields Rd. NG2: West Br . . .4F **123**
Oak Flatt NG9: Chil 3F **145**
Oakford Cl. NG8: Brox 5F **71**
Oak Gro. NG15: Huck 5A **26**
Oakham Cl. DE21: Chad 4C **108**
  NG5: Top V 5E **49**
Oakham Rd. NG11: Rudd 1C **174**
Oakham Way DE7: Ilk 4C **66**
Oakhurst Cl. DE56: Bel 3C **12**
Oakington Cl. NG5: Bestw 2A **74**
Oakland Av. NG10: Long E . . .1B **194**
Oakland Ct. NG9: Bram 4F **117**
Oakland Gro. NG14: Calv 2E **31**
Oaklands Av. DE23: Lit 1B **184**
  DE75: Hea 2F **41**
Oaklands Cl. DE5: Den 3B **38**
Oaklands Rd. DE65: Etw 2B **180**
Oakland St. NG7: H Grn 3D **97**
Oakland Ter. NG10: Long E . . .1B **194**
Oakleigh Av. DE21: Chad 2E **137**
  NG3: Mapp 5B **76**
Oakleigh St. NG6: Bulw 3C **72**
Oakley M. NG6: Bulw 1E **71**
Oakley's Rd. NG10: Long E . . .4D **169**
Oakley's Rd. W.
  NG10: Long E 5C **168**
Oak Lodge NG13: Bing 2F **131**
Oak Lodge Dr. NG16: Kimb . . .5E **45**
Oakmead Av. NG8: Bilb 2E **95**
Oakmere Cl. NG12: Edwal . . .4B **152**
Oakover Dr. DE22: All 2C **106**
Oakridge DE21: Chad 1A **138**
Oakridge Pk. DE74: C Don . . .4F **205**
Oak Rd. DE72: Thul 2E **189**
Oaks, The DE21: L Eat 2B **84**
  NG3: Nott 1F **5** (5C **98**)
Oakside Way DE21: Oak 2A **110**
Oak St. DE23: Der 1F **159**
  NG5: Sher 1A **98**
Oak Tree Av. NG12: Rad T . . .1E **127**
Oaktree Av. DE24: Der 4A **160**
Oak Tree Cl. NG2: West Br . . .5F **123**
  NG15: Huck 5C **24**
Oak Tree Ct. DE72: Bor 2B **164**
Oak Tree Dr. NG4: Ged 5F **77**
Oakvale Ho. DE23: Der 1F **159**
Oak Vw. NG7: Radf 4E **97**
Oakwell Cres. DE7: Ilk 2D **91**
Oakwell Dr. DE7: Ilk 2D **91**
OAKWOOD 3F **109**
Oakwood Cl. DE24: S Flds . . .4C **184**
Oakwood District Cen.
  DE21: Oak 4F **109**
Oakwood Dr. DE21: Oak 3A **110**
  NG8: Aspl 3B **96**
Oakwood Gdns. NG16: Nuth . .4C **70**
Oakwood M. DE21: Oak 3E **109**
Oatfield La. NG12: Rad T 3C **104**
Oban Rd. NG9: Chil 2B **146**
Oberon Cl. DE73: Chel 5D **187**

Oberon Retail Pk.
  DE56: Bel 1E **35**
Occupation Rd. NG6: Bulw . . .2A **72**
  NG15: Huck 4F **25**
OCKBROOK 4B **140**
Ockbrook Ct. DE7: Ilk 4E **67**
Ockbrook Dr. NG3: Mapp 5E **75**
Ockerby St. NG6: Bulw 1B **72**
Octavia Cl. DE73: Chel 4D **187**
Odeon Cinema
  Derby 4B **108**
  Nottingham 3A **4**
Odesa Dr. NG6: Bulw 3A **72**
Offerton Av. DE23: Der 3D **159**
Ogdon Ct. NG3: Nott 4E **99**
Ogle Dr. NG7: Nott 5A **4** (2A **122**)
Ogle St. NG15: Huck 2F **25**
Okehampton Cres.
  NG3: Mapp 1B **76**
Oldacres NG14: Woodbo 5C **32**
Old Bank Ct. NG6: Basf 5C **72**
Old Barn Cl. DE21: L Eat 2B **84**
OLD BASFORD 4D **73**
Old Blacksmiths Yd.
  DE1: Der 2C **6** (3F **135**)
Old Brickyard NG3: Nott 3F **99**
Old Bull Farm Cl.
  LE12: Sut B 2F **215**
Oldbury Cl. DE21: Oak 3F **109**
  NG11: Clif 4C **172**
Old Chester Rd. DE1: Der 5F **107**
Old Church Cl. DE22: Quar . . .1B **106**
Old Church St. NG7: Lent 3D **121**
Old Coach Rd. NG8: Bilb 4D **95**
  NG8: Woll 5E **95**
Old Coppice Side DE75: Hea . .4D **41**
  (Roper Av., not continuous)
  DE75: Hea 4E **41**
  (Sunningdale Av.)
Old Derby Rd. NG16: Eastw . . .1C **42**
Old Dr. NG9: Bee 5C **118**
Old Epperstone Rd.
  NG14: Lowd 5F **33**
Oldershaw Av. DE74: Keg . . .2B **214**
Old Farm Ct. NG11: Bart F . . .5D **171**
Old Farm Rd. NG5: Top V 4E **49**
Old Ga. Av. DE72: W Tre 4D **203**
Old Hall Av. DE23: Lit 2A **158**
  DE24: Alv 4A **162**
  DE56: Duff 4C **58**
Old Hall Cl. NG14: Calv 2D **31**
Old Hall Dr. NG3: Mapp P 1C **98**
Old Hall Mill Bus. Pk.
  DE21: L Eat 3B **84**
Old Hall Rd. DE23: Lit 2B **158**
Oldham Ct. NG9: Chil 4B **146**
Old Hartshay Hill DE5: Rip 4B **8**
Old Kiln La. NG16: Eastw 3F **43**
Oldknow St. NG7: H Grn 4E **97**
Old La. DE22: D Abb 3F **107**
OLD LENTON 2D **121**
Old Lenton St.
  NG1: Nott 2D **5** (5C **98**)
Old Lodge Dr. NG5: Sher 3C **74**
Old Main Rd. NG14: Bulc 2F **79**
  (not continuous)
Old Manor Cl.
  NG14: Woodbo 5C **32**
Old Mansfield Rd.
  DE21: Chad 4B **108**
Old Market Square Stop (NET)
  . . . . .3B **4** (1B **122**)
Old Melton Rd.
  NG12: Plum 4D **177**

Old Mill Cl. DE56: Duff 4D 59
  NG6: Bestw V 1C 48
  NG7: Radf 5E 97
  NG9: Toton 1F 169
Old Mill St. NG13: Bing . . .1D 131
Oldmoor Wood Nature Reserve
  . . . . .2E 93
Old Oak Rd. NG11: Clif 1F 173
Old Orchard Wlk.
  DE21: Spon 2E 139
Old Park, The NG12: Cotg . .4E 155
Old Park Cl. NG8: Bilb 3D 95
  NG11: Rat 3E 209
Old Pit La. DE7: Smal 1F 63
Old Pond, The DE75: Hea 4F 41
OLD RADFORD 4C 96
Old Rd. DE56: H'age 1C 14
  NG11: Rudd 2C 122
Old School Cl. NG11: Clif . . .3D 173
Old School Ct. DE56: H'age 1D 15
Old School La. NG16: Aws 2B 68
Old School M.
  DE72: Ast T 1A 204
Old Station Cl. DE65: Etw . . .2A 180
Old Station Dr.
  NG11: Rudd 4A 174
Old St. NG1: Nott 1C 4 (5B 98)
Old Tannery Dr. NG14: Lowd . . .3D 57
Old Tollerton Rd.
  NG2: Gam 1B 152
Old Vicarage Cl. DE23: Lit . .2B 158
Old Vicarage La.
  DE22: Quar 5B 42
Olga Ct. NG3: Nott 4E 99
Olga Rd. NG3: Nott 4E 99
  NG14: Bur J 2E 79
Oliver Cl. DE75: Hea 2A 42
  NG7: Radf 4F 97
Oliver Rd. DE7: Kirk H 5B 90
Oliver St. NG7: Radf 4F 97
Olive St. DE22: Der 4D 135
Olivier St. DE23: Der 2A 160
Ollerton Rd. NG5: Arn 5D 29
Olton Av. NG9: Lent A 4E 119
Olton Rd. DE3: Mick 4B 132
Olympus Cl. NG15: Huck 1C 46
Omer Ct. NG16: Want 5F 45
Onchan Av. NG4: Carl 4D 101
Onchan Dr. NG4: Carl 4D 101
Onslow Rd. DE3: Mick 4C 132
Opal Cl. DE21: Oak 3F 109
Open University, The 2A 98
OPENWOODGATE 1C 36
Openwoodgate DE56: Bel 1C 36
Openwood Rd. DE56: Bel 1C 36
Orange Gdns. NG2: Nott 3C 122
Orby Cl. NG3: Nott 4E 99
Orby Wlk. NG3: Nott 5E 99
Orchard, The DE5: God 5F 9
  DE7: H Woo 1C 62
  DE7: Stan D 5E 115
  DE56: Dcl 6E 13
Orchard Av. DE74: C Don 1F 211
  NG4: Carl 3D 101
  NG13: Bing 2C 130
Orchard Bus. Pk. DE7: Ilk 1C 90
Orchard Cl. DE5: Rip 2F 17
  DE7: West H 3D 89
  DE21: Bre 1C 108
  DE23: Lit 4B 158
  DE24: Alv 2B 188
  DE56: H'ook 4A 36

Orchard Cl. DE72: Brea 3E 167
  DE72: Ock 4B 140
  NG11: Clif 1B 172
  NG12: Rad T 2D 127
  NG12: Toll 3C 176
  NG14: Bur J 2E 79
  NG14: Gun 2F 81
Orchard Cotts. DE56: Duff 3D 59
Orchard Ct. DE21: Spon 3D 139
  NG4: Carl 3D 101
  NG4: Ged 5C 76
  NG8: Basf 2D 97
  NG15: Huck 3F 25
  NG16: Lang M 1A 42
Orchard Cres. NG9: Chil 3B 146
Orchard Dr. NG14: Calv 2F 31
Orchard Gro. NG5: Arn 1B 74
Orchard Pk. NG3: Mapp 1B 76
Orchard Pk. Ind. Est.
  NG10: Sand 2B 144
Orchard Pl. NG8: Stre 5B 70
Orchard Ri. DE75: Hea 2E 41
  NG4: Lamb 5B 54
Orchards, The DE22: All 2C 106
  NG4: Ged 1F 101
  NG14: Lowd 4D 57
Orchard St.
  DE1: Der 1B 6 (2E 135)
  DE3: Mick 2C 156
  DE7: Ilk 3E 91
  NG10: Long E 4D 169
  NG15: Huck 3F 25
  NG16: Kimb 1E 69
  NG16: Lang M 1A 42
  NG16: Newth 3F 43
Orchard Way DE73: Chel 4E 187
  NG10: Sand 5F 143
Orchid Cl. NG2: West Br 4B 150
Orchid Cft. NG15: Huck 5B 26
Ordish Av. DE21: Chad 3E 137
Ordnance Ct. NG9: Chil 5B 146
Oregon Way DE21: Chad 1A 138
Orford Av. NG11: Clif 4E 149
  NG12: Rad T 3D 127
Oriel Ct. DE1: Der 5A 136
Orient M. NG16: Want 5F 45
Orient Way DE24: Der 1D 161
Orion Cl. NG8: Bilb 3D 95
Orion Dr. NG8: Bilb 3D 95
Orkney Cl. DE24: Sin 3C 184
Orlando Ct. DE73: Chel 4D 187
Orlando Dr. NG4: Carl 2E 101
Orlock Wlk. NG5: Bestw 2A 74
Orly Av. DE74: C Don 2F 211
Ormonde St. NG16: Lang M . . .5A 20
Ormonde Ter. NG5: Sher 5B 74
  NG16: Lang M 5A 20
Ormskirk Ri. DE21: Spon 4E 139
Ornsay Cl. NG5: Top V 3D 49
Orpean Way NG9: Toton 1D 169
Orston Av. NG5: Arn 5F 51
Orston Dr. NG8: Woll 1B 120
Orston Grn. NG8: Woll 2C 120
Orton Rd. E. NG2: West Br 4F 123
Orston Rd. W.
  NG2: West Br 4D 123
Orton Av. NG9: Bram 2B 146
Orton Way DE56: Bel 3A 14
Ortzen Ct. NG7: Radf 4E 97
Ortzen St. NG7: Radf 4E 97
Orville Rd. NG5: Bestw 2D 73
Osborne Cl. NG10: Sand 4A 144
Osborne Gro. NG5: Sher 4B 74

Osborne St. DE23: Der 5B 136
  NG7: Radf 4D 97
Osbourne Cl. NG16: Want 5A 46
Osgood Rd. NG5: Arn 2B 76
Osier Rd. NG2: Nott 4B 122
Osiers, The DE74: Keg 2C 214
Osiers Cl. DE22: All 4B 106
Osman Cl. NG2: Nott 4A 122
OSMASTON 4C 160
Osmaston Cl.
  NG10: Long E 1E 193
Osmaston Pk. Ind. Est.
  DE24: Der 2C 160
               (Ellesmere Av.)
  DE24: Der 3D 161
    (Sandown Rd., not continuous)
Osmaston Pk. Rd.
  DE23: Der 4F 159
  DE24: Der 4F 159
Osmaston Rd.
  DE1: Der 4D 7 (4F 135)
  DE23: Der 5E 7 (4A 136)
  DE24: Der 4C 160
Osmaston St. NG7: Lent 2E 121
  NG10: Sand 3B 144
Osnabruck Sq.
  DE1: Der 3D 7 (3F 135)
Osprey Cl. DE24: Sin 4D 185
  NG11: Clif 2B 172
  NG13: Bing 3E 131
Ossington Cl. NG1: Nott 4B 98
Ossington St. NG7: Radf 4E 97
Osterley Grn. DE22: Mac 3F 133
Osterley Gro. NG16: Nuth 4C 70
Oswestry Cl. DE21: Oak 2A 110
Othello Dr. DE73: Chel 4C 186
Otterburn Dr. DE22: All 3B 106
Otter St. DE1: Der 1F 135
Oulton Cl. DE24: S Loc 2C 186
  NG5: Arn 1E 75
Oulton Lodge NG5: Top V 3C 48
Oundle Dr. DE7: Ilk 3A 92
  NG8: Woll 2B 120
Ousebridge Cres. NG4: Carl . . .2F 101
Ousebridge Dr. NG4: Carl 2F 101
Outram Cl. DE5: Rip 4D 9
Outram St. DE5: Rip 4D 9
Outram Wharf DE21: L Eat 4B 84
Outram Way DE24: S Flds 4D 185
Out Track, The DE7: Mapp 5D 65
               (off Church La.)
Oval Ct. DE23: Lit 3B 158
Oval Gdns. NG8: Aspl 2C 96
Overdale Cl. NG10: Long E . . .5E 167
Overdale Rd. DE23: Der 1D 159
  NG6: Basf 5B 72
Over La. DE56: Bel 1C 36
  DE56: S'gate 2A 34
Overstone Cl. DE56: Bel 5C 14
Overstrand Cl. NG5: Arn 1E 75
Owen Av. NG10: Long E 5F 169
Owers Av. DE75: Hea 5E 41
Owlers La. DE23: Lit 1B 158
Owlswick Cl. DE23: Lit 3F 157
Owsthorpe Cl. NG5: Top V 4F 49
Owthorpe Gro. NG5: Sher 5A 74
Owthorpe Rd. NG12: Cotg 1E 179
Oxborough Rd. NG5: Arn 5B 50
Oxbow Cl. NG2: Nott 4B 122
Oxbury Rd. NG16: Want 4E 45
Oxclose La. NG5: Arn 1A 74
Oxendale Cl. NG2: West Br . . .2B 152
Oxengate NG5: Arn 1B 74

Oxenhope Cl. DE23: Lit 4D 157
Oxford St. DE1: Der 1F 151
Oxford St. DE1: Der 5A 136
   DE5: Rip 5C 8
   DE7: Ilk 3E 91
   DE21: Spon 3D 139
   NG1: Nott 3A 4 (1A 122)
   NG4: Carl 1D 101
   NG10: Long E 3C 168
   NG16: Eastw 2E 43
Oxton Av. NG5: Sher 3B 74
Oxton Rd. NG5: Arn 2E 29
   NG14: Calv 2E 29
   NG14: Epp 1B 32
Oxton Way DE24: Sin 4E 185
Oxwich Cl. DE21: Oak 2A 110
Ozier Holt NG4: Colw 1D 125
   NG10: Long E 5B 168

P

Packington Hill DE74: Keg . . .1B 214
Packman Dr. NG11: Rudd 3C 174
Paddington M. NG3: Nott 3F 99
Paddock, The DE24: Alv 2C 188
   DE56: H'ook 1B 60
   DE72: Ock 4B 140
   NG9: Atten 1C 170
   NG13: Bing 2D 131
Paddock Cl. DE74: C Don 1D 211
   NG6: Bulw 2A 72
   NG12: Rad T 3D 127
   NG14: Calv 2E 31
Paddock Cft. DE21: Oak 3E 109
Paddock Farm Cotts.
   NG14: Epp 4F 33
Paddocks, The DE5: Rip 1E 17
   LE2: Sut B 5F 215
   NG10: Sand 3F 143
   NG12: Edwal 5A 152
   NG16: Nuth 2A 70
Paddocks Vw.
   NG10: Long E 3F 167
Padge Rd. NG9: Bee 2A 148
Padgham Ct. NG5: Top V 4F 49
Padley Cl. DE5: Rip 3B 8
   DE22: All 5F 83
Padley Ct. NG6: Bulw 1F 71
Padleys La. NG4: Lur J 2D 79
Padstow Cl. DE24: S Flds 3C 184
Padstow Rd. DE24: Alv 1B 188
   NG5: Bestw 1E 73
Page Av. NG5: Bestw 2F 73
Paget Cres. NG11: Rudd 3B 174
Pagett Cl. NG15: Huck 3B 26
Paignton Cl. NG8: Aspl 5A 72
Paisley Gro. NG9: Chil 2B 170
Palatine Gro. DE23: Lit 4E 157
Palatine St.
   NG7: Nott 5A 4 (2A 122)
Palin Ct. NG7: H Grn 3E 97
Palin Gdns. NG12: Rad T 2F 127
Palin St. NG7: H Grn 4E 97
Palladium Dr. DE23: Lit 5F 157
Pall Mall DE21: Bre 1D 109
Palm Cl. DE23: Lit 3F 157
Palm Cotts. NG5: Sher 4C 74
Palm Ct. NG7: Basf 1E 97
Palmer Av. NG15: Huck 1F 25
Palmer Cres. NG4: Carl 3C 100
Palmer Dr. NG9: Stap 3C 144
Palmerston Gdns. NG3: Nott . .4B 98
   (not continuous)

Palmerston Rd. DE7: Ilk 2E 91
Palmerston St. DE23: Der 2D 159
Palm St. NG7: Basf 1E 97
Palmwood Ct. NG6: Bulw 2B 72
PAPPLEWICK 3F 11
Papplewick La. NG15: Huck . . .2A 26
Parade, The DE3: Mick 2C 156
Parcel Ter. DE1: Der 3C 134
Parchment M. NG5: Sher 1A 98
Pares Way DE72: Ock 3B 140
Pargate Cl. DE5: Mare 4C 16
PARK, THE 1A 122
Park, The NG12: Cotg 4E 155
Park & Ride
   Daleside Road East 2A 124
   Hucknall 2A 26
   Meteor Centre 4B 108
   Moor Bridge 2C 48
   Phoenix Park 3F 71
   Pride Park 5D 137
   Queen's Drive 1F 149
   The Forest 3F 97
   Wilkinson Street 1D 97
Park Av. DE5: Rip 5E 9
   DE7: Ilk 2E 91
   DE7: S'ley 4B 88
   DE74: C Don 1E 211
   NG2: West Br 5E 123
   NG3: Mapp P 2B 98
   NG4: Carl 2E 101
   NG5: Woodt 2D 75
   NG12: Key 3C 198
       (Croft Rd.)
   NG12: Key 3C 198
       (Park Rd.)
   NG14: Bur J 3E 79
   NG14: Woodbo 5A 32
   NG15: Huck 2E 25
   NG16: Aws 2A 68
   NG16: Eastw 1D 43
   NG16: Kimb 3F 69
Park Av. E. NG12: Key 3C 198
Park Av. W. NG12: Key 3C 198
Park Chase NG6: Bulw 2A 72
Park Cl. DE7: Stan D 5E 115
   DE21: L Eat 2A 84
   DE56: Kil 4F 37
   NG3: Mapp 5D 75
Park Ct. DE75: Hea 3E 41
   NG7: Lent 4D 121
Park Cres. DE7: Ilk 2F 91
   DE56: H'age 1D 15
   NG8: Woll 1B 118
   NG16: Eastw 5E 21
Parkcroft Rd.
   NG2: West Br 2E 151
Parkdale Rd. NG3: Nott 4A 100
   NG4: Carl 4A 100
Park Dr. DE7: Ilk 3E 91
   DE23: Lit 2B 158
   DE55: Swan 1E 9
   NG7: Nott 1F 121
   NG10: Sand 5F 143
   NG15: Huck 4F 25
Parker Cen. DE21: Der 5A 108
Parker Cl. DE1: Der 2E 135
   NG5: Arn 4B 52
Parker Gdns. NG9: Stap 5E 117
Parker Ind. Est.
   DE21: Der 5A 108
Parker St. DE1: Der 1E 135
   NG15: Huck 2A 26
Park Farm Cen. DE22: All 3C 106
Park Farm Dr. DE22: All 3C 106

Parkfields Dr. DE22: Der 5D 107
Parkfields Vw. DE56: H'age . . .1D 15
Park Ga. DE23: Der 1A 160
Parkgate NG15: Huck 5D 11
Park Gro. DE23: Der 5D 107
Park Hall DE7: Mapp 4C 64
Park Hall La. DE7: Mapp 5C 64
   DE7: West H 2B 88
Park Hall Rd. DE5: Den 1F 37
Parkham Rd. NG16: Kimb 5E 45
Park Hgts. NG7: Nott 2F 121
   NG16: Aws 2A 68
Park Hill NG7: Nott 5F 97
Park Hill Dr. DE23: Der 4E 159
Park Homes DE24: S Loc 3C 186
Park Ho. Gates
   NG3: Mapp P 1C 98
Parkland Cl. NG11: Clif 5B 148
Parkland Dr. DE73: Chel 1E 201
Parklands Cl. NG5: Top V 3A 50
   DE22: All 1E 107
   DE23: Lit 2B 158
   DE56: H'age 1D 15
   DE72: W Tre 5D 203
   DE74: C Don 1A 210
   NG4: Lamb 5B 54
   NG6: Basf, Bulw 3D 73
   NG14: Epp 4F 33
Park La. Bus. Cen.
   NG6: Bulw 2D 73
Park Leys Ct. DE21: Spon 4D 139
Park Lodge Rd.
   NG16: Newth 5F 43
Park M. NG3: Mapp P 2B 98
PARK NOOK 2A 82
Park Ravine NG7: Nott 2F 121
Park Rd. DE3: Mick 1C 156
   DE5: Rip 5D 9
   DE7: Ilk 3E 91
   DE21: Spon 3C 138
   DE56: Bel 2F 35
   DE56: Duff 4C 58
   DE56: H'age 1D 15
   NG4: Carl 3E 101
   NG5: Woodt 2D 75
   NG6: Bestw V 5D 27
   NG7: Lent 2E 121
   NG9: Bram 5E 117
   NG9: Chil 2D 147
   NG12: Key 2E 199
   NG12: Rad T 1E 127
   NG14: Calv 1C 30
   NG15: Huck 2E 25
Park Rd. E. NG14: Calv 1E 31
Park Rd. Nth. NG9: Chil 2D 147
Park Rock NG7: Lent 2F 121
Park Row
   NG1: Nott 4A 4 (1A 122)
Park Side DE56: Bel 1F 35
Parkside DE56: H'age 1D 15
   NG8: Woll 2D 119
   NG12: Key 2E 199
Parkside Av. NG10: Long E . . .3A 168
Parkside Dr.
   NG10: Long E 3A 168
Parkside Gdns. Nth.
   NG8: Woll 2D 119
Parkside Gdns. Sth.
   NG8: Woll 3D 119
Parkside Ri. NG8: Woll 3D 119
Parkside Rd. DE21: Chad 3F 137
Parkstone Cl.
   NG2: West Br 3B 150
Parkstone Ct. DE3: Mick 2B 156

Park St. DE1: Der 5F **7** (4A **136**)
DE5: Rip 5D **9**
DE72: Brea 3E **167**
DE75: Hea 2C **40**
(not continuous)
NG7: Lent 1E **121**
NG9: Bee 2D **147**
NG9: Stap 2B **144**
NG10: Long E 2B **168**
Park Ter. NG1: Nott 3A **4** (1A **122**)
NG12: Key 1E **199**
Park Valley
NG7: Nott 4A **4** (1A **122**)
Park Vw. DE21: L Eat 2B **84**
DE72: Ast T 2A **204**
DE75: Hea 3C **40**
NG3: Mapp 5D **75**
NG15: Huck 4A **26**
NG16: Eastw 3E **43**
Park Vw. Cl. DE22: All 1E **107**
Park Vw. Ct.
NG1: Nott 2F **5** (5C **98**)
NG9: Chil 2C **146**
Parkview Dr. NG25: Bestw 5F **49**
Park Vw. Ho. DE21: Chad . . .2B **156**
Park Wlk. DE56: Kil 3E **37**
Park Way DE65: Etw 2B **180**
Parkway DE73: Chel 4D **187**
Parkway Ct. NG8: Bilb 5C **94**
Park W. NG7: Nott 5F **97**
(off Derby Rd.)
Park Wharf
NG7: Nott 5A **4** (2A **122**)
Parkwood Ct. NG6: Bulw 2D **73**
Parkwood Cres. NG5: Sher 4D **75**
Parkyn Rd. NG5: Arn 1C **74**
Parkyns St. NG11: Rudd 4B **174**
Parliament Cl. DE22: Der 4D **135**
Parliament St.
DE22: Der 5A **6** (4D **135**)
(not continuous)
Parliament St. Mills
DE22: Der 4D **135**
Parliament Ter.
NG1: Nott 2A **4** (5A **98**)
Parr Ct. NG12: Rad T 2E **127**
Parr Ga. NG9: Chil 3F **145**
Parrs, The NG9: Bee 2A **148**
Parry Ct. NG3: Nott 4F **99**
Parry Way NG5: Arn 4A **52**
Parsons Gro. DE5: Der 2C **38**
Parsons Mdw. NG4: Colw 1D **125**
Partridge Cl. NG13: Bing 3E **131**
Partridge Way DE3: Mick 5F **133**
Parwich Cotts. DE23: Der 1F **159**
Pasteur Av. DE5: Rip 4C **8**
Pasteur Ho. NG3: Mapp 5E **75**
Pasture Cl. NG2: Colw 1D **125**
Pasture La. LE12: Sut B 5F **215**
NG10: Long E 5F **169**
NG11: Rudd 5E **173**
Pasture Rd. NG9: Stap 4C **116**
Pastures, The DE56: Duff . . .3D **59**
DE72: W Trc 4E **203**
NG14: Calv 2C **30**
NG16: Gilt 4A **44**
Pastures Av. DE23: Lit 4E **157**
NG11: Clif 3C **172**
Pastures Hill DE23: Lit 3F **157**
Pasture Vw. NG14: Gun 2F **81**
Patchings Farm Art Cen. 1F **29**
Pateley Rd. NG3: Mapp 3F **75**
Paterson Av. DE21: Chad 2A **138**
Patmore Sq. DE23: Der 4E **159**

Paton Rd. NG5: Bestw 2D **73**
Patricia Dr. NG5: Arn 3F **51**
Patrick Rd. NG2: West Br 5D **123**
Patriot Cl. NG16: Want 5F **45**
Patten Ct. DE24: Sin 1F **185**
Patterdale Cl. NG2: Gam 1B **152**
Patterdale Ct. NG9: Chil 3F **145**
Patterdale Rd. DE24: Alv 2F **161**
NG5: Woodt 2E **75**
Patterson Rd. NG7: H Grn 3E **97**
Pavilion, The NG7: H Grn 3F **97**
Pavilion Cl. NG2: Nott 4C **122**
Pavilion Ct. DE7: West H 3C **88**
NG14: Lowd 4D **57**
Pavilion Rd. DE23: Lit 3B **158**
NG2: West Br 4D **123**
NG5: Arn 3A **50**
Pavior Rd. NG5: Bestw 2E **73**
Paxton Cl. DE3: Mick 2B **156**
Paxton Gdns.
NG3: Nott 1F **5** (5D **99**)
Payne Rd. NG9: Chil 5F **145**
Payne St. DE22: Der 2C **134**
Paytons Rd. DE23: Der 5A **136**
Peache Way NG9: Bram 1A **146**
Peachey St.
NG1: Nott 1B **4** (5B **98**)
Peach St. DE22: Der 3C **134**
DE75: Hea 3C **40**
Peacock Cl. NG11: Rudd 5A **174**
NG14: Gun 3F **81**
Peacock Cres. NG11: Clif 1D **173**
Peacock Gro. DE23: Lit 5A **150**
Peacock Pl. DE7: Ilk 3C **66**
Peak Cl. DE1: Der 1B **6**
Peakdale Cl. DE5: Mare 3C **16**
NG10: Long E 5F **167**
Peak Dr. DE24: Der 4F **159**
Pearce Dr. NG8: Bilb 3A **96**
Pearl Cl. DE21: Oak 3F **109**
Pearmain Dr. NG3: Nott 3E **99**
Pearson Av. NG9: Chil 3A **146**
Pearson Cl. NG9: Chil 3A **146**
Pearson Ct. NG5: Arn 5D **51**
NG9: Bram 5A **118**
Pearson St. NG4: Neth 4F **101**
NG7: Basf 5E **73**
PEAR TREE 3E **159**
Pear Tree Av. DE5: Rip 1C **16**
Peartree Cl. DE74: C Don . . .1F **211**
Pear Tree Ct. DE65: Etw 2A **180**
NG6: Basf 3D **73**
Pear Tree Cres. DE23: Der 3F **159**
Peartree Ho. NG12: Cotg 1E **179**
(off Manorwood Rd.)
Pear Tree Ind. Est.
DE23: Der 3A **160**
Peartree Orchard
NG11: Rudd 4B **174**
Pear Tree Rd. DE23: Der 1F **159**
Peartree Station (Rail) 4A **160**
Pear Tree St. DE23: Der 3F **159**
Peary Cl. NG5: Bestw 1E **73**
PEASEHILL 1E **17**
Peasehill DE5: Rip 1E **17**
Peasehill Rd. DE5: Rip 1D **17**
Peashill La. NG12: Cotg 3B **154**
Peas Hill Rd. NG3: Nott 4C **98**
Peatburn Av. DE75: Hea 2B **40**
Peatfield Ct. NG9: Stap 4C **116**
Peatfield Rd. NG9: Stap 4C **116**
Peckerdale Gdns.
DE21: Spon 5D **139**

Peckham Gdns. DE22: Mac . . .3F **133**
Peck La. NG1: Nott 3C **4** (1B **122**)
NG14: Gun 2F **81**
Pedestrian Way NG5: Top V . .4E **49**
Pedley St. DE7: Ilk 3E **91**
Pedmore Valley NG5: Bestw . .5F **49**
Peebles Cl. DE24: Sin 4D **185**
Peel St. DE22: Der 2C **134**
NG1: Nott 1A **4** (4A **98**)
NG10: Long E 3D **169**
NG16: Lang M 1A **42**
Peel Vs. NG3: Mapp 5D **75**
Peers Cl. DE21: Oak 3A **110**
Peet St. DE22: Der 5A **6** (4D **135**)
Pegasus Bus. Pk.
DE74: N Air 4E **213**
Peggs Wlk. DE23: Der 4D **159**
Pegwell Cl. DE23: Der 4C **158**
Pelham Av. DE7: Ilk 1D **91**
NG5: Sher 2A **98**
Pelham Cotts. NG7: Nott 1E **121**
(off Pelham Cres.)
Pelham Ct. NG5: Sher 5B **74**
(off Private Rd.)
Pelham Cres. NG7: Nott 1E **121**
NG9: Bee 1A **148**
Pelham Rd. NG5: Sher 2A **98**
Pelham St. DE7: Ilk 1D **91**
DE22: Der 5A **6** (4E **135**)
NG1: Nott 3C **4** (1B **122**)
Pellham Ct. NG5: Sher 2A **98**
Pemberton St.
NG1: Nott 4E **5** (1C **122**)
Pembrey Cl. NG9: Trow 3C **116**
Pembridge Cl. NG6: Basf 5C **72**
Pembroke Dr. NG3: Mapp P . .1B **98**
Pembroke St. DE21: Chad 1C **136**
Pembury Rd. NG8: Woll 5D **95**
Penalton Cl. DE24: A'ton 5D **161**
Penarth Gdns. NG5: Sher 4D **75**
Penarth Ri. NG5: Sher 4D **75**
Pencroft Gro. DE23: Lit 1B **184**
Pendennis Cl. DE24: Alv 5A **162**
NG4: Ged 1A **102**
Pendine Cl. NG5: Redh 3C **50**
Pendlebury Dr. DE3: Mick 2D **157**
(not continuous)
Pendle Cres. NG3: Nott 1E **99**
Pendleside Way DE23: Lit 4D **157**
Pendock La. NG11: Rudd 4E **197**
Penge Rd. DE22: Mac 1F **133**
Penhale Dr. NG15: Huck 4B **24**
Penhaligan's Cl.
DE73: Chel 5E **187**
Penhaligan's Wlk.
DE73: Chel 5E **187**
(off Penhaligan's Cl.)
Penhurst Cl. NG11: Wilf 4F **149**
Penllech Cl. NG5: Bestw 5F **49**
Penllech Wlk. NG5: Bestw 5F **49**
Pen Moor Cl.
NG10: Long E 5F **167**
Pennant Rd. NG6: Basf 5C **72**
Pennard Wlk. NG11: Clif 3C **172**
Penn Av. NG7: Lent 2D **121**
Pennhome Av. NG5: Sher 5B **74**
Pennie Cl. NG10: Long E 2C **194**
Pennine Cl. NG5: Arn 3A **50**
NG10: Long E 2F **167**
Pennine Vw. DE56: H'age 1D **15**
Penn St. DE56: Bel 5F **13**
Pennycress Cl. DE23: Lit 4F **157**
Pennyfields Blvd.
NG10: Long E 4F **167**

Pennyfoot St.
  NG1: Nott 4F **5** (1D **123**)
Penny Long La. DE22: Der . . .5D **107**
Penrhyn Av. DE23: Der 3C **158**
Penrhyn Cl. NG3: Nott 4C **98**
Penrhyn Cres. NG9: Chil 4A **146**
Penrith Av. NG12: Rad T 1F **127**
Penrith Cres. NG8: Aspl 5B **72**
Penrith Pl. DE21: Chad 3C **108**
Penshore Cl. NG11: Clif 2C **172**
Pentagon, The DE21: Der . . .2B **136**
Pentagon Trade Pk.
  DE21: Chad 2B **136**
  (off The Pentagon)
Pentewan Cl. DE22: D Abb . . .3D **107**
Pentland Cl. DE21: Oak 3F **109**
Pentland Dr. NG5: Arn 2A **50**
Pentland Gdns.
  NG10: Long E 2F **167**
PENTRICH 1A **8**
Pentrich Rd. DE5: Rip 4C **8**
Pentridge Dr. DE7: Ilk 4B **66**
Pentwood Av. NG5: Arn 2E **51**
Penzance Rd. DE24: Alv 1A **188**
Peoples Hall Cotts. NG1: Nott . .3D **5**
Peppercorn Gdns. NG8: Woll . . .4B **96**
Pepper La. DE7: Stan D 5D **115**
Pepper Rd. NG14: Calv 1D **31**
Peppers Dr. DE74: Keg 2A **214**
Pepper St.
  NG1: Nott 4C **4** (1B **122**)
Percival Rd. NG5: Sher 5A **74**
Percy St. DE7: Ilk 3E **91**
  DE22: Der 5D **135**
  NG6: Basf 4C **72**
  NG16: Eastw 2F **43**
Peregrine Cl. DE24: Sin 2C **184**
  NG7: Lent 1D **121**
Perivale Cl. NG16: Nuth 4C **70**
Perlethorpe Av. NG2: Nott . . .1E **123**
  NG4: Ged 5C **76**
Perlethorpe Cl. NG4: Ged 5D **77**
Perlethorpe Cres. NG4: Ged . .5D **77**
Perlethorpe Dr. NG4: Ged 5C **76**
  NG15: Huck 2A **26**
Perry Gro. NG13: Bing 2E **131**
Perry Rd. NG5: Sher 5E **73**
Perth Cl. DE3: Mick 4D **133**
Perth Dr. NG9: Stap 4D **117**
Perth St. DE21: Chad 4C **108**
  NG1: Nott 1C **4** (5B **98**)
Peter Baines Ind. Est.
  DE22: Der 5B **6** (4E **135**)
Peterborough St.
  DE21: Chad 5D **109**
Peterhouse Ter. DE23: Der . . .1F **159**
Peterlee Pl. DE24: Alv 1F **187**
Peters Cl. NG5: Arn 1B **76**
  NG16: Newth 2B **44**
Petersfield Cl. NG5: Top V . . .5E **49**
Petersgate NG10: Long E 2F **167**
Petersgate Cl.
  NG10: Long E 1F **167**
Petersham Ct.
  NG10: Long E 1A **168**
Petersham Dr. DE24: Alv 5B **162**
Petersham M. NG7: Lent 2E **121**
Petersham Rd.
  NG10: Long E 1F **167**
Petworth Av. NG9: Toton 5E **145**
Petworth Dr. NG5: Sher 3E **73**
Peveril Av. DE72: Bor 1B **164**
Peveril Ct. DE5: Rip 5B **8**
  NG2: West Br 1D **151**

Peveril Cres. DE7: West H 2D **89**
  NG10: Long E 1E **193**
Peveril Dr. DE7: Ilk 5C **66**
  NG2: West Br 5D **151**
  NG7: Nott 5A **4** (2A **122**)
Peveril M. NG7: Nott 1F **121**
  (off Alexander Rd.)
Peveril Rd. NG9: Bee 5E **119**
Peveril St. DE24: Der 5C **160**
  NG7: Radf 4E **97**
  NG15: Huck 1F **25**
Pheasant Fld. Dr.
  DE21: Spon 2F **139**
Philip Av. NG16: Eastw 3F **43**
  NG16: Nuth 1B **70**
Philip Gro. NG4: Ged 5D **77**
Philips Cft. NG16: Duff 3D **59**
Phoenix Av. NG4: Ged 5D **77**
Phoenix Cen. NG8: Cin 3F **71**
Phoenix Cl. NG2: Nott 3A **122**
Phoenix Ct. NG7: Lent 5E **121**
  NG16: Eastw 2F **43**
Phoenix Park Stop (NET) 3F **71**
Phoenix Pl. NG8: Cin 3A **72**
Phoenix Rd. NG16: Newth . . .5A **22**
Phoenix St.
  DE1: Der 1D **7** (2F **135**)
Phyllis Cl. NG15: Huck 5B **10**
Phyllis Gro. NG10: Long E . . .4E **169**
Piccadilly NG6: Bulw 1C **72**
Pickburn's Gdns. DE56: Kil . . .4E **37**
Pickering Av. NG16: Eastw . . .2E **43**
Pickering Ri. DE21: Chad . . .4B **108**
Pickford's House Mus.
  . . . . .2A **6** (3E **135**)
Pieris Dr. NG11: Clif 2B **172**
Pierrepont Av. NG4: Ged 1D **101**
Pierrepont Ct.
  NG2: West Br 4A **124**
Pierrepont Rd.
  NG2: West Br 5F **123**
Pilcher Ga.
  NG1: Nott 3C **4** (1C **122**)
Pilgrims Way DE24: S Flds . . .3B **184**
Pilkington Rd. NG3: Mapp 1F **99**
Pilkington St. NG6: Bulw 5A **48**
Pillar Ct. DE3: Mick 2D **157**
Pilsley Cl. DE56: Bel 3B **14**
Pimlico DE7: Ilk 2D **91**
  DE22: Mac 2A **134**
Pimlico Av. NG9: Bram 2A **118**
Pimlico Cl. NG12: Rad T 2D **129**
Pinchom's Hill Rd.
  DE56: Bel 1A **36**
Pinder St. NG1: Nott . . .4E **5** (1C **122**)
Pine Av. NG16: Lang M 1F **41**
Pine Cl. DE5: Rip 5C **8**
  DE7: Smal 2E **63**
  DE21: Chad 4A **138**
  DE65: Etw 2B **180**
Pinecroft Ct. DE21: Oak 4A **110**
Pine Gro. NG15: Huck 5A **26**
Pine Hill Cl. NG5: Top V 3E **49**
Pinehurst Av. NG15: Huck . . .4B **24**
Pines, The DE72: Dray 4A **166**
Pine Tree Wlk. NG16: Eastw . .2D **43**
Pine Vw. NG7: Radf 4E **97**
Pineview Gdns. DE23: Lit 2A **158**
Pinewood Av. DE5: Cod 2A **18**
  NG5: Arn 3A **50**
Pinewood Gdns. NG11: Clif . . .3C **172**
Pinewood Rd. DE56: Bel 3D **13**
Pinfold NG13: Bing 2E **131**

Pinfold, The DE56: Bel 4B **14**
  DE72: Thul 2E **189**
Pinfold Cl. NG12: Cotg 4E **155**
  NG14: Woodbo 5B **32**
Pinfold Cres.
  NG14: Woodbo 5B **32**
Pinfold La. NG9: Stap 1C **144**
  NG11: Wilf 2A **150**
  NG12: Plum 4E **177**
  NG12: Shel 1B **104**
Pinfold Rd. NG16: Gilt 3B **44**
Pinfold Trad. Est.
  NG9: Stap 1D **145**
Pingle DE22: All 1D **139**
Pingle, The DE21: Spon 4D **139**
  NG10: Long E 2C **168**
Pingle Cres. DE56: Bel 4E **13**
  NG5: Top V 4E **49**
Pinglehill Way DE73: Chel . . .4A **188**
Pingle La. DE56: Bel 4E **13**
  DE73: Swar 2D **201**
Pingreaves Dr. DE73: Chel . . .4F **187**
Pintail Cl. NG4: Neth 4A **102**
Pintail Dr. DE24: Sin 2C **184**
Pioneer Meadows Local
  Nature Reserve 1B **114**
Piper Cl. NG15: Huck 5D **11**
Pippin Cl. NG3: Nott 3E **99**
Pippin Gdns. DE24: Alv 4E **161**
Pippin Hill DE5: Den 3D **39**
Pitcairn Cl. NG2: Nott 4B **122**
Pitch Cl. NG4: Carl 2B **100**
Pit Cl. La. DE73: Chel 5F **187**
Pit La. DE5: Rip 5D **9**
  (Albion St.)
  DE5: Rip 2F **17**
  (Stoney La.)
  DE7: Ilk 1A **66**
  DE75: Ship 1A **66**
Pittar St. DE22: Der . . .5A **6** (5E **135**)
Plackett Cl. DE72: Brea 3C **166**
  NG9: Stap 5E **117**
Plains Farm Cl. NG3: Mapp . . .2B **76**
Plains Gro. NG3: Mapp 3F **75**
Plains La. DE56: B'ook 5A **12**
Plains Rd. NG3: Mapp 4E **75**
Plane Cl. NG6: Bulw 5E **47**
Plane Tree Ct. NG15: Huck . . .4A **26**
Plantagenet Ct.
  NG3: Nott 1E **5** (5C **98**)
Plantagenet St.
  NG3: Nott 1E **5** (5C **98**)
Plantain Gdns. DE23: Lit 1B **184**
Plantation, The DE23: Lit 2A **158**
Plantation Cl. NG5: Arn 3A **50**
Plantation Rd. NG8: Woll 1B **118**
  NG12: Key 3C **198**
Plantations, The
  NG10: Long E 3F **167**
Plantation Side NG7: H Grn . . .3D **97**
Plantin Rd. NG5: Sher 1A **98**
Plant La. NG10: Long E 2F **193**
Platform Ct. DE21: Spon 5C **138**
Platt La. NG12: Key 2E **199**
Platts Av. DE75: Hea 3B **40**
Player St. NG7: Radf 4D **97**
Plaza Gdns. NG6: Basf 3D **73**
Pleasant Ct. NG7: H Grn 3E **97**
Pleasant Pl. DE74: Keg 2C **214**
Pleasant Row NG7: H Grn 3E **97**
Plimsoll Ct. DE22: Der 5E **135**
Plimsoll St. DE22: Der 2B **134**
  NG7: H Grn 2D **97**
Ploughfield Cl. DE23: Lit 5A **158**

Plough Ga. DE22: D Abb 3E **107**
Plough La.
  NG1: Nott 4F **5** (1D **123**)
  NG14: Lowd 3C **56**
Ploughman Av.
  NG14: Woodbo 5C **32**
Plover Ct. DE3: Mick 4A **156**
Plover Wharf NG7: Lent 3F **121**
Plowman Ct. NG9: Stap 2C **144**
Plowright Ct. NG3: Nott 3C **98**
Plowright St. NG3: Nott 3C **98**
Plumb Rd. NG15: Huck 2E **25**
Plummer La. DE74: Keg 2B **214**
Plumptre Almhouses
  NG1: Nott 4E **5**
Plumptre Cl. NG16: Eastw 3E **43**
Plumptre Pl.
  NG1: Nott 4D **5** (1C **122**)
Plumptre Rd. NG16: Lang M . . .4A **20**
Plumptre Sq.
  NG1: Nott 4E **5** (1C **122**)
Plumptre St.
  NG1: Nott 4D **5** (1C **122**)
Plumptre Way NG16: Eastw . . .3E **43**
PLUMTREE 4D **177**
Plumtree Ct. NG12: Plum 4D **177**
Plumtree Gdns. NG14: Calv . . .2E **31**
PLUMTREE PARK 2E **199**
Plumtree Rd. NG12: Cotg . . .1C **178**
Plungar Cl. NG8: Bilb 4A **96**
Podder La. NG3: Mapp 1B **76**
Point, The NG1: Nott 4E **5**
  *NG2: West Br 1D **151***
  (off Loughborough Rd.)
  NG3: Mapp P 2C **98**
Pointers Ct. NG3: Nott 3F **99**
Pollard Ct. NG9: Bee 1E **147**
Pollards Oaks DE72: Bor 2A **164**
Polperro Way NG15: Huck 4B **24**
Pond End DE74: C Don 3A **206**
Pond Hills La. NG5: Arn 4E **51**
Pond Rd. DE56: H'ook 5B **36**
Ponsonby Ter.
  DE1: Der 2A **6** (3D **135**)
Pontefract St. DE24: Der 4C **160**
Pontypool Cl. DE21: Oak 3A **110**
Pool Cl. DE24: Alv 2B **188**
Poole St. DE24: A'ton 5D **161**
Pool Mdw. NG4: Colw 1E **125**
Popham Cl.
  NG1: Nott 4D **5** (1C **122**)
Popham St.
  NG1: Nott 4D **5** (1C **122**)
Poplar Av. DE5: Rip 1C **16**
  DE21: Spon 3D **139**
  NG5: Sher 5F **73**
  NG10: Sand 1F **143**
Poplar Cl. DE24: Alv 4A **162**
  NG4: Carl 4C **100**
  NG13: Bing 2F **131**
Poplar Cres. NG16: Nuth 1F **69**
Poplar Nook DE22: All 1F **107**
Poplars Rd. DE72: Brea 2E **167**
Poplar Row DE22. D Abb 4F **107**
Poplars, The DE22: All 1E **107**
  NG2: West Br 1E **151**
  NG7: H Grn 2D **97**
  NG9: Bee 1E **147**
  NG12: Plum 5D **177**
Poplars Av. NG14: Bur J 2F **79**
Poplars Cl. NG12: Key 2F **199**
Poplars Rd. NG7: Lent 3E **121**
Poplar St. NG1: Nott 4E **5** (1C **122**)
Poplar Way DE7: Kirk H 5C **90**

Poppyfields DE5: Rip 2C **16**
Poppy M. NG15: Huck 5C **26**
PORCHESTER 5A **76**
Porchester Cl. NG15: Huck 2B **26**
Porchester Ct. NG3: Nott 2F **99**
Porchester Rd. NG3: Mapp 5E **75**
  NG13: Bing 2D **130**
Porlock Cl. NG10: Long E 3F **167**
Porlock Cl. DE21: Oak 3F **109**
Portage Cl. NG12: Rad T 3D **127**
Port Arthur Rd. NG2: Nott 1F **123**
Porter Cl. NG11: Clif 3B **172**
PORTERHOUSE 5E **9**
Porterhouse Rd. DE5: Rip 5D **9**
Porter Pl. DE21: Spon 3C **138**
Porter Rd. DE23: Der 2D **159**
Porter's La. DE21: Oak 2E **109**
  DE65: Find 4B **182**
    (not continuous)
Porters Wlk. NG3: Nott 3F **99**
Porthcawl Pl. DE21: Oak 3B **110**
Portia Cl. DE21: Spon 5C **138**
Portico Rd. DE23: Lit 5F **157**
Portinscale Cl.
  NG2: West Br 3B **152**
Portland Cl. DE3: Mick 1C **156**
Portland Cl. NG5: Bestw 2A **74**
Portland Cres. NG9: Stap 2D **145**
Portland Gdns. NG15: Huck . . .2E **25**
Portland Grange
  NG15: Huck 2D **25**
Portland Hill NG7: Nott 4B **120**
Portland Leisure Cen. 4C **122**
Portland Pk. Cl. NG15: Huck . . .2E **25**
Portland Rd. DE7: Ilk 4E **67**
  NG2: West Br 2E **151**
  NG4: Carl 5B **76**
  NG7: Radf 5F **97**
  NG9: Toton 2E **169**
  NG10: Long E 2F **193**
  NG15: Huck 2A **26**
  NG16: Gilt 4A **44**
Portland St. DE23: Der 2F **159**
  DE65: Etw 2A **180**
  NG5: Arn 1C **74**
  NG9: Bee 1F **147**
Portman Chase
  DE24: S Flds 4C **184**
Portreath Dr. DE22: All 1D **107**
Portree Dr. NG5: Top V 3E **49**
Port Said Vs. NG7: Basf 1E **97**
Port Way DE21: Cox 1B **60**
  DE56: Cox, H'ook 1B **60**
Portway Cl. DE22: All 1F **107**
Posey La. DE72: Ast T 2F **203**
Postern St.
  NG1: Nott 3A **4** (1A **122**)
Potato Pit La. DE7: D Ab 4F **113**
Potomac M. NG7: Nott 1F **121**
Potters Cl. NG5: Top V 5F **49**
Potters Ct. NG9: Bram 4C **118**
Potters Hollow NG6: Bulw 2B **72**
Potter St. DE21: Spon 4C **138**
Pottery Way DE7: Ilk 2F **91**
Pottery Cl. DE56: Bel 4B **14**
Pottery La. DE5: Den 1B **38**
Pottery Way NG6: Bulw 5F **47**
Poulter Cl. NG7: Radf 3C **96**
Poulton Dr. NG2: Nott 2E **123**
Poultry Arc. NG1: Nott 3C **4**
Powell St. DE23: Der 1D **159**
Powerleague Soccer Cen.
  Nottingham 2D **149**
Powis St. NG6: Bulw 5A **48**

Powtrell Pl. DE7: Ilk 4A **92**
Poynter Cl. DE75: Hea 3B **40**
Poynton St.
  NG1: Nott 2A **4** (5A **98**)
Poyser Av. DE21: Chad 1F **137**
Poyser Cl. NG7: Basf 1F **97**
Premier Rd. NG7: H Grn 2F **97**
Prendwick Gdns.
  NG5: Bestw 4A **50**
Prescot Cl. DE3: Mick 2B **156**
Prestbury Cl. DE21: Oak 4A **110**
Prestwick Cl. NG8: Stre 5C **70**
Prestwick Way DE73: Chel . . .4D **187**
Prestwood Dr. NG8: Aspl 3A **96**
Pretoria Vs. NG8: Aspl 5B **72**
Previn Gdns. NG3: Nott 4E **99**
PRIDE PARK 5C **136**
Pride Pk. Stadium 5D **137**
Pride Parkway
  DE1: Der 4F **7** (4B **136**)
  DE24: Der 4B **136**
Pride Pl. DE24: Der 5C **136**
Pride Point Dr. DE24: Der 1C **160**
Priestland Av. DE21: Spon . . .4C **138**
Primary Cl. DE56: Bel 5F **13**
Prime Ent. Pk. DE1: Der 2A **136**
Prime Ind. Est. DE23: Der 1B **160**
Prime Parkway
  DE1: Der 1E **7** (1A **136**)
Primrose Bank DE65: Etw 1B **180**
  NG13: Bing 2C **130**
Primrose Cl. DE21: Oak 2E **109**
  NG3: Nott 3C **98**
Primrose Cotts. DE72: Ris 5C **142**
Primrose Cres. NG4: Carl 3E **101**
Primrose Dr. DE7: Mor 2B **86**
Primrose Gdns. NG15: Huck . .5C **26**
Primrose Hill DE7: Ilk 4D **67**
Primrose Ri. NG16: Newth 4F **43**
Primrose St. DE7: Ilk 4D **67**
  NG4: Carl 3E **101**
Primula Cl. NG11: Clif 1B **172**
Primula Way DE23: Lit 2C **184**
Prince Charles Av.
  DE22: Mac 2E **133**
Prince Edward Cres.
  NG12: Rad T 3C **126**
Princes Dr. DE23: Lit 1A **158**
Princess Alice Ct.
  DE1: Der 1A **6** (2E **135**)
Princess Av. NG9: Bee 2F **147**
Princess Cl. DE75: Hea 2C **40**
  NG4: Ged 5D **77**
Princess Dr. DE72: Bor 1F **163**
  NG10: Sand 4A **144**
Princess St. NG10: Long E . . .3C **168**
Princes St. DE23: Der 2F **159**
  NG16: Eastw 1E **43**
Prince St. DE7: Ilk 3D **67**
  NG10: Long E 3C **168**
Prioridge NG12: Cotg 1F **179**
Prior Rd. NG5: Arn 1C **74**
Priors, The NG14: Lowd 2C **56**
Priors Barn Cl. DE72: Bor 1C **164**
Priors Cl. NG13: Bing 1F **131**
Priorway Av. DE72: Bor 2B **164**
Priorway Gdns. DE72: Bor 2B **164**
Priory Av. NG12: Toll 2B **176**
Priory Cir. NG12: Toll 2B **176**
Priory Cl. DE7: Kirk H 4B **90**
  DE73: Chel 1E **201**
Priory Ct. NG3: Mapp 1D **99**
  NG4: Ged 1E **101**
  NG7: Lent 2D **121**

Priory Cres. NG4: Ged 1E **101**
Priory Gdns. DE21: Oak 2E **109**
Priory Hgts. Ct. DE23: Der . . .1C **158**
Priory M. NG7: Lent 3D **121**
Priory Rd. NG2: West Br 5E **123**
  NG4: Ged 1E **101**
  NG15: Huck 2D **25**
  NG8: Eastw 3E **43**
Priory St. NG7: Lent 3D **121**
Priory Way DE5: Rip 1D **17**
Pritchard Dr. NG9: Stap 2D **145**
Pritchett Dr. DE23: Lit 3D **157**
Private Rd. NG3: Mapp 5C **74**
  NG5: Sher 5B **74**
  NG14: Woodbo 4A **32**
  NG15: Huck 2D **25**
Private Rd. 1 NG4: Colw 4E **101**
Private Rd. 2 NG4: Colw 5E **101**
Private Rd. 3 NG4: Colw 5F **101**
Private Rd. 4 NG4: Colw 5A **102**
Private Rd. 5 NG4: Colw 5A **102**
Private Rd. 6 NG4: Colw 4E **101**
Private Rd. 7 NG4: Colw 4E **101**
Private Rd. 8 NG4: Colw 5E **101**
Prize Cl. NG11: Clif 2B **172**
Promenade NG3: Nott . . .1E 5 (5C **98**)
Prospect Cl. NG4: Carl 1F **99**
Prospect Dr. DE56: Bel 2E **35**
Prospect Pl. DE24: Der 4D **137**
  NG7: Lent 2E **121**
Prospect Rd. DE5: Den 3E **37**
  DE75: Hea 4F **41**
  NG4: Carl 1F **99**
Prospect St. NG7: Radf 4D **97**
Prospect Ter. NG7: Radf 4D **97**
Prospect Vs. NG14: Lowd 3C **56**
Providence Pl. DE7: Ilk 1D **91**
Providence St. DE5: Rip 1D **17**
Provident St. DE23: Der 1E **159**
Prudhoe Ct. NG2: Nott 4C **122**
Pulborough Cl. NG5: Sher 3E **73**
Pulborough Gdns. DE23: Lit . .5F **157**
Pullman Rd. DE21: Chad 4E **137**
  NG2: Nott 1E **123**
Pumping Sta. Cotts.
  NG2: Nott 2F **123**
Purbeck Cl. NG10: Long E . . .3F **167**
Purbeck Dr. NG2: West Br . . .3B **150**
Purchase Av. DE75: Los 2B **40**
Purdy Mdw. NG10: Long E . . .1E **193**
Putney Cl. DE22: Mac 3D **133**
Pyatt St. NG2: Nott 4C **122**
Pybus St. DE22: Der 2C **134**
Pykestone Cl. DE21: Oak 3E **109**
Pym Leys NG10: Long E 1E **193**
Pym St. NG3: Nott 4E **99**
Pym Wlk. NG3: Nott 1F 5 (4D **99**)
Pytchley Cl. DE56: Bel 5C **14**

Q

Q Arts Gallery 1C 6 (2F **135**)
QUAD 2D 7 (3F **135**)
Quadrangle, The
  NG15: News 1A **10**
Quantock Cl. DE24: S Flds . . .4C **184**
  NG5: Arn 2A **50**
Quantock Gro. NG13: Bing . . .2B **130**
Quantock Rd.
  NG10: Long E 2F **167**
QUARNDON 4B **82**
QUARNDON COMMON 3C **82**
Quarndon Hgts. DE22: All 3B **106**
Quarndon Vw. DE22: All 3B **106**

Quarn Dr. DE22: All 2B **106**
Quarn Gdns. DE1: Der 1E **135**
Quarn St. DE1: Der 2E **135**
  (not continuous)
Quarn Way DE1: Der 2E **135**
Quarry Av. NG6: Bulw 1A **72**
Quarrydale NG15: Huck 5B **10**
Quarry Hill DE7: Stan D 5E **115**
Quarry Hill Ind. Est.
  DE7: Ilk 1E **115**
Quarry Hill Rd. DE7: Ilk 5E **91**
Quarry La. NG15: Lin 1D **11**
Quarry Rd. DE7: Mor 2A **86**
  DE56: Bel 2E **35**
Quays, The NG7: Lent 2F **121**
Quayside Cl. NG2: Nott 4D **123**
Queen Elizabeth Rd.
  NG9: Chil 4F **145**
Queen Elizabeth Way
  DE7: Kirk H 5B **90**
Queen Mary Ct. DE22: Der . . .1E **135**
Queen Mary's Cl.
  NG12: Rad T 3C **128**
Queens Av. DE7: Ilk 5F **91**
  DE7: S'ley 4B **88**
  DE75: Hea 2C **40**
  NG4: Ged 5D **77**
Queensberry St. NG6: Basf . . .3D **73**
Queen's Bower Rd.
  NG5: Bestw 4A **50**
Queens Bri. Rd. NG2: Nott . . .2B **122**
Queensbury Av.
  NG2: West Br 5B **150**
Queensbury Chase
  DE23: Lit 5F **157**
Queens Ct. DE22: Der 5D **107**
  DE72: Dray 4F **165**
  NG13: Bing 1C **130**
Queens Dr. DE7: Ilk 2D **91**
  DE23: Lit 1B **158**
  DE56: Bel 4D **13**
  NG2: Nott 1F **149**
  NG9: Bee 2F **147**
  NG10: Sand 4A **144**
  NG16: Brins 2D **21**
  NG16: Nuth 1B **70**
Queensferry Gdns.
  DE24: A'ton 2D **187**
Queensgate Dr. DE73: Chel . . .1D **201**
Queens Gro. NG2: Nott 2B **122**
Queensland Cl. DE3: Mick . . .4D **133**
Queen's Leisure Cen.
  . . . . .1C 6 (2F **135**)
Queens Rd. DE74: Keg 1C **214**
  NG2: Nott 2B **122**
  NG9: Bee 3F **147**
  NG12: Rad T 1E **127**
Queen's Rd. E. NG9: Bee 1A **148**
Queens Rd. Nth.
  NG16: Eastw 2E **43**
Queens Rd. Sth.
  NG16: Eastw 3E **43**
Queen's Rd. W.
  NG9: Bee, Chil 4C **146**
Queen's Sq. NG16: Eastw 2E **43**
Queen St. DE1: Der 1C 6 (2F **135**)
  DE5: Rip 2E **17**
  DE7: Ilk 2D **91**
  DE56: Bel 1F **35**
  NG1: Nott 2B 4 (5B **98**)
  NG5: Arn 3E **51**
  NG10: Long E 4D **169**
  NG15: Huck 1E **25**
  NG16: Lang M 1B **42**

Queens Vw. Dr. DE5: Rip 2F **17**
Queens Wlk. NG2: Nott 4A **122**
Queensway DE22: Der 1C **134**
  DE74: C Don 5E **205**
Queen Ter. DE7: Ilk 2D **91**
Quenby La. DE5: Rip 5D **9**
Querneby Av. NG3: Mapp 5D **75**
Querneby Rd. NG3: Mapp 5D **75**
Quick Hill Rd. DE24: S Flds . . .4C **184**
Quillings Way DE72: Bor 2C **164**
Quinton Cl. NG11: Wilf 3F **149**
Quintyn Rd. DE24: Alv 3F **161**
Quorn Cl. NG9: Atten 5D **147**
Quorndon Cres.
  NG10: Long E 1C **194**
Quorn Gro. NG5: Sher 4F **73**
Quorn Ri. DE23: Der 5D **159**
Quorn Rd. NG5: Sher 4F **73**

R

Rabown Av. DE23: Lit 3C **158**
Racecourse Ind. Est.
  DE21: Der 5B **108**
Racecourse Rd.
  NG2: Colw, Nott 1A **124**
Radbourne Ga. DE3: Mick . . .3C **132**
Radbourne La. DE6: Rad 3B **132**
  DE22: Mac 2D **133**
Radbourne Rd. NG2: Nott 2E **123**
Radbourne St. DE22: Der 2B **134**
Radburn Ct. NG9: Stap 4D **117**
Radcliffe Av. DE21: Chad 1E **137**
Radcliffe Dr. DE22: Der 5C **134**
Radcliffe Gdns. NG4: Carl 2C **100**
Radcliffe Lodge
  NG12: Rad T 2D **127**
Radcliffe Mt. NG2: West Br . . .4E **123**
RADCLIFFE ON TRENT 2E **127**
Radcliffe Rd.
  NG2: Gam, West Br 4D **123**
  NG12: Crop Bu 5E **129**
  NG12: Hol P 5C **124**
Radcliffe Station (Rail) 2E **127**
Radcliffe St. NG2: Nott 4C **122**
RADFORD 5E **97**
Radford Blvd. NG7: Radf 4D **97**
Radford Bri. Rd.
  NG8: Aspl, Woll 4B **96**
Radford Ct. NG7: Basf 5E **73**
  (off Radford Rd.)
  NG7: Radf 5E **97**
Radford Ct. Ind. Est.
  NG7: Radf 5E **97**
Radford Cres. NG4: Ged 5D **77**
Radford Gro. La. NG7: Radf . . .4D **97**
Radford Mdw. DE74: C Don . . .1E **211**
Radford Rd. DE7: Smal 1E **63**
  NG7: Basf, H Grn 5E **73**
Radford Road Stop (NET) 2E **97**
Radford St. DE24: Alv 4E **161**
Radham Ct. NG5: Sher 5B **74**
Radley Sq. NG6: Bulw 2C **72**
Radmarsh Rd. NG7: Lent 2D **121**
Rad Mdws. NG10: Long E 5B **168**
Radnor Gro. NG13: Bing 2B **130**
Radnor St. DE21: Chad 5C **108**
Radstock Gdns.
  DE21: Chad 4D **109**
Radstock Rd. NG3: Nott 3F **99**
Radstone Cl. DE21: Oak 3A **110**
Radway Dr. NG11: Wilf 3F **149**
Raeburn Dr. NG9: Toton 1D **169**

Ragdale Rd. NG6: Bulw 4A 48
(not continuous)
Raglan Av. DE22: Der 3B 134
Raglan Cl. NG3: Nott 3C 98
Raglan Ct. NG9: Lent A 4F 119
Raglan Dr. NG4: Ged 1A 102
Raglan St. NG16: Eastw 3F 43
Raibank Gdns. NG5: Woodt . .2D 75
Railway Cotts. NG16: Kimb . . .1E 69
Railway Side DE5: Den 2F 37
Railway Ter.
DE1: Der 5F 7 (4B 136)
Rainham Gdns. DE24: Alv 1F 187
NG11: Rudd 5B 174
Rainier Dr. DE21: Chad 2F 137
Raithby Cl. NG5: Bestw 1F 73
Raleigh Cl. DE7: Ilk 4E 67
NG11: Clif 2B 172
Raleigh Ct. NG7: Radf 4F 97
Raleigh M. NG7: Radf 5F 97
Raleigh Pk. NG7: Lent 5C 96
Raleigh Sq. NG7: Radf 5F 97
Raleigh St. DE22: Der 2B 134
NG7: Radf 5F 97
Ralf Cl. NG2: West Br 4D 151
Ralph Way NG5: Sher 2B 74
Ramblers Cl. NG4: Colw 5D 101
Ramblers Dr. DE21: Oak 2B 110
Ramsdale Av. NG14: Calv 1C 30
Ramsdale Cres. NG5: Sher . . .4C 74
Ramsdale Pk.
NG14: Woodbo 3A 30
Ramsdale Rd. NG4: Carl 1D 101
Ramsdean Cl. DE21: Chad . . .5C 108
Ramsey Ct. NG9: Stap 3D 117
Ramsey Ct. NG5: Sher 1A 98
Ramsey Dr. NG5: Arn 3A 136
Ramshaw Way DE22: Der 4D 135
Ranby Wlk. NG3: Nott 4E 99
Rancliffe Av. NG12: Key 2C 198
Randal Gdns. NG7: H Grn 3E 97
Randall St. NG7: H Grn 3E 97
Randal St. NG7: H Grn 3D 97
Randolph Rd. NG23: Der 3E 159
Ranelagh Gdns. DE22: Mac . .1A 134
Ranelagh Gro. NG8: Woll 5F 95
Rangemore Cl. DE3: Mick 4D 133
Ranmere Rd. NG8: Bilb 3F 95
Ranmoor Rd. NG4: Ged 1E 101
Ranmore Cl. NG9: Bram 3A 118
Rannerdale Cl.
NG2: West Br 2A 152
Rannoch Cl. DE21: Spon 3E 139
DE22: All 2D 107
Rannoch Ri. NG5: Arn 3E 51
Rannock Gdns. NG12: Key . . .3E 199
Ranskill Gdns. NG5: Top V . . .4F 49
Ransom Dr. NG3: Mapp 1D 99
Ransom Rd. NG3: Nott 1D 99
Ranson Rd. NG9: Chil 2A 170
Ranworth Cl. DE24: S Loc 3C 186
Ratcliffe La. DE74: Lock 2A 208
RATCLIFFE ON SOAR 3E 209
Ratcliffe St. NG16: Eastw 2E 43
Rathgar Cl. NG8: Woll 1C 118
Rathmines Cl. NG7: Lent 2D 121
Rathvale Cl. NG9: Chil 4F 145
Rauche Ct. DE23: Der 5A 136
Raven Av. NG5: Sher 1A 98
Ravenhill Cl. NG9: Chil 4A 146
Raven Oak Cl. DE56: Bel 2F 35
Ravens Ct. NG5: Bestw 2A 74
Ravenscourt Rd.
DE22: Mac 1B 134

Ravenscroft Dr.
DE21: Chad 2E 137
Ravensdale Av.
NG10: Long E 1A 168
Ravensdale Dr. NG8: Woll 2B 118
Ravensdale Rd. DE22: All 2B 106
Ravensdene Ct.
NG3: Mapp P 2B 98
Ravensmore Rd.
NG5: Sher 5A 74
Ravenstone Ct. NG15: Huck . . .1D 47
Raven St. NG22: Der 5D 135
Ravenswood Rd. NG5: Arn . . .5E 51
Ravensworth Rd.
NG6: Bulw 4A 48
Rawdon Cl. DE74: C Don 5F 205
Rawdon St. DE23: Der 1E 159
Rawlinson Av. DE23: Der 4F 159
RAWSON GREEN 2E 37
Rawson Grn. DE56: Kil 3E 37
Rawson St. NG7: Basf 1E 97
Raymede Cl. NG5: Bestw 1E 73
Raymede Dr. NG5: Bestw 1D 73
Raymond Dr. NG13: Bing 2F 131
Rayner Ct. NG7: Lent 5E 97
Raynesway
DE21: Chad, Spon 2F 161
DE24: Alv 3A 162
Raynesway Pk.
DE21: Spon 2A 162
Raynesway Pk. Dr.
DE21: Spon 2A 162
Raynesway Vw.
DE21: Chad 4F 137
Raynford Av. NG9: Chil 4C 146
Rays Av. DE75: Hea 3D 41
Ray St. DE75: Hea 3C 40
Read Av. NG9: Bee 2F 147
Reader St. DE21: Spon 3D 139
Read Lodge NG9: Bee 1F 147
Readman Rd. NG9: Chil 5F 145
Realm Cl. NG73: Chel 1D 201
Rearsby Cl. NG8: Bilb 5C 94
Rebecca Ho. DE1: Der 2D 135
Recreation Rd.
NG10: Sand 2A 144
Recreation St.
NG10: Long E 3E 169
Recreation Ter. NG9: Stap . . .3D 145
(off Wellspring Dale)
NG9: Stap 2C 144
(Halls Rd.)
Rectory Av. NG8: Woll 1D 119
Rectory Cl. LE12: Sut B 5F 235
Rectory Cl. NG2: West Br 1E 151
Rectory Dr. NG4: Ged 5E 77
Rectory Farm M.
DE72: W Tre 5D 203
Rectory Gdns. DE72: Ast T . . .2F 203
NG8: Woll 1E 119
Rectory La. DE21: Bre 5C 84
Rectory M. DE72: Ast T 2F 203
Rectory Pl. NG11: Bart F 5D 171
Rectory Rd. DE72: Brea 3D 167
NG2: West Br 1D 151
NG4: Colw 5D 101
NG12: Cotg 5D 155
Reculver Ct. DE23: Der 4C 158
Redbourne Dr. NG8: Aspl 4B 96
Redbridge Cl. DE7: Ilk 3F 91
Redbridge Dr. NG16: Nuth 4C 70
Redbury Cl. DE1: Der 4D 135
Redcar Cl. NG4: Ged 5D 77

Redcar Gdns. DE21: Chad 4C 108
Redcliffe Gdns.
NG3: Mapp P 2B 98
Redcliffe Rd. NG3: Mapp P . . .2A 98
Redens, The NG10: Long E . . .2A 194
Redfern Av. DE5: Rip 4D 9
Redfield Rd. NG7: Lent 5D 121
Redfield Way NG7: Lent 4D 121
Redgates St. NG14: Calv 1C 30
REDHILL 3D 51
Redhill Cl. DE56: Bel 2A 36
Redhill Leisure Cen. 3D 51
Redhill Lodge Dr.
NG5: Redh 3C 50
Redhill Rd. NG5: Arn 3D 51
Redland Av. NG4: Carl 2E 101
Redland Cl. DE7: Ilk 4E 67
DE24: Sin 2E 185
NG9: Chil 4B 146
Redland Dr. NG9: Chil 5B 146
Redland Gro. NG4: Carl 2D 101
Red La. DE56: H'ook, Mil 2F 59
NG14: Lowd 3C 56
NG16: Brins 1D 21
Red Lion Sq. DE75: Hea 2D 41
Red Lion Yd. NG15: Huck 2F 25
(off High St.)
Redmays Dr. NG14: Bulc 1A 80
Redmile Rd. NG8: Aspl 5B 72
Redmires Dr. DE73: Chel 4F 187
Redmoor Cl. DE5: Cod 5F 9
Redoubt St. NG7: Radf 5D 97
Redruth Cl. NG8: Bilb 4B 94
Redruth Pl. DE24: Alv 1B 188
Redshaw St. DE1: Der 1D 135
Redstart Cl. DE21: Spon 2E 139
Redwing Cft. DE23: Der 4C 158
Redwood NG2: West Br 2A 150
Redwood Av. NG8: Woll 2C 118
Redwood Cl. NG7: Lent 1D 121
(off Faraday Rd.)
NG15: Huck 1E 25
Redwood Cres. NG9: Bee 3F 147
Redwood Rd. DE24: Sin 3D 185
Reedham Wlk. NG5: Bestw . . .4A 50
Reedman Rd.
NG10: Long E 2A 194
Rees Gdns. NG5: Top V 3F 49
Reeves Rd. DE23: Der 2A 160
Regal Ga. DE73: Chel 1D 201
Regan Way NG9: Chil 1A 170
Regatta Way NG2: West Br . . .5B 124
Regency Cl. DE23: Lit 4C 158
Regency Ct. NG9: Bee 1F 147
Regency Ho. DE56: Bel 1E 35
Regent M. NG1: Nott . . .2A 4 (5A 98)
Regents Pk. Cl.
NG2: West Br 3B 150
Regents Pl. NG11: Wilf 5A 150
Regent St. DE1: Der 5F 7 (5A 136)
DE7: Ilk 3E 91
NG1: Nott 3A 4 (1A 122)
NG7: Basf 1F 97
NG9: Bee 1F 147
NG10: Long E 3C 168
NG10: Sand 3B 144
NG16: Kimb 1E 69
NG16: Lang M 1A 42
Regina Cl. NG12: Rad T 3D 127
Reginald Rd. Nth.
DE21: Chad 1E 137
Reginald Rd. Sth.
DE21: Chad 2E 137
Reginald St. DE23: Der 1A 160

Regis Cl. DE21: Oak 3A **110**
Reid Gdns. NG16: Want 1A **70**
Reigate Cl. NG9: Atten 1D **171**
Reigate Dr. DE22: Mac 2E **133**
  NG9: Atten 1D **171**
Reigate Rd. NG7: Basf 5E **73**
Rempstone Dr. NG6: Bulw 2C **72**
Renals St. DE23: Der 5F **135**
Renals Way NG14: Calv 3E **31**
Renfrew Dr. NG8: Woll 1D **119**
Renfrew St. DE21: Chad 1D **137**
Rennie Hogg Rd. NG2: Nott ...4E **121**
Repton Av. DE23: Der 2C **158**
Repton Dr. DE7: Ilk 3A **92**
Repton Rd. NG2: West Br ...3D **151**
  NG6: Bulw 1C **72**
  NG10: Long E 2E **193**
Retford Cl. DE21: Chad 3C **108**
Retford Rd. NG5: Sher 4F **73**
Retlaw Ct. NG9: Chil 3C **146**
Revelstoke Way NG5: Top V ...3C **48**
Revelstoke Way NG5: Top V ...3C **48**
Revena Cl. NG4: Colw 4D **101**
Revesby Gdns. NG8: Aspl 3B **96**
Revesby Rd. NG5: Woodt 2E **75**
Revill Cl. DE7: Ilk 5B **66**
Revill Cres. NG9: Stap 5E **117**
Reydon Dr. NG8: Basf 1C **96**
Reynolds Av. DE5: Rip 5E **9**
Reynolds Dr. NG8: Woll 5E **95**
Rhodes Way NG6: Bestw V ...3A **28**
Rhyl Cres. NG4: Ged 5E **77**
Ribblesdale DE7: Kirk H 5B **90**
Ribblesdale Cl. DE22: All ...3B **106**
Ribblesdale Ct. NG9: Chil ...4F **145**
Ribblesdale Rd. NG5: Sher 2B **74**
  NG10: Long E 1F **193**
Riber Cl. DE7: West H 2D **89**
  NG10: Long E 1C **194**
Riber Cres. NG5: Bestw 2E **73**
Richardson Cl. NG11: Clif 2B **172**
Richardson Dr. DE7: Smal 1E **63**
Richardson St. DE22: Der 2C **134**
Richborough Pl. NG8: Woll ...3C **118**
Richey Cl. NG5: Arn 5A **52**
Richmond Av. DE7: Ilk 3E **67**
  DE23: Lit 3B **158**
  DE72: Brea 3F **167**
  NG3: Nott 3E **99**
  NG10: Sand 4F **143**
  NG14: Calv 1F **31**
  NG16: Newth 2A **44**
Richmond Cl. DE7: West H ...2C **88**
  DE23: Lit 4F **157**
Richmond Ct. NG9: Chil 3D **147**
Richmond Dr. DE56: Duff 2C **58**
  NG3: Mapp P 5C **74**
  NG9: Chil 3D **147**
  NG12: Rad T 1E **127**
Richmond Gdns. NG5: Redh ...3D **51**
Richmond Rd. DE21: Chad 2E **137**
  DE23: Der 2F **159**
  NG2: West Br 4E **123**
Richmond Ter.
  NG12: Rad T 2E **127**
Ricklow Cl. *NG5: Top V 4F **49**
  (off Gautries Cl.)*
Rick St. NG1: Nott 2D **5** (5C **98**)
Riddings DE22: All 1D **107**
Riddings, The *NG4: Neth 3F **101**
  (off Morris St.)*
Riddings St.
  DE22: Der 5A **6** (5E **135**)
Ridding Ter. NG3: Nott 4B **98**

Riddles Ct. NG16: Want 4F **45**
Ridgedale Vw. DE5: Rip 4C **8**
Ridge Hill NG14: Lowd 2C **56**
Ridge La. NG12: Rad T 5F **103**
Ridge Way NG5: Top V 5D **49**
Ridgeway DE73: Chel 1E **201**
  DE75: Hea 4E **41**
Ridgeway Av. DE23: Lit 5B **158**
Ridgeway Cl. DE23: Der 1C **158**
Ridgeway Dr. DE7: Kirk H 5A **90**
Ridgeway on the Hill
  DE56: Bel 1F **13**
Ridgeway Wlk. NG5: Top V ...4F **49**
Ridgewood Ct. DE21: Oak 3D **109**
Ridgewood Dr. NG9: Chil 4B **146**
Ridgmont Wlk. NG11: Clif 3C **172**
  (not continuous)
Ridgway Cl. NG2: West Br 3B **152**
Ridgway St. NG3: Nott 4D **99**
Ridings, The DE72: Ock 2B **140**
  NG12: Key 3F **199**
  NG14: Bulc 2F **79**
Ridsdale Rd. NG5: Sher 2B **74**
Rifle St. NG7: Radf 5D **97**
Rigga La. DE56: Duff 5F **59**
Rigg Hill Ct. NG6: Bulw 2F **71**
Rigley Av. DE7: Ilk 1E **91**
Rigley Dr. NG5: Top V 5D **49**
Rigsby Ct. DE3: Mick 5B **132**
Rimsdale Cl. DE24: Sin 2D **185**
Ring Leas NG12: Cotg 1E **179**
Ringstead Cl.
  NG2: West Br 3B **150**
Ringstead Wlk. NG5: Bestw ...4A **50**
Ringwood Cl. DE21: Chad 5D **109**
Ringwood Cres. NG8: Woll 5B **96**
Ringwood Rd. NG13: Bing ...2B **130**
RIPLEY 5C **8**
Ripley Heritage Cen. *5C **8**
  (off High St.)*
Ripley Ho. DE21: Spon 5D **139**
Ripley Leisure Cen. 5C **8**
Ripley Rd. DE5: L Har 2A **8**
  DE56: H'age 5A **8**
Ripon Cres. DE21: Chad 5D **109**
Ripon Rd. NG3: Nott 5A **100**
Risborow Cl. DE65: Etw 2D **181**
Rise, The DE22: D Abb 3D **107**
  NG5: Sher 4C **74**
Riseborough Wlk.
  NG6: Bulw 3A **48**
Rise Ct. NG5: Sher 2A **98**
Risegate NG12: Cotg 5E **155**
Risegate Gdns. NG12: Cotg ...5E **155**
Riseholme Av. NG8: Woll 2B **118**
RISE PARK 3D **49**
Rise Pk. Rd. NG5: Top V 3C **48**
Rise Pk. Shop. Cen.
  NG5: Top V 3D **49**
RISLEY 4E **143**
Risley Ct. DE7: Ilk 4E **67**
Risley Dr. NG2: Nott 3A **122**
Risley La. DE72: Brea, Ris ...5C **142**
Riste's Pl.
  NG1: Nott 3D **5** (1C **122**)
Ritchie Cl. NG12: Cotg 1F **179**
Ritson Cl. NG3: Nott 1E **5** (4C **98**)
Ritz Cinema, The *1E **35**
  (off King St.)*
Rivenhall Cl. DE23: Lit 4E **157**
Riverdale Pk. NG14: Gun 3A **81**
Riverdale Rd. NG9: Chil 1C **170**
Rivergreen NG11: Clif 5D **149**
Rivergreen Cl. NG9: Bram ...3B **118**

Rivergreen Cres.
  NG9: Bram 3B **118**
Riverlands Cl. NG14: Gun 2F **81**
Rivermead NG2: West Br 1C **150**
  NG12: Cotg 5E **155**
Rivermead Ho. DE1: Der 1F **135**
River Pk. Wlk. DE24: Alv 2F **161**
River Rd. NG4: Colw 1D **125**
Riverside NG14: Sto B 2E **103**
Riverside Cl. NG9: Bee 5A **148**
Riverside Ct. DE24: Der 4C **136**
Riverside Pk. DE21: Spon 5A **138**
Riverside Point NG7: Lent ...2D **121**
Riverside Retail Pk.
  NG2: Nott 5F **121**
Riverside Rd. DE24: Der 4C **136**
  NG9: Bee 5F **147**
Riverside Way NG2: Nott 4A **122**
River St. DE1: Der 2F **135**
River Vw. DE56: Mil 5E **35**
  NG2: Nott 4C **122**
  NG10: Long E 3F **193**
Riverway Gdns. NG2: Nott ...3C **122**
Rivington Rd. NG9: Toton 1D **169**
Road No. 2 NG4: Colw 5F **101**
Robbie Burns Rd.
  NG5: Bestw 4B **50**
Robbinetts La. NG8: Stre 1E **93**
Robert Ludlum Theatre 3E **107**
Roberts Cl. DE74: Keg 3C **214**
Roberts La. NG15: Huck 2E **25**
Roberts St. DE7: Ilk 4F **91**
  NG2: Nott 1D **123**
Robert St. DE1: Der 1E **7** (2A **136**)
Roberts Yd. NG9: Bee 1F **147**
Robey Cl. NG15: Lin 5D **11**
Robey Dr. NG16: Eastw 5E **21**
Robey Ter. NG7: H Grn 3E **97**
Robina Dr. NG16: Gilt 4B **44**
Robin Bailey Way
  NG15: Huck 3B **26**
Robincroft DE22: All 1D **107**
Robin Cft. Rd. DE22: All 1D **107**
Robinet Rd. NG9: Bee 3E **147**
Robinettes La.
  NG16: Babb, Coss 1C **92**
  (not continuous)
Robin Hood Chase
  NG3: Nott 3C **98**
Robin Hood Cl. NG16: Eastw ...3E **43**
Robin Hood Dr. NG15: Huck ...5D **25**
Robin Hood Ind. Est.
  NG3: Nott 1F **5** (5D **99**)
Robin Hood Rd. NG5: Arn 3B **50**
Robin Hood Statue **4A 4**
Robin Hood St.
  NG3: Nott 2F **5** (5D **99**)
Robin Hood Ter.
  NG3: Nott 1E **5** (5C **98**)
Robin Hood Way NG2: Nott ...4A **122**
Robinia Cl. DE21: Oak 2B **110**
Robinia Ct. NG2: West Br 3F **151**
Robin Rd. DE1: Der 1E **135**
Robins Cl. DE72: Elv 1C **188**
Robinscross DE72: Bor 2A **164**
Robinson Ct. NG9: Chil 1A **170**
Robinson Gdns. NG11: Clif ...2B **172**
Robinson Rd. NG3: Mapp 4E **75**
Robinsons Hill NG6: Bulw 5A **48**
Robinsons Ind. Est.
  DE23: Der 1A **160**
Robinswood Ho. NG8: Bilb ...3A **96**
Robins Wood Rd. NG8: Aspl ...4A **96**
Rob Roy Av. NG7: Lent 2E **121**

Robson Cl. DE24: Alv 4F 161
Roby Lea DE74: C Don 5E 205
Roche Cl. NG5: Arn 5B 52
Rochester Av. NG4: Neth 3F 101
Rochester Cl. DE24: Alv 1F 187
  NG10: Long E 4F 167
Rochester Ct. NG6: Bulw 1E 71
Rochester Wlk. NG11: Clif 2E 173
Rochford Ct. NG12: Edwal . . .5B 152
Rochley Cl. DE21: Oak 2E 109
Rockbourne Cl. DE24: Alv . . .5C 162
Rock Cl. NG6: Basf 4C 72
Rock Dr. NG7: Nott 2F 121
Rocket Cl. NG16: Want 5F 45
Rockford Ct. NG9: Stap 4D 117
Rockford Rd. NG5: Sher 4E 73
Rockhouse Rd. DE24: Alv 5F 161
Rockingham Cl. DE22: All . . .1F 107
Rockingham Gro.
  NG13: Bing 2B 130
Rockley Av. NG12: Rad T 1E 127
  NG16: Newth 3F 43
Rockley Cl. NG15: Huck 3B 24
Rockleys Vw. NG14: Lowd 2F 55
Rock Side NG16: Kimb 1E 69
           (off The Sidings)
Rockside Gdns. NG15: Huck . .2D 25
Rock St. NG6: Bulw 4F 47
Rockwell Ct. NG9: Stap 1D 145
Rockwood Cres. NG15: Huck . .3C 24
Rockwood Wlk. NG15: Huck . . .3D 25
Rodel Ct. NG3: Nott 1D 5 (4C 98)
Roden St. NG3: Nott . . .2F 5 (5D 99)
Roderick St. NG6: Basf 3C 72
Rodice Ct. NG7: Lent 5D 97
Rodney Ho. DE24: A'ton 5D 161
Rodney Rd. NG2: West Br 2F 151
Rodney Wlk. DE23: Lit 4D 157
Rodney Way DE7: Ilk 4E 67
Rodsley Cres. DE23: Lit 1C 184
Rodwell Cl. NG8: Aspl 4B 96
Roebuck Cl. NG5: Arn 4A 50
Roecliffe NG2: West Br 4D 151
Roe Farm La. DE21: Chad . . .1D 137
Roe Gdns. NG11: Rudd 4A 174
Roehampton Dr. DE22: Mac . . .1F 133
  NG9: Trow 3C 116
Roe Hill NG14: Woodbo 3B 32
         (not continuous)
Roe La. NG14: Woodbo 5B 32
Roes La. NG14: Calv 2F 31
Roe Wlk. DE23: Der 1F 159
Roker Cl. NG8: Aspl 1F 95
Roland Av. NG11: Wilf 1A 150
  NG16: Nuth 3D 71
Rollerworld
  Derby 5A 108
Rolleston Cl. NG15: Huck 4C 24
Rolleston Cres. NG16: Want . . .3E 45
Rolleston Dr. NG5: Arn 5F 51
  NG7: Lent 1E 121
  NG16: Newth 4F 43
Roman Ct. DE1: Der 1A 136
Roman Dr. NG6: Basf 3D 73
Roman Rd. DE1: Der 1A 136
Romans Ct. NG6: Basf 5D 73
Roman Way DE72: Bor 2B 164
Romilay Cl. NG9: Lent A 4F 119
Romney Av. NG8: Woll 3C 118
Romorantin Pl.
  NG10: Long E 4D 169
Romsley Cl. DE3: Mick 4C 132
Rona Cl. DE24: Sin 2D 185
Rona Ct. NG6: Bulw 2D 73

Ronald Cl. DE23: Lit 4D 157
Ronald St. NG7: Radf 5E 97
Rookery Gdns. NG5: Arn 4E 51
Rookwood Cl. NG9: Bee 2D 147
Roosa Cl. NG6: Bulw 2E 71
Roosevelt Av. DE21: Chad . . .2A 138
  NG10: Long E 1B 194
Roper Av. DE75: Hea 4D 41
Rope Wlk. DE5: Rip 1D 17
Ropewalk DE74: Keg 2B 214
Ropewalk, The DE7: Ilk 1F 91
  DE7: Stan C 1A 88
  DE75: Hea 4E 41
  NG7: Nott 3A 4 (5F 97)
Ropewalk Ct. NG1: Nott 5A 98
Ropewalk Ind. Est. DE7: Ilk . . .1F 91
Ropsley Cres.
  NG2: West Br 4F 123
Rosamond's Ride
  DE23: Der 3C 158
Roscoe Av. NG5: Redh 2D 51
Roseacre NG9: Bee 3F 147
Rose Ash La. NG5: Bestw 4A 50
Rose Av. DE7: Ilk 5D 67
  DE72: Bor 2B 164
Rosebank Dr. NG5: Arn 3A 52
Rosebay Av. NG7: H Grn 2D 97
Roseberry Ct. DE21: Oak 4A 110
Roseberry Gdns.
  NG15: Huck 3B 26
Rosebery Av. NG2: West Br . . .4D 123
Rosebery St. NG6: Basf 3D 73
Rose Cl. DE73: Chel 5D 187
  NG3: Nott 3C 98
Rose Cotts. NG14: Bur J 2D 79
Rose Ct. NG10: Long E 2A 168
Rosecroft Dr. NG5: Bestw 1B 74
Rosedale Av. DE24: Alv 5F 161
Rosedale Cl. NG10: Long E . . .5A 168
Rosedale Dr. NG8: Woll 1A 118
Rosedale Rd. NG3: Nott 4B 100
Rose Flower Gro.
  NG15: Huck 5B 26
Rosegarth Wlk. NG6: Basf 3C 72
Rose Gro. NG9: Bee 3A 148
  NG12: Key 2E 199
Rosegrove Av. NG5: Arn 3E 51
Roseheath Cl. DE23: Der 1D 185
ROSE HILL 5A 136
Rose Hill NG12: Key 3D 199
Rose Hill St. DE23: Der 1F 159
Roseland Cl. NG12: Key 4D 199
Roseleigh Av. NG3: Mapp 5A 76
Rosemary Cl. NG8: Brox 1D 95
Rosemary Dr. DE24: Alv 1F 187
Rosemoor La. DE21: Oak 4A 110
Rosemount Ct. DE22: All 2B 106
Rosengrave St.
  DE1: Der 5B 6 (4E 135)
Rosetta Rd. NG7: Basf 1E 97
         (not continuous)
Rosette Ct. DE21: Oak 2B 110
Rosewall Ct. NG5: Arn 5A 52
Rosewood Cl. DE24: Alv 4B 162
Rosewood Cres. DE75: Hea . . .2A 42
Rosewood Gdns.
  NG2: West Br 5B 150
  NG6: Bulw 5E 47
Roslyn Av. NG4: Ged 5D 77
Roslyn Ct. NG14: Bur J 2E 79
Ross Cl. NG14: Lowd 3D 57
Rossell Dr. NG9: Stap 3C 144
Rossendale DE7: Ilk 3D 67

Rosett Cl. NG2: Gam 2C 152
Rossington Dr. DE23: Lit 5E 157
Rossington Rd. NG2: Nott 5E 99
Ross La. NG4: Lamb 5B 54
Rosslyn Dr. NG8: Aspl 5F 71
  NG15: Huck 1B 26
Rosslyn Gdns. DE24: Alv 5F 161
Ross Wlk. DE21: Chad 4C 108
Rosthwaite Cl.
  NG2: West Br 3B 152
Rosyth Cres. DE73: Chel 5D 187
Rothbury Av. NG9: Trow 3C 116
Rothbury Gro. NG13: Bing . . .1B 130
Rothbury Pl. DE21: Chad 4D 109
Rothesay Av. NG7: Lent 5E 97
Rothesay Cl. DE24: Sin 2D 185
Rothley Av. NG3: Nott 5E 99
Rothwell Cl. NG11: Wilf 4F 149
Rothwell La. DE56: Bel 5A 14
Rothwell Rd. DE3: Mick 5C 132
Rough Heanor Rd.
  DE3: Mick 5F 133
Roughs Wood La.
  NG15: Huck 5C 24
Roughton Cl. DE3: Mick 3C 156
Roundhouse Rd.
  DE24: Der 4B 136
Roundwood Rd. NG5: Arn 5B 50
Routh Av. DE74: C Don 2A 212
Rovings Dr. DE21: Spon 1E 163
Rowallan Way DE73: Chel . . .5D 187
Rowan Av. DE5: Rip 1C 16
  NG9: Stap 3D 117
Rowan Cl. DE7: Ilk 5E 91
  DE21: Chad 3A 138
  DE24: S Flds 3C 184
  NG13: Bing 2F 131
  NG14: Calv 2C 30
Rowan Ct. NG16: Nuth 1A 70
Rowan Dr. DE56: Kil 4A 38
  NG11: Wilf 4F 149
  NG12: Key 4F 199
Rowan Gdns. NG6: Bulw 5E 47
Rowan Pk. Cl. DE23: Der 4C 158
Rowans Cres. NG6: Cin 3A 72
Rowan Wlk. NG3: Nott 2F 99
Rowditch Av. DE22: Der 4C 134
Rowditch Pl. DE22: Der 4C 134
Rowe Gdns. NG6: Bulw 1C 72
Rowena Cl. DE24: Alv 4E 161
Rowland Av. NG3: Mapp 5F 75
Rowland M. NG3: Nott 3D 99
Rowland St. DE24: A'ton 5D 161
Rowley Dr. NG5: Sher 5F 73
Rowley Gdns. DE23: Lit 4B 158
Rowley La. DE23: Lit 4B 158
Rowleys Mill
  DE1: Der 3A 6 (3E 135)
Rowsley Av. DE23: Der 3C 158
  NG10: Long E 1F 193
Roxburgh Av. DE21: Chad . . .1D 137
Roxby Ho. NG5: Arn 1F 75
Roxley Ct. NG9: Bee 1D 147
Roxton Ct. NG16: Kimb 5E 45
Royal Albert Ct.
  NG7: Radf 4F 97
      (off Russell St.)
Royal App. DE73: Chel 1D 201
Royal Av. NG10: Long E 2C 168
Royal Cen. NG1: Nott 2B 4
Royal Centre Stop (NET)
           . . . . .2B 4 (5A 98)
Royal Cl. DE72: Bor 2A 164
Royal Concert Hall 2B 4 (5B 98)

Royal Ct. NG5: Sher 5B **74**
   (off Haydn Rd.)
Royal Crown Derby Factory,
  Mus. & Vis. Cen. 5A **136**
Royal Ga. DE56: Bel 1C **36**
Royal Gro. DE21: Oak 2C **110**
Royal Hill Rd. DE21: Spon . . .2C **138**
  (not continuous)
Royal M. NG9: Chil 5B **146**
Royal Scot Rd. DE24: Der 1D **161**
Royal Standard Ho.
  NG1: Nott 4A **4** (1A **122**)
Royal Standard Pl. NG1: Nott . . .4A **4**
Royal Victoria Ct. NG7: Radf . . .4F **97**
Royal Way DE24: Der 5D **137**
Roy Av. NG15: Huck 4A **148**
Royce Av. NG15: Huck 5D **25**
Roydon Cl. DE3: Mick 4B **132**
Royston Cl. NG2: Nott 4A **122**
Royston Dr. DE56: Bel 4C **14**
RTC Bus. Pk. DE24: Der 1C **160**
Ruby Paddocks NG16: Kimb . . .2E **69**
RUDDINGTON 4B **174**
Ruddington Flds. Bus. Pk.
  NG11: Rudd 1C **196**
  (not continuous)
Ruddington Framework Knitters Mus.
  . . . . .5B **174**
Ruddington La. NG11: Wilf . . .2A **150**
Ruddington Station
  Great Central Railway . .1C **196**
Ruddington Village Mus. 4B **174**
Rudge Cl. NG8: Woll 5E **95**
Rudyard Av. DE21: Spon . . .2D **139**
Ruffles Av. NG5: Arn 2A **76**
Rufford Av. NG4: Ged 5C **76**
  NG9: Bram 5F **117**
Rufford Cl. NG15: Huck 3B **26**
Rufford Gro. NG13: Bing 2C **130**
Rufford Rd. NG5: Sher 4B **74**
  NG10: Long E 2A **194**
  NG11: Rudd 4C **174**
Rufford Wlk. NG6: Bulw 5A **48**
  NG11: Rudd 4C **174**
Rufford Way NG2: West Br . . .2A **152**
RUFFS 4D **25**
Ruffs Dr. NG15: Huck 4C **24**
Ruffstone Cl. DE56: H'ook 5B **36**
Rugby Cl. NG5: Top V 5D **49**
Rugby Ct. NG2: West Br 3D **151**
Rugby Rd. NG2: West Br 3B **150**
Rugby St. DE24: Alv 2D **161**
Rugby Ter. NG7: H Grn 3E **97**
Rugeley Av. NG10: Long E 4E **169**
Ruislip Cl. NG16: Kimb 5D **45**
Runcie Cl. NG12: Cotg 1E **179**
Runnymede Ct. NG7: Radf 5F **97**
  NG9: Bee 3F **147**
  (off Grove St.)
Runswick Dr. NG5: Arn 4E **51**
  NG8: Woll 5F **95**
Runton Dr. NG6: Basf 3E **73**
Rupert Rd. DE21: Chad 1F **137**
  NG13: Bing 2C **130**
Rupert St. DE7: Ilk 1F **91**
Ruscombe Pl. NG3: Nott 4C **98**
Rushcliffe Arena 2B **150**
Rushcliffe Av. DE21: Chad . . .2E **137**
  NG4: Carl 2C **100**
  NG12: Rad T 2E **127**
Rushcliffe Country Pk. 1B **196**
Rushcliffe Ct. NG6: Bulw 1C **72**
Rushcliffe Gdns.
  DE21: Chad 2E **137**

Rushcliffe Leisure Cen. 4E **151**
Rushcliffe Ri. NG5: Sher 2C **74**
Rushcliffe Rd. NG15: Huck 4D **25**
Rushdale Av. DE23: Lit 5C **158**
Rushford Dr. NG8: Woll 1B **144**
Rush Leys NG10: Long E 1C **194**
Rushmere Wlk. NG5: Woodt . . .2E **75**
Rushton Gdns. NG3: Nott 3D **99**
Rushup Cl. DE22: All 5F **83**
Rushworth Av.
  NG2: West Br 5D **123**
Rushworth Cl. NG3: Nott 3D **99**
Rushworth Ct.
  NG2: West Br 5D **123**
Rushy Cl. NG8: Bilb 5C **94**
Rushy La. DE72: Ris 3D **143**
  NG10: Sand 2D **143**
Ruskin Av. NG9: Chil 4C **146**
  NG10: Long E 1A **194**
Ruskin Cl. NG5: Arn 5C **50**
Ruskin Rd. DE1: Der 1E **135**
Ruskin St. NG7: Radf 5D **97**
Ruskin Way DE23: Lit 3A **158**
Russell Av. NG8: Woll 5E **95**
Russell Ct. NG10: Long E 2C **168**
Russell Cres. NG8: Woll 5E **95**
Russell Dr. NG8: Woll 5D **95**
Russell Pl. NG1: Nott 2A **4** (5A **98**)
Russell Rd. NG7: H Grn 2E **97**
Russell St. DE24: Der 2B **160**
  NG7: Radf 4F **97**
  NG10: Long E 2C **168**
Russet Av. NG4: Carl 3D **101**
Russet Cl. DE21: Oak 4A **110**
  NG14: Lowd 3D **57**
Russley Rd. NG9: Bram 5F **117**
Ruth Dr. NG5: Arn 3F **51**
Rutherford Ho. NG7: Nott 4C **120**
Rutherford Ri. DE21: Oak 3E **109**
Ruthwell Gdns. NG5: Top V . . .2F **49**
Rutland Av. DE5: Rip 2F **17**
  DE72: Bor 1B **164**
  NG9: Toton 1F **169**
Rutland Dr. DE3: Mick 5D **133**
Rutland Gro. NG10: Sand 3B **144**
Rutland Hall NG7: Nott 4A **120**
Rutland Rd. NG2: West Br 4E **123**
  NG4: Ged 4C **76**
  NG13: Bing 2E **131**
Rutland St. DE7: Ilk 1E **91**
  DE23: Der 2F **159**
  NG1: Nott 4A **4** (1A **122**)
Rutland Ter. DE7: Ilk 5E **67**
Rutland Vs. NG2: Nott 1E **123**
Ryal Cl. DE72: Ock 3B **140**
Ryan Cl. DE24: Sin 3D **185**
Ryan Way NG6: Bestw 5F **147**
Rycroft Rd. DE74: Hem 2C **206**
Rydal Av. NG10: Long E 1A **168**
Rydal Cl. DE22: All 1D **107**
Rydal Dr. NG9: Bram 5C **118**
  NG15: Huck 1E **25**
Rydale Rd. NG5: Sher 2B **74**
Rydal Gdns. NG2: West Br 3F **151**
Rydal Gro. NG6: Basf 4D **73**
Ryde Ho. DE24: Alv 4B **162**
Ryder St. NG6: Basf 3C **72**
Rye Butts DE73: Chel 5D **187**
Rye Cl. DE21: Oak 2D **109**
Ryecroft St. NG9: Stap 4D **117**
Ryedale Gdns. DE23: Lit 1B **184**
Ryefield Av. DE7: Ilk 2E **67**
Ryegrass Cl. DE56: Bel 5C **14**

Ryegrass Rd. DE21: Oak 3B **110**
Ryehill Cl. NG2: Nott 3C **122**
Ryehill Rd. NG2: Nott 3C **122**
Ryeland Gdns. NG2: Nott 3B **122**
Ryemere Cl. NG16: Eastw 2D **43**
Ryemere Ct. NG16: Eastw 2D **43**
  (off Ryemere Cl.)
Rye St. NG7: Basf 1E **97**
Rykneld Cl. DE23: Lit 5D **157**
Rykneld Dr. DE23: Lit 4E **157**
Rykneld Rd. DE3: Mick 1C **182**
Rykneld Way DE23: Lit 5D **157**
Ryknield Hill DE5: Den 1A **38**
Ryknield Rd. DE56: Kil 5A **38**
Ryknild St.
  DE7: Cox, Hors, H Woo 2A **62**
RYLANDS 3A **148**
Rylands Cl. NG9: Bee 4A **148**
Rylands Ct. NG9: Bee 3F **147**
Rymill Dr. DE21: Chad 4E **109**
Ryton Ct. NG2: Nott 4C **122**
Ryton Sq. NG8: Aspl 1A **96**

S

Sacheverel St.
  DE1: Der 5C **6** (4F **135**)
Sackville St. DE23: Der 3E **159**
Saddlers Ga. NG12: Rad T 2E **127**
Saddlers Yd. NG12: Plum 4D **177**
Saddleworth Ct. NG3: Nott 4B **98**
Saddleworth Wlk.
  DE24: S Loc 3D **187**
Sadler Ga. DE1: Der . . .2C **6** (3F **135**)
Sadler Ga. Bri.
  DE1: Der 2C **6** (3F **135**)
Saffron Dr. DE21: Oak 4F **109**
Saffron Gdns. NG2: Nott 3A **122**
St Agnes Av. DE22: All 1D **107**
St Agnes Cl. NG8: Bilb 2C **94**
St Aidans Ct. NG6: Basf 3D **73**
St Albans Cl.
  NG10: Long E 1D **195**
St Albans M. NG6: Bulw 1C **72**
St Albans Rd. DE22: Der 5B **134**
  NG5: Arn 5C **50**
  NG6: Bestw V 5D **27**
  NG6: Bulw 4B **48**
St Alkmunds Cl. DE56: Duff . . .3D **59**
St Alkmunds Way
  DE1: Der 1B **6** (2E **135**)
  DE56: Duff 3D **59**
St Andrews Cl. NG6: Bulw 5B **48**
  NG15: Huck 1F **25**
St Andrews Ct. NG6: Bulw 5C **48**
St Andrew's Dr. DE7: Ilk 2D **91**
St Andrews Ho. DE1: Der 5B **136**
  NG3: Mapp 4B **76**
St Andrew's Ri. DE74: Keg . . .3B **214**
St Andrew's Rd.
  NG3: Mapp P 3A **98**
St Andrew's Vw.
  DE21: Chad 3C **108**
St Anne's Cl. DE1: Der 2D **135**
St Anne's La. DE74: C Don . . .1A **212**
  LE12: Sut B 5F **215**
ST ANN'S 4C **98**
St Ann's Gdns. NG3: Nott 3D **99**
St Ann's Hill NG3: Nott 3B **98**
St Ann's Hill Rd. NG3: Nott . . .3B **98**
St Ann's St.
  NG1: Nott 1C **4** (5B **98**)

St Ann's Valley NG3: Nott 4D **99**
St Ann's Way NG3: Nott 4B **98**
St Ann's Well Rd.
   NG3: Nott 1D **5** (5C **98**)
St Anthony Ct. NG7: Lent . . .3D **121**
St Augustines Cl. NG7: Basf . . .1F **97**
St Augustine St. DE23: Der . . .2E **159**
St Austell Dr. NG11: Wilf . . .3A **150**
St Austins Ct. NG4: Carl 2E **101**
St Austins Dr. NG4: Carl 2E **101**
St Barnabas' RC Cathedral
   . . . . .2A **4** (1A **122**)
St Bartholomew's Rd.
   NG3: Nott 3E **99**
St Bride's Wlk. DE22: Mac . . .2A **134**
St Catherines St.
   NG12: Rad T 3D **127**
St Cecilia Gdns. NG3: Nott . . .4C **98**
St Chads NG4: Carl 3E **101**
St Chads Cl. DE72: Dray 4F **165**
St Chad's Rd. DE23: Der 1D **159**
   NG3: Nott 2F **5** (5D **99**)
St Christophers Ct.
   DE22: Der 2D **135**
St Christopher St.
   NG2: Nott 1E **123**
St Christopher's Way
   DE24: Der 5C **136**
St Clares Cl. DE22: Der 1C **158**
St Cuthbert's Rd.
   DE22: Der 5B **134**
   NG3: Nott 5D **99**
St David's Cl. DE22: Der 5C **134**
St Edmunds Cl. DE22: All . . .1E **107**
St Edward's Rd.
   DE74: C Don 2A **212**
St Emmanuel Vw. NG5: Arn . . .3A **50**
St Ervan Rd. NG11: Wilf 2A **150**
St George's Cl. DE22: All 2E **107**
St Georges Ct. NG15: Huck 1F **25**
St Georges Dr. NG2: Nott 3B **122**
   NG9: Toton 1E **169**
St Georges Est. DE21: Chad . . .2B **136**
St George's Pl. DE56: Bel 5E **13**
St Giles Rd. DE23: Der 2E **159**
St Helens Cres. NG9: Trow . . .1B **116**
   NG14: Bur J 3E **79**
St Helen's Gro. NG14: Bur J . . .4D **79**
St Helens Rd.
   NG2: West Br 2E **151**
St Helen's St.
   DE1: Der 1B **6** (2E **135**)
   NG7: Nott 5F **97**
St Helier NG7: Nott 1F **121**
St Hugh's Cl. DE22: D Abb . . .3E **107**
St James Av. DE7: Ilk 3F **91**
St James Cl. DE56: Bel 5C **14**
St James Ct.
   DE1: Der 2A **6** (3D **135**)
   NG3: Mapp 5A **76**
   NG10: Sand 5A **144**
   NG15: Huck 1F **25**
St James Dr. NG16: Brins 1C **20**
St James Rd. DE23: Dor 2E **159**
St James's Hall DE1: Der 2C **6**
St James's St.
   NG1: Nott 4A **4** (1A **122**)
St James's Ter.
   NG1: Nott 4A **4** (1A **122**)
St James St.
   DE1: Der 3C **6** (3F **135**)
   NG9: Stap 2B **144**
St James Ter. NG9: Stap 2B **144**
St John's Av. DE21: Chad . . .3A **138**

St Johns Cl. DE5: Rip 4E **9**
   DE22: All 2C **106**
   NG16: Brins 1C **20**
St John's Ct. NG4: Carl 3C **100**
St John's Cres. NG15: Huck . . .4B **26**
St John's Dr. DE21: Chad 3F **137**
   DE56: Kil 4E **37**
St Johns Rd. DE7: Ilk 3F **91**
   DE7: Smal 2E **63**
   DE56: Bel 5F **13**
   NG11: Rudd 4B **174**
St Johns St. NG10: Long E 4C **168**
St John's Ter.
   DE1: Der 1A **6** (2E **135**)
St Jude's Av. NG3: Mapp 5C **74**
St Judith's Ct.
   DE1: Der 2A **6** (3D **135**)
St Katherines Ct.
   DE22: Der 2C **134**
St Laurence Ct.
   NG10: Long E 5D **169**
St Laurence Gdns. DE56: Bel . .5E **13**
St Lawrence Blvd.
   NG12: Rad T 3C **126**
St Lawrence Cl. DE75: Hea 2E **41**
St Leonards Dr. NG8: Woll 1E **119**
St Leven Cl. NG8: Bilb 2C **94**
St Lukes Cl. NG2: West Br 3A **152**
St Luke's St.
   NG3: Nott 2F **5** (5D **99**)
St Lukes Way NG14: Sto B . . .2E **103**
St Margaret's Av. NG8: Aspl . . .2B **96**
St Mark's Rd. DE21: Chad . . .1C **136**
St Mark's St.
   NG3: Nott 1D **5** (5C **98**)
St Martins Cl. NG8: Stre 2D **95**
St Martin's Gdns. NG8: Stre . . .2C **94**
St Martin's Rd. NG8: Stre 2D **95**
St Mary's Av. DE72: Dray 4F **165**
   NG4: Ged 5D **77**
St Mary's Bri.
   DE1: Der 1D **7** (2F **135**)
St Mary's Church **4D 5**
   (off High Pavement)
   NG5: Arn 3E **51**
   NG9: Atten 2C **170**
   NG14: Lowd 2C **56**
St Mary's Ct.
   DE1: Der 1C **6** (2F **135**)
St Mary's Cres.
   NG11: Rudd 4B **174**
St Marys Ga.
   DE1: Der 2C **6** (3F **135**)
   NG1: Nott 3D **5** (1C **122**)
St Mary's M. DE1: Der 2F **135**
St Mary's Pl.
   NG1: Nott 3D **5** (1C **122**)
St Marys Rd. NG13: Bing 1E **131**
St Mary St. DE7: Ilk 2D **91**
St Marys Way NG15: Huck 1E **25**
St Mary's Wharf Rd.
   DE1: Der 1A **136**
St Matthew's Wlk
   DE22: D Abb 3E **107**
St Matthias Rd. NG3: Nott 4D **99**
St Mawes Av. NG11: Wilf 2A **150**
St Mawes Cl. DE22: All 1C **106**
St Mellion Cl. DE3: Mick 2E **157**
St Michaels LE12: Sut B 4F **215**
St Michael's Av. NG4: Ged 5D **77**
   NG8: Bilb 2C **94**
St Michael's Cl. DE24: Alv . . .4B **162**
   DE56: H'ook 1B **60**

St Michael's La.
   DE1: Der 1C **6** (2F **135**)
St Michaels Sq. NG9: Bram . .5A **118**
St Michaels Vw. DE24: Alv . . .4B **162**
   (off Branscome Av.)
   NG15: Huck 5D **11**
St Nicholas Cl. DE22: All 3C **106**
   NG5: Arn 5D **51**
St Nicholas M. DE1: Der 1E **135**
St Nicholas Pl. DE1: Der 1E **135**
St Nicholas St.
   NG1: Nott 4B **4** (1B **122**)
St Norbert Dr. DE7: Kirk H 5B **90**
St Pancras Way DE1: Der 1A **136**
   DE5: Rip 2D **9**
St Patrick's Rd. NG15: Huck . . .2E **25**
   NG16: Nuth 1A **70**
St Paul's Av. NG7: H Grn 3E **97**
St Pauls Ct. NG16: Kimb 1E **69**
St Paul's Rd. DE1: Der 1F **135**
St Paul's St. NG8: Radf 5C **96**
St Paul's Ter. NG7: H Grn 3E **97**
St Peters Chambers
   NG1: Nott *3C **4***
   (off Bank Pl.)
St Peter's Chu. Wlk.
   NG1: Nott 3C **4** (1B **122**)
St Peter's Chyd.
   DE1: Der 3C **6** (3F **135**)
St Peter's Cl. DE56: Bel 5E **13**
St Peters Ct. NG7: Radf 5C **96**
St Peters Cres.
   NG11: Rudd 4B **174**
St Peter's Cft. DE56: Bel 5F **13**
St Peter's Ga.
   NG1: Nott 3C **4** (1B **122**)
St Peter's Rd. DE73: Chel 5F **187**
St Peter's Sq. NG1: Nott 3B **4**
St Peter's St.
   DE1: Der 3D **7** (3F **135**)
   NG7: Radf 5D **97**
St Peter's Way
   DE1: Der 4D **7** (3F **135**)
St Quentin Cl. DE22: Der 5B **134**
St Ronan's Av. DE56: Duff 5D **59**
St Saviours Gdns.
   NG2: Nott 3C **122**
St Stephen's Av. NG2: Nott . . .1E **123**
St Stephens Cl. DE23: Der . . .5C **158**
   DE72: Bor 2A **164**
St Stephen's Rd. NG2: Nott . . .1D **123**
St Swithins Cl. DE22: Der 5C **134**
St Thomas Rd. DE23: Der 3F **159**
St Vincent Cl.
   NG10: Long E 5D **169**
St Werburgh's Chyd.
   DE1: Der 2B **6**
St Werburghs Cloisters
   DE1: Der 2B **6**
St Werburgh's Vw.
   DE21: Spon 3C **138**
St Wilfrid's Rd. DE7: West H . . .3D **89**
St Wilfrid's Sq. NG14: Calv 2E **31**
St Winifreds Ct.
   NG11: King 5E **209**
St Wystan's Rd. DE22: Der . .5B **134**
Salamander Cl. NG4: Carl 5C **76**
Salcey Dr. NG9: Trow 3C **116**
Salcombe Cir. NG5: Redh 3C **50**
Salcombe Cl. NG16: Newth . . .3B **44**
Salcombe Cres.
   NG11: Hudd 3C **174**
Salcombe Dr. NG5: Redh 3C **50**
Salcombe Rd. NG5: Sher 4E **73**

Sale St. DE23: Der 1A **160**
Salford Gdns.
  NG3: Nott 1E **5** (5C **98**)
Salisbury Ct. NG3: Mapp 5D **75**
Salisbury Dr. DE56: Bel 4C **14**
Salisbury Sq. NG7: Lent 1D **121**
Salisbury St. DE23: Der 5F **135**
  NG7: Lent 5D **97**
  NG9: Bee 1F **147**
  NG10: Long E 4D **169**
Sallywood Cl.
  DE24: S Flds 4C **184**
Salmon Cl. NG6: Bulw 5E **47**
Salop St. NG5: Arn 5C **50**
Saltburn Cl. DE21: Chad . . .4B **108**
Saltburn Rd. NG8: Bilb 4F **95**
Saltby Grn. NG2: West Br . . .5A **150**
Salter Cl. DE74: C Don 5E **205**
Salterford Av. NG14: Calv 1E **31**
Salterford Rd. NG15: Huck 4D **25**
Saltford Cl. NG4: Ged 5E **77**
Salthouse Cl. NG9: Bee 5F **119**
  (off Salthouse La.)
Salthouse Cl. NG9: Bee 5F **119**
Salthouse La. NG9: Bee 5F **119**
Saltney Way NG11: Wilf 5F **149**
Samantha Cl. DE21: Oak 4A **110**
Samson Ct. NG11: Rudd 3A **174**
Samuel Cl. DE5: Rip 1C **16**
Sancroft Ct. DE23: Lit 4A **158**
Sancroft Rd. DE21: Spon 2D **139**
Sandale Cl. NG2: Gam 2B **152**
Sandalwood Cl. DE24: Alv . . .4B **162**
Sandays Cl. NG2: Nott 4B **62**
Sandbach Cl. DE21: Oak 4F **109**
Sandbed La. DE56: Bel 3B **36**
Sandby NG1: Nott 1A **4**
Sandby Ct. NG9: Chil 3B **146**
Sanderling Heath
  DE3: Mick 4A **156**
Sanders Cl. DE7: Ilk 5B **66**
Sanderson Dr. NG3: Mapp 1C **76**
Sanderson Rd.
  DE21: Chad 2A **138**
Sandfield Cl. DE21: Oak 5A **110**
Sandfield Ct. NG6: Bulw 1F **71**
Sandfield Rd. NG5: Arn 1E **75**
  NG7: Lent 1E **121**
  NG9: Toton 1D **169**
Sandford Av.
  NG10: Long E 4D **169**
Sandford Rd. NG3: Mapp 5E **75**
Sandgate NG9: Bram 4C **118**
Sandgate Cl. DE24: Alv 5F **161**
Sandham La. DE5: Rip 5B **8**
Sandham Wlk. NG11: Clif 5D **149**
Sandhurst Dr. NG9: Chil 1B **170**
  NG11: Rudd 5A **174**
Sandhurst Rd. NG6: Bulw 3A **48**
SANDIACRE 3A **144**
Sandiacre Friesland Sports Cen.
  . . . . .3E **143**
Sandiacre Rd. NG9: Stap 2B **144**
Sandon St. NG7: Basf 1F **97**
Sandown Av. DE3: Mick 5A **132**
Sandown Rd. DE24: Der 3C **160**
  NG9: Toton 5E **145**
Sandpiper Cl. NG13: Bing 3E **131**
Sandpiper La. DE3: Mick 5A **156**
Sandpiper Way NG7: Lent 1D **121**
Sandringham Av.
  NG2: West Br 5D **123**
Sandringham Cres.
  NG8: Woll 5B **94**

Sandringham Dr.
  DE21: Spon 4E **139**
  DE75: Hea 2B **40**
  NG9: Bram 4B **118**
Sandringham Pl.
  DE7: Kirk H 5C **90**
  NG15: Huck 1A **26**
Sandringham Rd.
  DE21: Chad 4D **109**
  NG2: Nott 1E **123**
  NG10: Sand 5A **144**
Sands Cl. NG4: Colw 5D **101**
Sandside NG12: Cotg 1E **179**
Sandwell Cl. NG10: Long E . . .5F **167**
Sandyford Cl. NG6: Basf 4B **72**
Sandyhill Cl. DE73: Chel 4F **187**
Sandy La. DE21: Cox 3E **61**
  NG9: Bram 3C **118**
  NG12: Hol P 3A **126**
  NG15: Huck 2F **25**
Sandypits La. DE65: Etw 2B **180**
  (not continuous)
Sanger Cl. NG11: Clif 3B **172**
Sanger Gdns. NG11: Clif 3B **172**
Sankey Dr. NG6: Bulw 5F **47**
Santolina Dr. DE21: Oak 4E **109**
Sapele Cl. NG4: Ged 5F **77**
Sapperton Cl. DE23: Lit 1C **184**
Sapphire Dr. DE5: Den 2A **38**
Sarah Av. NG5: Sher 5F **73**
Sargent Gdns. NG3: Nott 4E **99**
Saskatoon Cl. NG12: Rad T . .3D **127**
Saunby Cl. NG5: Arn 5A **52**
Saundersfoot Way
  DE21: Oak 3A **110**
Saunton Cl. NG12: Edwal 4B **152**
Savages Rd. NG11: Rudd 3B **174**
Savages Row NG11: Rudd 3B **174**
Saville Cl. NG9: Stap 5D **117**
Saville Rd. NG5: Woodt 2E **75**
Savoy Workshops
  NG7: Lent 2E **121**
SAWLEY 2F **193**
Sawley Rd.
  DE72: B'ea, Dray 4D **167**
  DE72: Dray 4A **166**
Sawmand Cl. NG10: Long E . .5B **168**
Sawmills Ind. Pk. DE75: Los . .1C **40**
Saxby Ct. NG11: Rudd 4C **174**
Saxelby Gdns. NG6: Bulw 4A **48**
SAXONDALE 1E **129**
Saxondale Av. DE3: Mick 4B **132**
Saxondale Cl. NG6: Bulw 3B **48**
Saxondale Dr. NG6: Bulw 2C **72**
  NG12: Rad T 1C **128**
Saxon Grn. NG7: Lent 2D **121**
Saxon Way NG12: Cotg 2E **179**
Saxton Av. DE75: Hea 2E **41**
Saxton Cl. NG9: Bee 1A **148**
Saxton Ct. NG5: Arn 5B **52**
Scafell Cl. NG2: West Br 3B **152**
Scafell Way NG11: Clif 4C **172**
Scala Cinema
  Ilkeston 2D **91**
Scalby Cl. NG16: Eastw 2C **42**
Scalford Dr. NG8: Woll 1B **120**
Scarborough Av. DE7: Ilk 2C **90**
Scarborough Ri.
  DE21: Chad 4B **108**
Scarborough St.
  NG3: Nott 1E **5** (5C **98**)
Scarcliffe Cl. DE24: S Loc 3D **187**
Scarf Wlk. NG11: Wilf 1A **150**
Scargill Av. NG16: Newth 3A **44**

Scargill Cl. NG16: Newth 3A **44**
Scargill Rd. DE7: West H 2D **89**
Scargill Wlk. NG16: Eastw . . .1E **43**
Scarrington Rd.
  NG2: West Br 4E **123**
Scarsdale Av. DE22: All 2B **106**
  DE23: Lit 1B **158**
Scarsdale Rd. DE56: Duff 4D **59**
Sceptre St. NG5: Sher 5B **74**
School Av. NG15: Huck 5C **24**
School Cl. NG2: Nott 4C **122**
Schoolhouse Hill
  DE56: H'age 1C **14**
School La. DE5: Rip 5B **8**
  DE7: Stan D 1E **143**
  DE73: Chel 5F **187**
  DE74: C Don 5F **205**
  NG9: Chil 4B **146**
  NG13: Bing 1D **131**
School Sq. DE7: West H 3D **89**
School Wlk. NG6: Bestw V 5B **37**
School Way NG2: Nott 4C **122**
School Woods Cl.
  DE75: Ship 1F **65**
School Yd., The
  DE1: Der 1C **6** (2F **135**)
Science Rd. NG7: Nott 4C **120**
SCOTCHES 3E **13**
Scotches, The DE56: Bel 3E **13**
Scotholme Av. NG7: H Grn . . .2E **97**
Scotland Bank NG12: Cotg . . .5E **155**
Scotland Rd. NG5: Basf 4E **73**
Scott Av. NG9: Bee 2E **147**
Scott Cl. NG6: Bulw 2E **71**
Scott Dr. DE56: Bel 4D **15**
Scott St. DE23: Der 2E **159**
Scotts Yd. DE5: Rip 4C **8**
Scrimshire La. NG12: Cotg . . .5D **155**
Script Dr. NG6: Basf 3D **73**
Scrivelsby Gdns. NG9: Chil . . .4C **146**
Scrooby Row NG5: Top V 4F **49**
Scropton Wlk. DE24: S Loc . . .3D **187**
Seaburn Rd. NG9: Toton 5D **145**
Seaford Av. NG8: Woll 5A **96**
Seagrave Cl. DE21: Oak 5A **110**
Seagrave Ct. NG5: Arn 5D **51**
  NG8: Stre 1C **94**
Seagrave Rd. NG8: Stre 1C **94**
Seale St. DE1: Der 1F **135**
Seamer Rd. NG16: Kimb 5E **45**
Searl St. DE1: Der 1A **6** (2E **135**)
Seascale Cl. DE21: Chad 4C **108**
Seatallan Cl. NG2: West Br . . .2B **152**
Seathwaite Cl.
  NG2: West Br 4B **152**
Seatoller Cl. NG2: West Br . . .3B **152**
Seaton Cl. DE3: Mick 5B **132**
Seaton Cres. NG8: Aspl 1F **95**
Second Av. DE7: Ilk 3E **91**
  DE72: Ris 4E **143**
  DE73: Chel 1E **201**
  NG4: Carl 3B **100**
  NG4: Ged 1E **101**
  NG6: Bulw 5A **48**
  NG7: H Grn 2A **98**
  NG7: Nott 2B **98**
Sedgebrook Cl. DE21: Oak . . .3E **109**
  NG6: Basf 4B **72**
Sedgefield Grn. DE3: Mick . . .2B **156**
Sedgemoor Rd.
  NG10: Long E 1D **195**
Sedgemoor Way DE23: Lit 1F **183**
Sedgewood Gro. NG11: Clif . .5D **149**
Sedgley Av. NG2: Nott 5E **99**

Sedgley Rd. NG12: Toll 3C **176**
Sedgwick St. NG16: Lang M . . .1A **42**
Sedley Av. NG16: Nuth 1B **70**
Seeley Ho. NG1: Nott 4E **5**
(off Malin Hill)
Seely Av. NG14: Calv 1C **30**
Seely Rd. NG7: Lent, Radf 5E **97**
Sefton Av. NG9: Stap 5D **117**
Sefton Dr. NG3: Mapp P 1C **98**
Sefton Rd. DE21: Chad 2E **137**
Sefton Way DE56: Duff 3C **58**
Selborne St. DE24: Der 1C **160**
Selby Cl. NG9: Toton 5D **145**
Selby La. NG12: Key 4D **199**
Selby Rd. NG2: West Br 2E **151**
Selhurst Cl. NG7: H Grn 3E **97**
Selhurst St. NG7: H Grn 3E **97**
Selina Cl. DE74: C Don 5F **205**
Selkirk St. DE21: Chad 1D **137**
Selkirk Way NG5: Sher 1A **98**
Sellars Av. NG11: Rudd 5B **174**
Sellers Wood Dr. NG6: Bulw . . .4E **47**
Sellers Wood Dr. W.
NG6: Bulw 5D **47**
Seller's Wood Nature Reserve
. . . . .5D **47**
Selside Ct. NG9: Chil 4F **145**
Selston Dr. NG8: Woll 2B **120**
Selworthy Cl. DE21: Oak 3F **109**
Selwyn Cl. NG6: Bulw 2D **73**
Selwyn St. DE22: Der 2B **134**
Senso Ct. NG4: Ged 1A **102**
Serif Cl. NG5: Sher 1A **98**
Serina Av. DE23: Der 3C **158**
Serina Ct. NG2: West Br 1D **151**
NG9: Bee 1A **148**
Serlby Ri. NG3: Nott 4E **99**
Serlby Rd. NG16: Newth 1F **43**
Serpentine Cl.
NG12: Rad T 3C **128**
Settlement, The DE72: Ock . .3B **140**
Sevenlands Dr. DE24: Alv . . .2B **188**
Sevenoaks Av. DE22: Mac . . .3E **133**
Seven Oaks Cres.
NG9: Bram 4A **118**
Seven Oaks Rd.
DE7: Stan D 4F **115**
Seventh Av. NG7: Nott 3B **148**
Severals NG9: Stap 1E **145**
Severn St. DE24: Alv 3E **161**
NG6: Bulw 5A **48**
Severnvale Cl. DE22: All 5A **84**
Seymour Cl. DE7: Ilk 2E **67**
DE22: Der 2B **134**
Seymour Ct. NG7: Radf 4F **97**
Seymour Pl. NG2: West Br . . .4A **124**
Seymour Rd. NG2: West Br . .5A **124**
NG15: Huck 4D **26**
NG16: Eastw 3E **43**
Seymour St. NG3: Nott 5D **99**
SGCS Bus. Cen. NG9: Bee . . .3F **147**
SGCS Bus. Pk. NG9: Bee 4F **147**
SHACKLECROSS 2C **164**
Shacklecross Cl. DE72: Bor . .2B **164**
Shackleton Cl. NG8: Stre 5C **70**
Shacklock Cl. NG5: Arn 2F **49**
Shadwell Gro.
NG12: Rad T 2D **127**
Shady La. NG9: Atten 1C **170**
Shaftesbury Av.
NG10: Long E 2A **194**
NG10: Sand 3F **143**
NG12: Rad T 2C **128**
NG14: Bur J 2F **79**

Shaftesbury Cres.
DE23: Der 2A **160**
Shaftesbury Sports Cen. 2A **160**
Shaftesbury St. DE23: Der . . .2B **160**
NG7: Basf 1F **97**
Shaftesbury St. Sth.
DE23: Der 3A **160**
Shakespeare Cl.
NG4: Colw 5D **101**
Shakespeare Rd.
NG16: Aws 2B **68**
Shakespeare St. DE24: Sin . .1E **185**
NG1: Nott 1A **4** (5A **98**)
NG10: Long E 2B **168**
Shakespeare Vs.
NG1: Nott 1B **4** (5B **98**)
Shaldon Cl. NG5: Top V 3E **49**
Shaldon Dr. DE23: Lit 2C **158**
Shalfleet Dr. DE24: Alv 5B **162**
Shamrock St. DE23: Der 2D **159**
Shandwick Cl. NG5: Arn 3A **52**
Shandwick Ct. DE24: Sin 3C **184**
Shanklin Dr. NG9: Stap 1C **144**
Shanklin Ho. DE24: Alv 4B **162**
Shannon Cl. DE23: Der 5C **158**
Shannon Sq. DE21: Chad 4A **138**
Shanwell Cl. NG8: Stre 5C **70**
Shardale Gdns. NG6: Basf 3C **72**
SHARDLOW 4D **191**
Shardlow Bus. Pk.
DE72: Shar 5C **190**
Shardlow Heritage Cen. 5F **191**
Shardlow Rd. DE24: Alv 4A **162**
DE72: Ast T 2A **204**
SHARDLOW SERVICE AREA
. . . . .5C **190**
Sharnford Way NG9: Bram . . .1A **118**
Sharp Cl. DE7: Kirk H 4B **90**
NG10: Long E 5B **168**
Sharpes Way NG6: Bestw V . . .3A **28**
Sharphill Rd. NG12: Edwal . . .4A **152**
Shaw Cres. NG15: Huck 5D **25**
Shaw Gdns. NG4: Ged 2A **102**
NG11: Clif 3B **172**
Shaw La. DE56: Mil 4E **35**
Shaw Rd. NG9: Chil 1A **170**
Shaws Grn. DE22: Der 2C **134**
Shaw St. DE22: Der 2D **135**
NG11: Rudd 4B **174**
Shaw St. E. DE7: Ilk 4F **91**
Shaw St. W. DE7: Ilk 4F **91**
Shaw's Yd. DE56: Kil 4E **37**
Shearing Cl. NG4: Ged 1F **101**
Shearing Hill NG4: Ged 1F **101**
Shearwater Cl. DE23: Der 4C **158**
Sheepfold La. NG11: Rudd . . .5B **174**
Sheets Stores Ind. Est.
NG10: Long E 1C **194**
Sheffield Pl.
DE1: Der 5F **7** (4B **136**)
Shelby Cl. NG7: Lent 1D **121**
Sheldon Cl. NG10: Sand 5A **144**
Sheldon Ct. DE24: S Loc 3D **187**
Sheldon Rd. DE75: Los 4B **18**
SHELFORD 1B **104**
Shelford Cl. DE3: Mick 5B **132**
NG9: Chil 4C **146**
NG12: Rad T 1F **127**
Shelford Cres. NG14: Bur J . . .2F **79**
Shelford Dr. NG13: Bing 2C **130**
Shelford Hill NG12: Shel 2B **104**
Shelford Nurseries Cvn. Pk.
NG12: Shel 2B **104**
Shelford Ri. NG3: Nott 4F **99**

Shelford Rd. NG4: Ged 4B **76**
NG12: Rad T, Shel 2E **127**
NG13: Newton 2B **104**
Shellburne Cl. NG5: Top V 4D **49**
Shelley Av. NG11: Clif 5D **149**
Shelley Cl. NG15: Huck 3C **24**
NG16: Nuth 1A **70**
Shelley Dr. DE24: Sin 1F **185**
Shelley Rd. NG5: Arn 5C **50**
Shelmory Cl. DE24: A'ton 1D **187**
Shelt Hill NG14: Woodbo 5C **32**
Shelton Av. NG15: Huck 5B **26**
Shelton Dr. DE24: S Loc 3D **187**
Shelton Gdns. NG11: Rudd . . .4A **174**
Shelton Ga. Cl.
DE24: S Loc 1D **187**
SHELTON LOCK 3D **187**
Shelton St. NG3: Nott . . .1D **5** (4B **98**)
Shenfield Gdns. NG5: Top V . . .3C **48**
Shenington Way DE21: Oak . .3A **110**
Shepard Cl. NG6: Bulw 1E **71**
Shepherd Ct. NG15: Huck 5C **24**
Shepherd Ho. NG5: Bestw 2F **73**
Shepherds Cl. NG8: Bilb 3F **95**
Shepherd St. DE23: Lit 2B **158**
Shepherds Wood Dr.
NG8: Aspl 3B **96**
Shepherd Wlk. DE74: Keg . . .3B **214**
Shepton Cl. DE7: Ilk 4C **66**
Shepton Cres. NG8: Aspl 5A **72**
Sheraton Dr. NG8: Woll 2D **119**
Sherborne Rd.
NG2: West Br 3E **151**
NG8: Aspl 1F **95**
Sherbourne Dr. DE56: Bel 4C **14**
Sherbrook Av. NG5: Arn 1C **74**
Sherbrooke Cl. NG14: Calv . . .1D **31**
Sherbrooke Rd. NG5: Sher . . .1A **98**
Sherbrooke Ter. NG5: Sher . . .1A **98**
Sherbrook Rd. NG5: Arn 1B **74**
Sherbrook Ter. NG5: Arn 1C **74**
Sheridan Ct. NG1: Nott 1C **4**
NG9: Stap 4E **117**
Sheridan St. DE24: Sin 1E **185**
Sheridan Way NG5: Sher 4F **73**
NG15: Huck 4F **25**
Sheriffs Lea NG9: Toton 1D **169**
Sheriffs Way NG2: Nott 2B **122**
Sheringham Cl. NG5: Arn 1E **75**
Sherman Dr. NG9: Chil 1B **170**
Sherrington Cl. NG11: Clif 3B **172**
Sherroside Cl. DE22: All 1C **106**
Sherston Cl. DE21: Oak 3A **110**
Sherwin Gro. NG7: Lent 2D **121**
Sherwin Rd. NG7: Lent 2D **121**
NG9: Stap 4E **117**
Sherwin Sports Cen. 3A **160**
Sherwin St. DE22: Der 5D **107**
Sherwin Wlk. NG3: Nott 4B **98**
SHERWOOD 4A **74**
Sherwood Av. DE21: Chad . . .1E **137**
DE23: Lit 1C **184**
DE72: Bor 1C **164**
NG5: Sher 4C **74**
NG14: Calv 1C **30**
Sherwood Ct. NG9: Chil 5B **146**
NG14: Calv 1E **31**
Sherwood Gro.
NG13: Bing 2C **130**
NG14: Calv 1E **31**
Sherwood Hall NG7: Nott 4A **120**
SHERWOOD RISE 2A **98**
Sherwood Ri. NG7: Sher 1F **97**
NG16: Eastw 3E **43**

Sherwood St. DE22: Der 5D 135
  NG15: Huck 3B 26
Sherwood Va. NG5: Sher 4D 75
Sherwood Wlk. NG15: Lin 4C 10
Shetland Cl. DE21: Chad 1B 136
Shields Cres. DE74: C Don . .1E 211
Shilling Way
  NG10: Long E 4F 167
Shilo Way NG16: Aws 3A 68
SHIPLEY 1A 66
SHIPLEY COMMON 4B 66
Shipley Comn. La. DE7: Ilk . . .3B 66
Shipley Country Pk. 3D 65
Shipley Country Pk. Vis. Cen.
  . . . . .5D 41
Shipley Ga. NG16: Eastw 5D 43
Shipley La. DE75: Hea, Ship . .2E 65
Shipley Ri. NG4: Carl 3D 101
Shipley Rd. NG8: Brox 5E 71
Shipley Vw. DE7: Smal 1E 63
Shipley Wlk. DE7: S Loc . . .3D 187
Shipstone St. NG7: Basf 2E 97
Shipstone Street Stop (NET) . .2E 97
Shipstones Yd. NG6: Bulw 4B 48
  (off Filey St.)
Shirebrook Cl. DE7: Ilk 1E 67
  NG6: Basf 4B 72
Shiregate Gdns. DE23: Lit 1F 183
Shire Hall 4D 5 (1C 122)
Shireoaks DE56: Bel 4C 12
Shireoaks Cl. DE23: Lit 4B 158
Shirland Cl. DE7: Ilk 2E 67
Shirland Ct. DE24: S Loc . . .3D 187
Shirley Cl. DE74: C Don 5F 205
Shirley Ct. NG9: Toton 1F 169
Shirley Cres. DE72: Brea 3C 166
Shirley Dr. NG5: Arn 5A 52
Shirley Pk. DE72: Ast T 2A 204
Shirley Rd. DE5: Rip 5C 8
  DE21: Chad 4E 109
  NG3: Mapp P 2B 98
Shirley St. NG10: Long E 2F 193
Shop Stones DE72: Ock 3B 140
Shoreswood Cl. NG5: Bestw . .4A 50
Short Av. DE22: All 5E 83
Shortcross Av. NG3: Mapp . . .3E 75
Short Hill NG1: Nott . . .4E 5 (1C 122)
Shortlands DE56: Bel 5F 13
Short Row DE56: Bel 5E 13
Short Stairs
  NG1: Nott 4E 5 (1C 122)
Short St. DE56: Bel 5A 14
Shortwood Av. NG15: Huck . . .4E 25
Shortwood Cl.
  NG1: Nott 4D 5 (1C 122)
Shorwell Gdns. DE24: Alv 1B 188
Shorwell Rd. NG3: Nott 3B 100
Shottle Wlk. DE24: S Loc . . .3D 187
Shotton Dr. NG5: Arn 2F 51
Showcase Cinema
  Derby 4F 159
  Nottingham 5D 121
Shrewsbury Cl. DE21: Oak . . .3B 110
Shrewsbury Rd. NG2: Nott . . .1F 123
Shrimpton Ct. NG11: Rudd . . .5C 174
Shropshire Av. DE21: Chad . . .1D 137
Sibson Dr. DE74: Keg 2A 214
Sibson Wlk. NG5: Arn 2E 51
Siddals La. DE22: All 1E 107
Siddals Rd.
  DE1: Der 3E 7 (3A 136)
Siddons St. DE24: Alv 4F 161
Side Ley DE74: Keg 1B 214

Sidings, The DE21: Chad 4F 137
  NG14: Lowd 4D 57
  NG16: Kimb 1E 69
Sidings La. NG9: Bram 2F 117
Sidlaw Ri. NG5: Arn 2A 50
Sidmouth Cl. DE24: Alv 4B 162
  NG12: Key 2D 199
Sidney Ho. DE23: Lit 2B 158
Sidney Rd. NG9: Bee 1D 147
Sidney Robinson Bus. Pk.
  DE24: Der 2C 160
Sidney St. DE1: Der 5A 136
  NG10: Long E 5C 168
  NG16: Kimb 1E 69
Silbury Cl. NG11: Clif 4C 172
Silk Mill, The
  Derby's Mus. of
  Industry & History
  . . . . .1D 7 (2F 135)
Sillitoe Cl. NG7: Lent 5C 96
Sillitoe Way NG7: Lent 1C 120
Sills Rd. DE74: C Don 3F 205
Silver Birch Cl. NG6: Cin 3A 72
Silverburn Dr. DE21: Oak 3E 109
SILVERDALE 4F 149
Silverdale NG9: Stap 3D 145
Silverdale Cl. DE73: Chel 4F 187
Silverdale Rd. NG7: Basf 5E 73
Silverdale Wlk. NG11: Clif 5F 149
Silver Hill Rd. DE23: Der 1F 159
Silverhill Rd. DE21: Spon 5D 139
Silverhow Cl.
  NG2: West Br 3B 152
Silver La. DE72: Elv 1E 189
Silverton Dr. DE24: S Flds 4B 184
Silverwood Rd. NG9: Bee 2D 147
Silvey Gro. DE21: Spon 4C 138
Simcoe Leys DE73: Chel 4E 187
Simkin Av. NG3: Mapp 1F 99
Simone Gdns. NG11: Clif 1E 173
Simon Flds. Cl. DE7: Stan C . . .5F 63
Simons Ct. NG9: Bram 4C 118
Sims Av. DE1: Der 3D 135
Sinclair Cl. DE24: Sin 2D 185
  DE75: Hea 4C 40
SINFIN 2E 185
Sinfin Av.
  DE24: A'ton, S Loc 2C 186
Sinfin Central Bus. Pk.
  DE24: Sin 1E 185
Sinfin District Cen.
  DE24: Sin 3D 185
Sinfin Flds. Cres.
  DE24: A'ton 1C 186
Sinfin La. DE23: Der, Sin 2E 185
  DE24: Sin 2E 185
  DE73: Bar T 3A 200
Sinfin La. Ind. Est.
  DE24: Sin 1E 185
SINFIN MOOR 3A 186
Sinfin Moor La. DE24: Sin 3E 185
  (not continuous)
  DE73: Chel 4B 186
Sir Francis Ley Ind. Est.
  DE23: Der 2A 160
Sir Francis Ley Ind. Pk.
  DE23: Der 2B 160
Sir Frank Whittle Rd.
  DE21: Der 1F 7 (5B 108)
Sir John Robinson Way
  NG5: Arn 5C 50
Sir Peter Hilton Ct.
  DE1: Der 1A 6 (2E 135)

Siskin Cl. DE3: Mick 4A 156
Siskin Dr. DE24: Sin 2C 184
Sisley Av. NG9: Stap 2D 145
Sisters La. DE72: Ock 3B 140
Sitwell Cl. DE7: Smal 2E 63
  DE21: Spon 4C 138
Sitwell Dr. DE56: Kil 4F 37
Sitwell St. DE1: Der 4D 7 (4F 135)
  DE21: Spon 4C 138
Sixth Av. NG7: Nott 3B 148
Skeavingtons La. DE7: Ilk 2D 67
Skelwith Cl. NG2: West Br 3B 152
Sketchley Cl. NG6: Bulw 5F 47
Sketchley St. NG3: Nott 4E 99
Skiddaw Cl. NG2: West Br 3B 152
Skiddaw Dr. DE3: Mick 2D 157
Skipness Cl. DE73: Chel 5D 187
Skipton Cir. NG3: Nott 4F 99
Skipton Cl. DE7: Ilk 4C 66
Skipton Grn. DE21: Chad 4B 108
Skithorne Ri. NG14: Lowd 4C 56
Skylark Cl. NG13: Bing 3E 131
Skylark Dr. NG6: Basf 3C 72
Skylark Way DE24: Sin 2C 184
Slack Av. DE5: Rip 5C 8
Slack La. DE5: Rip 5C 8
  DE22: D Abb 3E 107
  DE22: Der 3C 134
  DE55: Rid 2F 9
  DE75: Hea 4D 41
Slack Rd. DE7: Mapp 4E 65
Slade Cl. DE7: Ilk 5F 91
  DE65: Etw 2B 180
Slade Lands Dr. DE73: Chel . . .4F 187
Slade La. DE73: Wils 5A 210
Slade Rd. NG9: Chil 3A 146
Slaidburn Av. NG11: Wilf 3F 149
Slaidburn Cl. DE3: Mick 2D 157
Slalom Run NG4: Carl 1B 100
Slaney Cl. DE24: A'ton 4D 161
Slater Av. DE1: Der 3D 135
Slaters Way NG5: Bestw 2E 73
Sledmere Cl. DE24: Alv 4B 162
Slindon Cft. DE24: Alv 5C 162
Sloan Dr. NG9: Bram 2A 118
Sloane Ct. NG2: West Br 5B 150
Sloane Rd. DE22: Mac 2F 133
Sloethorne Gdns. NG5: Arn . . .4C 50
SMALLEY 2E 63
SMALLEY COMMON 1F 87
Smalley Dr. DE21: Oak 2A 110
SMALLEY GREEN 3E 63
Smalley Mill Rd. DE21: Hors . .2F 61
Small Meer Cl. DE73: Chel . . .5E 187
Small's Cft. NG14: Woodbo . . .5B 32
Smedley Av. DE7: Ilk 3F 91
Smedley Cl. NG8: Aspl 5A 72
Smedley's Av. NG10: Sand . . .3A 144
Smeeton St. DE75: Hea 3A 42
Smisby Way DE24: S Loc 3D 187
Smite Ct. NG7: Radf 3C 96
Smith Av. DE5: Cod 5F 9
Smith Dr. NG16: Lang M 1F 41
Smithfield Av. NG9: Trow 1C 116
Smithurst Rd. NG16: Gilt 4F 43
Smithy Cl. NG11: Clif 1C 172
Smithy Cres. NG5: Arn 4E 51
Smithy Row
  NG1: Nott 3C 4 (1B 122)
Smithy Vw. NG6: Bestw V 4A 28
  NG14: Calv 2D 31
Smythson Dr. NG8: Woll 1D 119
Snake La. DE56: Duff 4C 58
Snape Nook Ct. NG6: Bulw . . .5E 47

Snape Wood Rd. NG6: Bulw . . .5E **47**
Snead Ct. NG5: Top V 3F **49**
SNEINTON 1E **123**
Sneinton Blvd. NG2: Nott 1E **123**
Sneinton Dale NG2: Nott 1E **123**
NG3: Nott 1E **123**
Sneinton Hermitage
NG2: Nott 5F **5** (2D **123**)
Sneinton Hollows
NG2: Nott 1E **123**
Sneinton Rd.
NG2: Nott 3F **5** (1D **123**)
Snelsmoor La. DE72: Thul . . .4A **188**
DE73: Chel 4A **188**
Snelston Cres. DE23: Lit 1C **158**
Snowberry Av. DE56: Bel 1A **36**
Snowdon Cl. NG5: Top V 3A **50**
Snowdrop Cl. NG15: Huck 5B **26**
Soarbank Cl. NG16: Kimb 5D **45**
Soar La. LE12: Sut B 4D **215**
Sobers Gdns. NG5: Arn 1A **76**
Society Pl. DE23: Der 1F **159**
Softwood Cl. NG6: Bulw 5E **47**
Soloman Pk. DE7: Ilk 5A **68**
Soloman Rd. DE7: Ilk 5A **68**
Solway Cl. DE21: Oak 3F **109**
NG9: Chil 3D **147**
Somercy Ct. NG9: Bram 1A **118**
Somerby Way DE21: Oak 3E **109**
Somerleyton Dr. DE7: Ilk 1F **115**
Somersal Cl. DE24: S Loc . . .3C **186**
Somersby Rd. NG3: Mapp 2E **75**
NG5: Woodt 2E **75**
Somerset Cl. NG10: Long E . .3F **169**
Somerset St. DE21: Chad 1C **136**
Somerton Av. NG11: Wilf 4F **149**
Somme Rd. DE22: All 2A **106**
Songthrush Av. NG6: Basf 3C **72**
Sophie Rd. NG7: H Grn 4E **97**
Sorrel Dr. NG13: Bing 2B **130**
Soudan Dr. NG2: Nott 4A **122**
Southampton St. NG3: Nott . . .4D **99**
South Av. DE21: Spon 4D **139**
DE22: D Abb 2F **107**
DE23: Lit 2C **158**
DE73: Chel 3E **187**
NG12: Rad T 1A **128**
Sth. Brae Cl. DE23: Lit 4C **158**
Southchurch Ct. NG11: Clif . .5E **149**
Southchurch Dr. NG11: Clif . . .2D **173**
Southcliffe Rd. NG4: Carl 3C **100**
South Ct. DE3: Mick 2C **156**
NG9: Bee 4A **148**
Southcroft DE23: Lit 1C **184**
Southdale Dr. NG4: Carl 3C **100**
Southdale Rd. NG4: Carl 3C **100**
(not continuous)
Sth. Devon Av. NG3: Mapp . . .5A **76**
Sth. Down Cl. DE24: S Flds . . .4B **184**
South Dr. DE1: Der 1E **135**
DE3: Mick 1F **157**
DE21: Chad 3F **137**
DE73: Chel 3E **187**
Southey St. NG7: Radf 4F **97**
Southfield Rd. NG8: Aspl 4C **96**
Southfields NG10: Long E 4D **169**
Southfields Ct. NG9: Chil 2A **146**
Southgate DE23: Der 5F **135**
Southgate Cl. DE3: Mick 5B **132**
Southglade Food Pk.
NG5: Bestw 1D **73**
Southglade Leisure Cen. 5E **49**
Southglade Rd. NG5: Bestw . .1D **73**
Southlea Rd. NG4: Carl 3C **100**

Southmead Way DE22: Der . . .5A **134**
South Pde.
NG1: Nott 3B **4** (1B **122**)
South Pl. DE5: Rip 5C **8**
Southport Ter. NG7: H Grn . . .3D **97**
South Rd. NG2: West Br 2D **151**
NG5: Sher 3A **74**
NG7: Nott 2F **121**
(Clumber Cres. Sth.)
NG7: Nott 3C **120**
(West Rd.)
NG9: Bee 4F **147**
South Row DE56: Mil 5F **35**
Sth. Sherwood St.
NG1: Nott 1B **4** (5B **98**)
Southside NG5: Arn 4B **52**
Sth. Snape Cl. NG6: Bulw 5E **47**
South St. DE1: Der 2A **6** (3D **135**)
DE7: Ilk 2D **91**
DE72: Dray 4F **165**
NG10: Long E 4D **169**
NG15: Huck 2F **25**
NG16: Eastw 2D **43**
NG16: Gilt 4B **44**
South Vw. DE23: Lit 2B **158**
DE56: Mil 5F **35**
South Vw. Rd. NG4: Carl 5C **76**
Southwark Cl. DE22: Mac 3A **134**
Southwark St. NG6: Basf 4D **73**
Southwell Hall NG8: Woll 1C **120**
Southwell Ri. NG16: Gilt 5A **44**
Southwell Rd.
NG1: Nott 3F **5** (1C **122**)
NG14: Gon, Lowd 3D **57**
Southwold Dr. NG8: Aspl 5B **96**
Southwood St. DE24: Alv 3E **161**
Sovereign Ct. NG9: Bee 3F **147**
Sovereign Gro.
NG10: Long E 4A **168**
Sovereign Way DE21: Oak . . .2C **110**
DE75: Hea 3C **40**
Sowbrook La.
DE7: D Ab, Stan D 1C **114**
Sowter Rd. DE1: Der 1D **7** (2F **135**)
Spa Cl. DE22: Der 5B **6** (5E **135**)
Spa La. DE22: Der 5B **6** (5E **135**)
Spalding Rd. NG3: Nott 5D **99**
Spaniel Row
NG1: Nott 4B **4** (1B **122**)
Sparrow Cl. DE7: Ilk 5F **91**
DE24: Sin 2C **184**
Spean Ct. NG8: Woll 5F **95**
Spean Dr. NG8: Aspl 3A **96**
Speedwell Cl. DE21: Oak 2B **110**
NG13: Bing 2B **130**
Speedwell La. NG16: Kimb . . .1D **69**
Spenbeck Dr. DE22: All 5F **83**
Spencer Av. DE24: A'ton 2C **186**
DE56: Bel 5A **14**
NG3: Mapp 2B **76**
NG10: Sand 1A **144**
Spencer Cl. NG11: Rudd 4A **174**
Spencer Ct. NG7: H Grn 2A **98**
Spencer Cres. NG9: Stap 5E **117**
Spencer Dr. NG16: Nuth 1B **70**
Spencer Rd. DE56: Bel 5F **13**
DE7: Stan C 1F **87**
DE24: Alv 3F **161**
Spey Cl. NG15: Huck 1C **46**
Spicer Cl. NG9: Chil 1B **170**
Spindle Gdns. NG6: Bulw 5F **47**
Spindle La. NG14: Woodbo . . .4B **30**
Spindletree Dr. DE21: Oak . . .3D **109**
Spindle Vw. NG14: Calv 3E **31**

Spinnaker Cl. DE5: Rip 2D **9**
Spinners Way DE56: Bel 3B **14**
Spinney, The DE5: Rip 3C **8**
DE7: Ilk 4D **91**
DE7: Ilk 5E **115**
DE7: Stan D 5E **115**
DE56: Bel 3F **13**
DE72: Bor 2B **164**
DE74: C Don 5F **205**
NG5: Woodt 3D **75**
NG6: Bestw V 4D **27**
NG14: Bulc 2A **80**
NG16: Nuth 4E **71**
(Harcourt Cres.)
NG16: Nuth 1A **70**
(Laurel Cres.)
Spinneybrook Way
DE3: Mick 4C **132**
Spinney Cl. DE22: D Abb 3F **107**
NG2: West Br 4A **152**
NG12: Cotg 1E **179**
Spinney Cres. NG9: Toton . . .5E **145**
Spinney Dr. NG10: Long E . . .1B **168**
Spinney Ri. NG9: Toton 5D **145**
Spinney Rd. DE7: Ilk 4D **91**
DE21: Chad 1E **137**
DE22: Der 5D **135**
NG10: Long E 1B **168**
NG12: Key 3C **198**
NG13: Bing 2C **130**
Spinney Way NG11: Wilf 4F **149**
Spinningdale NG5: Arn 3A **52**
Spital Hill DE74: C Don 5F **205**
Spittal, The DE74: C Don 5F **205**
SPONDON 3D **139**
Spondon Station (Rail) 5C **138**
Spondon St. NG5: Sher 5B **74**
Spoonley Wood Ct.
DE23: Lit 4E **157**
Spot, The DE1: Der . . .4D **7** (4F **135**)
Spray Cl. NG4: Colw 5D **101**
Spridgeon Cl.
NG10: Long E 1A **168**
Spring, The NG10: Long E . . .1C **194**
Spring Cl. DE56: Bel 3D **13**
DE72: Brea 3B **166**
NG16: Want 5F **45**
Spring Ct. NG2: West Br 5A **124**
NG9: Stap 1D **145**
Springdale Ct. DE3: Mick 2D **157**
Springdale Gdns.
NG9: Trow 3C **116**
Springfield DE23: Lit 1A **158**
DE74: Keg 2A **214**
Springfield Av. DE75: Los 4A **18**
NG10: Long E 3E **169**
NG10: Sand 5F **143**
NG16: Eastw 2F **43**
Springfield Cl. NG9: Stap 4E **117**
Springfield Dr. DE56: Duff 4C **58**
NG6: Bulw 1E **71**
Springfield Gdns. DE7: Ilk . . .5E **67**
Springfield Mill
NG10: Sand 2A **144**
SPRINGFIELD PARK 5A **144**
Springfield Retail Pk.
NG6: Bulw 4B **48**
Springfield Rd. DE21: Chad . .3A **138**
DE65: Etw 3A **180**
DE73: Chel 4D **187**
NG5: Redh 3D **51**
NG15: Huck 3C **24**
Springfields NG2: West Br . . .2C **150**
Springfield St. NG7: Basf 1E **97**
Springfield Ter. DE5: Rip 5D **9**

Springfield Vw. DE5: Rip 4C **8**
Spring Gdns. DE21: Chad 1E **137**
   NG8: Bilb 3B **94**
Spring Garden Ter. DE7: Ilk 5E **67**
Spring Grn. NG11: Clif 4D **173**
Springhead Ct. NG6: Bulw 1F **71**
Spring Heather Ct.
   NG12: Rad T 2D **127**
Spring Hill NG16: Kimb 2E **69**
Springhill Cl. NG6: Bulw 3A **48**
Springhill Way DE5: Cod 1F **17**
Spring Hollow DE56: Haz 5B **34**
Springland Farm Cotts.
   NG16: Nuth 1C **70**
        (off Watnall Rd.)
Spring La. DE75: Hea 3D **41**
   NG3: Mapp 1B **76**
   NG4: Lamb 1B **76**
Spring Mdw. NG12: Cotg 5F **155**
Spring Moor NG2: Colw 5C **100**
Spring Rd. NG6: Bulw 5B **48**
Spring St. DE22: Der . .5A **6** (4E **135**)
   NG15: Huck 1F **25**
Spring Ter. NG16: Nuth 2C **70**
Spring Ter. Gdns.
   NG16: Nuth 1C **70**
Springwood Cl. NG14: Calv 2F **31**
Springwood Dr. DE21: Oak . . .3F **109**
Springwood Gdns. DE56: Bel . . .5F **13**
   NG5: Woodt 4E **75**
Springwood Leisure Cen. 3F **109**
Spruce Gdns. NG6: Bulw 5F **47**
Spruce Gro. NG15: Huck 4A **26**
Sprydon Wlk. NG11: Clif 3E **173**
Square, The DE3: Mick 2C **156**
   DE22: D Abb 4F **107**
   NG6: Bestw V 5D **27**
   NG8: Woll 1D **119**
   NG9: Bee 2E **147**
   NG12: Key 4D **199**
Squires Av. NG6: Bulw 3A **48**
Squires Dr. NG6: Bestw V 3A **28**
Squires Way DE23: Lit 4F **157**
   NG2: West Br 2C **150**
Squirrel Wlk. DE56: Duff 5F **59**
Stables St. DE22: Der 3C **134**
Stacey Av. NG5: Top V 5E **49**
Stadium Bus. Ct.
   DE24: Der 4D **137**
Stadium Ind. Pk.
   NG10: Long E 3E **169**
Stadium Vw. DE24: Der 5D **137**
Stadmoor Ct. *DE73: Chel* 5E **187**
        (off Parkway)
Stafford Av. NG6: Bulw 1A **72**
Stafford Cl. DE7: Smal 1E **63**
Stafford Ct. NG6: Bulw 2E **71**
Staffords Acre DE74: Keg . . .2B **214**
Staffords Ct. NG4: Neth 3F **101**
Stafford St.
   DE1: Der 3A **6** (3E **135**)
   NG10: Long E 3E **169**
Stagsden Cres. NG8: Bilb 5B **94**
Staindale Cl. NG8: Aspl 1B **96**
Staindale Dr. NG8: Aspl 1B **96**
Staines Cl. DE3: Mick 1B **156**
Stainmore Gro. NG13: Bing . . .2B **130**
Stainsborough Rd.
   NG15: Huck 3B **24**
Stainsby Av. DE7: H Woo 1D **63**
   DE75: Hea 3D **41**
Staithes Wlk. DE21: Chad . . .4B **108**
Staker La. DE3: Mick 1C **182**
Staker Way DE3: Mick 4C **156**

Stamford Cl. NG10: Long E . . .2D **195**
Stamford Ct. NG5: Bestw 4A **50**
Stamford Rd. NG2: West Br . . .2F **151**
Stamford St. DE7: Ilk 1D **91**
   DE24: A'ton 5C **160**
   DE75: Hea 2D **41**
   NG16: Aws 3B **68**
   NG16: Newth 3B **44**
Stanage Grn. DE3: Mick 1E **157**
Stancliffe Av. NG6: Bulw 5B **48**
Standard Cl.
   NG1: Nott 4A **4** (1A **122**)
STANDARD HILL 4A **4** (1A **122**)
Standard Hill
   NG1: Nott 4A **4** (1A **122**)
Standhill Av. NG4: Carl 2A **100**
Standhill Rd. NG4: Carl 1F **99**
Stanesby Ri. NG11: Clif 2D **173**
Stanford Gdns.
   NG12: Rad T 1E **127**
Stanford St.
   NG1: Nott 4B **4** (1B **122**)
Stanhome Ct.
   NG2: West Br 4C **150**
Stanhome Dr.
   NG2: West Br 4C **150**
Stanhome Sq.
   NG2: West Br 4C **150**
Stanhope Av. NG5: Sher 1A **98**
Stanhope Cres. NG5: Arn 4D **51**
   NG14: Sto B 3E **103**
Stanhope Rd. DE3: Mick 5D **133**
   NG4: Ged 3C **76**
   NG5: Arn 4D **51**
Stanhope St. DE7: Ilk 4F **91**
   DE7: Stan D 5E **115**
   DE23: Der 1E **159**
   NG1: Nott 3E **5** (1C **122**)
   NG10: Long E 3C **168**
Stanhope Way NG13: Bing . .2D **131**
Stanier Way DE21: Chad 5F **137**
Staniland Cl. NG9: Chil 1B **170**
STANLEY 4B **88**
Stanley Av. DE5: Rip 4D **9**
   NG7: H Grn 2F **97**
Stanley Cl. DE7: Ilk 3D **91**
   DE22: Der 5E **107**
STANLEY COMMON 1B **88**
Stanley Ct. NG16: Eastw 3E **43**
Stanley Dr. NG9: Bram 5F **117**
Stanley Pl. NG1: Nott . . .2A **4** (5A **98**)
Stanley Rd. DE21: Chad 3F **137**
   DE24: Alv 5D **161**
   NG2: West Br 2E **151**
   NG3: Mapp 5F **75**
   NG7: H Grn 2F **97**
        (not continuous)
Stanley St. DE7: Ilk 3E **91**
   DE22: Der 3C **134**
   NG10: Long E 4D **169**
Stanmore Cl. NG16: Nuth 4D **71**
Stanmore Gdns. NG5: Arn 1D **75**
        (not continuous)
Stannier Way NG16: Want 5F **45**
Stansfield St. NG7: Lent 5D **97**
Stanstead Av. NG5: Top V 4C **48**
   NG12: Toll 3C **176**
Stanstead Rd. DE3: Mick 5B **132**
Stanthorne Cl. NG11: Wilf . . .4F **149**
Stanton Av. DE56: Bel 5A **14**
STANTON BY BRIDGE 5F **201**
STANTON-BY-DALE 5E **115**
Stanton Ga. DE7: Stan D 4B **116**

Stanton La. NG12: Stan W . . .4F **199**
Stanton Rd. DE7: Ilk 4E **91**
   NG10: Sand 1E **143**
Stanton St. DE23: Der 2E **159**
Stanway Cl. NG3: Nott 4B **100**
Stanwick Cl. NG8: Bilb 2D **95**
STAPLEFORD 1C **144**
Stapleford By-Pass
   NG10: Sand 4F **143**
Stapleford La. NG9: Toton . . .4E **145**
Stapleford Rd. NG9: Trow 1B **116**
Staplehurst Dr. NG5: Sher 3F **73**
Staples St. NG3: Mapp 5D **75**
Stapleton Rd. DE7: Ilk 3D **67**
Starch La. NG10: Sand 1A **144**
Starcross Ct. DE3: Mick 5B **132**
Starflower Way DE3: Mick . . .3C **132**
Starkie Av. DE74: C Don 1E **211**
Starthe Bank DE75: Hea 2E **41**
Starth Wood Rd.
   NG15: Huck 5C **24**
Statham St. DE22: Der 1D **135**
Stathern Wlk. NG5: Bestw 5A **50**
Station App.
   DE1: Der 3F **7** (3A **136**)
   DE56: Duff 3E **59**
Station Av. NG4: Ged 1F **101**
Station Cl. DE56: Kil 3E **37**
   DE73: Chel 5E **187**
Station Ct. *DE7: Ilk* 1D **91**
        (off Bath Rd.)
Station La. DE5: Cod 3A **18**
Station Rd. DE3: Mick 1C **156**
   DE5: Den 1A **38**
   DE7: Ilk 1E **91**
        (not continuous)
   DE7: S'ley, West H 5A **88**
   DE21: Bre 1C **108**
   DE21: L Eat 3B **84**
   DE21: Spon 5C **138**
   DE56: Duff 3E **59**
   DE72: Bor 2A **164**
   DE72: Dray 4A **166**
   DE73: Chel 5E **187**
   DE74: C Don 5A **206**
   DE74: Hem 3B **206**
   DE74: Keg 1C **214**
   LE12: Sut B 1D **215**
   NG4: Carl 3D **101**
   NG6: Bulw 1B **72**
   NG9: Bee 2E **147**
        (not continuous)
   NG10: Long E 3E **169**
   NG10: Sand 3B **144**
   NG11: King 5F **209**
   NG12: Key, Plum 5D **177**
   NG14: Bur J 4E **79**
   NG14: Lowd 3D **57**
   NG15: Huck 2A **26**
   NG15: News 1A **10**
   NG16: Aws 2B **68**
   NG16: Kimb 1E **69**
   NG16: Lang M 2F **41**
Station St. DE7: Ilk 5F **67**
   NG1: Nott 5C **4** (2B **122**)
   NG10: Long E 4D **169**
   NG13: Bing 1E **131**
Station Street Stop (NET)
   . . . . .5D **5** (2C **122**)
Station Ter. NG12: Rad T 2E **127**
   NG15: Huck 2A **26**
Station Vs. NG9: Bee 3F **147**
Staunton Av. DE23: Der 5D **159**
Staunton Cl. DE74: C Don . . .5F **205**

Staunton Dr. NG5: Sher 3B 74
Staveley Cl. DE24: S Loc 3D 187
Stavely Way NG2: Gam 1A 152
Staverton Dr. DE3: Mick 4C 132
Staverton Rd. NG8: Bilb 4C 94
Steadfold Cl. NG6: Bulw 1A 72
Steads Cl. NG4: Carl 3E 101
Steam Mill La. DE5: Rip 1F 17
Steedman Av. NG3: Mapp 3F 75
Steeles Way NG4: Lamb 5A 54
Steelyard Cl. DE5: Rip 2D 9
Steeple Cl. DE21: Oak 3D 109
Steeple Dr. DE5: Rip 1D 17
Steinbeck Rd. NG4: Carl 3B 100
Stella Av. NG12: Toll 3C 176
Stella Gro. NG12: Toll 3C 176
STENSON 5A 184
Stenson Av. DE23: Der 5D 159
Stenson Ct. DE5: Rip 5E 9
STENSON FIELDS 4C 184
Stenson Rd.
　DE23: Der, Lit 5C 158
　DE24: S Flds 3C 184
　DE73: Sten 5A 184
Stephensons Way
　DE21: Chad 5F 137
Stepney Ct. NG8: Brox 1E 95
Stepping Cl. DE1: Der 3D 135
Stepping La. DE1: Der 3C 134
Sterling Cl. DE5: Den 2A 38
Sterndale Ho.
　DE1: Der 5C 6 (4F 135)
Sterndale Rd.
　NG10: Long E 5A 168
Stevenage Cl. DE24: Alv 1E 187
Steven Cl. NG9: Toton 4E 145
Stevenholme Cres.
　NG5: Bestw 1F 73
Steven's La. DE72: Brea 3C 166
Stevenson Av.
　DE72: Brea 3A 166
Stevenson Gdns.
　NG11: Rudd 5C 174
Stevenson Pl. DE23: Lit 3A 158
Stevens Rd. NG10: Sand 3F 143
Stewart Cl. DE21: Spon 2D 139
Stewarton Cl. NG5: Arn 3A 52
Stiles Rd. DE24: Alv 4A 162
　NG5: Arn 1B 76
Stiles Wlk. DE56: Duff 3D 59
Stinsford Cl. NG5: Bestw 4B 50
Stirland St. DE5: Cod 5F 9
Stirling Cl. DE21: Chad 5B 108
Stirling Gdns. NG9: Chil 1A 170
Stirling Gro. NG11: Clif 3E 173
　NG16: Kimb 5D 45
Stockbrook Rd. DE22: Der 5C 134
Stockbrook St.
　DE22: Der 5A 6 (4D 135)
Stockdale Cl. NG5: Arn 2F 49
Stockdove Cl. DE24: Sin 2C 184
Stocker Av. DE24: Alv 4B 162
Stockgill Cl.
　NG2: West Br 2B 152
Stockhill Cir. NG6: Basf 4B 72
Stockhill La. NG6: Basf 4B 72
Stocks Rd. NG16: Kimb 5D 45
Stockton St. NG6: Bulw 5A 48
Stock Well NG6: Bulw 1A 72
Stoddard Dr. DE75: Hea 2E 41
STOKE BARDOLPH 2E 103
Stoke Cl. DE56: Del 5C 14
Stoke Ferry La.
　NG12: Shel 1E 103

Stoke La. NG4: Ged 1A 102
　NG14: Sto B 4E 79
　　　　　　　　　　　　　(Station Rd.)
　NG14: Sto B 2C 102
　　　　　　　　　　　　　(Top Row)
Stokesay Wlk.
　NG2: West Br 3E 151
Stolle Cl. NG5: Arn 1B 76
Stoneacre NG5: Bestw 4A 50
Stonebridge City Farm
　. . . . . .1F 5 (5D 99)
Stonebridge Ct. Ind. Est.
　NG3: Nott 1F 5 (5D 99)
Stonebridge Rd.
　NG3: Nott 1F 5 (5D 99)
Stonebroom Wlk.
　DE24: S Loc 3D 187
Stonechat Cl. DE3: Mick 1F 157
Stone Cl. DE21: Spon 2D 139
Stonehaven Cl. NG5: Arn 3A 52
Stonehill DE74: C Don 2A 212
Stonehill Rd. DE23: Der 1E 159
Stonehills DE74: Keg 2B 214
Stoneleigh Cl. NG9: Chil 3B 146
Stoneleigh St. NG7: Radf 5F 97
Stone Mdws.
　NG10: Long E 1D 195
Stonepit Cl. NG3: Nott 1E 99
Stonesby Cl. DE21: Oak 3E 109
Stonesby Va.
　NG2: West Br 5A 150
Stonesdale Ct. DE24: Alv 5B 162
Stoney Bank NG14: Lowd 2C 56
Stoneycroft Rd. NG6: Bulw . . .2D 73
Stoney Cross DE21: Spon 5D 139
Stoney Cross Ind. Pk.
　DE21: Spon 5C 138
Stoneyfield Bank DE56: Bel . . .4F 13
Stoney Flatts Cres.
　DE21: Chad 5F 109
STONEYFORD 2E 19
Stoney Ga. Rd.
　DE21: Spon 5C 138
Stoney Houghton Gdns.
　NG6: Bulw 4E 47
Stoneyhurst Ct.
　DE24: S Loc 3D 187
Stoney La. DE5: Rip 2F 17
　DE21: Spon 3D 139
　DE56: Bel 5F 13
　DE56: H'ook 1B 60
　NG9: Trow 4A 92
　NG16: Brins 4B 20
Stoney St.
　NG1: Nott 3D 5 (1C 122)
　NG9: Bee 1E 194
Stony Clouds Local Nature Reserve
　. .5A 116
Stoodley Pike Gdns.
　DE22: All 3B 106
Stoppard Cl. DE7: Ilk 5C 66
Stores Rd.
　DE21: Der 1F 7 (5A 108)
Storey Av. NG4: Ged 5D 77
Storm Extreme Sports Cen.
　. .2B 160
Stornoway Cl. DE24: Sin 3C 184
Stornoway Ct. NG9: Bee 3F 147
Storth Av. NG15: Huck 3F 25
Story Gdns. NG15: Huck 4B 26
Stotfield Rd. NG8: Bilb 5A 94
Sluurdale Cl. NG10: Long E . . .5F 167
Stourport Dr. DE73: Chel 3F 187
Stowe Av. NG2: West Br 3C 150

Stowmarket Dr.
　DE21: Chad 4C 108
STRAGGLETHORPE 1F 155
Stragglethorpe La.
　NG12: Rad T 4B 126
Strand, The
　DE1: Der 2C 6 (3F 135)
　NG9: Atten 2C 170
Strand Arc. DE1: Der . . .2C 6 (3F 135)
Stratford Cl. NG4: Colw 5D 101
Stratford Rd. DE21: Chad 3C 108
　NG2: West Br 1E 151
Stratford St. DE7: Ilk 3E 67
Strathaven Ct. DE21: Spon . . .3D 139
Strathglen Cl. NG16: Kimb . . .5D 45
Strathmore Av. DE24: Alv 5E 161
Strathmore Cl. NG15: Huck . . .4D 25
Strathmore Rd. NG5: Arn 3A 52
Streatham Rd. DE22: Mac 2F 133
STREET LANE 3F 15
Street La. DE5: Den, Rip 1F 15
STRELLEY 2B 94
Strelley Av. DE5: Rip 1B 16
Strelley La. NG8: Stre 2A 94
Strelley Rd. NG8: Bilb, Stre . . .2B 94
Strelley St. NG6: Bulw 5A 48
Stretton Cl. DE3: Mick 2C 156
Stretton St.
　NG3: Nott 1D 5 (4C 98)
Striding Edge Cl.
　NG10: Long E 1A 168
Stripes Vw. NG14: Calv 3E 31
Stroma Cl. DE24: Sin 2E 185
Strome Cl. NG2: Nott 3B 122
Strome Ct. NG2: Nott 3B 122
Strutt St. DE23: Der 1F 159
　DE56: Bel 1E 35
Stuart Cl. NG5: Arn 4A 52
Stuart St. DE1: Der 1D 7 (2F 135)
Studbrook Cl. DE74: C Don . . .1E 211
Studio Theatre, The 2A 152
Studland Way
　NG2: West Br 3B 150
Sturgeon Av. NG11: Clif 4E 149
Sturges La. DE72: Thul 2E 189
Sturton St. NG7: H Grn 2F 97
Styring St. NG9: Bee 2E 147
Sudbury Av. DE7: Ilk 3F 91
　NG10: Sand 1F 143
Sudbury Cl. DE1: Der 3D 135
Sudbury Ct. NG10: Long E 2E 193
Sudbury M. NG16: Eastw 3D 43
Sudbury St. DE1: Der 3D 135
Suez St. NG7: Basf 1E 97
Suffolk Av. DE21: Chad 1D 137
　NG9: Bee 4B 148
　NG15: Huck 4B 24
Sulleys Fld. DE22: Quar 3C 82
Sullivan Cl. NG3: Nott 3E 99
Sullivan St. NG7: Radf 5D 97
Sumburgh Rd. NG11: Clif 2F 173
Summerbrook Ct.
　DE22: Der 4E 135
Summerfields Way DE7: Ilk . . ,3B 66
Summerfields Way Sth.
　DE7: Ilk 5C 66
Summer Leys Rd.
　NG2: Nott 2C 122
Summers Ct. DE21: Spon 4C 138
Summerville Cl. DE23: Lit 5F 157
Summer Way
　NG12: Rad T 1D 127
Summer Wood Ct.
　DE23: Der 4C 158

Summerwood La.
   NG11: Clif 3C 172
Sunart Cl. DE24: Sin 4E 185
Sunbourne Ct. NG7: Radf 4F 97
Sunbury Gdns. NG5: Arn 3F 51
Sunderland Gro. NG8: Stre 5C 70
Sundew Cl. DE21: Spon 4E 139
Sundown Av. DE23: Lit 5C 158
Sundridge Pk. Cl.
   NG2: West Br 3B 150
Sunflower Cl. DE24: Alv 2F 161
Sunlea Cres. NG9: Stap 3E 145
Sunnindale Dr. NG12: Toll . . .2C 176
Sunningdale Av.
   DE21: Spon 3C 138
   DE75: Hea 4E 41
Sunningdale Dr. DE7: Kirk H . .5A 90
   NG14: Woodbo 4B 32
Sunningdale Rd. NG6: Bulw . . .1C 72
Sunninghill Cl. DE7: West H . . .2C 88
Sunninghill Dr. NG11: Clif . . .5D 149
Sunninghill Ri. NG5: Arn 3F 51
Sunny Bank Gdns. DE56: Bel . .2E 35
SUNNYDALE 4C 158
Sunnydale Rd. NG3: Nott 4A 100
Sunny Gro. DE21: Chad 3F 137
SUNNY HILL 5D 159
Sunny Hill DE56: Mil 5E 35
Sunnyhill Av. DE23: Der 5D 159
Sunny Hill Gdns. DE56: Mil . . .5E 35
Sunny Row NG8: Woll 5D 95
Sunnyside Rd. NG9: Chil 2B 146
Sunridge Ct. NG3: Mapp P 2B 98
Sunrise Av. NG5: Bestw 2E 73
   NG6: Bestw V 4A 28
Sun St. DE22: Der 5A 6 (4E 135)
Sun Valley Leisure Cen. . . .2D 173
Surbiton Cl. DE22: Mac 2F 133
Surbiton Ct. DE7: West H 2C 88
   NG3: Mapp 1D 99
Surbiton Sq. NG8: Cin 4A 72
Surfleet Cl. NG8: Woll 2B 118
Surgey's La. NG5: Arn 3E 51
Surrey Ct. NG3: Mapp 1D 99
Surrey St. DE22: Der 2C 134
Susan Cl. NG15: Huck 5D 11
Susan Dr. NG6: Bulw 3C 72
Sussex Cir. DE21: Chad 5D 109
Sussex Cl. NG16: Gilt 4F 43
Sussex St.
   NG1: Nott 4C 4 (1B 122)
Sussex Way NG10: Sand 3A 144
Sutherland Dr.
   NG2: West Br 4F 151
Sutherland Rd. DE23: Der 2E 159
   NG3: Nott 3A 100
Suthers Rd. DE74: Keg 2A 214
Sutton Av. DE73: Chel 3E 187
SUTTON BONINGTON 5F 215
Sutton Cl. DE22: Der 2C 134
Sutton Ct. NG16: Eastw 2E 43
Sutton Dr. DE24: S Loc 2D 187
Sutton Gdns. NG11: Rudd 5B 174
Sutton Ho. DE24: Alv 1B 188
Sutton La. DE65: Etw 1A 180
Sutton Passeys Cres.
   NG8: Woll 1A 120
Sutton Rd. DE74: Keg 3B 214
   NG5: Arn 2E 51
Swain's Av. NG3: Nott 4F 99
Swaledale Cl. NG8: Aspl 1C 96
Swaledale Ct. DE24: Alv 5B 162
Swallow Cl. DE3: Mick 1F 157
   NG6: Basf 3C 72

Swallow Ct. DE5: Mare 3C 16
Swallowdale Rd. DE24: Sin . . .2C 184
Swallow Dr. NG13: Bing 3B 131
Swallow Gdns. NG4: Carl 1A 100
Swan Cl. LE12: Sut B 5F 215
Swan Hill DE3: Mick 5A 156
Swan Mdw. NG4: Colw 1D 125
Swanmore Rd. DE23: Lit 3F 157
Swansdowne Dr. NG11: Clif . . .1E 173
Swanwick Gdns.
   DE21: Chad 4E 109
Swanwick Junction Station
  Midland Railway Centre . . .1F 9
Swanwick Rd. DE7: Ilk 2E 67
Swanwick Station
  Golden Valley Light Railway
   .2F 9
SWARKESTONE 3C 200
Swarkestone Boat Club 2D 201
Swarkestone Bri.
   DE73: S Bri, Swar 4C 200
Swarkestone Dr. DE23: Lit 1B 184
Swarkestone Rd.
   DE72: W Tre 3C 200
   DE73: Bar T 3A 200
      (not continuous)
   DE73: Chel 5E 187
   DE73: Chel, Swar 3C 200
Swayfield Cl. DE3: Mick 1B 156
Sweeney Ct. NG5: Top V 4F 49
Sweetbriar Cl. DE24: Alv 1F 187
Sweet Leys Rd. NG2: Nott 4B 122
Swenson Av. NG7: Lent 2D 121
Swift Cl. DE3: Mick 5F 133
Swift Ct. NG16: Eastw 2E 43
Swigert Cl. NG6: Bulw 2E 71
Swildon Wlk. NG5: Top V 4E 49
Swinburne St. DE1: Der 5F 135
   NG3: Nott 4E 99
Swinburne Way NG5: Arn 5B 50
Swindale Cl. NG2: Gam 1A 152
Swinderby Dr. DE21: Oak 4A 110
Swindon Cl. NG16: Gilt 5B 44
Swiney Way
   NG9: Chil, Toton 1E 169
SWINGATE 2F 69
Swingate NG16: Kimb 2F 69
Swinney Bank DE56: Bel 4F 13
Swinney La. DE56: Bel 4F 13
Swinscoe Gdns. NG5: Top V . . .4E 49
Swinscoe Ho.
   DE1: Der 4B 6 (4E 135)
Swinstead Cl. NG8: Bilb 1F 95
Swithland Dr. NG2: West Br . . .4D 151
Sycamore Av. DE5: Rip 1C 16
   DE22: All 2C 106
   DE65: Find 5C 182
Sycamore Cl. DE7: Mapp 4E 65
   DE65: Etw 2B 180
   NG12: Rad T 3E 127
   NG13: Bing 2F 131
   NG15: Huck 4D 25
Sycamore Ct. DE21: Spon 3D 139
   NG9: Bee 1F 147
Sycamore Cres.
   NG10: Sand 1F 143
Sycamore Dr. DE7: Ilk 3A 92
Sycamore Pl. NG3: Mapp P 2B 98
Sycamore Ri. NG6: Cin 3A 72
Sycamore Rd. DE74: C Don . . .4A 206
   NG10: Long E 1B 194
   NG16: Aws 2A 68
Sycamores, The
   NG16: Eastw 3D 43

Sydenham Rd. DE22: Mac 1F 133
Syderstone Wlk. NG5: Arn 2E 75
Sydney Cl. DE3: Mick 5E 133
Sydney Gro. NG12: Rad T 2D 127
Sydney Rd. DE72: Dray 4F 165
   NG8: Woll 5A 96
Syke Rd. NG5: Top V 4E 49
Synge Cl. NG11: Clif 3B 172
Syon Pk. Cl. NG2: West Br . . .3B 150

T

Taddington Cl. DE21: Chad . . .5D 109
Taddington Rd.
   DE21: Chad 4D 109
Taft Av. NG10: Sand 2A 144
Talbot Cl. NG12: Rad T 2D 127
Talbot Dr. NG9: Stap 3C 116
Talbot St. DE1: Der . . .3A 6 (3E 135)
   NG1: Nott 2A 4 (5A 98)
Tales of Robin Hood 3A 4
Talgarth Cl. DE21: Oak 3B 110
Tamar Av. DE22: All 1C 106
Tamarix Cl. NG4: Ged 5F 77
Tambling Cl. NG5: Arn 1A 76
Tame Cl. NG11: Clif 4D 149
Tamworth Gro. NG11: Clif 1E 173
Tamworth Ri. DE56: Duff 3D 59
Tamworth Rd. DE72: Shar 1C 206
   DE74: C Don 2B 206
      (not continuous)
   NG10: Long E 1C 206
Tamworth St. DE56: Duff 3D 59
Tamworth Ter. DE56: Duff 3D 59
Tanglewood Cl. DE56: Bel 3F 13
Tangmere Cres. NG8: Stre 1D 95
Tanners Wlk.
   NG1: Nott 4C 4 (1B 122)
Tannin Cres. NG6: Bulw 2B 72
Tansley Av. DE7: Stan C 1F 87
Tansley Ri. DE21: Chad 4E 109
Tansy Way NG13: Bing 3B 130
Tants Mdw. DE56: L Kil 1D 61
Tantum Av. DE75: Los 5B 18
Tanwood Rd. NG9: Toton 2A 170
Tanyard Cl. DE74: C Don 5A 206
Taplow Cl. DE3: Mick 1B 156
Tarbert Cl. NG2: Nott 3A 122
Target St. NG7: Radf 5D 97
Tarina Cl. DE73: Chel 5F 187
Tarn Cl. NG16: Lang M 5A 20
Tasman Cl. DE3: Mick 5E 133
Tatham's La. DE7: Ilk 5D 67
      (not continuous)
Tattershall Dr. NG7: Nott 1F 121
   NG9: Bee 1A 148
Tattle Hill DE7: D Ab 3D 113
Taunton Cl. DE24: Alv 4B 162
Taunton Rd. NG2: West Br 2E 151
Taupo Dr. NG15: Huck 4B 24
Tavern Av. NG8: Aspl 5B 72
Taverners Cres. DE23: Lit 3B 158
Tavistock Av. DE5: Rip 4B 8
   NG3: Mapp P 1B 98
Tavistock Cl. DE24: S Flds 3C 184
   NG15: Huck 4C 24
Tavistock Ct. NG5: Sher 1B 98
Tavistock Dr. NG3: Mapp P 1B 98
Tavistock Rd. NG2: West Br . . .2E 151
Tawny Way DE23: Lit 4F 157
Tayberry Cl. DE24: Alv 3D 161
Tay Cl. DE24: S Flds 4C 184
Taylor Cl. NG2: Nott 1F 123

Taylor Cres. NG9: Stap 5E **117**
Taylor La. DE75: Los 1C **40**
Taylor La. Ind. Est.
   DE75: Los 1C **40**
Taylors Cft. NG14: Woodbo 5A **32**
Taylor St. DE7: Ilk 1E **91**
   DE24: Der 1C **160**
Tayside Cl. DE24: S Flds 3C **184**
Tay Wlk. DE22: All 2D **107**
TDG Pinnacle DE7: West H . . .4D **89**
Teak Cl. NG3: Nott 3C **98**
Tealby Cl. NG6: Bulw 5E **47**
Teal Cl. NG4: Neth 3A **102**
Teal Wharf NG7: Lent 3F **121**
Teasels, The NG13: Bing 3C **130**
Technology Dr. NG9: Bee 3F **147**
Tedworth Av. DE24: S Flds . . .4C **184**
Teesbrook Dr. NG8: Woll 1A **118**
Teesdale Cl. NG9: Chil 4F **145**
Teesdale Rd. NG5: Sher 5F **73**
   NG10: Long E 5F **167**
Telford Cl. DE3: Mick 2D **157**
Telford Dr. NG16: Newth 1A **44**
Teme Ct. NG2: West Br 3E **151**
Templar Cl. DE24: S Flds 3B **184**
Templar Lodge NG9: Bee 2A **148**
Templar Rd. NG9: Bee 2A **148**
Templars Ct. _NG7: Radf_ 4D **97**
           (off New Rd.)
Templebell Cl. DE23: Lit 5F **157**
Temple Cres. NG16: Nuth 3C **70**
Temple Dr. NG16: Nuth 3D **71**
Templeman Cl.
   NG11: Rudd 3A **174**
Templeoak Dr. NG8: Woll 2B **118**
Temple St. DE23: Der 5F **135**
Tenants Hall Cl.
   NG9: Lent A 4F **119**
Tenant St. DE1: Der . . .2D **7** (3F **135**)
Tenbury Cres. NG8: Aspl 1A **96**
Tenby Dr. DE21: Oak 3B **110**
Tene Cl. NG5: Arn 2E **51**
Tennessee Rd. DE21: Chad . . .1F **137**
Tennis Ct. Ind. Est.
   NG2: Nott 2F **123**
Tennis Dr. NG7: Nott 1F **121**
Tennis M. NG7: Nott 1F **121**
Tennis Vw. NG7: Nott 1F **121**
Tennyson Av. NG4: Ged 1E **101**
Tennyson Ct. NG5: Sher 4A **74**
   NG15: Huck 3C **24**
Tennyson Dr. NG9: Atten 1C **170**
Tennyson Rd. NG5: Woodt . . .3D **75**
Tennyson Sq. NG16: Aws 3B **68**
Tennyson St. DE7: Ilk 4D **67**
   DE24: Der 4C **160**
   NG7: Radf 4F **97**
          (not continuous)
Tenter Cl. NG5: Top V 4E **49**
   NG10: Long E 1C **194**
Terrace St. NG7: H Grn 3E **97**
Terrian Cres. NG2: West Br . . .1E **151**
Terry Pl. DE24: Alv 5E **161**
Terton Rd. NG5: Top V 4E **49**
Tetney Wlk. NG8: Bilb 3F **95**
Tettenbury Rd. NG5: Sher 4E **73**
Teversal Av. NG7: Lent 1E **121**
Tevery Cl. NG9: Stap 5D **117**
Teviot Pl. DE21: Oak 3F **109**
Teviot Rd. NG5: Bestw 2E **73**
Tewkesbury Cl.
   NG2: West Br 2F **151**
Tewkesbury Cres.
   DE21: Chad 5C **108**

Tewkesbury Dr. NG6: Basf 3D **73**
   NG16: Kimb 5D **45**
Tewkesbury Rd.
   NG10: Long E 2D **195**
Thackeray's La. NG5: Woodt . . .2C **74**
Thackeray St. DE24: Sin 1F **185**
   NG7: Radf 5E **97**
Thales Dr. NG5: Arn 5B **52**
Thames Cl. DE22: Mac 3E **133**
Thames St. NG6: Bulw 5A **48**
Thane Rd. NG7: Lent, Nott . . .2C **148**
Thanet Dr. DE24: Alv 5F **161**
Thatch Cl. DE22: D Abb 3E **107**
Thatchmarsh Cl. DE7: Ilk 1E **67**
Thaxted Cl. NG8: Bilb 4C **94**
The . . . .
   Names prefixed with 'The' for
   example 'The Aerodrome' are
   indexed under the main name
   such as 'Aerodrome, The'
Theatre Royal **2B 4** (5B **98**)
Theatre Sq.
   NG1: Nott 2B **4** (5B **98**)
Theatre Wlk.
   DE1: Der 3E **7** (3A **136**)
Thelda Av. NG12: Key 3D **199**
Thetford Cl. NG5: Arn 1F **75**
Third Av. DE7: Ilk 3E **91**
   NG4: Carl 2A **100**
          (not continuous)
   NG4: Ged 1E **101**
   NG6: Bulw 5A **48**
   NG7: H Grn 2A **98**
   NG7: Nott 2B **148**
Thirlmere NG2: West Br 3B **152**
Thirlmere Av. DE22: All 2D **107**
Thirlmere Cl. NG3: Nott 3E **99**
   NG10: Long E 1A **168**
Thirlmere Rd.
   NG10: Long E 1A **168**
Thirsk Pl. DE24: Der 4C **160**
Thirston Cl. NG6: Bulw 5E **47**
Thistle Cl. NG16: Newth 4A **44**
Thistledown Cl.
   DE22: D Abb 3F **107**
Thistledown Rd. NG11: Clif 4D **173**
Thistlegreen Cl. DE75: Hea . . .3A **42**
Thistle Gro. DE73: Chel 5D **187**
Thistle Rd. DE7: Ilk 1F **115**
Thomas Av. NG12: Rad T 1B **128**
Thomas Cl. NG3: Nott 4C **98**
Thomas Ct. DE1: Der 4D **135**
Thomas Forman Ct.
   NG5: Sher 1A **98**
Thomas Rd. DE74: Keg 3B **214**
Thompson Cl. NG9: Chil 5B **146**
Thompson Ct. NG9: Chil 2A **170**
Thompson Gdns. NG5: Top V . . .3F **49**
Thompson St.
   NG16: Lang M 1A **42**
Thomson Dr. DE5: Cod 1A **18**
Thomson Wlk. _DE5: Cod_ 1F **17**
         (off Thomson Dr.)
Thoresby Av. NG2: Nott 2E **123**
   NG4: Ged 5C **76**
Thoresby Cl. DE5: Rip 5D **9**
   DE21: Oak 4A **110**
   NG12: Rad T 1F **127**
Thoresby Ct. NG3: Mapp P . . .2C **98**
Thoresby Cres. DE72: Dray . . .4E **165**
Thoresby Dale NG15: Huck 2A **26**
Thoresby Rd. NG9: Bram 4B **118**
   NG10: Long E 5A **168**
   NG13: Bing 2B **130**

Thoresby St.
   NG2: Nott 4F **5** (1D **123**)
Thor Gdns. NG5: Top V 3E **49**
Thornbury Way NG5: Top V . . .5E **49**
Thorncliffe Ri. NG3: Mapp P . . .2B **98**
Thorncliffe Rd.
   NG3: Mapp P 2B **98**
Thorn Cl. DE22: All 1C **106**
Thorndale Rd. NG6: Basf 5B **72**
   NG14: Calv 2E **31**
Thorndike Av. DE24: Alv 4E **161**
Thorndon Cl. DE3: Mick 3C **156**
Thorn Dr. NG16: Newth 4A **44**
Thorndyke Cl. NG9: Bee 4A **148**
Thorner Cl. NG6: Bulw 2D **73**
Thorness Cl. DE24: Alv 1B **188**
Thorney Hill NG3: Nott 3E **99**
THORNEYWOOD 2F **99**
Thorneywood Mt. NG3: Nott . . .3E **99**
Thorneywood Ri. NG3: Nott . . .3E **99**
Thorneywood Rd.
   NG10: Long E 3E **169**
Thornfield Ind. Est.
   NG3: Nott 5E **99**
Thornfield Sq.
   NG10: Long E 3E **169**
Thorn Gro. NG15: Huck 5A **26**
Thornhill Cl. NG9: Bram 3A **118**
Thornhill Rd. DE22: Der 4B **134**
   DE23: Lit 2B **158**
Thornley St. NG7: H Grn 3D **97**
Thorn St. DE23: Der 1E **159**
Thornthwaite Cl.
   NG2: West Br 2B **152**
Thornton Av. NG5: Redh 3C **50**
Thornton Cl. NG8: Woll 1D **119**
Thorntons Cl. NG12: Cotg 5F **155**
Thorntons Holt Camping Pk.
   NG12: Rad T 5C **126**
Thornton Ter. NG7: H Grn 3E **97**
Thorntree Cl. DE72: Brea 2E **167**
Thorn Tree Gdns.
   NG16: Eastw 5E **21**
Thorntree La.
   DE1: Der 3D **7** (3F **135**)
Thorold Cl. NG11: Clif 1D **173**
Thoroton Rd. NG2: West Br . . .4E **123**
Thoroton St. NG7: Radf 5F **97**
Thorpe Cl. NG5: Top V 4E **49**
   NG9: Stap 1B **144**
Thorpe Cres. NG3: Mapp 5A **76**
Thorpe Dr. DE3: Mick 5D **133**
Thorpe Hill Dr. DE75: Hea 5D **41**
Thorpelands Dr. DE22: All 4D **107**
Thorpe Lea NG14: Gun 2E **81**
Thorpe Leys NG10: Long E . . .1C **194**
Thorpe Rd. NG16: Eastw 5E **21**
Thorpe's Rd. DE75: Hea 3C **40**
Thorpes Rd. Ind. Est.
   DE75: Hea 4C **40**
Thorpe St. DE/: Ilk 4D **67**
Thorpe Way DE56: Bel 4A **14**
Thrapston Av. NG5: Arn 2E **51**
Thraves Yd. NG12: Rad T 2D **127**
Three Gates DE56: Bel 2E **35**
Three Tuns Rd. NG16: Eastw . . .2F **43**
Threlkeld Cl. NG2: West Br . . .2B **152**
Thrumpton Av.
   NG10: Long E 4E **169**
Thrumpton Dr. NG2: Nott 4A **122**
Thrushton Cl. DE65: Find 5B **182**
Thruxton Cl. DE24: Alv 5B **162**
THULSTON 2E **189**
Thurcroft Cl. DE22: Der 2B **134**

Thurgarton Av. NG2: Nott 1E **123**
Thurgarton St. NG2: Nott 1E **123**
Thurland St.
  NG1: Nott 3C **4** (1B **122**)
Thurlbeck NG12: Cotg 2F **179**
Thurlestone Dr. NG3: Mapp 1B **76**
Thurloe Ct. NG2: West Br 5B **150**
Thurlow Ct. DE21: Oak 4F **109**
Thurman Dr. NG12: Cotg 5E **155**
Thurman St. DE7: Ilk 4F **91**
  NG7: H Grn 4E **97**
Thurrows Way DE73: Chel 4A **188**
Thursby Rd. NG11: Clif 5D **149**
Thurstone Furlong
  DE73: Chel 5D **187**
Thyme Cl. DE23: Lit 1C **184**
Thymus Wlk. NG11: Clif 2B **172**
Thyra Ct. NG3: Nott 1D **99**
Thyra Gro. NG3: Nott 1C **98**
  NG9: Bee 2F **147**
Tiber Cl. DE24: Alv 1C **188**
Tickham Av. DE24: S Flds 4C **184**
Ticknall La. DE5: Den 2A **38**
Ticknall Wlk. DE23: Der 5D **159**
Tideswell Rd. DE21: Chad 4E **109**
Tidworth Cl. NG8: Bilb 4F **95**
Tilberthwaite Cl.
  NG2: Gam 2B **152**
Tilbury Pl. DE24: Alv 1F **187**
Tilbury Ri. NG8: Cin 4F **71**
Tilford Gdns. NG9: Stap 2D **145**
Tiller Cl. DE23: Lit 5A **158**
Tilstock Ct. NG16: Want 4F **45**
Tilton Gro. DE7: Kirk H 5B **90**
Timbersbrook Cl.
  DE21: Oak 4F **109**
Tim La. NG11: Bur J 3E **79**
Timsbury Ct. DE21: Oak 3D **109**
Tindall Cl. NG3: Chil 1A **170**
Tinderbox La. DE65: Burn 1E **181**
Tinker Cft. DE7: Ilk 3D **91**
Tinkers Way NG7: Lent 2A **122**
Tinsley Rd. NG16: Eastw 3C **42**
Tintagel Cl. DE23: Der 1A **160**
Tintagel Grn. NG11: Clif 2D **173**
Tintern Dr. NG8: Basf 5C **72**
Tipnall Rd. DE74: C Don 1F **211**
Tippett Ct. NG3: Nott 4E **99**
Tip Tree Cl. NG16: Kimb 5E **45**
Tiree Cl. DE24: Sin 2E **185**
  NG9: Trow 3C **116**
Tishbite St. NG6: Bulw 5A **48**
Tissington Cl. NG7: H Grn 2F **97**
  NG9: Chil 2B **170**
Tissington Dr. DE21: Oak 2A **110**
Tissington Rd. NG7: H Grn 2F **97**
Titchfield Ct. NG15: Huck 3F **25**
Titchfield St. NG15: Huck 2A **26**
Titchfield Ter. NG15: Huck 2A **26**
Tithby Dr. NG5: Sher 3C **74**
Tithby Rd. NG13: Bing, Tith . . .3D **131**
Tithe Gdns. NG5: Top V 3F **49**
Tithe La. NG14: Calv 2E **31**
Tiverton Cl. DE3: Mick 4C **132**
  NG8: Aspl 5A **72**
  NG15: Huck 4C **24**
Tivoli Gdns. DE1: Der 1D **135**
Toad La. DE21: L Eat 5C **60**
  NG14: Epp 4F **33**
Tobermory Way DE24: Sin . . .3C **184**
Tobias Cl. NG5: Top V 4E **49**
Todd Cl. NG11: Clif 3B **172**
Todd Ct. NG11: Clif 3B **172**
Toft Cl. NG12: Cotg 1D **179**

Toft Rd. NG9: Chil 5F **145**
Token Ho. Yd. NG1: Nott 3C **4**
TOLLERTON 2C **176**
Tollerton Grn. NG6: Bulw 2C **72**
Tollerton La. NG12: Toll 3C **176**
Tollerton Pk. Cvn. Pk.
  NG12: Toll 2D **153**
Tollerton Rd. NG12: Toll 2C **152**
Tollhouse Hill
  NG1: Nott 2A **4** (5A **98**)
Tom Blower Cl. NG8: Woll 5F **95**
Tomlinson Ct. DE24: Alv 4E **161**
Tomlinson Ind. Est.
  DE21: Der 3B **108**
Tonbridge Dr. DE24: Alv 1F **187**
Tonbridge Mt. NG8: Woll 3C **118**
Ton La. NG14: Lowd 2C **56**
Tonnelier Rd. NG7: Lent 4D **121**
Top Farm Ct. DE56: Kil 4E **37**
Topley Gdns. DE21: Chad 3E **109**
Topliff Rd. NG9: Chil 1B **170**
Top Mnr. Cl. DE72: Ock 3B **140**
Top Rd. NG11: Rudd 5B **174**
Top Row NG14: Sto B 3C **102**
TOP VALLEY 4D **49**
Top Valley Dr. NG5: Top V 4F **49**
Top Valley Way NG5: Top V . . .5D **49**
Torbay Cres. NG5: Bestw 1A **74**
Top Valley Cl. NG5: Top V 4E **49**
Torridon Cl. DE24: Sin 2D **185**
Torrington Ct. NG5: Sher 5C **74**
Torvill Dr. NG8: Woll 5D **95**
Torvill Hgts. NG8: Woll 5D **95**
Toston Dr. NG8: Woll 1B **120**
Totland Dr. NG8: Basf 5C **72**
Totland Rd. NG9: Bram 3B **118**
Totley Cl. NG6: Bulw 2B **48**
Totnes Cl. NG15: Huck 3C **24**
Totnes Rd. NG3: Nott 5A **100**
TOTON 1F **169**
Toton Cl. NG6: Bulw 2C **72**
Toton La. NG9: Stap 1C **144**
Tottle Gdns. NG7: Radf 4C **96**
Tottle Rd. NG2: Nott 5F **121**
Touchstone Ct. DE73: Chel . . .4C **186**
Tourist Info. Cen.
  Derby 2D **7** (3F **135**)
  Nottingham 3C **4** (1B **122**)
  Ripley 4C **8**
  Trowell Service Area 4D **93**
Tower Cres. NG16: Kimb 3F **69**
Tower St. DE24: Der 4C **160**
Tower's Mt. NG4: Carl 3D **101**
Towle Cl. DE72: Bor 2A **164**
Towles Pastures
  DE74: C Don 1F **211**
Towle St. NG10: Long E 2F **193**
Towlson Ct. NG9: Chil 5C **146**
Towlsons Cft. NG6: Basf 4C **72**
Town, The DE21: L Eat 3B **84**
Town End Cotts.
  NG12: Plum 4D **177**
Town End Rd. DE72: Dray 4A **166**
Townsend Ct. NG5: Top V 3F **49**
Townsend Gro. DE73: Chel 4F **187**
Townside Cl. NG10: Long E . . .2A **194**
Town St. DE56: Duff 4D **59**
  DE56: H'ook 1B **60**
  NG9: Bram 5A **118**
  NG10: Sand 3A **144**
Town Vw. NG16: Kimb 5E **45**
Towson Av. NG16: Lang M 2B **42**
Towyn Ct. NG5: Bestw 5F **49**
Tracy Cl. NG9: Bram 4D **119**

Trafalgar Cl. NG7: Radf 4E **97**
Trafalgar Rd. NG9: Bee 4F **147**
  NG10: Long E 5C **168**
Trafalgar Sq. NG10: Long E . . .4E **169**
Trafalgar Ter.
  NG10: Long E 4D **169**
Traffic St. DE1: Der 4E **7** (4A **136**)
  NG2: Nott 2B **122**
Trafford Gdns. NG8: Aspl 3C **96**
Trafford Way DE23: Lit 3B **158**
Tranby Gdns. NG8: Woll 1E **119**
Travers Rd. NG10: Sand 2F **143**
Tredegar Dr. DE21: Oak 3A **110**
Treegarth Sq. NG5: Top V 3A **50**
Tree Vw. Cl. NG5: Arn 3B **50**
Trefan Gdns. NG5: Bestw 5F **49**
Trefoil Cl. NG13: Bing 3C **130**
Trefoil Ct. DE23: Lit 4F **157**
Tregaron Cl. DE21: Oak 3B **110**
Tregoning Gallery 1C **6**
Tregony Way DE24: S Flds . . .3C **184**
Trelawn Cl. NG5: Sher 5C **74**
Tremadoc Ct. NG5: Sher 2A **98**
Tremayne Rd. NG8: Bilb 4B **94**
Trent Av. NG11: Rudd 3B **174**
Trent Blvd. NG2: West Br 4E **123**
Trent Bridge 4D **123**
Trent Bri.
  NG2: Nott, West Br 4D **123**
Trent Bri. Bldgs.
  NG2: West Br 4D **123**
Trent Bri. Ct. DE23: Lit 3B **158**
Trent Bus. Cen.
  NG10: Long E 1B **168**
Trent Cl. DE24: S Flds 4C **184**
Trent Cotts. NG10: Long E 5E **169**
Trent Ct. NG2: West Br 4F **123**
Trent Cres. NG9: Atten 5D **147**
Trentdale Rd. NG4: Carl 4C **100**
Trent Dr. DE23: Lit 5C **158**
  NG15: Huck 1C **46**
Trent Gdns. NG14: Bur J 3F **79**
Trentham Dr. NG8: Aspl 3B **96**
Trentham Gdns.
  NG8: Aspl 3B **96**
  NG14: Bur J 4C **78**
Trent Ho. NG10: Long E 2F **193**
Trent La. DE72: W Tre 5D **203**
  DE74: C Don 4F **205**
  NG2: Nott 2E **123**
  NG10: Long E 2D **195**
  NG13: East B 3F **81**
  NG14: Bur J 3E **79**
  NG14: Gun 3E **81**
Trent La. Ind. Est.
  DE74: C Don 4A **206**
TRENTLOCK 3D **195**
Trenton Cl. NG9: Bram 4F **117**
Trenton Dr. DE21: Chad 2A **138**
  NG10: Long E 3F **169**
Trenton Grn. DE21: Chad 2A **138**
Trent Ri. DE21: Spon 4E **139**
Trent Rd. DE7: Kirk H 1C **114**
  NG2: Nott 1E **123**
  NG9: Bee 4F **147**
Trentside DE73: Swar 3C **200**
  NG2: West Br 5D **123**
  *NG9: Bee 5F **147***
  (off Riverside)
  NG14: Gun 3F **81**
Trentside Nth.
  NG2: West Br 4D **123**
Trent Sth. Ind. Pk.
  NG2: Nott 2F **123**

Trent St. DE24: Alv 4F 161
  NG2: Nott 5D 5 (2C 122)
  NG10: Long E 3D 169
Trent Va. Rd. NG9: Bee 4F 147
Trent Valley Sailing Club
  . . . . .3D 195 & 2F 195
Trent Valley Vw. NG3: Mapp . . .1F 99
Trentview Ct. NG2: Nott 3E 123
Trent Vw. Gdns.
  NG12: Rad T 5F 103
Tresillian Cl. DE22: D Abb . . .3D 107
Tressall Cl. DE7: Ilk 2F 91
Trevelyan Rd.
  NG2: West Br 4E 123
Treveris Cl. DE21: Spon 4E 139
Trevino Gdns. NG5: Top V 3F 49
Trevone Av. NG9: Stap 2D 145
Trevone Ct. DE24: Alv 1B 188
Trevor Rd. NG2: West Br 2F 151
  NG9: Bee 3E 147
Trevose Gdns. NG5: Sher 4C 74
Treyford Cl. NG11: Wilf 4F 149
Triangle, The DE7: Ilk 4F 91
  (not continuous)
  DE56: Bel 5D 13
  NG2: Nott 3F 121
Tricornia Dr. NG6: Cin 3A 72
Tring Va. NG5: Sher 3F 73
Trinity Av. NG7: Lent 2D 121
Trinity Cl. DE7: Ilk 4D 67
Trinity Cres. NG4: Lamb 5B 54
Trinity Row NG1: Nott . . .2B 4 (5B 98)
Trinity Sq. NG1: Nott . . .2C 4 (5B 98)
  (not continuous)
Trinity St. DE1: Der . . .5F 7 (4A 136)
Trinity Vw. NG10: Long E 3D 169
Trinity Wlk.
  NG1: Nott 2C 4 (5B 98)
Trinity Way DE75: Hea 4D 41
Trinstead Way NG5: Bestw . . .5B 50
Triumph Rd. NG7: Lent 1C 120
Trivett Sq. NG1: Nott 4E 5
Trocadero Ct. DE1: Der 5F 135
Troon Cl. DE23: Lit 3F 157
  NG16: Kimb 5D 45
Trough La. NG16: Want 4E 45
Trough Rd. NG16: Want 4E 45
Troutbeck NG12: Cotg 5F 155
Troutbeck Cres. NG9: Bram . .5B 118
Troutbeck Gro. DE23: Lit 4F 157
Trowbridge Cl. DE21: Oak 3D 109
TROWELL 1B 116
Trowell Av. DE7: Ilk 5F 91
  NG8: Woll 5A 94
Trowell Gdns. NG8: Bilb 5B 94
Trowell Gro. NG9: Trow 2C 116
  NG10: Long E 1A 168
TROWELL MOOR 5A 94
Trowell Pk. Dr. NG9: Trow . . .3C 116
Trowell Rd. NG8: Woll 1A 118
  NG9: Stap 3D 117
TROWELL SERVICE AREA 4D 93
Trowels La. DE22: Der 4B 134
Trueman Gdns. NG5: Arn 1A 76
Trueman St. DE7: Ilk 3E 67
Truman Cl. NG3: Nott . . .1D 5 (4C 98)
Truman Dr. NG15: Huck 3F 25
Trumans Rd. NG2: Nott 4C 122
Truman St. NG16: Kimb 5C 44
Truro Cres. DE21: Chad 5D 109
  NG7: Radf 3D 97
Trusley Gdns. DE23: Lit 1C 184
Tudor Cl. NG4: Colw 5D 101
  NG10: Long E 2D 169

Tudor Ct. DE72: Dray 2D 165
  NG9: Stap 3C 144
  NG15: Huck 4B 24
Tudor Falls DE75: Hea 1D 41
Tudor Fld. Cl. DE73: Chel 5F 187
Tudor Gro. NG1: Nott 3A 98
Tudor Rd. DE21: Chad 2F 137
  NG2: West Br 1E 151
Tudor Sq. NG2: West Br 1E 151
Tudwal Cl. NG5: Bestw 5F 49
Tudwal Wlk. NG5: Bestw 5F 49
Tudwell Gdns. DE22: Mac 1A 134
Tulip Av. NG3: Nott 3C 98
Tulip Rd. NG16: Aws 2A 68
Tulla Cl. DE24: S Flds 4D 185
Tumbling Hill DE56: H'age 1D 15
Tunnel Rd. NG7: Nott 1F 121
Tunstall Cres. NG8: Aspl 1F 95
Tunstall Dr. NG5: Sher 3E 73
Tunstall Rd. NG5: Woodt 3E 75
Tuphall Rd. DE73: Chel 4A 188
Turnberry Cl. DE7: Ilk 5B 66
  NG9: Bram 2B 146
Turnberry Ct. NG12: Edwal . . .5B 152
Turnberry Rd. NG6: Bulw 1C 72
Turner Av. NG16: Lang M 1F 41
Turner Cl. NG5: Sher 2A 74
  NG9: Stap 2D 145
Turner Dr. NG16: Gilt 5A 44
Turner Rd. NG10: Long E 2B 194
Turner's Almshouses
  DE22: Der 2C 134
Turner St. DE24: A'ton 5D 161
  NG15: Huck 2F 25
Turneys Ct. NG2: Nott 4D 123
Turney St. NG2: Nott 4C 122
Turnoak Av. DE7: Ilk 2E 67
Turnpike La. NG9: Bee 5F 119
Turnpike Village NG9: Bee 5F 119
Turnstone Wharf NG7: Lent . . .3E 121
Turpin Av. NG4: Ged 4C 76
Turton Cl. NG16: Lang M 1F 41
Turton Dr. NG5: Arn 5D 51
Tuxford Cl. DE21: Oak 4A 110
Tuxford Wlk. NG3: Nott 4E 99
Tweedsmuir Cl. DE21: Oak . . .3E 109
Twells Cl. NG3: Nott 1A 98
Twelve Houses
  DE7: Stan D 2D 115
Twickenham Dr. DE22: Mac . . .2F 133
Twin Oaks Cl. DE23: Lit 4E 157
Twitchell, The NG9: Chil 4D 147
Twycross Rd. NG5: Bestw 5A 50
Twyford Cl. DE7: West H 2C 88
  DE75: Hea 4B 40
Twyford Gdns. NG11: Clif 4D 149
Twyford Rd. DE73: Bar T 3A 200
  NG10: Long E 2E 193
Twyford St. DE23: Der 5F 135
Tyburn Cl. NG5: Arn 3F 49
Tynedale Chase
  DE24: S Flds 4B 184
Tynedale Cl. NG8: Aspl 1C 96
  NG10: Long E 5F 167
Tynefield Cl. DE65: Etw 4A 180
Tynefield M. DE65: Etw 4A 180
Tyne Gdns. NG15: Huck 1C 46

U

Uffa Magna DE3: Mick 2C 156
Ulldale Ct. NG9: Chil 4A 146

Ullscarf Cl. NG2: West Br 3B 152
Ullswater Cl. DE21: Chad 3C 108
  NG2: Gam 2C 152
  NG4: Ged 5E 77
Ullswater Cres. NG9: Bram . .4B 118
Ullswater Dr. DE21: Spon 2D 139
  NG15: Huck 2E 25
Underhill Av. DE23: Der 4E 159
Underhill Cl. DE23: Der 5D 159
Underpass, The
  DE1: Der 1E 7 (2A 136)
Union Ct. NG15: Lin 4C 10
Union Rd. DE7: Ilk 3D 91
  NG1: Nott 1C 4 (5B 98)
  NG3: Nott 1D 5 (5C 98)
Union St. NG9: Bee 2E 147
  NG10: Long E 3D 169
  NG13: Bing 2D 131
Unity Cres. NG3: Mapp 5B 76
University Blvd. NG7: Nott . . .5A 120
  NG9: Bee 5A 120
University of Derby
  Britannia Mill Campus
  .2D 135
  Green Lane Campus 4C 6
  Kedleston Road Campus
  .5C 106
University of Nottingham
  Jubilee Campus 1C 120
University of Nottingham, The
  University Pk. 3B 120
University of Nottingham
  School of Agriculture . . .3F 215
University Pk. NG7: Nott 4A 120
Upchurch Cl. DE3: Mick 5B 132
Uplands Av. DE23: Lit 5B 158
Uplands Cl. NG8: Woll 4E 95
Uplands Gdns. DE23: Der 1D 159
Upminster Dr. NG5: Arn 3E 51
  NG16: Nuth 3C 70
Up. Bainbrigge St.
  DE23: Der 1E 159
Up. Barn Cl. DE75: Hea 2E 41
Up. Boundary Rd.
  DE22: Der 4D 135
Upper Canaan NG11: Rudd . . .3C 174
Up. College St.
  NG1: Nott 2A 4 (5A 98)
Up. Dale Rd. DE23: Der 2E 159
Up. Dunstead Rd.
  NG16: Lang M 1A 42
Up. Eldon St.
  NG2: Nott 3F 5 (1D 123)
Up. Hall Cl. DE56: H'ook 1B 60
UPPER HARTSHAY 5A 8
Upper Hollow DE23: Lit 2B 158
Up. Marehay Rd.
  DE5: Mare 3B 16
Up. Moor Rd. DE24: A'ton 5D 161
Up. Orchard St. NG9: Stap . . .1D 145
Up. Parliament St
  NG1: Nott 2A 4 (5A 98)
UPPER SAXONDALE 2D 129
Up. Wellington St
  NG10: Long E 2B 168
Uppingham Cres.
  NG2: West Br 3C 150
Uppingham Gdns.
  NG2: Nott 3C 122
Upton Cl. DE74: C Don 5A 206
  DE75: Hea 3F 41
Upton Dr. NG5: Sher 2C 74
Upton M. NG3: Nott 2A 100
Utile Gdns. NG6: Bulw 5F 47

Uttoxeter New Rd.
DE22: Der 3A **6** (5A **134**)
Uttoxeter Old Rd. DE1: Der . . .4C **134**
Uttoxeter Rd. DE3: Mick . . .2C **156**

Vale, The DE7: Ilk 4D **67**
Valebrook Rd. NG5: Sher 2B **74**
Vale Cl. NG16: Eastw 2A **44**
Vale Cres. Nth. NG8: Aspl 4C **96**
Vale Cres. Sth. NG8: Aspl 4C **96**
Vale Gdns. NG4: Colw 5C **100**
Vale Mills DE22: Der 5E **135**
Valerian Way NG13: Bing 2B **130**
Valerie Rd. DE72: Ast T 2E **203**
Vale Rd. NG4: Colw 5D **101**
Valeside Gdns.
NG4: Colw 5D **101**
Valetta Rd. NG5: Arn 5A **52**
Valley Ct. NG4: Carl 1A **100**
NG5: Sher 2C **74**
Valley Dr. NG16: Newth 2A **44**
Valley Farm Ct. NG5: Top V . . .4F **49**
Valley Gdns.
NG2: West Br 3B **152**
Valley Rd. DE7: Kirk H 5D **91**
DE21: Chad 2A **138**
DE23: Lit 2C **158**
NG2: West Br 3F **151**
NG4: Carl 1A **100**
(not continuous)
NG5: Basf, Sher 5E **73**
NG9: Chil 3F **145**
NG12: Rad T 5F **103**
NG16: Kimb 5C **44**
Valley Vw. DE7: Kirk H 5D **91**
DE56: Bel 2F **35**
Valley Vw. Dr. DE7: Stan C 1A **88**
Valmont Rd. NG5: Sher 4F **73**
NG9: Bram 5F **117**
Vancouver Av.
DE21: Spon 5C **138**
NG12: Rad T 3D **127**
Vanguard Rd. DE74: N Air 4F **211**
NG10: Long E 1C **194**
Vantage, The NG7: H Grn 2A **98**
Varden Av. NG9: Lent A 4F **119**
Varley St. DE24: Der 4C **160**
Varney Rd. NG11: Clif 5E **149**
Vaughan Av. NG15: Huck 5E **11**
Vaughan Rd. NG9: Chil 4F **145**
Vauxhall Av. DE22: Mac 1F **133**
Vedonis Pk. NG15: Huck 4F **25**
Venn Ct. NG9: Bee 2E **147**
Ventnor Ho. DE24: Alv 4B **162**
Ventnor Ri. NG5: Sher 3E **73**
Ventura Dr. NG6: Bulw 3B **48**
Venus Cl. NG6: Basf 2D **73**
Verbena Cl. NG3: Nott 3C **98**
Verbena Dr. DE23: Lit 2C **184**
Verder Gro. NG5: Top V 4D **49**
Vere St. NG6: Bulw 5A **48**
Vermont Dr. DE21: Chad 2B **138**
Verne Cl. NG4: Carl 3B **100**
Vernon Av. NG4: Carl 2E **101**
NG6: Basf 4D **73**
NG9: Bee 2E **147**
NG11: Wilf 5A **122**
Vernon Ct. NG12: Rad T 2E **127**
NG16: Nuth 4E **71**
Vernon Dr. DE21: Spon 4E **139**
NG16: Nuth 4E **71**

Vernon Ga. DE1: Der 3D **135**
(not continuous)
Vernon Pk. Dr. NG6: Basf 4D **73**
Vernon Pl. NG6: Basf 3C **72**
Vernon Rd. NG6: Basf 3C **72**
Vernon St.
DE1: Der 2A **6** (3D **135**)
DE7: Ilk 3E **67**
NG1: Nott 2A **4** (5A **98**)
Verona Av. NG4: Colw 4E **101**
Verona Way DE73: Chel 4D **187**
Veronica Dr. NG4: Carl 1C **100**
NG16: Gilt 4B **44**
Veronica Wlk. NG11: Clif 2B **172**
Versailles Gdns.
NG15: Huck 4F **25**
Vestry Rd. DE21: Oak 3D **109**
Vetchfield Cl. DE24: Sin 4E **185**
Vicarage Av. DE7: Ilk 3C **66**
DE23: Der 1D **159**
Vicarage Cl. DE7: Smal 1E **63**
DE56: Bel 5F **13**
NG5: Sher 4E **73**
Vicarage Ct. DE3: Mick 2C **156**
Vicarage Dr. DE21: Chad 1F **137**
NG14: Bur J 3D **79**
Vicarage Gdns. DE75: Hea 3E **41**
Vicarage Grn.
NG12: Edwal 5A **152**
Vicarage La. DE21: L Eat 2A **84**
DE56: Duff 3D **59**
NG11: Rudd 4B **174**
NG12: Rad T 2D **127**
Vicarage Rd. DE3: Mick 1B **156**
DE56: Mil 4E **35**
DE73: Chel 4E **187**
Vicarage St. DE7: Ilk 3C **66**
NG9: Bee 2D **147**
Vicarwood Av.
DE22: D Abb 4E **107**
DE56: H'ook 5B **36**
Vickers St. NG3: Mapp P 2C **98**
Vickery Way NG9: Chil 1A **170**
Victor, The NG7: Lent 3D **121**
(off Leen Ct.)
Victor Av. DE22: Der 5E **107**
Victor Cres. NG10: Sand 4B **144**
Victoria Av. DE72: Bor, Ock . . .1A **164**
DE72: Dray 4F **165**
DE75: Hea 3C **40**
NG2: Nott 1E **123**
NG14: Lowd 4D **57**
(not continuous)
Victoria Bus. Pk.
NG4: Neth 4A **102**
Victoria Cen.
NG1: Nott 1C **4** (5B **98**)
Victoria Cen. Sth. NG1: Nott 2C **4**
(off Clinton St. E.)
Victoria Cl. DE3: Mick 4D **133**
NG5: Arn 2E **51**
Victoria Ct. DE7: Ilk 1D **91**
NG10: Long E 3D **169**
Victoria Cres. NG5: Sher 5C **74**
Victoria Emb. NG2: Nott 4B **122**
Victoria Gdns.
NG16: Want 3F **45**
Victoria Gro. NG15: Lin 4D **11**
Victoria Hall NG3: Nott 1D **5**
Victoria Leisure Cen. . .2E **5** (5C **98**)
Victoria Mkt.
NG1: Nott 2C **4** (5B **98**)
Victoria Mill DE72: Dray 4A **166**
Victoria Pk. Leisure Cen. 1D **91**

Victoria Pk. Way
NG4: Neth 4A **102**
Victoria Rd. DE5: Rip 4C **8**
DE72: Dray 4F **165**
NG2: West Br 1D **151**
NG4: Neth 3E **101**
NG5: Sher 4A **74**
NG10: Sand 3A **144**
NG11: Bunny 5D **197**
NG13: Bing 1F **131**
Victoria St. DE1: Der . . .3C **6** (3F **135**)
DE5: Rip 4E **9**
DE7: Ilk 4E **67**
DE74: C Don 4A **206**
NG1: Nott 3C **4** (1B **122**)
NG4: Ged 1E **101**
NG9: Stap 1C **144**
NG10: Long E 1A **194**
NG12: Rad T 2E **127**
NG15: Huck 1E **25**
NG16: Eastw 1E **43**
NG16: Kimb 1F **69**
NG16: Lang M 1B **42**
Victoria Ter.
NG2: Nott 3F **5** (1D **123**)
Victoria Way DE24: Der 5D **137**
Victor Ter. NG5: Sher 5B **74**
Victory Av. DE5: Rip 5E **9**
Victory Cl. NG10: Long E 1C **194**
Victory Rd. DE24: Der 4A **160**
NG9: Bee 4F **147**
View, The NG9: Bram 1A **146**
Village, The DE7: D Ab 3E **113**
DE7: West H 3C **88**
Village Cl. NG12: Edwal 5A **152**
Village Ct. DE56: Duff 4E **59**
Village Rd. NG11: Clif 1B **172**
Village St. DE23: Der 3D **159**
NG12: Edwal 5F **151**
Villa Rd. NG3: Mapp P 3B **98**
NG12: Key 2E **199**
Villa St. DE72: Dray 4A **166**
NG9: Bee 1E **147**
Villiers Rd. NG2: West Br 2F **151**
NG5: Woodt 3C **74**
Vincent Av. DE7: Ilk 2E **91**
DE21: Spon 5D **139**
NG9: Bee 3E **147**
Vincent Cl. DE56: Kil 4F **37**
Vincent Gdns. NG7: H Grn 3D **97**
Vincent St. DE23: Der 2E **159**
Vine Cl. DE23: Lit 4A **158**
Vine Cres. NG10: Sand 2A **144**
Vine Farm Cl. DE7: Kirk H 4C **90**
NG12: Cotg 5D **155**
Vines Cross NG8: Woll 3D **119**
Vine Ter. NG15: Huck 2A **26**
Viola Cl. DE21: Oak 2B **110**
Violet Av. NG16: Newth 4A **44**
Violet Cl. NG6: Basf 4C **72**
Violet Gro. NG15: Huck 2B **26**
Violet Rd. NG2: West Br 5F **123**
NG4: Carl 5C **76**
Violet St. DE23: Der 2E **159**
Virgin Active 2B **136**
Viscount Rd. DE74: N Air 5A **212**
Vision Bus. Cen. NG6: Bulw . . .3F **47**
Vista, The NG9: Stap 3D **145**
Vivian Av. NG5: Sher 2A **98**
Vivian Ct. NG5: Sher 2A **98**
Vivian St. DE1: Der 5A **108**
Viyella Gdns. NG15: Huck 4F **25**
Viyella M. NG15: Huck 3F **25**
Voce Gdns. NG15: Huck 3B **26**

Vulcan Cl. NG6: Basf 3D **73**
Vulcan St. DE23: Der 2A **160**
Vyse Dr. NG10: Long E 5A **168**

W

Waddington Dr.
　NG2: West Br 4C **150**
Wade Av. DE7: Ilk 3F **91**
　DE23: Lit 1B **158**
Wadebridge Gro. DE24: Alv . . .1B **188**
Wade Dr. DE3: Mick 1D **157**
Wades Av. NG7: H Grn 2D **97**
Wade St. DE23: Lit 2B **158**
Wades Way NG13: Bing 3F **131**
Wadham Rd. NG5: Woodt 2D **75**
Wadhurst Gdns. NG3: Nott 4C **98**
Wadhurst Gro. NG8: Woll 3C **118**
Wadsworth Rd. NG9: Stap 5E **117**
Wagtail Cl. DE24: Sin 2C **184**
Wainfleet Cl. DE7: Ilk 4B **66**
Wainfleet Cl. NG5: Arn 2F **51**
Waingrove NG11: Wilf 5F **149**
WAINGROVES 2F **17**
Waingroves Rd. DE5: Cod 3A **18**
　DE5: Rip 1E **17**
Wakami Cres. DE73: Chel 3F **187**
Wakefield Av. NG12: Rad T . . .1F **127**
Wakefield Ct. DE74: C Don . . .5B **206**
Wakefield Cft. DE7: Ilk 4B **66**
Wakelyn Cl. DE72: Shar 5E **191**
Walbrook Cl. NG8: Cin 4F **71**
Walbrook Rd. DE23: Der 2E **159**
Walcote Cl. DE56: Bel 4B **14**
Walcote Dr. NG2: West Br 4B **150**
Walcott Grn. NG11: Clif 2C **172**
Waldeck Rd. NG5: Sher 1A **98**
Waldemar Gro. NG9: Bee 2F **147**
Waldene Dr. DE24: Alv 5F **161**
　(not continuous)
Waldorf Av. DE24: Alv 4F **161**
Waldorf Cl. DE24: Alv 4F **161**
Waldron Cl. NG2: Nott 3C **122**
Walesby Cres. NG8: Aspl 4B **96**
Walgrave Cl. DE56: Bel 3A **14**
Walgrave Wlk. NG5: Bestw 5A **50**
Walk, The DE23: Der 1D **185**
　DE56: Kil 4A **38**
Walk Cl. DE72: Dray 4F **165**
Walker Av. DE5: Rip 4D **9**
Walker Bldgs. DE73: Chel 5F **187**
Walker Cl. DE7: Ilk 1F **115**
Walker Gro. NG9: Stap 2D **145**
Walker La. DE1: Der 1B **6** (2E **135**)
Walkers Cl. NG13: Bing 2D **131**
Walker St. NG2: Nott . . .2F **5** (5D **99**)
　NG16: Eastw 2F **43**
Walker's Yd. NG12: Rad T 2E **127**
Walk Mill Dr. NG15: Huck 5D **11**
Wallace Av. NG4: Carl 3E **101**
　NG7: Radf 4E **97**
Wallace Gdns. NG9: Toton 1E **169**
Wallace St. DE22: Der 3B **134**
Wallan St. NG7: Radf 4D **97**
Wallet St. NG2: Nott 3C **122**
　NG4: Neth 3F **101**
Wallett Av. NG9: Bee 5E **119**
Wallfields Cl. DE65: Find 3C **182**
Wallis Cl. DE72: Dray 4F **165**
Wallis St. NG6: Basf 3D **73**
Wallsend Cl. DE7: Ilk 3E **67**
Wall St. DE5: Rip 4C **8**
Walnut Av. DE24: Alv 4A **162**

Walnut Cl. DE7: Ilk 3F **91**
　DE65: Burn 1E **181**
　DE72: Ast T 1A **204**
　DE73: Chel 1E **201**
　NG2: West Br 4B **124**
Walnut Dr. NG9: Bram 5A **118**
Walnut Gro. NG12: Cotg 5E **155**
　NG12: Rad T 2E **127**
　NG14: Calv 1E **31**
Walnut Rd. DE56: Bel 1A **36**
Walnut St. DE24: Der 4B **160**
Walnut Tree Gdns.
　NG6: Bulw 5E **47**
Walpole St. DE21: Chad 2C **136**
Walsham Cl. NG9: Chil 1B **170**
Walsham Ct. DE21: Chad 4C **108**
Walsingham Rd.
　NG5: Woodt 2F **75**
Walters Av. NG16: Brins 3D **21**
Walter St. DE1: Der 1D **135**
　DE72: Dray 3E **165**
　NG7: Radf 4F **97**
Waltham Av. DE24: Sin 2E **185**
Waltham Cl. NG2: West Br . . .2A **152**
Walthamstow Dr.
　DE22: Mac 2A **134**
Walton Av. DE24: A'ton 2D **187**
　NG3: Nott 5E **99**
Walton Cl. DE7: West H 2C **88**
　DE74: Keg 1B **214**
　NG4: Carl 3D **101**
　　(not continuous)
　NG12: Key 3E **199**
Walton Cres. NG4: Carl 3D **101**
Walton Dr. DE23: Der 4D **159**
　NG12: Key 3E **199**
Walton Hill DE74: C Don 5F **205**
　DE74: I Wal 5C **210**
Walton M. NG3: Nott 3E **99**
Walton Rd. DE21: Chad 3E **137**
　NG5: Arn 3F **51**
Walton St. NG10: Long E 3C **168**
Wansbeck Cl. NG7: Radf 5F **97**
Wansfell Cl. DE3: Mick 2D **157**
Wanstead Av. NG5: Arn 2E **51**
Wanstead Way NG5: Top V . . .3D **49**
Warburton Ct. NG15: Huck 3A **26**
Ward Av. NG3: Mapp 4A **76**
　NG15: Huck 5B **10**
Wardle Gro. NG5: Arn 4F **51**
Wardlow Av. DE21: Chad 5F **109**
Wardlow Rd. DE7: Ilk 4D **67**
Ward's La. DE72: Brea 3C **166**
　DE73: S Bri 5F **201**
Ward St. DE22: Der 4A **6** (4D **135**)
　NG7: Basf 2E **97**
Wardwick DE1: Der 2C **6** (3F **135**)
Wareham Cl. NG2: West Br . . .3B **150**
　NG8: Cin 4F **71**
Warehouse, The NG1: Nott 4D **5**
Warke Flatt DE74: C Don 3A **206**
Warkton Cl. NG9: Chil 3B **146**
Warmwells La.
　DE5: Mare, Rip 2C **16**
Warner St. DE3: Mick 2C **156**
　DE22: Der 5E **135**
　NG7: Radf 5D **97**
Warren, The NG12: Cotg 1E **179**
Warren Av. NG5: Sher 5F **73**
　NG9: Stap 1C **144**
Warren Ct. NG9: Stap 1C **144**
Warrendale Ct. DE73: Chel . . .4F **187**
Warrender Cl. NG9: Bram 4B **118**
Warrener Gro. NG5: Top V 4D **49**

Warren Hill Cl. NG5: Arn 5B **50**
Warren La. DE74: Lock 3F **207**
　NG10: Long E 4F **193**
Warren Rd. NG15: Huck 4C **24**
Warren St. DE24: Alv 3E **161**
Warrington Rd. NG6: Bulw 5B **48**
Warser Ga.
　NG1: Nott 3D **5** (1C **122**)
Warsop Cl. NG8: Stre 5C **70**
Warton Av. NG3: Nott 2E **99**
Warwick Av. DE23: Der 2C **158**
　NG5: Woodt 2D **75**
　NG9: Bee 5E **119**
Warwick Dr. DE7: Ilk 4B **66**
Warwick Gdns. DE56: Bel 4C **14**
　NG12: Cotg 2E **179**
Warwick Rd. NG3: Mapp P 5C **74**
　NG10: Long E 4E **169**
Warwick St. DE24: Der 1C **160**
　NG7: Lent 3D **121**
Wasdale Cl. NG2: West Br 3B **152**
Washdyke La. NG15: Huck 5A **10**
Washington Av.
　DE21: Chad 1A **138**
　　(not continuous)
Washington Cotts.
　DE72: Bor 2B **164**
Washington Ct. NG5: Arn 5E **51**
Washington Dr. NG9: Stap 4E **117**
Wasnidge Cl.
　NG3: Nott 1E **5** (5C **98**)
Wasnidge Wlk. NG3: Nott 1E **5**
Watchwood Gro. NG14: Calv . . .1E **31**
Watcombe Cir. NG5: Sher 5A **74**
Watcombe Rd. NG5: Sher 1B **98**
Watendlath Cl.
　NG2: West Br 3B **152**
Waterdown Rd. NG11: Clif 2C **172**
Waterford Dr. DE21: Chad 4F **137**
Waterford St. NG6: Basf 4D **73**
Waterfront Plaza
　NG2: Nott 5E **5** (2C **122**)
Waterfurrows La.
　NG12: Shel 1C **104**
Watergo La. DE3: Mick 4C **156**
Waterhouse La. NG4: Ged 5F **77**
Watering La. DE56: H'ook 1C **60**
Water La. NG12: Rad T 2D **127**
　NG12: Shel 1B **104**
Waterloo Ct. DE1: Der 1A **136**
Waterloo Cres. NG7: Radf 4F **97**
Waterloo La. NG9: Trow 4D **93**
Waterloo Prom. NG7: Radf 4F **97**
　　(not continuous)
Waterloo Rd. NG7: Radf 4F **97**
　NG9: Bee 3F **147**
　NG15: Lin 4C **10**
Watermeadow Rd.
　DE24: Alv 1F **187**
Watermeadows, The
　DE73: Swar 3C **200**
　NG10: Long E 3F **167**
Watermint Cl. DE23: Lit 5A **158**
Water Orton Cl.
　NG9: Toton 5D **145**
Waters Edge NG11: Wilf 1A **150**
Waterside Cl. DE22: D Abb . . .3F **107**
　NG2: Gam 2B **152**
　NG10: Sand 5A **144**
Waterside Gdns. NG7: Lent . . .4D **121**
Waterside Retail Pk.
　DE7: Ilk 1F **91**
Waterway, The
　NG10: Sand 4B **144**

Waterway St. NG2: Nott 3C **122**
(Newthorpe St.)
NG2: Nott 3B **122**
(Wallet St.)
Waterway St. W. NG2: Nott . . .3B **122**
Watford Rd. NG8: Aspl 5A **72**
Watkinson St. DE75: Hea 2C **40**
Watkin St. NG3: Nott . . .1C **4** (4B **98**)
WATNALL 4F **45**
WATNALL CANTELUPE 5E **45**
WATNALL CHAWORTH 3F **45**
Watnall Rd. NG15: Huck 2C **46**
NG16: Nuth 1B **70**
Watnall Rd. Factory Units
NG15: Huck 4E **25**
Watson Av. DE75: Hea 2E **41**
NG3: Nott 4A **100**
Watson Gdns. DE1: Der 2E **135**
Watson Rd. DE7: Ilk 5B **66**
Watson St. DE1: Der 1D **135**
(not continuous)
Watten Cl. DE24: Sin 4E **185**
Waveney Cl. DE22: All 5A **84**
NG5: Arn 1F **75**
NG9: Bee 2F **147**
Waverley Av. NG4: Ged 1F **101**
NG9: Bee 2F **147**
Waverley Mt. NG7: Nott 4F **97**
Waverley St. DE24: Der 4C **160**
NG1: Nott 1A **4** (4F **97**)
NG7: Nott 4F **97**
NG10: Long E 3D **169**
Waverley Ter.
NG1: Nott 1A **4** (5A **98**)
Wayfaring Rd. DE21: Oak 4F **109**
Wayford Wlk. NG6: Bulw 4A **48**
Wayne Cl. NG11: Clif 2D **173**
Wayte Cl. NG11: Rudd 2D **175**
Wayzgoose Dr. DE21: Chad . .2B **136**
Weardale Rd. NG5: Sher 5F **73**
Wearmouth Gdns.
NG5: Top V 3F **49**
Weaver Row DE7: Ilk 2E **91**
Weavers Cl. DE56: Bel 4B **14**
DE72: Bor 2C **164**
Weavers Cft. DE5: Rip 1C **16**
Weavers Grn. DE3: Mick 2B **156**
Weaverthorpe Rd.
NG5: Woodt 2F **75**
Webb Rd. NG8: Bilb 3A **96**
Webb St. NG15: News 1A **10**
Webster Av. NG16: Eastw 3E **43**
Webster St.
DE1: Der 5B **6** (4E **135**)
Weedon Cl. NG3: Nott 4F **99**
Weekday Cross
NG1: Nott 4C **4** (1B **122**)
Weetman Gdns. NG5: Top V . .4F **49**
Weightman Dr. NG16: Gilt 5A **44**
Weirfield Rd. DE22: D Abb . . .3F **107**
Welbeck Av. DE7: Kirk H 5C **90**
NG4: Ged 5C **76**
Welbeck Cl. NG5: Woodt 3F **75**
Welbeck Gdns. NG5: Woodt . . .3F **75**
NG9: Toton 5E **145**
Welbeck Gro. DE22: All 2B **106**
NG13: Bing 2B **130**
Welbeck Rd. NG2: West Br . . .5D **123**
NG10: Long E 5A **144**
NG12: Rad T 1F **127**
Welbeck Wlk. NG3: Nott 4B **98**
Welby Av. NG7: Lent 1E **121**
Welch Av. NG9: Stap 5E **117**
Weldbank Cl. NG9: Chil 4A **146**
Welham Cres. NG5: Arn 5F **51**

Welland Cl. DE3: Mick 4C **132**
Welland Ct. NG3: Nott 4E **99**
Welldon St. DE5: Den 5F **17**
Wellesley Av. DE23: Der 4C **158**
Wellesley Cres. NG8: Stre 5C **70**
Wellin Cl. NG12: Edwal 5A **152**
Wellin Ct. NG12: Edwal 5A **152**
Wellington Cir.
NG1: Nott 3A **4** (1A **122**)
Wellington Ct. DE56: Bel 5E **13**
NG16: Eastw 2E **43**
Wellington Cres.
DE1: Der 5F **7** (4A **136**)
NG2: West Br 1E **151**
Wellington Pl. NG16: Eastw . .2E **43**
Wellington Rd. NG14: Bur J . .2F **79**
Wellington Sq. NG7: Nott 5F **97**
Wellington St.
DE1: Der 5F **7** (5A **136**)
DE5: Rip 5D **9**
DE75: Hea 2C **40**
NG3: Nott 4B **98**
NG9: Stap 2B **144**
NG10: Long E 5B **144**
NG16: Eastw 1E **43**
Wellington Ter. NG7: Radf 5F **97**
Wellington Vs. NG7: Lent 5F **97**
Wellin La. NG12: Edwal 5A **152**
Well La. DE56: Mil 5E **35**
Wells Ct. DE23: Lit 4E **157**
Wells Gdns. NG3: Nott 2E **99**
Wellspring Dale NG9: Stap . . .3D **145**
Wells Rd. DE3: Mick 1D **157**
Wells Rd., The
NG3: Mapp, Nott 5D **75**
Well St. DE1: Der 1F **135**
DE5: Rip 5C **8**
Well Yd. DE56: Bel 4F **13**
DE56: H'ook 1B **60**
Welney Cl. DE3: Mick 3C **156**
Welshpool Rd. DE21: Chad . .4C **108**
Welstead Av. NG8: Aspl 5F **71**
Welton Av. DE56: Bel 3A **14**
Welton Gdns. NG6: Bulw 4F **47**
Welwyn Av. DE22: All 2C **106**
DE24: S Loc 2D **187**
Welwyn Rd. NG8: Woll 5D **95**
Wembley Gdns. DE22: Mac . . .2F **133**
NG9: Bram 3A **118**
Wembley Rd. NG5: Arn 2A **76**
Wemyss Gdns. NG8: Woll 2C **120**
Wendling Gdns. NG5: Bestw . .5A **50**
Wendover Cl. DE3: Mick 2B **156**
Wendover Dr. NG8: Aspl 5A **72**
Wenlock Cl. DE3: Mick 2D **157**
NG16: Gilt 4B **44**
Wenlock Dr. NG2: West Br . . .3E **151**
Wensleydale Cl. NG8: Aspl 1C **96**
Wensleydale Rd.
NG10: Long E 5A **168**
Wensleydale Wlk.
DE24: Alv 4B **162**
Wensley Dr. DE21: Spon 5E **139**
Wensley Rd. NG5: Woodt 2D **75**
Wensor Av. NG9: Lent A 5E **119**
Wentworth Cl. DE3: Mick 2E **157**
Wentworth Cft. DE75: Hea 1F **41**
Wentworth Rd. NG5: Sher 5A **74**
NG9: Chil 2B **146**
Wentworth St. DE7: Ilk 5F **67**
Wentworth Way
NG12: Edwal 5A **152**
Werburgh Cl. DE21: Spon 4C **138**

Werburgh St.
DE22: Der 4A **6** (4E **135**)
Wesleyan Chapel Wlk.
NG9: Stap 1C **144**
Wesley Ct. NG5: Sher 5B **74**
(off Drayton St.)
Wesley Gro. NG5: Sher 1A **98**
Wesley La. DE72: Ock 3B **140**
Wesley Pl. NG9: Stap 5D **117**
Wesley Rd. DE24: Alv 1A **188**
Wesley St. DE7: Ilk 3D **67**
NG5: Sher 1A **98**
NG16: Lang M 1B **42**
Wesley Way NG11: Rudd 5C **174**
Wessex Dr. NG16: Gilt 4F **43**
Wessington M. DE22: All 4D **107**
West Av. DE1: Der 2E **135**
DE5: Rip 5B **8**
DE72: Dray 3E **165**
NG2: West Br 1D **151**
NG9: Stap 5D **117**
NG10: Sand 2F **143**
West Av. Nth. DE73: Chel 3D **187**
West Av. Sth. DE73: Chel 4D **187**
W. Bank Av. DE22: Der 5D **107**
W. Bank Cl. DE22: Der 5D **107**
W. Bank M. DE74: Keg 2B **214**
W. Bank Rd. DE22: All 5D **83**
Westbourne Ct. NG9: Bram . .4E **117**
Westbourne Pk.
DE22: Mac 2E **133**
WEST BRIDGFORD 2D **151**
Westbury Cl. NG9: Chil 4B **146**
Westbury Ct. DE22: Der 5D **135**
Westbury Gdns. DE56: Bel 4B **14**
Westbury Rd. NG5: Sher 5E **73**
Westbury St. DE22: Der 5C **134**
Westby La.
NG16: Babb, Coss 3B **68**
Westcliffe Av. NG4: Ged 4C **76**
NG12: Rad T 1F **127**
West Cl. DE72: Rad T 1F **127**
NG12: Key 4D **199**
West Cres. NG9: Bee 4A **148**
Westcroft Av. DE23: Lit 1C **184**
W. Cross Av. NG9: Stap 5D **117**
Westdale Cl. NG10: Long E . . .1F **193**
Westdale Ct. NG4: Carl 5C **76**
Westdale Cres. NG4: Carl 1D **101**
Westdale La. E. NG4: Carl 5B **76**
Westdale La. W. NG3: Mapp . .4F **75**
Westdene Av. DE24: A'ton 1C **186**
West Dr. DE3: Mick 1B **156**
NG7: Nott 5A **120**
West End NG9: Bee 3E **147**
NG14: Calv 1B **30**
West End Arc.
NG1: Nott 3A **4** (1A **122**)
West End Cres. DE7: Ilk 2C **90**
West End Dr. DE7: Ilk 2C **90**
DE72: Shar 5D **191**
West End St. NG9: Stap 2B **144**
West End Vs. NG12: Rad T 2D **127**
NG14: Lowd 1B **56**
Westerfield Way
NG11: Wilf 4F **149**
Westerham Cl. NG8: Bilb 3C **94**
Westerham Rd.
NG11: Rudd 5A **174**
Westerhope Cl.
NG12: Edwal 4B **152**
Westerlands NG9: Stap 3E **145**
Western Av. NG13: Bing 1C **130**

Western Blvd.
NG8: Aspl, Basf 2B **96**
Western Dr. DE75: Hea 4E **41**
Western Flds. NG11: Rudd 5A **174**
Western Gdns. NG8: Aspl 2C **96**
Western Rd. DE3: Mick 1C **156**
DE23: Der 5E **135**
Western St.
NG1: Nott 2D **5** (5C **98**)
Western Ter. NG7: Nott 1F **121**
Westfield Av. DE75: Hea 4E **41**
Westfield Cl. DE7: Kirk H 4B **90**
Westfield Dr. DE7: Ilk 5C **66**
Westfield Gro. DE22: Der 4C **134**
Westfield La.
NG14: Woodbo 5F **31**
Westfield Rd. NG13: Bing . . .2C **130**
Westfields Derby
DE1: Der 4E **7** (4A **136**)
West Furlong NG12: Cotg 1F **179**
West Ga. NG10: Long E 4D **169**
Westgate Ct. NG9: Chil 3D **147**
Westgate St. NG3: Nott 4D **99**
Westgreen Av. DE7: A'ton 1C **186**
West Gro. DE24: A'ton 1C **186**
WEST HALLAM 2C **88**
WEST HALLAM COMMON . . .1A **88**
Westhall Rd. DE3: Mick 5C **132**
Westhay Ct. NG8: Woll 5B **96**
West Hill DE5: Cod 2A **18**
Westholme Gdns. NG8: Aspl . . .4B **96**
Westhorpe Av. NG3: Nott 5E **99**
Westhorpe Dr.
NG10: Long E 3B **168**
Westland Av. NG15: Huck 5C **24**
West Lawn DE65: Find 4C **182**
Westleigh Av. DE22: Der 2B **134**
Westleigh Rd. NG8: Brox 5D **71**
Westley Cres. DE21: L East 5C **60**
Westmanor Ct. NG9: Chil 3C **146**
West Mdws. Ind. Est.
DE21: Der 2F **7** (3B **136**)
Westminster Av.
NG10: Sand 3B **144**
Westminster Cl. NG3: Nott . . .3D **99**
Westminster Dr.
NG12: Rad T 2C **128**
Westminster St. DE24: Alv . . .3E **161**
West Moor NG2: Colw 1C **124**
Westmoore Cl. NG3: Mapp . . .4A **76**
Westmoore Ct. NG3: Mapp . . .4A **76**
Westmoreland Ct.
NG5: Sher 1A **98**
Westmorland Cl.
DE21: Chad 2B **136**
Weston Av. NG7: Radf 4F **97**
Weston Cl. NG5: Woodt 3D **75**
Weston Cotts. NG7: Radf 4D **97**
Weston Ct. DE24: S Loc 3D **186**
DE72: W Tre 5D **203**
Weston Cres.
NG10: Long E 2E **193**
WESTON-ON-TRENT 4E **203**
Weston Pk. Av.
DE24: S Loc 3C **186**
Weston Pk. Gdns.
DE24: S Loc 3C **186**
Weston Ri. DE73: Chel 1E **201**
Weston Rd.
DE72: Ast T, W Tre 4E **203**
Weston Spot Cl. DE5: Rip 2C **16**
Weston St. DE75: Hea 4F **41**
Weston Ter. NG5: Sher 4B **74**
West Pk. Ct. NG10: Long E . . .4C **168**

West Pk. Leisure Cen. 4A **168**
West Pk. Rd. DE22: Der 5D **107**
Westpoint NG2: West Br 1C **150**
Westray Cl. NG9: Bram 2A **118**
West Rd. DE21: Spon 3C **138**
NG7: Nott 3C **120**
West Row DE22: D Abb 4F **107**
W. Service Rd. DE21: Spon . . .1F **161**
West St. DE7: Ilk 3D **91**
DE75: Hea 2C **40**
NG2: Nott 3F **5** (1D **123**)
NG5: Arn 5D **51**
NG12: Shel 1B **104**
NG15: Huck 2F **25**
NG16: Kimb 3F **69**
NG16: Lang M 1A **42**
West Ter. DE7: Ilk 1E **91**
DE56: Mil 4F **35**
NG15: Huck 2F **25**
West Vw. NG2: West Br 3C **150**
West Vw. Av. DE23: Lit 4A **158**
West Vw. Ct. NG15: Pap 3F **11**
Westview Cl. NG4: Carl 2E **101**
West Vw. Rd. NG4: Carl 2E **101**
WESTVILLE 5C **24**
Westville Cl. NG2: West Br . . .2D **151**
Westville Dr. NG15: Huck 1D **47**
Westville Gdns. NG3: Nott . . .3C **98**
West Wlk. NG2: Nott . . .3F **5** (1D **123**)
Westward Av. NG9: Bee 2F **147**
Westway NG12: Cotg 1E **179**
Westwick Rd. NG8: Bilb 4B **94**
Westwick St. DE7: Ilk 4F **91**
Westwood Dr. DE24: A'ton 1C **186**
Westwood Rd. NG2: Nott 1E **123**
Wetherby Cl. NG8: Aspl 1A **96**
NG16: Kimb 5D **45**
Wetherby Rd. DE24: Der 4C **160**
Wetherlam Cl. NG2: Nott 3B **122**
Weyacres DE72: Bor 2B **164**
Weybridge Cl. DE7: West H . . .2C **88**
Wharf, The DE72: Shar 5F **191**
(not continuous)
Wharfedale NG8: Woll 2A **118**
Wharfedale Cl. DE22: All 1A **118**
Wharfedale Rd.
NG10: Long E 5F **167**
Wharf La. NG12: Rad T 2D **127**
Wharf Rd. NG7: Nott . . .5A **4** (2A **122**)
Wharncliffe Rd. DE7: Ilk 2D **91**
Whateley Ct. DE23: Lit 4F **157**
Whatton Dr. NG2: West Br . . .5A **150**
Whatton Ri. NG5: Sher 3A **74**
Whatton Rd. DE74: Keg 3B **214**
Wheatacre Rd. NG11: Clif 2E **173**
Wheat Cl. NG8: Bilb 5C **94**
Wheatcroft Vw.
NG2: West Br 5B **150**
Wheatcroft Way DE21: Der . . .3B **108**
Wheatfields Rd. NG3: Nott . . .3F **99**
Wheatgrass Rd. NG9: Chil . . .3A **146**
Wheathill Gro. DE23: Lit 5F **157**
Wheatland Cl.
DE24: S Flds 4B **184**
Wheatley Cl. NG11: Rudd 1B **196**
Wheatley Dr. NG4: Carl 3B **100**
Wheatley Gro. NG9: Chil 4E **147**
Wheatsheaf Cl. DE21: Oak . . .3B **110**
Wheatsheaf Ct. NG14: Bur J . . .3E **79**
Wheeldale Cl. NG8: Woll 1A **118**
Wheeldon Av. DE22: Der 1D **135**
DE56: Bel 5A **14**
Wheeldon Cl. DE7: Ilk 1E **67**
Wheeldon Rd. NG7: Basf 1E **97**

Wheeldon Mnr. DE22: Der 5D **107**
Wheeler Av. NG16: Eastw 3A **44**
Wheeler Ga.
NG1: Nott 3B **4** (1B **122**)
Wheelwright Way
DE24: Der 5C **136**
Wheldon Av. NG4: Carl 5B **76**
Whenby Cl. DE3: Mick 1B **156**
Whernside Cl. DE24: Alv 5C **162**
Whernside Rd. NG5: Woodt . .2D **75**
Whetstone Cl. NG16: Nuth . . .5C **70**
Whickham Cl. NG2: Nott 4C **122**
Whilton Cl. DE56: Bel 5C **14**
Whilton Cres. DE7: West H . . .2C **88**
Whimsey Pk. NG4: Carl 4E **101**
Whinbush Av. DE24: A'ton 1D **187**
Whinfell Cl. NG11: Clif 1E **173**
Whinlatter Dr.
NG2: West Br 2B **152**
Whistlestop Cl. DE3: Mick . . .4C **132**
Whiston Cl. NG5: Bestw 1F **73**
Whiston St. DE23: Der 1F **159**
Whitaker Gdns. DE23: Der . . .1D **159**
Whitaker Rd. DE23: Der 1C **158**
Whitaker St. DE23: Der 1F **159**
Whitbread St. NG7: Basf 2E **97**
Whitburn Rd. NG9: Toton 5D **145**
Whitby Av. DE21: Chad 4B **108**
Whitby Cl. NG8: Woll 1A **118**
Whitby Cres. NG5: Woodt 2F **75**
Whitby Rd. NG16: Newth 1F **43**
Whitchurch Cl. NG5: Top V . . .4E **49**
Whitcliffe Gdns.
NG2: West Br 3E **151**
Whitcombe Gdns.
NG5: Top V 4F **49**
Whitcombe Pl. DE5: Rip 4C **8**
Whiteacre NG14: Bur J 2D **79**
Whitebeam Gdns.
NG6: Bulw 5E **47**
Whitechapel St. NG6: Basf . . .5C **72**
White City Trad. Est.
NG2: Nott 2F **123**
Whitecross Gdns. DE1: Der . . .1D **135**
Whitecross Ho. DE1: Der 2D **135**
Whitecross St. DE1: Der 2D **135**
White Furrows NG12: Cotg . . .1D **179**
White Gates DE5: Cod 1A **18**
Whitegate Va. NG11: Clif 2C **172**
Whitehall Cl. NG12: Rad T . . .2D **129**
White Hart Yd. DE56: Kil 4E **37**
Whitehaven Gro.
DE73: Chel 3F **187**
Whitehead Cl. DE7: Ilk 5C **66**
Whitehead Dr. NG16: Brins . . .1C **20**
Whitehouse Cl.
DE24: S Loc 3C **186**
Whitehouse Ri. DE56: Bol 3D **13**
Whitehurst St. DE24: A'ton . . .4C **160**
Whitelands NG12: Cotg 1F **179**
WHITELEY 2E **17**
Whiteley Rd. DE5: Rip 2E **17**
White Lion Sq. DE7: Ilk 3E **91**
White Lodge Gdns.
NG8: Bilb 3C **94**
Whitely Av. DE7: Ilk 2E **67**
Whitely Cl. NG9: Stap 5D **117**
WHITE MOOR 4C **14**
WHITEMOOR 2C **96**
Whitemoor Av. NG8: Aspl 2C **96**
NG8: Basf 2C **96**
Whitemoor Ct. NG8: Aspl 2C **96**
Whitemoor Ct. Ind. Est.
NG8: Aspl 2C **96**

Whitemoor Hall DE56: Bel 4C 14
Whitemoor La. DE56: Bel 5B 14
Whitemoor Rd. NG6: Basf 5C 72
Whitemoss Cl. NG8: Woll 2D 119
White Rd. NG5: Basf 4D 73
White's Av. NG3: Nott 4A 100
Whites Cft. NG14: Woodbo 5A 32
White St. DE22: Der 1D 135
Whiteway DE22: D Abb 3D 107
Whiteways Ct. NG11: Clif . . .2D 173
Whitewells La. DE56: Bel 1B 12
Whitfield Cl. NG11: Wilf 2A 150
Whiting Av. NG9: Toton 1E 169
Whitmore Rd. DE21: Chad 2E 137
Whitstable Cl. DE23: Der 4C 158
Whittaker La. DE71: E Lat 5C 60
DE56: Duff 5F 59
(not continuous)
Whittaker Rd. NG9: Chil 5F 145
Whitt Cl. DE72: Bor 2B 164
Whittier Rd. NG2: Nott 2F 123
Whittingham Ct. NG3: Mapp . . .4F 75
Whittingham Rd. NG3: Mapp . . .4F 75
Whittington St. DE24: A'ton . . .1C 186
Whittlebury Dr. DE23: Lit 4E 157
Whitton Cl. NG5: Top V 3A 50
NG9: Chil 1B 170
Whitwell Cl. DE7: Ilk 1D 67
NG8: Brox 1E 95
Whitwell Gdns. DE24: Alv 1B 188
Whitworth Dr. NG12: Rad T . . .3D 127
NG14: Bur J 5B 78
Whitworth Ri. NG5: Top V 4E 49
Whitworth Rd. DE7: Ilk 4E 91
Whyburn La. NG15: Huck 2B 24
Whyburn St. NG15: Huck 3B 26
Whysall Dr. NG10: Long E 4A 168
Whysall St. DE75: Hea 2D 41
Whyston Ct. NG15: Huck 4B 24
Whyteleafe Gro. DE21: Oak . . .4A 110
Wibberley Dr. NG11: Rudd . . .4A 174
Wichal Farm Cl. DE5: Rip 2C 16
Wichnor Cl. NG11: Clif 4D 149
Wickens Wlk. NG3: Nott 4D 99
Wickersley Cl.
DE22: D Abb 3E 107
Wicket Gro. NG7: Lent 1D 121
Wickets, The NG2: West Br . . .4E 123
Wickstead Cl. NG5: Woodt 4E 75
Wicksteed Cl. DE56: Bel 4C 14
Widdowson Cl. NG6: Bulw 4E 47
Widdowson Rd.
NG10: Long E 1A 194
Widdowson's Row
NG11: Rudd *4B 174*
(off Easthorpe St.)
Widdybank Cl. DE22: All 3B 106
Widecombe La. NG11: Clif . . .3C 172
Widmerpool La. NG12: Key . . .4F 199
WIGHAY 5B 10
Wighay Rd. NG15: Huck 5B 10
Wigley Cl. NG3: Nott 4D 99
Wigman Rd. NG8: Bilb 2C 94
Wigmore Cl. DE3: Mick 5B 132
Wigwam Gro. NG15: Huck 2B 26
Wigwam La. NG15: Huck 2B 26
Wilcock Ho. DE21: Chad 2B 136
Wilcocksons Yd.
NG15: Huck *2F 25*
(off Baker St.)
Wilden Cres. NG11: Clif 5D 149
Wilderbrook La. DE56: Shot . . .1A 12
Wilders Lea Ct. DE56: Bel 2F 35

Wildersley Rd. DE56: Bel 2F 35
Wildman St. NG7: Radf 4F 97
Wildsmith St. DE24: Alv 3F 161
Wild St. DE1: Der 3C 134
WILFORD 3F 149
Wilford Cres. NG11: Rudd 3B 174
Wilford Cres. E. NG2: Nott . . .4C 122
Wilford Cres. W. NG2: Nott . . .4B 122
Wilford Gro. NG2: Nott 3B 122
(not continuous)
WILFORD HILL 4D 151
Wilford Hill Crematorium
NG2: West Br 5C 150
Wilford La. NG2: West Br 2A 150
NG11: Wilf 2A 150
Wilford Rd. NG2: Nott 3A 122
(not continuous)
NG11: Rudd 5A 150
Wilford St.
NG2: Nott 5B 4 (2B 122)
Wilfred St. DE23: Der 1A 160
Wilfrid Gro. NG2: West Br 5D 151
Wilkins Dr. DE24: A'ton 4D 161
Wilkins Gdns. NG11: Clif 2B 172
Wilkinson Av. NG9: Bee 2E 147
Wilkinson Cl. NG9: Chil 1A 170
Wilkinson St. NG7: Basf 1C 96
NG8: Basf 1C 96
Wilkinson Street Stop (NET)
. . . . .2D 97
Willaston Cl. NG6: Cin 3B 72
Willbert Rd. NG5: Arn 4F 51
Willerby Rd. NG5: Woodt 2F 75
Willersley Dr. NG2: Nott 3B 122
Willesden Av. DE22: Mac 1F 133
Willesden Grn. NG16: Nuth . . .4C 70
Willetts Rd. DE21: Chad 1F 137
Willey La.
NG16: Newth, Unde 1F 21
William Av. NG16: Eastw 2E 43
William Bancroft Bldg.
NG3: Nott 1F 5
William Birk Flats DE5: Rip . . .5E 9
William Booth Birthplace Mus.
. . . . .3F 5 (1D 123)
William Booth Rd.
NG2: Nott 1F 123
William Cl. DE56: Duff 3C 58
NG4: Ged 2A 102
William Lee Bldgs.
NG7: Nott 5C 120
William Olds Ct. NG8: Woll . . .5F 95
William Rd. NG2: West Br . . .5D 123
NG9: Stap 1C 144
Williamson Gdns.
NG16: Lang M 2F 41
Williamson Row
NG5: Bestw *2F 73*
(off Arnold Rd.)
Williams Rd. NG9: Chil 5F 145
(not continuous)
William St. DE1: Der 2E 135
DE56: Bel 5E 13
NG10: Long E 1B 168
NG15: Huck 2F 25
Willington Rd. DE65: Etw 2A 180
DE65: Find 5C 182
Willn St. DE23: Der 2E 159
Willoughby Av. NG7: Lent 1E 121
NG10: Long E 1B 168
Willoughby Cl. DE72: Brea . . .3E 167
NG7: Nott 5A 120
Willoughby Ct. NG7: Lent 2E 121
Willoughby Hall NG7: Nott . . .5F 119

Willoughby Rd.
NG2: West Br 2E 151
Willoughby St. NG7: Lent 2E 121
NG9: Bee 1E 147
Willow Av. DE5: Rip 2C 16
NG4: Carl 2F 101
NG9: Stap 2C 144
NG10: Long E 2C 168
NG15: Huck 5C 24
Willow Brook NG12: Key 4F 199
Willowbrook Ct. NG2: Nott . .4B 122
Willowbrook Grange
DE73: Chel 5F 187
Willow Cl. DE7: Stan C 5F 63
DE22: D Abb 3E 107
DE72: Ast T 2A 204
NG2: West Br 4C 124
NG12: Rad T 3E 127
NG14: Bur J 2E 79
NG16: Lang M 1A 42
Willow Cotts. NG8: Bilb 3F 95
Willow Cl. DE5: Rip 5C 8
NG2: West Br 3C 150
Willow Cres. NG4: Ged 5F 77
NG4: Lamb 5A 54
Willow Cft. DE24: Alv 2B 188
Willowcroft Rd.
DE21: Spon 5C 138
Willowdene NG12: Cotg 5F 155
Willow Farm Bus. Pk.
DE74: C Don 3A 206
Willow Farm Ct.
DE65: Find 4C 182
Willow Gro. DE56: Bel 2F 35
Willowherb Cl. DE24: Sin 4E 185
Willow Hill Cl. NG6: Bulw 1F 71
Willow Holt NG14: Lowd 3D 57
Willow Ho. DE21: Chad 2B 136
Willow La. NG4: Ged 5E 77
Willow Pk. Way
DE72: Ast T 2F 203
Willow Ri. NG10: Sand 3A 144
Willow Rd. DE74: C Don 4A 206
NG2: West Br 4D 151
NG4: Carl 2F 101
NG7: Lent 4D 121
NG13: Bing 2F 131
Willow Row
DE1: Der 1B 6 (2E 135)
(not continuous)
Willows, The NG8: Bilb 3F 95
NG9: Bee 2E 147
Willows Ct. *DE5: Rip* *4C 8*
(off Cromford St.)
Willowsend Cl. DE65: Find . . .5C 182
Willowside Grn.
DE21: Spon 5C 138
Willow Sports Cen. . . .1B 6 (2E 135)
Willowtree Dr. DE21: Chad . . .1F 137
Willow Vw. NG7: Radf 4E 97
Willow Wong NG14: Bur J 2E 79
Willow Wong Cotts.
NG14: Bur J 2E 79
Willson Av. DE23: Lit 3B 158
Willson Rd. DE23: Lit 4B 158
Willwell Dr. NG2: West Br . . .5B 150
Wilmington Av. DE24: Alv . . .1A 188
Wilmington Gdns. NG5: Arn . . .1C 74
Wilmore Rd. DE24: Der 1F 185
Wilmot Av. DE21: Chad 3E 137
DE72: W Tre 4D 203
Wilmot Dr. DE7: Smal 2E 63
Wilmot La. NG9: Bee 3E 147
Wilmot Rd. DE56: Bel 5F 13

Wilmot St.
DE1: Der 5C **6** (4F **135**)
DE7: Ilk 1D **91**
DE75: Hea 3D **41**
NG10: Long E 1F **193**
Wilmslow Dr. DE21: Oak 4A **110**
Wilne Av. NG10: Long E 2F **193**
Wilne Cl. NG10: Long E 2E **193**
Wilne La. DE72: Dray 2B **192**
DE72: Shar 5F **191**
NG10: Long E 2B **192**
Wilne Mill DE72: Dray 2A **192**
Wilne Rd. DE72: Dray 5F **165**
NG10: Long E 2E **193**
Wilson Av. DE75: Los 5A **18**
Wilson Cl. DE3: Mick 3B **156**
NG5: Arn 1A **76**
Wilson Rd. DE21: Chad 5E **109**
NG16: Eastw 3E **43**
Wilsons Ct. NG11: Rudd 4B **174**
Wilson St.
DE22: Der 4B **6** (4E **135**)
WILSTHORPE 3A **168**
Wilsthorpe Rd.
DE21: Chad 1E **137**
DE72: Brea 3D **167**
NG10: Long E 3A **168**
Wilton Cl. DE24: S Flds 4B **184**
Wilton Pl. DE7: Ilk 1E **91**
Wilton Rd. NG7: Radf 4D **97**
Wilton St. DE7: Ilk 1E **91**
NG6: Basf 3D **73**
Wilton Ter. NG6: Basf 3D **73**
Wiltra Gro. DE56: Duff 4E **59**
Wiltshire Rd. DE21: Chad . . .5C **108**
Wimbledon Dr. NG16: Nuth . . .4D **71**
Wimbledon Rd. DE22: Mac . . .2F **133**
NG5: Sher 4F **73**
Wimborne Cl.
NG2: West Br 3B **150**
Wimbourne Cl. DE22: Mac . . .2A **134**
Wimbourne Rd. NG7: Radf . . .4E **97**
WIMORTON 2D **161**
Wimpole Gdns. DE22: Mac . . .2A **134**
Wimpole Rd. NG9: Bram 4C **118**
Wincanton Cl. DE24: Der 2C **160**
Winchcombe Way
DE21: Oak 3F **109**
Winchester Av. NG9: Bee 5D **119**
Winchester Ct. NG5: Sher 4D **75**
Winchester Cres. DE7: Ilk 2F **91**
DE21: Chad 5C **108**
Winchester St. NG5: Sher 4B **74**
Winchester Ter. NG5: Sher 4B **74**
Windermere Av. DE7: Kirk H . . .5B **90**
Windermere Cl. NG2: Gam . . .1C **152**
NG4: Ged 5E **77**
Windermere Cres.
DE22: All 2D **107**
Windermere Dr.
DE21: Spon 3D **139**
Windermere Gdns.
NG10: Long E 1A **164**
Windermere Rd. NG7: H Grn . . .2F **97**
NG9: Dram 4C **118**
NG10: Long E 1F **167**
NG15: Huck 2E **25**
Windings, The NG4: Carl 3C **100**
(off Chesterfield St.)
Windles Sq. NG14: Calv 2F **31**
Windley Cres. DE22: D Abb . .4E **107**
Windley Dr. DE7: Ilk 4C **66**
Windmill Av. DE56: Kil 4F **37**
NG15: Huck 3F **25**

Windmill Cl. DE24: Alv 2C **188**
DE72: Ock 3B **140**
DE74: C Don 2A **212**
NG3: Nott 5E **99**
Windmill Ct. NG12: Key 4E **199**
Windmill Gro. NG15: Huck . . .2F **25**
Wind Mill Hill La.
DE22: Der 2B **134**
Windmill Hill Wlk.
DE22: Mac 3D **133**
Windmill La. DE56: Bel 5F **13**
NG2: Nott 1D **123**
NG3: Nott 1D **123**
Windmill Mdw.
DE21: Spon 3C **138**
Windmill Ri. DE56: Bel 4F **13**
Windmill Rd. DE65: Etw 3A **180**
Windmill Vw. DE56: H'age . . .1D **15**
NG2: Nott 1F **123**
Windrush Cl. DE22: All 5A **84**
NG9: Bram 4C **118**
Windsmoor Rd.
NG16: Brins 1C **20**
Windsor Av. DE23: Lit 3A **158**
Windsor Cl. DE72: Bor 2B **164**
DE75: Hea 1D **41**
NG9: Trow 5A **92**
NG15: Huck 1A **26**
Windsor Ct. DE3: Mick 5C **132**
DE7: West H 2C **88**
NG10: Long E 4D **169**
NG10: Sand 4A **144**
NG13: Bing 2B **130**
Windsor Cres. DE7: Kirk H . . .5C **90**
NG5: Woodt 1F **75**
NG9: Stap 1D **145**
Windsor Dr. DE21: Spon 2E **139**
Windsor St. NG9: Bee 2F **147**
NG9: Stap 1D **145**
Windy La. DE21: L Eat 1B **84**
Wing All. NG1: Nott . . .3D **5** (1C **122**)
Wingate Cl. NG8: Bilb 4E **95**
Wingbourne Wlk. NG6: Bulw . .3B **48**
Wingerworth Pk. Rd.
DE21: Spon 3D **139**
Wingfield Dr. DE7: Ilk 4C **66**
DE21: Chad 4E **109**
NG9: Lent A 4F **119**
Wings Dr. NG15: Huck 5C **24**
Winifred Cres. NG14: Bur J . . .3E **79**
Winifred St. NG15: Huck 3A **26**
Winrow Gdns. NG6: Basf 4B **72**
Winscale Av. NG5: Top V 4F **49**
Winscale Gdns. NG5: Top V . .4F **49**
Winscombe Mt. NG11: Clif . . .3C **172**
Winsford Cl. NG8: Aspl 5A **72**
Winslow Grn. DE21: Chad . . .2B **138**
Winster Av. NG4: Carl 1C **100**
Winster Cl. DE56: Bel 4A **14**
NG9: Lent A 4E **119**
Winster Rd. DE21: Chad 1D **100**
Winster Way NG10: Long E . . .1E **193**
Winston Cl. NG3: Mapp 2B **76**
NG9: Stap 5D **117**
Winterbourne Dr.
NG9: Stap 4D **117**
Winter Closes NG16: Unde . . .1E **21**
Wintergreen Dr. DE23: Lit 5E **157**
Winterton Cl. NG5: Arn 1E **75**
Winterton Ri. NG5: Bestw 5A **50**
Winthorpe Rd. NG5: Arn 5F **51**
Wintringham Cres.
NG5: Woodt 2F **75**

Wirksworth Rd. DE7: Kirk H . . .5A **90**
DE56: Duff 4C **58**
DE56: Haz 2A **58**
Wisa Ter. NG5: Sher 4C **74**
Wisgreaves Rd. DE24: Alv . . .3E **161**
Wishford Av. NG7: Lent 2D **121**
Wisley Cl. NG2: West Br 5B **150**
Wistow Cl. NG8: Basf 2D **97**
Witham Dr. DE23: Lit 5C **158**
Withern Rd. NG8: Brox 1E **95**
Witney Cl. DE24: Der 3B **160**
NG5: Top V 4D **49**
Wittering Cl. NG10: Long E . . .1D **195**
Witton Ct. DE24: S Flds 3D **184**
Wiverton Rd. NG7: H Grn 2F **97**
NG13: Bing 2D **131**
Woburn Cl. NG12: Edwal 4B **152**
Woburn Cft. NG10: Sand 4F **143**
Woburn Pl. DE22: Mac 3A **134**
Woburn Ri. NG5: Woodt 2A **76**
Wolds Dr. NG12: Key 4E **199**
Wolds La. NG12: C'ton 3C **178**
NG12: Key 5D **199**
NG12: Norm W 4A **178**
Wolds Ri. NG12: Key 3E **199**
Wolfa St. DE22: Der . . .4A **6** (4E **135**)
WOLLATON 1D **119**
Wollaton Av. NG4: Ged 4C **76**
Wollaton Ct. NG6: Bulw 1D **73**
Wollaton Cres. NG9: Bee 5D **119**
Wollaton Hall 2F **119**
Wollaton Hall Dr.
NG8: Woll 2C **120**
Wollaton Paddocks
NG8: Woll 1B **118**
Wollaton Ri. NG8: Woll 3D **119**
Wollaton Rd. DE21: Chad 5E **109**
NG8: Radf, Woll 1D **119**
NG9: Bee 4D **119**
Wollaton Rd. Nth.
DE21: Chad 4E **109**
Wollaton St.
NG1: Nott 2A **4** (5A **98**)
NG15: Huck 2A **26**
Wollaton Va. NG8: Woll 1A **118**
Wolsey Av. NG7: Radf 5E **97**
Wolverley Grange
DE24: Alv 5C **162**
Woodale Cl. DE23: Lit 5E **157**
Wood Av. NG10: Sand 2F **143**
Woodbank Dr. NG8: Woll 3C **118**
Woodbeck Ct. DE21: Oak 3A **110**
WOODBOROUGH 5B **32**
Woodborough La.
NG3: Mapp 1A **52**
NG5: Arn 1A **52**
Woodborough Rd.
NG3: Mapp, Nott 4B **98**
Woodbridge Av. NG11: Clif . . .5D **149**
Woodbridge Cl. DE73: Chel . . .5E **187**
DE75: Hea 3A **42**
Woodchester Dr. DE24: Alv . . .5C **162**
Woodchurch Rd. NG5: Arn 3A **50**
Woodcock Sq. DE3: Mick 3B **156**
Woodcote Way DE23: Lit 4F **157**
Wood Cft. DE23: Lit 3C **158**
Wood End Rd. DE75: Hea 2D **41**
Woodfall La. DE22: Quar 1A **82**
Woodfield Dr. DE5: Rip 1F **71**
Woodfield Rd. NG8: Brox 1D **95**
Woodford Cl. NG5: Top V 3D **49**
Woodford Rd. DE22. Mac 1F **133**
NG5: Woodt 2F **75**
NG15: Huck 3A **26**

Woodgate Cl. NG12: Cotg 5D 155
Woodgate Ct. NG7: Radf 5F 97
Woodgate Dr. DE73: Chel 5F 187
Woodgate La. NG12: Cotg . . .4C 154
Wood Gro. NG14: Calv 1E 31
Woodhall Dr. DE23: Lit 3D 157
Woodhall Rd. NG8: Woll 5A 96
Woodhedge Dr. NG3: Nott . . .2F 99
Woodhouse Rd. DE7: H Woo . .4E 37
DE56: Kil 4E 37
Woodhouse St. NG3: Nott . . .5E 99
Woodhouse Way NG8: Stre 1C 94
NG16: Nuth 1C 94
Woodhurst Cl. DE21: Chad . . .5C 108
Woodkirk Rd. NG11: Clif 1E 173
Woodland Av. DE7: Ilk 3C 66
DE72: Bor 1B 164
DE72: Brea 3E 167
NG6: Bulw 2B 72
Woodland Cl. NG12: Cotg . . .1E 179
NG12: Rad T 2A 128
NG16: Want 5F 45
Woodland Ct. NG9: Bee 1F 147
Woodland Dr. NG3: Mapp P . . .1C 98
NG16: Nuth 3E 71
Woodland Gro. NG4: Colw . . .4E 101
NG5: Sher 3C 74
NG9: Chil 3C 146
Woodland Rd. DE22: Der 5D 107
NG2: West Br 4E 123
Woodlands, The
NG12: Rad T 2D 127
Woodlands Av.
DE24: S Loc 2D 187
Woodlands Cl. DE21: L Eat . . .2A 84
Woodlands Farm Cl.
NG15: Huck 5C 24
Woodlands Gro. NG15: Huck . .5C 24
Woodlands La. DE22: Quar . . .3C 82
DE73: Chel 1E 201
Woodlands Pk. DE72: Dray . . .1A 166
Woodlands Rd. DE22: All 5D 83
Woodlands Yd. DE73: Chel . . .1A 202
Woodland Way NG16: Eastw . .2D 43
Wood La. DE5: Pen 2A 8
DE7: H Woo 1C 62
DE56: Mil 1E 59
NG4: Ged 1F 101
NG15: Huck 2D 25
Woodlane Gdns. NG3: Nott . . .3E 99
Woodlark Ho. NG3: Nott 3E 99
Woodlea Gro. DE21: L Eat 2B 84
Woodleigh NG12: Key 4D 199
Woodleigh Gdns.
NG3: Mapp 5A 76
Wood Leys NG3: Nott 3F 99
Woodley Sq. NG6: Bulw 2B 48
Woodley St. NG11: Rudd 4B 174
Wood Link NG6: Bulw 5D 47
WOODLINKIN 3D 19
Woodminton Dr.
DE73: Chel 3E 187
Woodpecker Cl.
NG13: Bing 3E 131
Woodpecker Hill DE7: D Ab . .3F 113
Woodridge, The DE56: Mil 1E 59
Woodrising Cl. DE21: Oak . . .2F 109
Wood Rd. DE21: Chad 4E 109
DE21: Spon 2F 139
Woodroffe Wlk. DE23: Der . . .4D 159
Woodrow Av. NG8: Bilb 2E 95
Woodsend Cl. NG14: Bur J . . .3E 79
Woodsford Gro. NG11: Clif . . .1D 173
Woodshop La. DE73: Swar . . .3C 200

WOODSIDE 4C 62
Woodside DE7: Mor 4C 62
NG16: Eastw 2D 43
Woodside Av. DE5: Rip 1C 16
NG12: Rad T 2A 128
NG16: Nuth 1F 69
Woodside Cres. DE7: Ilk 2C 66
NG10: Long E 3A 168
Woodside Dr. DE22: All 1F 107
NG5: Arn 4C 50
Woodside Rd.
NG9: Bee, Lent A 4E 119
NG9: Chil 4F 145
NG10: Sand 3F 143
NG12: Rad T 2A 128
NG14: Bur J 4C 78
Woods La.
DE22: Der 5A 6 (5E 135)
NG14: Calv 2D 31
Woods Mdw. DE72: Elv 1C 188
Woodsorrel Dr. DE21: Oak . . .2A 110
Woodstock Av. NG7: Radf 4D 97
Woodstock Cl. DE22: All 1C 106
Woodstock Rd. NG9: Toton . .5D 145
Woodstock St. NG15: Huck . . .3A 26
Woodstock St. W.
NG15: Huck 2A 26
Woodston Wlk. NG5: Arn 2F 51
Wood St. DE1: Der . . .1D 7 (2A 136)
DE5: Rip 4C 8
DE7: Ilk 1E 91
NG5: Arn 4E 51
NG7: Radf 5F 97
NG16: Eastw 2E 43
Woodthorne Av.
DE24: S Loc 2D 187
WOODTHORPE 2E 75
Woodthorpe Av.
DE21: Chad 2E 137
NG5: Woodt 3D 75
Woodthorpe Ct. NG5: Sher . . .4D 75
Woodthorpe Dr. NG3: Mapp . .3C 74
NG5: Woodt 3C 74
Woodthorpe Gdns.
NG5: Sher 4E 75
Woodthorpe Grange
NG5: Woodt 4D 75
Woodthorpe M. NG5: Woodt . .3C 74
Woodthorpe Rd. NG3: Mapp . .4E 75
Woodvale NG8: Woll 1A 118
Woodview NG12: Cotg 5F 155
NG12: Edwal 5A 152
Woodview Bus. Cen.
NG5: Top V 3F 49
Woodview Ct. NG3: Nott 5B 100
Woodview Gdns.
DE22: D Abb 5D 107
Woodville Cl. NG9: Chil 2B 146
Woodville Dr. NG5: Sher 4B 74
Woodville Rd. NG5: Sher 5B 74
Woodward Av. NG9: Chil 1A 170
Woodwards Rd. DE72: Bor . . .2C 164
Woodward St. NG2: Nott 4C 122
Woodyard La. NG8: Woll 5F 95
Woolacombe Cl. NG3: Mapp . .2C 76
Wooliscroft Cl. DE7: Ilk 5B 66
Woolmer Rd. NG2: Nott 4B 122
Woolpack La.
NG1: Nott 3D 5 (1C 122)
(not continuous)
Wool Pk. La.
NG1: Nott 3E 5 (1C 122)
Woolrych St. DE23: Der 1E 159

Woolsington Cl. NG8: Stre . . .5C 70
Woolsthorpe Cl. NG8: Bilb . . .4E 95
Woolsthorpe Cres.
DE7: Kirk H 1C 114
Wootton Cl. NG8: Bilb 3C 94
Worcester Cl. NG14: Lowd . . .3D 57
Worcester Cres.
DE21: Chad 5C 108
Worcester Gdns.
NG5: Woodt 1D 75
Worcester Rd. NG5: Woodt . . .2D 75
Wordsworth Av. DE24: Sin . . .1D 185
NG15: Huck 3C 24
Wordsworth Dr. DE24: Sin . . .1F 185
Wordsworth Rd.
NG2: West Br 2D 151
NG5: Arn 5C 50
NG7: Radf 4D 97
NG16: Aws 2B 68
Worksop Rd. NG3: Nott 5E 99
Worrall Av. NG5: Arn 5E 51
NG10: Long E 2D 169
Worth St. NG4: Carl 2D 101
Worthy Row NG5: Bestw 2F 73
(off Arnold Rd.)
Wortley Av. NG9: Trow 2C 116
Wortley Cl. DE7: Ilk 2F 91
Wortley Hall Cl. NG7: Nott . . .3B 120
Worwood Dr. NG2: West Br . .4B 150
Woulds Fld. NG12: Cotg 2E 179
Wragby Rd. NG7: Lent 5D 97
Wragley Way DE24: S Flds . . .4B 184
Wray Cl. NG3: Nott 1F 5 (5D 99)
Wren Ct. NG10: Long E 2F 193
Wren Pk. Cl. DE56: Bel 4C 12
DE65: Find 5C 182
Wrenthorpe Va. NG11: Clif . . .2D 173
Wren Way DE3: Mick 4A 156
Wretham Cl. DE3: Mick 3C 156
Wright Av. DE5: Rip 5E 9
Wrights Orchard
NG12: Key 4D 199
Wright St. DE5: Cod 1A 18
NG4: Neth 3F 101
Wroughton Ct. NG16: Eastw . .2F 43
Wroxham Cl. DE24: S Loc . . .2C 186
Wroxham Dr. NG8: Woll 2C 118
Wyaston Cl. DE22: D Abb 4D 107
Wyatts Way DE5: Rip 3E 9
Wychwood Dr. NG9: Trow . . .3C 116
Wychwood Rd. NG13: Bing . . .2B 130
Wycliffe Gro. NG3: Mapp 5D 75
Wycliffe St. NG7: Basf 1E 97
Wycombe Cl. NG11: Clif 3C 172
Wye Gdns. NG7: Radf 4C 96
Wye St. DE24: Alv 3F 161
Wykeham Rd. NG5: Woodt . . .2F 75
Wykes Av. NG4: Ged 5E 77
Wymondham Cl. NG5: Arn . . .1F 75
Wynbreck Dr. NG12: Key 3E 199
Wyndale Dr. DE7: Kirk H 4B 90
Wyndham Ct. NG9: Chil 4A 146
Wyndham M. NG3: Mapp P . . .3A 98
Wyndham St. DE24: Alv 4F 161
Wyndings, The NG5: Woodt . . .3E 75
Wynhill Ct. NG13: Bing 1B 130
Wynndale Dr. NG5: Sher 4F 73
Wynton Av. DE24: Alv 3E 161
Wynwood Cl. NG9: Toton 1A 170
Wynwood Rd. NG9: Toton 1A 170
Wynyard Cl. DE7: Ilk 4B 66
Wyrale Dr. NG8: Stre 1D 95
Wysall La. NG11: Bunny 5A 198
NG12: Key 5C 198

Wyton Cl. NG5: Bestw 2F 73
Wyvelle Cres. DE74: Keg 1B 214
WYVER 3D 13
Wyver La. DE56: Bel 2E 13
Wyvern Av. NG10: Long E ...5C 168
Wyvern Bus. Pk.
 DE21: Chad 5F 137
Wyvern Cl. NG16: Newth 4F 43
Wyvern Retail Pk.
 DE21: Chad 4F 137
Wyvernside DE21: Chad 4E 137
Wyvern Way DE21: Chad 4E 137
Wyville Cl. NG7: Radf 5D 97

Y

Yalding Dr. NG8: Woll 1B 118
Yalding Gdns. NG8: Woll 1B 118
Yard, The NG7: H Grn 4E 97
 (off Sophie Rd.)
Yard Gallery, The 2F 119
Yardley Way DE56: Bel 5C 14
Yarmouth Ho. DE24: Alv 4B 162
 (off Durley Cl.)
Yarrow Cl. DE24: Sin 4D 185
Yarwell Cl. DE21: Chad 4C 108
 NG3: Nott 3B 100

Yates Av. DE72: Ast T 2F 203
Yatesbury Cres. NG8: Stre 2D 95
Yates Dr. DE23: Der 2F 159
Yates Gdns. NG5: Top V 4F 49
Yates St. DE23: Der 2F 159
Ye Olde Trip To Jerusalem Inn
 ....5B 4
 (off Castle Rd.)
Yeoman Av. NG6: Bestw V 5E 27
Yeomans Pde. NG4: Carl 3E 101
Yeovil Cl. DE24: Alv 4B 162
Yewbarrow Cl.
 NG2: West Br 3B 152
Yew Cl. NG5: Sher 5C 74
Yewdale Cl. NG2: West Br ...3B 152
 NG11: Clif 3C 172
Yewdale Gro. DE21: Oak 2A 110
Yews Dr. DE73: Chel 5F 187
 NG5: Sher 1B 98
Yew Tree Av. DE72: Ock 3C 140
 NG12: Rad T 2C 126
Yew Tree Cl. DE24: Alv 4B 162
Yew Tree Ct. NG5: Sher 1B 98
 NG9: Bee 2E 147
Yew Tree La. DE72: Thul 2E 189
 NG4: Ged 5F 77
 NG11: Clif 1B 172
Yew Tree Rd. NG15: Huck 4A 26

Yonge Cl. NG12: Rad T 3D 127
York Av. NG9: Chil 4E 147
 NG10: Sand 3F 143
York Cl. NG4: Ged 5E 77
York Dr. NG8: Stre 5C 70
Yorke St. NG15: Huck 2F 25
York Rd. DE21: Chad 1E 137
 NG10: Long E 2B 168
York St. DE1: Der ...2A 6 (3D 135)
 NG3: Nott 1C 4 (4B 98)
 NG4: Neth 3F 101
Youlgreave Cl. DE21: Chad ..4E 109
Young Cl. NG6: Bulw 2E 71
Young St. DE23: Der 2E 159
Yoxall Dr. DE22: Der 4B 134
Ypres Rd. DE22: All 3B 106
Yvonne Cres. NG4: Carl 3E 101

Z

Zetland Cres. DE24: S Flds ...4B 184
Zone, The NG1: Nott 2D 5
Zulla Rd. NG3: Mapp P 2B 98
Zulu Rd. NG7: Basf 5E 73

HOSPITALS and HOSPICES
covered by this atlas.

N.B. Where Hospitals and Hospices are not named on the map, the reference given is for the road in which they are situated.

BABINGTON HOSPITAL 2E **35**
Derby Road
BELPER
DE56 1WH
Tel: 01773 824171

DERBY CITY GENERAL HOSPITAL
....................1A **158**
Uttoxeter Road
DERBY
DE22 3NE
Tel: 01332 340131

DERBY NUFFIELD HOSPITAL
...................4E **157**
Rykneld Road
Littleover
DERBY
DE23 4SN
Tel: 01332 540100

DERBYSHIRE CHILDREN'S HOSPITAL
(WITHIN DERBY CITY
GENERAL HOSPITAL) 1A **158**
Uttoxeter Road
DERBY
DE22 3NE
Tel: 01332 340131

DERBYSHIRE ROYAL INFIRMARY
...............5E **7** (5A **136**)
London Road
DERBY
DE1 2QY
Tel: 01332 347141

HAYWOOD HOUSE MACMILLAN
SPECIALIST PALLIATIVE
CARE UNIT 3A **74**
Nottingham City Hospital
Hucknall Road
NOTTINGHAM
NG5 1PB
Tel: 0115 962 7619

HEANOR MEMORIAL HOSPITAL
...................3E **41**
Ilkeston Road
HEANOR
DE75 7EA
Tel: 01773 710711

HIGHBURY HOSPITAL 2B **72**
Highbury Road
Bulwell
NOTTINGHAM
NG6 9DR
Tel: 0115 9770000

ILKESTON COMMUNITY HOSPITAL
...................3C **66**
Heanor Road
ILKESTON
DE7 8LN
Tel: 0115 9305522

KINGSWAY HOSPITAL 4A **134**
Kingsway
DERBY
DE22 3LZ
Tel: 01332 362221

LINGS BAR HOSPITAL 2C **152**
Beckside
Gamston
NOTTINGHAM
NG2 6PR
Tel: 0115 945 5577

NHS WALK-IN CENTRE
(NOTTINGHAM)
...................5E **5** (2C **122**)
City Link
NOTTINGHAM
NG2 4LA

NHS WALK-IN CENTRE
(STAPLEFORD) 1C **144**
Stapleford Care Centre
Church Street
Stapleford
NOTTINGHAM
NG9 8DB

NOTTINGHAM CITY (UNIVERSITY)
HOSPITAL 2A **74**
Hucknall Road
NOTTINGHAM
NG5 1PB
Tel: 0115 969 1169

NOTTINGHAM NUFFIELD
HOSPITAL, THE 2C **74**
748 Mansfield Road
Woodthorpe
NOTTINGHAM
NG5 3FZ
Tel: 0115 9209209

NOTTINGHAMSHIRE HOSPICE
...................2C **98**
384 Woodborough Rd
NOTTINGHAM
NG3 4JF
Tel: 0115 910 1008

QUEENS MEDICAL CENTRE HOSPITAL
PALLIATIVE CARE TEAM
...................3C **120**
E Floor East Block
Derby Road
NOTTINGHAM
NG7 2UH
Tel: 0115 919 4402

QUEEN'S MEDICAL CENTRE
(UNIVERSITY HOSPITAL,
NOTTINGHAM)
...................3C **120**
Derby Road
NOTTINGHAM
NG7 2UH
Tel: 0115 9249924

RIPLEY HOSPITAL 5C **8**
Sandham Lane
RIPLEY
DE5 3HE
Tel: 01773 743456

TREETOPS HOSPICE 4D **143**
Derby Rd.
Risley
DERBY
DE72 3SS
Tel: 0115 9491264

The representation on the maps of a road, track or footpath is no evidence of the existence of a right of way.
The Grid on this map is the National Grid taken from Ordnance Survey® mapping with the permission of the Controller of Her Majesty's Stationery Office.
No reproduction by any method whatsoever of any part of this publication is permitted without the prior consent of the copyright owners.

Printed and bound in the United Kingdom by Polestar Wheatons Ltd., Exeter.